Practical Instructional Features

Ideas, examples, strategies, and activities for the classroom and ongoing professional development

P9-ELP-168

MODEL ACTIVITIES — Multiple Meanings of Words

Give the students a list of sentences, drawn from their textbooks, that contain words with specialized meanings for that subject. Have them use the dictionary or the textbook's glossary to discover the specialized meanings that fit the context of the sentences. After the students have completed the task independently, go over the sentences with them and discuss reasons for right and wrong responses.

The material you give to the students may look something like this:

Directions: Some words mean different things in your textbooks from what they mean in everyday conversation. In each of the following sentences, find the special meanings for the words and write these meanings on the lines provided.

1. Frederick Smith has decided to *run* for mayor.

2. The park was near the *mouth* of the Little Bear River.

3. The management of the company was unable to avert a *strike*.

4. That song is hard to sing because of the high *pitch* of several notes.

Model Activities for all levels

FOCUS ON STRATEGIES — Finding Main Ideas

Mrs. Braswell wrote the following paragraph on the chalkboard:

Edward Fong is a good family man. He is well educated, and he keeps his knowledge of governmental processes current. He has served our city well as a mayor for the past two years, exhibiting his outstanding skills as an administrator. Edward Fong has qualities that make him an excellent choice as our party's candidate for governor.

She said, "I am going to try to locate the topic sentence, the one to which all of the other sentences are related. The topic sentence provides one type of main idea for the paragraph. ... Now, let's see, is it the first sentence? No. None of the other sentences appears to support his being a good family man. ... Is it the second sentence? No. That idea isn't supported by the first sentence. ... Is it the third sentence? No. That sentence may be supported by the second sentence, but not by the others. ... Is it the fourth sentence? Yes, I think it is. A candidate for governor would do well to be a good family man, to be well educated and knowledgeable about government, and to have experience as a city administrator. All the other sentences support the last one, which is broad enough in its meaning to include the ideas expressed in the other sentences."

After this demonstration, Mrs. Braswell let one student "think aloud" the reasoning behind his or her choice of a topic sentence for another paragraph. Finally, she had students work on this process in pairs, "thinking aloud" to each other.

Focus on Strategies

CLASSROOM SCENARIO — Inclusion

Danny, who has cerebral palsy, has been admitted to Alan Stanton's third-grade class. Danny can move only his head and is unable to speak, but his IQ has been placed at 110. By moving his head and using his eyes, Danny indicates his wishes and answers questions. He also holds a stylus in his teeth to type written work, which is displayed along with the work of his peers, and he reads from an open book placed on a music stand.

Alan's positive attitude toward Danny and the students' eagerness to include him in *everything* they did created a positive learning environment. A larger child pushed his wheelchair so that Danny could go with them on field trips, take his turn as class leader, and participate in activities on the playground. When paired with a student of lower academic ability, Danny supplied the "brains" for a project while the other student carried out the plan. When the class learned some folk dances, Danny was the hub of the wheel and a classmate turned his chair. The students were protective, respectful, and accepting.

Classroom Scenarios

The For Your Journal... And Your Portfolio feature includes questions that link to the video clips on the new Student CD

For your journal...

1. Reflect on your own home environment. How did it support, or fail to support, your progress in reading?

2. Think back about your involvement in elementary school reading groups. How were you grouped? How did your group placement make you feel?

3. How can you promote self-esteem in students who struggle with the reading process?

4. Think about effective teachers you know or have known. What characteristics did they possess?

5. Reflect on the video that accompanies this chapter on your CD. Would you use student-led parent conferences in your own classroom? Why or why not?

...and your portfolio

1. Brainstorm a list of ideas for thematic units for which you have resource materials and special knowledge.

2. Conduct your own mini-research project by focusing on a student in your classroom or in one where you are observing. How does this student respond to different types of motivation to read? What works best, and

Teaching Reading
in Today's
Elementary Schools

Teaching Reading in Today's Elementary Schools

Ninth Edition

Betty D. Roe
Tennessee Technological University

Sandy H. Smith
Tennessee Technological University

Paul C. Burns
Late of University of Tennessee at Knoxville

Houghton Mifflin Company   Boston   New York

KH

Dedicated to Michael H. Roe and David, Dusty, and Tyler Smith

Publisher, Editor-in-Chief: Patricia Coryell
Senior Sponsoring Editor: Sue Pulvermacher-Alt
Senior Development Editor: Lisa Mafrici
Senior Project Editor: Ylang Nguyen
Associate Project Editor: Reba Libby
Editorial Assistant: Rachel Zanders
Senior Production/Design Coordinator: Jodi O'Rourke
Manufacturing Coordinator: Renée Ostrowski
Marketing Manager: Jane Potter
Senior Designer: Henry Rachlin

Cover image © Allan Davey/Masterfile

Printed in the U.S.A.

Library of Congress Control Number: 2003109904

ISBN: 0-618-34900-6

56789-FFG-10 09 08 07

8/28/09

Brief Contents

Contents

8 Language and Literature 313

9 Reading/Study Techniques 343

13 Classroom Organization and Management 491

Preface

Today's teachers are faced with a great many challenges when making decisions regarding instruction. We would like to empower teachers to become informed decision makers rather than merely followers of plans provided by others. Therefore, we offer information about many methods and materials for reading instruction, along with principles to help teachers choose among these options for their specific students and situations.

Most schools today are incorporating authentic literature, active learning techniques, technological applications, and alternative assessment into their reading instruction periods. They are also integrating instruction in all of the language arts and integrating the language arts across the curriculum. Teachers are employing many audiovisual aids and incorporating computers into instructional sessions, including both use of appropriate instructional software and use of Internet resources. Teachers are also working to meet more effectively the needs of diverse populations. In addition, teachers are making sure their instruction is addressing the standards to which they are being held accountable. This ninth edition of *Teaching Reading in Today's Elementary Schools* addresses all of these areas of concern. It also includes new information on theory, research, and techniques, while retaining solid, time-tested ideas and procedures—all within the familiar and practical framework of previous editions. As always, we have included new concepts, materials, techniques, and positions and tried to integrate them with valid traditional ideas in a balanced, even-handed way.

● Audience and Purpose

Teaching Reading in Today's Elementary Schools is intended for use in introductory reading education courses for both preservice and inservice elementary school classroom teachers. It will also be beneficial in introductory courses for teachers preparing to become reading specialists, and it contains much information that will help administrators direct their schools' reading programs.

This book is designed to familiarize teachers with all the important aspects of elementary reading instruction. It presents much practical information about the process of teaching reading. Theoretical background and the research base behind suggestions have also been included to give the teacher or prospective teacher a balanced perspective.

The primary aim of the book is to prepare teachers to develop their students' abilities to read fluently and to foster their students' enjoyment of reading. The large amount of the school day spent on reading instruction in the primary grades makes this content especially important to the primary grade teacher. In the intermediate grades students must handle reading assignments in the content areas as well as in reading periods. Our book—particularly the chapters on content area reading and reading/study techniques—contains information that will help teachers implement reading instruction across the curriculum.

● Revisions in This Edition

This edition represents a substantial revision. As always, the research base for understandings about reading instruction has been fully updated. A number of topics of recent concern, such as standards-based instruction, technology uses in reading instruction (especially Internet applications), authentic assessment, high-stakes testing, family involvement, and ways to help diverse populations learn to read are given special attention in this edition.

Each chapter has undergone thorough revision. Up-to-date theoretical and practical information has been added, and outdated information has been deleted. Material about diverse learners and students with special needs that was previously in a separate chapter has been integrated into all of the appropriate chapters, making its application more obvious to students.

Chapter 1 has increased emphasis on the relationship between technology and reading. It also has expanded information related to students with special needs. **Chapter 2** now contains information on guided reading and additional suggestions for meeting the needs of young students who are struggling with the reading process. **Chapters 3 and 4** have new headings to make the material more accessible as well as increased coverage of methods for helping diverse populations of students learn word recognition and vocabulary. **Chapter 3** also has a new chapter appendix including teaching strategies for phonics instruction. **Chapters 4, 5, and 6** have new examples, especially for use of new literature selections, and they also have more emphasis on family involvement. **Chapter 5** has new material on strategy prompts. In **Chapter 6** there is expanded coverage of critical literacy and questioning. This chapter also has information about some of the problems related to Internet use. **Chapter 7** has new material on guided reading and use of sketching as a strategy. It also has expanded material about literature-based reading instruction, meeting the needs of struggling readers, students who have nonstandard dialects, and English language learners. **Chapter 8** provides additional information on how literature is used to meet the instructional needs of diverse learners. **Chapter 9** has expanded suggestions for the use of graphic organizers and updated information about the role of technology in content area instruction. **Chapter 10** has new material on scientific literacy and a new strategy for use with social studies. New suggestions for literature to use are also presented. The material on determining the difficulty of texts through use of cloze tests and readability formulas has been moved from this chapter to Chapter 12. **Chapter 11** has new material on Internet Workshop, WebQuests, and iREAP. It offers definitions for technological literacy, media literacy, and digital literacy. It has new references to websites and computer software and expanded coverage of diverse students, especially English language learners. **Chapter 12** includes information on current assessment trends. It describes tools that can be used as multiple measures of assessment to collect student data and outlines assessment strategies that can be used effectively by diverse learners. It now has a section on assessing the difficulty of texts. **Chapter 13** provides new information on the 4-Blocks Literacy Model as an organizational framework for the classroom. In addition, it outlines practical suggestions for developing an inclusive learning environment that meets the needs of all students and establishes a strong partnership between home and school.

All chapters have increased emphasis on five topics that have extensive application across the entire reading curriculum—literature, technology, standards and assessment, diversity, and family involvement—although these topics are also represented more fully in Chapters 8, 11, 12, and 13. Marginal icons that represent textual ties among these topics and between these topics and other book topics are described under "Features of the Text."

Two new appendixes are included:

- The appendix to Chapter 3 on **Phonics Teaching Strategies** provides a ready reference for teaching strategies that reflect best practice in the teaching of phonics.

- The **Teaching Strategies Reference Guide** located at the end of the book in Appendix B outlines a selected list of effective teaching strategies for pre-, during, and postreading. This appendix will provide a quick, visually accessible guide for teacher education candidates preparing for pedagogy in reading examinations such as the PRAXIS Series.

The **Technology Resources** appendix that appeared in the previous edition has been moved to the accompanying website, to provide live links to the resources mentioned and to allow for regular updating.

Coverage

Chapter 1 discusses components of the reading act, theories related to reading, and principles of teaching reading. Chapter 2 presents information on emergent literacy. The next two chapters are devoted to techniques of teaching word recognition and meaning vocabulary. Comprehension strategies and skills are covered in Chapters 5 and 6. Major approaches and materials for reading instruction are described in Chapter 7. Chapter 8 deals with language and literature; Chapter 9 discusses methods of teaching reading/study techniques; and Chapter 10 tells how to present the reading skills necessary for reading in individual content areas. Chapter 11 addresses use of technology for literacy instruction and learning. Assessment of student progress and text materials is discussed in Chapter 12, and classroom management and organization are treated in Chapter 13. Information on students with special needs is integrated throughout the book. Appendix A contains answers to Test Yourself quizzes. Appendix B is a teaching strategies reference guide.

● Features of the Text

This text provides an abundance of practical activities and strategies for improving students' reading performance. *Illustrative lesson plans, classroom scenarios, focus on strategies vignettes, learning-center ideas, model activities, instructional games,* and *new textual ties* are all presented.

To help students study effectively, we have included the following features:

Setting Objectives, part of the opening material in each chapter, provides objectives to be met as the chapter is read.

Key Vocabulary, a list of important terms that readers should know, is included to help students focus on key chapter concepts. Vocabulary can be reviewed using the Flashcards available on the textbook website.

Introductions to each chapter help readers develop a mental set for reading the chapter and give them a framework into which they can fit the ideas they will read about.

Marginal icons indicate the **five textual ties** that provide cross references to topics that are integral to the entire text. The textual ties are

Literature   Standards and Assessment
Technology   Diversity
Family

Examples, Model Activities, Classroom Scenarios, and **Focus on Strategies** sections clarify the material in the text and put it into perspective.

Time for Reflection is a feature located at strategic points throughout each chapter to encourage readers to think about the subject matter that has been presented and decide where they stand on debated issues.

Test Yourself, a section at the end of each chapter, includes questions that check retention of the chapter's material as a whole; these questions may also serve as a basis for discussion.

For Your journal... presents topics the readers can write about in order to further their understanding of the ideas and methods presented in the chapter.

...And Your portfolio presents ideas to include in a portfolio for assessment purposes. Included in this feature are questions that link to video clips offered on the new *Teaching Reading* student CD.

A **Glossary** contains meanings of specialized terms used in this book.

Appendixes contain answers to Test Yourself questions, and a teaching strategies reference guide.

● Accompanying Teaching and Learning Resources

Instructor's Resource Manual with Test Items   This teaching aid provides supplementary material including model syllabi, chapter outlines, key vocabulary terms and definitions, instructional media selections, suggested teaching strategies, and suggested readings. It also includes listings of resources for independent reading activities, multimedia materials, and computer software. In addition, essay and objective questions are provided for each chapter, as well as ideas for implementing authentic assessment.

Computerized Test Bank   Questions from the *Instructor's Resource Manual* are available in computerized format as well.

Teaching Reading Student CD-ROM   Free with every student text, this CD contains videos of classroom situations accompanied by questions to stimulate student reflection and critical thinking.

Companion Website   This site (go to **http://education.college.hmco.com**) provides additional pedagogical support and resources for both instructors and students using the text, including self-testing questions, case studies, links to technology resources, PowerPoint slides, and more.

● Acknowledgments

We are indebted to many people for their assistance in the preparation of this text. In particular, we would like to recognize the contribution that Paul C. Burns made to the first and second editions of this book and the contribution that Elinor P. Ross made to the third through seventh editions of the book.

Although we would like to acknowledge the many teachers and students whose inspiration was instrumental in the development of this book, we cannot name all of them. We offer grateful recognition to the following reviewers, whose constructive advice and criticism helped greatly in the writing and revision of the manuscript: Linda Aulgur, Westminster College; Beverly Joan Boulware, Western Kentucky University; Barbara Decker, Southeastern Oklahoma State University; Laurie Elish-Piper, Northern Illinois University; Francine Falk-Ross, Northern Illinois University; Marcia Stewart Froemke, Bryan College; Caroline M. Hagen, Jamestown College; Amy Huffman, Guilford Technical Community College; Lijun Jin, Towson University; Louise F. Karther, Northwest Christian College; Isabelle Medina Sandoval, College of Santa Fe; Katharyn E. K. Nottis, Bucknell University; Tim Toops, Florida Southern College; Betty Ann Watson, Harding University.

In addition, we express appreciation to those who have granted permission to use sample materials or citations from their respective works. Credit for these contributions has been given in the source lines.

The invaluable assistance provided by Michael Roe in proofreading is greatly appreciated. Grateful acknowledgment is also given to our editors — Sheralee Conners, Lisa Mafrici, Sue Pulvermacher-Alt, Reba Libby, and Rachel Zanders—for their assistance throughout the development and production of the book.

Betty D. Roe
Sandy H. Smith

The Reading Act

SETTING OBJECTIVES

When you finish reading this chapter, you should be able to

● Discuss the reading product.

● Describe the reading process.

● Explain three types of theories of the reading process: subskill, interactive, and transactive.

● Describe a balanced approach to reading instruction.

● Name some principles on which effective reading instruction is based.

● Discuss standards for the English language arts that were developed by professional organizations.

Few adults would question the importance of reading to effective functioning in our complex technological world. Educators have long made reading instruction a priority in the school curriculum, especially in the primary grades. As students enter the middle grades, a systematic approach to reading instruction often decreases.

Many children come to school with a sense of the importance of reading in their lives. Unfortunately, however, not all students have this vision. One of the tasks teachers face is to help students see the importance of acquiring reading ability for performing everyday tasks effectively and the value of reading as a source of information, enjoyment, and recreation. To accomplish this task effectively, teachers need to know something about the reading act, some useful principles of reading instruction, and some of the theories on which instructional practices in reading are based. They should understand the need for a balanced approach to reading instruction. They also need to understand the standards movement that has arisen from concerns about students' reading performance.

Reading is a highly complex act. It includes two major components—a process and a product—each of which is itself complicated. Teachers need to be aware of these components and their different aspects in order to respond effectively to their students' reading needs.

Chapter 1 Organization

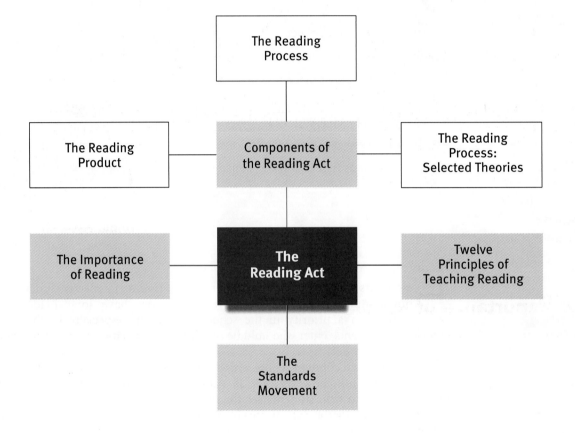

The Reading Process

The Reading Product

Components of the Reading Act

The Reading Process: Selected Theories

The Importance of Reading

The Reading Act

Twelve Principles of Teaching Reading

The Standards Movement

Students may read for relaxation, vicarious adventure, or aesthetic pleasure, as well as to gain information.
(© Laimute E. Druskis/Stock Boston)

This chapter analyzes the reading product and process. It describes three theories of the reading process; presents some sound principles for reading instruction, with explanatory comments; and offers information on the standards movement.

The Importance of Reading

The ability to read is vital to functioning effectively in a literate society such as ours. However, children who do not attach importance to learning to read will not be motivated to learn. Learning to read takes effort, and children who fail to see the value of reading in their personal activities will be less likely to work hard than those who do see the benefits.

Teachers should have little trouble demonstrating to children that reading is important. Every aspect of life involves reading. Road signs direct travelers to particular destinations, inform drivers of hazards, and remind people about traffic regulations. There are menus in restaurants, labels on cans, printed advertisements, newspapers, magazines, insurance claim forms, income tax forms, and campaign and travel brochures. These reading situations are inescapable. Even very young children can be helped to see the need to read the signs on rest rooms, the labels on individual desks in their classrooms, and the labeled areas for storing supplies. In fact, these young children are often eager to learn to read and are ready to attack the task enthusiastically. However, children do not automatically recognize the "profusion of literacy activities in the nonschool world" (Kotrla, 1997, p. 702).

Reading tasks become increasingly complex as students advance through the grades, and attention must be given to these tasks continually. Anderson (1988) suggests sparking the interest of middle-grade students through career education activities, helping them in this way to see that reading is a life skill that is relevant to their future success. The children can choose occupations that interest them and list the reading skills each occupation requires. They can take one or more field trips to businesses to see workers using reading to do their jobs, and they can hear resource people speak to their classes about how they personally need reading in their jobs. These resource people may bring to class examples of the reading materials they must use to perform their daily tasks. The students may also interview parents and others to learn about reading demands in a wide variety of careers. In many cases, the reading activities involve such applications as use of computer databases and electronic mail.

FAMILY

TECHNOLOGY

As important as functional reading is to everyday living, another important goal of reading is enjoyment. Teachers must attempt to show students that reading can be interesting to them for reasons other than strictly utilitarian ones. Students may read for relaxation, vicarious adventure, or aesthetic pleasure as they immerse themselves in tales of other times and places or those of the here and now. They may also read to obtain information about areas of interest or hobbies to fill their leisure time. To help children see reading as a pleasurable activity, teachers should read to them each day on a variety of themes and topics, in a variety of genres, and from the works of many authors. They should also make many books available for children to look at and read for themselves, and they should set aside time for children to read from self-selected materials. Students should be given opportunities to share information from and reactions to their reading in both oral and written forms. They should be encouraged to think about the things they are reading and to relate them to their own experiences.

TIME for REFLECTION

What can you add to the list of ways to demonstrate to students the importance of reading? Can you think of more suggestions to show students the enjoyment of reading?

Components of the Reading Act

The reading act is composed of two parts: the reading process and the reading product. Nine aspects of the reading process — sensory, perceptual, sequential, experiential, thinking, learning, associational, affective, constructive — combine to produce the reading product. When these aspects blend and interact harmoniously, good communication between the writer and reader is the product. But the sequences involved in the reading process are not always exactly the same, and they are not always performed in the same way by different readers. Because the goal of communication is central to reading instruction, we will discuss the reading product first.

● The Reading Product

The product of the reading act is the communication of thoughts and emotions by the writer to the reader, resulting in the reader's own understanding of ideas that the writer has put into print. Communication results from the reader's construction of meaning through integrating his or her prior knowledge with the information presented in the text.

Today's readers have a wealth of knowledge available to them because they are able to read material that others wrote in years past. Americans can read of events and accomplishments that occur in other parts of the world. Knowledge of great discoveries need not be laboriously passed from person to person by word of mouth; such knowledge is available to all who can read.

In addition to being a means of communicating generally, reading is a means of communicating specifically with friends and acquaintances. A note may tell a child that Mother has gone to the store or inform a baby-sitter about where to call in case of an emergency. A memo from a person's employer can identify the work to be done. Reading can be a way to share another person's insights, joys, sorrows, or creative endeavors. Reading can also enable a person to find places he or she has never visited before (through maps and directional signs), to take advantage of bargains (through advertisements), or to avert disaster (through warning signs). It is difficult to imagine what life would be like without this vital means of communication.

Communication depends on comprehension, which is affected by all aspects of the reading process. Word recognition strategies, a part of the associational aspect of the reading process, are essential, but comprehension involves much more than decoding symbols into sounds; the reader must construct meaning while interacting with the printed page. Some people mistakenly view reading as a single skill, that of pronouncing words, rather than as a combination of many skills that lead to the derivation of meaning. Thinking of reading in this way may have fostered the misguided practice of using a reading period for extended drill on word calling, in which the teacher asks each child to "read" aloud while classmates follow in their books. Some students may be good pronouncers in such a situation, but are they readers? They may pronounce words perfectly but fail to understand anything they have read. Although pronunciation is important, reading involves much more.

TIME for REFLECTION

Some people believe that just teaching children to pronounce words enables them to achieve communication with the authors of written materials. What do *you* think, and why?

Teachers who realize that all aspects of the reading process affect comprehension of written material will be better able to identify children's reading difficulties and, as a result, offer effective instructional programs based on children's needs. Faulty performance related to any aspect of the reading process may result in an inferior product or in no product at all.

● The Reading Process

Reading is an extremely complex process. When they read, children must be able to

- perceive the symbols set before them (sensory aspect);
- follow the linear, logical, and grammatical patterns of the written words (sequential aspect);
- interpret what they see (perceptual aspect);

- relate words to direct experiences to give the words meaning (experiential aspect);

- make inferences from and evaluate the material (thinking aspect);

- remember what they learned in the past and incorporate new ideas and facts (learning aspect);

- recognize the connections between symbols and sounds, between words and what they represent (associational aspect);

- deal with personal interests and attitudes that affect the task of reading (affective aspect); and

- put everything together to make sense of the material (constructive aspect).

Reading seems to fit into the category of behavior called a skill, which Frederick McDonald has defined as an act that "demands complex sets of responses—some of them cognitive, some attitudinal, and some manipulative" (Downing, 1982, p. 535). Understanding, rather than simple motor behavior, is essential. The key element in skill development is integration of the processes involved, which "is learned through practice. Practice in integration is supplied only by performing the whole skill or as much as is a part of the learner's 'preliminary fix.' … one learns to read by reading" (Downing, 1982, p. 537). Whereas reading can be broken down into subskills, reading takes place only when these subskills are put together into an integrated whole. Performing subskills individually is not reading (R. C. Anderson et al., 1985).

TECHNOLOGY 🖥️   Technology has affected the teaching of reading and other literacy skills by serving as a vehicle for such instruction. However, it has also added to the literacy strategies needed for functioning in today's society. El-Hindi (1998, p. 694) says, "Literacy now involves being able to make sense of information including images, sounds, animation, and ongoing discussion groups." It involves navigating hypertext and hypermedia environments that deviate radically from the sequential text found in print sources. (See Chapter 11 for discussions of hypertext and hypermedia.)

Not only is the reading process complex, but each aspect of the process is complex as well. As Example 1.1 shows, the whole process can be likened to a series of books, with each aspect represented by a hefty volume. A student would have to understand the information in every volume to have a complete grasp of the subject. Therefore, the student would have to integrate information from all of the volumes in order to perform effectively in the area of study. The series would be more important than any individual volume.

Sensory Aspects of Reading

DIVERSITY 🌐   The reading process begins with a sensory impression, either visual (sight) or *tactile* (touch). A normal reader perceives the printed symbol visually; a blind reader uses the tactile sense. (Discussion of the blind reader is beyond the scope of this text.) The auditory sense is also very important, because a beginning stage in reading is the association of printed symbols with spoken language. A person with poor auditory discrimination may find some reading skills, especially those involved with phonics, difficult to master.

EXAMPLE 1.1   Aspects of the Reading Process

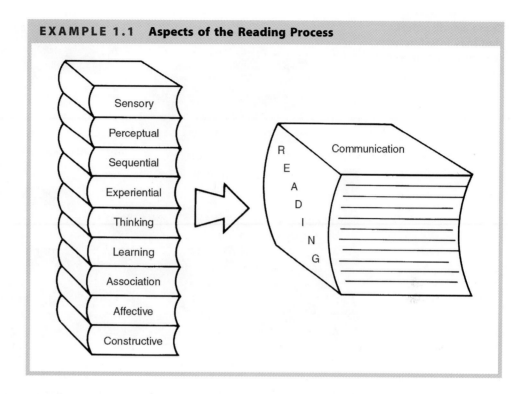

Vision.   The reading act imposes many visual demands on children. They must be able to focus their eyes on a page of print that is generally fourteen to twenty inches away, as well as on various signs and visual displays that may be twenty or more feet away. Besides possessing *visual acuity* (sharpness of vision), children must learn to discriminate visually among the graphic symbols (letters or words) that are used to represent spoken language. Reading is impossible for a person who cannot differentiate between two unlike graphic symbols. Because of these demands, teachers should be aware of the way in which a child's sight develops and of the physical problems that can handicap reading.

DIVERSITY 🌐   Many first graders have not yet attained 20/20 vision. Farsighted first graders may learn reading skills more easily by working on charts and chalkboards than by using workbooks and textbooks. Teachers should avoid requiring farsighted children to do a great deal of uninterrupted reading, and they should also use large print for class handouts. Although nearsighted children may do well when working with books, they are often unable to see well enough to respond to directions or exercises written on charts or chalkboards.

Some children may have an eye disorder called *astigmatism*, which results in blurred vision. This problem, as well as nearsightedness and farsightedness, can generally be corrected by glasses.

If a child's eyes do not work well together, he or she may see two images instead of one. Sometimes when this occurs, the child manages to suppress the image from one eye. If suppression continues over a period of time, he or she may lose sight in

Some eye disorders that may interfere with reading can be corrected by glasses. *(© Mug Shots/ Corbis)*

that eye entirely. If suppression occurs for only short periods, the child may lose the appropriate place on the page when reading, becoming confused and frustrated.

It takes time for children to learn to move their eyes across a page in a left-to-right progression and to execute a return sweep from the end of one line to the beginning of the next line. This is a difficult maneuver. Children who have not yet mastered the process will find themselves rereading lines and skipping lines, both of which hamper comprehension. Although teachers often attempt to correct faulty eye movements, such movements may be symptoms of other problems (for example, poor muscle coordination or poor vocabulary) rather than causes of problems. When the other problems are removed, these symptoms usually disappear.

DIVERSITY   Uncorrected nearsightedness or farsightedness, astigmatism, problems with dual-eye coordination, and problems with tracking lines are all *visual impairments*. A child who is visually impaired has difficulty, but is able to learn to read print, in contrast to a child who is blind and must learn to read Braille. Teachers can make provisions for children with visual impairments by adjusting lighting and seating, providing tape-recorded stories and books with large print, and reading orally to the whole class frequently. Students who have trouble tracking print with their eyes can be encouraged to follow along the line of print through the use of a pointer. The teacher can use a pointer when sharing big books and when reading material from the board. Student-held pointers and highlight tape can also be used to assist students in following print during reading. Teachers should refer children to vision specialists if they observe such symptoms as squinting, closing or covering one eye, rubbing eyes frequently, or making frequent errors when copying board work.

Hearing. A child who cannot discriminate among the different sounds (*phonemes*) represented by graphic symbols will be unable to make the sound-symbol associations necessary for decoding unfamiliar words. Of course, before a child can discriminate among sounds, he or she must be able to hear them; that is, *auditory acuity* must be adequate. Therefore, children who are deaf or hearing-impaired are deprived of some methods of word identification. Children whose hearing is temporarily impaired by problems related to colds or allergies may also experience difficulties.

DIVERSITY   The term *hearing impaired* applies to individuals whose sense of hearing is defective but adequate for ordinary purposes, with or without a hearing aid. When providing reading instruction for children with hearing impairments, teachers should speak slowly, clearly, and with adequate volume; seat the child as far as possible from distracting sounds; and supplement reading lessons with visual aids. As we'll discuss in Chapters 2 and 3, teachers of students with hearing impairments should also use a whole-word approach to word recognition rather than a phonics approach because the child cannot hear sounds well and should use the language experience approach described in Chapter 2 to connect meaningful experiences to words. Teachers should refer students to hearing specialists if they observe such symptoms as inattentiveness in class, requests for repetition of verbal information, frowning when trying to listen, or turning the head so that one ear always faces the teacher.

Perceptual Aspects of Reading

Perception involves interpretation of the sensory impressions that reach the brain. Each person processes and reorganizes sensory data in accordance with his or her background of experiences. When a person is reading, the brain receives a visual sensation of words and phrases from the printed page. It recognizes and gives meaning to these words and phrases as it associates them with the reader's previous experience with the objects, ideas, or emotions represented.

Because readers' experiences vary, different readers may interpret a single text differently (R. C. Anderson et al., 1985). For example, seeing the printed words *apple pie* can result not only in a visual image of a pie but also in a recollection of its smell and taste. Of course, the person must have prior experience with the thing named by the word(s) in order to make these associations. Since different people have had different experiences with apple pies, and apple pies can vary in smell, taste, and appearance, people will attach different meanings to *apple pie*. Therefore, individuals will have slightly different perceptions when they encounter these or any other words.

The clusters of information that people develop about things (such as apple pies), places (such as restaurants or airports), and ideas (such as justice or democracy) are sometimes referred to as *schemata*. Every person has many schemata. Reading comprehension has been described as the act of relating textual information to existing schemata (Pearson et al., 1979). Chapter 5 provides more information about this relationship.

Visual Perception. Visual perception involves identification and interpretation of the size, shape, and relative position of letters and words. *Visual discrimination*, the ability to see likenesses and differences in visual forms (for example, between the printed words *big* and *dig*), is an important part of visual perception because many letters and words are very similar in form but very different in pronunciation and meaning. Accurate identification and interpretation of words result from detecting the small variations in form. A child may have good visual acuity (see images clearly) but be unable to discriminate well visually. Teachers can help children develop this skill through carefully planned activities (discussed in Chapter 2). The final step in visual perception, of course, is attaching meaning to the words by using past experiences, as described earlier.

Auditory Perception. Auditory perception involves *auditory discrimination*, detecting likenesses and differences in speech sounds (for example, recognizing the difference between the spoken words *big* and *dig*) and interpreting the result. Children must be able consciously to separate a phoneme (sound) from one spoken word and compare it with another phoneme separated from another word. As is true of visual discrimination, a child can have good auditory acuity (hear sounds clearly) but be unable to discriminate well auditorily. The skill can be taught, however. (Instructional activities for enhancing auditory discrimination are discussed in Chapter 2.) The final step in auditory perception is using past experiences to attach meaning to the words a person has heard.

Sequential Aspects of Reading

DIVERSITY 🌐 English-language printed material generally appears on a page in a left-to-right, top-to-bottom sequence. A person's eyes must follow this sequence in order to read. Learning to follow this sequential pattern can be a new challenge for children who have not been exposed to many printed materials or who have experience with different sequences used in other languages. Readers occasionally regress, or look back to earlier words and phrases, as they read. Although these regressions momentarily interrupt the reading process as the reader checks the accuracy of initial impressions, the reader eventually returns to the left-to-right, top-to-bottom sequence.

TECHNOLOGY 🖥 The sequence of reading text from page to page in a book, front to back, has predominated in years past. Today, hypertext and hypermedia (see Chapter 11) computer materials allow random access to information in an electronic document and offer new challenges to students who must learn to navigate multiple sequences of text and still retain the organizational sense necessary for understanding the topic. (However, on any individual page of hypertext material, the print is generally still arranged in a left-to-right, top-to-bottom sequence.) Chapter 11 addresses, to some extent, the challenge of reading hypertext and hypermedia materials, but much research is needed to help teachers understand how to assist students with reading in this different manner. Current textbooks also have begun to vary from standard formats somewhat with more use of sidebars, and some children's literature selections, such as *The Magic School Bus* series, have several levels and types of texts presented on the same page.

Another reason why reading is a sequential process is that oral language is strung together in a sequential pattern of grammar and logic. Since written language is a way of representing speech, it is expressed in the same manner. The reader must be able to follow the grammatical and logical patterns of spoken language in order to understand written language.

Experiential Background and Reading

As indicated in the section on perceptual aspects, meaning derived from reading is based on the reader's experiential background. Children with rich background experiences have had more chances to develop understanding of the vocabulary and concepts they encounter in reading than have children with limited experiences. For example, a child who has actually been in an airport is more likely to be able to attach appropriate meaning to the word *airport* when he or she encounters it in a reading selection than a child who has not been to an airport. Direct experiences with places, things, and processes described in reading materials make understanding of the materials much more likely. Students from different cultures comprehend and remember best the texts that are most culturally familiar and that have characters who are like them (Drucker, 2003).

Vicarious (indirect) experiences also enhance conceptual development, although they are probably less effective than concrete experiences. Hearing other people tell of or read about a subject; seeing photos or a movie of a place, event, or activity; and reading about a topic are examples of vicarious experiences that can build concept development. Because vicarious experiences involve fewer senses than do direct, concrete experiences, the concepts gained from them may be developed less fully.

FAMILY

Some parents converse freely with their children, read to them, tell them stories, show them pictures, and take them to movies and on trips. These parents are providing rich experiences. Other parents do not offer these experiences to their children. Teachers can help broaden children's concrete experiences through

TECHNOLOGY

field trips, displays of objects, and class demonstrations. They can also help by providing rich vicarious experiences, such as photographs, videos, CD and tape recordings, computer software, classroom discussions, and story-telling and story-reading sessions.

If reading materials contain vocabulary, concepts, and sentence structures that are unfamiliar to children, teachers must help them develop the background they need to understand the materials. Because children's experiential backgrounds differ, some need more preparation for a particular selection than others do.

Teachers can help children learn the Standard English found in most books by telling and reading stories, encouraging show-and-tell activities, leading or encouraging class discussions, using language experience stories (accounts that are developed cooperatively by teacher and class members about actual events), and encouraging dramatic play (enactment of roles or imitation of people or things). (Language experience stories are described further in Chapters 2 and 7.) The new words encountered during field trips and demonstrations will also be valuable.

Good readers can skillfully integrate information in the text with prior knowledge about the topic, but poor readers may either overemphasize the symbols in the text or rely too heavily on their prior knowledge. Poor readers who focus primarily on the text may produce nonsense words that are graphically similar to the ones in the text. This occurs because such readers are not attempting to connect what they read to their experiences and are not demanding sense from reading. Poor readers who depend too much on prior knowledge may not make enough use of clues in the text to come close to the intended message (R. C. Anderson et al., 1985).

The Relationship Between Reading and Thinking

Reading is a thinking process. The act of recognizing words requires interpretation of graphic symbols. To comprehend a reading selection thoroughly, a person must be able to use the information to make inferences and read critically and creatively—to understand the figurative language, determine the author's purpose, evaluate the ideas presented, and apply those ideas to actual situations. All of these skills involve thinking processes.

Teachers can guide students' thinking by asking appropriate questions. Students will be more likely to evaluate the material they are reading if they have been directed to do so. *How* and *why* questions are particularly good. Appropriate questions can help involve a reader in the material and help the reader make personal connections with it. Questions can also limit thinking, however; if children are asked only to locate isolated facts, they will probably not be very concerned about main ideas in a passage or about the author's purpose. Test questions also affect the way students read assignments: if the usual test questions ask for evaluation or application of ideas, children will be apt to read the material more thoughtfully than they will if they are asked to recall isolated facts.

STANDARDS AND
ASSESSMENT

The Relationship of Reading to Learning

Reading is a complex act that must be learned. It is also a means by which further learning takes place. In other words, a person learns to read *and* reads to learn.

Learning to read depends on motivation, practice, and reinforcement. Teachers must show children that being able to read is rewarding in many ways: it increases success in school, helps in coping with everyday situations outside of school, bestows status, and provides recreation. Children are motivated by the expectation that they will receive these rewards, which then provide the reinforcement that encourages them to continue to make associations between printed words and the things to which they refer and to practice the skills they need for reading.

After children have developed some facility in reading, it becomes a means through which they learn other things. They read to learn about science, mathematics, social studies, literature, and all other subjects, a topic treated in depth in Chapter 10.

We should clarify one additional idea at this time. Teachers sometimes assume the existence of a dichotomy: that children "learn to read" in the primary grades and "read to learn" in the intermediate and upper grades. Although it may be true that teachers devote less attention to the actual process of learning to read at the intermediate level, there is still a need there for attention to primary, as well as higher-level, strategies. In addition, primary students can and do read for information.

Reading as an Associational Process

Learning to read depends on a number of types of associations. First, children learn to associate objects and ideas with spoken words. Next, they are asked to build up associations between spoken words and written words. In some cases—for instance, when a child encounters an unfamiliar written word paired with a picture of a familiar object—the child makes a direct association between the object or event and the written word without an intermediate connection with the spoken word. In teaching phonics, teachers set up associations between graphic symbols (*graphemes*) and sounds (phonemes).

When children practice the associations through classroom activities, immediate positive *reinforcement*, or support, of correct answers and correction of wrong ones can help to establish the associations. Positive reinforcement can include simple feedback about the correctness of an answer or a reward such as praise, a smile, or even tangible items like stickers or gold stars. The sooner the teacher provides the reinforcement after the child makes the response, the more effective the reinforcement is likely to be. For example, the teacher might show a child the word *time* and say that this printed word is *time*. Then the teacher would show the word again and ask the child to respond with the word *time*, followed by feedback on the correctness of the response. The teacher may offer the child opportunities for repetition of this response in a variety of situations, and the child can respond appropriately, using the association each time he or she sees that word.

Practice in and of itself, however, is not always enough to set up lasting associations. The more meaningful an association is to a child, the more rapidly he or she will learn it. Children can learn words after only a single exposure if the words have vital meaning for them (Ashton-Warner, 1963).

Affective Aspects of the Reading Process

Interests, attitudes, and self-concepts are three *affective* aspects of the reading process. These aspects influence how hard children will work at the reading task. For example, children who are interested in the materials presented to them will put forth much more effort in the reading process than will children who have no interest in the available reading materials.

FAMILY

In the same manner, children with positive attitudes toward reading will expend more effort on the reading process than children with negative attitudes. Positive attitudes are nurtured in homes where the parents read for themselves and to their children and where reading materials are provided for children's use. In the classroom, teachers who enjoy reading, who seize every opportunity to provide pleasurable reading experiences for their students, and who allow time for recreational reading during school hours are encouraging positive attitudes. Reading aloud to the children regularly can also help accomplish this objective, and this activity should continue beyond the primary grades (Daisey, 1993; Duchein and Mealey, 1993; Schumm and Saumell, 1994). Also, if a child's peers view reading as a positive activity, that child is likely to view reading in the same way.

Ruddell (1992) believes internal ***motivation*** and identification with a piece of literature can take several forms: seeing oneself as a successful problem solver, viewing oneself as a person of significance, evoking an aesthetic sense, finding escape from daily life, piquing intellectual curiosity, and understanding oneself. These types of internal motivation all invite the reader to "step into the story" and be a part of it. External motivations for reading may include peer pressure, teacher expectations, and meeting one's responsibilities.

 **FAMILY** Negative attitudes toward reading may develop in a home environment where parents, for a variety of reasons, do not read. Children from some homes may be given the impression that reading is a female activity. They may bring this idea to the classroom and spread it among children who have not previously been exposed to it. This attitude affects everyone in the classroom negatively, regardless of gender. (See the Focus on Strategies.)

Maudeville (1994) believes that when readers make decisions about what interested them or what information was important to them in a selection they have just read, they understand and retain that information better. Reflecting on changes in attitude about the topic may also help. Discussion of these personal responses is also important. Giving students opportunities for self-expression is a key to intrinsic motivation (Oldfather, 1995). Open-ended tasks promote student motivation because they allow personal choices, challenges, and control. Social interaction

---

FOCUS ON STRATEGIES **Attitude Toward Reading**

James, a sixth grader, grumbled about being asked to participate in any reading activities. One day he told Mr. Hyde, his teacher, "I don't need to be able to read. My dad is a construction worker who drives heavy equipment, and that's what I'm going to be. I won't need to read to do that."

Mr. Hyde responded, "What will you do if you are given written instructions to get to the construction site? Won't you need to read then?"

"I'll ask somebody," James replied.

"What if nobody else is there?" Mr. Hyde persisted.

"I don't think that will happen," James countered.

"Well, what if you can't read the road signs to find the place that you are going? You might even need to read a map to find the place. Or what will you do if you get letters from people? You may not want to ask someone else to read them to you. They could be private. Can't you see some advantages to being able to read, even if you don't have to read a lot at work?"

"I guess so," James mumbled reluctantly.

Mr. Hyde had some arguments that were difficult to refute, but he probably did not change James's attitude with this one conversation. James needed to be shown repeatedly the benefits that could accrue from reading ability. He also needed to be helped to see that reading can be fun. Mr. Hyde found an informational book containing lots of pictures of heavy equipment and gave James the book to look through whenever he had some time. He did not choose to look at it immediately, but a couple of days later, when the children were having a supervised study time, he took out the book in preference to doing mathematics homework. At first he just thumbed through the pages, but eventually he began to pay closer attention to specific parts of the book. After a day or two, he returned the book and remarked that it was "okay." Mr. Hyde saw a possible avenue to helping James become a reader and pursued it for the rest of the year.

during literacy tasks, book-rich environments, and teachers who model reading also enhance motivation (Gambrell, 1996; Turner and Paris, 1995).

Children with poor opinions of themselves may be afraid to attempt a reading task because they are sure they will fail. They find it easier to avoid the task altogether and to develop "don't care" attitudes than to risk looking "dumb." Children with positive *self-concepts*, on the other hand, are generally not afraid to attack a reading task, since they believe they are going to succeed.

There are several ways to help children build positive self-concepts. First, in every possible way, the teacher should help the children feel accepted. A definite relationship exists between a teacher's attitude toward a child, as the child perceives it, and the child's self-concept. One of the best ways to make children feel accepted is for the teacher to share their interests, utilizing those interests in planning for reading instruction. Second, the teacher can help children feel successful by providing activities that are simple enough to guarantee satisfactory completion. Third, the teacher should avoid comparing a child with other children. Instead, reading progress should be compared with the child's own previous work.

Constructive Aspect of the Reading Process

The reader puts together input from sensory and perceptual channels with experiential background and affective responses and thereby constructs a personal meaning for the text. This meaning is based on the printed word but does not reside completely in it; rather, it is transformed by the information the reader brings to the text, the reader's feelings about the material, the purposes for the reading, and the context in which the reading takes place. Readers with different backgrounds of experience and different affective reactions will derive different meanings from the same text, as may those with divergent purposes and those reading under varying

DIVERSITY conditions. A person from the Middle East will understand an article about dissension among Middle Eastern countries differently than one from the United States. A person reading to find a single fact or a few isolated facts will derive a different meaning from an article than someone reading to get an overall picture of the topic. A person reading a horror story alone in the house at night may well construct a different understanding of the text from one reading the same story in broad daylight in a room full of family members.

● The Reading Process: Selected Theories

A theory is a set of assumptions or principles designed to explain phenomena. Theories that are based on good research and practical observations can be helpful when teachers are planning reading instruction, but teachers should not lose sight of the fact that current theories do not account for all aspects of this complex process. In addition, theories grow out of hypotheses—educated guesses. New information may be discovered that proves part or all of a theory invalid.

It would not be practical to present all the theories related to reading in the introductory chapter of a survey textbook. We have chosen to discuss three theoretical approaches—*subskill, interactive,* and *transactive theories*—to give you a feeling for the complexities inherent in choosing a theoretical stance. The choices that teachers make about types of instruction and emphases in instructional programs are affected by their theoretical positions concerning the reading process.

Subskill Theories

Some educators see reading as a set of subskills that children must master and integrate. They believe that, although good readers have learned and integrated these subskills so well that they use them automatically, beginning readers have not learned them all and may not integrate well those that they have learned. Beginning readers, therefore, may exhibit slow, choppy reading and perhaps have reduced comprehension, because the separate skills of word recognition take so much concentration. Teaching these skills until they become automatic and smoothly integrated is thus the approach these educators take to reading instruction (Weaver and Shonhoff, 1984). *Automaticity* is "the ability to perform a task with little attention" (Samuels, 1994, p. 819). It is evident when a high level of accuracy is combined with speed, and readers who read orally with good expression are exhibiting automaticity in word recognition.

Richard Smith and his colleagues (1978) assert that teachers need to teach specific skills in order to focus instruction. Otherwise, instruction in reading would be reduced to assisted practice—a long, laborious trial-and-error approach. Weaver and Shonhoff (1984) state that "although some research suggests that skilled reading is a single, holistic process, there is no research to suggest that children can learn to read and develop reading skill if they are taught using a method that treats reading as if it were a single process. Therefore, for instructional purposes, it is probably best to think of reading as a set of interrelated subskills" (p. 36).

There is research to support this approach. Samuels and Schachter (1984) report a study of one decoding subskill, recognizing words in isolation (sight words), which showed that "roughly 50 percent of the variability in oral reading of connected words is associated with how well one can read these words in isolation" (p. 40). Similarly, LaBerge and Samuels (1985) point out that a child who is slow in learning to read "often must be given extensive training on each of a variety of tasks, such as letter discrimination, letter-sound training, blending, etc. In this manner, a teacher becomes aware of the fact that letter recognition can be considered a skill itself" (p. 713). LaBerge and Samuels's hierarchical model of perceptual learning suggests that students master smaller units before larger ones and integrate them into larger units after mastery (Samuels and Schachter, 1984).

Since fluent readers have mastered each of the subskills to the point where they use and integrate the subskills automatically, they do not clearly see the dividing lines among these skills during their daily reading. "One of the hallmarks of the reader who learned the subskills rapidly is that he was least aware of them at the time, and therefore now has little memory of them as separate subskills" (LaBerge and Samuels, 1985, p. 714). Guthrie (1973) found that reading subskills correlated highly with one another for students who were good readers. The correlations among reading subskills for poor readers were low. These students seemed to be operating at a level of separate rather than integrated skills. Guthrie's findings led to the conclusion that "lack of subskill mastery and lack of integration of these skills into higher order units" were sources of disability among poor readers (Samuels and Schachter, 1984, p. 39).

Whereas beginning readers first focus on decoding and then switch their attention to comprehension, fluent readers decode automatically and thus can focus attention on comprehension. Samuels (1994) points out that although the meanings of familiar words may be automatic for skilled readers, "the ability to get the meaning of each word in a sentence, however, is not the same as the ability to comprehend a sentence. In comprehending a sentence one must be able to interrelate and combine the separate meanings of each of its words. From this point of view, comprehension is a constructive process of synthesis and putting word meanings together in special ways, much as individual bricks are combined in the construction of a house" (p. 820).

Those who teach a set of subskills as a means of instructing children in reading generally recognize the importance of practicing the subskills in the context of actual reading in order to ensure integration. But some teachers overlook this vital phase and erroneously focus only on the subskills, overlooking the fact that they are the means to an end and not an end in themselves. Samuels (1994) points out that students can build automaticity only by spending much time reading. Although he acknowledges the need for practice with important subskills, he cautions that practice time must also be "spent on reading easy, interesting, meaningful material" (p. 834).

Adams (1994) feels much the same way. She says, "Deep and ready working knowledge of letters, spelling patterns, and words, and of the phonological translations of all three, are of inescapable importance to both skillful reading and its acquisition—not because they are the be all or the end all of the reading process, but because they enable it" (p. 859). She points out that frequent broad reading is important in developing reading proficiency.

Interactive Theories

An interactive theoretical model of the reading process depicts reading as a combination of two types of processing—*top-down* (reader-based) and *bottom-up* (text-based)—in continuous interaction. In top-down processing, the act of reading begins with the reader generating hypotheses or predictions about the material, using visual cues in the material to test these hypotheses as necessary (Walberg, Hare, and Pulliam, 1981). For instance, the reader of a folktale that begins with the words "Once upon a time there was a man who had three sons …" forms hypotheses about what will happen next, predicting that there will be a task to perform or a beautiful princess to win over and that the older two sons will fail but the youngest will attain his goal. Because of these expectations, the reader may read the material fairly quickly, giving attention primarily to words that confirm the expectations. Close reading occurs only if the hypothesis formed is not confirmed and an atypical plot unfolds. Otherwise, the reader can skip many words while skimming for key words that move the story along. Processing of print obviously cannot be a totally top-down experience, because a reader must begin by focusing on the print (Gove, 1983).

In bottom-up processing, reading is initiated by examining the printed symbols and requires little input from the reader (Walberg, Hare, and Pulliam, 1981). Gove (1983) says, "Bottom-up models assume that the translation process begins with print, i.e., letter or word identification, and proceeds to progressively larger linguistic units, phrases, sentences, etc., ending in meaning" (p. 262). A reader using bottom-up processing might first sound out a word letter by letter and then pronounce it, consider its meaning in relation to the phrase in which it is found, and so on.

An interactive model assumes that students are simultaneously processing information from the print they are reading and information from their background knowledge. Recognition and comprehension of printed words and ideas are the result of using both types of information (Gove, 1983). Rumelhart's early model indicated that "at least for skilled readers, top-down and bottom-up processing occur simultaneously. ... Because comprehension depends on both graphic information and the information in the reader's mind, it may be obstructed when a critical skill or a piece of information is missing" (Harris and Sipay, 1985, p. 10). For example, a reader who is unable to use clues from the sentences or pictures that surround an unfamiliar word may fail to grasp the meaning of a word that is central to understanding the passage. Similarly, a reader who has no background knowledge about the topic may be unable to reconstruct the ideas the author is trying to convey.

Ruddell and Unrau (1994) consider a wider range of potential interactions by bringing social context into the picture, along with the reader and the text. They assert that "meaning results from the reader's meaning-construction process. That meaning is not entirely in either the text or the reader but is created as a result of the interactions among reader, text, teacher, and classroom community" (p. 1032).

Transactive Theories

Rosenblatt (1994) believes that "every reading act is an event, or a transaction involving a particular reader and ... a text, and occurring at a particular time in a particular context. ... The meaning does not reside ready-made 'in' the text or 'in' the reader but happens or comes into being during the transaction between reader and text" (p. 1061). Meaning results during the transaction. McGee (1992) points out that readers employ knowledge gained through past experiences to help them select interpretations, visualize the message, make connections between the new information and what they know, and relate affectively to the material. The transaction between reader and text is dynamic. Thus a single reader may construct an entirely different meaning from the same passage if he or she reads it at one time and then rereads it later, after gaining relevant personal experience that changes his or her interpretation. The context of the reading event has changed between these two transactions.

The reader is highly important when reading is viewed as a transaction, and the stance the reader chooses must be considered. The reader may focus on obtaining information from the text (an efferent stance) but may also focus on the experience lived through during the reading, the feelings and images evoked and the memories aroused by the text (an aesthetic stance). Both stances are appropriate at times, and it is up to the reader to choose the approach to the reading. Even when reading a single work, readers may shift their stances from more efferent to more aesthetic, or vice versa, but fiction and poetry should involve a more aesthetic stance (Probst, 1988; Rosenblatt, 1978, 1991; McGee, 1992). Beach and Hynds (1991) believe that reading must be viewed as constructing an evolving experience, instead of as ferreting out a static meaning. The readers' stances, beliefs, and attitudes affect their responses, as does the context.

Rosenblatt's idea of an efferent–aesthetic continuum helps teachers see that there are both cognitive and affective aspects of all reading activities for both fiction and nonfiction and that the relative importance of each aspect will vary with the text and the reading situation. Frager (1993) suggests encouraging a wider range of aesthetic responses to content area reading by asking readers what feelings the text aroused in them. Students should both think about the concepts and experience the feelings evoked by the words.

Goodman (1973, p. 31) sees reading as a psycholinguistic guessing game in which readers "select the fewest, most productive cues necessary to produce guesses which are right the first time." Goodman believes that, although the ability to combine letters to form words is related to learning to read, it has little to do with the process of fluent reading. A person who is reading for meaning does not always need to identify individual words; a reader can comprehend a passage without having identified all the words in it. The more experience a reader has had with language and the concepts presented, the fewer clues from visual configurations (graphophonic clues) he or she will need to determine the meaning of the material. Fluent readers make frequent use of *semantic clues* (meaning) and *syntactic clues* (word-order) within the material as well (Cooper and Petrosky, 1976). Goodman points out the importance of the reader's ability to anticipate material that he or she has not yet seen. He also stresses that readers bring to their reading all their accumulated experience, language development, and thought in order to anticipate meanings in the printed material (p. 34).

TIME for REFLECTION

Some people believe that, for the reader, meaning resides in the text. Others believe that the reader brings meaning to the text. Still others believe that, for the reader to comprehend the meaning fully, reading must involve using both the information in the text and the information that the reader brings to the text in the context in which the reading takes place. **What do *you* think, and why?**

Goodman acknowledges that Rosenblatt (1938/1983) has influenced his thinking (Aaron et al., 1990), and he has moved from a strictly psycholinguistic focus to embrace a transactive focus. "The reader … constructs a text during reading through transactions with the published text and the reader's schemata are also transformed in the process. … In the receptive processes (listening and reading), meaning is constructed through transactions with the text and indirectly through the text with the writer" (K. S. Goodman, 1985, p. 814). He now asserts that the text a writer constructs has a meaning potential, although the text itself does not have meaning. Readers will use this meaning potential to construct their own meaning (Goodman, 1994).

The transactive theory appeals to advocates of a whole language philosophy toward reading. These educators want students to be involved with authentic reading, writing, listening, and speaking activities; that is, they advocate activities that are not just contrived to teach particular skills but are designed to communicate. Whole language is a curricular philosophy, or belief system, in which the teacher is an initiator and mediator of learning experiences, a kidwatcher (observer of children), and a curriculum developer who links the curriculum to the learner. The social context for whole language instruction is a collaborative, mutually supportive, learner-centered classroom in which all learners are viewed positively and accepted as a part of the community of learners, regardless of individual differences. Language is seen as central to learning; whole literature selections are used in reading programs; writing and reading are connected; functional language, reading comprehension, and written expression are emphasized; and teachers and students, rather than textbooks and tests, are in control of the curriculum. There is no packaged set of materials to rely on. The teacher, with student input, must be the decision maker. Students are involved in making choices, self-evaluating, and taking responsibility for their learning (Goodman, 1992; Cullinan, 1992; Pahl and Monson, 1992; Oldfather, 1993; Walmsley and Adams, 1993; Moss and Noden, 1993/1994; Church, 1994; Watson, 1994). Students are motivated to learn when they are given opportunities to express themselves and have choices about their learning. They need to know that they will have a chance to share their ideas and products with others and that the teacher and other students will listen and respond to their spoken and written ideas (Oldfather, 1993).

As we discuss in Chapter 3, whole language classrooms are not devoid of skills instruction. Teachers can blend holistic instructional activities with systematic direct instruction (Spiegel, 1992; Yatvin, 1991). Phonics is taught, but not separately from reading and writing. Spelling and grammar are viewed as means to an end (Newman and Church, 1990).

LITERATURE

Many of the approaches to reading instruction mentioned in this book are frequently used by whole language teachers, as well as teachers who embrace other philosophies of language instruction. Many of these teachers use the language experience approach (discussed in Chapter 7) and some computer applications to learning (discussed in Chapter 11). These teachers make much use of literature with such teaching techniques as thematic literature units, literature circles, some variations of whole-class reading of a core book, and the individualized reading approach. Literature-based reading approaches are discussed in Chapters 7 and 8. Sustained Silent Reading, a technique in which everyone reads a self-selected book without interruption for a predetermined period of time, is a particularly appropriate technique for use in a school that embraces a whole language philosophy. (See more about this in Chapter 8.) The Classroom Scenario on page 21 describes a successful sustained silent reading period.

Resolving the Teacher's Dilemma: Taking a Balanced Approach

STANDARDS AND
ASSESSMENT

The current educational situation in many areas can pose a dilemma for teachers. As we discuss later in this chapter, teachers and students are held accountable for meeting standards of performance set by their state or school districts. In many cases, performance is monitored by standardized tests. In general, the standardized tests of reading consist of performance of isolated skill activities rather than reading of whole pieces of text and responding to the text in a variety of ways. To prepare their students to score well on standardized tests, teachers may choose to follow a subskill approach to reading, even if they would otherwise be more likely to follow an interactive or a transactive theory. Such teachers might have set up classrooms filled with activities related to reading and writing whole pieces of literature, rather than

Sustained Silent Reading

A group of educators visited a middle school in West Tennessee shortly after 8 o'clock one morning. When they entered the school, it was extremely quiet. They went directly to the office, where they found the secretary reading a paperback book. One member of the group explained that they had entered the building during the sustained silent reading period and would not be able to talk to anyone until it was over, because interruptions to the reading of students, teachers, and staff members were not allowed. The visitors walked quietly through the school, observing the reading that was going on in every classroom. In some classrooms, students were sitting in chairs in a variety of postures or were sprawled on the carpet on their backs or stomachs. All seemed to be completely absorbed in reading books, magazines, or newspapers. At the end of the period a bell rang, and the students, many reluctantly, put aside their reading materials and readied themselves for classwork. Some whispered excitedly to their neighbors, perhaps about the materials they had been reading. The overall impression the visitors received was that children and adults alike were pleased with the opportunity to read self-chosen material without interruption.

Analysis of Scenario

The use of sustained silent reading in this school obviously gave students the opportunity to read entire stories independently. The students were also allowed to select their own reading material, making it more likely that the material would be meaningful to them. Motivation to read was high under these conditions.

activities that focus on isolated skills, if they had been able to make their own decisions about what would be best for the students. Mosenthal (1989) suggests that researchers need to focus on the complementarity between the approaches (subskills and holistic) rather than on their incompatibility, in order to help teachers see how the two approaches can work together.

Today, many teachers employ a balanced approach to reading instruction in which they combine elements of direct skills instruction and elements of holistic instruction. They offer authentic literacy activities in the classroom but teach skills directly to help students succeed in those activities. Spiegel (1992) sees direct instruction as teaching children strategies to be used flexibly to meet reading needs and suggests blending the best of whole language and systematic direct instruction in reading strategies to help all children reach their full literacy potential. Strategies may be taught and then practiced using authentic materials, rather than worksheets or other forms of isolated drill.

The need for balance is recognized by educators from many philosophical backgrounds. For example, constructivist theory emphasizes student autonomy, student construction of meaning, and student interest. It depicts learners as active, involved, and creative, with the teacher coordinating and critiquing student construction. Airasian and Walsh (1997) point out that students can engage in construction of meaning as part of any teaching approach and that even memorization and rote learning may be useful parts of learning activities under some circumstances. "One's task is to find the right balance between the activities of constructing and receiving knowledge, given that not all aspects of a subject can or should be taught in the same way or be acquired solely through 'hands-on' or

Some people think that skills instruction is unnecessary if students are surrounded by print and immersed in a literacy-rich environment. Others think that systematic, direct skills instruction is necessary for a successful reading program. **What do *you* think, and why?**

student-centered means" (Airasian and Walsh, 1997, p. 447). Airasian and Walsh (1997) also advocate a balance between teacher involvement and noninvolvement in constructions.

Instruction should also maintain a balance between focusing on word recognition and focusing on comprehension, with word recognition viewed as a means to enable comprehension, not as an end in itself. Comprehension instruction should be emphasized from the very beginning. Children should not have to wait until they can sound out most words to have an emphasis on meaning.

Twelve Principles of Teaching Reading

Principles of teaching reading are generalizations about reading instruction based on research in the field of reading and on observation of reading practices. The principles listed here are not all-inclusive; many other useful generalizations about teaching reading have been made in the past and will continue to be made in the future. They are, however, the ones we believe are most useful in guiding teachers who are planning reading instruction.

> *Principle 1*   ***Reading is a complex act with many factors that must be considered.***

The discussion earlier in this chapter of the nine aspects of the reading process makes this principle clear. The teacher must understand all parts of the reading process in order to plan reading instruction wisely.

> *Principle 2*   ***Reading involves construction of the meaning represented by printed symbols.***

A person who fails to derive meaning from a passage has not been reading, even if he or she has pronounced every word correctly. Chapters 4, 5, and 6 focus on constructing meaning from reading materials. "In addition to obtaining information from the letters and words in a text, reading involves selecting and using knowledge about people, places, and things, and knowledge about texts and their organization. A text is not so much a vessel containing meaning as it is a source of partial information that enables the reader to use already-possessed knowledge to determine the intended meaning" (R. C. Anderson et al., 1985, p. 8).

Readers construct the meanings of passages by using both the information conveyed by the text and their prior knowledge, which is based on their past experiences. Obviously, different readers construct meaning in somewhat different ways because of their varied experiential backgrounds. Some readers do not have enough background knowledge to understand a text; others fail to make good use of the knowledge they have (R. C. Anderson et al., 1985). For example, suppose a text mentions how mountains can isolate a group of people living in them. Students familiar with mountainous areas will picture steep grades and rough terrain, which make road building difficult, and will understand the source of the isolation,

DIVERSITY

although the text never mentions it. Because students from different cultures may come to school with widely varying backgrounds of experiences, teachers must learn about the cultures from which their students come in order to understand the students' perspectives. In addition, language and culture are so tightly connected that "nothing comes from separating them because they have no meaning apart from each other" (Gunderson, 2000). Affective factors, such as the reader's attitudes toward the subject matter, also influence the construction of meaning, as does the context in which the reading takes place.

TECHNOLOGY   Student talk is important in constructing meaning. Through use of the Internet, student talk can be extended around the world, and the social aspect of constructing meaning can be taken to extended dimensions. The Internet is also helpful in encouraging construction of meaning because it supports the natural curiosity of the students by putting a large source of information within their reach, enhancing their opportunities to discover ideas for themselves (El-Hindi, 1998).

FAMILY   One problem with asking students to construct meaning actively, rather than "feeding" the "correct" meaning to them, arises when this approach to instruction and learning runs counter to parents' beliefs about education and the purpose of schooling. Constructivist approaches focus on the process of meaning construction,

DIVERSITY   rather than on products that demonstrate acquisition of information. Parents from other cultures may see this emphasis on process, rather than product, as the teacher's

STANDARDS AND ASSESSMENT   failure to do the "teaching." They may want their children to focus on the accumulation of knowledge that will lead to high test scores and the chance for higher education (Gunderson, 2000), rather than focusing on higher-order thinking and on constructing meaning from printed sources and experience.

Principle 3   *There is no one correct way to teach reading.*

Some methods of teaching reading work better for some children than for others. Each child is an individual who learns in his or her own way. Some children are visual learners; some are auditory learners; some are ***kinesthetic/tactile*** learners, who learn better through their senses of movement and touch. Some need to be instructed through a combination of ***modalities***, or avenues of perception, in order to learn. The teacher should differentiate instruction to fit the diverse needs of the students. Of course, some methods also work better for some teachers than they do for others.

TECHNOLOGY   Teachers need to be acquainted with a variety of methods, including ones that involve technology, so that they can help all of their students. Chapter 7 covers a number of approaches to reading instruction, and Chapter 11 discusses the use of technology in literacy instruction.

Principle 4   *Learning to read is a continuing process.*

Children learn to read over a long period of time, acquiring more advanced reading skills after they master prerequisite skills. Even after they have been introduced to all reading skills, the process of refinement continues. No matter how old they are or how long they have been out of school, readers continue to refine their reading skills. Reading skills require practice. If readers do not practice, their skills deteriorate; if they do practice, their skills continue to develop.

Principle 5 ***Students should be taught word recognition strategies that will allow them to unlock the pronunciations and meanings of unfamiliar words independently.***

Children cannot memorize all the words they will meet in print. Therefore, they need to learn techniques for figuring out unfamiliar words so that they can read when the assistance of a teacher, parent, or friend is not available. Chapter 3 focuses on word recognition strategies that children need.

Principle 6 ***The teacher should assess each student's reading ability and use the assessment as a basis for planning instruction.***

STANDARDS AND
ASSESSMENT

Teaching all children the same reading lessons and hoping to deal at one time or another with all the difficulties students encounter is a shotgun approach and should be avoided. Such an approach wastes the time of those children who have attained the skills currently being emphasized and may never meet some of the desperate needs of other children. Teachers can avoid this approach by using assessment instruments and techniques to pinpoint the strengths and weaknesses of each child in the classroom. Then they can either divide the children into needs groups for pertinent instruction or give each child individual instruction. Chapter 12 describes many useful tests and other assessment procedures.

Principle 7 ***Reading and the other language arts are closely interrelated.***

FAMILY

Reading—the interaction between a reader and written language through which the reader tries to reconstruct the writer's message—is closely related to the other language arts (listening, speaking, writing, viewing, and visually presenting). People learn to speak before they learn to read and write. Learning to read should be treated as an extension of the process of learning spoken language, a process that generally takes place in the home with little difficulty if children are given normal language input and feedback on their efforts to use language. Children's reading vocabularies generally consist largely of words in their oral language (listening and speaking) vocabularies. These are words for which they have previously developed concepts and therefore can comprehend.

A special relationship exists among listening, reading, and viewing, which are receptive phases of language, as opposed to the expressive phases of speaking, writing, and visually presenting. Mastering listening skills is important in learning to read, for direct association of sound, meaning, and word form must be established from the start. The ability to identify sounds heard at the beginning, middle, or end of a word and the ability to discriminate among sounds are essential to successful phonetic analysis of words. Listening skills also contribute to the interpretation of reading material.

Students' listening and viewing comprehension are generally superior to their reading comprehension in the elementary school years. Although receptive skills are not identical and each has its own advantages, they are alike in many ways. For example, all three are constructive processes. In reading, the reader constructs the message from a printed source with the help of background knowledge; in listening, the listener constructs the message from a spoken source with the help of that same background knowledge; and in viewing, the viewer constructs the message from a visual source, using the background knowledge.

Speaking, writing, and visually presenting are also constructive processes. The speaker puts together words in an attempt to convey ideas to one or more listeners; the writer combines words in print to convey ideas to readers; and the person giving a visual presentation puts together images, and sometimes words and sounds, to convey meaning to the viewer.

The connection between reading and writing is particularly strong. Readers must evaluate the accuracy of their message construction as they monitor their reading processes; they may revise the constructed meaning if the need is apparent in order to establish communication with the writer.

Starting with purposes for writing that affect their choice of ideas and the way these ideas are expressed, writers work to create written messages for others to read. In completing the writing task, they draw on their past experiences and their knowledge of writing conventions. As they work, they tend to read and review their material in order to evaluate its effectiveness and to revise it, if necessary.

One means of relating early writing experiences to reading experiences — the language experience approach—is described in Chapter 7. Chapters 7 and 8 describe having children construct written responses to their reading of literature. Writing is also sometimes used as a follow-up or enrichment activity in basal reading lessons.

The strategies and skills needed for the language arts are interrelated. For example, the need to develop and expand concepts and vocabulary, which is essential to reading, is evident in the entire language arts curriculum. Spoken, written, and visual messages are organized around main ideas and supporting details, and people listen, read, and view to identify the main ideas and supporting details conveyed in the material. Chapter 6 contains many examples of reading skills that have parallel listening skills and related writing and speaking skills.

Principle 8   *Using complete literature selections in the reading program is important.*

LITERATURE   Students need to experience the reading of whole stories and books to develop their reading skills. Reading isolated words, sentences, and paragraphs does not give them the opportunity to use their knowledge of language and story structure to the fullest, and reading overly simplified language both reduces the opportunities to use their language expertise and dampens interest in reading the material. Whole pieces of literature can include students' own writing and the writing of other children, as well as the works of commercial authors.

Principle 9   *Reading is an integral part of all content area instruction within the educational program.*

Teachers must consider the relationship of reading to other subjects within the curriculum of the elementary school. Frequently, other curricular areas provide applications for the skills taught in the reading period. Textbooks in the various content areas are often the main means of conveying concepts to students. Students also frequently are required to read library materials, magazines, and newspapers. If they are unable to read these materials with comprehension, they may fail to master important ideas in science, mathematics, social studies, and other areas of the curriculum. Students who have poor reading skills may therefore face failure in other

TECHNOLOGY 🖥️   areas of study because of the large amount of reading these areas often require. In addition, the need to write reports in social studies, science, health, and other areas can involve many reading and study skills: locating information; organizing information; and using the library and multimedia reference sources, including the Internet. Chapter 11 addresses the use of multimedia references and the Internet.

Teachers who give reading and writing instruction only within isolated periods and treat reading and writing as separate from the rest of the curriculum will probably experience frustration rather than achieving student change and growth. Although a definite period scheduled specifically for language instruction (listening, speaking, reading, writing, viewing, and visually presenting) may be recommended, this does not mean that teachers should ignore these areas when teaching content subjects. The ideal situation at any level is not "reading" and "writing" for separate time periods, followed by "study" of social science or science for the next period. Instead, although the emphasis shifts, language learning and studying should be integrated during all periods at all levels. Chapters 9, 10, and 13 elaborate on these points.

Principle 10   *The student needs to see that reading can be an enjoyable pursuit.*

It is possible for our schools to produce capable readers who do not read; in fact, today this is a common occurrence. Reading can be entertaining as well as informative. Teachers can help students realize this by reading stories and poems to them daily and setting aside a regular time for pleasure reading, during which many good books of appropriate levels and from many interest areas are readily available. Teachers can show children that reading is a good recreational pursuit by describing the pleasure they personally derive from reading in their spare time and by reading for pleasure in the children's presence. When the children read recreationally, the teacher should do this also, thereby modeling desired behavior. Pressures of tests and

LITERATURE 📚   reports should not be a part of recreational reading times. Students in literature-based reading instructional programs that include self-selection of reading materials and group discussion of chosen reading materials are likely to discover the enjoyable aspects of reading for themselves. Chapter 7 discusses such programs.

Principle 11   *Reading should be taught in a way that allows each child to experience success.*

The stage of the child's literacy development should be considered for all instructional activities throughout the grades. Not only when reading and writing instruction begins, but whenever instruction in any language strategy takes place, at all grade levels, teachers should consider each child's readiness for the instructional activity. If the child's literacy development is not adequate for the task, the teacher should adjust the instruction so that it is congruent with the student's literacy level. This may involve instruction to prepare the child to incorporate the new learning into his or her store of concepts.

Asking children to try to learn to read from materials that are too difficult for them ensures that a large number will fail. Teachers should give children instruction at their own levels of achievement, regardless of grade placement. Success generates success. If children are given a reading task at which they can succeed, they gain the confidence to attack in a positive way the other reading tasks they must perform. This greatly increases the likelihood of their success at these later tasks. In addition, some studies have shown that if a teacher expects students to be successful readers, they will in fact be successful. As Cambourne (2001, p. 785) has pointed out, "We usually achieve what we expect to achieve (or are expected to achieve by others); we fail when we expect to fail (or are expected by others to fail); we are more likely to engage with the demonstrations by those whom we regard as significant and who hold high expectations for us." Therefore, teachers should always provide instruction with the expectation that the students will be successful.

Teachers tend to place poor readers in materials that are too hard for them more frequently than they place good readers in such materials. Children who are given difficult material to read use active, comprehension-seeking behaviors less often than do children who are reading material they can understand with a teacher's assistance. Placing poor readers on levels that are too high tends to reinforce the inefficient reading strategies that emerge when material is too difficult, making it less likely that these readers will develop more efficient strategies. Although they do not have high expectations of success under any circumstances, their expectations of success decrease more after failure than do those of good readers (Bristow, 1985).

Teachers should provide poor readers with material they can read without undue focus on word recognition. This approach allows poor readers to focus on comprehending the text. Poor readers must be convinced that they will gain greater understanding during reading if they apply strategies they have learned (Bristow, 1985).

DIVERSITY ⊕   Asking children to read from materials that are not related to their backgrounds of experiences can also result in less successful experiences. In view of the wide cultural diversity found in schools today, teachers must be particularly sensitive to this problem and must provide relevant materials for children that offer them a chance for success.

Principle 12   *Encouragement of self-direction and self-monitoring of reading is important.*

Good readers direct their own reading, making decisions about how to approach particular passages, what reading speed is appropriate, and why they are reading the passages. They are able to decide when they are having difficulties with understanding and can take steps to remedy their misunderstandings (R. C. Anderson et al., 1985). When they do this, they are using ***metacognitive strategies***. Chapters 5 and 9 present more information about the way good readers read flexibly and monitor their reading.

Some people think reading should be taught only during reading class. Others think reading instruction should take place, as needed, throughout the entire day. What do *you* think, and why?

No matter what teaching approaches are used in a school or what patterns of organization predominate, these principles of teaching reading should apply. Each teacher should consider carefully his or her adherence or lack of adherence to such principles.

The Standards Movement

STANDARDS AND
ASSESSMENT

Many people, concerned that students are not achieving at high enough levels in reading, have developed, or have turned to educators to develop, standards that "define what students should learn" (Agnew, 2000, p. 1). Many states have developed literacy standards for students at each grade level.

Schmoker and Marzano (1999, p. 21) point out the importance of establishing "standards and expectations for reaching them that are clear, not confusing; essential, not exhaustive." Some states have standards that cover so much that it is not realistic to expect to meet them in the available time.

Professional organizations have also sought to develop standards in their curricular areas. The National Council of Teachers of English and the International Reading Association cooperatively developed a set of standards for the English language arts from kindergarten through twelfth grade. (See Example 1.2.) These standards specify a range of areas in the English language arts in which students must be proficient, rather than specifying levels of achievement (Smagorinsky, 1999).

SUMMARY

The reading act is composed of two major parts: the reading process and the reading product. The reading process has nine aspects — sensory, perceptual, sequential, experiential, thinking, learning, associational, affective, and constructive—that combine to produce the reading product, communication.

Three of the many types of theories about the reading process are subskill theories, interactive theories, and transactive theories. Subskill theories depict reading as a series of subskills that children must master so that they become automatic and smoothly integrated. Interactive theories depict reading as the interaction of two types of processing: top-down and bottom-up. Both types of processing are used to recognize and comprehend words. According to the bottom-up view, reading is initiated by the printed symbols (letters and words) and proceeds to larger linguistic units until the reader discovers meaning. According to the top-down view, reading begins with the reader's generation of hypotheses or predictions about the material and proceeds as the reader uses the visual cues in the material to test these hypotheses. Therefore, according to interactive theories, both the print and the reader's background are important in the reading process. Transactive theories depict every reading act as a transaction involving a reader and a text at a particular time in a specific context. Readers generate and test hypotheses about the reading material and get feedback from the material. Whole language activities fit well with the transactive theoretical stance, since the whole language philosophy embraces the idea

EXAMPLE 1.2   Standards for the English Language Arts

Sponsored by NCTE and IRA

The vision guiding these standards is that all students must have the opportunities and resources to develop the language skills they need to pursue life's goals and to participate fully as informed, productive members of society. These standards assume that literacy growth begins before children enter school as they experience and experiment with literacy activities — reading and writing, and associating spoken words with their graphic representations. Recognizing this fact, these standards encourage the development of curriculum and instruction that make productive use of the emerging literacy abilities that children bring to school. Furthermore, the standards provide ample room for the innovation and creativity essential to teaching and learning. They are not prescriptions for particular curriculum or instruction. Although we present these standards as a list, we want to emphasize that they are not distinct and separable; they are, in fact, interrelated and should be considered as a whole.

1. Students read a wide range of print and non-print texts to build an understanding of texts, of themselves, and of the cultures of the United States and the world; to acquire new information; to respond to the needs and demands of society and the workplace; and for personal fulfillment. Among these texts are fiction and nonfiction, classic and contemporary works.

2. Students read a wide range of literature from many periods in many genres to build an understanding of the many dimensions (e.g., philosophical, ethical, aesthetic) of human experience.

3. Students apply a wide range of strategies to comprehend, interpret, evaluate, and appreciate texts. They draw on their prior experience, their interactions with other readers and writers, their knowledge of word meaning and of other texts, their word identification strategies, and their understanding of textual features (e.g., sound-letter correspondence, sentence structure, context, graphics).

4. Students adjust their use of spoken, written, and visual language (e.g., conventions, style, vocabulary) to communicate effectively with a variety of audiences and for different purposes.

5. Students employ a wide range of strategies as they write and use different writing process elements appropriately to communicate with different audiences for a variety of purposes.

6. Students apply knowledge of language structure, language conventions (e.g., spelling and punctuation), media techniques, figurative language, and genre to create, critique, and discuss print and non-print texts.

7. Students conduct research on issues and interests by generating ideas and questions, and by posing problems. They gather, evaluate, and synthesize data from a variety of sources (e.g., print and non-print texts, artifacts, people) to communicate their discoveries in ways that suit their purpose and audience.

8. Students use a variety of technological and information resources (e.g., libraries, databases, computer networks, video) to gather and synthesize information and to create and communicate knowledge.

9. Students develop an understanding of and respect for diversity in language use, patterns, and dialects across cultures, ethnic groups, geographic regions, and social roles.

10. Students whose first language is not English make use of their first language to develop competency in the English language arts and to develop understanding of content across the curriculum.

11. Students participate as knowledgeable, reflective, creative, and critical members of a variety of literacy communities.

12. Students use spoken, written, and visual language to accomplish their own purposes (e.g., for learning, enjoyment, persuasion, and the exchange of information).

Source: Standards for the English Language Arts, by the International Reading Association and the National Council of Teachers of English. Copyright 1996 by the International Reading Association and the National Council of Teachers of English. Reprinted with permission.

of encouraging authentic transactions with text. This philosophy also encourages collaborative, learner-centered classroom environments, much reading and writing of whole selections, and student choice.

Standards for literacy and other language arts have been developed by many states. The National Council of Teachers of English and the International Reading Association have cooperatively developed a set of standards for the English language arts.

Some principles related to reading instruction that may be helpful to teachers include the following:

❶ Reading is a complex act with many factors that must be considered.

❷ Reading involves construction of the meaning represented by printed symbols.

❸ There is no one correct way to teach reading.

❹ Learning to read is a continuing process.

❺ Students should be taught word recognition skills that will allow them to unlock the pronunciations and meanings of unfamiliar words independently.

❻ The teacher should assess each student's reading ability and use the assessment as a basis for planning instruction.

❼ Reading and the other language arts are closely interrelated.

❽ Using complete literature selections in the reading program is important.

❾ Reading is an integral part of all content area instruction within the educational program.

❿ The student needs to see that reading can be an enjoyable pursuit.

⓫ Reading should be taught in a way that allows each child to experience success.

⓬ Encouragement of self-direction and self-monitoring of reading is important.

TEST YOURSELF

True or False

_____ 1. Over a period of time a single, clear-cut definition of reading has emerged.

_____ 2. Reading is a complex of many skills.

_____ 3. Faulty eye movements usually cause serious reading problems.

_____ 4. Perception involves interpretation of sensation.

_____ 5. Prereading questions can affect the way students think while reading.

_____ 6. The more meaningful learning is to a child, the more rapidly associative learning takes place.

_____ 7. Word calling and reading are synonymous.

_____ 8. Teachers go to school so that they can learn the one way to teach reading.

_____ 9. People can continue to refine their reading skills long after their formal schooling is over.

_____ 10. Assessing the reading problems of every child in a class is a waste of a teacher's valuable time.

_____ 11. Assessment can help a teacher plan appropriate instruction for all children in a class.

_____ 12. Reading and the other language arts are closely interrelated.

_____ 13. Content area instruction should not have to be interrupted for teaching of reading strategies; reading instruction should remain strictly within a special reading period.

_____ 14. Understanding the importance of reading is not important to a child's reading progress.

_____ 15. Teachers should stress reading for enjoyment as well as for information.

_____ 16. Reading seems to fit in the "skill" category of behavior.

_____ 17. Current theories about reading account for all aspects of the reading process.

_____ 18. No research supports the view that reading is a set of subskills that must be mastered and integrated.

_____ 19. A bottom-up model of the reading process assumes that reading is initiated by the printed symbols, with little input required from the reader.

_____ 20. According to an interactive model of reading, parallel processing of information from print and from background knowledge takes place.

_____ 21. Reading involves constructing the meaning of a written passage.

_____ 22. Reading and writing are both constructive processes.

_____ 23. Teachers give good readers materials that are too hard for them more often than they give poor readers such materials.

_____ 24. Metacognitive processes are self-monitoring processes.

_____ 25. Whole language teachers personally make all of the decisions about classroom materials and activities.

_____ 26. Transactive theories of the reading process take into account the reader, the text, and the context in which the reading takes place.

_____ 27. A transactive theory would support the position that the meaning resides solely in the text.

_____ 28. Professional organizations have played a part in developing standards for the English language arts.

For your journal …

❶ Study the following definitions of reading, which have been suggested by well-known authorities. Indicate in your journal which aspect or combination of aspects of the reading process each definition emphasizes most.

a. "Reading is a process in which information from the text and the knowledge possessed by the reader act together to produce meaning." (Richard C. Anderson et al., *Becoming a Nation of Readers.* Washington, D.C.: National Institute of Education, 1985, p. 8.)

b. Reading is "a sampling, selecting, predicting, comparing and confirming activity in which the reader selects a sample of useful graphic cues based on what he sees and what he expects to see." (Kenneth Goodman, quoted in *The Literacy Dictionary: The Vocabulary of Reading and Writing,* edited by Theodore L. Harris and Richard E. Hodges. Newark, Del.: International Reading Association, 1995, p. 207.)

c. "Reading means getting meaning from certain combinations of letters. Teach the child what each letter stands for and he can read." (Rudolph Flesch, *Why Johnny Can't Read and What You Can Do About It.* New York: Harper & Row, 1986, pp. 2–3.)

d. "Reading is a process of looking at written language symbols, converting them into overt or covert speech symbols, and then manipulating them so that both the direct (overt) and implied (covert) ideas intended by the author may be understood." (Lawrence E. Hafner and Hayden B. Jolly, *Teaching Reading to Children,* 2d ed. New York: Macmillan, 1982, p. 4.)

e. "Reading is thinking … reconstructing the ideas of others." (Robert Karlin, *Teaching Elementary Reading: Principles and Strategies,* 3d ed. New York: Harcourt Brace Jovanovich, 1980, p. 7.)

f. "Reading involves the identification and recognition of printed or written symbols which serve as stimuli for the recall of meaning built up through past experience, and further the construction of new meanings through the reader's manipulation of relevant concepts already in his possession. The resulting meanings are organized into thought processes according to the purposes that are operating in the reader." (Miles A. Tinker and Constance M. McCullough, *Teaching Elementary Reading,* 4th ed. Englewood Cliffs, N.J.: Prentice-Hall, 1975, p. 9.)

g. "Reading involves nothing more than the correlation of a sound image with its corresponding visual image, that is, the spelling." (Leonard Bloomfield and Clarence L. Barnhart, *Let's Read: A Linguistic Approach.* Detroit: Wayne State University Press, 1961, dustjacket.)

h. "Reading typically is the bringing of meaning to rather than the gaining of meaning from the printed page." (Henry P. Smith and Emerald V. Dechant, *Psychology in Teaching Reading.* Englewood Cliffs, N.J.: Prentice-Hall, 1961, p. 22.)

❷ Note the points of agreement in the various definitions given in item 1.

❸ Find more recent definitions of reading in this text or in journal articles, and compare them with the definitions in item 1.

❹ After studying the principles of reading instruction presented in this chapter, see if you can formulate other principles based on your reading in other sources.

... and your portfolio

Write a description of the theoretical stance on reading instruction that makes the most sense to you. Give reasons for your position.

2 Emergent Literacy

SETTING OBJECTIVES

When you finish reading this chapter, you should be able to

- Discuss the relationship between cognitive development and language learning.
- Understand the concept of *emergent literacy*.
- List some features of a literacy-rich classroom environment.
- Explain the influence of the home on a child's early literacy development.
- Discuss the roles of listening comprehension and oral expression in the development of literacy.
- Identify some ways in which children learn to read in an emergent literacy classroom.
- Explain how children's growth in writing occurs.

This chapter opens with a discussion of the close relationship between cognitive development and language learning. Jean Piaget's and Lev Vygotsky's theories are considered, and attention is given to developmentally appropriate practice. The whole chapter is based on a current view of beginning reading, a view supporting the position that during early childhood and beyond, youngsters go through a period of **emergent literacy**, or a developing awareness of the interrelatedness of oral and written language (Teale and Sulzby, 1989). The word *emergent* implies that development occurs from within the child, that it happens gradually over time, that some fundamental abilities for making sense of the world must already exist within the child, and that *literacy* (the ability to read and write) will emerge when conditions are right (Hall, 1987).

The teacher in an emergent literacy classroom provides many opportunities for language development. A central emergent literacy concept is that most children know a great deal about literacy from early experiences in the home, and the teacher should build on this knowledge when planning classroom learning activities. Literacy-rich environments nurture growth in reading and writing and should offer children authentic purposes for learning language. As in the home, reading and writing should develop concurrently through the use of a wide variety of literacy experiences and materials.

Chapter 2 Organization

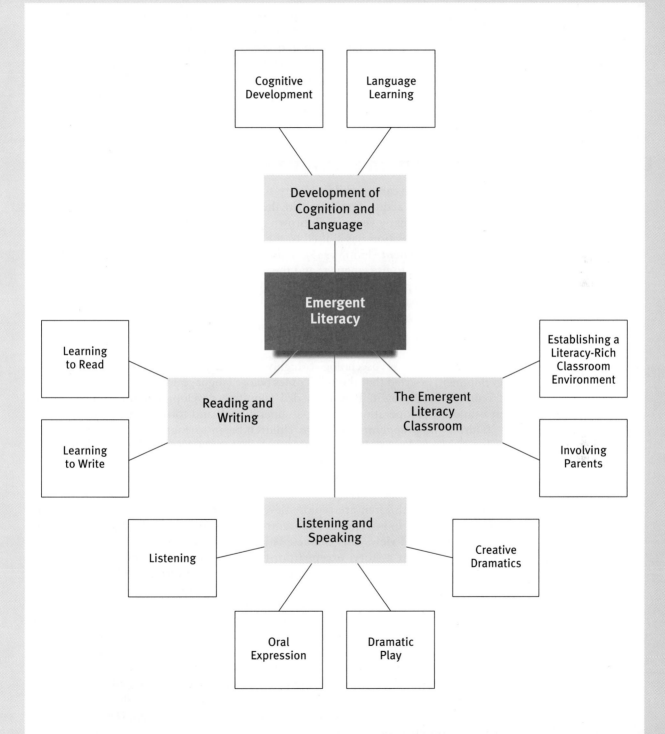

Cognitive Development

Language Learning

Development of Cognition and Language

Emergent Literacy

Learning to Read

Learning to Write

Reading and Writing

The Emergent Literacy Classroom

Establishing a Literacy-Rich Classroom Environment

Involving Parents

Listening and Speaking

Listening

Oral Expression

Dramatic Play

Creative Dramatics

The chapter presents a variety of ways that teachers can facilitate language development in young children. It discusses ideas for enhancing listening comprehension and oral expression and gives special attention to informal drama as a means of stimulating such development. Then it examines the ways that children learn to read and write by applying knowledge they have gained from their background experiences and their familiarity with print. Strategies for encouraging children to use invented spellings are considered for promoting both writing and reading.

Development of Cognition and Language

During preschool years, a child's ability to understand and use language develops rapidly. Language acquisition has held the interest and attention of linguists and psychologists for many years (Lightbrown and Spada, 1999). The study of language development in isolation has shifted to the study of language learning in relation to ***cognitive development*** (Finn, 1985). This means there is a connection between the way children learn to use language and the way they grow in their ability to know and understand concepts or ideas. Thought and language are closely related; language is a vehicle for understanding and communicating thoughts.

● Cognitive Development

Jean Piaget, a Swiss psychologist highly respected for his theory of cognitive development, asserted that thought comes before language and that language is a way of representing thought. Piaget divided cognitive development into four periods: sensorimotor, preoperational, concrete-operational, and formal-operational.

During the ***preoperational stage***, children begin to engage in symbolic thought by representing ideas and events with words and sentences, drawings, and dramatic play (Parkay, 1998). As they begin to use symbols to stand for spoken words, they realize that writing represents meaning, a concept that is basic to reading comprehension (Waller, 1977).

In this stage, children are rapidly developing concepts but are limited in their ability to use adult logic. They are egocentric; that is, they consider things only from their own points of view. This characteristic prevents children from thinking clearly about the events in a story, except from their own limited perspectives. Although most children at this stage are unable to state the rules governing the syntax of their primary language, they do demonstrate syntactic or grammatical awareness in their speech; that is, they are able to use words in a logical order as they form sentences.

Children at the preoperational level lack many of the concepts needed to understand reading and writing processes, and they are often frustrated when teachers expect them to perform such beginning reading tasks as memorizing rules and deciding which words follow a rule, understanding that a single letter can represent multiple sounds, and changing letters to sounds and back to letters (Harp, 1987). Children at this level would probably be more successful in classrooms with a wide variety of language materials and experiences that would allow them to form their own concepts about print.

DIVERSITY 🌐

Not all children go through Piaget's stages at the same ages; in fact, children may be advanced in some areas, displaying many of the skills characteristic of one stage, while they have not mastered other skills characteristic of that same stage (Sameroff and McDonough, 1996–1997). Such factors as the child's individual traits, the home environment, the type of support given, and the child's sensory-perceptual experiences, cultural context, and emotional involvement account for much of the variability in the ages at which children move from one stage to another (Fortson and Reiff, 1995; Sameroff and McDonough, 1996–1997; Snow, Burns, and Griffin, 1998).

STANDARDS AND ASSESSMENT 🖊

Realizing that children in any classroom are at a variety of levels, the teacher should apply *developmentally appropriate practice*, a framework or an approach for working with young children in which the teacher considers each child's competencies and adjusts instruction accordingly (Gestwicki, 1995; Richey and Wheeler, 2000). This practice is based on Piaget's theory that a child's education depends on finding a match between the curriculum and the child's level of thinking (Elkind, 1989). Knowledge of developmental stages indicates which practices are appropriate for beginning readers and writers (such as dictating stories, illustrating a field trip, and enjoying picture books) and which practices (such as isolated skill development and worksheets) are inappropriate (Gestwicki, 1995).

Developmentally appropriate activities promote self-esteem because children feel good about themselves when they complete tasks successfully. Self-esteem affects how well a child performs in school, and it should be established early because self-concept becomes more difficult to change as the child grows older (Sameroff and McDonough, 1996–1997). Negative influences on self-esteem include too-difficult learning tasks, teaching methods that ignore natural learning styles, and

> **TIME for REFLECTION**
>
> Some researchers believe that environmental factors greatly influence a child's language acquisition and cognitive development. What factors do *you* believe affect language development, and why?

unreasonably high expectations (Gestwicki, 1995). Some teaching procedures cover a range of abilities so that each child can experience success within a whole-class setting. For example, during shared book reading, some children may simply be learning directionality (directional orientation) by following the pointer from left to right; others may be acquiring letter-sound correspondences; and a few may be matching printed words to spoken words. Because each child participates at some level, each can feel successful.

FAMILY 👥

The Russian developmental theorist Lev Vygotsky stated that childhood experiences give rise to two different groups of concepts—*spontaneous* and *scientific* (Dixon-Krauss, 1996; Vygotsky, 1986). Vygotsky defines spontaneous concepts as those that children learn informally in the course of everyday concrete experiences at home and elsewhere. Verbal interactions with parents and others help children gain meaning from these experiences. Vygotsky defines scientific concepts as those that children learn during systematic classroom instruction when teachers present information. In other words, spontaneous concepts result from what children directly see or manipulate, and scientific concepts help children formalize their understandings as the teacher transmits knowledge verbally. Therefore, children need exposure to a wide variety of experiences, combined with structured class activities, in order to advance in cognitive development.

Vygotsky also suggested that children's cognitive development occurs through social experiences with others, especially those who can help children expand their thinking or other skills. Vygotsky's **zone of proximal development** is the span between a child's actual skill level and his or her potential level with assistance, or the difference between what a child can do alone and what the child can do with help (Vygotsky, 1986). The teacher can be most effective by serving as a mediating adult within this zone. As such, the teacher provides **scaffolding**, offering support that is gradually withdrawn as learners become capable of doing for themselves. With beginning readers, one way that a teacher creates a scaffold is by taking the lead during interactive storybook reading and then gradually turning the responsibility for interaction over to the students (Dixon-Krauss, 1996).

● Language Learning

Developmental learning occurs naturally, with minimal instruction, as a child grows up. It "is highly individual and noncompetitive; it is short on teaching and long on learning; it is self-regulated rather than adult-regulated; it goes hand in hand with the fulfillment of real life purposes; it emulates the behavior of people who model the skill in natural use" (Holdaway, 1979, p. 14). Speech develops in this way, and many educators argue that literacy should develop in a similar manner.

Language learning is a continuous, interactive, and purposeful process (Loughlin and Martin, 1987). Children learn to speak without instruction by imitating speech sounds and observing the interactions of language users. Language learning is more than imitation, however, because each individual constructs language according to personal needs and motivations. The child acquires speech through immersion in a language environment that provides speech models, motivation for speaking, and interactions with other speakers. The beginning speaker engages in trial and error and takes risks to establish communications with others.

A child's early attempts at language are intuitive; that is, the child uses language reasonably well but lacks *metalinguistic awareness,* the ability to think about language and manipulate it objectively. For example, a youngster may say, "I want some candy," but may be unable to tell how many words were spoken or recognize that this group of words is called a *sentence.* Many children can use language that they cannot describe in linguistic terms, such as *word, sentence, sound,* and *letter* (Hare, 1984; Lightbrown and Spada, 1999). A teacher who wishes to develop children's skill in recognizing words as basic elements of speech might use the Model Activity on page 39.

It is important to realize that children develop an understanding of the concept of *word* gradually through many experiences. Also, because individual children are at various developmental levels for acquiring this concept, for some the lesson will confirm what they were already beginning to realize, whereas for others, who are less ready, the lesson will have little or no meaning.

Because many children fail to understand linguistic terminology, they cannot make sense of instruction based on these terms. If a child does not understand the meanings of language-related terms, he or she must experience considerable confusion when a teacher says, "Look at the *middle letter* of this *word.* The *vowel* has its *short sound* because it is followed by a *consonant.*"

MODEL ACTIVITIES

Recognition of the Concept of *Word*

Make two copies of a chart story based on an experience that children have shared. Run your fingers under the first sentence on one of the charts as you say to the children: "Read this sentence with me." Then use your hands to block off individual words as you say to them: "Look at the groups of letters between the spaces. We call each group of letters a *word*." Ask them: "How many words are in this sentence?" Do the same thing with the other sentences on the chart. Then cut the sentences into strips and ask several children to cut the strips into words. Give each child a word. Say to the children: "Can you find your word on our other chart? If you can, put your word with the word on the chart."

LITERATURE   Having children perform isolated drills and memorize rules without understanding their meanings is unlikely to help them learn to read. Beginning reading instruction should be based on language experiences and predictable or repetitive stories. It is the teacher's responsibility to provide a literacy-rich environment, ask questions about language and help children discover answers, read to and with the children, provide authentic reading and writing tasks, and encourage and guide children in their developing sense of language.

The Emergent Literacy Classroom

FAMILY   Emergent literacy is based on the assumption that language learning occurs naturally in the home and community as children see print and understand its function in their environment. They learn about literacy from adult models, particularly family members, and their knowledge of reading and writing develops concurrently. Before they understand letter-sound associations, they scribble messages or draw letterlike forms that have meaning for them and then "read" their messages to others. Children who have quite naturally acquired basic concepts about print are members of the literacy club (F. Smith, 1988), and researchers have found that many kindergarten children do indeed understand a great deal about how language works, as in the following examples (Mavrogenes, 1986; McLane and McNamee, 1990):

1 They make sense out of the writing in their environment by relating words (such as *McDonald's*) to corresponding places (a restaurant).

2 They expect print to be meaningful and to communicate ideas.

3 They understand some characteristics of written language, such as directionality, spacing, sequencing, and form.

4 They have some knowledge of letter names, auditory and visual discrimination, and correspondence between written and spoken words. (Auditory and visual discrimination were introduced in Chapter 1.)

5 They know what books are and how to use them.

FAMILY What the child learns about language at home should be the foundation for literacy learning in the classroom, and it makes sense for continued language growth to occur in much the same way that it did during the preschool years. In other words, language learning in the classroom should grow out of the child's natural curiosity about language, functional use of language in authentic situations, and experimentation with ways to use language for effective communication.

Early experiences with written language that may occur during the first year of life, such as playing with alphabet blocks and listening to stories read from books, lay the foundation for a lifelong process of learning to read and write (Teale and Sulzby, 1989). Children progress through developmental stages in oral language (from babbling to mature speech) and written language (from scribbling to legible writing), moving toward ever-higher levels of language proficiency. Thus, literacy evolves in a natural, connected way over an extended period of time as the learner discovers new insights into language and how it works.

Reading and writing develop concurrently, with teacher guidance and encouragement. This does not mean skills are unimportant; indeed, children must learn them to become successful readers, writers, and speakers. The teacher's role is one of setting conditions that enable children to explore language and make discoveries that will lead them to internalize reading and writing skills. The teacher is there both to provide *direct instruction*, teacher-initiated strategy instruction, and to assist learners and intervene when they need help.

DIVERSITY The teacher must build on children's existing knowledge about language by understanding each child and providing developmentally appropriate literacy experiences. It is important to remember that every child who enters school is an individual with a unique personality, a specific set of experiences, and special interests. Diversity is on the rise in today's classrooms. Children vary in their racial, ethnic, cultural, and economic backgrounds, as well as in their physical and mental abilities (Jasmine, 1995). Although most children come to the classroom using oral language, they are likely to have many misconceptions and incompletely formed concepts about written language. Some children may be learning oral, as well as written, English for the first time.

Some students fail to acquire the skills they need to achieve success. Circumstances that place them at risk include (1) low teacher expectations; (2) failure to achieve in a competitive school structure, particularly for children with academic, functional, or physical disabilities; and (3) family stress or instability, low socioeconomic background, and low self-perception regarding school (Bertrand, 1995). According to Kenneth Goodman (1986), teachers should accept children as natural and curious learners, recognize their special competencies and needs, find ways to serve them, and support them with patience and encouragement.

Children value their ability to make choices—what to do, with whom to work, where to work, which books to read, and how best to do chosen tasks (Rasinski, 1988). Freedom to choose enables children to make decisions and self-direct their learning. From a study involving six year olds, Fresch (1995) found that children select books and activities that meet special needs, such as facing a new challenge, talking with friends about reading and writing, and building confidence through familiar reading. Children can even help create curriculum if their teacher considers

CLASSROOM SCENARIO

Freedom to Choose

Following a unit on giants that included a section on whales, a prefirst grader chose to draw pictures of whales during language workshop. Sprawled on the floor in a corner of the room, Danny carefully sketched a different kind of whale in each of six frames of large segmented paper to be used for a roll movie. He marked the distinguishing features of each whale and then labeled each picture by copying the name of the type of whale. For Danny, such sustained attention was unusual, but whales fascinated him.

Analysis of Scenario

When children are free to choose their activities, their concentration and determination enable them to accomplish remarkable tasks.

their interests, concerns, and inquiries when planning instruction (Fallon and Allen, 1994). The Classroom Scenario above illustrates the value of allowing children to make choices.

● Establishing a Literacy-Rich Classroom Environment

By establishing literacy-rich environments, teachers can encourage children to become aware of purposes for reading and writing. Charts on which teachers record dictations about students' experiences, as well as labels for identifying objects, remind students that print communicates meaning. Attractively displayed books invite children to read, and writing materials at play centers encourage them to write lists and memos (Booth, 1994).

FAMILY Many children learn to read ***environmental print*** — words they frequently see around them — long before they enter school. Teachers can link the home/community environment with that of the classroom by displaying environmental print, including advertisements and promotional materials for familiar products such as toothpaste and popular cereals (Neuman and Roskos, 1993; Sabey and Squier, 1993). Another advantage of using environmental print is that it is free and readily available. Often children bring examples to share, read them, and display them for others to read. Using the children's knowledge of environmental words, the teacher can begin teaching letter-sound relationships. See the Model Activity on page 42.

The classroom environment should provide opportunities for language growth that are similar to those provided in a natural home environment (Holdaway, 1979; Cunningham and Allington, 1999). Here are some guidelines based on this concept (Fisher, 1989; Wood and Nurss, 1988; Fortson and Reiff, 1995; Salinger, 1996).

❶ Provide a wide variety of materials for purposeful writing and reading.

❷ Place labels and key words around the room at the children's eye level.

❸ Organize the room so that children can follow the classroom routine and take care of their belongings independently.

❹ Display children's work so that they can see it and discuss it with others.

MODEL ACTIVITIES   Environmental Print

Since you have been encouraging the children to share examples of environmental print, they have responded enthusiastically. Today, as the children present their treasures, you notice a teaching opportunity. Say: "Tina and Jeff, will you please tell us what you brought?" (Tina has a label from a pizza box, and Jeff has an empty bag of potato chips.) Then say: "Who can tell me the name of the letter we see at the beginning of *pizza*? What letter do we see at the beginning of *potato chip*? Now let's say these words and listen to see if they sound alike at the beginning."

When the children have identified the letter and realized that the words begin with the same sound, say: "Can you find another word in the room that starts with the same letter?" When Carole finds the word *party* in a chart story about last week's Halloween party, ask: "Does *party* begin with the same sound we hear at the beginning of *pizza* and *potato chip*?" When the children reply affirmatively, put the letter *p* at the top of a chart and write *pizza*, *potato chip*, and *party* under the letter. Say: "Let's read these words again and listen for the sound that *p* makes. When we find other words that begin with the letter *p*, we can add them to our chart."

TIME for REFLECTION

Some teachers believe they should decorate the classroom with attractive displays so that children enter an intriguing, welcoming room on the first day of school. Other teachers prefer to leave the classroom nearly bare until the children create their own displays and charts; these teachers feel that children will develop a sense of ownership and pride if their contributions are recognized. What do *you* think, and why?

5 Encourage children to compose stories from wordless picture books and to respond creatively to literature.

6 Provide opportunities for expressing ideas, thoughts, and feelings through talk.

7 Immerse children in literature and in early drawing, writing, and read-along experiences.

8 Organize areas of the classroom into learning centers that contain varied and interesting materials that invite students to become engaged in a particular theme. (Learning centers are discussed in more detail in Chapter 13.)

FAMILY ● **Involving Parents**

It is important that parents provide a positive environment for their children's emerging literacy. Parents need to become aware that they are their children's first teachers and that the language experiences they provide will have a powerful effect on the children's growth in literacy. Teachers can help parents better understand and execute their critical role in promoting early literacy by encouraging them to respond enthusiastically to their children's curiosity about print. The continuity — or lack of continuity—between literacy experiences at home and in school strongly affects learning (McLane and McNamee, 1990; Routman, 1988; National Reading Panel, 2000).

DIVERSITY 🌐 Nistler and Maiers (2000) suggest strengthening the connection between home and school through innovative family literacy programs. Consistent interaction between parents and teachers, recognition of the diversity of family backgrounds, and viewing the role of parents and teachers as partners are some characteristics of an effective family literacy program. Many educators promote family literacy programs that encourage adult learners to enhance their own literacy skills while promoting the literacy of their children (Morrow and Neuman, 1995). One school-based family literacy program, in which 95 percent of the families are members of minority groups with low socioeconomic backgrounds, offers support in language and literacy development as it increases parental awareness of the importance of reading books to further their children's education. Specifically, the program involves parents in planning, includes workshops, invites parent volunteers to read or tell stories to children, provides books for children to take home and share with parents, and encourages teachers to communicate with parents regularly and to suggest ideas for them to try at home (Come and Fredericks, 1995).

Teachers can offer parents the following suggestions for guiding literacy development at home:

1. Read picture books, beginning at infancy.
2. Listen patiently and supportively when the child struggles to express an idea, and respond appropriately.
3. Share letters that come in the mail so that the child understands that writing can communicate messages.
4. Point out and read familiar signs, such as ones that say *Wal-Mart, Wendy's,* and *Stop.* Encourage the child to read them too.
5. Provide writing materials (including computers, if possible) and encourage their use for writing messages, shopping lists, and letters.
6. Model good reading practices by reading books for your own pleasure. Explain why you are enjoying your book.
7. Carry on conversations with the child. Answer questions and explain "why" and "how."
8. Share newspapers and magazines. Encourage the child to find familiar words that appear in advertisements.
9. Sing songs, do finger plays, recite nursery rhymes, and play guessing games.
10. Take the child with you on visits and trips. Use specific terms when discussing the experience, such as *flight attendant, pilot, gate,* and *baggage area.*
11. Involve the child in activities around the home, such as cooking, gardening, and paying bills. Point out the usefulness of recipes, instructions on seed packets, and checkbooks.
12. Visit the children's section of the library; let the child get a library card and check out books frequently.
13. Read together cereal boxes, menus, place mats, street signs, coupons, and other forms of print.
14. Encourage the child to "talk like a book" when sharing a storybook with you.

DIVERSITY 🌐   ⓯ Listen to stories or books recorded on audiotapes. These are especially helpful for parents who do not speak English at home.

LITERATURE 📖   Because of the importance of story reading with children, teachers might offer parents some specific pointers. Story reading can be a pleasurable experience for both the reader and the child, especially when accompanied by a lively verbal exchange about the story and the illustrations. Research on home storybook reading has supported the following interactive behaviors for their positive effects on literacy: questioning, praising, offering information, directing discussion, relating concepts to life experiences, modeling dialogue and responses, and sharing personal reactions (Strickland and Morrow, 1990). Here are examples of appropriate questions and comments based on *The Three Little Pigs:*

> How is this little pig's house different from our house?
>
> Uh-oh, that wolf is going to cause trouble! Can you read this part with me? (*I'll huff, and I'll puff, and I'll blow your house down.*)
>
> What do you think will happen next?
>
> That's a good idea! Let's read so that we can find out for sure.
>
> I think this third little pig is pretty smart. What do you think?

By sharing books with their children, parents can make them aware of many print conventions. Behaviors such as pointing to words and letters, talking about words with similar sounds, and observing upper- and lower-case letters occur naturally during parent-child reading. Smolkin and Yaden (1992) found that when parents read with their children, the children were learning to use correct linguistic terms (for example, *letter* and *word*) and becoming aware of directionality, letter forms, and sound-letter relationships. In addition, they were learning new word meanings and using prior knowledge to make sense of text.

Students in an emergent literacy classroom are often encouraged to draw and write, or *drite*, a combination of the two. Students are also encouraged to write without corrections made for spelling or handwriting. Teachers in emergent literacy classrooms recognize the importance of allowing students in the early scribbling stage to share their writing efforts without the demands of revisions (Cunningham and Allington, 1999). Parents unaccustomed to emergent literacy classrooms may expect their children to bring home graded worksheets and may be dismayed by child-created stories using invented spelling. The teacher should communicate with parents, perhaps through weekly newsletters or regular parent workshops, to inform them about classroom practices (Enz, 1995).

Listening and Speaking

The language skills children have learned at home are the foundation for their further language development. Throughout the school day, children should have many opportunities to develop oral communication skills. In the Classroom Scenario on

Sharing Time

At the beginning of school, Paula Franck modeled sharing time with her kindergartners, but now they are conducting it themselves. Paula and the children are sitting on the rug with Kelly, today's leader, on a chair in front of them. Kelly begins by saying: "Who has something to share today?" Jenny's hand goes up, and Kelly invites her to share. Jenny begins: "This is what my dad brought me from Washington." She shows a model of the Washington Monument and continues to talk about it. When Jenny finishes, she calls on the listeners to make comments and ask questions. Ted says: "I really like what you told us. What is it made of?" Jenny answers and then calls on Chris, who says: "That is very interesting. How big is the real one?"

Analysis of Scenario

Children who speak must be prepared to share and then be able to direct the discussion that follows. Basing their responses on careful listening, members of the audience must say something positive and then ask questions or make comments. Paula intervenes only when no one has a question or comment, which rarely occurs.

sharing time above, the children follow a procedure for sharing time that stresses courtesy in both speaking and listening behaviors.

● Listening

In teaching children to listen, the teacher should choose topics that interest them and make use of words and concepts they understand. To be members of an audience, children need to learn to concentrate and become good listeners.

DIVERSITY Teachers can help children improve their listening comprehension by reading both storybooks and informational books to them. For English language learners, comparing literature selections written in English with the same titles written in the child's primary language is an effective listening comprehension activity. When reading these books to the class, teachers should relate the children's experiences to the content of the books. They should read relevant books and make them available to children before and after visiting various places on field trips.

TECHNOLOGY Dedicated listening centers or areas are often visible in literacy-rich classrooms. These dedicated listening areas should be equipped with computers, early literacy software, tape recorders, headsets, story tapes, and multiple copies of read-along books. By recording themselves reading stories to the children, teachers can provide a wide variety of tapes easily and inexpensively (Ollila and Mayfield, 1992). Tapes of nonfiction books introduce children to expository text, and recorded commentaries on field trips help students recall special events with appropriate specialized vocabulary. Other ideas for listening center tapes include jump rope rhymes, riddles and jokes, interviews, tongue twisters, and poems or jingles.

● Oral Expression

Children learn about using language through informal conversations, which they may engage in while working together at centers or on class projects. Teachers' recognition of the value of talk reflects Vygotsky's theory that children develop intellectually as they interact socially with other children and with mediating adults (Fortson and Reiff, 1995). The classroom environment provides many subjects and opportunities for descriptive talk. Children can compare different building blocks and note their relationships (size, weight, color); they can observe several kinds of animals and consider differences in the animals' feet, skin covering, and size; and they can compare a variety of fabrics in terms of texture, weight, and purpose.

Opportunities for oral expression occur frequently during the day. Teachers should encourage children to use these opportunities to develop their skills in oral communication. Here are some good ideas for class activities that develop oral expression:

making the daily schedule

choosing a current event to record on the chalkboard

planning projects, activities, or experiences

discussing a new bulletin board display

interpreting pictures

discussing what to include in a language experience story (LEA, described in more detail later in this chapter and in Chapter 7)

brainstorming ideas from "What if ..." situations (Example: "What if we had four arms instead of two arms?")

acting out stories

carrying on pretend telephone conversations with toy telephones

reviewing the day's events

engaging in dramatic play

Some teachers may wish to set up language centers to combine verbal communication with cognitive development (Hunter-Grundin, 1990). An adult (teacher, parent, or teaching assistant) leads a small group of children in a discussion that enables them to express opinions, justify points of view, challenge the opinions of others, or suggest possible alternatives. Appropriate topics include ideas for books that children will coauthor, solutions to problems, and subjects related to a theme. The discussion is not a question-answer session but an open expression of thoughts and ideas. It should help students gain confidence in their ability to communicate, and it should stimulate them to think deeply about matters that concern them.

● Dramatic Play

Dramatic play occurs when children simulate real experiences, such as cooking dinner or being a cashier. It requires both speaking and listening but often incorporates reading and writing as well. It is spontaneous and unrehearsed, and children assume the roles of people they have observed in real life. They think, feel, move, react, and speak according to their interpretations of how these people perform their roles. Both Piaget and Vygotsky believe that children construct knowledge and develop intellectually through play (Wortham, 1996).

After the children have discussed their experiences at various fast-food restaurants, say to them: "How could we make a pretend fast-food restaurant in our own classroom? Where could we put it? What are some things we would need? How could we get these things?" Have the children come up with answers and develop a plan. Ask some children to bring in cups, napkins, bags, and Styrofoam containers from a fast-food restaurant, and have others paint a sign. You can provide a toy cash register.

Make an illustrated price list to place above an improvised counter. Help the children learn to read the food words and the prices by asking: "What is the first item on the list? How much does it cost?" Keep the list simple at first, and add new items later. When the fast-food center is ready, different children can assume the roles of customers and workers.

In the Model Activity above, children are able to practice language skills as they play the roles of customer, cashier, food preparer, and order taker. They learn to follow directions, fill out forms, and recognize the words for menu items. They also develop mathematical skills as they use play money to pay for their orders and make change.

Ideally, themes for dramatic play centers originate from the children's interests and ideas, with the teacher facilitating the development of the centers. A field trip to a grocery store or fire station may be the stimulus for a dramatic play center. Other typical centers are a kitchen, bakery, post office, bank, business office, hospital, beauty parlor, travel agency, aquarium, and restaurant (Dailey and Owen, 1994; Fields and Hillstead, 1990; Fisher, 1991).

Children can plan and prepare each center by bringing supplies, arranging the area, and painting cardboard walls or counters. The teacher should see that materials are available to stimulate the use of written language for communication, such as

recipes	note paper
writing tools	envelopes
file folders	newspapers
coupons	menus
grocery lists	junk mail

Only a few materials should be available at first, and others may be added as needed. Props should be safe for children to handle and should have an authentic use in dramatic play.

During dramatic play, the teacher acts primarily as an observer but may also participate briefly to model appropriate behaviors and promote interaction. For instance, at a grocery store, the teacher might ask, "Do you have any specials today?" or "May I use my coupon to buy this soap?"

Dramatic play has many benefits. Because children need to carry on conversations, they must use good language skills. Frequently children use printed words in their play, and these words later become sight words. These words may be found on package labels, order forms, street signs, or ticket booths. Children discover the need to read when they have to recognize words to play the situation. Perceiving this need stimulates their interest in learning to read.

● Creative Dramatics

Spontaneous story reenactments, or *creative dramatics*, heighten children's awareness of story structure and characterization, which in turn helps them to comprehend and recall stories (Martinez, 1993). Acting out stories spontaneously builds interest in reading because children love to hear stories and then perform them. As the teacher reads a story, the children need to pay close attention to the sequence of events, the personalities of the characters, the dialogue, and the mood. Before acting out the story, the class reviews what happened and identifies the characters. As they act, the children must use appropriate vocabulary, enunciate distinctly, speak audibly, and express themselves clearly. Children will want to dramatize some stories several times, switching roles each time. The rest of the class forms the audience and must listen carefully. There is little or no need for props, sets, or costumes. Here are some good stories to dramatize:

LITERATURE

Polar Bear, Polar Bear, What Do You Hear? by Bill Martin, Jr. New York: Henry Holt, 1991.

Caps for Sale by Esphyr Slobodkina. New York: William R. Scott, 1947.

The Three Billy Goats Gruff by Peter Asbjornsen and Jorgan Moe. New York: Harcourt Brace Jovanovich, 1957.

Joseph Had a Little Overcoat by Simms Tabaak. New York: Viking, 1999.

Seven Blind Mice by Ed Young. New York: Philomel, 1992.

Stone Soup by Marcia Brown. New York: Macmillan, 1975.

Puppets are also useful in creative dramatics. Some shy children who are unwilling to speak as themselves are willing to talk through puppets. Children develop good language skills as they plan puppet shows and spontaneously speak their lines.

Reading and Writing

Several concepts are basic to understanding how growth in reading and writing occurs in the classroom (Strickland and Morrow, 1988):

❶ Children construct their own knowledge of reading and writing through experimentation and discovery. By bringing the knowledge they already have to new situations, they make connections and look for patterns in printed words.

❷ Growth in reading and writing occurs jointly and along with growth in oral language. Each language art supports the others in an interrelated way.

❸ Children learn reading and writing by actively using them for real purposes. A major task for the teacher is to structure the environment so that children can explore language in meaningful ways.

Kindergarten Literacy Activities

Before the school day officially begins in Linda Edwards's kindergarten, the children are sitting at tables writing journal entries, gathering around the incubator watching newly hatched ducklings, or sharing books at the reading center. When Linda calls the children together, they discuss the date and the weather. They mark the calendar, and one child calculates the number of 1s and 10s in May 17. Linda then reads them a story from a big book, moving a pointer under the words as she reads. The children sing a song from the big book, with a parent using the pointer while the teacher plays the autoharp. When Linda questions the children about

their favorite part, they respond enthusiastically. Then they read the story with her as she moves the pointer below the words again.

Analysis of Scenario

The classroom described in this scenario contains many opportunities for observing and discussing, writing purposefully, and reading independently, as well as learning math concepts, singing songs, and making decisions as a class. Reading and writing are not lessons to be taught during specific time periods but, rather, occur in various forms throughout the day.

❹ Teachers need to consider individual differences in children's abilities, interests, and experiences when planning instruction.

❺ When necessary, teachers intervene in language learning to help children make connections and move ahead.

❻ Reading and writing activities take place throughout the school day, not in separate instructional periods.

In the Classroom Scenario "Kindergarten Literacy Activities," the teacher is using many of these concepts.

It is important to keep in mind that reading and writing are complementary processes; children learn them interrelatedly. To give each process due consideration, however, we will examine them separately.

● Learning to Read

STANDARDS AND ASSESSMENT

The National Reading Panel (2000), in response to a United States congressional mandate, identified specific competencies and methodologies important for student achievement in reading. The report outlined five key areas of reading instruction: phonemic awareness, phonics, fluency, vocabulary, and text comprehension. The first of these is a key goal in emergent literacy classrooms, as we explain in this section. We discuss phonics and fluency in Chapter 3, vocabulary development in Chapter 4, and comprehension in Chapters 5 and 6. The report further suggested that the most successful teachers explicitly teach specific reading skills, actively engage their students with authentic tasks, and help students develop metacognitive skills, which include the ability to select strategies that will help them as they are reading (Taylor et al., 2002). As we explain in this chapter, teachers can begin these processes at the very earliest stages of reading instruction.

Learning to read does not happen all at once when children enter school; it is a process that builds gradually from an early age as children acquire new understandings about reading and writing as communication. Some of the factors involved in a child's learning to read are discussed next.

Physical Features

It takes time for children to learn to move their eyes across a page in a left-to-right progression and to execute a return sweep from the end of one line to the beginning of the next. This is a difficult maneuver. Children who have not yet mastered the process will find themselves rereading lines and skipping lines, both of which affect comprehension.

Eye movements back to a previously read word or phrase in order to reread are called *regressions*. Although regressions can become an undesirable habit, they are useful if the reader performs them to correct false first impressions.

Although teachers often attempt to correct faulty eye movements, such movements may be *symptoms* of other problems (for example, poor muscle coordination or poor vocabulary) rather than *causes* of problems. When the other problems are resolved, these symptoms usually disappear.

Experiential Background

A broad experiential background is essential for success in reading, because children must be familiar with the concepts and vocabulary they will see in written form in order to gain meaning from them. Through their individual experiences, children gain an understanding of concepts and learn words, or labels, for them. As children encounter a variety of experiences, they modify and refine their perceptions until they get a clear picture of each concept they have acquired. A child may need many experiences to attain a well-rounded impression of a single idea. *School,* for example, is a concept that children do not completely understand until they have experienced it in different ways.

Experiences may be either direct or vicarious. Children generally best remember ***direct experiences*** (active participation in events) that entail actual physical involvement, but it may not always be feasible to provide such direct experiences. TECHNOLOGY ▣ Good ***vicarious experiences*** (indirect participation in events), such as listening to stories, watching videos, and using interactive software, provide opportunities to expand concepts and vocabulary indirectly. Some appropriate experiences of both types are

field trips	videos, slides, tapes, and computer programs
resource people	selected television programs
story reading	photographs, pictures, and posters
demonstrations	neighborhood walks
exhibits	

MODEL ACTIVITIES — Direct Experience

Start by saying to the children: "Tomorrow we will make some vegetable soup. Remember to bring a vegetable to put in the soup. Now we will write a chart story about the ingredients we will need for our soup."

The next morning, say: "Tell us about your vegetable. What is it called? What color is it? How does it feel? How does it smell?" Give each child a chance to handle and talk about the vegetables. Then ask: "What do we need to do first to make the soup? What must we do to the vegetables before we put them in the pot? What else should we add?" (Answers include getting and heating the water, washing and cutting up the vegetables, and adding seasonings.) The teacher should cut the vegetables.

When the soup is ready to eat, give each child a cupful. As the children eat, ask: "How does your soup taste? Are the colors of the vegetables the same as when we put them into the soup?" After they have finished eating, let the children dictate another chart story about the sequence of making the soup and/or their reactions to eating it, or have the children write their own stories.

Some of the concepts you can help children acquire from this experience and related discussions are (1) soup can be made from a variety of vegetables; (2) after they are cooked, the vegetables change in texture and appearance; (3) it takes time to heat water and cook soup; (4) the water absorbs flavor and color from the vegetables; (5) cold water becomes hot when it is placed on a heated surface; (6) certain foods are classified as vegetables.

As a result of the experience, children's vocabularies might now include *boil, simmer, dissolve, ingredients, squash, celery, slice, chop, shred, dice, tomatoes, carrots, corn, peas, liquid,* and *flavor.*

A class project like the Model Activity above can promote growth in vocabulary and concept development and can provide the prerequisite involvement for a language experience approach (LEA) to writing, discussed later in this section and in Chapter 7.

LITERATURE Wordless picture books and pictures can provide vicarious experiences. By looking at the pictures in wordless picture books, children can use their own words to describe events and characters, thus building their experiences along with vocabulary and concepts. Pictures, particularly those that tell a story, are extremely fruitful sources of new ideas and experiences.

Teachers should read aloud to children several times a day, because story sharing creates far-reaching benefits for the listener. Stories introduce children to new vocabulary, language patterns, concepts, cultures, and lifestyles. Children develop an awareness of story structure by listening to stories and discussing them. Hearing stories read aloud may foster an interest in reading and a desire to learn to read. Well-chosen stories can be the basis for creative expression such as drama, music, and art.

Having a news period can be useful. The teacher can make a chart of classroom news, including items like "We had a fire drill today" or "We talked about the farm." Students can help compile the week's news, decide on headlines, and make illustrations for some items.

Story writing can be a logical extension of either direct or vicarious experiences. If a class writes a story after a field trip, the students should first discuss the trip. By asking carefully selected questions, the teacher can encourage them to form valid

A teacher's daily reading aloud to children helps them develop an awareness of story structure, acquaints them with new words, and fosters their interest in reading. *(Ron Chapple/Taxi/Getty Images)*

concepts and use appropriate vocabulary words. The students then dictate sentences for the teacher to write on an *experience chart* like that in Example 2.1. A coordinated language experience approach (LEA) involves the following steps:

1. Participation in a shared experience
2. Discussion of the experience
3. Cooperative writing of the story on a chart, board, or computer
4. Participation in extension activities related to the story

Stories about an experience may be dictated by a whole class, a group, or a single child. When individual children tell stories, parents, teaching assistants, older children, classroom volunteers, or teachers can act as scribes. These stories should be about things that are important to the children, such as their families, pets, or favorite activities. The children may illustrate them and combine them into booklets that are then shared around the library table and eventually taken home by the authors. Following are some appropriate experiences for story writing:

taking a field trip	observing an animal
watching an experiment	popping corn
visiting a science or book fair	experimenting with paints
tasting unusual foods	planting seeds or bulbs
entertaining a visitor	building a pretend space ship

EXAMPLE 2.1 Experience Chart Story

Our Trip to the Zoo

We rode in the school bus.
Mr. Spring was the bus driver.
The bus took us to the zoo.
We saw many animals.
We ate popcorn and peanuts.
We thanked Mr. Spring.
Our trip was fun.

Perhaps the most important reason for story writing is that it helps children realize that speech can be recorded and that print makes sense. This awareness occurs as the teacher reads the story back to the children in the words they have just dictated. After repeated readings by the teacher, the children may also be able to "read" the story. The teacher can make copies of the story for all the children to take home and share with their families. As a result of their involvement with the story, children may learn to recognize some high-interest words and some words used more than once (such as *we, zoo,* and *bus* in the experience chart story).

Children learn many literacy concepts through story writing. They watch as the teacher forms letters that make up words. They notice that language consists of separate words that are combined into sentences. They see the teacher begin at the left side and move to the right and go from top to bottom. They become aware that dictated stories have titles in which the first letter of each important word is capitalized. They realize that sentences begin with capital letters and end with punctuation marks. Besides becoming familiar with mechanical writing skills, children develop their thinking skills. The teacher's questions help them develop skill in organizing and summarizing. As the children retell events in the order of occurrence, they begin to understand sequence. As they recall the important points, they begin to form a concept of *main idea.*

TIME for REFLECTION

Some educators say that children learn reading and writing naturally, just as they have learned to speak, and that a supportive environment and a wide variety of experiences are all they need to figure out the writing system on their own. Others, however, say that children need direct instruction in skills. What do *you* think, and why?

Print Conventions

Many children, especially those who have been read to often, begin to "talk like a book" at a very young age (Clay, 1979; Dickinson, 1987; Hall, 1987; Cunningham and Allington, 1999). They pretend to read by imitating literary style and content instead of using conversational style. Illustrations and previous readings by adults help children construct the text they pretend to read, but of course these children are not yet able to read the actual words. Youngsters often practice "pretend reading" to a younger sibling or a grandparent. "Talking like a book" is an important step in learning to read, because it shows acquisition of basic literacy concepts, such as realizing that print can be turned into spoken words and that books use a special type of language. These and similar concepts are sometimes called *print conventions*, that is, generally accepted concepts about reading and writing. The reader expects the writer to use certain conventions involving placement of words on a page, directionality, capitalization, and punctuation, and the writer assumes the reader will follow them (Butler and Turbill, 1987).

Sight Words

Children who enter school are rapidly acquiring *sight words*, words they recognize instantly without analyzing them. Teachers can encourage sight word recognition by exposing children to commonly used words, such as names, number and color words, and environmental words.

Sight vocabulary can be learned in a number of meaningful ways. Ashton-Warner (1963) described the use of *organic words,* words that are meaningful or emotionally charged, such as *ghost, kiss,* and *Mother.* Each child chooses a word that has special personal meaning, and the teacher writes that word on a card and gives it to the child. A word card is kept as long as the word is known; when a word is forgotten or is no longer meaningful to the child, the card is discarded. Other strategies for teaching sight words include the creation of a "word wall" and participation in "word sorts," as described in Chapter 4, using vocabulary that children find interesting or important.

Letters and Sounds

To learn to read, children must acquire knowledge of letters and their corresponding sounds. This requires them to use auditory and visual discrimination abilities.

Auditory Discrimination. "Auditory discrimination is the ability to hear phonetic likenesses and differences in phonemes and words" (Harris and Hodges, 1995, p. 15). Through auditory discrimination and phonemic awareness, which is discussed later in this chapter, students recognize that speech is composed of separate sounds, or phonemes. Students must be able to hear sounds within words, or they will be unable to form mental connections between sounds and letters (Adams, 1990; Ball and Blachman, 1991; Beck and Juel, 1995; Gill, 1992; Griffith and Olson, 1992; Juel, 1988, 1991; Lundberg, Frost, and Peterson, 1988; Pearson, 1993).

Introducing children to simple rhymes is an effective way to sensitize them to the likenesses and differences among verbal sounds. The teacher can ask children to pick

Auditory Discrimination

Name several puppets with double names to stress initial consonant sounds (Molly Mouse, Freddie Frog, Dolly Duck, and Bennie Bear). While holding a puppet, say: "I'd like you to meet Molly Mouse. Molly Mouse only likes things that begin the same way that her name begins. Molly Mouse likes milk, but she doesn't like water. I am going to name some things that Molly Mouse likes or doesn't like. You must listen closely to the way each word begins. Raise your hand if I say something that Molly Mouse likes. Keep your hand down if I say something that Molly Mouse doesn't like. Let's begin. Molly Mouse likes meat." The children should raise their hands. If they don't seem to understand why she likes meat, talk about the beginning sound and give additional examples. Then say: "Molly Mouse likes potatoes." The children should keep their hands down.

out the words that rhyme and to supply words that rhyme with a given word. This ability is fundamental to the construction of "word families." The Model Activity above should help children develop auditory discrimination abilities.

Visual Discrimination. Visual discrimination is the process of visually identifying similarities and differences. Students need practice with simultaneous and successive visual discrimination of letters and words. Simultaneous discrimination occurs when children match printed symbols that are alike while they can see both symbols. Successive discrimination occurs when children find a duplicate symbol after a stimulus symbol is no longer visible. Activities requiring children to discriminate among letter and word forms are more useful to beginning readers than activities requiring them to identify similarities and differences among geometric forms (Sippola, 1985). Unless children need practice in developing the concepts of *like* and *different*, it is pointless to have them make distinctions among shapes and forms. The Model Activity on page 56 should help children develop visual discrimination abilities.

Letter Recognition. Teachers need to keep several points in mind while helping beginning readers learn letters and words. Children should learn letter names early so that the teacher and the class have a common referent—for example, understanding when the teacher talks about the letter *f* or the letter *n* (Farr and Roser, 1979). Knowledge of letter *names* is important for talking about similarities and differences among printed words, but knowledge of letter *sounds* is more useful in decoding words. Children who learn both the names and the sounds of letters can read better than children who learn only letter names (R. C. Anderson et al., 1985).

Phonemic Awareness. *Phonemic awareness*, an understanding that spoken language consists of a series of small sound units, or phonemes, is a powerful predictor of success in reading (Adams, 1990; Pearson, 1993; Stanovich, 1993/1994; Yopp, 1992; Armbruster, Lehr, and Osborn, 2001). It is both a prerequisite for learning to read and a consequence of the increased awareness of language that comes from learning to read (Yopp, 1992).

MODEL ACTIVITIES   Visual Discrimination

Write on the board some letters that are similar in appearance (*b, d,* and *p,* for example). Say to the children: "Let's look at these letters. Are any of them alike? How are the first two letters different? What is different about the other letter?"

Then say to them: "Now I am going to give you a copy of a page of the story that we read today. Look at the first letter on the board. [Point to the letter.] Then look at the page from the story. Every time you see this letter in the story, circle it with your green crayon. [Give them time to search for the letter *b* and mark their pages.] Now look at the second letter. [Point to it.] Every time you see this letter in the story, circle it with your red

crayon. [Give them time to do this.] Now look at the third letter. [Point to it.] Every time you see this letter in the story, circle it in yellow. [Give them time to do this.]" Then display a large copy of the story and let individuals come up and point to the letters that should have been circled in the different colors, while children check their own papers.

Repeat the activity with a set of words containing these letters, such as *big, pet,* and *dog.* Ask the same questions about the words. Then have the children perform a similar activity with the words, using fresh pages from the story so that their previous marks will not confuse them.

Yopp (1995b, p. 20) says, "Most youngsters enter kindergarten lacking phonemic awareness. Indeed, few are conscious that sentences are made up of individual words, let alone that words can be segmented into phonemes." Phonemic awareness can be taught directly, and training in phonemic awareness has been shown to be effective and to have a positive effect on reading acquisition (Lundberg, Frost, and Peterson, 1988; Yopp, 1992). Use of read-aloud books is a way to integrate phonemic awareness into the instructional program, because many books have rhyme, alliteration, assonance, and other features that allow children to play with the sounds of language (Yopp, 1995a; Yopp, 1992; Griffith and Olson, 1992).

As suggested by the National Reading Panel (2000) described earlier in this chapter, phonemic awareness is an important component of a balanced literacy program. Teachers can help students develop phonemic awareness by encouraging them to identify, from a set of words, those words that begin with the same sound; identify the initial and final sounds in words; combine and blend sounds to say a word and segment a word into separate sounds (Armbruster, Lehr, and Osborn, 2001); and use invented spellings so that they become conscious of the sounds that make up words (Pearson, 1993). Exposing them to literature that plays with the sounds of language (Griffith and Olson, 1992) and involving them in songs and games that draw attention to the sounds of language (Yopp, 1992) are additional strategies for the development of phonemic awareness. When youngsters pay close attention to speech sounds and use their discoveries about letter-sound relationships to guide their writing and reading, they increase their functional and meaningful use of written language (Richgels et al., 1996).

Richgels, Poremba, and McGee (1996) suggest a "What Can You Show Us?" activity to develop phonemic awareness in a holistic context. They describe it as a "functional, contextualized, social literacy activity" (p. 641). It accompanies shared reading activities. Before shared reading, a *preparation* step involves selecting reading materials and displaying them appropriately; for example, if the text is copied onto a chart, the features of words that the teacher wants to emphasize can be highlighted in some way. The next step involves the children's *preview* of the text and discussion of what they see. Next, *student demonstrations* of what they know about the text (for example, identifying letters of words) take place. The shared reading (teacher reading, joint reading, and student activities) comes next. During and after this activity, the students apply what they know about the text. There may be further student demonstrations.

Alphabetic Principle.   It is critical that beginning readers understand the **alphabetic principle**, the concept that letters represent speech sounds (Pikulski, 1989). Some children learn this principle intuitively, but most need help. Holdaway (1979) suggests introducing two contrasting letter-sound combinations, such as *m* and *f,* and having children find these letters in familiar stories that the teacher has read with them. After they find many examples, which they can readily identify because of their familiarity with the stories, they work with other letter-sound relationships, including *b, g, s,* and *t*. Because of the insights they have gained, many children are now able to learn the remaining initial consonants and consonant blends on their own.

Reading Support

Establishing a literacy-rich classroom, as described earlier in this chapter, provides an environment that supports teachers' strategies for helping children learn to read. Literacy-rich classrooms are print-rich environments. In literacy-rich classrooms words are everywhere—on bulletin boards and walls, on children's work and book jackets, and as labels on objects around the room. There are charts dictated by the children and books on shelves and at centers.

Reading Aloud.   Within the literacy-rich classroom environment, the foundation of early literacy support is the reading aloud, by the teacher, of well-chosen texts. In the early primary grades, daily time dedicated to reading aloud encourages the understanding of story elements and of the organization of expository texts for students.

LITERATURE   *Big books* with enlarged pictures and print that the entire class can read together offer an excellent way for children to learn to read, even on the first day of school. (See the Classroom Scenario "First Day of School.") Many big books have **predictable or patterned stories**—stories that use repetition, rhythmic language patterns, and familiar concepts. Even during a first reading by the teacher, children join in on the repetitive lines or familiar chants. For example, when the teacher reads, "And the little red hen said —," the children respond, "I'll do it myself!" This procedure enables a child to "confirm the predictability of written language" (Wiseman, 1984, p. 343). Stories such as Bill Martin, Jr.'s *Brown Bear, Brown Bear* and Audrey Wood's *The Napping House* contain familiar sequences of this sort. Children will soon read these books by themselves if the teacher has reread them and pointed out the corresponding words.

CLASSROOM SCENARIO First Day of School

Early in the day, Oliver Jordan calls the children to the story rug and introduces the big book version of Bill Martin, Jr.'s *Brown Bear, Brown Bear, What Do You See?* Eagerly the children listen as he reads and watch as he turns the brightly colored pages. Soon they are chiming in on some of the words, helped along by the picture clues. When they beg him to read it again, he does so and invites all of them to read it with him. In additional readings throughout the day, children read pages by themselves and with partners. They listen with headphones as they follow along in small book versions, and by the end of the day they believe they are readers.

Across the hall, Mary Hill is also introducing her children to reading, but she does so by asking them to return to their seats and giving them new workbooks. She tells them to turn to the first page and explains the directions for marking the words that begin with the same letter. "Our letter today is the letter *m*," she says, "and I'd like you to take your pencil or crayon and mark each word that begins with this letter." The children finish the exercise, watch as Mary shows them how to print the letter *m*, and then make rows of *m*s.

Analysis of Scenario

Many children come to school eager to learn to read. In Oliver's class, the children were excited because they believed they were really reading. In Mary's class, the children were disappointed because they had not learned to read; they were unable to see any connection between their work and reading stories. According to Booth (1994), the way children encounter print at the beginning of school may determine their attitudes toward reading for the rest of their lives.

As children read and reread stories—by themselves and to one another—and engage in reading and writing activities related to the stories, they are participating in what Holdaway (1979) calls the **shared-book experience**. Teachers may use the following procedure for sharing big books with their children; it is an extension of the bedtime story shared between parent and child (Holdaway, 1979; Strickland, 1988a):

1 Introduce the story by stimulating a discussion that relates students' experiences to the text, presenting the title and author (using these terms), guiding the children to make predictions about the story, and showing eager anticipation for reading the story.

2 Read the story with lively expression. Run a pointer slowly under the words as you read them so that the children can match the spoken words with the print and observe the directionality. While reading, think aloud about aspects of the story ("I wonder what will happen now!" or "Little Bear must feel very happy!"). Encourage children to make predictions and read familiar parts with you.

3 When the story is over, guide a discussion about major points; then find and reread corresponding parts of the text to confirm the points. Help the children reread the text together until they become fluent and confident.

A number of optional variations and follow-up activities are also useful. To focus on meaning, the teacher may use adhesive notes or flaps to cover meaningful, predictable words and then ask the children to identify the words underneath. The teacher may also select certain phonic or structural elements that are well represented in the story, call the children's attention to them, and lead the children to discover word recognition strategies for decoding words with these elements. The children may wish to illustrate parts of the text, write their own versions, find other books

TECHNOLOGY 🖥 related to the same topic, or extend the text in some other way. Since many big books have accompanying audiotapes and sets of small books, the children may read a small version to a listener or listen to a tape of the big book while following along in the smaller one.

Guided Reading.   Guided reading is another form of support that places the student in a more formal instructional situation (Fountas and Pinnell, 1996). *Guided reading* is a framework that involves explicit modeling of reading strategies by the teacher while students are actively engaged in reading trade books (books marketed to the general public) appropriate for their instructional reading levels. Often students participate in guided reading groups three to five days each week. While in the group, students interact with new books each time. A student's assignment to the group is flexible, and student progress is assessed regularly. Leveled books are often used to meet the individual readability needs of the students as they participate in the group.

Choice Time.   Believing that children gain confidence and skill in reading from free selection, Fisher (1991) explains her procedure for daily *choice time* reading. The children may choose whatever they wish to read: big books or small versions of them, trade books, magazines, books published by other children, poems, or songs written on charts around the room. They may follow along in a book as they listen to a tape of a familiar story, or they may read with her, with a friend, with a visitor, or alone. Sometimes they role-play a shared-reading session, taking turns being the teacher and inviting a small group to respond.

Independent reading, the chance for students to read books on their own, provides further support for the development of skill and confidence. The reading and rereading of familiar texts is a regular event in a literacy-rich classroom. Independent reading also encourages students to read a variety of materials available throughout the classroom (Fountas and Pinnell, 1996).

Pocket Charts.   The McCrackens (1987) use a *pocket chart* for supporting literacy development. This consists of a large chart with rows of "pockets" that hold words, pictures that represent words, and sentence strips. The teacher has the children manipulate the words and sentences so that they can learn the story, become aware of print, match words, and build the story or sequence of events. See the Classroom Scenario on page 60 for example.

Early Intervention for Struggling Readers

Many early intervention programs for students who are experiencing difficulty in learning to read emphasize prevention rather than correction. Intensive early intervention followed by long-term, effective instruction appears to bring about lasting and substantial gains in reading achievement.

Reading from a Pocket Chart

As part of the morning activities, Tina DeStephen's prefirst graders read their daily schedule from a pocket chart.

Morning	Afternoon
Attendance/Tally	Lunch
Pledge/Song	Storytime
Calendar/Weather	Quiet self-selected reading
Language workshop	Buddy reading
Author's Chair	Reading conferences
Something Special	Self-selection
Recess	Clean-up
Math	Time to go home

Tina discusses the day's schedule with the children and talks about "something special," which may be a visitor, a trip, or an invitation to see another class perform a play. "Self-selection" refers to such options as playing with blocks, doing handwriting, making a puppet show, playing instruments, painting at the easel, using math manipulatives, and playing in the house-keeping center. Before releasing the children to work independently, Tina makes sure that each child has decided what to do.

Analysis of Scenario

This daily ritual serves many purposes. Tina and the children anticipate the day's events together as they read and discuss the activities. The children are comfortable and secure in this familiar routine, and they consider their choices and make decisions about what they will do. They realize that reading is purposeful, they reread now-familiar words, and they become aware of sequence.

Intervention should begin as soon as a student shows signs of difficulty, usually in first grade. Typically, an intensive program is provided by a trained instructor and lasts for a short period of time, although some students may need additional intensive support beyond first grade. Two early intervention programs are briefly described here: Reading Recovery and Success for All.

Reading Recovery, developed in New Zealand by Marie Clay, is a temporary intervention program intended for first graders who are at risk of early reading failure (Clay, 1979; Sensenbaugh, 1995). A specialist works daily with each child for thirty minutes, usually for a period of twelve to sixteen weeks, until the child has developed effective strategies for independent learning and can function adequately in the regular classroom. From a selection of approximately 500 "little books," the tutor selects those that meet a student's particular interests and needs. Each lesson consists of having the child read many little books and compose a brief story or message. Research evidence indicates that Reading Recovery has enabled children to retain initial gains in reading and continue to make progress.

Success for All focuses on low-achieving urban populations. This program involves school reorganization to provide excellent instruction from preschool through the primary grades (Slavin et al., 1994). Its three premises are innovative curriculum and instruction in reading, intensive one-on-one tutoring if reading problems emerge, and regrouping by reading level across the grades for ninety-minute reading instructional periods. The tutor reinforces the direct instruction provided by the regular classroom teacher but also seeks to identify problems and find different strategies. In addition, a family support team attempts to involve parents, making them feel welcome in the school and providing special services.

● Learning to Write

We have stressed that many youngsters know a great deal about written language before entering school. Children actually perceive themselves as writers long before they can write conventionally. They experiment with making scribbles, sometimes interspersing pictures and letterlike shapes, and believe that their "writing" conveys messages.

When teachers invite children to write in kindergarten, they should follow certain basic guidelines (based on Sulzby, Teale, and Kamberelis, 1989; Sulzby, 1994; Ollila and Mayfield, 1992):

1. Accept the form of writing the child can use; it does not have to be adult writing.

2. Allow children to share their writing and respond to what other children have written.

3. Let children "write" their own names on their work to give them a sense of ownership.

4. Encourage children to use writing to communicate with other people.

5. Provide a variety of writing materials that are readily available.

6. Be a model by letting children see you writing purposefully.

7. Provide ample time for children to write.

8. Help children realize the importance of writing in their lives.

Early Writing Strategies

For young children, writing is often a social event. Children confer with one another, sharing their skills and searching for resources and examples (Loughlin and Martin, 1987). They may tentatively compose stories and tell them to their friends before writing them. When children actually get down to the serious business of writing, Donald Graves claims, they talk to themselves, audibly or subaudibly (Walshe, 1986). They verbalize as they physically form letters and words in the process of formulating their stories.

When children begin kindergarten and are given opportunities to write, some are in the prephonetic stage and place letters on paper without regard for the sounds they make, as in Example 2.2. They tell the teacher what they have written, and the teacher records what they dictate while helping them see relationships between spoken and written words (Coate and Castle, 1989). In kindergarten most children continue to scribble, draw, *drite*, and use nonphonetic strings of letters (Sulzby, Teale, and Kamberelis, 1989; Cunningham and Allington, 1999).

Once children have a sense of letter-sound relationships, they begin to use **invented spellings**. Harris and Hodges (1995, p. 123) define invented spelling as "an attempt to spell a word whose spelling is not already known, based on a writer's knowledge of the spelling system and how it works." Writing with invented spellings enables children to apply their knowledge of letter-sound relationships for their own purposes. Example 2.3 shows how a kindergartner reacted to a dinosaur theme by drawing a picture and writing a story with invented spellings. Example 2.4 shows a first grader's use of invented spellings in a message to a friend.

Close observation of children's invented spellings provides insights into their awareness of letter-sound relationships. Because consonant sounds are more distinctive than vowel sounds, children often use them to represent the key sounds in the words they are trying to spell, either omitting or misrepresenting vowel sounds. Sometimes, in fact, beginning spellers use only the initial consonant of the word they wish to spell. In Example 2.3, Taylor shows considerable knowledge of phonics by systematically sounding through each word and representing each sound with the letter he hears, as in *dinaswrs*. Taylor also mixes some conventional spelling (i.e., *of*

EXAMPLE 2.2   Nonphonetic String of Letters

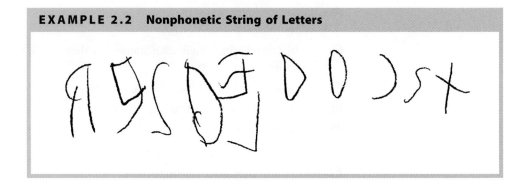

EXAMPLE 2.3   Kindergartner's Use of Invented Spellings

This story reads as follows: The meat eater of the dinosaurs. Will Tyrannosaurus Rex survive?

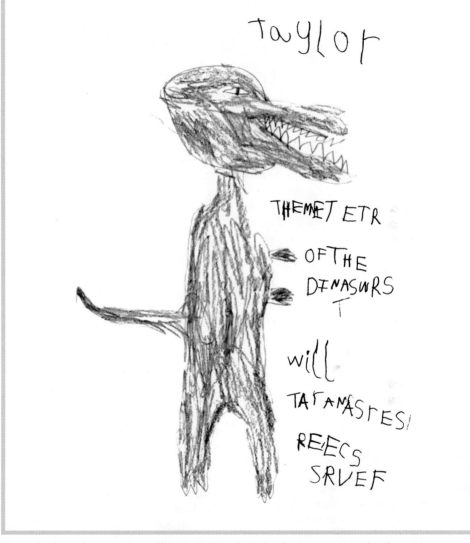

Source: Taylor Bennett, Sycamore Elementary School, Cookeville, Tennessee. Used with permission.

and *the*) with his spelling inventions. Trudy (Example 2.4) also reveals excellent awareness of letter-sound relationships in the word *dadokaded*.

With each writing sample, the teacher can learn a great deal about a child's beginning reading and writing competencies. In Example 2.5, the teacher observes that Sheila, a kindergartner, writes from left to right, leaves spaces between words,

EXAMPLE 2.4   First Grader's Use of Invented Spellings

This story reads as follows: Roses are red. Violets are blue. These golden flowers remind me of you. Dedicated to Janet.

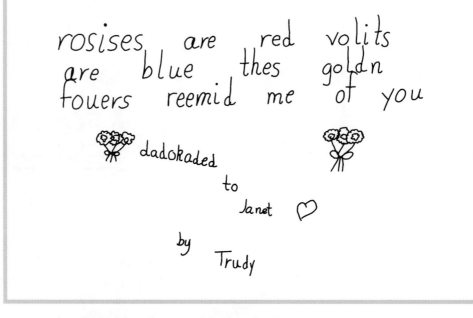

Source: Trudy Walker, Capshaw Elementary School, Cookeville, Tennessee. Used with permission.

and writes in complete sentences. She has a good sense of sound-letter relationships, although she sometimes omits some sounds (*WH* or *WIt* for *went*). She spells the *ing* ending correctly. She is not sure about when to use upper- and lower-case letters, however, and she does not use punctuation.

Knowledge of which letters represent certain sounds within words is useful not only for writing but also for decoding words in reading. Using invented spelling helps children develop phonemic awareness and understanding of the alphabetic principle (Adams, 1990). According to Cunningham and Cunningham (1992, p. 106), research indicates that "invented spelling and decoding are mirror-like processes that make use of the same store of phonological knowledge." Thus, as children learn to associate sounds with letters, they advance their knowledge of both reading and writing. The Model Activity on invented spelling on page 65 and the Focus on Strategies on page 67 demonstrate ways in which teachers can help children begin to write and read.

EXAMPLE 2.5   Beginning Writing

The story reads as follows: I went to get a present for my mom. Everybody was shouting hurrah and singing happy birthday.

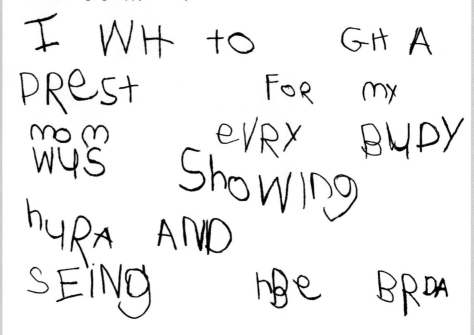

Source: Sheila Vogel, Kingston Elementary School, Kingston, Tennessee. Used with permission.

MODEL ACTIVITIES   Demonstrating Invented Spelling

Say to the children: "We've been talking about going camping, and today we set up a tent in our room. Some of you may want to write about tents in your journals. Can you help me spell *tent*?" The children agree. "Let's say *tent* slowly together and listen for the sounds. What letter makes the sound we hear at the beginning?" Most children suggest *t*, so write *t* on the board. Then ask: "Let's say *tent* again and stretch it out. Think about the sound we hear next. What letter makes that sound?" The children aren't quite sure; some say *t*; some say *n*; and a few offer other letters. For now, write *n*. Then say: "Is there another sound? Let's say *tent* once more, very slowly." After repeating the word, the children say: "*t*, another *t* at the end." Complete the word for them by adding *t*.

To reinforce the sound-letter relationships, ask: "Can you find a word in our room that begins like *tent*?" The children turn to the charts and labels. Jamie finds *turtle*, and Allyson sees *ten*. She says excitedly: "*Tent* and *ten* sound almost alike! Can we put an *e* in *tent*?" Ask Allyson to come to the board and put the *e* where it should go; then ask the other children if they agree. After receiving an affirmative answer, ask the children to say the letters in *tent* and remind them to use these letters if they write about tents.

Invented spelling enables children to apply their knowledge of letter-sound relationships for their own purposes. *(©Elizabeth Crews)*

Writing Support

When children write to communicate meaning, their writing is purposeful. Some classes support postal system/penpal programs with individual mailboxes for receiving letters and a central mailbox for sending letters. Many reasons for writing also emerge at dramatic play centers, where children write telephone messages, take orders for food, make shopping lists, and so on. Other purposeful writing activities include sending messages to school personnel, making greeting cards, sending thank-you notes, writing stories, writing letters, and recording information. Journal writing and writing workshops are two other ways to support students who are learning to write.

Journal Writing.   Journal writing offers another purposeful writing activity and often gives the teacher insights into the child's understandings and misinterpretations (Fallon and Allen, 1994). The teacher gives each child a booklet, often made of folded unlined sheets of paper stapled together, to write in during a special time each day. Children may copy, scribble, print, or draw anything they wish in their journals, and sometimes the teacher records in conventional print what the children dictate.

Writing Workshops.   Writing workshops provide a support framework that includes a minilesson designed to improve writing skills, a writing and conference time when students are authentically engaged in composing while the teacher meets individually with each student, and a sharing time when students read or listen to the sharing of a student's written selection. The writing workshop encourages the process of continuous growth with valuable feedback from both the teacher and peers (Fountas and Pinnell, 1996).

Getting Children Started in Writing

Ms. McLoughlin paused a moment as she moved from one kindergartner to another, offering encouragement as they worked in their journals. She thought back to the beginning of the year when only a few of them could even print their names. For the first few weeks, she had to write in their journals a sentence or two that they had dictated to her to help them grasp the concept that what they said could be written down.

When she had first asked the children to write, they told her they didn't know how. She supplied them with paper and a variety of writing tools, however, and encouraged them to draw a picture first and then write something about it. Some did this with scribbles, some with pictures only, and some with a few letters strewn haphazardly on the page. She accepted their work and asked them to read their stories to her, but she realized she would have to help them discover sound-letter relationships so that they could begin using the letters they needed to make words.

Ms. McLoughlin helped her children discover associations between sounds and letters by pointing them out during shared book reading and having the children pay attention to the letters and sounds in the environmental words at play centers. When the children had developed some knowledge of sound-letter relationships, she demonstrated how to spell words. Even though it took time, she shared individually with each of the children every day and noted in their journals if she helped them sound the words.

In a few weeks, some children were still scribble writing or drawing pictures, but a few had begun to string letters together, often using invented spelling to make words. Ms. McLoughlin remembered the day Tony asked her to spell *duck* and she had said, "What sounds do you hear? Stretch out the word so that you can hear all of its sounds." Slowly, Tony said the word and then wrote *dk* — a real breakthrough for him. As the children discovered sound-letter relationships, they eagerly attempted to spell any word they wanted to use in their stories.

Now, near the end of the school year, Ms. McLoughlin found that most of her students were writing longer and more readable journal entries. They were working on refining sentence structure, making sure there were spaces between words, and placing punctuation marks correctly. She looked at Hank's story and asked him to read it to her. He read:

Once upon a time there was a tree that wanted to be yellow and he could not decide. So he waited for fall. ... And he turned yellow. The end. By Hank.

Ms. McLoughlin complimented him on the way his story had a beginning, a middle, and an end — something she encouraged her students to consider as they wrote. They often discussed story structure as they read stories together.

Looking over at Judy's paper, Ms. McLoughlin could see that Judy still had not made the breakthrough to understanding the relationship between sounds and letters. She looked frustrated, so Ms. McLoughlin asked Hank to help Judy with the words she needed. Ms. McLoughlin smiled to herself as she heard Hank using her exact words: "Think of the sounds in *dinner*. What letter makes the sound you hear at the beginning of the word?"

Moving on, Ms. McLoughlin overheard two children conferring. Al said, "You know, when we write *running*, all we have to do is think how to spell *run* and add *ing*. That's easy." When Chris asked Karen how to spell a word, Karen reminded him he could copy the word he needed from yesterday's chart. Ms. McLoughlin was pleased to hear that exchange, because she always encouraged the children to use the words displayed in the room to get the correct spelling. Tara wanted someone to listen to her story, and Joshua was asking Jeff to help him write his next word. *The children learn so much from each other*, Ms. McLoughlin thought as she watched them work.

When most of the children had finished, Ms. McLoughlin told them she was ready for them to read

Continued

Continued

THETREE ETHeT COd hotbs
Ohce apon a time. Theyr
Wus a tree thet Wott too
be. Yellow and he Cob hot
b.sieb. So be Waebb for
foll....
Ahb He
turb Yellow. The Ead
By Hank

Source: Hank Replogle, Carthage Elementary School, Carthage, Tennessee. Used with permission.

their journals to her. Martha came first with a two-page story about her big sister's birthday party. After letting Martha stamp the date on her story, Ms. McLoughlin asked her to select a book to read while the others came to her with their journals. Chuck came next with four pages filled with writing. He eagerly read her a long, involved story about dinosaurs, but she noted that his words were made of letters that had no relationship to the sounds in them. Chuck was a bright child and knew a great deal about dinosaurs, but he still could not use letter-sound relationships.

Even though Ms. McLoughlin sometimes asked the children to write about special topics related to holidays or themes, she often let them choose their own topics. Free choice worked well for Matt; his last entry had only been three words, but today he produced a full-page story about his camping trip with his dad.

Continued

Continued

Glancing around, Ms. McLoughlin could see that nearly all the children had read their journals to her and were comfortably looking at books. Establishing this routine had taken considerable time and effort, but most of the children now understood the schedule and responded well. Even better, many of them were now able to write simple, well-constructed stories with invented spelling.

SUMMARY

Cognitive development and language learning occur together. Children learn language naturally by observing and imitating language users and then constructing language to meet their needs. Educators must nurture *emergent literacy,* a continuum of literacy growth beginning at birth. Children already possess knowledge about reading and writing before entering school. Teachers should build on and expand children's growing awareness of language as purposeful communication.

In the emergent literacy classroom, the teacher acts as a facilitator of learning by creating activities that involve both direct and vicarious experiences to meet the children's needs and interests. A print-rich environment with books, charts, labels, environmental print, and centers provides a further stimulus for language development. Realizing the value of a literate home environment, the teacher may suggest strategies to parents for guiding their children's literacy development.

Many children's listening and speaking skills are well developed when they enter school, and teachers provide opportunities for further growth in listening comprehension and oral expression. Through exposure to reading and writing materials and experiences, children gain knowledge of print conventions and sight words. Children's growth in reading and writing, based on what they already know, occurs concurrently and interrelatedly through experiences with big books, journal writing, and listening to stories. Participation in guided reading groups supports the development of early reading skills. The development of phonemic awareness and the use of invented spelling help children to connect letters with sounds, while writing workshops continue to provide scaffolding and support for early writing attempts.

TEST YOURSELF

True or False

_____ 1. Language learning begins at birth and is continuous.

_____ 2. The term *emergent literacy* refers to a child's language development only after the child enters school.

_____ 3. A child's phonemic awareness is a good predictor of future reading success.

_____ 4. A close relationship exists between cognitive development and the growth of concepts about language.

_____ 5. The preferred frequency for teachers to read aloud to children is once a week.

_____ 6. Picture reading is an example of a direct experience through which a child can learn concepts and vocabulary.

_____ 7. According to Piaget, children at the preoperational level are more likely to be successful in child-centered classes than in classes where they are required to memorize rules.

_____ 8. According to Piaget, language comes before thought.

_____ 9. The only way children can learn language is by imitation.

_____ 10. Many children engage in unconventional forms of reading and writing before they enter school.

_____ 11. Dramatic play centers should include materials for motivating written communication.

_____ 12. Young children need direct instruction in how to speak when they first begin talking.

_____ 13. Home environment has little or no effect on language learning.

_____ 14. In shared big book reading, children take turns reading from a large book.

_____ 15. When children "talk like a book," they are most likely reading the exact words.

_____ 16. Interactive story reading is a more worthwhile literacy experience than simply reading a story aloud without comments or questions.

_____ 17. Parents should discourage a child who wants to read before entering school.

_____ 18. Auditory discrimination has no relationship to the development of phonemic awareness.

_____ 19. Guided reading support involves the assignment of students to fixed groups for instruction during reading.

_____ 20. Children use invented spellings to express the ways in which they perceive letter-sound associations.

_____ 21. Isolated drills and memorization of rules are better than language experiences for helping children understand written communication.

_____ 22. Early reading of environmental words helps children realize that print represents meaning.

_____ 23. A teacher should intervene in language learning by providing help when students are having problems.

_____ 24. Many big books have predictable language patterns.

_____ 25. Piaget created the concept of zone of proximal development.

For your journal ...

❶ Respond to any practicum experiences with literacy in early childhood education.

❷ Reflect on one or more of the following concepts: invented spelling, developmentally appropriate practice, shared book reading, phonemic awareness, zone of proximal development, and emergent literacy.

❸ Observe one child carefully. How could you provide scaffolding that would move this child through the zone of proximal development?

❹ Reflect on the video that accompanies this chapter on your CD. How does a shared-book experience support early literacy development? Refer to the video to support your answer, and include other examples of activities that promote the development of emergent literacy.

... and your portfolio

❶ Start an annotated bibliography of read-aloud, predictable, and repetitive books that you would like to use with your class.

❷ Create a file of pictures that might stimulate children to tell or write their own stories.

❸ On a continuing basis, observe a child's emergent literacy and suggest developmentally appropriate practices for providing instruction.

CHAPTER APPENDIX

Predictable/Repetitive/Alliterative/Rhyming Books

Aardema, V. *Why Mosquitoes Buzz in People's Ears.* New York: Dial, 1978.

Aliki. *Go Tell Aunt Rhody.* New York: Macmillan, 1974.

Baer, G. *THUMP, THUMP, Rat-a-Tat-Tat.* Singapore: Harper & Row, 1989.

Barrett, J. *Animals Should Definitely Not Act Like People.* New York: Aladdin, 1987.

Carle, E. *Today Is Monday.* New York: Scholastic, 1993.

Carle, E. *The Very Busy Spider.* New York: Philomel, 1985.

Carle, E. *The Very Hungry Caterpillar.* Cleveland: Collins World, 1969.

Cowley, J. *Mrs. Wishy-Washy.* San Diego: The Wright Group, 1987.

Cronin, D. *Click, Clack, Moo: Cows That Type.* New York: Simon & Schuster, 2000.

Cronin, D. *Giggle, Giggle, Quack.* New York: Simon & Schuster, 2002.

Degen, B. *Jamberry.* New York: Scholastic, 1983.

Emberley, D. *Drummer Hoff.* Englewood Cliffs, N.J.: Prentice-Hall, 1967.

Galdone, P. *The Teeny, Tiny Woman.* New York: Clarion, 1984.

Grossman, B. *My Little Sister Ate One Hare.* New York: Crown, 1996.

Hutchins, P. *The Doorbell Rang.* New York: Greenwillow, 1986.

Hutchins, P. *Rosie's Walk.* New York: Macmillan, 1968.

Johnson, T. *Yonder.* New York: Dial, 1988.

Kent, J. *The Fat Cat.* New York: Scholastic, 1987.

Langstaff, J. *Oh, A-Hunting We Will Go.* New York: Atheneum, 1974.

Livingston, M. C. *Dilly Dilly Piccalilli.* New York: McElderry, 1988.

Lobel, A. *The Rose in My Garden.* New York: Greenwillow, 1984.

Martin, B. *Brown Bear, Brown Bear.* New York: Holt, Rinehart and Winston, 1970.

Martin, B. *Fire! Fire! Said Mrs. McGuire.* New York: Holt, Rinehart and Winston, 1970.

Martin, B., and J. Archambault. *The Braggin' Dragon.* Allen, Tex.: DLM, 1988.

Mayer, M. *What Do You Do with a Kangaroo?* New York: Scholastic, 1973.

Munsch, R. *Mud Puddle.* Scarborough, Ontario: Firefly, 1982.

Nelson, J. *Peanut Butter and Jelly.* Cleveland: Modern Curriculum Press, 1989.

Quackenbush, R. *She'll Be Coming 'Round the Mountain.* New York: Lippincott, 1973.

Sendak, M. *Pierre.* New York: Harper & Row, 1962.

Shaw, C. B. *It Looked Like Spilt Milk.* New York: Harper & Row, 1947.

Shaw, N. *Sheep on a Ship.* Boston: Houghton Mifflin, 1989.

Stevens, J. *The House That Jack Built.* New York: Holiday House, 1985.

Westcott, N. *I Know an Old Lady Who Swallowed a Fly.* New York: Little, Brown, 1980.

Wood, A. *King Bidgood's in the Bathtub.* New York: Harcourt Brace Jovanovich, 1985.

Wood, A. *The Napping House.* San Diego: Harcourt Brace Jovanovich, 1984.

Yolen, J. *Owl Moon.* New York: Philomel, 1987.

3

Word Recognition

SETTING OBJECTIVES

When you finish reading this chapter, you should be able to

● Describe some ways to help a child develop a sight vocabulary.

● Describe some activities for teaching the use of context clues.

● Discuss the role of phonics in the reading program.

● Define each of the following terms: *consonant blend, consonant digraph, vowel digraph, diphthong.*

● Explain how to teach a child to associate a specific sound with a specific letter or group of letters.

● Discuss ways to teach the various facets of structural analysis.

● Identify the skills children need in order to use a dictionary as an aid in word recognition.

● List the steps readers should take when trying to recognize an unfamiliar word.

Good readers differ from poor readers in both the number of words they recognize instantly and their ability to decode words. Good readers tend to have larger sight vocabularies than poor readers, and this reduces their need to stop and analyze words. When they do need to analyze words, good readers often have a more flexible approach than poor readers do because they generally have been taught several strategies and have been encouraged to try a new one if the first strategy that they try fails (Jenkins et al., 1980). Poor readers frequently know only a single strategy for decoding words. No one strategy is appropriate for all words, however, so these children are at a disadvantage when they encounter words for which their strategy is not useful. Even if they have been taught several strategies, poor readers may have failed to learn a procedure that will enable them to decode unfamiliar words as efficiently as possible.

This chapter presents a variety of methods of word recognition and stresses a flexible approach to decoding unfamiliar words, encouraging application of those word recognition strategies that are most helpful at the moment. It also explains ways

Chapter 3 Organization

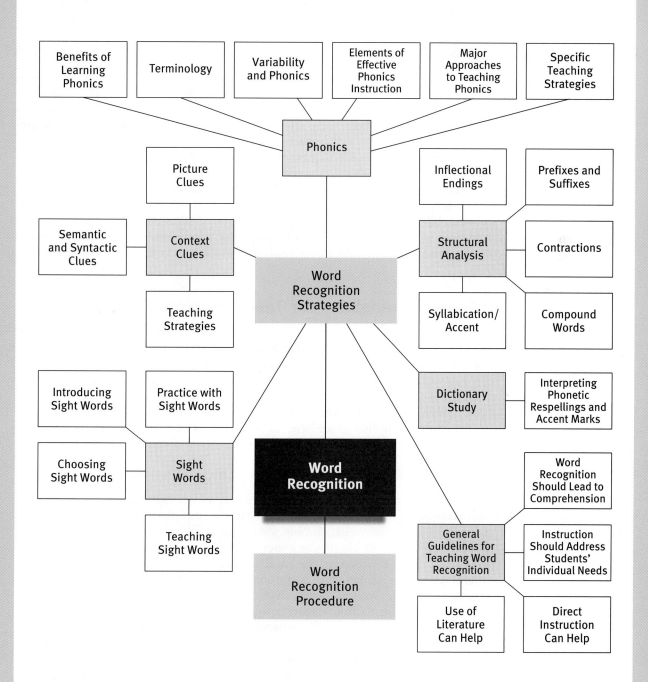

- Benefits of Learning Phonics
- Terminology
- Variability and Phonics
- Elements of Effective Phonics Instruction
- Major Approaches to Teaching Phonics
- Specific Teaching Strategies

Phonics

- Picture Clues
- Semantic and Syntactic Clues
- **Context Clues**
- Teaching Strategies

Word Recognition Strategies

- Inflectional Endings
- Prefixes and Suffixes
- **Structural Analysis**
- Contractions
- Syllabication/Accent
- Compound Words

Dictionary Study
- Interpreting Phonetic Respellings and Accent Marks

- Introducing Sight Words
- Practice with Sight Words
- Choosing Sight Words
- **Sight Words**
- Teaching Sight Words

Word Recognition

Word Recognition Procedure

- Word Recognition Should Lead to Comprehension
- **General Guidelines for Teaching Word Recognition**
- Instruction Should Address Students' Individual Needs
- Use of Literature Can Help
- Direct Instruction Can Help

to show children how to use a number of word recognition strategies in combination to help them decode words.

Word Recognition Strategies

Word recognition strategies and skills help a reader recognize written words. They include development of a store of words that can be recognized immediately on sight and the ability to use context clues, phonics, structural analysis, and dictionaries for word identification where each strategy is appropriate. The last four types are sometimes referred to as *word attack* strategies or skills.

Children need to be able to perform all of the word recognition strategies because some will be more helpful than others in certain situations. Teaching a single approach to word identification is not wise, because children may be left without the proper tools for specific situations. In addition, depending on their individual abilities, children find some word recognition strategies easier to learn than others. A child who has a hearing loss, for example, may not become very skillful at using phonics but may learn sight words easily and profit greatly from the use of context clues.

DIVERSITY

● General Guidelines for Teaching Word Recognition

Instruction in word recognition should not dominate reading time. Much time should be spent in reading connected text; Stahl (1992) suggests half of the time or more. Attention to comprehension instruction should also receive ample time.

"Research suggests that, no matter which strategies are used to introduce them to reading, the children who earn the best scores on reading comprehension tests in the second grade are the ones who made the most progress in fast and accurate word identification in the first grade" (R. C. Anderson et al., 1985, pp. 10–11). Several factors contribute to effective teaching of word recognition.

Word Recognition Should Lead to Comprehension

Samuels (1988) sees word recognition skills as "a necessary prerequisite for comprehension and skilled reading" and points out that "we need a balanced reading program, one which combines decoding skills and the skills of reading in context" (pp. 757, 758). He has long supported the idea that accurate and automatic word recognition is necessary for reading fluency. This automaticity (application without conscious thought) in word recognition is achieved through extended practice (*Struggling Readers, Day 1*, 2000). Repeated readings of the same passages can help move students from accuracy to automaticity in word recognition.

Adams (Adams et al., 1991) also endorses the need for word recognition skills along with strategies for acquiring meaning. She encourages "thorough overlearning of letters, spelling patterns, and spelling-sound correspondences—and also of vocabulary, syntactic patterns, rhetorical devices, text structures, conceptual under-pinnings, and modes of thought on which the full meaning of text depends." However, she denounces "'ponderous drills' on 'isolated skills'" (Adams et al., 1991,

LITERATURE

p. 394). She also emphasizes the need for automaticity in decoding to free students' attention for comprehension ("A Talk with Marilyn Adams," 1991). Allen (1998) also believes that decoding needs to be automatic but cautions that children must develop motivation to read—motivation that results from participation in purposeful literacy tasks. This development requires time for reading, book choice, and a chance to discuss the reading material with others.

Instruction Should Address Students' Individual Needs

Students who are having difficulties need high-interest materials that they are capable of using successfully. They should not be given material with which they have previously failed. Gill (1992, p. 450) warns that instruction in word recognition "hinders progress when it places the child in reading material on his frustration level," because this prevents the child from extracting information from patterns that he or she is capable of detecting in the text.

DIVERSITY

When working with all students, but especially with students with special needs, learning styles and modalities should be considered when instruction is planned. Auditory learners learn readily with phonics instruction, visual learners learn sight words more easily, and kinesthetic-tactile learners need to use touch and movement in order to learn best. English language learners require instruction in use of the English language while they receive instruction in reading. They must build vocabulary and knowledge about English Language features before progressing to learning sound-symbol correspondences (*Struggling Readers, Day 1,* 2000).

Direct Instruction Can Help

All students also must be provided with appropriate materials and direct instruction, as needed, for skills that they lack. Many researchers have found that direct, systematic instruction in skills and strategies benefits students who have difficulty grasping important reading-writing concepts on their own (Adams, 1990; French, Ellsworth, and Amoruso, 1995; Gaskins, 1988; Wong-Kam and Au, 1988; Sears, Carpenter, and Burstein, 1994). These children seem to learn best when direct instruction in basic skills is part of their instructional program. Direct instruction is defined as instruction with clearly stated goals that students understand, carefully sequenced and structured materials, detailed explanations and extensive modeling of reading processes, and monitoring of student work with immediate feedback. It is generally continued until skill mastery is achieved.

Direct instruction focuses on academics and is teacher-directed. Such instruction is not a matter of asking children to complete skill sheets; instead, it is a planned instructional sequence of explaining and modeling. By modeling, the teacher is helping readers understand the "invisible mental processes which are at the core of reading" (Duffy, Roehler, and Herrmann, 1988, p. 762). Direct instruction enables students to become independent readers by providing them with additional strategies for attacking unknown words and applying higher-level comprehension skills.

Direct instruction is particularly helpful for students who have difficulty acquiring phonics and decoding skills that are essential for learning to read. After reviewing research on phonics skills, Lyon (1991) concluded that systematic, phonics-based instruction produces more positive outcomes than approaches that rely on contextual reading for students who cannot intuitively learn the alphabetic code. A potential danger with direct instruction of reading skills in isolation, however, is that children may learn to recognize and pronounce words but be unable to comprehend what they read.

According to Stahl (1994), direct instruction in phonics seems most effective when integrated into a meaningful reading-writing program, and Sears and her colleagues (1994) recommend teaching strategies explicitly or directly, but within the context of authentic reading activities. A literacy program that integrates direct instruction and holistic approaches emphasizes reading and writing with many regular opportunities for students to be actively engaged. Direct instruction in phonics can occur in holistic classrooms within the context of story reading. For example, the teacher reads a big book with the class and, on later readings, calls attention to beginning sounds of words or to rhyming words. Minilessons (direct instruction) drawn from words in the story follow. (See the "Focus on Strategies" later in this chapter for ways to teach phonics through literature.)

Use of Literature Can Help

LITERATURE When students are taught with materials that emphasize repetitions of spelling patterns, such as predictable books, stories, and poetry, they tend to develop strategies based on alphabetic principles. This is particularly helpful for struggling readers. The students need to be exposed to texts that contain unchanging patterns that they are able to detect. Some students also need assistance in detecting these patterns. Students may eventually write their own pieces using these patterns (Walker, 2000).

● Sight Words

Young readers also need to develop a store of *sight words*, words that are recognized immediately without having to resort to analysis. The larger the store of sight words a reader has, the more rapidly and fluently he or she can read a selection. Comprehension and reading speed suffer if a reader has to pause too often to analyze unfamiliar words. The more mature and experienced a reader becomes, the larger his or her store of sight words becomes. (Most, if not all, of the words used in this textbook, for example, are a part of the sight vocabularies of college students.) Therefore, one goal of reading instruction is to turn all the words students continuously need to recognize in print into sight words.

FAMILY Most children know some sight words when they first come to school. They have learned the names of some of their favorite fast-food restaurants and other businesses from signs, the names of some of their favorite foods and drinks from the packages or labels, or both categories of words, as well as others, from television commercials. Children who have been read stories while sitting on their parents' laps may well have picked up vocabulary from favorite stories that were repeatedly shared. Still, the sight vocabularies of beginning students are meager compared with those that mature readers need.

Young readers need to develop a store of sight words. *(© David Young Wolff/Photo Edit)*

Teaching Sight Words

Before children begin to learn sight words, they must have developed visual discrimination skills; that is, they must be able to see likenesses and differences among printed words. It is also helpful, although not essential, for them to know the names of the letters of the alphabet, because this facilitates discussion of likenesses and differences among words. For example, a teacher could point out that, whereas *take* has a *k* before the *e, tale* has an *l* in the same position.

Artley (1996) suggests development of a basic stock of sight words first, then teaching of other methods of word recognition. This allows students to reason inductively about sound-symbol associations and other word elements, such as prefixes and suffixes, coming to understand generalizations and rules through experience with specific examples. There are a number of reasons why sight words need to be taught:

❶ The English language contains a multitude of irregularly spelled words—that is, words that are not spelled the way they sound. Many of these are among the most frequently used words in our language. The spellings of the following common words include highly irregular sound-symbol associations: *of, through, two, know, give, come,* and *once.* Rather than trying in vain to sound out these words, children need to learn to recognize them on sight as whole configurations.

❷ Learning several sight words at the very beginning of reading instruction gives the child a chance to engage in a successful reading experience very early and consequently promotes a positive attitude toward reading.

❸ Words have meaning for youngsters by the time they arrive at school, but single letters have no meaning for them. Therefore, presenting children with whole words at the beginning allows them to associate reading with meaning rather than with meaningless memorization.

❹ After children have built up a small store of sight words, the teacher can begin phonics instruction with an analytic approach, which is described later in this chapter.

Choosing Sight Words

A teacher must carefully choose which words to teach as sight words. Extremely common irregularly spelled words (*come, to, two*) and frequently used regularly spelled words (*at, it, and, am, go*) should be taught as sight words so that children can read connected sentences early in the program. The first sight words should be useful and meaningful. A child's name should be one of those words; days of the week, months of the year, and names of school subjects are other prime candidates. Words that stand for concepts unfamiliar to youngsters are poor choices. Before children learn *democracy* as a sight word, for example, they need to understand what a democracy is; therefore, this is not a good word to teach in the primary grades.

Lists of basic sight words may give teachers an indication of the words that are most frequently used in reading materials and therefore are needed most frequently by students. The Dolch list of the 220 most common words in reading materials (excluding nouns), though first published in the 1930s, has repeatedly been found to be relevant and useful in more recent materials (Mangieri and Kahn, 1977; Palmer, 1985). Another well-known list of basic sight words is Fry's "Instant Words" (Fry, 1977a). This list presents the words most frequently used in reading materials.

Teaching some words that have regular spelling patterns as sight words is consistent with the beliefs of linguists who have become involved in developing reading materials (see Chapter 7 for further details). Words with regular spelling patterns are also a good base for teaching "word families" in phonics; the *an* family, for example, includes *ban, can, Dan, fan, man, Nan, pan, ran, tan,* and *van.*

Veatch (1996) suggests that the Key Vocabulary approach, developed by Ashton-Warner, is efficient and reliable in developing sight vocabulary. Children pick words that have intense meaning for them. The teacher writes the words on cards and gives the cards to the children. The children say the letters in the words, trace them (moving left to right), and use the words (to write stories, to play games, and so on).

Creating a Word Wall of terms and phrases found in public places, such as *Wet Paint*, *No Trespassing*, *Danger*, and so on, allows students to learn, through repetition, words that are important to them in daily life. This technique can be helpful to students who have reading difficulties. (Instructions for creating a Word Wall appear later in this chapter.)

Introducing Sight Words

A potential sight word must initially be identified for learners. A teacher should show the children the printed word as he or she pronounces it or pair the word with an identifying picture. Reading aloud to children as they follow along in the book is one way to identify vocabulary for children within a meaningful context.

LITERATURE

The language experience approach, in which students' own language is written down and used as the basis for their reading material, is good for developing sight vocabulary. This approach (described in detail in Chapter 7) provides a meaningful context for learning sight words, and it can be used productively with individuals or groups. The word-bank and word-sort activities associated with this approach are particularly helpful.

Teachers may also present words in conjunction with pictures or with the actual objects the words name, such as chairs and tables, calling attention to the fact that the labels name the items. These names can be written on the board so that youngsters can try to locate the items in the room by finding the matching labels.

Constructing picture dictionaries, in which children illustrate words and file the labeled pictures alphabetically in a notebook, is a good activity for helping younger children develop sight vocabulary. This procedure has been effective in helping children whose primary language is not English learn to read and understand English words.

DIVERSITY

Regardless of the method of presentation, one factor is of paramount importance: The children must *look* at the printed word when it is identified in order to associate the letter configuration with the spoken word or picture. If children fail to look at the word when it is pronounced, they have no chance of remembering it when they next encounter it.

Teachers should also encourage children to pay attention to the details of the word by asking them to notice ascending letters (such as *b, d, h*), descending letters (such as *p, g, q*), word length, and particular letter combinations (such as double letters). Careful scrutiny of words can greatly aid retention.

Children learn early to recognize some sight words by their visual **configurations**, or shapes. Teachers should not overly stress this technique, because many words have similar shapes. But since many children seem to use the technique in the early stages of reading, regardless of the teacher's methods, a teacher can use configuration judiciously to develop early sight words. One way to call attention to shape is to have the children frame the words to be learned:

The limitation of configuration as a sight word recognition clue is demonstrated by the following words:

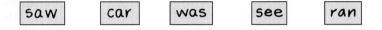

Teachers can call attention to word makeup through comparison and contrast, comparing a new word to a similar known word: *fan* may be compared with *can* if the children already have *can* in their sight vocabularies. Either the teacher can point out that the initial letters of the words are different and the other letters are the same, or the students can discover this on their own. The latter method is preferable, because the students are likely to remember their own discoveries longer than something the teacher has told them.

Few words are learned after a single presentation, although Ashton-Warner (1963) claims that children will instantly learn words that are extremely important to them. Generally, a number of repetitions are necessary before a word actually becomes a sight word.

Practice with Sight Words

The teacher should carefully plan practice with potential sight words. This practice should be varied and interesting, because children will more readily learn those things that interest them. Games, such as those we discuss later in this section, are useful if they emphasize the words being learned rather than the rules of the game.

Practice with potential sight words should generally involve using the words *in context*. Children cannot pronounce many words out of context with certainty—for example, *read*. The following sentences indicate the importance of context:

I *read* that book yesterday. I can't *read* without glasses.

Another reason for using context when presenting sight words is that many commonly used words have little meaning when they stand alone. Prime examples are *the, a,* and *an.* Context for words may be a sentence (*The* girl ate *a* pear and *an* apple) or short phrases (*the* girl, *a* pear, *an* apple). Context is also useful if pronunciation is less clear than it should be. Children may confuse the word *thing* with *think* unless the teacher has presented context for the word: "I haven't done a useful thing all day."

LITERATURE   The most natural, holistic approach to sight word instruction is reading to children as they follow along. Teachers may use this approach with groups of students when big books are available; this approach enables all children in the group to see the words. They may also read from books that are available in multiple copies in the classroom, with each child or pair of children following along on individual

TECHNOLOGY   copies of the story. Books with accompanying tapes or electronic books (discussed in Chapter 11) can promote sight vocabulary in a similar way. McGill-Franzen (1993) points out the value of highly predictable books, such as those used in the Reading Recovery Program, for beginning readers. Peterson (1991) has arranged a continuum of Reading Recovery books from easy to more complex, based partially on the context provided. The books at the easiest levels are highly predictable from the pictures and repetitive sentence patterns. Saccardi (1996a, 1996b) also recommends the use of predictable books for many literacy activities and suggests particular books and appropriate uses for each.

Using Basal Readers. Much teaching of sight word recognition takes place as a part of basal reader lessons.

- The teacher frequently introduces the new words, possibly in one of the ways described here, before reading, discussing meanings at the same time.

- Then students have a guided silent reading period during which they read material containing the new words in order to answer questions asked by the teacher.

- Purposeful oral rereading activities offer another chance to use the new words.

- Afterward, teachers generally provide practice activities suggested in the teacher's manual of the basal reading series.

- Follow-up activities may include skill sheets, games, manipulative devices, and special audiovisual materials. Writing new words is helpful for some learners, especially for kinesthetic learners (those who learn through muscle movement).

Learning Names. Teachers can use labels to help children learn to recognize their own names and the names of some of their classmates. On the first day of school, the teacher can give each child a name tag and label each child's desk with his or her name. The teacher may also label the area where the child is supposed to hang a coat or to store supplies. The teacher should explain to the children that the letters written on the name tags, desks, and storage areas spell their own names and that no one else is supposed to use these areas. The children should be encouraged to look at the names carefully and try to remember them when locating their belongings. Although the children may initially use the name tags to match the labels on the desks and storage areas, by the time the name tags are worn out or lost, the children should be able to identify their printed names without assistance.

The teacher can generally accelerate this process by teaching children how to write their names. Children may first trace the name labels on their desks with their fingers. Next, they can try to copy the names on sheets of paper. At first, the teacher should label all students' work and drawings with the students' names, but as soon as the children are capable of writing their names, they should label their own papers. From the beginning, the children's names should be written in capital and lower-case letters, rather than all capitals, since this is the way names most commonly appear in print.

The days of the week can also be taught as sight words. Each morning, the teacher can write "Today is" on the chalkboard and fill in the name of the appropriate day. At first the teacher may read the sentence to the children at the beginning of each day, but soon some children will be able to read the sentence successfully without help.

Learning Function Words.   Function words—words, such as *the* and *or,* that have only syntactic meaning rather than concrete content—are often particularly difficult for children to learn because they lack concrete meaning and because many of them are similar in physical features. These words need to be presented in context repeatedly so that the surrounding words can provide meaning. Jolly (1981) suggests teaching these troublesome words by presenting only one word at a time of a pair of words that are likely to be confused (for example, *was* and *saw*). He also suggests teaching words with more obvious differences in features first, then those with subtler differences. For example, teach *that* with words like *for* and *is* before presenting it with *this* and *the*. Teachers can also delete the words from passages, leaving blanks for the students to fill in with the target words.

Using Practice Aids.   Nicholson (1998) suggests using flashcards to foster automaticity in word recognition. He further points out that recent research indicates that "teaching children to read words faster can improve reading comprehension dramatically" (p. 188).

Another technique is to list sight words on a circular piece of cardboard and have children paper-clip pictures to appropriate words. The teacher can make this activity self-scoring by printing the matching words on the backs of the pictures, as shown here.

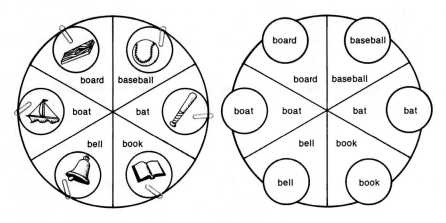

Using Games.   Games such as word bingo are useful for practice with sight words. The teacher or a leader calls out a word, and the children who recognize that word on their cards cover it. When a child covers an entire card, he or she says, "Cover," and the teacher or leader checks the card to see if all the covered words were actually called.

Dickerson (1982) compared the use of physically active games, passive games, and worksheets in an attempt to discover which would be most effective in increasing the sight vocabularies of remedial first graders. The physically active games proved to be most effective, followed by the passive games. Worksheets were the least effective, although the children who used the worksheets did gain some sight vocabulary.

CLASSROOM SCENARIO

Developing Sight Vocabulary

Mr. Barkley, a first-grade teacher, found that three children were having trouble remembering the action words in the stories they were reading. He called these children over to a corner of the room near the chalkboard and wrote these words on the board: *jump, walk, run*. He introduced the words by saying, "We have seen these words in our stories this week, but they have been hard for you to remember, so we are going to practice reading them as we play a game. This word is *jump*. Can you jump for me?" The children jumped. Then he said, "Good. Whenever you read the word *jump* for this game, I want you to jump just like that."

Mr. Barkley introduced *walk* and *run* in the same way. The students readily demonstrated each one.

Then Mr. Barkley brought out a board game with a racetrack oval drawn on it. Each space in the path around the oval had a simple sentence containing either *jump, walk,* or *run* written on it. The children took turns spinning a spinner and moving the number of spaces indicated around the racetrack with a personally selected token (one of several different miniature race cars). A child who landed on a space had to read the sentence, tell what it meant, and perform the action in the sentence. For example, the child might read, "Mary can jump," and then say, "That means Mary can do this." Then the child would stand up and jump. If a child could not read the sentence or tell/show what it meant, another player could "steal his or her play" by reading the sentence and performing the action. The player who got to try this would be determined by having the opponents of the player who missed spin the spinner for a high number.

The first child around the track won the game, but all three children were actively involved with the action words and made progress in reading them correctly as the game continued.

Analysis of Scenario

Mr. Barkley used a physically active game to develop the children's sight vocabularies after more passive reading activities had failed to be effective with these children. He targeted the activity for the children who were having difficulty, rather than forcing repetitive practice on those who had mastered the words. He also presented the words in sentence contexts to encourage children to recognize the words in typical reading situations, rather than as isolated entities.

Teachers may consider increasing their use of more active games, such as those in which children stand and act out action verbs. The Classroom Scenario above describes such an activity.

Ceprano (1981) reviewed research on methods of teaching sight words and found that no one method alone was best for every student. She found evidence that teaching the distinctive features of words helped children learn. She also found evidence that use of picture clues along with specific instruction to focus attention on the words facilitated learning. She reported, however, that some research indicates that teaching words in isolation or with pictures does not ensure that children will acquire the ability to read words in context. In fact, indications are that "most learners need directed experience with written context while learning words in order to perceive that reading is a language process and a meaning-getting process" (p. 321). Therefore, when teachers are working with sight-word instruction, it seems wise to present words in context rather than just in isolation.

TIME for REFLECTION

Some people believe sight words should be taught in context. Others believe they should be taught in isolation. **What procedures would *you* use?**

● Context Clues

Context clues — the words, phrases, and sentences surrounding the words to be decoded—help readers determine what the unfamiliar words are. Here we will focus on the function of context clues as *word recognition* aids; Chapter 5 considers the function of context clues as *comprehension* aids.

Since research has found that syntactic and semantic context influence readers' identification of words, it is important that word recognition skills be introduced and practiced in context (Jones, 1982). Much of the written material to which primary-level readers are introduced falls well within their comprehension as far as vocabulary and ideas are concerned, but these youngsters cannot always recognize in printed form the words that are familiar in oral form. Context clues can be extremely helpful in this process. Research also shows that context clues help younger and poorer readers recognize words more than they help older and better readers (Gough, 1984; Daneman, 1991).

Picture Clues

Picture clues are generally the earliest context clues that children use. Picture Walks (going through the selection and analyzing the pictures for information) may be used as a strategy before reading a story to help develop concepts and vocabulary. If children are exposed to many pictures of a character, such as one named Julie, in beginning reading materials, they may come to recognize the character instantly. When they are shown a page containing a picture of Julie and a single word, they may naturally assume that the word names the picture and that the word is *Julie.* If they do not relate the picture to the word in this manner, the teacher can ask a question such as "Who is in the picture?" to lead them toward understanding the relationship. If a child responds, "A girl," the teacher might ask, "What kind of letter is at the beginning of the word?" The response "A capital letter" would prompt the question "What kinds of words have we talked about that begin with capital letters?" After eliciting the answer "Names," the teacher can then ask, "What is the name of the girl in the picture?" This question should produce the response "Julie." Finally, the teacher asks, "Now what do you think the word is?" At this point, a correct response is extremely likely. The teacher should use a procedure that encourages the use of picture clues *along with,* rather than apart from, the clues available in the printed word.

Teachers should not overemphasize picture clues. These clues may be useful in the initial stages of instruction, but they become less useful as the child advances to more difficult material, which has a decreasing number of pictures and an increasing proportion of print. Encouraging too much reliance on pictures may result in too little time spent on developing word analysis skills.

Semantic and Syntactic Clues

As soon as possible, teachers should encourage first-grade children to use written context as a clue to unknown words. The idea of using context clues can be

MODEL ACTIVITIES — Use of Oral Context

Read sentences such as the following to the children, leaving out words as indicated by the blanks. Sentences can be drawn from books the teacher plans to share later in class. After reading each sentence, ask the children what word they could use to finish the sentence in a way that would make sense. The children will find that the sentences that have missing words at the end are easier. In some cases, the children may suggest several possibilities, all of which are appropriate. Accept all of these contributions with positive comments.

Sample Sentences

1. Jane went out to walk her _____.

2. John was at home reading a _____.

3. They were fighting like cats and _____.

4. I want toast and _____ for breakfast.

5. Will you _____ football with me?

introduced by oral activities like the Model Activity above. The sentences can often be drawn from stories that have just been read or listened to in class.

In the sample sentences in the Model Activity, children can use both semantic (meaning) and syntactic (grammar) clues in choosing words to fill in the blanks. Youngsters generally use these two types of clues in combination, but to clarify the differences between them, we will consider them separately first.

Semantic clues are clues derived from the meanings of the words, phrases, and sentences surrounding the unknown word. In the examples in the Model Activity, children can ask themselves the following questions to decide what words would make sense:

Sentence 1. What are things that can be walked?

Sentence 2. What are things that can be read?

Sentence 3. What expression do I know about fighting that has *like cats and* in it?

Sentence 4. What food might be eaten with toast for breakfast?

Sentence 5. What things can you do with a football?

Syntactic clues are provided by the grammar or syntax of our language. Certain types of words appear in certain positions in spoken English sentences. Therefore, word order can give readers clues to the identity of an unfamiliar word. Because most children in schools in the United States have been speaking English since they were preschoolers, they have a feeling for the grammar or syntax of the language. Syntactic clues help them discover that the missing words in sentences 1 through 4 in the oral-context model activity are nouns, or naming words, and that the missing word in sentence 5 is a verb, or action word.

Looking at each item, we find various clues. In sentence 1, for example, we expect *her* to be followed by a noun. *A* is usually followed by a singular noun, as in sentence 2. Sentences 3 and 4 both employ *and,* which usually connects words of the same type. In sentence 3, children are likely to insert a plural animal name because of the absence of an article (*a, an, the*) and because the animals already mentioned, *cats,* are plural. Similarly, in sentence 4, *and* will signal insertion of another food. Sentence 5 has the verb marker *will*, which is often found in the sequence "Will you (verb)...?"

As we pointed out earlier, semantic and syntactic clues should be used *together* to unlock unknown words.

Teaching Strategies

Early exercises with context clues may resemble the oral-context exercise. It is good practice for a teacher to introduce a new word in context and let children try to identify it, rather than simply telling them what the word is. Then children can use any phonics and structural analysis knowledge they have, along with context clues, to help them identify the word. The teacher should use a context in which the only unfamiliar word is the new word; for example, use the sentence "My *umbrella* keeps me from getting wet when it rains" to present the word *umbrella*. The children will thus have successful examples of the value of context clues in identifying unfamiliar words.

When a child encounters an unfamiliar word when reading orally to the teacher, instead of supplying the word, the teacher can encourage the child to skip it for the time being and read on to the end of the sentence (or even to the next sentence) to see what word would make sense. Although most of the examples in this section show only a single sentence as the context, children should be encouraged to look for clues in surrounding sentences as well as in the sentence in which the word occurs. Sometimes an entire paragraph will be useful in defining a term.

Using Syntactic Clues.   The teacher can encourage use of the sound of the initial letter or cluster of letters, sounds of other letters in the word, or known structural components, along with context. In a sentence where *hurled* appears as an unknown word in the phrase *hurled the ball*, a child might guess *held* from the context. The teacher could encourage this child to notice the letters *ur* and try a word that contains those sounds and makes sense in the context. Of course, this approach will be effective only if the child knows the meaning of *hurled*. Encouraging the child to read subsequent sentences could also be helpful, since these sentences might disclose a situation in which *held* would be inappropriate but *hurled* would fit.

Cloze and Maze Activities.   A cloze passage, in which words have been systematically deleted and replaced with blanks of uniform length, can be a good way to work on using context clues. For this purpose, the teacher may also use a modified cloze passage, deleting certain types of words (nouns, verbs, adjectives, etc.), rather than using regularly spaced deletions. The students should discuss their reasons for choosing the words to be inserted in the blanks, and the teacher should accept synonyms and sometimes nonsynonyms for which the students have a good rationale. The point of the exercise is to have the students think logically about what makes sense in the context. (Other uses for the **cloze procedure** and more details about it are found in Chapters 5, 10, and 12.) An easier task for the students is to use a maze passage, in which the deleted words are replaced by three choices. This task may work better with younger students and those who are having difficulty with reading tasks. (The *maze procedure* is discussed in Chapter 12.)

A modified cloze procedure can be used with a story summary to develop children's skill in decoding in a meaningful context. The first letter of the deleted word is provided, which helps children use their knowledge of sound-symbol relationships in addition to choosing words that make sense in the context (Johnson and Louis, 1987). A child who encountered the following sentence with a blank instead of a word at the end might fill in the blank with either *bat* or *glove*:

> *Frank said, "If I am going to play Little League baseball this year, I need a new ball and _____."*

If the sentence indicated the initial sound of the missing word by presenting the initial letter *g*, the child would know that *glove*, rather than *bat*, was the appropriate word.

> *Frank said, "If I am going to play Little League baseball this year, I need a new ball and g_____."*

Structural analysis clues can be used in the same way. In the following sentence, a child might insert such words as *stop* or *keep* in the blank.

> *I wouldn't want to _____ you from going on the trip.*

The child who had the help of the familiar prefix *pre-* to guide his or her choice would choose neither. The word *prevent* would obviously be the proper choice.

> *I wouldn't want to pre_____ you from going on the trip.*

Suffixes and ending sounds are also very useful in conjunction with context to help in word identification. Sample sentences for practice activities can be drawn from stories that the children are about to read in class.

Using Context Clues to Teach Homographs. Some words are difficult to pronounce unless they appear in context. Many *homographs* — words that look alike but have different meanings and sometimes different pronunciations, such as *row, wind, bow, read, content, rebel, minute, lead, record,* and *live* — are prime examples. Here are some sentences that demonstrate how context can clarify the pronunciations of such words:

❶ The *wind* is blowing through the trees.

❷ Did you *wind* the clock last night?

❸ She put a *bow* on the gift.

❹ You should *bow* to the audience when you finish your act.

❺ Would you *rebel* against that law?

❻ I have always thought you were a *rebel*.

❼ Did your father *record* his gas mileage?

❽ Suzanne broke Jill's *record* for the highest score in one game.

Using Basal Readers to Teach Context Clues.   DeSerres (1990) introduces basal reader stories' mastery vocabulary by presenting each word on the board in sentence context, having students write the word in another sentence or phrase context on 3" x 5" word cards for their word banks, and letting them share their sentences. Later she uses modified cloze stories (in which selected words, rather than regularly spaced words, are deleted) with the mastery words as the words chosen for omission. Students fill in the blanks by choosing from their word cards as the class reads the story together. Then they fill in the blanks on individual copies of the stories and read them to partners. Partners point out parts that do not make sense. Later, students produce their own stories. This procedure gives practice with using context.

Combining Word Recognition Techniques.   Context clues are best used with the skills we'll discuss next, phonics and structural analysis skills. Context clues help children identify words more quickly than phonics or structural analysis clues alone would by helping them make educated guesses about the identities of unfamiliar words. But without the confirmation of phonics and structural analysis, context clues provide only guesses. As we mentioned earlier, when a blank is substituted for a word in a sentence, students can often use several possibilities to complete the sentence and still have it make sense. When children encounter unknown words, they should make educated guesses based on the context and verify those guesses by using other word analysis skills.

● Phonics

Before you read this section, go to "Test Yourself" at the end of the chapter and take the multiple-choice phonics test. It will give you an idea of your present knowledge of phonics. After you study the text, go back and take the test again to see what you have learned.

Phonics is the association of speech sounds (*phonemes*) with printed symbols (*graphemes*). In some languages, this sound-symbol association is fairly regular, but not in English. A single letter or combination of letters in our alphabet may stand for many different sounds. For example, the letter *a* has a different sound in each of the following words: *cape, cat, car, father, soda.* On the other hand, a single sound may be represented by more than one letter or combination of letters. The long *e* sound is spelled differently in each of the following words: *me, mien, meal, seed,* and *seize.* To complicate matters further, the English language abounds with words that contain letters that stand for no sound, as in is**l**and, **k**ni**gh**t, **w**rite, lam**b**, **g**nome, **p**salm, and **rh**yme.

The existence of these spelling inconsistencies does not imply that phonics is not useful in helping children decode written English. We discuss inconsistencies to counteract the feeling of some teachers that phonics is an infallible guide to pronouncing words in written materials. In addition, teaching phonics does not constitute a complete reading program. Phonics is a valuable aid to word recognition when used in conjunction with other skills, but it is only *one* useful skill among many. Mastering this skill, and thus gaining the ability to pronounce most unfamiliar words, should not be considered the primary goal of a reading program. Children can pronounce words without understanding them, and deriving *meaning* from the printed page should be the objective of all reading instruction. Still, Groff (1998, p. 139) states that "the consensus of pertinent empirical investigations is that the more phonics information that children acquire, and learn to apply to decode written words, the better."

Benefits of Learning Phonics

Phonics techniques are not intended to be ends in themselves; rather, they are means to the end of successful reading. Maclean (1988) sees phonics as "a catalyst which triggers the process of learning to read" (p. 517). It helps students pair spoken and written words and lays the groundwork for them to develop their own decoding routines, which may bear little resemblance to the rules used in phonics instruction. In order for the phonics catalyst to produce a reaction, children must be allowed to do large amounts of reading in appropriate materials.

As Heilman (2002, p. 1), emphasizing the benefits of using phonics in conjunction with context clues, points out, "English spelling patterns being what they are, children will sometimes arrive at only a close approximation of the needed sounds. ... Fortunately, if they are reading for meaning, they will instantly correct these errors."

Groff (1986) found that, if beginning readers can attain an approximate pronunciation of a written word by applying phonics generalizations, they can go on to infer the true pronunciation of the word. He found, for example, that "100% of the second graders tested could infer and produce the *o* of *from* as /u/ after first hearing it as /o/. The pronunciation /from/ was close enough to /frum/ for these young pupils to infer its correct pronunciation" (p. 921). Groff concluded that children need practice in making such inferences. First, they need to apply phonics generalizations to unfamiliar words, producing approximate pronunciations of the words. Then they can infer the real pronunciations of the words by thinking of words they know that are close in sound to the approximations achieved by the generalizations.

Skilled readers appear to identify unfamiliar words by finding similarities to known words (R. C. Anderson et al., 1985). For example, a reader might work out the pronunciation of the unknown word *lore* by comparing it with the known word *sore* and applying the knowledge of the sound of *l* in other known words, such as *lamp.* Cunningham (1978, 1979) and Allen (1998) suggest using a similar approach to identify polysyllabic words as well as single-syllable words.

TIME for REFLECTION

Some people think phonics is all that a child needs for a word recognition program. Others think that several different word attack methods are needed. **What do *you* think, and why?**

Carnine (1977) studied the transfer effects of phonics and whole word approaches to reading instruction and found superior transfer to new words among the students who were taught phonics. The phonics group even had greater transfer to irregular words, although it was not extensive. Research with adults has been interpreted as indicating that teachers should present *several* sound-symbol correspondences for each grapheme, rather than one-to-one correspondences, thereby providing their students with a set for diversity. If such a procedure had been used in this study, it might have produced more transfer to irregular words. The following Classroom Scenario shows one way that phonics principles begin to form in classes.

Development of Phonics Knowledge

Marty, a first grader, was turning the pages of a calendar in his classroom, finding numbers that he recognized on each page. Suddenly he called to his teacher excitedly, "Mrs. Overholt, this is almost like my name!"

Mrs. Overholt joined Marty at his table. "Yes, it is," she replied. "Show me the part that is the same."

Marty pointed to the letters *M, a, r,* in sequence.

"That's right," Mrs. Overholt said. "Can you tell me what month this is?"

"No," Marty said.

"The month is March," said Mrs. Overholt. "Does it sound a little like your name, too?"

"Yes," Marty almost squealed. "The beginning of it sounds like the beginning of my name."

"You really listened carefully to hear that," Mrs. Overholt said. "Those letters stand for the same sounds in your name and in the word *March*. Keep your eyes open for other words like this. You may be able to figure out what they are by remembering what you found out about letters and sounds."

Analysis of Scenario

Mrs. Overholt used a teachable moment with Marty. He had made a discovery about words that excited him, and his teacher helped him to expand it.

Terminology

To understand written material about phonics, teachers need to be familiar with the following terms.

Phoneme. The smallest unit of sound in a language is called a phoneme.

Grapheme. A written symbol for a phoneme is called a grapheme.

Vowels. The letters *a, e, i, o,* and *u* represent vowel sounds, and the letters *w* and *y* take on the characteristics of vowels when they appear in the final position in a word or syllable. The letter *y* also has the characteristics of a vowel in the medial (middle) position in a word or syllable.

Consonants. Letters other than *a, e, i, o,* and *u* generally represent consonant sounds. *W* and *y* have the characteristics of consonants when they appear in the initial position in a word or syllable.

Consonant Blends (or Clusters). Two or more adjacent consonant letters whose sounds are blended together, with each individual sound retaining its identity, constitute a consonant blend. For example, although the first three sounds in the word *strike* are blended smoothly, listeners can detect the separate sounds of *s, t,* and *r* being produced in rapid succession. Other examples are the *fr* in *frame,* the *cl* in *click,* and the *br* in *bread,* to mention only a few. Many teaching materials refer to these letter combinations as consonant clusters rather than consonant blends.

Consonant Digraphs. Two adjacent consonant letters that represent a single speech sound constitute a consonant digraph. For example, *sh* is a consonant digraph in the word *shore* because it represents one sound and not a blend of the sounds of *s* and *h*. Additional examples of consonant digraphs appear on page 94.

Vowel Digraphs. Two adjacent vowel letters that represent a single speech sound constitute a vowel digraph. In the word *foot, oo* is a vowel digraph. Additional examples of vowel digraphs appear on pages 94–95.

Diphthongs. Vowel sounds that are so closely blended that they can be treated as single vowel units for the purposes of word identification are called *diphthongs*. Unlike vowel digraphs, in which the two vowels produce a single sound, diphthongs are actually vowel blends, since the vocal mechanism produces two sounds. An example of a diphthong is the *ou* in *out*. Additional examples of diphthongs appear on page 95.

Variability and Phonics

As we have mentioned, the English language contains a great deal of variability, so students must use additional strategies to confirm the pronunciation guesses they arrive at by applying the principles of phonics. There are many exceptions to general rules and principles.

Consonants. Although consonant letters are more consistent in the sounds they represent than vowel letters are, they are not perfectly consistent. The following list shows some examples of variations with which a child must contend.

Consonant	Variations	Consonant	Variations
b	board, lamb	n	never, drink
c	cable, city, scene	p	punt, psalm
d	dog, jumped	q(u)	antique, quit
f	fox, of	s	see, sure, his, pleasure,
g	go, gem, gnat		island
h	hit, hour	t	town, listen
j	just, hallelujah	w	work, wrist
k	kitten, knee	x	fox, anxiety, exit
l	lamp, calf	z	zoo, azure, quartz

Consider the cases in which *y* and *w* take on vowel characteristics. Both of these letters represent consonant sounds when they are in the initial position in a word or syllable, but they represent vowel sounds when they are in a final or medial position. For example, *y* represents a consonant sound in the word *yard* but a vowel sound in the words *dye, myth,* and *baby*. Notice that three different vowel sounds are represented by *y* in these words. *W* represents a consonant sound in the word *watch* but a vowel sound in the word *cow*.

Consonant Digraphs.   Several consonant digraphs represent sounds not associated with either of the component parts. These are as follows:

Consonant Digraph	Example	Consonant Digraph	Example
th	then, thick	ph	telephone
ng	sing	gh	rough
sh	shout	ch	chief, chef, chaos

Other consonant digraphs generally represent the usual sound of one of the component parts, as in **wr**ite, **pn**eumonia, and **gn**at. Some sources consider one of the letters in each of these combinations as a "silent" letter and do not refer to these combinations as digraphs.

Vowels.   The variability of the sounds represented by vowels has been emphasized before. Some examples of this variability are as follows:

Vowel Letter	Variations
a	ate, cat, want, ball, father, sofa
e	me, red, pretty, kitten, her, sergeant
i	ice, hit, fir, opportunity
o	go, hot, today, women, button, son, work, born
u	use, cut, put, circus, turn

In the examples here, the first variation listed for each vowel is a word in which the long vowel sound, the same as its letter name, is heard. In the second variation, the short sound of the vowel is heard. These are generally the first two sounds taught for each vowel.

Another extremely common sound that children need to learn is the schwa sound, a very soft "uh" or grunt usually found in unaccented syllables. It is heard in the following words: sof**a**, kitt**e**n, opportun**i**ty, butt**o**n, circ**u**s. As you can see, each of the vowel letters can represent the schwa sound in some words. Three types of markings represent the three types of vowel sounds we have discussed:

Marking	Name of Mark	Designation
ā, ē, ī, ō, ū	macron	long vowel sound
ă, ĕ, ĭ, ŏ, ŭ	breve	short vowel sound
ə	schwa	soft "uh" sound

Many dictionaries place no mark at all over a vowel letter that represents the short sound of the vowel.

Vowel Digraphs.   Some vowel digraphs represent sounds not associated with either of the letters involved. These are as follows:

Vowel Digraph	Example
au	taught

Vowel Digraph	Example
aw	saw
oo	food, look

Other vowel digraphs generally represent the usual sound of one of the component parts, as in br**ea**k, br**ea**d, b**oa**t, s**ee**d, and **ai**m. Some sources treat one of the letters in these combinations as "silent" and do not refer to them as digraphs.

Diphthongs.   There are four common diphthongs, or vowel blends.

Diphthong	Example	Diphthong	Example
oi	foil	ou	bound
oy	toy	ow	cow

Notice that the first two diphthongs listed (*oi* and *oy*) stand for identical sounds, as do the last two (*ou* and *ow*). Remember that the letter combinations *ow* and *ou* are *not always diphthongs*. In the words *snow* and *blow, ow* is a vowel digraph representing the long *o* sound. In the word *routine, ou* represents the $\overline{oo}$ sound, and in the word *shoulder, ou* represents the long *o* sound.

As we have mentioned, these variations do not imply that phonics is not useful in helping children decode written English, but they do indicate that children should learn other word recognition strategies to use when they cannot be sure of pronunciation from their use of phonics.

Elements of Effective Phonics Instruction

For phonics instruction to be effective, students need to be ready to learn phonics, and teachers need to provide context and reinforcement—a reason to learn phonics. Teachers also need to target key phonics generalizations and decide how to communicate them.

Prerequisites for Phonics Instruction.   There seems to be agreement that good auditory and visual discrimination are prerequisites for learning sound-symbol relationships. We know that children must be able to distinguish one letter from another and one sound from another before they can associate a given letter with a given sound. *Visual discrimination* is the ability to distinguish likenesses and differences among forms, and *auditory discrimination* is the ability to distinguish likenesses and differences among sounds. To achieve these skills, children must first understand the concepts of *like* and *different.* Also, to achieve auditory discrimination, children must have **phonemic awareness**, or the awareness that speech is composed of separate sounds (phonemes). They must be able to hear sounds within words, or they will be unable to form mental connections between sounds and letters (Beck and Juel, 1995; Griffith and Olson, 1992; Juel, 1988, 1991; Ball and Blachman, 1991; Lundberg, Frost, and Peterson, 1988; Pearson, 1993; Adams, 1990; Gill, 1992). They must also understand the **alphabetic principle** (the concept that letters are symbols for phonemes, or sounds). Information on visual and auditory discrimination and on phonemic awareness and the alphabetic principle is found in Chapter 2.

Reinforcement and Context. A good phonics program provides sufficient reinforcement for a skill that is being taught and offers a variety of reinforcement opportunities. The practice activities in this text offer some ideas for reinforcement opportunities. Although reinforcement in phonics instruction may include practice with single letters and sounds, it must include application of the strategy or skill with whole words and longer pieces of discourse, such as sentences and paragraphs. Spiegel (1990b) suggests the following sequence: "auditory discrimination of the sound of interest, visual discrimination of the letter pattern, and then work with words, sentences, and short paragraphs" (p. 328). We believe this practice should be expanded to include work with whole selections, such as predictable books that contain the letter-sound association that is being emphasized. In fact, a whole selection, in the form of a big book, may be shared with the children orally, with children chiming in on the highly predictable parts wherever possible. From this beginning, the teacher may have students locate the letter representing the sound under consideration, listen for the sound as he or she reads portions of the story aloud again, and make their own generalizations about the relationship between the sound and the letter that represents it. The children will not state their personal generalizations in the same form as the rules that would be found in a reading text, of course, but they will understand the connection more deeply and retain it better if they have discovered it themselves. Lapp and Flood (1997) point out that when children are taught language skills and strategies in a context that includes the exploration of books, a balanced approach to literacy instruction has been attained.

When considering the use of predictable books, be aware that Johnston (1998, p. 670) "concluded that while beginners are more likely to learn words that repeat and are easily decodable, these were not the most common words in the predictable books [she] used." Although predictable text offers context clues, the ease of reading through context may detract from careful processing of print.

Decodable text has simple sentence structure, controlled letter-sound correspondences, controlled spelling patterns, and controlled use of high-frequency irregular sight words. Decodable books may or may not be predictable. The text difficulty increases gradually as the grade level increases (Brown, 1999/2000). Teachers may use decodable texts that contain regular letter-sound relationships (but are not necessarily predictable texts) to provide scaffolding for students who are just moving from partial-alphabetic to full-alphabetic reading. Decodable texts can give students a place to practice the sound-symbol associations they are learning (Mesmer, 1999).

Reading alphabet books can help children learn some letter-sound associations. These books should be chosen with care to ensure that they represent common sounds for the letters, present multiple words that begin with each letter, have words with which children are familiar, and provide clear illustrations for the words.

If students are to learn phonics associations effectively, they need to see a reason for doing so. The relevance of learning sound-symbol associations is much clearer when students can see the letters and sounds as a part of a meaning-bearing system, rather than as isolated bits of meaningless information.

If basal reading series consistently designed the stories and phonics instruction to support each other, the connection between the phonics instruction and achieving meaning when reading might be much clearer. Richard Anderson and colleagues

TIME for REFLECTION

Some people believe children should learn basic skills before they begin reading stories, but others believe they should learn skills as they encounter the need for them within stories. **What do *you* think, and why?**

(1985, p. 47) found that "a high proportion of the words in the earliest selections children read should conform to the phonics they have already been taught."

Adams sees the instructional goal of phonics as students' understanding of the alphabetic principle in written English. She points out that participating in language experience activities, writing with invented spelling, sharing books, and reading interesting texts can help in reaching this goal ("A Talk with Marilyn Adams," 1991). The National Reading Panel report showed "that helping children invent spellings is one of the best ways to teach phonemic awareness and phonics" (Yatvin, Weaver, and Garon, 2003, p. 32).

Phonics Generalizations. Some teachers believe that good phonics instruction is merely a matter of the teacher presenting a series of principles, or general rules, that children are expected to internalize and use in the process of word identification. Difficulties arise from this conception, however.

First, pupils tend to internalize a phonics generalization more rapidly and effectively when they can arrive at it inductively. That is, by analyzing words to which a generalization applies and by deriving the generalization themselves from this analysis, children will understand it better and remember it longer than if the teacher provides the generalization.

Second, the irregularity of the English spelling system results in numerous exceptions to phonics generalizations. Children must be helped to see that generalizations help them to derive *probable* pronunciations rather than infallible results. When applying a generalization does not produce a word that makes sense in the context of the material, readers should try other reasonable sound possibilities. For example, in cases where a long vowel sound is likely according to a generalization but results in a nonsense word, the child should be taught to try other sounds, such as the short vowel sound, in their search for the correct pronunciation. Some words are so totally irregular in their spellings that even extreme flexibility in phonic analysis will not produce close approximations of the correct pronunciations. In such situations, the child should be taught to turn to the dictionary for help in word recognition. Further discussion of this approach to word recognition can be found later in this chapter.

DIVERSITY 🌐 Third, students can be so deluged with rules that they cannot memorize them all. This procedure may result in their failure to learn any generalization well. The task of applying phonics generalizations is often even harder for children learning English who have learned different sound-symbol associations in their first language. Teachers can enhance a phonics program by presenting judiciously chosen phonics generalizations to youngsters, as long as they are taught, not as unvarying rules, but as guides to best guesses. Authorities vary on which generalizations to present (Bailey, 1967; Burmeister, 1968; Clymer, 1996; Emans, 1967), but they agree on some. Considering the findings of phonics studies and past teaching experience, we believe the following generalizations are among the most useful.

❶ When the letters *c* and *g* are followed by *e, i,* or *y,* they generally have soft sounds: the *s* sound for the letter *c* and the *j* sound for the letter *g.* (Examples: *cent, city, cycle, gem, ginger, gypsy.*) When *c* and *g* are followed by *o, a,* or *u,* they generally have hard sounds: *g* has its own special sound, and *c* has the sound of *k*. (Examples: *cat, cake, cut, go, game, gum.*)

❷ When two like consonants are next to each other, only one is sounded. (Examples: *hall, glass.*)

❸ *Ch* usually has the sound heard in *church,* although it sometimes sounds like *sh* or *k*. (Examples of usual sound: *child, chill, china.* Examples of *sh* sound: *chef, chevron.* Examples of *k* sound: *chemistry, chord.*)

❹ When *kn* are the first two letters in a word, the *k* is not sounded. (Examples: *know, knight.*)

❺ When *wr* are the first two letters in a word, the *w* is not sounded. (Examples: *write, wrong.*)

❻ When *ck* are the last two letters in a word, the sound of *k* is given. (Examples: *check, brick.*)

❼ The sound of a vowel preceding *r* is usually neither long nor short. (Examples: *car, fir, her.*)

❽ In the vowel combinations *oa, ee, ai,* and *ay,* the first vowel is generally long and the second one is not sounded. (Examples: *boat, feet, rain, play.*) This may also apply to other double vowel combinations.

❾ The double vowels *oi, oy,* and *ou* usually form diphthongs. The *ow* combination may also form a diphthong, although it frequently stands for the long *o* sound. (Examples: *boil, boy, out, now.*)

❿ If a word has only one vowel and that vowel is at the end of the word, the vowel usually represents its long sound. (Examples: *me, go.*)

⓫ If a word has only one vowel and that vowel is *not* at the end of the word, the vowel usually represents its short sound. (Examples: *set, man, cut, hop, list.*)

⓬ If a word has two vowels and one is a final *e,* the first vowel is usually long and the final *e* is not sounded. (Examples: *cape, cute, cove, kite.*)

Rosso and Emans (1981) tried to determine whether knowledge of phonic generalizations helps children decode unrecognized words and whether children have to be able to state the generalizations to use them. They found statistically significant relationships between knowledge of phonic generalizations and reading achievement, but they pointed out that this link does not necessarily indicate a cause-and-effect relationship. They also discovered that "inability to state a phonics rule did not seem to hinder these children's effort to analyze unfamiliar words. ... this study supports Piaget's theory that children in the concrete operations stage of development may encounter difficulty in describing verbally those actions they perform physically" (p. 657). Teachers may need to investigate techniques for teaching phonics generalizations that do not require children to verbalize the generalizations.

It is wise to teach only one generalization at a time, presenting a second only after students have thoroughly learned the first. The existence of exceptions to generalizations should be freely acknowledged, and children should be encouraged to treat the generalizations as *possible* rather than *infallible* clues to pronunciation.

In their summary of *Beginning to Read: Thinking and Learning About Print* by Adams (1990), Stahl, Osborn, and Lehr (1990) emphasize that rote learning of abstract generalizations will not produce a skillful decoder. They point out the importance of the connection of generalizations with experience. "Rules are intended to capture the patterns of spelling. But productive use of those patterns depends on relevant experience, not on rote memorization" (p. 83). They conclude that phonics generalizations have only temporary value; in fact, "Once a child has learned to read the spellings to which they pertain, they are superfluous" (p. 126).

Finally, teachers should keep in mind a caution about the teaching of phonics generalizations that involve the use of such terms as *sound* and *word*. Studies by Reid and Downing indicate that young children (five year olds) have trouble under-standing terms used to talk about language, such as *word, letter,* and *sound* (Downing, 1973), and Meltzer and Herse (1969) found that first-grade children do not always know where printed words begin and end. In addition, Tovey (1980) found that the group of second through sixth graders he studied had difficulty in dealing with abstract phonics terms such as *consonant, consonant blend, consonant digraph, vowel digraph, diphthong, possessive, inflectional ending,* and others. His study also showed that the children had learned sound-symbol associations without being able to define the phonics terms involved. Before teaching a lesson using linguistic terms, the teacher should check to be sure that students grasp such concepts. Technical terminology should be deemphasized when working with students who have not mastered the terms.

Major Approaches to Teaching Phonics

There are two major approaches to phonics instruction: the synthetic and the analytic. A third approach, based on "word families," has been developed to combine features of both approaches.

Synthetic Approach. In the ***synthetic approach***, the teacher first instructs children in the speech sounds that are associated with individual letters. Because letters and sounds have no inherent relationships, this task is generally accomplished by repeated drill on sound-symbol associations. The teacher may hold up a card on which the letter *b* appears and expect the children to respond with the sound ordinarily associated with that letter. The next step is to blend the sounds together to form words. The teacher encourages the children to pronounce the sounds associated with the letters in rapid succession so that they produce a word or an approximate pronunciation of a word, which they can then recognize and pronounce accurately. This blending process generally begins with two- and three-letter words and proceeds to much longer ones.

Although blending ability is a key factor in the success of a synthetic phonics approach, many commercial materials for reading instruction give little attention to its development. Research indicates that children must master both segmentation of words into their component sounds and blending before they are able to apply phonics skills to the decoding of unknown words and that the ability to segment is a

The teacher reads a literature selection with a specific phonic element to the class.
(© Tony Freeman/Photo Edit)

prerequisite for successful blending. Research also indicates that a teacher cannot assume children will automatically transfer the skills they have been taught to unknown words. Direct instruction for transfer is needed to ensure that it will occur (Johnson and Baumann, 1984).

In the synthetic phonics approach, children are sometimes asked to pronounce nonsense syllables because these syllables will appear later in written materials as word parts. Reading words in context does not generally occur until these steps have been repeatedly carried out and the children have developed a moderate stock of words.

Analytic Approach.   The ***analytic approach*** involves teaching some sight words, followed by teaching the sounds of the letters within those words. Many educators prefer this approach, and it is used in many basal reader series, partly because it avoids the distortion that occurs when consonants are pronounced in isolation. For example, trying to pronounce a *t* in isolation is likely to result in the sounds *tə*. Pronouncing a schwa sound following the consonant can adversely affect the child's blending, because the word *tag* must be sounded as *tə-a-gə*. No matter how fast children make those sounds, they are unlikely to come very close to *tag*. With an analytic approach, the teacher would refer to "the sound you hear at the beginning of the word *top*" when cueing the first sound in *tag*. The same process may be used to introduce other consonants, consonant blends, consonant digraphs, vowels, diphthongs, and vowel digraphs in initial, medial, and final positions. One possible problem with the use of analytic phonics, however, is that children may not be able to extract an individual sound just from hearing it within a word. Partly for this reason, and partly because some analytic phonics instruction is worded in a confusing manner, Adams's (1990) findings seem to indicate that even though trying to isolate phonemes can result in distortion, the advantages of asking students to produce phonemes in isolation can outweigh the disadvantages.

To help children sound out unfamiliar one-syllable words, first have them isolate the vowel sound and produce it; then have them blend the initial consonant or consonant cluster with that vowel sound; and then have them blend the remaining consonants at the end of the word with the onset-vowel chunk that has already been pronounced. This approach avoids the distortion of consonant sounds that results when single consonant sounds are isolated.

STANDARDS AND ASSESSMENT

LITERATURE

Whole language teachers often teach phonics with an analytic approach. Phonics is taught in whole language classrooms, but according to Dahl and Scharer (2000, p. 588), it is "not a separate curriculum; instead it [is] woven into daily whole language activities." Much of it takes place while children are doing writing activities. It also takes place during independent reading time. Teachers can engage in ongoing informal assessment so that instruction can match the individual student's needs. Trachtenburg (1990) suggests a procedure that is basically an analytic approach in which phonics instruction occurs within the context of reading quality children's literature. Here the progression is from the whole literature selection to the phonic element within the selection and back to another whole literature selection for application of the new knowledge. This procedure is consistent with Harp's (1989b) point of view: "While the process may be broken down to examine individual pieces, before the instruction ends the process should be 'put back together' so that the children see the relationship between the part and the whole" (p. 326).

Trachtenburg's method proceeds as follows:

- First, the teacher reads to the class a literature selection that contains many examples of the phonic element in question. Students may discuss or dramatize the story when the teacher has finished.

- The teacher introduces the phonic element that is the target for the lesson (long *a, e, i, o,* or *u;* short *a, e, i, o,* or *u;* or some other element) by explaining that the children are going to learn one of the sounds for a specific letter or letter combination.

- Then the teacher writes a portion of the story that contains the target element on the chalkboard or a transparency. The teacher reads this portion of the story aloud, underlining the words containing the target element as he or she reads.

- The teacher identifies the sound involved and asks the children to read the story portion with him or her and listen for the sound. The teacher may suggest a key word that will help them remember the sound in the future.

● The teacher guides practice with the new sound, using a mechanical device in which initial consonants can be varied while the medial vowel remains stationary or a similar device in which both initial and final consonants can be varied. An example of such a device is shown in Activity 3 (page 108) for phonics practice in this chapter. The teacher may also provide practice with a similar device that allows sentence parts to be substituted, which enables children to practice the sound in larger language chunks. For example, adjectives, verbs, or adverbs could be varied, as could prepositional phrases, verb phrases, or any other sentence part.

● Finally, the teacher presents another book that has numerous examples of the phonic element. Children may then be allowed to read this book independently, read it in unison from a big book, or read it with a partner, depending on their individual achievement levels.

Trachtenburg (1990) recommends many trade books that repeat long and short vowel sounds, including *The Cat in the Hat* (Seuss, 1957) for short *a, The Paper Crane* (Bang, 1985) for long *a, Caps for Sale* (Slobodkina, 1940) for long and short *a, Elephant in a Well* (Ets, 1972) for short *e, Ten Sleepy Sheep* (Keller, 1983) for long *e, Whistle for Willie* (Keats, 1964) for short *i, Why Can't I Fly?* (Gelman, 1976) for long *i, Fox in Socks* (Seuss, 1965) for short *o, The Giant's Toe* (Cole, 1986) for long *o, Thump and Plunk* (Udry, 1981) for short *u,* and *The Troll Music* (Lobel, 1966) for long *u.* Consonants can also be studied in literature contexts. Kane (1999) suggests *Circus* (Ehlert, 1992) for the soft and hard *c* sound, for example.

Oleneski (1992) used the jump-rope rhyme "Teddy Bear" to teach sounds in an analytic manner with authentic material. She duplicated the rhyme, which the children knew well, and let them engage in activities such as reading it and sequencing its parts with sentence strips. Next she covered up certain words and had the children figure out what these words were. She then asked them to predict which letters would represent the beginning and ending sounds of the target words. Students continued to use the poem for reading and writing activities to keep the phonics instruction in context. This procedure could be used with other jump rope rhymes or ball-bouncing rhymes.

The Focus on Strategies on page 103 tells how a teacher introduced the long *e* sound in story context, thus using an analytic approach to phonics.

The two sample lesson plans on page 104 further illustrate the analytic method. The first one is inductive: the children look at a number of specific examples related to a generalization and then derive the generalization. The second is deductive: the teacher states a generalization, and then the children apply the generalization in decoding unfamiliar words.

Combining Approaches: Onsets and Rimes. An approach that has some aspects of both the synthetic approach and the analytic approach is the teaching of **onsets** and **rimes.** In this approach, the teacher breaks down a syllable into the part of the syllable before the vowel (onset) and the remainder of the syllable (rime) that begins with the vowel (Allen, 1998; Johnston, 1999; Moustafa and Maldonado-Colon, 1999). In the past, these rimes were referred to as *phonograms* or *word families.* (See Example 3.1.)

FOCUS ON STRATEGIES: Teaching Phonics Through Literature

Ms. Mahan started her class by reading the predictable book *Peanut Butter and Jelly* (JoAnne Nelson, Modern Curriculum Press, 1989) to her first graders. By the time she got to page 13, the children were chiming in on the repeated line "But peanut butter and jelly is my favorite thing to eat," as she always encouraged the children to do when they discovered the predictable pattern. When the story had been completed, the teacher responded to requests to "read it again" by doing so. This time the children joined in on the repeated line from the beginning.

The children discussed the story, and Ms. Mahan made a list on the board of the children's personal favorite things to eat.

Then Ms. Mahan wrote the letter combination *ea* on the board. One of the words on the list of the children's favorite foods was *beans*. Another one was *peanuts*. She pronounced each of these words and pointed out that both contained a long *e* sound. Then she displayed transparencies of pages from the story *Peanut Butter and Jelly*. As she read page 5, she underlined the words *meat, peanut,* and *eat*. She then reread each underlined word and asked the children to listen to the sounds. She told the class that the letter combination *ea* often has the long *e* sound. Then she read the words again as they listened specifically for the long *e* sound.

She proceeded to display subsequent pages from the story, asking the children to watch for the *ea* combination in the words and raise their hands when they saw it. When hands were raised, she let the children identify the words with the *ea* combination. Then the children listened for the long *e* sound in each word. The following words from the story fit this pattern: *eat, meat, peanut, cream, wheat, treat, heat,* and *beat*. They also found the word *cereal* and recognized that they heard the long *e* sound. Since they had not yet had instruction on syllabication or schwa sounds, Ms. Mahan simply agreed that there was a long *e* sound after the *r* and went on to the next word. On page 18 they saw a word with the *ea* combination that did not have the long *e* sound: *bread*. The presence of this word allowed Ms. Mahan to point out that letter-sound relationships are not always consistent and that the letter-sound clues only helped the children make "best guesses" about pronunciations, not absolute certainties.

Ms. Mahan then encouraged the children to play with the words that had been located. She wrote *eat* on the board and asked them how to turn it into *meat*. She let Tammy come to the board and add the needed letter. Then she wrote *eat* again and asked who could turn it into *wheat*, then *treat*, then *heat*, then *beat*. Finally, she branched out from words that were found directly in the story and let the children form *neat* and *seat*. She also let them transform *cream* into *team*, *seam*, and *dream* by removing the initial blend and replacing it with other letters.

Then Ms. Mahan pointed out that sometimes there are several ways to spell a particular sound. She used the transparencies of the story again, encouraging the children to listen for the long *e* sound in words other than the ones already underlined. They located *sweet, street, beet, even,* and *cheese*. Ms. Mahan asked if they could suggest any other letter patterns that could spell the long *e* sound. They quickly identified the *ee* combination, and eventually Tommy said that the *e* by itself could also spell the sound.

Ms. Mahan then shared the books *Ten Sleepy Sheep* (Holly Keller, Greenwillow, 1983) and *Never Tease a Weasel* (Jean C. Soule, Parents' Magazine Press, 1964) with the children and put them in the reading center, along with *Peanut Butter and Jelly,* for the children to reread independently or with partners.

The children were then given time to write their own stories about favorite foods. Ms. Mahan asked them to notice which words had the long *e* sound as they wrote. She let them share their stories orally with small groups of their peers.

MODEL ACTIVITIES — Analytic-Inductive Lesson Plan for Initial Consonant

Write on the chalkboard the following words, all of which the children have learned previously as sight words:

dog	did
daddy	donkey
do	Dan

Ask the children to listen carefully as you pronounce the words. Then ask: "Did any parts of these words sound the same?" If you receive an affirmative reply, ask: "What part sounded the same?" This should elicit the answer that the first sound in each word is the same or that the words sound alike at the beginning.

Next, ask the children to look carefully at the words written on the board. Ask: "Do you see anything that is the same in all these words?" This should elicit the answer that all of the words have the same first letter or all of the words start with *d*.

Then ask what the children can conclude about words that begin with the letter *d*. The expected answer is that words that begin with the letter *d* sound the same at the beginning as the word *dog* (or any other word on their list).

Next, invite the children to name other words that have the same beginning sound as *dog*. Write each word on the board. Ask the children to observe the words and draw another conclusion. They may say, "Words that sound the same at the beginning as the word *dog* begin with the letter *d*."

Ask the children to watch for words in their reading that begin with the letter *d* to check the accuracy of their conclusions.

Johnston (1999) suggests initially teaching one word family (rime) at a time, blending different onsets with the chosen rime as words that fit the pattern are found in literature selections that contain the repeated rime. Children should spell words with familiar onsets and the target rime and should read other literature selections containing this word part. Later, more than one word family with the same vowel may be introduced together. The children can compare and contrast different rimes, such as -*at* and -*an*, as soon as both have been presented. Eventually, students will be

MODEL ACTIVITIES — Analytic-Deductive Lesson Plan for Soft Sound of *c*

Tell the children: "When the letter *c* is followed by *e, i,* or *y,* it generally has its soft sound, which is the sound you have learned for the letter *s*." Write the following examples on the chalkboard: *city, cycle,* and *cent*. Point out that in *cycle,* only the *c* that is followed by *y* has the soft sound. Follow this presentation with an activity designed to check the children's understanding of the generalization. The activity might involve a worksheet with items like this:

Directions: Place a check beside the words that contain a soft *c* sound.

_____cite	_____cider
_____cape	_____cord
_____cede	_____cymbal
_____cut	_____cod
_____cell	

The soft *c* sound is the sound we have learned for the letter _____.

EXAMPLE 3.1   Onsets and Rimes

Word	Onset	Rime
black	bl–	–ack
may	m–	–ay
am	—	am

---

ready to contrast word families that have different vowels, such as -*at* and -*ut*. The children need to be able to sort the families by sound and by sight.

Gunning (1995) proposes a system for phonics instruction called Word Building that uses onsets and rimes. The class first builds words by adding onsets to rimes and then by adding rimes to onsets. This is followed by reading that allows practice with the patterns under consideration. Gunning also suggests having the students make words with magnetic letters, mix the letters up and reassemble the words, and then observe how each word changes as letters are added and removed, a process advocated by Clay (1993). Students are shown how to decode hard words by using phonic elements that they have learned. This approach can be used with multisyllabic words as well as with single-syllable words.

Analogy Approach.   In one rime-based instructional program, the Benchmark Word Identification Program, children compare an unknown word to familiar words in order to decode the words by analogy. Then they use context to check their predictions (Allen, 1998; Stahl, 1992; Gaskins et al., 1988; Gaskins et al., 1991; Gaskins et al., 1997). Such an approach is called an *analogy approach,* a *phonogram approach,* or a *word family approach.* The children are taught an initial set of "key words" containing the phonograms or rimes. After comparing the unknown word to a known one and coming up with a tentative decision about the pronunciation of the unknown word, a child would be expected to check to see whether the new word produced made sense in the sentence in which it was found. According to Adams (1990), the letter-sound correspondences in rimes are more stable than the correspondences found when the letters are taken in isolation. Fry (1998) discovered that 654 different one-syllable words can be formed with just 38 phonograms and added beginning consonants.

Gaskins and colleagues (1991) found that direct instruction was useful in teaching phonics through the analogy approach. In every lesson, teachers inform the children about "*what* they are going to teach, *why* it is important, *when* it can be used, and *how* to use it" (p. 215). After this explanation, the teacher models the relevant skill and provides group and individual guided practice for the students. Every-pupil response activities and teacher feedback are important program features. Key words are introduced through a structured language experience activity (the writing of a group story with the key words just presented). (The language experience approach is discussed in detail in Chapter 7.) Phonemic awareness activities are also included to facilitate the learning of onsets such as the initial consonant *f* and the initial consonant blend *fr*. Gaskins and colleagues (1996/1997; 1997) stress the need for students to be reflective and analytic about words and spelling patterns. They also emphasize that the students must learn the importance of analyzing all letters in a word and relating the letters to sounds so that they can retrieve the word later. Students do this by matching sounds to letters as they "stretch out" the pronunciation of the words. Self-talk about the procedure is encouraged. The following Model Activity below illustrates the use of an analogy or compare/contrast approach.

Ehri and Robbins (1992) found that students needed some knowledge of phoneme-grapheme correspondences in order to be able to use onset-rime units. Bruck and Treiman (1992) discovered that beginning readers can use analogies but that they tend to rely more on individual phoneme-grapheme correspondences to decode new words. Their findings suggest that students need instruction on individual phoneme-grapheme correspondences, especially for vowels, rather than just on relationships between groups of phonemes and groups of graphemes. They warn that rime instruction is not sufficient by itself.

As Fox (2003, p. 97) points out, "Letter patterns are more generalizable than word family rimes. Our alphabet represents speech at the sound level, and letter patterns give us clues as to how to pronounce sounds. For example, children who understand the VC [Vowel-Consonant] letter pattern sound out *mat, beg, bun, cop,* and *miss* with equal ease. … They do not need to know five different word families."

Johnson and Baumann (1984) cite research indicating that "programs emphasizing a phonics or code approach to word identification produce superior word-calling ability when compared to programs applying an analytic phonics or meaning emphasis" (p. 590). But, they continue, "there seem to be distinct differences in the quality of error responses made by children instructed in the two general methodologies — readers' errors tend to be real words, meaningful, and

MODEL ACTIVITIES | **Analogy or Compare/Contrast Approach**

The teacher writes the key words *be* and *rain* on the board and pronounces them. Then he or she writes: "The student hopes to remain in that group." The teacher verbalizes the thought pattern needed to decode the word in this way: "If this (pointing to *be*) is *be*, then this is probably *re*. If this (pointing to *rain*) is *rain*, then this is probably *main*." (The sounds of the initial consonants *r* and *m* must have been taught previously.) The teacher continues: "The word is *remain*. Does that make sense in the context?" After receiving an affirmative reply, the teacher says: "Yes, *remain* means to stay."

Then the teacher provides a list of key words that the students have already studied and turned into sight words, as well as several paragraphs, preferably from a story they are about to read, with difficult words underlined. The teacher asks the students to decode these underlined words, using the key words and the strategy that has just been modeled. After the children have worked at this task independently, the teacher calls on several students to verbalize their strategies for the difficult words.

syntactically appropriate when instruction emphasizes meaning, whereas code-emphasis word-identification instruction results in more nonword errors that are graphically and aurally like the mispronounced words" (p. 590). Because the goal of reading is comprehension, not word calling, the analytic approach, which uses meaning-emphasis techniques, seems to be the better choice for instruction.

The choice of approach, however, may not matter as much as the fact that the teacher systematically includes phonics in his or her lesson plans. Research published by the Center for the Improvement of Early Reading Achievement (CIERA) indicated that "systematic and explicit phonics instruction makes a bigger contribution to children's growth in reading than non-systematic or no phonics instruction" (Armbruster, Lehr, and Osborn, 2001, p. 13). Systematic, explicit instruction can take place through synthetic, analytic, analogy-based, or onset-rime phonics instruction. "A program of systematic phonics instruction clearly identifies a carefully selected and useful set of letter-sound relationships and then organizes the introduction of these relationships into a logical instructional sequence" (Armbruster, Lehr, and Osborn, 2001, p. 16).

Specific Teaching Strategies

A variety of strategies can be used with all of the major approaches to teaching phonics. They include using key words, consonant and vowel substitution activities, Word Walls, and games.

Key Words. Cordts (1965) suggests using key words to help children learn the sounds associated with vowels, consonants, vowel digraphs, consonant digraphs, diphthongs, and consonant blends. In all cases, these words should already be part of the children's sight vocabularies. Cordts suggests that a key word for a vowel sound should be one that contains that vowel sound and can be pictured, whereas a key word for a consonant sound should be one that can be pictured and has that consonant sound at the end. She believes that consonant sounds can be heard more clearly at the ends than at the beginnings of words.

Other authorities also encourage the use of key words, but most suggest using words with the consonant sounds at the beginning. The sounds may be harder to distinguish, but usable key words are much easier to find when initial sounds are used.

Key words are valuable in helping children remember sound-symbol associations that are not inherently meaningful. People remember new things through associations with things they already know. The more associations a person has for an abstract relationship, such as the letter *d* and the sound of *d*, the more quickly that person will learn to link the sound and the symbol. The person's retention of this connection will also be more accurate. L. M. Schell (1978) refers to a third-grade boy who chose as key words for the consonant blends *dr*, *fr*, and *sp* the character names *Dracula*, *Frankenstein*, and *Spiderman*. These associations were both concrete and personal for him. The characters were drawn on key-word cards to aid his memory of the associations.

Consonant Substitution. Consonant substitution activities are useful for helping students see how their knowledge of some words helps them to decode other words. Below is a Model Activity for teaching consonant substitution.

LITERATURE

Word Wall. For students learning sound-symbol associations, a Word Wall may be helpful. Words found in the predictable books that students are reading can be written on construction paper and placed on the Word Wall, clustered with other words with the same beginning sounds, vowel sounds, or other salient features, such as rimes (Wagstaff, 1997/1998).

Games. Drill on letter-sound associations need not be dull. Teachers can use many game activities, and activities that are more formal will not become boring if they are not overused. When planning games, teachers should always remember that, although competitive situations are motivational for some youngsters, other children can be adversely affected by being placed in win/lose situations, especially if they have little hope of being winners at least part of the time. Game situations in which children cooperate or in which they compete with *their own previous records* rather than with one another are often more acceptable. Following are some practical examples of both competitive and noncompetitive games. (See the next Activities section.)

To be effective, practice exercises should always be preceded by instruction and followed by feedback on results. The absence of prior instruction may cause students to practice the wrong response. Feedback, which should come either directly from the teacher or through a self-correcting procedure (posted answers, for example), will inform students of errors immediately so that they do not learn incorrect responses. When students fail to see reasons for their errors, the teacher will need to provide explanations and reteach the strategy or skill.

ACTIVITIES

1. Give each child a sheet of paper that is blank except for a letter at the top. Have the children draw pictures of as many items as they can think of that have names beginning with the sound of the letter at the top of the page. Declare the child with the most correct responses the winner.

MODEL ACTIVITIES | **Consonant Substitution**

Write a known word, such as *pat*, on the board and ask the students to pronounce the word. Then write on the board a letter for which the sound has been taught (for example, *m*). If the letter sound can be pronounced in isolation without distortion, ask the students to do so; if not, ask for a word beginning with this sound. Then ask the students to leave the *p* sound off when they pronounce the word on the board. They will respond with *at*. Next, ask them to put the *m* sound in front of the *at*, and they will produce *mat*. The same process is followed with other sounds, such as *s*, *r*, and *b*.

This procedure is also useful with sounds at the ends of words or in medial positions. Vowel substitution activities, in which you may start with a known word and have the students omit the vowel sound and substitute a different one (for example: *sat*, *set*, *sit*; *pat*, *pet*, *pit*, *pot*), can also be helpful.

2. Make five decorated boxes, and label each box with a short vowel. Have the children locate pictures of objects whose names contain the short vowel sounds and file them in the appropriate boxes. Each day take out the pictures, ask the children to pronounce the names, and check to see if the appropriate sounds are present. Do the same thing with long vowel sounds, consonant sounds, consonant blends, digraphs, diphthongs, and rhyming words.

3. Place a familiar word ending on a cardboard disk like the one pictured here. Pull a strip of cardboard with initial consonants on it through an opening cut in the disk. Show the children how to pull the strip through the disk, pronouncing each word that is formed.

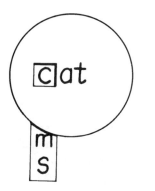

4. Divide the children into two groups. Give half of them initial consonant, consonant blend, or consonant digraph cards. Give the other half word-ending cards. Instruct the children to pair up with other children holding word parts that combine with their parts to form real words. Have each pair hold up their cards and pronounce the word they have made when they have located a combination. Then let them search for other possible combinations for their word parts.

5. Use riddles. For example: "I have in mind a word that rhymes with *far*. We ride in it. It's called a _____."

6. Let the children find a hidden picture by shading in all the spaces that contain words with long vowel sounds.

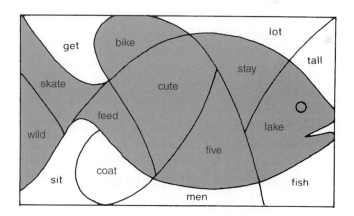

7. Have students read sentences made of alliterative words beginning with a sound that you just taught and then write their own alliterative sentences with that sound; for example, Betty Baxter bought big bowls.

8. Have the class make a phonogram tree (*Struggling Readers, Day 1*, 2000).

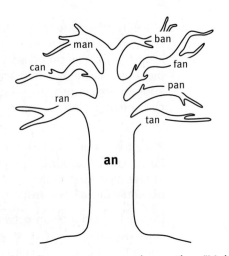

9. Try a spelling-decoding strategy such as the "Making Words" strategy developed by Cunningham (1991) and described in detail in Aiken and Bayer (2002). Aiken and Bayer (2002, p. 68) say, "Making Words allows each student to manipulate a set of six to eight letters to construct words dictated by the teacher. Each lesson begins with two-letter words and gradually builds to the final word, which uses all of the letters." Subsequently, students sort word cards of the words they have made by sounds or spelling patterns, and later they discover transfer words that have the same spelling patterns.

A phonics strategy or skill is a means to an end, not an end in itself. Readers who can recognize words without resorting to letter-by-letter sounding will recognize them more quickly than those who must sound out the words, and the process will interfere less with their train of thought than sounding out the words would have. When the words to be recognized are seen in context, as in most normal reading activities, the sound of the first letter alone may elicit recognition of the whole word. Context clues can provide a child with an idea about the word's identity, and the initial sound can be used to verify an educated guess. This procedure is efficient and is a good way to identify unfamiliar words quickly. Of course, the ultimate goal of instruction in phonics and other word identification skills is to turn initially unfamiliar words into automatically recognized sight words.

● Structural Analysis

Structural analysis is closely related to phonics and has several significant facets:

1 Inflectional endings

2 Prefixes and suffixes

3 Contractions

4 Compound words

5 Syllabication and accents

The first four are related to meaningful word parts and are also referred to as morphemic analysis.

Structural analysis strategies and skills enable children to decode unfamiliar words by using units larger than single graphemes; this procedure generally expedites the decoding process. Structural analysis can also help in understanding word meanings, a function discussed in Chapter 4.

Inflectional Endings

Inflectional endings are added to nouns to change number, case, or gender; are added to verbs to change tense or person; or are added to adjectives to change degree. They may also change a word's part of speech. Since inflectional endings are letters or groups of letters added to the endings of root words, some people call them *inflectional suffixes*. Here are some examples of words with inflectional endings:

Root Word	New Word	Change
boy	boys	Singular noun changed to plural noun
host	hostess	Gender of noun changed from masculine to feminine
Karen	Karen's	Proper noun altered to show possession (change of case)
look	looked	Verb changed from present tense to past tense
make	makes	Verb changed from first or second person singular to third person singular
mean	meaner	Simple form of adjective changed to the comparative form
happy	happily	Adjective changed to adverb

Generally, the first inflectional ending to which children are exposed is *-s*. This ending often appears in early reading materials and should be learned early in the first grade. Other inflectional endings that children are likely to encounter in these early materials are *-ing* and *-ed.*

A child can be shown the effect of the addition of an *-s* to a singular noun through use of illustrations of single and multiple objects. An activity such as that shown in the Model Activity on page 112 can be used to practice this skill. A second Model Activity for various inflectional endings on page 112 demonstrates further possibilities for practice with different inflectional endings.

Children in the primary grades are frequently exposed to the possessive case formed by *-'s.* The activity on page 113 is designed for work with this inflectional ending.

Prefixes and Suffixes

Prefixes and suffixes are *affixes,* letters or sequences of letters that are added to root words to change their meanings and/or parts of speech. A *prefix* is placed before a root word, and a *suffix* is placed after a root word.

MODEL
ACTIVITIES **Recognizing Inflectional Ending -s**

Give the practice sheet to the right to the children.

Ask the children to read and follow the directions. Then go over the practice sheet with them orally, asking how each word that shows more than one thing looks different from the word that shows only one thing. They should come to the conclusion that *-s* at the ends of the words indicates more than one thing.

Directions: Circle the word that describes two things.

bell   bells

car   cars

dogs   dog

book   books

**MODEL
ACTIVITIES** **Recognizing Inflectional Endings**

Write on the board sentences containing inflectional endings that have already been discussed, taken from a book that has been shared in class. Ask the children to read the sentences silently, looking for the inflectional endings they have studied in class. After the silent reading, let volunteers go to the board, circle the inflectional endings in the sentences, and tell how each ending affects word meaning or word use.

You may not wish to use all possible examples from the book in this activity. Instead, you can encourage students to go back to the book itself, either individually or in pairs, locate the inflectional endings under consideration, and make a list of the words they find. These words can be discussed later in a group discussion, with the students finding the words in the story and reading the sentences in which they appear.

As an example, *Ox-Cart Man* (Hall, Puffin Books, 1979) could be used for sentences containing the words *backed, filled, packed, sheared, spinning, pairs, mittens, candles, shingles, brooms, carved, borrowed, potatoes, counted, apples, honeycombs, turnips, cabbages, maples, tapped, boiled, feathers, collected, waved, walked, ox's, days, hills, valleys, streams, farms, villages, kissed, pockets, coins, pounds, candies, tucked, kettle's, waiting, stitching, whittling, cooked, sawed, embroidered, trees, knitted, planted, blossoms, bloomed, bees, starting, squawked, dropping,* and *clouds.* From this short book, you could effectively review the inflectional endings *-ed, -s, -'s,* and *-ing.* You may decide to handle each inflectional ending in a separate lesson.

MODEL ACTIVITIES — Using -'s for the Singular Possessive

Tell the children: "When I say, 'This is the book of my brother,' I mean that the book belongs to my brother. Another, shorter way to say the same thing is 'This is my brother's book.' The *apostrophe s* on the end of the word *brother* shows that the noun following *brother* (*book*) belongs to *brother*."

Have the children examine stories they have read recently for examples of the use of -'s. Let them read the sentences they found that contained -'s and tell the meanings of the phrases in which it occurs.

Children can learn the pronunciations and meanings of some common prefixes and suffixes. Good readers learn to recognize common prefixes and suffixes instantly; this helps them recognize words more rapidly than they could if they had to resort to sounding each word letter by letter. Knowledge of prefixes and suffixes can help readers decipher the meanings as well as the pronunciations of unfamiliar words.

The suffixes *-ment, -ous, -tion,* and *-sion* have especially consistent pronunciations and thus are particularly useful to know. The suffixes *-ment* and *-ous* generally have the pronunciations heard in the words *treatment* and *joyous*. The suffixes *-tion* and *-sion* have the sound of *shun,* as heard in the words *education* and *mission*.

Whereas prefixes simply modify the meanings of the root words, suffixes may change the parts of speech as well as modify the meanings. Some of the resulting modifications are listed here.

Root Word	Affix	New Word	New Meaning or Change
happy	un-	unhappy	not happy
amuse	-ment	amusement	verb is changed to noun
worth	-less	worthless	meaning is opposite of original meaning

Use activities like the Model Activity on page 114.

In the third and fourth grades, children begin to encounter more words that contain prefixes, suffixes, or both (White, Sowell, and Yanagihara, 1989; Nagy and Anderson, 1984). White, Sowell, and Yanagihara (1989) have identified nine prefixes (*un-; re-; in-, im-, ir-* [meaning *not*]; *dis-; en-, em-; non-; in-, im-* [meaning *in* or *into*]; *over-* [meaning *too much*]; and *mis-*) that cover 76 percent of the prefixed words in the *Word Frequency Book* (Carroll, Davies, and Richman, 1971). They recommend that these prefixes be taught systematically during grades three through five, beginning with *un-*, which alone accounts for 26 percent of the prefixed words. An analysis of their word counts would lead us to add *sub-, pre-, inter-,* and *fore-* to the recommended list, since they occur as frequently as *over-* and *mis-,* thereby covering 88 percent of the prefixed words.

MODEL ACTIVITIES — Recognition of Prefixes and Suffixes

After instruction in prefixes and suffixes, give the students duplicated sheets containing paragraphs from a story that has just been shared in class. Ask them to circle the prefixes and suffixes they see in the paragraphs, working independently. Then divide them into small groups, and have them compare and discuss their responses. Each group should come to an agreement about the correct answers. Finally, check the group responses in a whole-class discussion, calling on small-group representatives to give each group's responses to various items.

For example, in *Nadia the Willful* (Alexander, Knopf, 1983), the following words appear: *stubbornness, willful, kindness, graciousness, return, emptiness, punishment, remind, uneasily, hardness, coldness, unhappiness, bitterness, inside, recall, recalled, unbidden, happiness, sharpness,* and *forward.* Some of the words occur several times. The paragraphs in which these words appear can be duplicated for this exercise.

Not all of the words need to be used in a single lesson. You may wish to use one prefix or suffix at a time.

White, Sowell, and Yanagihara (1989) have identified ten suffixes and inflectional endings that are part of 85 percent of the suffixed words in the *Word Frequency Book:* -s, -es; -ed; -ing; -ly; -er, -or (agentive); -ion, -tion, -ation, -ition; -ible, -able; -al, -ial; -y; and -ness. The three inflectional endings –s, -es, -ed, and -ing alone account for 65 percent of the incidences of suffixed words in the sample.

Contractions

The apostrophe used in contractions indicates that one or more letters have been left out when two words were combined into one word. Children need to be able to recognize the original words from which the contractions were formed. The following are common contractions, with their meanings, that teachers should present to children:

can't/cannot	I'd/I had or I would	I'll/I will	shouldn't/should not
couldn't/could not	they'd/they had or they would	I'm/I am	we've/we have
didn't/did not	they'll/they will	I've/I have	won't/will not
don't/do not	they're/they are	isn't/is not	wouldn't/would not
hadn't/had not	they've/they have	let's/let us	you'll/you will
hasn't/has not	wasn't/was not	she'd/she would or she had	you're/you are
he'll/he will	we're/we are	she'll/she will	you've/you have
he's/he is or he has	weren't/were not	she's/she is or she has	

The teacher may wish to teach contractions in related groups — for example, those in which *not* is the reduced part, those in which *have* is the reduced part, and so on. Students should locate these contractions and their uncontracted referents in context and use them in writing to enhance their learning.

Compound Words

Compound words consist of two (or occasionally three) words that have been joined together to form a new word. The original pronunciations of the component words are usually maintained, and their meanings are connected to form the meaning of the new word: *dishpan,* for example, is a pan in which dishes are washed. Children can be asked to underline or circle component parts of compound words or to put together familiar compound words as practice activities. Below is an exercise for compound words.

Syllabication/Accent

Since many phonics generalizations apply not only to one-syllable words but also to syllables within longer words, many people believe that breaking words into syllables can help determine pronunciation. Some research indicates, however, that syllabication is usually done after the reader has recognized the word and that readers use the sounds to determine syllabication rather than syllabication to determine the sounds (Glass, 1967). If children normally attack words using sounds first, then syllabication would seem to be of little use in a word analysis program. On the other hand, many authorities firmly believe that syllabication is helpful in decoding words. For this reason, a textbook on reading methods would be incomplete without discussions of syllabication and a related topic, stress or accent.

A *syllable* is a letter or group of letters that forms a pronunciation unit. Every syllable contains a vowel sound. In fact, a vowel sound may form a syllable by itself (*a/mong*). Only in a syllable that contains a diphthong is there more than one vowel sound. Diphthongs are treated as single units, although they are actually vowel blends. Although each syllable has only one vowel sound or diphthong, a syllable may have more than one vowel letter. Letters and sounds should not be confused. The word *peeve,* for example, has three vowel letters, but the only vowel sound is the long *e* sound. Therefore, *peeve* contains only one syllable.

There are two types of syllables: open and closed. Open syllables end in vowel sounds; closed syllables end in consonant sounds. Syllables may in turn be classified as accented (given greater stress) or unaccented (given little stress). Accent has much

---

MODEL ACTIVITIES | **Recognizing Parts of Compound Words**

Display a page from a big book (or a transparency made from a regular-size book) that contains several compound words. Let students come to the book (or the projected image) and point out the words that are made up of two or more words. For example, *Song and Dance Man* (Ackerman, Knopf, 1988) includes the words

Grandpa, Grandma, cardboard, leather-trimmed, inside, half-moon, spotlight, woodpecker, somebody's, bathroom, gold-tipped, and *stairway.* Write the words on the chalkboard. Let volunteers come to the board and circle the separate words that make up each compound word. Have a class discussion about the way to decide how to pronounce compound words.

to do with the vowel sound we hear in a syllable. Multisyllabic words may have primary (strongest), secondary (second strongest), and even tertiary (third strongest) accents. The vowel sound of an open accented syllable is usually long (*mī′ nus, bā′ sin*); the second syllable of each of these example words is unaccented, and the vowel sound represented is the schwa, often found in unaccented syllables. A single vowel in a closed accented syllable generally has its short sound, unless it is influenced by another sound in that syllable (*căp′ sule, cär′ go*).

Following are several useful generalizations concerning syllabication and accent:

❶ Words contain as many syllables as they have vowel sounds (counting diphthongs as a unit). Examples: *se/vere* (final *e* has no sound); *break* (*e* is not sounded); *so/lo* (both vowels are sounded); *oil* (diphthong is treated as a unit).

❷ In a word with more than one sounded vowel, when the first vowel is followed by two consonants, the division is generally between the two consonants. Examples: *mar/ry, tim/ber.* If the two consonants are identical, the second one is not sounded.

❸ Consonant blends and consonant digraphs are treated as units and are not divided. Examples: *ma/chine, a/bridge.*

❹ In a word with more than one sounded vowel, when the first vowel is followed by only one consonant or consonant digraph, the division is generally after the vowel. Examples: *ma/jor, ri/val* (long initial vowel sounds). There are, however, many exceptions to this rule, which make it less useful. Examples: *rob/in, hab/it* (short initial vowel sounds).

❺ When a word ends in *-le* preceded by a consonant, the preceding consonant and *-le* together constitute the final syllable of the word. This syllable is never accented, and the vowel sound heard in it is the schwa. Examples: *can/dle, ta/ble.*

❻ Prefixes and suffixes generally form separate syllables. Examples: *dis/taste/ful, pre/dic/tion.*

❼ A compound word is divided between the two words that form the compound, as well as between syllables within the component words. Examples: *snow/man, thun/der/storm.*

❽ Prefixes and suffixes are usually not accented. Example: *dis/grace′ ful.*

❾ Words that can be used as both verbs and nouns are accented on the second syllable when used as verbs and on the first syllable when used as nouns. Examples: *pre/sent′*—verb; *pres′ ent*—noun.

❿ In two-syllable root words, the first syllable is usually accented, unless the second syllable has two vowel letters. Examples: *rock′ et, pa/rade′.*

⓫ Words containing three or more syllables are likely to have secondary (and perhaps tertiary) accents, in addition to primary accents. Example: *reg′ i/men/ ta′ tion.*

Readiness for learning syllabication includes the ability to hear syllables as pronunciation units. Below is an early exercise on syllabication.

Generalizations about syllabication can be taught using the same process as that for phonic generalizations, described earlier in this chapter. The teacher can present many examples of a particular generalization and lead the children to state the generalization.

In dictionaries it is the syllable divisions in the phonetic respellings, rather than the ones indicated in the boldface entry words, that are useful to students in pronouncing unfamiliar words. The divisions of the boldface entry words are a guide for hyphenation in writing, not for word pronunciation.

Accentuation generally is not taught until children have a good background in word attack skills and is often presented in conjunction with dictionary study as a tool for word attack. More will be said on this topic in the next section of this chapter.

● Dictionary Study

Dictionaries are valuable tools that can help in completing many kinds of reading tasks. They can help students determine pronunciations, meanings, derivations, and parts of speech for words they encounter in reading activities. They can also help with word spellings if children have some idea of how the words are spelled and need only to confirm the order of letters within the words. Picture dictionaries are used primarily for sight word recognition and spelling assistance. Children can be introduced to picture dictionaries as early as the first grade. They can learn how dictionaries are put together and how they function by making their own picture dictionaries. Intermediate-grade pupils can develop dictionaries of special terms, such as *My Science Dictionary* or *My Health Dictionary*. From these they can advance to beginning and intermediate dictionaries.

This section deals mainly with the role the dictionary plays in helping children with word recognition; Chapter 4 discusses the dictionary as an aid to comprehension of word meanings. Study skills related to dictionary use, such as the use of guide words, are covered in Chapter 9.

MODEL ACTIVITIES | **Syllabication**

Teachers can have children as young as first graders listen to words and clap for every syllable heard. Ask the children to say words aloud and listen for the syllables. Let them clap once for each syllable as it is pronounced. Include both single-syllable and multi-syllabic words in the exercise.

Some example words you may use are as follows:

1. rule
2. table
3. meaningful
4. middle
5. disagreement
6. person
7. fingertip
8. name

Although the dictionary is undeniably useful in determining the pronunciation of unfamiliar words, students should turn to it only as a last resort for this purpose. They should consult it only after they have applied phonics and structural analysis clues, along with knowledge of context clues. There are two major reasons for following this procedure. First, applying the appropriate word recognition skills immediately, without having to take the time to look up the word in the dictionary, is less of a disruption of the reader's train of thought and therefore less of a hindrance to comprehension. Second, a dictionary is not always readily available; thoroughly mastered word recognition skills, however, will always be there when they are needed.

When using other word attack skills has produced no useful or clear result, children should turn to the dictionary for help. Obviously, before children can use the dictionary for pronunciation, they must be able to locate words in it. This skill is discussed in Chapter 9.

After children have located particular words, they need two more skills to pronounce the words correctly: the ability to interpret phonetic respellings and the ability to interpret accent marks.

Interpreting Phonetic Respellings and Accent Marks

The pronunciation key, along with knowledge of sounds ordinarily associated with single consonants, helps in interpreting phonetic respellings in dictionaries. A pronunciation key is present somewhere on every page spread of a good dictionary. Students should not be asked to memorize the diacritical (pronunciation) markings used in a given dictionary, because different dictionaries use different markings; learning the markings for one could cause confusion when students use another. The sounds ordinarily associated with relatively unvarying consonants may or may not be included in the pronunciation key. Because they are not always included, it is important that children have a knowledge of phonics.

Here are four activities related to interpretation of phonetic spellings:

ACTIVITIES

1. Have the students locate a given word in their dictionaries (example: *cheat* [*chēt*]). Call attention to the phonetic respelling beside the entry word. Point out the location of the pronunciation key and explain its function. Have the children locate each successive sound-symbol in the key—*ch, ē, t.* (If necessary, explain why the *t* is not included in the key.) Have the children check the key word for each symbol to confirm its sound value. Then have them blend the three sounds together to form a word. Repeat with other words. (Start with short words and gradually work up to longer ones.)

2. Code an entire paragraph or a joke using phonetic respellings. Provide a pronunciation key. Let groups of children compete to see who can write the selection in the traditional way first. Let each group of students who believe they have done so come to your desk. Check their work. If it is correct, keep it and give it a number indicating the order in which it was finished. If it is incorrect, send the students back to work on it some more. Set a time limit for the activity. The activity may be carried out on a competitive or a noncompetitive basis.

3. Give the children a pronunciation key, and let them encode messages to friends. Check the accuracy of each message before it is passed on to the friends to be decoded.

4. Use an activity such as the Model Activity below.

Some words will have only one accent mark, whereas others will have marks showing different degrees of accent within a single word. Children need to be able to translate the accent marks into proper stress when they speak the words. Here are two ideas for use in teaching accent marks:

1. Write several familiar multisyllabic words on the board. (*Bottle* and *apartment* are two good choices.) Explain that when words of more than one syllable are spoken, certain syllables are stressed or emphasized by the speaker's breath. Pronounce each of the example words, pointing out which part or parts of each word receive stress. Next, tell the class that the dictionary uses accent marks to indicate which parts of words receive stress. Look up each word in the dictionary, and write the dictionary divisions and accent marks for the word on the board. Pronounce each word again, showing how the accent marks indicate the parts of the words that you stress when you pronounce them. Then have the children complete the Model Activity on page 120.

2. Introduce the concept of accent in the same way described in the procedure just suggested. Then distribute sheets of paper with a list of words such as the following.

   (1) des' ti na' tion
   (2) con' sti tu' tion

MODEL ACTIVITIES | **Pronunciation Key**

Write the following hypothetical pronunciation key on the board. Tell the children: "Pretend that this list of words is part of the pronunciation key for a dictionary. Choose the key word or words that would help you pronounce each of the words listed below it. Hold up your hand when you have written the number of the appropriate key word on your paper beside the number of each entry word." (You may form the list of words from a book the children are about to read, thereby giving them some advance preparation for the words that they will meet in the book.)

When all the children have made their choices, call on a volunteer to reply to each one, telling why he or she chose a particular answer.

Pronunciation Key: (1) cat, (2) āge, (3) fär, (4) sōfə, (5) sit

1. cape (kāp)
2. car (kär)
3. ago (ə/gō)
4. aim (ām)
5. fad (fad)
6. race (rās)
7. rack (rak)
8. affix (ə/fiks)

(3) mys' ti fy'

(4) pen' nant

(5) thun' der storm'

Ask volunteers to read the words, applying the accents properly. When they have done so, give them a list of unfamiliar words with both accent marks and diacritical (pronunciation) marks inserted. (Lists will vary according to the children's ability. Use of words from their classroom reading material is preferable to use of random words.) Once again, ask the children to read the words, applying their dictionary skills.

Word Recognition Procedure

DIVERSITY ⊕ It is helpful for all children to know a strategy for decoding unfamiliar words independently. For a student with special needs, the instruction often needs to be more direct and explicit. A child may discover the word at any point in the following procedure; he or she should then stop the procedure and continue reading. Sometimes it is necessary to try all of the steps.

> Step 1. Apply context clues. This may involve reading to the end of the sentence or paragraph in which the word is found to take in enough context to draw a reasonable conclusion about the word.
>
> Step 2. Try the sound of the initial consonant, vowel, or blend, along with context clues.
>
> Step 3. Check for structure clues (prefixes, suffixes, inflectional endings, compound words, or familiar syllables).
>
> Step 4. Begin sounding out the word using known phonics generalizations. (Go only as far as necessary to determine the word.)
>
> Step 5. Consult the dictionary.

MODEL ACTIVITIES | **Accent Marks**

Write the following words on the board.

1. truth ful
2. lo co mo tion
3. fric tion
4. at ten tion
5. ad ven ture
6. peo ple
7. gig gle
8. emp ty
9. en e my
10. ge og ra phy

Call on volunteers to pronounce these words and decide where the accent is placed in each one. Have them come to the board and indicate placements of the accents by putting accent marks (') after the syllables where they think the accents belong. Then have all the students look up the words in the dictionary and check the placements of the accents. Anyone who finds an incorrectly marked word can come to the board, make the correction, and pronounce the word with the accent correctly placed.

A teacher may explain this five-step strategy in the following way:

❶ First, try to decide what word might reasonably fit in the context in which you found the unfamiliar word. Ask yourself: "Will this word be a naming word? A word that describes? A word that shows action? A word that connects two ideas?" Also ask yourself: "What word will make sense in this place?" Do you have the answer? Are you sure of it? If so, continue to read. If not, go to Step 2.

❷ Try the initial sound(s) along with the context clues. Does this help you decide? If you are sure you have the word now, continue reading. If not, go to Step 3.

❸ Check to see if there are familiar word parts that will help you. Does the word have a prefix or suffix that you know? If this helps you decide on the word, continue reading. If not, go to Step 4.

❹ Begin sounding out the word, using all of your phonics skills. If you discover the word, stop sounding and go back to your reading. If you have sounded out the whole word and it does not sound like a word you know, go to Step 5.

❺ Look up the word in the dictionary. Use the pronunciation key to help you pronounce the word. If the word is one you have not heard before, check the meaning. Be sure to choose the meaning that fits the context.

For example, a reader who is confronted with the unfamiliar word *chamois* might apply the strategy in the following way:

❶ "'He used a chamois to dry off the car.' I've never seen the word *c-h-a-m-o-i-s* before. Let's see. … Is it a naming word? … Yes, it is, because *a* comes before it. … What thing would make sense here? … It is something that can be used to dry a car. Could it be *towel?* … No, that doesn't have any of the right sounds. Maybe it is *cloth?* … No, *cloth* starts with *cl.*"

❷ "*Ch* usually sounds like the beginning of *choice.* … I can't think of anything that starts that way that would fit here. … Sometimes it sounds like *k.* … I can't think of a word that fits that either…. *Ch* even sounds like *sh* sometimes. … The only word I can think of that starts with the *sh* sound and fits in the sentence is *sheet,* and I can tell that none of the other sounds are right."

❸ "I don't see a prefix, suffix, or root word that I recognize, either."

❹ "Maybe I can sound it out. *Chămois.* No, that's not a word. *Kămois.* That's not a word either. *Shămois.* I don't think so. … Maybe the *a* is long. *Chāmois.* No. *Kāmois.* No. *Shāmois.* No."

❺ "I guess I'll have to use the dictionary. What? *Shăm′ē?* Oh, I know what that is. I've seen Dad use one! Why is it spelled so funny? Oh, I see! It came from French."

A crucial point for teachers to remember is that children should not consider use of word recognition skills important only during reading classes. They should apply these skills whenever they encounter an unfamiliar word, whether it happens during reading class, science class, a free reading period, or in out-of-school situations. Teachers should emphasize to their students that the strategy explained here is applicable to *any* situation in which an unfamiliar word occurs. Teachers should also encourage students to self-correct their reading errors when the words they read do not combine to make sense.

SUMMARY

Word recognition skills help readers identify words while reading. One skill is sight word recognition, the development of a store of words a person can recognize immediately on sight. Use of context clues to help in word identification involves using the surrounding words to decode an unfamiliar word. Both semantic and syntactic clues can be helpful. Phonics, the association of speech sounds (phonemes) with printed symbols (graphemes), is very helpful in identifying unfamiliar words, even though the sound-symbol associations in English are not completely consistent. Structural analysis skills enable readers to decode unfamiliar words by employing units larger than single graphemes. The process of structural analysis involves recognition of prefixes, suffixes, inflectional endings, contractions, and compound words, as well as syllabication and accent. Dictionaries can also be used for word identification. The dictionary respelling that appears in parentheses after the word supplies the word's pronunciation, but the reader has to know how to use the dictionary's pronunciation key to interpret the respellings appropriately.

Children need to learn to use all of the word recognition skills. Because they will need different skills for different situations, they must also learn to use the skills appropriately.

An overall strategy for decoding unfamiliar words is useful. The following five-step strategy is a good one to teach: (1) use context clues; (2) try the sound of the initial consonant, vowel, or blend, in addition to context clues; (3) check for structure clues; (4) use phonics generalizations to sound out as much of the word as necessary; and (5) consult the dictionary.

TEST YOURSELF

True or False

_____ 1. It is wise to teach only a single approach to word attack.

_____ 2. All word recognition strategies are learned with equal ease by all children.

_____ 3. Sight words are words that readers recognize immediately without needing to resort to analysis.

_____ 4. The English language is noted for the regularity of sound-symbol associations in its written words.

_____ 5. Teaching a small store of sight words can be the first step in implementing an analytic approach to phonics instruction.

_____ 6. Early choices for sight words to be taught should be words that are extremely useful and meaningful.

_____ 7. Games with complex rules are good ones to use for practice with sight words.

_____ 8. Most practice with sight words should involve the words in context.

_____ 9. If teachers teach phonics well, they do not need to bother with other word recognition strategies.

_____ 10. Consonant letters are more consistent in the sounds they represent than vowel letters are.

_____ 11. Phonics generalizations often have numerous exceptions.

_____ 12. It is impossible to teach too many phonics rules, since these rules are extremely valuable in decoding unfamiliar words.

_____ 13. In a word that has only one vowel letter at the end, the vowel letter usually represents its long sound.

_____ 14. It is wise to teach only one phonics generalization at a time.

_____ 15. Structural analysis skills include the ability to recognize prefixes and suffixes.

_____ 16. The addition of a prefix to a root word can change the word's meaning.

_____ 17. Inflectional endings can change verb tenses.

_____ 18. The apostrophe in a contraction indicates possession or ownership.

_____ 19. Every syllable contains a vowel sound.

_____ 20. There is only one vowel letter in each syllable.

_____ 21. Open syllables end in consonant sounds.

_____ 22. The vowel sound in an open accented syllable is usually long.

_____ 23. The schwa sound is often found in unaccented syllables.

_____ 24. When dividing words into syllables, we treat consonant blends and consonant digraphs as units and do not divide them.

_____ 25. Prefixes and suffixes generally form separate syllables.

_____ 26. Prefixes and suffixes are usually accented.

_____ 27. Picture clues are the most useful word recognition clues for sixth-grade students.

_____ 28. Context clues used by themselves provide only educated guesses about the identities of unfamiliar words.

_____ 29. Children should be expected to memorize the diacritical markings used in their dictionaries.

_____ 30. Accent marks indicate which syllables are stressed.

_____ 31. Some words have more than one accented syllable.

_____ 32. Writing new words is helpful to some learners in building sight vocabulary.

_____ 33. The language experience approach is good for developing sight vocabulary.

_____ 34. One method of teaching sight words is best for all students.

_____ 35. For students with special needs, instruction often needs to be more direct and explicit.

Multiple Choice

(Take this quiz before you read the phonics section of the chapter. Try again after you have read the section.)

_____ 1. In the word *myth,* the *y*
   a. has the characteristics of a vowel.
   b. is silent.
   c. has the characteristics of a consonant.

_____ 2. When it occurs in the initial position in a syllable, the letter *w*
   a. stands for a vowel sound.
   b. is silent.
   c. stands for a consonant sound.

_____ 3. In the word *strong,* the letters *str*
   a. represent a consonant blend.
   b. are silent.
   c. represent a single sound.

_____ 4. Consonant digraphs
   a. represent two blended speech sounds.
   b. represent a single speech sound.
   c. are always silent.

_____ 5. The word *sheep* is made up of
   a. five sounds.
   b. four sounds.
   c. three sounds.

_____ 6. In the word *boat,* the *oa* is a
   a. vowel digraph.
   b. diphthong.
   c. blend.

_____ 7. In the word *boy*, the *oy* is a
    a. vowel digraph.
    b. consonant digraph.
    c. diphthong.

_____ 8. The word *diphthong* contains
    a. three consonant blends.
    b. three consonant digraphs.
    c. a consonant digraph and two consonant blends.

_____ 9. In the word *know*, the *ow* is a
    a. diphthong.
    b. vowel digraph.
    c. consonant blend.

_____ 10. In the word *his*, the letter *s* has the sound usually associated with the letter(s)
    a. *s.*
    b. *z.*
    c. *sh.*

_____ 11. Which type of accent mark indicates the heaviest emphasis?
    a. primary
    b. secondary
    c. tertiary

For your journal . . .

❶ Write a description of how you would teach sight recognition of function words that do not represent concrete images, words such as *for* and *which*.

❷ React to the following statement: "Going back to teaching basic phonics skills will cure all of our country's reading ills."

❸ After observing a teacher teaching a synthetic phonics lesson and a teacher teaching an analytic phonics lesson, write an evaluation of the two approaches on the basis of your observations. Be sure to evaluate the methods, not the instructors.

❹ React to the following statement: "I do not believe in teaching children to use context clues. It just produces a group of guessers."

❺ Reflect on the video that accompanies this chapter on your CD. Which approach to word recognition can you identify in this video?

. . . and your portfolio

❶ Plan a lesson to teach one or more word recognition strategies, using a popular picture book that contains appropriate examples of phonic and structural analysis elements.

❷ Develop a collection of rhymes and poems to use in working with onsets and rimes.

CHAPTER APPENDIX

Teaching Strategies for Phonics Instruction

The National Reading Panel (2000) reviewed numerous approaches to the teaching of phonics and concluded that, although there were no significant differences found when results of the approaches were compared statistically, the more successful ones were implemented in an explicit and systematic way.

Students develop an understanding that the spoken word is made up of sounds, or phonemes. This realization enables readers to recognize patterns and develop knowledge of sound-symbol relationships. Along with semantic and syntactic knowledge of language, the ability to apply grapho-phonic cues enables readers to recognize words and decode print.

The following strategies and techniques supplement those found in Chapter 3. They provide students with practice at a variety of levels in a systematic phonics instruction program. These lists include suggestions for the development of phonemic awareness and the use of patterns and analogy for decoding.

Sound Play

- Take nature walks or share tape recordings of everyday sounds.
- Listen to and identify sounds in the environment.
- Play taped rhythms or model rhythms for students to duplicate by clapping or tapping out the patterns using percussion instruments.
- Share literature selections that include predictable language.
- Share tongue twisters that feature specific phonemes.

Rhyming

- Share nursery rhymes, poems, finger plays, and songs that demonstrate rhyming, repetition, and alliteration.
- Display a picture or an object from a story, nursery rhyme, poem, finger play, or song. Have students identify as many words as possible that rhyme with the name of the object.
- Construct a list of rhyming words drawn from reading materials that are familiar to the students. Assign a word to each student. Call out two rhyming words, and ask the students who have those words to act out the two words.
- Construct rhyming couplets. Read the stem and ask students to complete with a rhyming word. An example of a couplet follows:

  I went to the circus in town
  To see the funny _____ (clown).

- Sit in a circle and ask students to imagine going on a class trip. Then give one student a ball. That student begins a rhyming couplet by completing the following frame:

"We're going on a trip and I'm taking a _____ (hat)."

The ball is tossed to a second student, who responds, "We're going on a trip and I'm taking a _____ (bat, mat, etc.)"

The ball is tossed to another student who continues by starting a new couplet with a different ending.

Identifying Sounds

- Give students individual mirrors and tell them to look at the positions of their lips, tongue, and teeth when they are pronouncing certain sounds and words. Use these observations to discuss how certain sounds are produced.

- Create a list of word pairs. Some should have the same number of phonemes, others different numbers. Pronounce the word pairs, and ask students to indicate which pairs have the same number of phonemes and which do not.

- Create a list with pairs of words. Some should end with the same phoneme. Pronounce each word pair, and ask students to indicate if the members of the pair end with the same sound or with different sounds.

- Prepare a class picture dictionary. Write the upper-case and lower-case letter that represents the initial phoneme of each word you enter. Collect pictures for each of the letter-sounds.

- Create a mobile or collage that features words or pictures of words that begin or end with a specific sound (phoneme).

- Play a consonant riddle game by presenting the riddle in the following frame: "I'm thinking of something that rhymes with dish but starts with /f/. What can it be?" Use Word Walls to display words that feature specific sounds or patterns.

Segmenting Words into Sounds

- Have students use letter tiles or small objects to represent the phonemes in a word.

- Ask students to pronounce a word. Then ask them to repeat the same word without one of the sounds. Begin by having them delete the initial consonant sound, and conclude by having them delete the final consonant sound.

- Using a large rubber band as a visual, stretch it as you slowly pronounce a particular word. Instruct the students to pretend to stretch a rubber band when they pronounce words to identify the individual phonemes, or sounds.

- Use magnetic letters or colored chalk or markers to visually differentiate segments of words by syllables.

- After students have been introduced to word families, construct manipulatives such as word wheels or flip-books to create various words.

Blending Sounds into Words

● Identify the phonemes in a blending riddle that provides a clue to the meaning. One example might be: "I am thinking of a small, furry animal that meows." The sounds are /k/a/t/.

● Assign each student a specific phoneme. Form teams of students to create words from the blending of their assigned sounds. The words can be shared orally or visually by spelling the words on the board or charts.

● Construct a cloze passage from familiar material that has been read to the students or that the students have read. Delete every fifth word by covering it with a sticky note or select key words with particular sounds or patterns that you want to review. As students read the material, encourage them to "guess" the missing word, using clues that you provide. Start by providing the initial letter, and continue giving letters for them to use by blending their sounds until the word is identified.

Combining Phonics Skills

● Incorporate repeated readings of familiar passages or stories with previously taught spelling patterns to develop fluency and increase rate.

● Use a stamp and stamp pad to create words. Once the words are constructed, vocalize each phoneme, blending the sounds, and then discuss the meaning of the word. A picture of the word may also be drawn.

● When teaching words with common spelling patterns, use word sorts to encourage students to sort according to the common patterns. *Open sorts* involve presenting the students with the list of words to be sorted in any way they choose. *Closed sorts* involve presenting the students with a list and instructions on how to sort them.

● Demonstrate the connection of phonics with spelling by using dictation and free-writing activities.

● Include in learning center areas commercially prepared children's games that support sound/spelling relationships, such as *Hangman, Scrabble,* and *Got-A-Minute.*

● Make words. Begin by choosing a word from which shorter words can be made. Create a list of shorter words that can be constructed using letters from the larger word. Provide the students with individual letter tiles or cards. Prompt the students to construct two-letter words. Pronounce the words and use each one in a sentence. Continue constructing smaller words, gradually increasing the number of letters used. Prompt the students to look for patterns as the words are created. Finally, review all the words that were created, and encourage students to use the words in authentic writing activities (Cunningham and Allington, 1999).

Resources

The following references provide additional strategies for phonemic awareness and phonics instruction.

Armstrong, Thomas. *The Multiple Intelligences of Reading and Writing: Making Words Come Alive.* Alexandria, Va.: Association for Supervision and Curriculum Development, 2003.

Blevins, Wiley. *Phonics from A to Z: A Practical Guide.* New York: Scholastic, 1998.

Cunningham, Patricia M., and Richard L. Allington. *Classrooms that Work: They Can All Read and Write.* New York: Longman, 1999.

Ericson, Lita, and Moira Fraser Juliebo. *The Phonological Awareness Handbook for Kindergarten for Primary Teachers.* Newark, Del.: International Reading Association, 1998.

Farstrup, Alan, and S. Jay Samuels, eds. *What Research Has to Say About Reading Instruction.* Newark, Del.: International Reading Association, 2002.

Heilman, Arthur W. *Phonics in Proper Perspective.* Upper Saddle River, N.J.: Merrill, 2002.

National Reading Panel. *Teaching Children to Read: An Evidence-based Assessment of the Scientific Research Literature on Reading and Its Implications for Reading Instruction.* Washington, D.C.: National Institute of Child Health and Human Development, 2000.

Meaning Vocabulary

SETTING OBJECTIVES

When you finish reading this chapter, you should be able to

- Discuss some factors involved in vocabulary development.

- Name and describe several techniques of vocabulary instruction.

- Identify some special types of words and explain how they can cause problems for children.

In Chapter 3 we examined the importance of decoding words and developing a sight vocabulary, but these abilities have little value if students do not understand the words. Children's sight vocabularies should be built from words they already comprehend, words that are a part of their meaning vocabularies. This chapter focuses on the development of extensive meaning vocabularies and the difficulties that certain types of words may present to youngsters.

Meaning vocabulary (words for which meanings are understood) is essentially the set of labels for the clusters of concepts that people have learned through experience. These clusters of concepts, or knowledge structures, are called *schemata.* (Schemata are also discussed in Chapter 5.) Because students must call on their existing schemata in order to comprehend, meaning vocabulary development is an important component of comprehension (Dixon-Krauss, 2001/2002). Therefore, direct instruction in word meanings is a valuable part of reading instruction. Research indicates that preteaching new vocabulary terms (teaching students the terms before they read a selection) can result in significant gains in students' comprehension of that selection (Roser and Juel, 1982; Carney et al., 1984) and that long-term vocabulary instruction, in which words are taught and reinforced over a period of time, enhances comprehension of materials containing those words (Beck, Perfetti, and McKeown, 1982; McKeown et al., 1983; Robinson et al., 1990).

Chapter 4 Organization

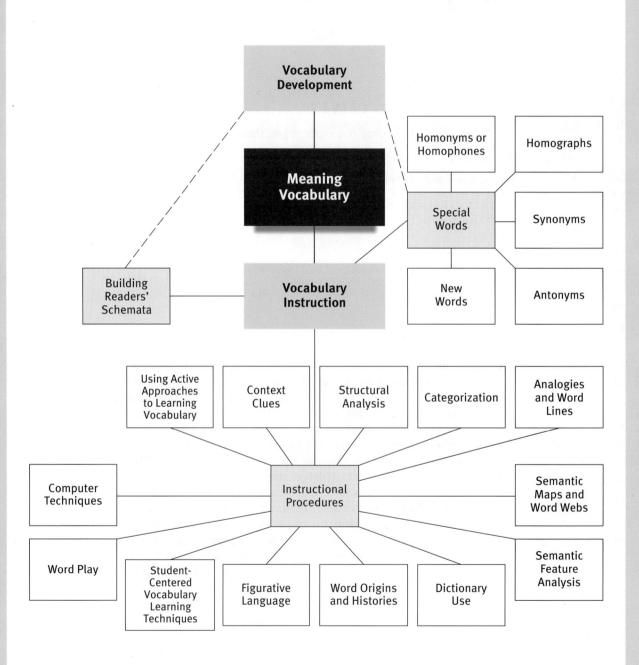

Vocabulary Development

Meaning Vocabulary

Homonyms or Homophones

Homographs

Special Words

Synonyms

Building Readers' Schemata

Vocabulary Instruction

New Words

Antonyms

Using Active Approaches to Learning Vocabulary

Context Clues

Structural Analysis

Categorization

Analogies and Word Lines

Computer Techniques

Instructional Procedures

Semantic Maps and Word Webs

Word Play

Student-Centered Vocabulary Learning Techniques

Figurative Language

Word Origins and Histories

Dictionary Use

Semantic Feature Analysis

Vocabulary Development

It is difficult to pinpoint the age at which children learn the precise meanings of words. Early in the language development process, they learn to differentiate between *antonyms* (opposites), making more discriminating responses as they grow older. Sometimes they overgeneralize about word meanings: a very young child who learns the word *car*, for example, may apply it to any motor vehicle, making no discrimination among cars, trucks, vans, and other kinds of vehicles. Some children as old as nine years have trouble distinguishing between the meanings of *ask* and *tell*, and some children as old as ten years have not yet differentiated between the words *brother* and *boy* and the words *sister* and *girl* (McConaughy, 1978). As children mature, they learn more about choosing specific words.

Children increase their vocabularies at a rapid rate during the elementary school years. Vocabulary building is a complex process involving many kinds of words: words with *multiple meanings* (Joe's money is in the *bank*. Mike and Jim sat on the *bank* to fish.); words with *abstract definitions* (*Justice* must be served.); **homonyms** (She will take the *plane* to Lexington. He has on *plain* trousers.); *homographs* (I will *read* the newspapers. I have *read* the magazine.); **synonyms** (Marty was *sad* about leaving. Marty was *unhappy* about leaving.); and *antonyms* (Bill is a *slow* runner. Mary is a *fast* runner.). Children must also acquire meanings for a number of relational terms, such as *same/different, more/less, taller/shorter, older/ younger, higher/ lower,* and so on. In content area instruction, students must deal with *technical vocabulary* (words whose only meanings are specific to the content areas, for example, *photosynthesis*) and *specialized vocabulary* (words with general meanings as well as specialized meanings that are specific to the content area, for example, *pitch* in the area of music). Content area materials also abound with special *symbols* and *abbreviations* that children must master in order to read the materials successfully.

FAMILY Wide reading is a prime method of vocabulary building. Many studies have shown that students' vocabularies increase when they read materials with many new words (Pressley, 2002). Students have many vicarious experiences through read-alouds by parents and teachers and reading for themselves. These experiences offer them a multitude of words and concepts that are not often found in their daily language interactions or experiences (Brabham and Villaume, 2002). "If we can substantially increase the reading students do, we can substantially increase the words they learn," according to Graves and Watts-Taffe (2002, p. 142). Developing enthusiasm for pleasure reading is therefore a worthy goal for teachers. Teachers can also encourage their students' parents and guardians to model the enjoyment of reading and provide opportunities for pleasurable reading at home.

Vocabulary Instruction

FAMILY Children learn much vocabulary by listening to the conversations of those around them. Therefore, a language-rich environment promotes vocabulary acquisition (Anderson and Nagy, 1991; Brabham, Greene, and Villaume, 2002). Teachers can provide such environments in their classrooms, and they can encourage parents to do so at home. They can greatly influence children's vocabulary development simply by being good models of vocabulary use. For example, when teachers read aloud or give explanations to the class, they should discuss any new words used and encourage the children to use them. Teachers should not "talk down" to children but, rather, should use appropriate terminology in describing things to them and participating in discussions with them. Graves and Watts-Taffe (2002, p. 144) also cite the importance of word consciousness—"awareness of and interest in words and their

LITERATURE meanings"—in a vocabulary program. Modeling precise word usage and calling attention to particularly appropriate word choices in literature encourage word consciousness. A teacher may want to have the students read the book *Miss Alaineus: A Vocabulary Disaster* (Frasier, 2000) for an entertaining introduction to learning word meanings and possibilities for misunderstanding word meanings.

Learning new vocabulary may just involve acquisition of a new label for a concept that is already known. In this case, the teacher's task is simple. The teacher provides the new term (such as *journey*) and tells the children it means the same thing as a familiar term (such as *trip*) (Armbruster and Nagy, 1992).

Most teachers recognize the importance of vocabulary instruction as a part of reading and language arts classes. The importance of teaching word meanings and encouraging variety in word choice and exactness in expressing thoughts is generally accepted. Teachers therefore usually give attention to many aspects of vocabulary instruction—such as structural analysis; use of context clues; and use of reference books, such as dictionaries and thesauruses—during language classes. During these lessons, teachers also need to help the children understand the real-world purpose for building vocabulary: a rich vocabulary helps us to communicate effectively. The more words we know and use appropriately, the better we are able to communicate our knowledge and our feelings to others and to understand what others try to communicate to us.

TIME for REFLECTION

Whereas some teachers stress the need for vocabulary instruction throughout the day, others argue that such instruction logically belongs in a reading or language arts class. What do *you* think, and why?

Vocabulary instruction should take place throughout the day, however, not just during the language arts or reading period. Vocabulary knowledge is important in all subject areas covered in the curriculum. Children need to develop their vocabularies in every subject area so that the specialized or technical words they encounter will not be barriers to learning. Rupley, Logan, and Nichols (1998/1999, p. 339) point out that "teaching and reviewing of key concept words prior to reading help students activate their background knowledge, relate this knowledge to new concepts, and understand how new words and concepts are related." Nelson-Herber (1986) suggests intensive direct teaching of vocabulary in specific content areas to help students read the content materials successfully. She endorses building from the known to the new, helping students understand the interrelationships among words in concept clusters (groups of related concepts), and encouraging students to use new words in reading, writing, and speaking. Leading students to construct word meaning from context, experience, and reasoning is basic to her approach. At times the students work in cooperative groups on vocabulary exercises, and they are involved with vocabulary learning before, during, and after reading of assigned material. The techniques described in this chapter and the ideas presented in Chapter 10 will help teachers plan effectively for vocabulary instruction in various content areas.

Choosing words to teach can be a problem for teachers. Blachowicz and Lee (1991); Rupley, Logan, and Nichols (1998/1999); and Dixon-Krauss (2001/2002) suggest choosing terms from classroom reading materials. The terms should be central to the selections in which they appear. The teacher should activate prior knowledge related to the words before the reading begins and should have students use the new vocabulary in postreading discussion. Words that students still do not understand well need further attention and elaboration. For further experiences, the students might use the words in retellings, dramatizations, or writings based on the story or selection.

DIVERSITY 🌐

Davis and McDaniel (1998) urge teachers to include "essential" vocabulary words in their instruction. These are words that are important to survival in our complex society. This instruction is particularly important to struggling readers and English language learners. Davis and McDaniel stress teaching *recognition* of these words, but many are words that appear to require instruction in meanings as well: *hazardous, prohibited, expiration, evacuate, infectious,* and *ventilation,* for example.

Teachers can approach vocabulary instruction in a variety of ways, but some vocabulary instructional techniques appear to be more effective than others. The most desirable instructional techniques are those that

❶ Assist students in integrating the new words with their background knowledge.

❷ Assist students in developing elaborated (expanded) word knowledge.

❸ Actively involve students in learning new words.

❹ Help students acquire strategies for independent vocabulary development.

❺ Provide repetition of the words to build ready accessibility of their meanings.

❻ Have students engage in meaningful use of the words (Carr and Wixson, 1986; Nagy, 1988; Blachowicz and Lee, 1991; Beck and McKeown, 1991b).

We will now look at several common methods of vocabulary development.

● Building Readers' Schemata

Vocabulary terms are labels for *schemata,* or the clusters of concepts each person develops through experience. Sometimes children cannot understand the terms they encounter in books because they do not know the concepts to which the terms refer. In this case, concept or schemata development involving the use of direct and vicarious experiences is necessary.

A good technique for concept development is to offer as concrete an experience for the concept as possible. The class should then discuss the attributes of the concept. The teacher should give *examples* and *nonexamples* of the concept, pointing out the attributes that distinguish examples from nonexamples. Next, the students should try to identify other examples and nonexamples that the teacher supplies and give their reasons. Finally, the students should suggest additional examples and nonexamples.

For example, to develop the concept of *banjo,* the teacher could bring a banjo to class. The teacher would show it to the students, play it for them (or get someone else to do so), and let them touch it and pluck or strum the strings. A discussion of its attributes would follow. The children might decide that a banjo has a circular body and a long neck, that it has a tightly stretched cover over the body, that it has strings, and that one can play music on it. The teacher might show the children pictures or real examples of a variety of banjos, some with five and some with four strings, and some with enclosed backs and some with open backs. Then the teacher might show the children a guitar, pointing out the differences in construction (different shape, different material forming the front of the instrument, different number of strings, etc.). The teacher might also show several other instruments, at first following the same procedure and then letting the students identify how they are different from and similar to banjos. The students can provide their own examples of banjos by bringing in pictures or actual instruments. They will note that, although there may be some variation in size and appearance, the essential attributes are present. They can also name and bring pictures or actual examples of instruments that are not banjos, such as harps, mandolins, or violins, and explain why these instruments do not fit the concept.

As students progress in school, they are introduced to a growing number of abstract concepts. Concrete experiences for abstract concepts are difficult to provide, but the teacher can use approximations. For example, to develop the concept of *freedom*, the teacher can say, "You may play with any of the play equipment in the room for the next ten minutes, or you may choose not to play at all." After ten minutes have passed, the teacher can tell the class that they were given the freedom to choose their activity; that is, they were not kept from doing what they chose to do. The teacher may then offer several examples of freedom. One might be the freedom to choose friends. No one else tells the children who their friends have to be; they themselves choose on the basis of their own desires. The teacher should also offer several nonexamples of freedom, perhaps pointing out that during a game players are restrained by a set of rules and do not have the freedom to do anything they might want to do. Then the teacher should ask the students to give examples of freedom and to explain why these examples are appropriate. A student may suggest that the freedom we have in this country to say what we think about our leaders is a good example, because we are not punished for voicing our views. After eliciting several examples, the teacher can ask the students for nonexamples. Students may suggest that people in jail do not have freedom, because they cannot go where they wish or do what they wish. After students have offered a number of nonexamples, the teacher may ask them to be alert for examples and nonexamples of freedom in their everyday activities and to report their findings to the class. Some may discover that being "grounded" by their parents is a good nonexample of freedom.

Firsthand experiences, such as field trips and demonstrations, can help students associate words with real situations. These experiences can be preceded and followed by discussion of the new concepts, and written accounts of the experiences can help students gain control of the new vocabulary. Before a field trip, for example, a teacher may discuss the work that is done at the target location. During the field trip, the teacher or the field trip host can explain each activity to students as they watch it. This explanation should include the proper terms for the processes and personnel involved. After the trip, the students can discuss the experience. They can make

Field trips and demonstrations provide first-hand experiences that help students increase their schemata and expand their vocabularies.
(Elizabeth Crews)

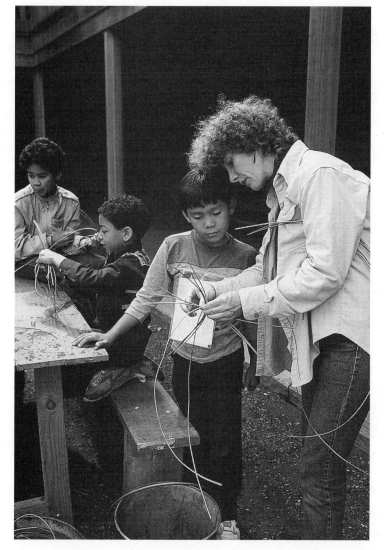

graphic displays of the new terms (see the sections later in this chapter on semantic maps and word webs), classify the new terms (see the section on categorization), make comparison charts for the words (see the section on semantic feature analysis), analyze the structure of the words (see the section on structural analysis), or manipulate the new terms in some other way. They may write individual summaries of the experience or participate in writing a class summary. They may wish to use reference books or the Internet to expand their knowledge about some of the new things they have seen. All of these activities will build both the children's concepts and their vocabularies, thereby enhancing their comprehension of material containing this vocabulary.

TECHNOLOGY 🖥️   Vicarious experiences can also help to build concepts and vocabulary. Audiovisual aids, such as pictures, films, videotapes, and computer displays, can be used to illustrate words that students have encountered in reading and to provide other words for discussion. Books such as thesauruses, children's dictionaries, and trade books about words are also useful sources of information about words.

LITERATURE 📖   Story telling and story reading are good ways to provide vicarious experiences. Studies by Roe (1985, 1986) and Pigg (1986) showed that a seven-week program of daily one-hour story telling/story reading sessions with language follow-up activities could improve vocabulary skills of kindergarten, first-grade, and second-grade students. Language follow-up activities included creative dramatics, creative writing (or dictation), retelling stories with the flannel board, and illustrating scenes from the stories and describing them to the teacher. When the students who participated in these studies were asked to produce their own stories, those in the experimental groups used more words, more different words, and more multisyllabic words in their stories than students in the control groups did. The Classroom Scenario below is drawn from one of Roe's experiences.

Thelen (1986) found that meaningful learning is enhanced by teaching general concepts before specific concepts. Using this approach, the teacher presents the concept of *dog* before the concept of *poodle,* for example. In this way, the children have the schemata they need to incorporate new facts they encounter. For example, they have a prior pool of information about dogs to which they can relate the new information about *poodle.* Isabel Beck has stated that *ownership* of a word, or the ability to relate the word to an existing schema, is necessary for meaningful learning.

CLASSROOM SCENARIO   ## Using Literature Selections to Develop Vocabulary

📖 Dr. Roe (1985), a visiting teacher, was presenting the song "The Old Woman Who Swallowed a Fly" in a first-grade class. After she sang the line "How absurd to swallow a bird," she asked the students, "What does *absurd* mean?" None of them knew.

Dr. Roe told them that *absurd* meant *silly* or *ridiculous.* Then she asked them, "Would it be silly for a woman to swallow a bird?"

The children answered, "Yes," in unison.

"Would it be absurd for me to wear a flowerpot on my head to teach the class?" she then asked.

Again the children answered, "Yes!"

"What are some other absurd things that you can think of?" Dr. Roe finally asked.

Each child gave a reply. If the reply showed understanding of the term, Dr. Roe provided positive reinforcement. If it did not show understanding of the term, her questioning led the child to see why the thing mentioned was not absurd, and the child was given another chance to answer.

Weeks later, when these children encountered the word again in the story *Horton Hatches the Egg,* they remembered its meaning.

Analysis of Scenario

The children encountered a word in the context of a familiar song. The word's meaning was unclear to them, so the teacher supplied both a definition and other examples of the concept that the term named. To ensure that the children really understood the term, the teacher asked them to supply their own examples. This activity helped the children make the word their own through active involvement with it.

That is, students need to relate the word to information they already know. Semantic mapping and semantic feature analysis (discussed later in this chapter) are two particularly good methods for accomplishing this goal.

● Instructional Procedures

Although procedures for vocabulary development vary widely, many of them have produced good results, and teachers should be familiar with a variety of approaches. A number of the programs described here combine several approaches, and good teachers will also use combinations of approaches in their classrooms. Graves and Prenn (1986) point out that "there is no one best method of teaching words. ... various methods have both their costs and their benefits and will be very appropriate and effective in some circumstances and less appropriate and effective in others" (p. 597).

As described earlier in this chapter, wide reading can help students increase their vocabularies. However, research on vocabulary instruction indicates that "extensive reading can increase vocabulary knowledge, but direct instruction that engages students in construction of word meaning, using context and prior knowledge, is effective for learning specific vocabulary and for improving comprehension of related materials" (Nelson-Herber, 1986, p. 627). McKeown and colleagues (1985) also offer support for this assessment.

Some research findings indicate that "vocabulary instruction improves comprehension only when both definitions and context are given, and has the largest effect when a number of different activities or examples using the word in context are used" (Stahl, 1986, p. 663). Techniques requiring students to think deeply about a term and its relationships to other terms are most effective. Class discussion seems to make students think more deeply about words as they make connections between their prior knowledge and new information. Multiple presentations of information about a word's meaning and multiple exposures to the word in varying contexts both enhance comprehension. In addition, the more time spent on vocabulary instruction, the better the results. Vocabulary programs that extend over a long period of time give students a chance to encounter the words in a number of contexts and to make use of them in their own language (Stahl, 1986).

When commercial materials are employed, teachers should use discussion to relate word meanings to the students' own experiences. Then students should use the words in some way to demonstrate their understanding of the meanings. Because multiple experiences with each word are necessary for complete learning, the number of words presented should not be overwhelming. Spaced reviews of the words over a long period of time will increase students' retention of the word meanings.

Using Active Approaches to Learning Vocabulary

We will now look at a number of carefully researched instructional techniques and the studies related to them. Then we will describe several common methods of vocabulary development.

Relating Vocabulary to Background Knowledge and Experiences. Several instructional approaches encourage teachers to be aware of and use their students' experience base when they teach new word meanings, to avoid situations where students are expected to acquire a store of words for which they have only superficial understanding. Duffelmeyer (1985) suggests four techniques to link word meaning and experience: use of synonyms and examples, use of positive and negative instances of the concepts, use of examples and definitions, and use of definitions together with sentence completion. All of these techniques are teacher-directed and involve verbal interaction between the teacher and the students.

Brainstorming about words and webbing the responses (as described later in this chapter in the section on semantic mapping and word webbing) can be a good way to tie vocabulary instruction to background experiences. Children learn new connections as their classmates contribute new related words.

Beck and McKeown (1983) described a program of vocabulary instruction that emphasized relating vocabulary to students' preexisting word knowledge and experiences. Students generated their own context for the terms being taught by answering questions about the words (for example, the teacher might say, "Tell about something you might want to *eavesdrop* on" [p. 624]). The program also helped students to further their word knowledge by introducing new words in global semantic, or meaning, categories, such as *people* or *places,* and by requiring the students to work with the relationships among words. The children were asked to differentiate among critical features of words and to generalize from one word to similar ones. They were also asked to complete analogies involving the words and to pantomime words. These activities were in keeping with suggestions 2 and 3 about vocabulary instruction presented in the list on page 135; the students were active participants in the activities described, rather than passive observers. Students were given a number of exposures to each word in a variety of contexts. The final aspect of the program was development of rapid responses to words by using timed activities, some of which were gamelike. These activities kept the students actively involved and probably increased their interest as well.

The children involved in Beck and McKeown's program learned the words taught, developed speed and accuracy in making semantic decisions, and showed comprehension of stories containing the target words superior to that of a control group. They also learned more than the specific words taught, as indicated by the size of their gains on a standardized measure of reading comprehension and vocabulary.

Constructing Definitions. A closely related procedure, developed by Blachowicz (1986), also helps teachers focus on vocabulary instruction. First, teachers activate what the students know about the target words in the reading selection, using either exclusion brainstorming (in which students exclude unrelated words from a list of possible associated words) or knowledge rating (in which students indicate their degree of familiarity with the words). Then the teachers can elicit predictions about "connections between words or between words and the topic and structure of the selection" (p. 644), emphasizing the words' roles in semantic networks. (Word webs or semantic feature analysis, discussed later in this chapter, may be used.) Next, the

There are several active approaches to learning vocabulary, including relating vocabulary to students' previous experiences, constructing definitions, dramatizing words, using manipulatives to demonstrate words, creating learning aids, expanding sentences, and creating illustrations of words.
(Elizabeth Crews)

students are asked to construct tentative definitions of the words. They read the text to test these definitions, refining them as they discover additional information. Finally, the students use the words in other reading and writing tasks to make them their own.

Blachowicz (1985, p. 877) points out that "the harder one works to process stimuli ... the better one's retention." Blachowicz's approach causes the students to work harder, predicting and constructing definitions rather than merely memorizing the material presented.

Dramatizing Words. Another active way to clarify word meanings by associating situations with them is dramatization of words. This technique is more effective than mere verbal explanations of terms. Under some circumstances, dramatization of words has proved more effective than use of context clues, structural analysis, or dictionaries (Duffelmeyer, 1980; Duffelmeyer and Duffelmeyer, 1979).

Expanding Sentences. Cudd and Roberts (1993/1994) use sentence expansion activities to work on vocabulary. They create sentence stems composed of syntactic structures and vocabulary that the children have encountered in classroom reading materials. Then they display the stems on the board and lead a discussion of them. Students supply endings for the sentences and then read the completed sentences. Students write their own sentences based on the stems, working with peer-editing partners. Then they illustrate one or two of their sentences. In this way, students become actively involved in using the target vocabulary.

Using Manipulatives. Manipulatives are helpful in explaining or demonstrating meanings of content area vocabulary. Teachers can use tape measures to show the meanings of certain lengths (*foot, yard,* etc.), use cotton balls and water to demonstrate *absorption,* and use a rubber band to demonstrate the concept of *elasticity* (Petrick, 1992).

Concept Cards. Students can also become highly involved in learning vocabulary through creating their own learning aids. Davis (1990) has pairs of students construct "concept cards" for new vocabulary terms. On the cards they list definitions, synonyms, and examples for the terms. She has the students supplement their own knowledge by consulting dictionaries and thesauruses. Then she has them discuss the various connotations of the synonyms provided. Following the discussion, the class is divided into teams that compete to supply the most definitions, synonyms, or examples for words from the cards.

Making Possible Sentences. A technique called Possible Sentences is effective in teaching content area vocabulary. In this activity, the teacher chooses six to eight difficult words and four to six familiar words that are important to a reading selection. The teacher writes these words on the board and may offer a definition of each one. Students are asked to supply "possible sentences" that include at least two of the words. This causes them to think about the relationships among the terms. When all words are represented in possible sentences, the students read the selection. After reading, each possible sentence is discussed and either accepted as true or changed to make it true. This technique requires much active processing of the vocabulary (Stahl and Kapinus, 1991).

LITERATURE *Connecting to Literature.* Iwicki (1992) and her colleagues found that they could enhance vocabulary learning through an activity called Vocabulary Connections. They put the vocabulary terms and definitions on wall charts and then asked students to relate each term to situations in the literature selection they were reading and to situations in previously read books. For example, the word *pandemonium* is used in

Welcome Home, Jelly Bean (Shyer, 1988). It can later be related to events in *The Black Stallion* (Farley, 1941). This activity can be motivational and can encourage use of higher-level thinking skills.

DIVERSITY 🌐 *Illustrating Words.* Primary-grade children and children whose primary language is not English can be asked to draw pictures to illustrate new vocabulary words and thereby demonstrate their understanding. Then the children's illustrations can be shown to a small group of other class members, who try to identify the word being illustrated in each picture and record it on their papers. Finally, each artist tells which word each of his or her pictures represented. This procedure gets the children very actively involved with words (Baroni, 1987).

Context Clues

In Chapter 3, we discussed the use of *context clues* to help children recognize words that are familiar in speech but not in print. Context clues can also help students learn the meanings of unfamiliar words.

Locating Context Clues. Several types of context clues are found in written materials. These include

❶ *Definition clues.* A word may be directly defined in the context.

The *dictionary* is a book in which the meanings of words can be found.

❷ *Appositive clues.* An appositive may offer a synonym or a description of the word that will cue its meaning. Children need to be taught that an *appositive* is a word or phrase that restates or identifies the word or expression it follows and that it is usually set off by commas, dashes, or parentheses.

They are going to *harvest*, or gather in, the season's crops.

That model is *obsolete* (outdated).

The *rodents*—rats and mice—in the experiment learned to run a maze.

❸ *Comparison clues.* A comparison of the unfamiliar word with a word the child knows may offer a clue. In the examples, the familiar words *sleepy* and *clothes* provide the clues for *drowsy* and *habit*, respectively.

Like her sleepy brother, Mary felt *drowsy*.

Like all the clothes she wore, her riding *habit* was very fashionable.

❹ *Contrast clues.* A contrast of the unknown word with a familiar one may offer a clue. In the examples, the unfamiliar word *temporary* is contrasted with the familiar word *forever*, and the unfamiliar word *occasionally* is contrasted with the familiar word *regularly*.

It will not last forever; it is only *temporary*.

She doesn't visit regularly; she just comes by *occasionally*.

❺ *Example clues.* Sometimes examples are given for words that may be unfamiliar in print, and these examples can provide the clues needed for identification.

Mark was going to talk about *reptiles*—for example, snakes and lizards.

Andrea wants to play a *percussion* instrument, such as the snare drum or bells.

Although the preceding examples have clues in the sentences in which the new words are found, context can also offer clues in sentences other than the one in which the new words appear, so children should be encouraged to read surrounding sentences for clues to meaning. Sometimes an entire paragraph embodies the explanation of a term, as in the following example:

I've told you before that the flu is contagious! When Johnny had the flu, Beatrice played with him one afternoon, and soon Beatrice came down with it. Joey caught it from her, and now you tell me you have been to Joey's house. I hope you don't come down with the flu and have to miss the party on Saturday.

LITERATURE   Context clues are available in both text and illustrations in many trade books. *A Gaggle of Geese,* by Philippa-Alys Browne (Atheneum Books for Young Readers, 1996); *A Gaggle of Geese,* by Eve Merriam (Knopf, 1960); and *A Cache of Jewels and Other Collective Nouns,* by Ruth Heller (Grosset & Dunlap, 1987) put collective terminology for groups into an interesting context. Teaching children to recognize the context clues in these meaningful settings encourages them to use such clues in DIVERSITY   their independent reading. Illustrations often provide strong context clues for both beginning readers and English language learners.

TECHNOLOGY   Some researchers have found that using closed-caption television programs to provide readers with both auditory and visual context was effective with below-DIVERSITY   average readers and bilingual students (Koskinen et al., 1993; Neuman and Koskinen, 1992). They found that such programs provided readers with print to read in a motivational format. Videotaping the programs allows repetition of the reading for different purposes and use of small segments (only a few minutes each) of video in a lesson. (Teachers must study copyright laws, however, to ensure that use is in compliance with these laws.) Teachers and students could discuss words from the programs while the students were viewing video images. Later, students could read the words again, from handouts prepared with sentences drawn from the captioned video, and finally from magazines and books on the same topic. They could also use the words in written retellings of the viewed episode. The captions presented some challenges for readers: the match between the audio and the captions seen was not exact, the captions were presented at a rapid rate for poor readers (about 120 words per minute), and the captions were in all capital letters. Nevertheless, the results that teachers obtained were impressive.

Teaching Students to Use Context Clues. It is estimated that average ten- to fourteen-year-old students could acquire from 750 to 8,250 new words each year

Intermediate-Level Lesson on Context Clues

Write on the board or display on a transparency the following sentence: "Rather than encountering hostile natives, as they had expected, many settlers found the natives to be amicable." Read the sentence aloud and say: "I wonder what *amicable* means? Let's see; the sentence says, '*Rather than* encountering hostile natives.' That means the natives weren't hostile. *Hostile* means *unfriendly*; so maybe *amicable* means *friendly*."

through incidental, rather than directed, contextual learning (Schwartz, 1988; Herman et al., 1987; Nagy, Herman, and Anderson, 1985; Wysocki and Jenkins, 1987). Helping students learn to use context more efficiently should therefore greatly enhance their vocabulary learning.

Teachers can use a "think-aloud" strategy to help students see how to use context clues. (Think-aloud strategies are valuable in teaching several aspects of reading.) The Model Activity above makes use of this strategy.

After several example "think-aloud" activities in which the teacher models the use of context clues, the teacher can ask student volunteers to "think aloud" the context clues for specific words. Students may work in pairs on a context clues activity and verbalize their context usage strategies to each other. Finally, the students should work alone to determine meanings from context clues.

Teachers can create their own sentences to introduce new words in context. Use sentences that students can relate to their own experiences and that have only one unfamiliar word each. It is best not to use the new word at the very beginning of the sentence, since the children will not have had any of the facilitating context before they encounter it (Duffelmeyer, 1982).

Context can also come from reading selections. Edwards and Dermott (1989) select difficult words from material about to be assigned, take a quotation using each word in good context from the material, and provide written comments to the students to help them use appropriate context clues or other strategies (primarily structural analysis or dictionary use). The students try to use the clues available to decide on the meanings of the words before reading. Class discussion helps the students to think through their use of the strategy.

ACTIVITIES Using a selection that the students are about to read, take an unfamiliar word, put it into a title, and construct several sentences that offer clues to its meaning. Show the title on the overhead projector; then show one sentence at a time, letting the students guess the meaning of the word at each step (Kaplan and Tuchman, 1980).

Gipe (1980) expanded a context method (in which students read new words in meaningful contexts) to include having children apply the words on the basis of their own experiences. She then studied the effectiveness of this method by comparing it with three other methods: an association method (in which an unknown word is paired with a familiar synonym), a category method (in which students place words in categories), and a dictionary method (in which students look up the word, write a definition, and use the word in a sentence). The expanded context method was found to be the most effective of the four. The application of the new words may have been the most important aspect of the context method that Gipe used. After the students derived the meaning of the word from a variety of contexts, including a definition context, they *applied* the word to their personal experiences in a written response. Therefore, the instruction exhibits the first of the desirable qualities listed on page 135 of this chapter: it assists students in integrating the new words with their background knowledge.

Teachers need to help students learn *why* and *when* to use context clues (Blachowicz and Zabroske, 1990). Context clues are useful when the context is explicit about word meaning, but they are less useful when the meaning is left unclear. If the clues are too vague, they may actually be misleading. Furthermore, if the word is not important to understanding the passage, the explicitness of the context is not important. Teachers should model through think-alouds their decision-making processes about the importance of determining the meaning of the word, the usefulness of the context, and the kinds of clues available there. Students need to realize that the meanings they attribute to the words must make sense in the context.

Instruction that gradually moves the responsibility for determining new word meanings from the teacher to the student helps students become independent learners. Teachers can guide students to use context clues to define words independently by using a four-part procedure. First, students are given categorization tasks (described later in this chapter). Second, they practice determining meanings from complete contexts. Third, they practice determining meaning in incomplete contexts. Finally, they practice defining new vocabulary by means of context clues (Carr and Wixson, 1986).

As mentioned earlier in this chapter, good teachers combine a variety of approaches when teaching vocabulary. Combining contextual and definitional approaches to vocabulary instruction, for example, is more effective than using a contextual approach alone. In fact, "it would be hard to justify a contextual approach in which the teacher did not finally provide an adequate definition of the word or help the class arrive at one" (Nagy, 1988, p. 8). In addition, teachers can have students apply context clues in conjunction with structure clues, which we will discuss next, to help them decide whether or not a meaning suggested by the context is reasonable.

Structural Analysis

Like context clues, structural analysis, which was discussed in Chapter 3 as a word recognition skill, can also be used as an aid in discovering meanings of unknown words.

Children begin to learn about word structure very early. First, they deal with words in their simplest, most basic forms — as **morphemes**, the smallest units of meaning in a language. (The word *cat* is one morpheme.) Then they gradually learn to combine morphemes. If an *s* is added to form the plural, *cats*, the final *s* is also a morpheme, because it changes the word's meaning. There are two classes of

MODEL ACTIVITIES	Prefix *un-*

Have the students read the book *Fortunately* by Remy Charlip (New York: Aladdin Paperbacks, 1964). Discuss with them the meanings of *fortunately* and *unfortunately,* using the situations from the book to make the discussion concrete and clear. When they have stated that *unfortunately* means *not fortunately* or *the opposite of fortunately,* have them decide what part of the word means *not.* After they identify the *un-* as the part that means *not,* have them name other words they know that begin with *un-*. Discuss the meanings of these words, pointing out that the prefix means *not* or *the opposite of* in each case in which the remainder of the word forms a root word or a root word and a word ending (as in *unfortunately*), but not when the beginning two letters are not a prefix attached to a root word (such as *under*). Ask them to look in their reading assignments for words starting with *un-* in which *un-* is a prefix added to a root word. Have them use their knowledge of the meaning of *un-* to determine the meaning of each of these words.

morphemes, distinguished by function: *free* morphemes, which have independent meanings and can be used by themselves (*cat, man, son*), and *bound* morphemes, which must be combined with another morpheme to have meaning. Affixes and inflectional endings are bound morphemes; the *-er* in *singer* is an example.

Knowing meanings of common affixes and combining them with meanings of familiar root words can help students determine the meanings of many new words. For example, if a child knows the meaning of *joy* and knows that the suffix *-ous* means *full of,* he or she can conclude that the word *joyous* means *full of joy.*

Practice activities such as the above Model Activity can help children see how prefixes and suffixes change the meanings of words. *Un-* is the most common prefix

CLASSROOM SCENARIO	Use of Structural Analysis Skills

A middle-school science textbook presented two theories of the solar system: a geocentric theory and a heliocentric theory. Two diagrams were provided to help the students visualize the two theories, but the diagrams were not labeled. Mrs. Brown, the teacher, asked the students, "Which diagram is related to each theory?"

Matt's hand quickly went up, and he accurately identified the two diagrams.

"How did you decide which was which?" asked Mrs. Brown.

"You told us that *geo-* means *earth. Centric* looks like it comes from *center.* This diagram has the earth in the center. So I decided it was geocentric. That would mean the other one was heliocentric. Since the sun is in the center in it, I guess *helio-* means *sun.*"

Analysis of Scenario

Mrs. Brown had taught an important science word part the first time it occurred in her class. She had encouraged her students to use their knowledge of word parts to figure out unfamiliar words. Matt followed her suggestions and managed to make decisions about key vocabulary on the basis of his knowledge of word parts.

appearing in the *Word Frequency Book* (Carroll, Davies, and Richman, 1971; White, Sowell, and Yanagihara, 1989).

White, Sowell, and Yanagihara (1989) caution teachers that prefixes may have more than one meaning. *Un-, re-, in-,* and *dis-,* the four most frequently used prefixes, have at least two meanings each. *Un-* and *dis-* may each mean either *not* or *do the opposite. In-* may mean either *not,* or *in,* or *into. Re-* may mean either *again* or *back.* Both the word parts and the context of the words should be considered in determining the meanings of prefixed words. The Classroom Scenario on page 147 shows an application of structural analysis in the classroom.

The students can study word cards that contain words derived from Latin or Greek word parts, such as *prescription* and *scripture.* They can be encouraged to think of other examples and asked to use the derived words in sentence context.

Students can often determine the meanings of compound words by relating the meanings of the component parts to each other (*watchdog* means a *dog* that *watches*). After some practice, they can be led to see that the component parts of a compound word do not always have the same relationships to each other (*bookcase* means a *case* for *books*). See the Focus on Strategies on page 149 for an activity that can offer practice in determining meanings of compound words.

Categorization

Categorization is the grouping together of things or ideas that have common features. Classifying words into categories can be a good way to learn more about word meanings. An activity such as this is referred to as a *word sort.* Young children can begin learning how to place things into categories by grouping concrete objects according to their traits. Once the children have developed some sight vocabulary, it is a relatively small step for them to begin categorizing the words they see in print according to their meanings. Very early in their instruction, children will be able to look at the following list and classify the words into such teacher-supplied categories as "people," "things to play with," "things to eat," and "things to do."

Word List

doll	bicycle	ball	run	girl
candy	cookie	boy	baby	sit
toy	dig	sing	mother	banana

The children may discover that they want to put a word in more than one category. This desire will provide an opportunity for discussion about how a word may fit in two or more places for different reasons. The children should give reasons for all of their placements.

Classifying words into categories supplied by the teacher is a *closed-ended sort.* After the children become adept doing closed-ended sorts, they are ready for the more difficult task of generating the categories needed for classifying the words presented. The teacher may give them a word list such as the one that follows and ask

Compound Words

Mr. Clay based his lesson on the book *The Seal Mother* by Mordicai Gerstein (Dial, 1986). He introduced the story by saying that it was an old Scottish folktale. He wrote the word *folktale* on the board. Then he asked, "What can you tell me about this word?"

Bobby said, "It is made up of two words: *folk* and *tale*. That makes it a compound word."

"Good, Bobby," Mr. Clay responded. "What does that make you believe this word means?"

"A tale is a story," LaTonya replied.

"That's right," said Mr. Clay. "Can anyone add anything else to what we know about the word's meaning? What does *folk* mean?"

Carl answered tentatively, "A kind of music?"

"There is folk music, just as there are folktales, but we still need a meaning for the word *folk*," Mr. Clay responded.

After he got only shrugs, he explained, "A folktale is a tale, or story, told by the folk, or common people, of a country. Folktales were passed down orally from older people to younger ones over the years. See how both parts of the compound word give something to the meaning?

"Listen as I read this story to you. When I finish, we will try to retell the story by listing the main events."

The children listened intently. When he finished the story, Mr. Clay asked them to list the events in the story in order. As they suggested events, he wrote each one on the board. When he had listed all of the events that they could remember, they discussed how to put some of the events in the proper order. Mr. Clay erased and moved the sentences around until the children were satisfied.

Then Mr. Clay asked the children, "Did you use any compound words to retell the story?"

Hands shot up all over the room. Mr. Clay called on them one by one, and they pointed out *fisherman, sealskin, without, oilcloth, inside, rayfish, everywhere,* *grandfather,* and *whenever.* The children who mentioned the words were allowed to go to the board and circle them, identify the two words that made up each compound, and try to define each compound word, using the meanings of the two component words. Other students helped in determining the definitions, and sometimes the dictionary was consulted.

Finally, the children were asked to copy the compound words from the board into their vocabulary study notebooks. "I'm putting three copies of *The Seal Mother* in the reading center for the rest of this week," Mr. Clay said. "When you have time, take your vocabulary notebook to the center and read the book to yourself or with a partner. Each time you find one of our compound words, put a checkmark by the word in your notebook. When you find a compound word that we didn't use in our retelling, copy it into your notebook, and write a definition for it, using the meanings of the two words and the context of the sentence in which you found it. We'll discuss the other words that you found on Friday."

On Friday, the children had found a number of words in the book that they hadn't used in their retelling, including *moonlit, moonlight, everything, wide-eyed, tiptoed, another,* and *into.* A discussion of the words and their meanings followed. Mr. Clay asked how the author's use of some of these words added to the children's understanding of the story.

"*Moonlit* and *moonlight* give you a picture in your mind of the scene," Jared said.

"*Wide-eyed* lets us know how his parents' talk made the boy feel," Marissa added.

"*Tiptoed* showed us how he walked quietly," Tyrone said.

"Watch for compound words in other books that you read, and use the meanings of the two words in each compound to help you with meanings that you don't already know," Mr. Clay told them as he ended the lesson.

them to place the words in groups of things that are alike and to name the trait that the items have in common. This activity is an *open-ended sort*.

Word List

horse	cow	goose	stallion	foal
gosling	mare	filly	chick	calf
colt	gander	bull	hen	rooster

Children may offer several categories for these words: various families of animals; four-legged and two-legged animals; feathered and furred animals; winged and wingless animals; or male animals, female animals, and animals that might be either sex. They may also come up with a classification that the teacher has not considered. As long as the classification system makes sense and the animals are correctly classified according to the stated system, it should be considered correct. Teachers should encourage students to discover various possibilities for classifications.

There are several benefits to a classification task such as this. Discussion of the different classification systems may help to extend the children's concepts about some of the animals on the list, and it may help some children develop concepts related to some of the animals for the first time. The classification system enables them to relate the new knowledge about some of the animals to the knowledge they already have about these animals or others. If some of the animal terms are new to students, putting these new words into categories can help students remember their meanings. The usefulness of categorization activities is supported by research indicating that presenting words in semantically related clusters can lead to improvement in students' vocabulary knowledge and reading comprehension (Marzano, 1984).

A classification game such as the one in the Model Activity below provides an interesting way to work on categorization skills.

MODEL ACTIVITIES | **Classification Game**

Divide the class into groups of three or four, and make category sheets like the one shown here for each group. When you give a signal, the children start writing as many words as they can think of that fit in each category; when you signal that time is up, a child from each group reads the group's words to the class. Have the children compare their lists and discuss why they placed particular words in particular categories.

Appropriate categories in addition to the ones used below are meats, fruits, and vegetables; mammals, reptiles, and insects; and liquids, solids, and gases.

Cities	States	Countries

The ability to classify is a basic skill that applies to many areas of learning. Many of the other activities described in this chapter, including those for analogies, semantic maps, and semantic feature analysis, depend on categorization.

Analogies and Word Lines

Analogies compare two relationships and thereby provide a basis for building word knowledge. Educators may teach analogies by displaying examples of categories, relationships, and analogies; asking guiding questions about the examples; allowing students to discuss the questions; and applying the ideas that emerge.

Students may need help in grouping items into categories and understanding the relationships among items. For example, the teacher might write *nickel, dime,* and *quarter* on the board and ask, "How are these things related? What name could you give the entire group of items?" (Answer: *money.*) Teachers can use pictures instead of words in the primary grades; in either case, they can ask students to apply the skill by naming other things that would fit in the category (*penny* and *dollar*). Or the teacher could write *painter* and *brush* and ask, "What is the relationship between the two items?" (Answer: A *painter* works with a *brush.*) Teachers should remember to simplify their language for discussions with young children and to have students give other examples of the relationship (*dentist* and *drill*). After working through many examples such as these, the students should be ready for examples of simple analogies, such as "Light is to dark as day is to night," "Glove is to hand as sock is to foot," and "Round is to ball as square is to block." Students can discuss how analogies work: "How are the first two things related? How are the second two things related? How are these relationships alike?" They can then complete incomplete analogies, such as "Teacher is to classroom as pilot is to _____." Younger children should do this orally; older ones can understand the standard shorthand form of *come:go::live:die* if they are taught to read the colon (:) as *is to* and the double colon (::) as *as* (Bellows, 1980).

Huff-Benkoski and Greenwood (1995) taught second graders how to use analogies. These authors modeled their reasoning processes for the students through think-alouds as they analyzed analogies. They also had students explain their reasoning processes. The children came up with a definition for *analogies.* Attention then was given to classification activities—choosing words that did or did not belong with a given set of words related to a theme study. Next, the children were asked to state the relationship between two words. Following that, students completed analogies that had one part missing. Finally, students produced their own analogies in groups and individually.

Dwyer (1988) suggests mapping analogies, as shown in Example 4.1. Teachers might use analogy maps as part of an instructional sequence such as the one developed by Huff-Benkoski and Greenwood. The map in Example 4.1 provides the relationship involved, a complete example, two incomplete examples for the students to complete, and one space for an example that comes entirely from the student.

Teachers may use word lines to show the relationships among words, just as they use number lines for numbers. They can arrange related words on a graduated line that emphasizes the relationships among the words. Teachers of young children can

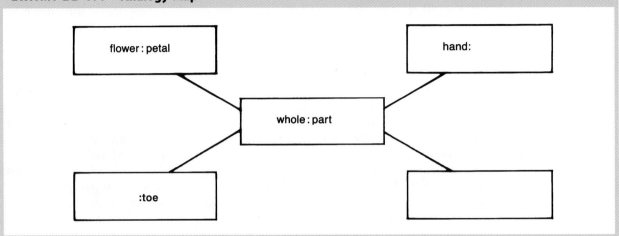

EXAMPLE 4.1   Analogy Map

use pictures and words for students to match or ask students to locate or produce appropriate pictures. Upper-grade students can be asked to arrange a specified list of words on a word line themselves. Word lines can concretely show antonym, synonym, and degree analogies, as in this example:

| enormous | large | medium | small | tiny |

The teacher can eventually have the students make their own word lines and analogies. Analogies that they could develop based on the word line example above include "enormous is to large as small is to tiny" (synonym); "enormous is to tiny as large is to small" (antonym); and "large is to medium as medium is to small" (degree).

Semantic Maps and Word Webs

Semantic maps are diagrams that show how words are connected in meaning to each other (Johnson and Pearson, 1984; Johnson, Pittelman, and Heimlich, 1986; Heimlich and Pittelman, 1986). They can be used to teach related concepts or to expand or activate students' knowledge about a single concept. To construct a semantic map with a class, the teacher writes, on the board or a chart, a word that represents a concept that is central to the topic under consideration. The teacher asks the students to name other words related to this concept. The teacher groups the students' words into broad categories while listing them on the board or chart. Then students name the categories. They may also suggest additional categories. A discussion of the central concept, the listed words, the categories, and the interrelationships among the words follows.

The discussion step appears to be the key to the effectiveness of this method, because it allows the students to be actively involved in the learning. After the class

EXAMPLE 4.2 Semantic Map of the Concept *Tennis*

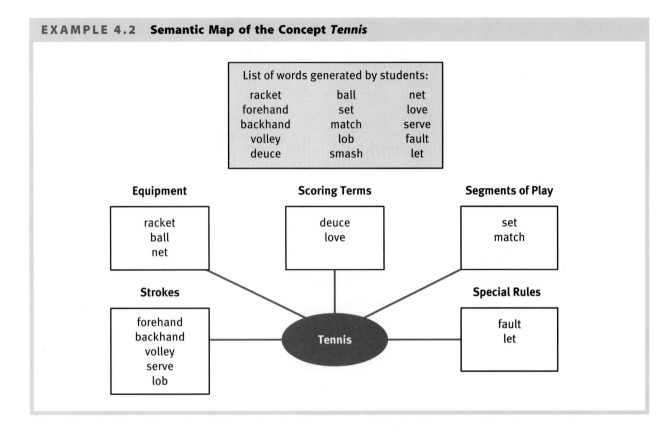

List of words generated by students:

racket	ball	net
forehand	set	love
backhand	match	serve
volley	lob	fault
deuce	smash	let

Equipment
racket
ball
net

Scoring Terms
deuce
love

Segments of Play
set
match

Strokes
forehand
backhand
volley
serve
lob

Special Rules
fault
let

Tennis

has discussed the semantic map, the teacher can give the children an incomplete semantic map and ask them to fill in the words from the map on the board or chart and add any categories or words that they wish. The children can work on their maps as they do the assigned reading related to the central concept. Further discussion can follow the reading, and more categories and words can be added to the maps. The final discussion and mapping allow the children to recall and graphically organize the information they gained from the reading (Johnson, Pittelman, and Heimlich, 1986; Stahl and Vancil, 1986). Example 4.2 shows a semantic map constructed by one class.

Because a semantic map shows both familiar and new words under labeled categories, the process of constructing one helps students make connections between known and new concepts (Johnson, Pittelman, and Heimlich, 1986). The graphic display makes relationships among terms easier to see. Discussion of the map enables the teacher to assess the children's background knowledge, to clarify concepts, and to correct misunderstandings.

Schwartz and Raphael (1985) used a modified approach to semantic mapping to help students develop the concept of *definition*. The students learned what types of information are needed for a definition and learned how to use context clues and background knowledge to help them better understand words. Word maps are really graphic representations of definitions. The word maps that Schwartz and Raphael

EXAMPLE 4.3 **Word Map for Definition**

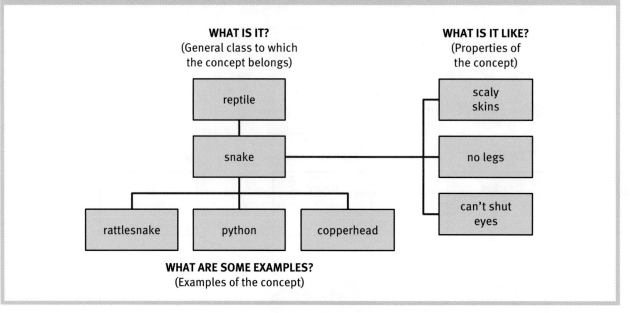

WHAT IS IT?
(General class to which
the concept belongs)

reptile

snake

WHAT IS IT LIKE?
(Properties of
the concept)

scaly
skins

no legs

can't shut
eyes

rattlesnake

python

copperhead

WHAT ARE SOME EXAMPLES?
(Examples of the concept)

used were like the one in Example 4.3, which defines the concept *snake*. The maps contained information about the general class to which the concept belonged, answering the question "What is it?"; the properties of the concept, answering the question "What is it like?"; and examples of the concept.

With the basic information contained in such a map, students have enough information to construct definitions. This procedure for understanding the concept of definition is effective from the fourth-grade level through college. The approach used by Schwartz and Raphael started with strong teacher involvement, but control was gradually transferred to the children. Children were led to search the context of a sentence in which the word occurred for the elements of definition needed to map a word. Eventually, the teachers provided only partial context for the word, leading the children to go to outside sources, such as dictionaries, for information to complete the maps. Finally, teachers asked the students to write definitions, including all the features previously mapped, without actually mapping the word on paper. *Word webs* are another way to represent the relationships among words graphically. Students construct these diagrams by connecting related words with lines. The words used for the web may be taken from material students have read in class.

Semantic Feature Analysis

Semantic feature analysis is a technique that can help children understand the uniqueness of a word as well as its relationships to other words (Johnson and Pearson, 1984). To perform such an analysis, the teacher lists, in a column on the board or a chart, some known words with common properties. Then the children generate a list of features possessed by the various items in the list. A feature needs to apply to only one item to be listed. The teacher writes these features in a row across the top of the board or chart, and the students fill in the cells of the resulting matrix with pluses or minuses to indicate the presence or absence of each feature.

Example 4.4 shows a partial matrix developed by children for various buildings. "Walls" and "doors" were other features the children suggested for the matrix; they were omitted from the example only to save space. Both of these features received a plus for each building, an outcome that emphasized the similarities of the terms *jail, garage, museum,* and *church.*

EXAMPLE 4.4   Semantic Feature Analysis Chart

	barred windows	exhibits	steeple	cross	cars	lift-up doors	guards	oil stains
jail	+	–	–	–	–	–	+	–
garage	?	–	–	–	+	+	–	+
museum	?	+	–	–	?	–	+	–
church	–	–	+	+	–	–	–	–

The children discussed the terms as they filled in the matrix. In the places where the question marks occur, the children said, "Sometimes it may have that, but not always. It doesn't have to have it." The group discussion brought out much information about each building listed and served to expand the children's existing schemata.

Students can continue to expand such a matrix after initially filling it out by adding words that share some of the listed features. For example, the children added *grocery store* to the list of buildings in Example 4.4 because it shared the walls and doors, and they added other features showing characteristics that differentiate it from the other buildings, such as *food, clerks,* and *checkout counters.* Johnson and Pearson (1984) suggest that after gaining experience with these matrices, children may begin to realize that some words have different degrees of the same feature. At this time, the teacher may want to introduce a numerical system of coding, using 0 for *none,* 1 for *some,* 2 for *much,* and 3 for *all.* Under the feature "fear," for example, *scared* might be coded with a 1, whereas *terrified* might be coded with a 3.

Dictionary Use

TECHNOLOGY
The dictionary can be an excellent source for discovering meanings of unfamiliar words, particularly for determining the appropriate meanings of words that have multiple definitions or specific, technical definitions. Either print or computerized dictionaries can be used. Hand-held computerized dictionaries are as portable as print dictionaries. In some instances, children may be familiar with several common meanings of a word, but not with a word's specialized meaning found in a content area textbook. For example, a child may understand a reference to a *base* in a baseball game but not a discussion of a military *base* (social studies material), a *base* that turns

litmus paper blue (science material), or a character's *base* motives (literature). Words that have the greatest number of different meanings, such as *run* and *bank,* are frequently very common.

There are some problems related to dictionary use. As Rhoder and Huerster (2002, p. 730) point out, "Definitions are short, abstract generalizations often written in dense embedded text. No concrete examples are offered, and ideas are never repeated in different words." The student may have to look up other words that are in the definition in order to decipher the meaning expressed in the definition. Teaching word meanings through dictionary use has been widely criticized for these and other reasons. Nevertheless, as research shows, it is a useful technique for vocabulary development if it is applied properly (Graves and Prenn, 1986).

Teachers should not simply assume that being able to recite a dictionary definition means that the students actually understand the word's meaning. They should point out the potential problems with dictionary definitions and should model strategies for determining word meaning.

Teachers should instruct children to consider the context surrounding a word, to read the different dictionary definitions, and to choose the definition that makes the most sense in the context. Without such instruction, children have a strong tendency to read only the first dictionary definition and try to force it into the context. The teacher should model the choice of the correct definition for the students so that they can see what the task is. Students will then need to practice the task under teacher supervision. As Nagy (1988) points out, combining a definitional approach to vocabulary instruction with a contextual approach is more effective than using a definitional approach in isolation. Sentences that illustrate meanings and uses of the defined words can help immensely.

The Model Activities below and on page 157 are good to use for practice immediately after instruction in dictionary use and for later independent practice.

Chapter 9 presents information about the mechanics of dictionary use. Chapter 3 discusses using the dictionary for word recognition.

MODEL ACTIVITIES **Appropriate Dictionary Definitions**

Write the following sentences on the board. Ask the children to find the dictionary definition of *sharp* that fits each sentence. You may ask them to jot down each definition and have a whole-class or small-group discussion about each one after all meanings have been located, or you may wish to discuss each meaning as it is located. The students may read other definitions for *sharp* in the dictionary and generate sentences for these as well.

1. Katherine's knife was very sharp.
2. There is a sharp curve in the road up ahead.
3. I hope that, when I am seventy, my mind is as sharp as my grandmother's is.
4. We are leaving at two o'clock sharp.

MODEL ACTIVITIES — Multiple Meanings of Words

Give the students a list of sentences, drawn from their textbooks, that contain words with specialized meanings for that subject. Have them use the dictionary or the textbook's glossary to discover the specialized meanings that fit the context of the sentences. After the students have completed the task independently, go over the sentences with them and discuss reasons for right and wrong responses.

The material you give to the students may look something like this:

Directions: Some words mean different things in your textbooks from what they mean in everyday conversation. In each of the following sentences, find the special meanings for the words and write these meanings on the lines provided.

1. Frederick Smith has decided to *run* for mayor.
   _____

2. The park was near the *mouth* of the Little Bear River.
   _____

3. The management of the company was unable to avert a *strike*.
   _____

4. That song is hard to sing because of the high *pitch* of several notes.
   _____

5. That number is written in *base* two.
   _____

Students can also use dictionaries to study *etymology*, the origin and history of words. Dictionaries often give the origin of a word in brackets after the phonetic respelling (although not all dictionaries do this in the same way), and archaic or obsolete definitions are frequently given and labeled so that students can see how words have changed.

Word Origins and Histories

Children in the intermediate grades can enjoy learning about the histories and origins of words and the kinds of changes that have taken place in the English language. They can learn more about etymology by studying words and definitions that appear in very old dictionaries and by studying differences between American English and British English. Charles Earle Funk's *Curious Word Origins, Sayings and Expressions* (Galahad, 1993) is a good reference.

Teachers need to help children understand the different ways in which English words have been created. *Portmanteau* words are formed by merging the sounds and meanings of two different words (for example, *smog*, from *smoke* and *fog*). *Acronyms* are words formed from the initial letters of a name or by combining initial letters or parts from a series of words (for example, *radar*, from *ra*dio *d*etecting *a*nd *r*anging). Some words are just shortened forms of other words (for example, *phone*, from *telephone; flu*, from *influenza;* and *piano*, from *pianoforte*). Both shortened forms and acronyms represent ways in which our language has become more compact (Richler, 1996). Some words are borrowed from other languages (for example, *lasso*, from the Spanish *lazo*). The teacher can discuss the origins of such terms when they occur in students' reading materials. In addition, students should try to think of other words that have been formed in a similar manner. The students can combine structural analysis and etymology by studying words derived from Latin or Greek word parts, such as *prescription* and *scripture*. They can be encouraged to think of other examples and asked to use the derived words in sentences. The teacher may also wish to contribute other examples from familiar sources.

Figurative Language

Figurative language, or nonliteral language, can be a barrier to understanding written selections. Children tend to interpret literally many expressions that have meanings different from the sums of the meanings of the individual words. For example, the expression "the teeth of the wind" does not mean that the wind actually has teeth, nor does "a blanket of fog" denote a conventional blanket. Context clues indicate the meanings of such phrases in the same ways that they cue the meanings of individual words. English language learners have special difficulties interpreting figurative language because they lack background exposure to such usage in English.

DIVERSITY

Adults often assume that children have had exposure to expressions that in fact are unfamiliar to them. Children need substantial help in order to comprehend figurative language. Even basal readers present many of these expressions. Some common figures of speech that cause trouble follow.

❶ *Simile*—a comparison using *like* or *as*

❷ *Metaphor*—a direct comparison without the word *like* or *as*

❸ *Personification*—giving the attributes of a person to an inanimate object or abstract idea

❹ *Hyperbole*—an extreme exaggeration

❺ *Euphemism*—substitution of a less offensive term for an unpleasant term or expression

❻ *Allusion*—an indirect reference to a person, place, thing, or event considered to be known to the reader

Teaching children to recognize and understand similes is usually not too difficult, because the cue words *like* and *as* signal the presence of a comparison. Metaphors, however, may cause more serious problems. A metaphor is a comparison between two unlike things that share an attribute. Sometimes children do not realize that the language in metaphors is figurative; sometimes they do not have sufficient background knowledge about one or both of the things being compared; and sometimes they simply have not learned a process for interpreting metaphors.

The two things compared in a metaphor may seem to be incompatible, but readers must think of past experiences with each, searching for a match in attributes that could be the basis of comparison. For example, a man might be compared to a mouse on the basis of the characteristic of timidity.

Readence, Baldwin, and Head (1986, 1987) suggest the following instructional sequence for teaching metaphorical interpretation:

❶ The teacher can display a metaphor, such as "Her eyes were stars," together with a more explicit simile, such as "Her eyes were as bright as stars," and explain that metaphors have missing words that link the things being compared (such as *bright* does). Other sentence pairs can also be shown and explained.

❷ Then the students can be asked to find the missing word in a new metaphor, such as "He is a mouse around his boss." They can offer guesses, explaining their reasons aloud.

❸ The teacher can explain that people have lists of words related to different topics stored in their minds. Examples can be modeled by the teacher and then produced by the students. At this point, the students can try to select the attribute related to the new metaphor. If there are two incorrect guesses, the attribute *timid* can be supplied and the reason for this choice given. This process can then be repeated with another metaphor.

❹ As more metaphors are presented, the teacher can do less modeling, turning over more and more control of the process to the students.

LITERATURE After explaining each type of figurative language, modeling its interpretation, and having students interpret it under supervision, the teacher may provide independent practice activities such as the following ones. Ideally, the teacher should take examples of figurative expressions from literature that the children are currently reading and use these expressions in constructing practice activities. For instance, *Maniac Magee* by Jerry Spinelli contains an abundance of good examples, such as "The book came flapping like a wounded duck," "He's paralyzed, a mouse in front of the yawning maw of a python," and "The phantom Samaritan ... hauled him out of there like a sack of flour." All of these were found in the first nineteen pages, and there are many more throughout the book.

1. Show students pictures of possible meanings for figurative expressions found in their reading materials, and ask them to accept or reject the accuracy of each picture. Have them look carefully at the context in which the expression was found before answering. (For example, if you illustrate the sentence "She worked like a horse" with a woman pulling a plow, children should reject the picture's accuracy.)

2. Give each child a copy of a poem that is filled with figures of speech, and have the class compete to see who can "dig up" all the figures of speech first. You may require students to label all figures of speech properly as to type and to explain them.

Teachers can also use an activity like the Model Activity on page 160 to illustrate the use of a figure of speech.

Figures of Speech

Display the following cartoon on a transparency.

"I hear you been through the mill.....what do they DO there?"

Source: DENNIS THE MENACE® used by permission of Hank Ketcham Enterprises and © by North America Syndicate.

Lead a discussion about the cartoon, using the following questions as a guide.

1. What does "been through the mill" really mean, as Dennis's mother used it?

2. What does Dennis think it means?

3. How is the woman likely to react to Dennis's question?

4. How does Dennis's mother probably feel about the question?

5. Can misunderstanding figurative language cause trouble at times? Why do you say so?

Have the children suggest other figurative expressions that could produce misunderstandings. Then, as a follow-up activity, let them draw funny scenes in which the misunderstandings occur.

Also have the children look for other examples in newspaper comics. Ask them to cut out the examples and bring them to school for discussion.

Student-Centered Vocabulary Learning Techniques

Some vocabulary learning techniques focus on students and their individual needs and interests. Explanations of several of these techniques follow.

Vocabulary Self-Collection Strategy (VSS). Some educators believe that "vocabulary instruction should feature student-selected words" (Brabham, Greene, and Villaume, 2002, p. 266). Haggard (1986) suggests the following approach for general vocabulary development:

❶ Ask each child to bring to class a word that the entire class should learn. (The teacher brings one, too.) Each child should determine the meaning of his or her word from its context, rather than looking it up in the dictionary.

❷ Write the words on the board. Let each participant identify his or her word and tell where it was found, the context-derived meaning, and why the class should learn the word. The class should then discuss the meaning of the word, in order to clarify and extend it and to construct a definition on which the class agrees. The result may be checked against a dictionary definition, if desired.

3 Narrow the list down to a manageable number, and have the students record the final list of words and definitions in their vocabulary journals. Some students may want to put eliminated words on their personal lists.

4 Make study assignments for the words.

5 Test the students on the words at the end of the week.

Ruddell and Shearer (2002, p. 354) believe that "students learn new words not by hearing them explained with other new words, but rather from ongoing and extended transaction with the words, their peers, and their teacher within the context of life and classroom experience." It increases word awareness and word-learning strategies. They used the VSS as a vehicle to accomplish these goals with at-risk middle-school students. The word study during the week involved such techniques as discussion, semantic mapping, and semantic feature analysis. Students chose many words from their content area classes, but they also chose words from nonschool sources. Ruddell and Shearer (2002) found that the students chose important and challenging words, learned these words, and retained the words over time.

Rosenbaum (2001) used eight techniques for clarifying word meanings of self-selected words for students that Harmon (1998) had identified. Rosenbaum developed a word map for her students to use daily with words they located during independent reading. They included "synonyms, brief descriptions, examples and nonexamples, rephrasing, repetition, associations, and unique expression" (Rosenbaum, 2001, p. 45). Example 4.5 shows an example of this word map.

Word Banks or Vocabulary Notebooks. Students can form their own word banks by writing on index cards words that they have learned, the words' definitions, and sentences showing the words in meaningful contexts. They may also want to illustrate the words or include personal associations with or reactions to the words. Students can carry their word banks around and practice the words in spare moments, such as while waiting for the bus or the dentist, or at home with their families. In the classroom, the word banks can be used in word games and in classification and other instructional activities.

FAMILY

Vocabulary notebooks are useful for recording new words found in general reading or words heard in conversations or on radio or television. New words may be alphabetized in the notebooks and defined, illustrated, and processed in much the same way as word-bank words.

Both word banks and vocabulary notebooks can help children maintain a record of their increasing vocabularies. Generally, word banks are used in primary grades and notebooks in intermediate grades and above, but there are no set limits for either technique.

TIME for REFLECTION

Some teachers think that having students learn the dictionary definitions of weekly teacher-chosen vocabulary words is a good approach to vocabulary instruction. Others believe in more use of student-centered methods to help students acquire meaning vocabulary. What do *you* think, and why?

EXAMPLE 4.5   Word Map Completed by Student

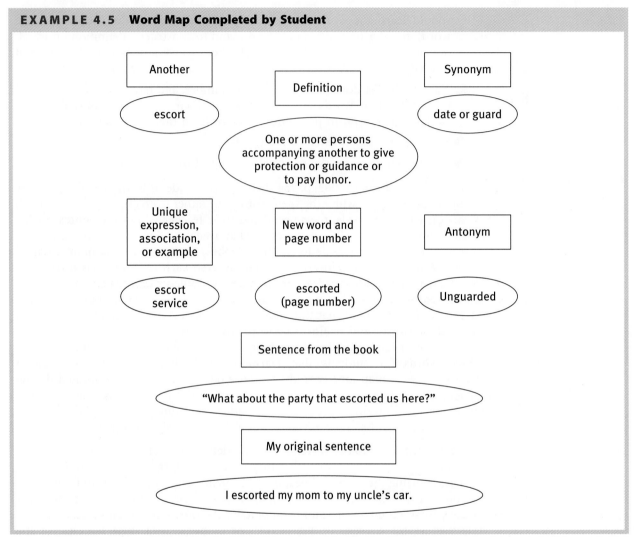

Source: Catherine Rosenbaum, "A Word Map for Middle School: A Tool for Effective Vocabulary Instruction," *Journal of Adolescent & Adult Literacy* 45 (1) (September 2001), p. 44–49.

Word Play

Word play is an enjoyable way to learn more about words. It can provide multiple exposures to words in different contexts that are important to complete word learning. Silly songs and rhymes are among the types of word play that "promote a love of words" (Brabham and Villaume, 2002, p. 265). Gale (1982, p. 220) states, "Children who play with words show a stronger grasp of meaning than those who do not. To create or comprehend a pun, one needs to be aware of the multiple meanings of a word."

Vocabulary Instruction **163**

The following activities present some other ways in which teachers can engage children in word play.

ACTIVITIES

1. Have students write words in ways that express their meanings; for example, they may write *backward* as *drawkcab,* or *up* slanting upward and *down* slanting downward.

2. Ask them silly questions containing new words. Example: "Would you have a terrarium for dinner? Why or why not?"

3. Discuss what puns are and give some examples. Then ask children to make up or find puns to bring to class. Let them explain the play on words to classmates who do not understand it. Example: "What is black and white and read all over?" Answer: A newspaper (word play on the homonyms *red* and *read*).

4. Use Hink Pinks, Hinky Pinkies, and Hinkety Pinketies—rhyming definitions for terms with one, two, and three syllables, respectively. Give a definition, tell whether it is a Hink Pink, a Hinky Pinky, or a Hinkety Pinkety, and let the children guess the expression. Then let the children make up their own terms. Several examples follow.

   Hink Pink: Unhappy father—Sad dad

   Hinky Pinky: Late group of celebrators—Tardy party

   Hinkety Pinkety: Yearly handbook—Annual manual

5. Give the students a list of clues ("means the same as …," "is the opposite of …," and so forth) to words in a reading selection, along with page numbers. Tell them to go on a scavenger hunt for the words and write the words beside the appropriate clues (Criscuolo, 1980).

6. Students might also enjoy crossword puzzles that highlight new words in their textbooks or other instructional materials.

7. Mountain (2002) has students start with four syllables on two poker chips—two prefixes on one and two roots on the other, or two suffixes on one and two roots on the other. The students flip the two chips until they form four different words. They discuss the meanings of the words and then place them in appropriate blanks in a cloze passage. (See Chapter 12 for an explanation of cloze passages.) Later the students can make their own Flip-Chip pairs and cloze passages.

Riddles are a very effective form of word play. To use riddles, children must interact verbally with others; to create riddles, they have to organize information and decide on significant details. Riddles can help children move from the literal to the interpretive level of understanding (Gale, 1982). Tyson and Mountain (1982) point out that riddles provide both context clues and high-interest material. Both of these factors promote vocabulary learning.

TIME for REFLECTION

What forms of word play are particularly effective in enhancing vocabulary development? Why do you believe this is so?

Riddles can be classified into several categories: those based on homonyms, on rhyming words, on double meanings, and on figurative/literal meanings, for example. (See the section "Special Words" later in this chapter.) Here is an example of a homonym riddle: "What does a grizzly *bear* take on a trip? Only the *bare* essentials" (Tyson and Mountain, 1982, p. 170).

Riddles work best with children who are at least six years old (Gale, 1982), and they continue to be especially effective with children through eleven years of age. After that, interest in this form of word play wanes.

TECHNOLOGY ## Computer Techniques

Computers are present in many elementary school classrooms in this age of high technology, and the software available includes many programs for vocabulary development. Although some of them are simply drill-and-practice programs, which are meant to provide practice with word meanings the teacher has already taught, some tutorial programs provide initial instruction in word meanings. (These programs may also include a drill-and-practice component.) Programs that focus on synonyms, antonyms, homonyms, and words with multiple meanings are available, as are programs that provide work with classification and analogies. Semantic mapping programs allow students to work with word relationships.

Word-processing programs can be profitably used in vocabulary instruction. A child may be given a disk that has files containing paragraphs with certain words used repeatedly. The child may use the find-and-replace function to replace all instances of a chosen word with a synonym and then read the paragraph to see if the synonym makes sense in each place it appears. If it does not, the child can delete the synonym in the inappropriate places and either choose more appropriate replacements for the original word or put the original word back into the paragraph. Then the child can read the file again to see if the words chosen convey the correct meanings and if the variation in word choices makes the paragraph more interesting to read.

A paragraph such as the following one could be a starting place:

Shonda had to run to the store for her mother because, just before the party, her mother got a run in her pantyhose. Shonda had to listen to her mother run on and on about her run of bad luck that day before she was able to leave the house. When she arrived at the store, she saw her uncle, who told her he had decided to run for office, delaying her progress further. She finally bought the last pair of pantyhose in the store. There must have been a run on them earlier in the day.

See Chapter 11 for more information on computer use.

● Special Words

Special types of words, such as those discussed in the following sections, need to be given careful attention.

Homonyms or Homophones

Many *homonyms* or *homophones* can cause trouble for young readers because they are spelled differently but pronounced the same way. Some common homonyms are found in the following sets of sentences.

I want to *be* a doctor.
That *bee* almost stung me.

She has *two* brothers.
Will you go *to* the show with me?
I have *too* much work to do.

I can *hear* the bird singing.
Maurice, you sit over *here*.

Mark has a *red* scarf.
Have you *read* that book?

I *ate* all of my supper.
We have *eight* dollars to spend.

LITERATURE Fred Gwynne's *The King Who Rained* (Windmill, 1970) and *A Chocolate Moose for Dinner* (Windmill/Dutton, 1976) both have homonyms in their titles, as well as throughout their texts. Pettersen (1988) suggests letting the students look for homonyms in all of their reading materials. Students can construct lists of homonym pairs that mean something to them because they discovered at least one of the qualifying words in each pair themselves. If you would like to try this for yourself, the paragraph you are currently reading is a good one to use as a starter for such an exercise. (Hint: *all-awl* is a good start.) Expanding Pettersen's activity to require the use of each homonym in a meaningful sentence is one way to keep the focus on meaning.

1. Have children play a card game to work on meanings of homonyms. Print homonyms on cards and let the children take turns drawing from each other, as in the game of Old Maid. A child who has a pair of homonyms can put them down if he or she gives a correct sentence using each word. The child who claims the most pairs wins.

2. Have students web homonyms in the following way:

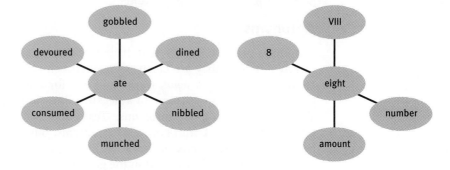

Homographs

Homographs are words that have identical spellings but not the same meanings. Their pronunciations may or may not be the same. Readers must use context clues to identify the correct pronunciations, parts of speech, and meanings of homographs. Examples include

I will *read* my newspaper. (pronounced as though it were *reed)*

I have *read* my newspaper. (pronounced like the color *red*)

I have a *contract* signed by the president. (noun: pronounced *con' trakt;* means a document)

I didn't know it would *contract* as it cooled. (verb: pronounced *cən/trakt;* means to reduce in size)

LITERATURE   The books by Fred Gwynne mentioned in the section on homonyms are also rich sources of homographs.

Synonyms

Synonyms are words that have the same or very similar meanings. Work with synonyms can help expand children's vocabularies.

Study of the sports page of the newspaper for ways in which writers express the ideas of *win* and *lose* can be a good way to introduce synonyms. The teacher should take this opportunity to show the students the way that synonyms can convey different shades of meaning. For example, the headlines "Cats Maul Dogs" and "Cats Squeak By Dogs" both mean that the Cats beat the Dogs, but one indicates a win by a large margin, whereas the other indicates a close game. In addition, some synonyms are on varying levels of formality (for example, *dog* and *pooch*) (Breen, 1989).

LITERATURE   *Sylvester and the Magic Pebble* by William Steig (Simon & Schuster, 1969) offers several good opportunities for discussion of synonyms used in describing the rain's cessation, the lion's movement, and the lion's feelings. In *Alexander and the Terrible, Horrible, No Good, Very Bad Day* by Judith Viorst (Atheneum, 1972), the synonyms are right there in the title, ready for discussion (Howell, 1987).

A teacher can also provide a stimulus word and have the students find as many synonyms as they can. The class can discuss the small differences in meaning of some words suggested as synonyms. For example, the teacher can ask, "Would you rather be called *pretty* or *beautiful*? Why?"

Antonyms

Antonyms are two words that have opposite meanings. Their meanings are not merely different; they are balanced against each other on a particular feature. In the continuum *cold, cool, tepid, warm,* and *hot,* for example, *cold* is the opposite of *hot,* being as close to the extreme in a negative direction as *hot* is in a positive direction. Thus, *cold* and *hot* are antonyms. *Tepid* and *hot* are different, but they are not opposites. *Cool* and *warm* are also antonyms. Similarly, *buy* and *sell* are antonyms because one is the reverse of the other. But *buy* and *give* are not antonyms, because no exchange of money is involved in the giving. The words are different, but they are not opposites. Powell (1986) points out that the use of opposition (citing antonyms) in defining terms can help to establish the extremes of a word's meaning and provide its shadings and nuances. Research has shown that synonym production is improved by antonym production, although the reverse has not been shown to be true. Therefore, work with antonyms may enhance success in synonym exercises.

LITERATURE *Big Dog . . . Little Dog: A Bedtime Story* by P. D. Eastman (Random House, 1973) provides students with examples of antonyms to discuss in an interesting context. Teachers may wish to locate other trade books that could be used for meaningful exposures to antonyms.

New Words

New words are constantly being coined to meet the changing needs of society and are possible sources of difficulty. Have students search for such words in their reading and television viewing and then compile a dictionary of words so new that they are not yet in standard dictionaries. The class may have to discuss these words to derive an accurate definition for each one, considering all the contexts in which the students have heard or seen it. These new words may have been formed from Latin and Greek word elements, from current slang, or by shortening or combining older words (Richek, 1988).

SUMMARY

Acquiring a meaning vocabulary involves developing labels for the schemata, or organized knowledge structures, that a person possesses. Because vocabulary is an important component of reading comprehension, direct instruction in vocabulary can enhance reading achievement. Although pinpointing the age at which children learn the precise meanings of words is difficult, children generally make more discriminating responses about word meanings as they grow older, and vocabulary generally grows with increasing age.

There are many ways to approach vocabulary instruction. The best techniques link new terms to the children's background knowledge, help them expand their word knowledge, actively involve them in learning, help them become independent in acquiring vocabulary, provide repetition of the words, and have them use the words meaningfully. Techniques that cause children to work harder to learn words tend to aid retention. Teachers may need to spend time on schema development before working with specific vocabulary terms.

Vocabulary development should be emphasized throughout the day, not just in reading and language classes; children can learn much vocabulary from the teacher's modeling of vocabulary use. Context clues, structural analysis, categorization, analogies and word lines, semantic maps and word webs, semantic feature analysis, dictionary use, study of word origins and histories, study of figurative language, a number of student-centered learning techniques, word play, and computer techniques can be helpful in vocabulary instruction.

Some special types of words can cause comprehension problems for children. They include homonyms, homographs, synonyms, antonyms, and newly coined words.

TEST YOURSELF

True or False

_____ 1. Context clues are of little help in determining the meanings of unfamiliar words, although they are useful for recognizing familiar ones.

_____ 2. Structural analysis can help readers determine the meanings of new words that contain familiar prefixes, suffixes, and root words.

_____ 3. When looking up a word in the dictionary to determine its meaning, a child needs to read only the first definition listed.

_____ 4. Homonyms are words that have identical, or almost identical, meanings.

_____ 5. Antonyms are words that have opposite meanings.

_____ 6. Word play is one good approach to building vocabulary.

_____ 7. Children sometimes make overgeneralizations in dealing with word meanings.

_____ 8. The development of vocabulary is essentially a child's development of labels for his or her schemata.

_____ 9. Work with analogies bolsters word knowledge.

_____ 10. Semantic maps show how words are connected to each other in meaning.

_____ 11. Instruction in vocabulary that helps students relate new terms to their background knowledge is helpful.

_____ 12. Active involvement in vocabulary activities has little effect on vocabulary learning.

_____ 13. Pantomiming word meanings is one way to produce active involvement in word learning.

_____ 14. Children should have multiple exposures to words they are expected to learn.

_____ 15. Working hard to learn words results in better retention.

_____ 16. There is no one best way to teach words.

_____ 17. Both concrete and vicarious experiences can help to build concepts.

_____ 18. Vocabulary instruction should receive attention during content area classes.

_____ 19. "Think-aloud" strategies can help students see how to use context clues.

_____ 20. Although the use of categorization activities is motivational, current research findings suggest that it is not an effective approach.

_____ 21. Semantic mapping can help students develop a concept of definition.

_____ 22. Semantic feature analysis is the same thing as structural analysis.

_____ 23. Semantic feature analysis can help students see the uniqueness of each word studied.

_____ 24. The study of word origins is called *etymology*.

_____ 25. Word banks can help students maintain a record of their increasing vocabularies.

_____ 26. At present, no computer programs are available for vocabulary development.

_____ 27. A word-processing program can facilitate certain types of vocabulary instruction.

_____ 28. Children instinctively understand figures of speech; therefore, figurative language presents them with no special problems.

_____ 29. Wide reading is a prime method of vocabulary building.

_____ 30. Being able to recite a dictionary definition means that the students understand the word's meaning.

For your journal . . .

❶ Reflect on the value of context clues for vocabulary development.

❷ React to commercial computer software for vocabulary development that you have used. Include strengths and weaknesses of the programs. Which one would you recommend to parents who ask about buying software for home use? Why?

❸ Reflect on the video that accompanies this chapter on your CD. Are these teachers' approaches examples of student-centered methods of vocabulary instruction? Why or why not? Do these approaches offer advantages over other methods? Explain.

. . . and your portfolio

❶ Plan a lesson on dictionary use that requires the students to locate the meaning of a word that fits the context surrounding that word.

❷ Plan a lesson designed to teach the concept of *justice* to a group of sixth-grade students.

❸ After collecting examples of figurative language from a variety of sources, use them as the basis for a lesson on interpreting figurative language.

5

Comprehension: Part 1

**KEY
VOCABULARY**

*Pay close attention to these
terms when they appear in the
chapter.*

anticipation guides

cloze procedure

InQuest

K-W-L Teaching Model

knowledge-based
processing

metacognition

multiple intelligences

reciprocal teaching

relative clauses

schema

semantic webbing

story grammar

story mapping

text-based processing

think-alouds

SETTING OBJECTIVES

When you finish reading this chapter, you should be able to

● Explain how schema theory is related to reading comprehension.

● Explain how a reader's purpose and other aspects of the situation in which reading takes
place affect comprehension.

● Describe some characteristics of text that affect comprehension.

● Discuss some prereading, during-reading, and postreading activities that can enhance
comprehension.

The objective of all readers is, or should be, comprehension of what they read.
Comprehension is understanding. Wiggins and McTighe (1998) point out that
understanding involves the abilities to explain, interpret, apply, have
perspective, empathize, and have self-knowledge. Shanklin and Rhodes (1989) see
comprehension as an evolving process, one that often begins before a book is opened,
changes as the material is read, and continues to change even after the book is
completed. This developmental nature of comprehension is enhanced when the child
interacts with others about aspects of the material after reading it. Therefore,
classroom interaction related to reading materials is important to comprehension
development and should be planned carefully.

As Pearson and Johnson (1978) point out, "reading comprehension is at once a
unitary process and a set of discrete processes" (p. 227). We discuss the individual
processes separately; yet teachers must not lose sight of the fact that there are many
overlaps and interrelationships among the processes. Close relationships even exist
between comprehension and decoding. Research has shown that good comprehend-
ers are able to decode quickly and accurately ("A Talk with Marilyn Adams," 1991).
Thus, developing decoding strategies to the automatic stage is important. Teachers
should always keep in mind, however, that use of decoding strategies is merely a
means of accessing the meaning of the written material.

When good decoders have problems with comprehension, for example, they
need help in developing language proficiency and listening comprehension. Teachers
can help them develop these skills by combining vocabulary and comprehension

Chapter 5 Organization

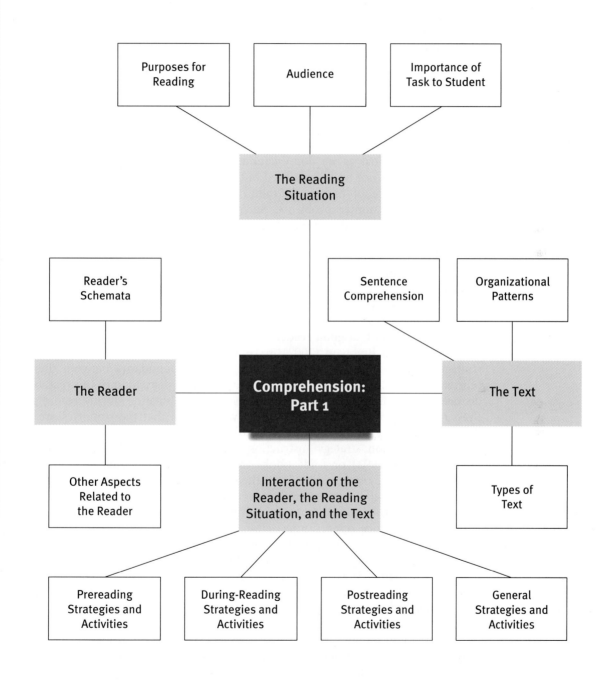

strategy instruction with encouragement to increase their reading of material written at levels that currently yield good comprehension (Dymock, 1993).

Allington (2002) and his colleagues studied effective teachers of reading and writing. These teachers spent much of the school day having their students actually read and write. This extensive practice gives the students a chance to internalize the skills and strategies that they have been taught. Much of this reading should be done in materials that the students can read with accuracy, fluency, and understanding. The lowest achievers benefited most from this exemplary teaching, in which they were given material that they could read with ease.

Villaume and Brabham (2002, p. 673) point out that "[t]hrough strategic reading, students gain access to the rights, responsibilities, and benefits accorded to skillful readers." Just as we do, Villaume and Brabham see the need for explicit instruction that is not heavily scripted but is *clear*, involving modeling of strategies, supervised practice of them, and follow-up assistance that clarifies areas where students may encounter problems. Such effective comprehension instruction is presented in a logical and purposeful manner; the interrelated strategies are addressed over time, and learning is monitored, with instruction based on exhibited student needs. Strategy instruction should center on tasks that are of appropriate difficulty for the particular students. Practice with the strategies in the context of real-world tasks is especially important. Strategy use should be practiced until it becomes automatic (Pressley, 1995; Rhoder, 2002). Allington (2002, p. 743) says that the exemplary teachers in his study "routinely gave direct explicit demonstrations of the cognitive strategies that good readers use when they read."

Villaume and Brabham (2002) make a good point when they remind us "that strategies do not exist in neat boxes and that the boundaries between them are blurred" (p. 647). We isolate strategies for purposes of discussion in this text, but we do *not* mean to imply that they are not used in combination during reading. Like Pressley (1995) and Rhoder (2002), however, we feel that the strategies are more durable when they are initially learned individually.

Comprehension strategy instruction should make use of the students' own textbooks (Roe, 1992) or trade books they are reading (Baumann, Hooten, and White, 1999). The teacher should tell the students what strategy they are going to learn and how it will help them in their reading. Then the teacher should describe the strategy, model it, provide teacher-guided practice with it, and offer cooperative and independent practice opportunities (Roe, 1992). About one-fifth of each reading period should be spent on explicit strategy instruction, and the rest should be spent on reading, responding to, analyzing, and discussing the reading material (Baumann, Hooten, and White, 1999).

Readers approach a text with much background knowledge concerning their world, and they use this knowledge along with the text to construct the meanings represented by the printed material that meet their purposes for reading. To access the information supplied by the text, they must use word recognition strategies (covered in Chapter 3) and comprehension strategies (covered in Chapter 4, this chapter, and Chapter 6). They combine their existing knowledge with new information supplied by the text in order to achieve understanding of the material.

This chapter discusses the importance to comprehension of the interaction among the reader, the reading situation, and the text. It explores the importance of the reader's prior knowledge, the reader's purposes for reading, the audience for reading, and the characteristics of the text to be read. It also presents strategies to be used before, during, and after reading.

This chapter is a logical continuation of Chapter 4, "Meaning Vocabulary," because vocabulary knowledge is a vital component of comprehension. Therefore, these chapters cannot truly be considered separately and are divided here only for convenience of presentation. The coverage of the types of comprehension in Chapter 6 is also a continuation of the topic, separated only for ease of treatment.

The Reader

This section discusses factors related to the reader that affect his or her comprehension, including the reader's background knowledge, sensory and perceptual abilities, thinking abilities, word recognition strategies, and affective aspects, such as attitudes, self-concepts, and interests.

● The Reader's Schemata

Educators have long believed that if a reader has not been exposed to a writer's language patterns or to the objects and concepts to which the writer refers, the reader's comprehension will be incomplete. This belief is supported by theories holding that reading comprehension involves relating textual information to preexisting knowledge structures, or schemata (Pearson et al., 1979). *Schemata* are a person's organized clusters of concepts related to objects, places, actions, or events. Each schema represents a person's knowledge about a particular concept and the interrelationships among the known pieces of information. For example, a schema for *car* may include a person's knowledge about the car's construction, its appearance, and its operation, as well as many other facts about it. Two people may have quite different schemata for the same basic concept; for example, a racecar driver's schema for *car* (or, to be more exact, his or her cluster of schemata about cars) will differ from that of a seven-year-old child.

Types of Schemata

People may have schemata for objects, events, abstract ideas, story structure, processes, emotions, roles, conventions of writing, and so forth. In fact, "schemata can represent knowledge at all levels — from ideologies and cultural truths ... to knowledge about what patterns of excitations are associated with what letters of the alphabet" (Rumelhart, 1981, p. 13). Each schema a person has is incomplete, as though it contained empty slots that could be filled with information collected from new experiences. Reading of informational material is aided by the existing schemata and also fills in some of the empty slots in them (Durkin, 1981).

Students need schemata of a variety of types to be successful readers. They must have concepts about the arrangement of print on a page, about the purpose of

Story reading is an excellent way to develop children's schemata related to stories or other materials that they will be expected to read.
(© Bill Paxson/Courtesy of Des Moines Public Schools)

printed material (to convey ideas), and about the relationship of spoken language to written language. They need to be familiar with vocabulary and sentence patterns not generally found in oral language and with the different writing styles associated with various literary genres.

A *story schema* is a set of expectations about the internal structure of stories (Mandler and Johnson, 1977; Rand, 1984). Readers find well-structured stories easier to recall and summarize than unstructured passages. Possession of a story schema appears to have a positive effect on recall, and good readers seem to have a better grasp of text structure than poor readers. Having children retell stories is a good way to discover their grasp of a story schema (Rand, 1984). (A rubric for analyzing retelling is found in Chapter 12.)

Having many experiences with well-formed stories helps children develop a story schema. Story telling and story reading are excellent ways to develop children's

STANDARDS AND
ASSESSMENT

LITERATURE

schemata related to stories or other materials they will be expected to read. Hearing a variety of stories with standard structures helps children develop a story schema that enables them to anticipate or predict what will happen next. This ability allows children to become more involved in stories they read and better able to make and confirm or reject predictions—a process that fosters comprehension. The sentence structures in the stories that are told and read to children expose them to patterns they will encounter when they read literature on their own and will help make these patterns more understandable (Rand, 1984; Nessel, 1985; Pigg, 1986; Roe, 1985, 1986). Another way to help develop children's story schemata is direct teaching of story structure and story grammars, covered later in this chapter in the section "Story Grammar Activities."

Perhaps the most important concept that children need to have in their "reading schema" is the understanding that reading can be fun and can help them do things. They also need extensive background knowledge about the nature of the reading task and general background knowledge on the topics about which they are reading (Roney, 1984). Often children do not comprehend well because they know very little about their world (Cunningham, 1982).

Research Findings About Schemata

Many research studies have supported schema theory. Anderson and colleagues, for example, discovered that recall and comprehension of passages with two possible interpretations (in one case, wrestling versus a prison break; in another, card playing versus a music rehearsal) were closely related to the readers' background knowledge and/or the testing environment (cited in Pearson et al., 1979). Bransford and Johnson discovered that recall of obscure passages increased if a statement of the passage's topic or a picture related to the passage was provided.

Studies have shown that providing background information on a topic before reading is likely to enhance reading comprehension, especially inferential comprehension (Pearson et al., 1979; Stevens, 1982). These findings indicate that teachers should plan experiences that will give children background information to help them understand written material they are expected to read and to help them choose appropriate schemata to apply to the reading. When children have trouble using their experiential backgrounds to assist in reading comprehension, teachers need to find out whether the children lack the necessary schemata or whether they possess the needed schemata but cannot use them effectively when reading (Jones, 1982). If the children lack the schemata, the teacher should plan direct and vicarious experiences to build them, such as having the children examine and discuss pictures that reveal information about the subject, introducing new terminology related to the subject, taking field trips, giving demonstrations, or having students read about particular topics in other books. Poor readers frequently need more help with concept development and more discussion time before reading than teachers provide (Bristow, 1985). If children already know about the subject, letting them share their knowledge, preview the material to be read, and predict what might happen can encourage them to draw on their existing schemata (Jones, 1982).

Readers vary in the relative degree to which they use two processes of comprehension (Spiro, 1979). *Text-based processes* are those in which the reader is primarily trying to extract information from the text. ***Knowledge-based processes*** are those in which the reader primarily brings prior knowledge and experiences to bear on the interpretation of the material. For example, consider this text: "The children were gathered around a table on which sat a beautiful cake with *Happy Birthday* written on it. Mrs. Jones said, 'Now, Maria, make a wish and blow out the candles.'" Readers must use a text-based process to answer the question "What was written on the cake?" because the information is directly stated in the material. They must use a knowledge-based process to answer the question "Whose birthday was it?" Prior experience will provide them with the answer, "Maria," because, at parties they have attended, they have consistently seen candles blown out by the child who is celebrating the birthday. Of course, before they use the knowledge-based process, they must use a text-based process to discover that Maria was told to blow out the candles.

Skilled readers may employ one type of process more than the other when the situation allows them to do this without affecting their comprehension. Less able readers may tend to rely too heavily on one type of processing in all situations, a habit that results in poorer comprehension (Walker, 2000). Unfortunately, some students have the idea that knowledge-based processing is not an appropriate reading activity, so they fail to use knowledge they have.

Rystrom (as cited in Strange, 1980) presents a good argument that reading cannot be exclusively knowledge-based, or "top-down": if it were, two people reading the same material would rarely arrive at the same conclusions, and the probability that a person could learn anything from written material would be slight. Rystrom makes an equally convincing argument that reading is not exclusively text-based, or "bottom-up": if it were, all people who read a written selection would agree about its meaning. It is far more likely that reading is interactive, involving both information supplied by the text and information brought to the text by the reader, which combine to produce the reader's understanding of the material. (See Chapter 1 for a detailed discussion of this idea.) Example 5.1 illustrates this process.

If reading performance results from interaction between information in the text and information the reader possesses, anything that increases a reader's background knowledge may also enhance reading performance. Increased exposure to social studies, science, art, music, mathematics, and other content areas should therefore enhance reading achievement. In general, this seems to be the case: students at schools with broad curricular scopes have been found to score higher on inferential reading comprehension than students at schools with narrow curricular scopes FAMILY (Singer, McNeil, and Furse, 1984). Teachers can also encourage family members to involve students in a wide variety of activities outside of school.

Helping Students Use Their Schemata

Teachers need to help students activate whatever background knowledge they already possess about a selection to be read, as well as help them develop important concepts, related to the reading material, that they do not currently possess. The students need to understand that they can use what they already know to help comprehend reading materials.

EXAMPLE 5.1   Flow of Information During Reading

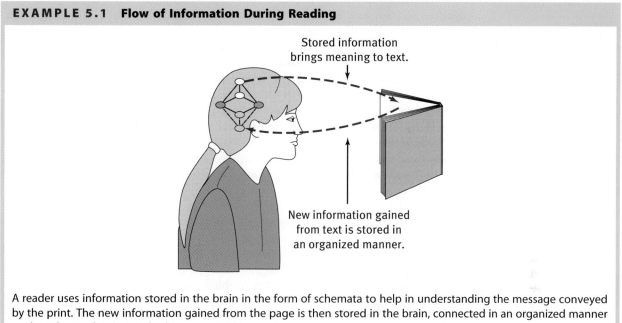

Stored information brings meaning to text.

New information gained from text is stored in an organized manner.

A reader uses information stored in the brain in the form of schemata to help in understanding the message conveyed by the print. The new information gained from the page is then stored in the brain, connected in an organized manner to the schema that it enriched.

Teachers can "think aloud" for the students the process that they use in activating schemata for a passage being read, modeling the mental process so that the students can emulate it. (An example of a think-aloud session appears on pages 196–197.) Some other techniques that may be used for schema activation include the prediction strategies in a Directed Reading-Thinking Activity (described in Chapters 7 and 10), the preview step of the SQ3R study method (described in Chapter 9), and the purpose questions of the Directed Reading Activity (described in Chapter 7).

Teachers should make sure that the material students are asked to read is not too difficult for them. Difficult materials tend to work against students' use of meaning-seeking activities, because they cause students to focus too much on decoding and not enough on comprehension.

● Other Aspects Related to the Reader

Experiential background is the basis for readers' schemata. The discussion in Chapter 1 of the many aspects of the reading process includes this vital aspect, as well as a number of other aspects related to the reader that affect comprehension. These additional aspects are readers' sensory and perceptual abilities, their thinking abilities, and such affective aspects as self-concepts, attitudes, and interests. Readers' attitudes and interests affect motivation to read, and readers who are not motivated to read are not likely to give the reading task the degree of attention required for high levels of comprehension. Facility with word recognition strategies also enhances

DIVERSITY 🌀 comprehension, because it releases the students' attention from the word recognition task and allows the students to apply it to the task of comprehension (Irwin, 1991). Some educators have been concerned that nonstandard dialects could be a major barrier to comprehension. Goodman and Buck (1997, p. 459) assert that "dialect-involved miscues do not interfere with the reading process or the construction of meaning, since they move to the readers' own language."

Teachers may also find Howard Gardner's theory of **multiple intelligences** of interest. Gardner recognizes several distinct areas of potential that readers possess to different degrees (Gardner, 1995; Armstrong, 1994; Lazear, 1992). These areas of potential are *linguistic intelligence*, the ability to use written and spoken words effectively; *logical-mathematical intelligence*, the ability to reason, think deductively, and use numbers effectively; *spatial intelligence*, the capacity to perceive visual-spatial aspects of the world accurately and to create mental images; *bodily-kinesthetic intelligence*, knowledge of one's body and its physical movements; *musical intelligence*, recognition of tonal patterns and sensitivity to rhythm; *interpersonal intelligence*, the capacity to understand and relate to other people; *intrapersonal intelligence*, knowledge of self, including metacognition, spirituality, and self-reflection; and *naturalist intelligence*, the ability to solve problems, observe, classify, and categorize. Lessons that incorporate the use of more than one type of intelligence, or potential, are likely to be appropriate for more students than lessons that involve only one. Several of the techniques described later in this chapter encourage students to use multiple intelligences.

TIME for REFLECTION

Gardner does not believe that every topic can be taught through all intelligences, yet some teachers disagree. Gardner, for example, doesn't believe that the mathematical skill of a person who is strong in musical intelligence is enhanced by music being played in the background while the person is doing math problems. **What do** *you* **think, and why?**

Gardner (1995, p. 202) defines an intelligence as follows: "an *intelligence* is a biological and psychological potential; that potential is capable of being realized to a greater or lesser extent as a consequence of the experiential, cultural, and motivational factors that affect a person." It is not the same as a learning style; it is applied to a more narrow range of activities. Gardner asserts that there is not one "right way" to use the multiple intelligences theory in education. Furthermore, he says that not every topic can be taught through all intelligences. Trying to teach every topic that way is a waste of time, and some efforts to force attention on particular intelligences are pointless. Playing music in the background while students work in areas other than music does not use musical intelligence, for example. Gardner (1995) does believe that concepts should be taught in a variety of *appropriate* ways, so that more students will be reached.

The Reading Situation

The reading situation includes purposes for the reading, both self-constructed and teacher-directed; the audience for the reading; and the importance the reading task has for the individual.

● Purposes for Reading

All of the reading that children do should be purposeful, because children who read with a purpose tend to *comprehend* what they read better than those who have no purpose. This result may occur because the children are attending to the material, rather than just calling words. For this reason, teachers should set purposes for youngsters by providing them with pertinent objectives for the reading or help them set their own purposes by deciding on their own objectives. Objectives may include reading

- for enjoyment;

- to perfect oral reading performance or use of a particular strategy;

- to update knowledge about a topic in order to link new information to that already known;

- to obtain information for an oral or written report;

- to confirm or reject predictions;

- to perform an experiment or apply information gained from the text in some other way;

- to learn about the structure of a text; or

- to answer specific questions (Blanton, Wood, and Moorman, 1990; Dowhower, 1999; Irwin, 1991).

Teacher-constructed purpose questions can help students focus on important information in the selection and should replace such assignments as "Read Chapter 7 for tomorrow." Providing specific purposes avoids presenting children with the insurmountable task of remembering everything they read and informs them whether they are reading to determine main ideas, locate details, understand vocabulary terms, or meet some other well-defined goal. As a result, they can apply themselves to a specific, manageable task. However, if teachers always use the same types of purpose questions and do not guide children to set their own purposes, children may not develop the ability to read for a variety of purposes. Purpose-setting activities can help students activate their existing schemata about the topic of the material.

Cunningham and Wall (1994, p. 481) suggest always setting a purpose for student reading that is either "(a) a clear and precise statement of what the students are to focus on while they read or (b) a clear preview of the task they will be asked to perform after reading." This allows students to use the purpose to help them choose reading strategies. Cunningham and Wall also suggest making purposes more specific for more difficult texts to guide the students to the important and challenging content.

For maximum effectiveness, Blanton and colleagues (1990) recommend setting a single purpose for reading, rather than multiple purposes. A single purpose may be especially effective for poor readers, because it can help to avoid cognitive confusion from the overload of multiple purposes. The purpose should be one that is sustained throughout the entire selection, not met after reading only a small portion of the material; in other words, the purpose should be fairly broad in scope. Purposes should be formed carefully, because poor ones can actually misdirect the students' attention by focusing on information that is not essential to the passage and slighting important information. Purposes should help readers differentiate between relevant and irrelevant information.

Even when teachers set purposes for students initially, responsibility for setting purposes should gradually shift from the teacher to the students. Students are capable of setting their own purposes, and they will be more committed to purposes they themselves have set than to those set by the teacher. When teachers set purposes for reading, they may then "think aloud" how the purpose was developed, thus modeling the purpose-setting procedure for later independent use by students. Having students predict what will happen in a story or what information will be presented in an informational selection is a step in helping students set for themselves the purpose of reading to find out if their predictions are accurate. Such purposes engage the students in the reading more than teacher-generated ones. The Directed Reading-Thinking Activity, described further in Chapters 7 and 10, encourages such personal purpose setting through predictions on the part of the students. Fielding and colleagues (1990) found that prediction questions were more effective than traditional basal reader questions if the predictions were compared with the actual text after reading (Pearson and Fielding, 1991). Therefore, teachers should be sure to follow up on predictions when this type of purpose is used. Actually, all purposes should be discussed immediately after the reading is completed. Neglecting this procedure may cause students to ignore the purposes and merely try to pronounce all the words in the selection.

Commercial reading materials tend to offer a variety of types of purpose questions. However, teachers sometimes do not make use of these ready-made questions, or they may paraphrase them. If teachers are going to use self-constructed questions, they should give careful thought to the desired outcomes of the reading and to the types of purpose questions most likely to lead to these outcomes.

Prereading questions should focus on predicting and on relating text to prior knowledge. Students should be asked about the details that are related to problems, goals, attempts to solve problems, characters' reactions, resolutions, and themes (Pearson, 1985). (More about this type of questioning appears in the section "Story Grammar as a Basis for Questioning" in Chapter 6.)

Even when teachers do not provide purpose questions, children are often guided in the way they approach their reading assignments by the types of questions that teachers have used in the past on tests. If a teacher tends to ask for factual recall of small details in test questions, children will concentrate on such details and perhaps overlook the main ideas entirely. In class discussion, the teacher may be bewildered by the fact that the children know many things that happened in a story without knowing what the basic theme was. Teachers need to be aware that their testing

TIME for REFLECTION

Some teachers believe that students should always set their own purposes for reading. Others believe that teachers should set the purposes. Still others believe that sometimes it is appropriate for teachers to set purposes, but that much of the time, students should do the purpose setting. What do *you* think, and why?

STANDARDS AND
ASSESSMENT

In school, a common audience is the reading group. Some children, however, may comprehend less well in such a setting than when reading independently. For this reason, it is important for teachers to assess reading comprehension in a variety of settings. *(Owen Franken/Corbis)*

procedures affect the purposes for which children read content material in their classrooms.

● Audience

The audience for the reading may consist of only the reader, reading alone for personal or teacher-directed purposes. In this case, the reader is free to use his or her available reading strategies as needed to meet the purposes. The degree to which the reader has accepted the purposes as valid will affect his or her comprehension of the material.

Sometimes the audience for the reading is the teacher. Teachers have been found to focus more on word recognition concerns with lower-achieving groups of students and more on meaning with higher-achieving groups (Irwin, 1991), a tendency that could be detrimental to the students in lower groups. Richard Anderson and colleagues (1983) found that a meaning focus was more effective than a word recognition focus with both poor and good readers.

Sometimes the audience is other children. In school, a common audience is the reading group. However, some children may comprehend less well when reading to perform in a reading group than when reading independently. They may even react differently to different groups of children—for example, younger students as

STANDARDS AND
ASSESSMENT

opposed to students of their own age. Teachers should be aware of this possibility and assess reading comprehension in a variety of settings.

● Importance of Task to Student

STANDARDS AND
ASSESSMENT

The degree to which students embrace the purposes for reading the material will affect the attention they give to the task and the perseverance with which they attempt it. The level of risk involved will also affect the results of the reading. Mosenthal and Na (1980a) found that students performed differently on reading tasks in high-risk situations, such as tests, than in low-risk situations, such as normal classroom lessons. In high-risk situations, low-ability and average-ability students tended to reproduce the text, whereas high-ability students tended to reproduce and embellish it. In low-risk situations, the students tended to respond according to their typical verbal interaction patterns with the teacher (Mosenthal and Na, 1980b).

The Text

Reading a text involves dealing with its specific characteristics and deriving information from it by using word recognition and comprehension strategies. Texts are made up of words, sentences, paragraphs, and whole selections. Because vocabulary is one of the most important factors affecting comprehension, Chapter 4 was devoted to vocabulary instruction. Sentence difficulty and organizational patterns are other text characteristics. Although some suggestions in this section focus on comprehension of sentences or paragraphs, comprehension is a unitary act, and eventually all the procedures discussed here must work together for the reader to achieve comprehension of the whole selection.

People who choose texts and supplementary material for children must be aware of the level of difficulty of the material they choose, especially when students will use it independently. The directions provided for students and the instructional language used in such materials should be of high quality. The language of the directions should be clearer than the language of the exercises (Spiegel, 1990a).

● Sentence Comprehension

Children may find complicated sentences difficult to understand, so they need to know ways to derive sentence meanings. Research has shown that systematic instruction in sentence comprehension increases reading comprehension. For example, Weaver (as cited in Durkin, 1978/1979) had students arrange cut-up sentences in the correct order by finding the action word first and then asking *who, what, where,* and *why* questions. This activity may work especially well when the sentences are drawn from literature selections that the teacher has shared with the students. Another approach is to have children discover the essential parts of sentences by writing them in telegram form, as illustrated in the Model Activity on page 183.

MODEL ACTIVITIES | Telegram Sentences

Write on the board a sentence like this one: "The angry dog chased me down the street." Tell the children that you want to tell what happened in the fewest words possible because, when you send a telegram, each word used costs money. Then think aloud about the sentence: "Who did something in this sentence? Oh, the dog did. My sentence needs to include the dog. ... What action did he perform? He chased. I'll need that action word, too. 'Dog chased . . .' That doesn't make a complete thought, though. I'll have to tell whom he chased. He chased me. Now I have a complete message that leaves out the extra details. My telegram is: 'Dog chased me.'"

Then let the students write a telegram based on some story they have read or heard. For example, have them write the telegram that Little Red Riding Hood might have sent to her mother after the woodcutter rescued her and her grandmother. This telegram might contain several pared-down sentences.

Teachers should help children learn that sentences can be stated in different ways without changing their meanings. For example, some sentence parts can be moved around without affecting the meaning of the sentence, as in these two sentences:

On a pole in front of the school, the flag was flying.

The flag was flying on a pole in front of the school.

On the other hand, teachers should acknowledge that moving sentence parts *can* affect the meaning. For example, the following two sentences have distinctly different meanings:

Carla helped Teresa.

Teresa helped Carla.

Sentence Difficulty Factors

A number of types of sentences are difficult for children to comprehend. They include

- sentences with relative clauses,
- other complex sentences,
- sentences with missing words,
- sentences in the passive voice, and
- sentences that express negation.

Children understand material better when the syntax is like their oral language patterns, but the text in some primary-grade reading material is syntactically more complex than the students' oral language.

Relative clauses are among the syntactic patterns that do not appear regularly in young children's speech. Relative clauses either restrict the information in the main clause by adding information or simply add extra information. Both types may be troublesome. In the example "The man *who called my name* was my father," the relative clause indicates the specific man to designate as "my father" (Kachuck, 1981).

Teachers should ask questions that assess children's understanding of particular syntactic patterns in the reading material and, when misunderstanding is evident, they should point out the clues that can help children discover the correct meanings (Kachuck, 1981). Teachers may find it necessary to read aloud, to the children, sentences from assigned passages and to explain the functions of the relative clauses found in the sentences. Then they may give other examples of sentences with relative clauses and ask the children to explain the meanings of these clauses. Feedback on correctness or incorrectness and further explanation should be given at this point. Finally, teachers should provide children with independent practice activities to help them set the new skill in memory.

Students who need more work with relative clauses can be asked to turn two-clause sentences into two sentences (Kachuck, 1981). Teachers can model this activity also, as in the earlier example: "The man called my name. The man was my father." Supervised student practice with feedback and independent practice can follow, with progressively more difficult sentences. Students can move from this activity into sentence combining, which we will examine next. Finally, they should apply their understanding in reading whole passages (Kachuck, 1981). Until they have used the skill in interpreting connected discourse, it is impossible to be sure they have mastered it.

Sentence combining involves giving students two or more short sentences and asking them to combine the information into a single sentence. (For example, they might be asked to combine these two sentences: "Joe has a bicycle. It is red." Responses might include "Joe has a red bicycle," "Joe has a bicycle, and it is red," "Joe has a bicycle that is red," and "Joe's bicycle is red.") Wilkinson and Patty (1993) have found that students can learn to attend to elements of text related to connectives through sentence-combining practice, but not just through reading texts written by other students during sentence-combining practice activities.

Discussion of a number of sentence combinations may reveal much about the children's syntactic knowledge. Sentence-combining activities also bring out the important fact that there are always multiple ways of expressing an idea in English (Pearson and Camperell, 1981).

Punctuation

Punctuation can greatly affect the meaning a sentence conveys; it represents pauses and pitch changes that would occur if the passage were read aloud. Although punctuation marks represent the inflections in speech imperfectly, they greatly aid in turning written language into oral language.

Commas and dashes indicate pauses within sentences. Periods, question marks, and exclamation points all signal pauses between sentences and also alter the meaning:

He's a crook. (Making a statement)

He's a crook? (Asking a question)

He's a crook! (Showing surprise or dismay at the discovery)

To help students see how punctuation can affect the meaning of the material, use sentences such as the following:

Mother said, "Joe could do it."   We had ice cream and cake.

Mother said, "Joe could do it?"   We had ice cream and cake?

"Mother," said Joe, "could do it."   We had ice, cream, and cake.

Discuss the differences in meaning among the sentences in each set, highlighting the function of each punctuation mark.

Underlining and italics, which are frequently used to indicate that a word or group of words is to be stressed, are also clues to underlying meaning. Here are several stress patterns for a single sentence:

Pat ate one snail.

Pat *ate* one snail.

Pat ate *one* snail.

Pat ate one *snail.*

In the first pattern, the stress immediately indicates that Pat, and no one else, ate the snail. In the second variation, stressing the word *ate* shows that the act of eating the snail was of great importance. In the third variation, the writer emphasizes that only one snail was eaten. The last variation implies that eating a snail was unusual and that *snail* is more important than the other words in the sentence.

Teachers need to be sure that children are aware of the aids to comprehension that punctuation provides and that they practice interpreting punctuation marks. To make students more aware of punctuation such as quotation marks, periods, and commas, teachers can have students read stories in parts, as they would a play, with a narrator (Carr, 1991).

TIME for REFLECTION

Some teachers think there should be much work with sentence-level comprehension before moving on to whole selections. Others think they should address sentence-level comprehension only within the context of whole selections. What do *you* think, and why?

● Organizational Patterns

The internal organization of paragraphs in informational material can have a variety of patterns (for example, listing, chronological order, comparison and contrast, and cause and effect). In addition, paragraphs of each of these types also generally have an underlying organization that consists of the main idea plus supporting details. Whole selections contain these same organizational patterns and others, notably a topical pattern such as the one used in this textbook. Students' comprehension of informational material can be increased if they learn these organizational patterns. The Model Activities on page 186 show two examples of procedures for teaching

LITERATURE

paragraph patterns. Similar exercises may be constructed with longer selections as well, preferably excerpts drawn from books available for the children to read. Kane (1998) suggests books like *The Philharmonic Gets Dressed* (Kuskin, 1982) and *A Year Down Yonder* (Peck, 2000) for straight chronological order, and time-travel books like *The Devil's Arithmetic* (Yolen, 1988) to show movement back and forth in time; *Animals Should Definitely Not Wear Clothing* (Barrett, 1970) and *Who Really Killed*

MODEL ACTIVITIES Chronological-Order Paragraphs

Write the following paragraph on the chalkboard:

> Jonah wanted to make a peanut butter sandwich. First, he gathered the necessary materials—peanut butter, bread, and knife. Then he took two slices of bread out of the package and opened the peanut butter jar. Next, he dipped the knife into the peanut butter, scooping up some. Then he spread the peanut butter on one of the slices of bread. Finally, he placed the other slice of bread on the peanut butter he had spread, and he had a sandwich.

Discuss the features of this paragraph, pointing out the functions of the sequence words, such as *first, then,* *next,* and *finally*. Make a list on the board, showing the sequence of events, numbering the events appropriately, or numbering them directly above their positions in the paragraph. Next, using another passage of the same type (preferably from a literature or content area selection that the students have already read), have them discover the sequence under your direction. Sequence words should also receive attention during this discussion. Then have the students detect sequence in other paragraphs from literature or content area selections that you have duplicated for independent practice. Discuss these independent practice paragraphs in class after the students have completed the exercises. Finally, alert students to watch for sequence as they do their daily reading.

Cock Robin (George, 1991) for cause and effect; and *Christmas in the Big House,* *Christmas in the Quarters* (McKissack and McKissack, 1994) for comparison and contrast. Examples of several patterns may be located in a single book, as well. Teachers may introduce complex structures through read-alouds.

● Types of Text

Narrative (storylike) selections generally consist of a series of narrative paragraphs that present the unfolding of a plot. They have a number of elements (setting,

MODEL ACTIVITIES Cause-and-Effect Paragraphs

Write the following paragraph on the board:

> Jean lifted the box and started for the door. Because she could not see where her feet were landing, she tripped on her brother's fire truck.

Discuss the cause-and-effect relationship presented in this paragraph by saying: "The effect is the thing that happened, and the cause is the reason for the effect. The thing that happened in this paragraph was that Jean tripped on the fire truck. The cause was that she could not see where her feet were landing. The word *because* helps me to see that cause."

Then lead class discussions related to the cause-and-effect paragraph pattern by using other cause-and-effect paragraphs with different key words (such as *since* or *as a result of*) or with no key words at all. These examples should preferably be chosen from the children's classroom reading materials.

characters, theme, and so on) that have been described in story grammars (discussed later in this chapter). Although they are usually arranged in chronological order, paragraphs may be flashbacks—that is, narrations of events from an earlier time—to provide readers with the background information they need to understand the current situation.

Expository (explanatory) selections are composed of a variety of types of paragraphs, usually beginning with one or more introductory paragraphs and composed primarily of a series of topical paragraphs, with transition paragraphs to indicate shifts from one line of thought to another and illustrative paragraphs to provide examples to clarify the ideas. These selections generally conclude with summary paragraphs. Most content area textbooks are made up primarily of expository text.

Teaching students to make use of paragraphs that have specific functions can be beneficial. For example, students can be alerted to the fact that *introductory paragraphs* inform the reader about the topics a selection will cover. These paragraphs usually occur at the beginnings of whole selections or at major subdivisions of lengthy readings.

If children are searching for a discussion of a particular topic, they can check the introductory paragraph(s) of a selection to determine whether or not they need to read the entire selection. (The introductory sections that open each chapter in this book are suitable for use in this manner.) Introductory paragraphs can also help readers establish a proper mental set for the material to follow; they may offer a framework for categorizing the facts that readers will encounter in the selection.

Summary paragraphs occur at the ends of whole selections or major subdivisions and summarize what has gone before, stating the main points of the selection in a concise manner and omitting explanatory material and supporting details. They offer a tool for rapid review of the material. Students should be encouraged to use these paragraphs to check their recall of the important points in the selection.

To carry the reader through the author's presentation of an idea or a process, the topical paragraphs within an expository selection are logically arranged in one of the organizational patterns discussed earlier in this chapter. The writer's purpose will dictate the order in which he or she arranges the material—for example, chronologically or in terms of cause and effect. A history textbook may present the causes of the Civil War and lead the reader to see that the war was the effect of these causes. At times, a writer may use more than one form of organization in a single selection, such as combining chronological order and cause-and-effect organization in history materials.

One way to work on recognition of text patterns is to write examples of text patterns on index cards and give them to small, cooperative groups of students to sort into the patterns represented. Discussion of the reasons for the classifications can take place in a whole-class setting. Students can then move from this activity to locating the patterns in their content textbooks (Kuta, 1992).

Regardless of the approach, attention needs to be given to text structure. Pearson and Fielding (1991, p. 832) state, "It appears that any sort of systematic attention to clues that reveal how authors attempt to relate ideas to one another or any sort of systematic attempt to impose structure upon a text … facilitates comprehension as well as both short-term and long-term memory for the text." Chapter 10 discusses various text patterns in more detail.

EXAMPLE 5.2   Interaction of Reader, Reading Situation, and Text

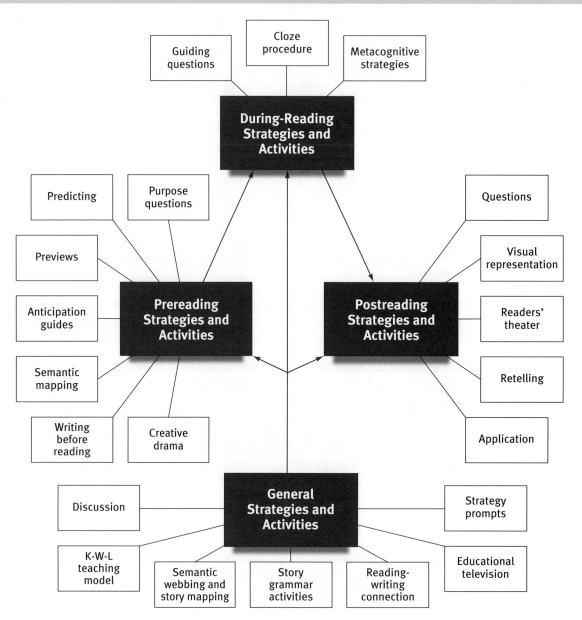

Interaction of the Reader, the Reading Situation, and the Text

Factors related to the reader, the reading situation, and the text all interact as the student reads in instructional settings. To encourage comprehension of whole selections, teachers usually incorporate prereading, during-reading, and postreading activities into lessons. Some techniques are more general and include activities for more than one of these lesson parts. Example 5.2 on page 188 shows some techniques applicable to various parts of a lesson.

● Prereading Strategies and Activities

Prereading activities are often intended to activate students' problem-solving behavior and their motivation to examine the material. The making of predictions in the Directed Reading-Thinking Activity described in Chapter 7 is a good example of this type of activity. The use of purpose questions as described earlier in this chapter is another example. The following activities can also enhance comprehension of the material by activating schemata related to the subject or type of text to be read, or they can be used to help students expand their schemata by building background for topics covered by the reading material.

Previews

Story previews, which contain information related to story content, can enhance comprehension. Research has shown that having students read story previews designed partially to build background knowledge about the stories increases students' learning from the selections impressively and that story previews can help students make inferences when they read. The previews help children to activate their prior knowledge and to focus their attention before reading (Tierney and Cunningham, 1984). Story previews of trade books are often found on the back cover of the book. For other selections, teachers may have to write short previews.

Anticipation Guides

LITERATURE 📖 *Anticipation guides* can be useful prereading devices. Designed to stimulate thinking, they consist of declarative statements related to the material about to be read. Some of the statements are true and some are not. Before the children read the story, they respond to the statements according to their own experiences and discuss them (Wiesendanger, 1985). The value of anticipation guides can be extended into the postreading part of the lesson by repeating the process after reading, considering the input from the reading; this results in a combination anticipation/reaction guide.

Anticipation Guide

Directions: Read each statement below and make a checkmark on the line under *Yes* if you agree with the statement or on the line under *No* if you disagree with the statement.

Yes   *No*

_____   _____   1. You should have to work for your rewards.

_____   _____   2. You should be generous to others with your possessions.

Anticipation Guide

| | | 3. It is important to cooperate to get work done in the fastest and easiest way. |
| | | 4. Some people should work to support others who do not want to work. |

Merkley (1996/1997) suggests adding an "I'm Not Sure" column to anticipation guides. She thinks it causes students who choose this option to attend more carefully to the text to discover the answer. (See the Classroom Scenario on page 191 for an example of an anticipation/reaction guide.)

Semantic Mapping

Semantic mapping (discussed in Chapter 4) is a good prereading strategy because it introduces important vocabulary that students will encounter in the passage and activates their schemata related to the topic of the reading assignment. This makes it possible for them to connect new information in the assignment to their prior knowledge. The procedure may also motivate them to read the selection (Johnson, Pittelman, and Heimlich, 1986).

Writing Before Reading

Hamann and her colleagues (1991) found that having students write about relevant personal experiences before they read a selection resulted in more on-task behavior, more sophisticated responses to characters, and more positive reactions to the selections. This helped the students become more involved with their reading.

Creative Drama

Although creative drama is most often used as a postreading activity, it also may be used *before* a story is read to enhance comprehension. The teacher may describe the situation developed in the story and let the children act out their own solutions. Then they can read the story to see how their solutions compared with the actual story. The teacher can take the parts of various characters to help move the drama along and to pose questions related to setting, characters, emotions, and critical analysis (Flynn and Carr, 1994). Drama may be particularly effective with students who have strong interpersonal skills and are kinesthetic learners.

● During-Reading Strategies and Activities

Some strategies and activities can be used during reading to promote comprehension.

Metacognitive Strategies

Metacognition refers to a person's knowledge of the intellectual functioning of his or her own mind and that person's conscious efforts to monitor or control this functioning. It involves analyzing the way thinking takes place. In reading tasks, the reader who displays metacognition selects skills and reading techniques that fit the particular reading task (Babbs and Moe, 1983).

CLASSROOM SCENARIO	**Use of Anticipation/Reaction Guide**

Ms. Bucholtz's sixth-grade class had been studying the many cultures that make up the United States culture. To introduce the Chinese culture to a group of children who had no Chinese-American classmates, she decided to have them read *Child of the Owl* by Laurence Yep, a book for which she had a classroom set. She had prepared an anticipation/reaction guide that was designed to help them banish stereotypes and see the commonalities among all people.

Ms. Bucholtz began the lesson by holding up the book. She said, "Look at the cover of the book I have just given to you. From what you see on the cover, what do you think the book will be about?"

Blake said, "Maybe it will be about a baby owl."

Krystal looked at him disdainfully and said, "Oh, don't be silly. The picture is of a Chinese girl and an owl necklace. She's in front of a Chinese store. I think it's about her getting that necklace."

Ms. Bucholtz looked at Krystal and said, "Your prediction is reasonable, but you shouldn't say someone else's is silly. We don't have enough information yet to know if live owls will be in the story."

"I'm sorry, Blake," Krystal said. "Sometimes the cover does fool you, and it almost looks like an owl is flying behind her."

"That looks like a ghost owl. It looks spooky," said DeRon. "Maybe this is a ghost story."

"*Yep* sounds Chinese," Marie said.

"It is," Pete replied. "This guy wrote *Dragonwings* too, and it was great. It was about Chinese who came to America. I guess this one will be too, but the main character will be a girl in this one."

"You'll have to read the book to see if your predictions are right," said Ms. Bucholtz, "but first I want you to turn over that paper I put on your desk."

The children turned over the following anticipation/reaction guide:

Anticipation/Reaction Guide

Directions: As you read *Child of the Owl* by Laurence Yep, you will find out some things about Chinese and Chinese-American people and some things about people in general. Before you read the book, write *Yes, No,* or *Sometimes* on the line under the word *Before* to show what you believe to be true at this time. After you read the book, write *Yes, No,* or *Sometimes* on the line under the word *After* to show what you believe then.

Before   *After*

——— ———   1. Chinese-Americans can speak Chinese.

——— ———   2. Chinese-Americans can write Chinese.

——— ———   3. Chinese-Americans live in Chinatowns.

——— ———   4. Chinese-Americans are very close to family members and take care of them when they need help.

——— ———   5. Chinese-Americans live just like other Americans.

——— ———   6. Chinese-Americans are wealthy.

——— ———   7. All it takes to "fit in" in Chinatown is to look Chinese.

——— ———   8. Chinese owls are supposed to be evil.

——— ———   9. Chinese-Americans eat with chopsticks, instead of forks and knives.

——— ———   10. People can hurt people whom they care about.

——— ———   11. The way people look and act on the outside is the way they are inside.

Continued

Anticipation/Reaction Guide (cont.)

_____	_____	12. Chinese-Americans have feelings that are like other Americans' feelings.
_____	_____	13. People make sacrifices for people whom they love.
_____	_____	14. Chinese-Americans have been treated fairly since they came to this country.

"Bryan, read the directions for us," Ms. Bucholtz requested.

Bryan read the directions.

Then Ms. Bucholtz said, "Please follow the directions and fill in the *Before* column now. Then break into your cooperative groups and discuss the reasons for your answers with your classmates. When all of you have discussed your answers, you may begin reading. A few minutes before the period ends today, I'll stop you and let you discuss your predictions with your group and set new ones if your old ones no longer seem likely. You'll be reading this book all week. We'll discuss and revise predictions every day and jot down our new predictions. When you finish reading, fill in the *After* column on your guide. You may want to look back in the book to find evidence for your responses to share later. When your entire group is finished, discuss those responses with your classmates. Then we'll talk about the guide as a whole class. Happy reading!"

The children quickly read and completed the guide, but their small-group discussions were filled with uncertainty about the items that specified Chinese-Americans, since none of the children knew any. Statements such as the following were heard: "Of course, a person who looked Chinese would 'fit in' in Chinatown. I'd stick out like a sore thumb, though." "The Chinese in that book I read weren't wealthy, but that was a long time ago." "Sure, they do; they always have chopsticks in Chinese restaurants." "They can speak Chinese, because we can speak American." They were quick to support the answers they had given for more general categories with statements such as the following: "Mr. Woolly looks mean, but he gives us candy when we are in his store."

"But Mr. Lynn looks nice, and he is super." "Guess that means 'Sometimes,' right?" "Yeah, 'Sometimes.'" "My Mom bought me a boom box with her new dress money because she felt sorry for me." "My brother spent *all* of his paycheck to buy flowers for this girl he is crazy about, even though he couldn't go to the ballgame with his friends after he did it."

Predictions were quickly revised after the day's reading, and they continued to be revised every day.

On Friday, the children independently filled out the *After* column on the guide, some of them mumbling about how wrong they had been. Their discussions of the responses in their small groups were lively, with reading from the text to support many points. Some of the comments were as follows: "*Casey* couldn't even speak Chinese." "Her Uncle Phil and his family were wealthy, but her grandmother wasn't. So 'Sometimes.'" "Look at how different Gilbert was than he seemed to be." (This was followed by the reading of several example passages.) The whole-class discussion was rich, featuring comments such as the following: "People are a lot alike in how they feel, even if they look different on the outside." "I felt like she did when her grandmother was in the hospital when my Dad got hurt on the job." "Gilbert is like my cousin. He wants to act cool, too."

Ms. Bucholtz ended the focus on the book by inviting the children to read individually other books about the Chinese or Chinese-American culture for comparisons and contrasts with this book the next week.

Analysis of Scenario

Ms. Bucholtz began the lessons by eliciting from the students predictions, based on the book cover, that activated the schemata they had for the story. Then she gave them an anticipation/reaction guide that elicited further predictions and led them to commit their predictions to paper. The small-group discussions of the predictions and the adjustment of predictions throughout the week kept the students involved in the reading. Returning to the anticipation/reaction guide at the end caused them to revise their predictions on the basis of the reading. They were encouraged to be ready to defend their answers with evidence.

Much attention has been given to students' use of metacognitive strategies during reading. Certainly, effective use of metacognitive techniques has a positive effect on comprehension. Since learning metacognitive strategies enhances study skills, this topic will be covered in detail in Chapter 9. Some information related to the use of metacognitive skills during reading as an aid to comprehension is included here to show the interrelationship of these two aspects of reading.

Part of the metacognitive process is deciding what type of task the reader needs to complete in order to achieve understanding. Readers need to ask themselves:

❶ Is the answer that I need stated directly? (If so, the reader looks for the author's exact words for an answer.)

❷ Does the text imply the answer by giving strong clues that help determine it? (If so, the reader searches for clues related to the question and then actively reasons about the information provided to determine an answer.)

❸ Does the answer have to come from my own knowledge and ideas as they are related to the story? (If so, the reader relates what he or she knows and thinks about the topic to the information given and includes both sources of information in the reasoning process in order to come to a decision about an answer.)

Direct instruction in which teachers model reasoning processes to help students understand how reading works may be particularly effective for helping struggling readers become more strategic. It is not possible, however, to reduce the mental processes associated with strategic reading to a fixed set of steps, because, for example, "what an expert reader does when encountering an unknown affixed word in one text situation may differ from what is done when an unknown affixed word is met in another textual situation" (Duffy, Roehler, and Herrmann, 1988, p. 765). Poor readers often do not grasp the need for variation from situation to situation. After demonstrating their own metacognitive strategies, teachers may ask the students to explain how they made sense of material they have read and then may provide additional help if the students' responses indicate the need (Herrmann, 1988).

Teaching students to combine the two metacognitive strategies of self-questioning and prediction can result in better comprehension scores for middle-school students reading below grade level than using only a self-questioning strategy or traditional vocabulary instruction. This may be because the combination strategy causes them to monitor the information more actively as they read to confirm predictions (Nolan, 1991).

Good readers monitor their comprehension constantly and take steps to correct situations when they fail to comprehend. They may reread passages or adjust their reading techniques or rates. Poor readers, on the other hand, often fail to monitor their understanding of the text. They make fewer spontaneous corrections in oral reading than good readers do and also correct miscues that affect meaning less frequently than do good readers. They seem to regard reading as a decoding process, whereas good readers see it as a comprehension-seeking process (Bristow, 1985).

Studies have shown that gifted students tend to be more efficient in the use of strategies, learn new strategies more easily, are more apt to transfer them to new situations, and are better at discussing their understanding of their cognitive processes than average students. There are, however, indications that gifted students, like other students, can benefit from metacognitive instruction (Borkowski and Kurtz, 1987; Cheng, 1993).

Englot-Mash (1991) helps students learn to tie strategies together in a usable manner by presenting them with the flow chart in Example 5.3 on page 195. This chart helps the students to think about their fix-up strategies in a concrete way.

Baumann and his colleagues (1993) advocate using **think-alouds** to enhance children's comprehension monitoring: "Think alouds involve the overt, verbal expression of the normally covert mental processes readers engage in when constructing meaning from texts" (p. 185). They studied the teaching of think-alouds using an instructional format in which teachers tell the students *what* the strategy is, *why* it is important and helpful for them to know, *how* it functions, and *when* it should be used (Baumann and Schmitt, 1986). In their study, Baumann and colleagues used think-alouds to model for the students the asking of questions about the material, accessing prior knowledge about the topic, asking if the selection is making sense, making predictions and verifying them, making inferences, retelling what they have already read, and rereading or reading further to clear up confusion. They had the students use think-alouds as they applied the strategies to their own reading. At times, the students were divided into small groups or pairs to apply the think-alouds, and this collaborative activity appeared to be especially helpful. The researchers helped build student interest by comparing the students as readers to newspaper or television reporters: they interview writers as they read, just as reporters interview people. A sample think-aloud is on pages 196–197.

Palincsar and Brown (1986) suggest **reciprocal teaching** as a way to promote comprehension and comprehension monitoring. In this technique, the teacher and the students take turns being the "teacher." The "teacher" leads the discussion of material the students are reading. The participants have four common goals: "predicting, question generating, summarizing, and clarifying" (p. 772). When using reciprocal teaching, the teacher must explain to the students each component strategy and the reason for it:

❶ The predictions that the students make provide them with a purpose for reading: to test their predictions. Text features such as headings and subheadings help students form predictions.

❷ Generating questions provides a basis for self-testing and interaction with others in the group.

❸ Summarizing, which can be a joint effort, helps students to integrate the information presented.

❹ Clarifying calls attention to reasons why the material may be hard to understand. Students are encouraged to reread or ask for help when their need for clarification becomes obvious.

Instruction in each strategy is important. At first, the teacher leads the discussion, modeling the strategies for the children. The children add their predictions, clarifications, and comments on the teacher's summaries and respond to the teacher's

EXAMPLE 5.3   Strategy Use

Example: A Skilled Reader's Possible "Flow Chart"

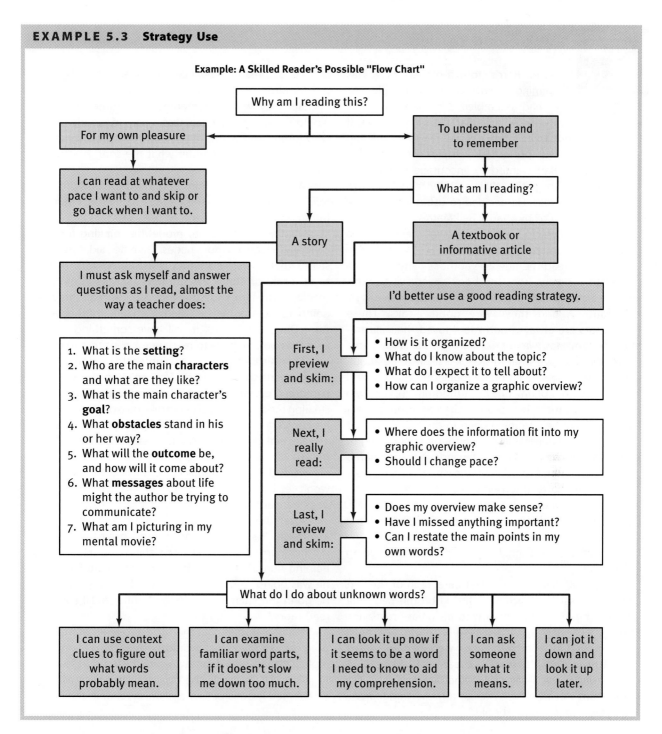

Why am I reading this?

For my own pleasure

I can read at whatever pace I want to and skip or go back when I want to.

To understand and to remember

What am I reading?

A story

A textbook or informative article

I must ask myself and answer questions as I read, almost the way a teacher does:

I'd better use a good reading strategy.

1. What is the **setting**?
2. Who are the main **characters** and what are they like?
3. What is the main character's **goal**?
4. What **obstacles** stand in his or her way?
5. What will the **outcome** be, and how will it come about?
6. What **messages** about life might the author be trying to communicate?
7. What am I picturing in my mental movie?

First, I preview and skim:

- How is it organized?
- What do I know about the topic?
- What do I expect it to tell about?
- How can I organize a graphic overview?

Next, I really read:

- Where does the information fit into my graphic overview?
- Should I change pace?

Last, I review and skim:

- Does my overview make sense?
- Have I missed anything important?
- Can I restate the main points in my own words?

What do I do about unknown words?

I can use context clues to figure out what words probably mean.

I can examine familiar word parts, if it doesn't slow me down too much.

I can look it up now if it seems to be a word I need to know to aid my comprehension.

I can ask someone what it means.

I can jot it down and look it up later.

Source: Christine Englot-Mash, "Tying Together Reading Strategies," *Journal of Reading,* 35 (2) (October 1991), 151. Reprinted with permission of the International Reading Association.

Think-Aloud Session

Mr. Barr's fourth-grade class was beginning a unit on elderly people. Mr. Barr had assembled a number of books featuring elderly characters for the unit of study. The books covered a wide range of reading levels, and some presented complex or unfamiliar concepts. Mr. Barr wanted to encourage students to use their metacognitive skills as they read from this collection of books. He decided to use one book, *The Hundred Penny Box* by Sharon Bell Mathis, for which he had a class set, to model his own metacognitive processes when reading texts.

First he read the title, the author's name, and the illustrators' names from the book cover. "I'll bet this will be a good book," he said. "I've read other books by this author, and they were good books. These illustrators are always good too. I loved their illustrations in *Why Mosquitoes Buzz in People's Ears* by Verna Aardema. Let's see what this book is likely to be about. The picture shows a little boy looking into a box and either getting a penny out or putting one in, while an elderly woman sits in a chair in the background. That box must be the one mentioned in the title. I guess it has a hundred pennies in it. I wonder if they belong to the boy or to the woman, and I wonder if the woman is his grandmother. Maybe she has saved the pennies for him. I'll have to read to find out."

Opening the book to the first page of text, Mr. Barr remarked about the facing page, "I liked the picture on the front better than this one. This one looks a little depressing. I wonder if the book is going to be sad."

Then Mr. Barr read the first paragraph of the text aloud and said, "If Michael is sitting on the bed 'that used to be his' in the room with his great-great-aunt, he probably had to let her have his room. She must have moved in with his family. I wonder how he felt about giving up his bed? … Great-great-aunt. … A great-aunt is the sister of a grandparent, so a great-great-aunt must be the sister of a great-grandparent. Aunt Dew must be pretty old."

Mr. Barr read the next paragraph and said, "I guess the hundred penny box is Aunt Dew's, and she lets Michael play with it sometimes. … Sometimes she would forget who Michael was. I had an elderly uncle who forgot who we were sometimes. He called me by my daddy's name. I wonder what the song has to do with forgetting."

After he read the third and fourth paragraphs, he said, "She called him by his daddy's name too. I think it irritated Michael's mother."

Mr. Barr continued to model his thinking for the children for several more pages. Then he said, "So far it seems that Michael's mother is frustrated with trying to take care of Aunt Dew, but Michael likes to get her to play with him with the box. I think that there is going to be trouble between Michael's mother and Aunt Dew, and I think it will have something to do with that box. I'll have to read on if I want to find out."

Then Mr. Barr asked for a volunteer to read and think aloud about the next part. After reading the second paragraph on page 14, Susan said in alarm, "Is Michael stealing the box? He didn't seem like he would steal from his aunt. I don't think that's it. I'll read on to see."

Several paragraphs later, Susan exclaimed, "Oh, no! His mother is going to burn the box!"

After the next paragraph, Susan said, "But Michael won't let her have it. Is he protecting it from her, or does he want it for himself? I think he's protecting it."

After the next paragraph, Susan said with more assurance, "He *is* protecting it. But I can't believe his mother burned someone else's things up. He's been helping Aunt Dew hide some of her other stuff. Maybe he was going to hide the box. But, if he was, why did he go in the kitchen with it? I'm confused. I'll have to read more."

Mr. Barr stopped her there. He asked her to make a prediction about what would happen next, and she replied, "I think he will run away with the box and save it."

Then Mr. Barr told the class to break up into pre-established groups of four and finish reading the book

Continued

Continued

aloud, taking turns reading and thinking aloud about it as they read. At the end of each person's turn (about two pages each time), that person would summarize the situation and make a prediction about what would happen next.

Eager to read on, the children quickly formed their groups and began to read. The book was short enough to be completed that day.

The next day the children were reminded of the questioning, predicting, connecting to prior knowledge, and summarizing that they had done in the think-alouds the day before. Mr. Barr encouraged them to continue to do these things silently as they read their individually chosen selections for that day.

DIVERSITY

questions. Gradually, the responsibility for the process is transferred from the teacher to the students. The teacher participates, but the students take on the "teacher" role, too. The interactive aspect of this procedure is very important. Rosenshine and Meister (1994) reviewed research on reciprocal teaching and concluded that such instruction should be incorporated into ongoing practice. The reciprocal teaching procedure may need to be modified for English language learners. Some of them may be unable to assume the role of "teacher" but may serve different useful functions, such as translator for other English language learners. Some English language learners may need to answer questions by drawing pictures or pointing (Herrell, 2000).

Richards and Gipe (1992) describe another very active during-reading strategy. They suggest asking students to consider, after each paragraph, an idea they know about, appreciate, or understand and an idea they dislike, dispute, or don't understand. They must also give reasons for these reactions. They may share their responses with other students "as they go" or record them to share after the entire selection has been read. For each paragraph, students may also indicate a connection with their own experiences by telling what the paragraph reminds them of. All of these activities help students connect their knowledge to the text and expand their comprehension.

Simply reminding and encouraging children to use metacognitive strategies, such as making connections between different reading selections, can also lead to their increased use. The Classroom Scenario below shows how one child used her metacognitive skills.

CLASSROOM SCENARIO **Metacognition**

As Ina Maxwell works at her desk one January morning, a student comes by to share a discovery about her reading. The girl is currently reading *Dark Hour of Noon*.

"*Dark Hour of Noon* reminds me of *Number the Stars*, that book we read last fall," she says. "In *Number the Stars*, the Nazis came and told the Jews to move to camps. They took butter and other foods. The Nazis were killing Jews. Adolf Hitler was in charge of the Germans."

Analysis of Scenario

Ms. Maxwell encourages her students to make connections with life experiences and previous reading material as they read. Her encouragement and openness to students' comments lead students to share these connections with her, even when they are unsolicited.

Guiding Questions

During reading, guiding questions are often used to enhance comprehension. Research indicates that questions posed by the teacher when students are reading seem to facilitate comprehension (Tierney and Cunningham, 1984). Some authorities have suggested that extensive use of self-questioning while reading also will facilitate comprehension. Teachers can enhance students' learning of the factual information by showing them how to turn each factual statement they need to remember into a *why* question that they then attempt to answer. (For example: "Why did Davy Crockett leave Tennessee to fight at the Alamo?") Better answers to the *why* questions result in better memory for the facts (Menke and Pressley, 1994).

Shoop (1986) describes the ***Investigative Questioning Procedure (InQuest)***, a comprehension strategy that combines student questioning with creative drama and encourages reader interaction with text. In this technique, the teacher stops the reading at a critical point in the story. One student takes the role of a major character, and other students take the roles of investigative reporters "on the scene." The reporters ask the character interpretive and evaluative questions about story events. More than one character may be interviewed to delve into different viewpoints. Then the children resume reading, although the teacher may interrupt their reading several more times for other "news conferences." When first introducing the procedure, the teacher may occasionally participate as a story character or a reporter, in order to model the processes involved. The class should evaluate the process when the entire story has been covered.

InQuest lets students monitor comprehension. They actively keep up with "what is known." Before this procedure can be effective, however, students must have had **TECHNOLOGY** 🖥 some training in generating questions. One means to accomplish this training is to give students opportunities to view and evaluate actual questioning sessions on television news shows. They need to learn to ask questions that produce information, evaluations, and predictions, and they need to ask a variety of types of questions and to use *why* questions judiciously to elicit in-depth responses.

Cloze Procedure

The *cloze procedure* is sometimes used as a strategy for teaching comprehension. In using the cloze procedure, the teacher deletes some information from a passage and asks students to fill it in as they read, drawing on their knowledge of syntax, **DIVERSITY** 🌐 semantics, and graphic clues. (See Chapter 12 for an example of a cloze passage.) Use of cloze techniques can help English language learners understand that a reader does not have to be able to read every word of a passage to grasp the meaning (Herrell, 2000).

Cloze tasks can involve deletions of letters, word parts, whole words, phrases, clauses, or whole sentences. In macrocloze activities, entire story parts are deleted. The deletions are generally made for specific purposes to focus on particular skills. Although either random or regularly spaced deletions can lead students to make predictions and confirm predictions on the basis of their language knowledge, such systems of deletion will not focus on one particular skill.

To focus on specific skills, teachers can vary the sizes of blanks. When a whole word is deleted and a standard-size blank is left, the readers must use semantic and syntactic clues to decide on a replacement. If the blanks vary in length according to word length, word recognition skill also can be incorporated. Teachers can make the task of exact replacement easier by providing the additional clue of a short underline for each letter in the deleted words. However, the discussion of alternatives likely to be generated when standard-size blanks are used can be extremely beneficial in developing comprehension skills. Teachers should always ask students to state their reasons for making particular choices and should give positive reinforcement for good reasoning.

Teachers can offer a multiple-choice set of answers for completing each blank, a task referred to as a *maze* procedure. Maze techniques are probably less effective in encouraging learners to use their linguistic resources (Valmont, 1983). However, they may simplify the task for readers who need scaffolding and may prepare students for participating in cloze activities. (See Chapter 12 for more on the cloze and maze procedures.)

● Postreading Strategies and Activities

Postreading strategies help students integrate new information into their existing schemata. They also allow students to elaborate on the learning that has taken place. Students should be given an opportunity to decide what further information they would like to have about the topic and where they can find out more. They may read about the topic and share their findings with the class.

Questions

Prereading questions may focus children's learning more than postreading questions do, but research indicates that postreading questions may facilitate learning for all information in the text. There appears to be an advantage to using higher-level, application-type, and structurally important questions, rather than questions that focus on facts or details. Children obtain greater gains from postreading questions if feedback on answers is provided, especially feedback on incorrect answers (Tierney and Cunningham, 1984).

Visual Representation

After reading, students may be asked to sketch or paint what they learned from the text or what it made them think about and then to share their sketches with a group, explaining how the sketches are related to the text. The sharing can extend the comprehension of all participants (Shanklin and Rhodes, 1989).

Quiocho (1997) had students work in groups. One student would read a section of a text aloud while other group members made sketches based on what they were hearing. Group members discussed the accuracy of each sketch, and the sketches were revised on the basis of the discussion.

Readers' Theater

After the students read a story, they can work together, or with the teacher's guidance, to transform the story into a readers' theater script. The act of developing the script from a story involves deciding on important dialogue and narration and thereby increases comprehension (Walker, 2000). Once the script is designed, the students take specific parts and practice reading the script together. Finally, they read the script for an audience.

Retelling

Talking about reading material has been shown to have a positive effect on reading comprehension. Therefore, an appropriate comprehension enhancement technique is *retelling* of the important aspects of the material read. To retell a story or selection, the reader must organize the material for the presentation (Walker, 2000). Students are generally paired with partners for this activity. After silent reading of a section from the text, one child retells what has been read, while the other listens. Tellers and listeners alternate. This technique has been used with intermediate grade students, with whom it resulted in better comprehension than did producing illustrations or answering questions about the text.

Teachers should introduce the retelling technique by explaining that it will help the children become better storytellers, in the case of presentation of narrative retellings, and help them see how well they understand the reading selections. They should model good retellings for the students, provide guided practice, and then allow independent practice. When the procedure is first used, short, well-constructed reading selections should be chosen. Prereading and postreading discussions of the story frequently help students improve their retellings. The teacher may wish to tape retellings and play them back to allow students to identify their strengths and weaknesses (Koskinen et al., 1988; Morrow, 1989).

TECHNOLOGY

FAMILY

STANDARDS AND ASSESSMENT

Children can retell stories for teachers, classmates, or younger children in the school, or they can retell stories into a tape recorder. They can also practice and improve their retelling skills at home with family members. Story retellings can be done unaided or with the assistance of the pictures in the book. Retellings can also be done with flannel boards, with props (for example, stuffed animals), as chalk talks, or as sound stories in which sound effects are added to the telling of the story. These retellings make children more familiar with the use of "book language" (Morrow, 1989). Teachers can also use retelling to assess student progress (this approach is discussed in Chapter 12).

Application

A good postreading activity for use with content area selections that explain how to do something (for example, how to work a certain type of math problem or how to perform a science experiment) is to have the students perform the task, applying the information that was read. Postreading activities that are often appropriate for social studies reading include constructing time lines of events described in the reading selection and creating maps of areas discussed. Many of the activities described in the "Creative Reading" section of Chapter 6 are good postreading activities that ask the students to go beyond the material they have read and create something new based on the reading.

TIME for REFLECTION

How can comprehension strategies be integrated into authentic learning situations across the curriculum?

● General Strategies and Activities

Some types of strategies are useful throughout the reading process: before, during, and after reading. Several of these are discussed next.

Discussion

Goldenberg (1992/1993) advocates what he calls "instructional conversations." Basically, these are highly interactive discussions among the teacher and the students. Students focus on a topic chosen by the teacher and are gently guided by the teacher's questions and probing for elaboration and for text support for their positions, but the discussions are not dominated by the teacher. Students are encouraged to use their background knowledge to contribute to the discussion, and in some cases the teacher provides needed background information that the students do not have. Sometimes the teacher offers direct teaching of a needed skill or concept.

The discussions generally center on questions for which a number of correct answers may exist. The teacher encourages participation from the students but does not determine the order of speaking. Ideas are built on previously shared ones, and the teacher is responsive to students' contributions in order to build a positive climate for students' attempts to construct meaning. It can be helpful for the teacher or students to record on the board, in a list or on a semantic map, the key points that students make during the discussion. Having students write about the topic after the discussion can show what they have learned.

LITERATURE Informational storybooks that present facts through fictional situations have been found to enhance discussion more than books that were all fiction or all fact (Leal, 1993). The children discussed these books more, made more predictions about them, and connected more outside information to them.

Cornett (1997) allows only students who have read the material to participate in story discussions. Before the discussion, students think of parts of the story that are exciting or puzzling or that connect to their lives to read aloud or discuss. They also list questions they have about the book, to ask the others. They look for special language in the book and decide what truths the book holds. Then they meet with three to five other students for student-led discussions.

K-W-L Teaching Model

Ogle (1986, 1989) has devised what she calls the *K-W-L teaching model* for expository text. The *K* stands for "What I *Know*," the *W* for "What I *Want* to Learn," and the *L* for "What I *Learned*." The *K* and *W* steps take place before reading. In the first step, the teacher and the students discuss what the group already knows about the topic of the reading material. The teacher may ask the students where they learned what they know or how they could verify the information. Students may also be asked to think of categories of information that they expect to find in the material they are about to read. The second step involves class discussion of what the students want to learn. The teacher may point out disagreements about the things that the students think they already know and may call attention to gaps in their knowledge. Then each student writes down personal questions to be answered by the reading. Students then read the material. After they have finished reading, they record what they have learned from the reading. If the reading did not answer all of their personal questions, students can be directed to other sources for the answers. (Example 5.4 below shows a K-W-L study sheet that was filled out by a fourth-grade girl who was working with teacher Gail Hyder.) Weissman (1996) adapts paragraph frames (as described in Chapter 10) to help her first graders complete the "What I Learned" step of the K-W-L, and Sippola (1995) adds a column labeled "What I Still Need to Learn" to the original three columns.

Semantic Webbing and Story Mapping

Semantic webbing is a way of organizing terms into categories and showing their relationships through visual displays that can help students integrate concepts. Each web consists of a core question, strands, strand supports, and strand ties. The teacher chooses the core question, which becomes the center of the web, to which the entire web is related. The students' answers are web strands; facts and inferences taken from

---

EXAMPLE 5.4   Completed K-W-L Sheet

K-W-L Welcome to the Green House by: Jane Yolen		
What I <u>Know</u>	What I <u>Want</u> to Know	What I <u>Learned</u>
a lot of animal live there.	What kind of animal live there.	butter flys, snakes, frogs, bats, fish, bees,
Plant live there.	What kind of plants grow there.	wild pigs, tamarin toucan, herons, Ocelot, lizirds,
A Green house is very hot.	How hot it is in there.	humingbirds, sloth.
		<u>flowers</u>
		crimson, orchid
		trees, vines
		lianas, very hot
		A wet house,

Source: Stephanie Hunsucker, fourth grade, Crossville, Tennessee.

the story and students' experiences are the strand supports; and the relationships of the strands to one another are strand ties (Freedman and Reynolds, 1980).

LITERATURE   Example 5.5 below shows a semantic web based on *Prince Caspian* by C. S. Lewis, developed by Winter Howard, a sixth grader. Before constructing webs like this one, the children in Winter's class read a portion of the book to a point where the hero found himself in a difficult situation. At this point the teacher, Natalie Knox, asked the children to predict what would happen next. The core question ("What will the Old Narnians do with or to Prince Caspian?") focuses on this prediction. Students answered the question individually, and their answers became web strands (for example, "Nikabrik will try to kill Caspian"). They drew support for strands from the story and from their own experiences. Then the strands were related through strand ties (shown with broken lines in the example). Finally, students used the webs as a basis for reading the end of the story to see what really happened.

EXAMPLE 5.5   Semantic Web

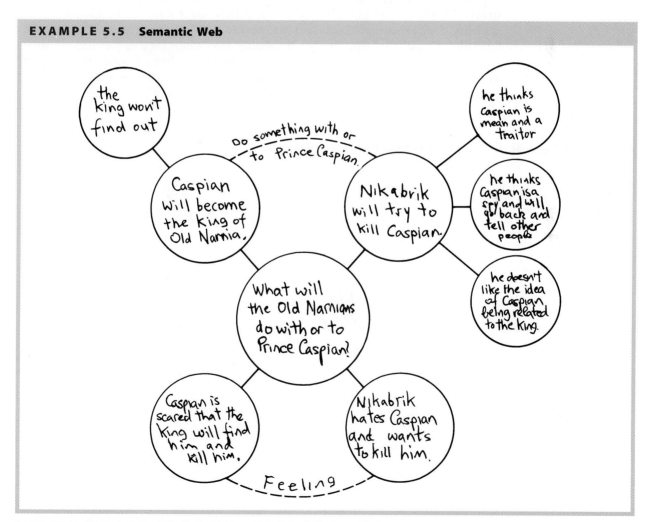

Source: Winter Howard, sixth grade, Central Intermediate School, Harriman, Tennessee.

LITERATURE   Instruction in story structure can benefit reading comprehension. *Story mapping* provides mental representations of story structures that can aid reading comprehension (Fitzgerald, 1989; Gordon and Pearson, 1983; Davis and McPherson, 1989). A story map is "a graphic representation of all or part of the elements of a story and the relationships between them" (Davis and McPherson, 1989, p. 232). In addition to representing plots, settings, characterizations, and themes of stories visually, these maps (which are sometimes called *literature webs*) can emphasize the authors' writing patterns in predictable books.

Some webs are based on plot structure or story grammar (discussed in the next section), but some are more like structured overviews. One way to construct story maps is to put the theme in the center and arrange main events or settings sequentially in a second level of circles. Circles with characters, events, and actions may be connected to these second-level circles, and each may have additional circles attached to them, arranged in a clockwise order. Teaching readers to fill in story structure components on story maps while they are reading is beneficial to the students' comprehension (Davis and McPherson, 1989). Primary-grade students can learn about basic story elements by developing story maps for a single element, such as the characters of a story. Younger students may work at first with pictures and later with written phrases (Felber, 1989; Munson, 1989). Example 5.6 shows one first grader's mapping of just the characters in a story. Bluestein (2002) suggests another

EXAMPLE 5.6   Semantic Mapping of the Characters in a Story

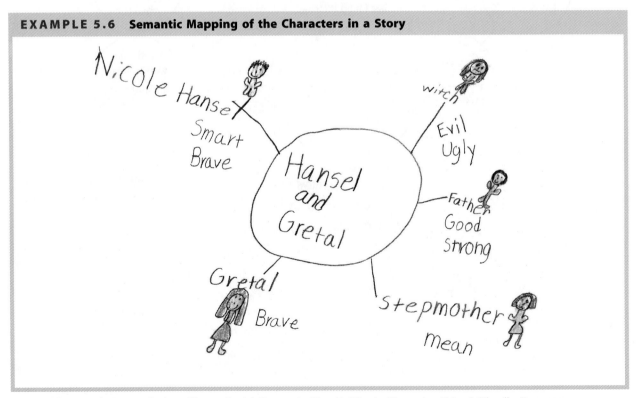

Source: Tiffany Nicole Reagan, Bethany Vincent Frady's first grade, Mary V. Wheeler Elementary School, Pikeville, Tennessee.

type of story map. She asks students to create word webs to describe characters. The map would include a character's words, feelings, and actions that show what he or she is like.

Staal (2000) has developed an adaptation of the story mapping strategy called the Story Face. It is especially useful with grades one through five, because it is easy to construct and remember. The technique is based on the shape of a face, with two circles for the eyes, which contain the setting and the main characters, respectively. Eyelashes (radiating lines) can be added to the eyes for descriptive words about the setting and other characters. The nose is a square in which the problem is written. The mouth is a semicircle of small circles that contain the main events and solution. This semicircle can curve up for a happy story or down for a sad one, and the number of circles for events can vary. This graphic can serve as a visual aid for retelling a story or as a framework for narrative writing. As a framework for narrative writing, the graphic is filled in with the student's own story plan.

Story maps resemble semantic maps or webs (described in Chapter 4 and in this chapter). Story maps help readers perceive the way their reading material is organized. They can be used to activate schemata for a story that is about to be read, to help students follow the sequence during reading, or as a way to focus postreading discussion. When the story map is used to activate schemata, the students may try to predict the contents of the story from it and then read to confirm or reject their predictions. Students may also refer to the map as reading progresses to help them keep their thoughts organized. After reading, the students can try to reconstruct the map from memory or can simply discuss it and its relationship to the story events.

Story Grammar Activities

STANDARDS AND
ASSESSMENT

A *story schema* is a person's mental representation of story structures, the elements that make up a story, and the way they are related. Knowledge of such structures appears to facilitate both comprehension and recall of stories. Children's written stories can serve as a source for understanding their concepts of story, and their retellings of stories also reveal story knowledge (Golden, 1984).

A ***story grammar*** provides rules that define these story structures. Educational researchers have developed different story grammars. Jean Mandler and Nancy Johnson include six major structures in their story grammar: setting, beginning, reaction, attempt, outcome, and ending (Whaley, 1981). In a simplified version of Perry Thorndike's story grammar, the structures are setting, characters, theme, plot, and resolution (McGee and Tompkins, 1981). Teachers may be able to help students develop a concept of story by using these or other story grammars. They can also help students focus on particular elements of a story grammar, including setting, character, and themes.

Teachers can use many activities to develop the concept of story. For instance, they can read stories and talk about the structure in terms that children understand (folktales and fairy tales make good choices because they have easily identifiable parts), or they can have children retell stories. Reading or listening to stories and predicting what comes next is a good activity, as is discussion of the predicted parts. Teachers may give students stories in which whole sections are left out, indicated by blank lines in place of the material (macrocloze activity), ask the students to supply the missing material, and then discuss the appropriateness of their answers. By dividing a story into different categories and scrambling the parts, teachers can give students the opportunity to rearrange the parts to form a good story. Or they can give the children all of the sentences in the story on strips of paper and ask them to put together the ones that fit together (Whaley, 1981).

Students may enjoy a turn-taking activity for working on the concept of story. Each student starts by writing a setting for a story and then passing his or her paper to a classmate, who adds a beginning and passes the paper along to another classmate. As the papers are passed from student to student, each child contributes a reaction, attempt, outcome, or, finally, an ending. When the stories are complete, they are read aloud to the class (Spiegel and Fitzgerald, 1986).

Fowler (1982) suggests the use of *story frames* to provide a structure for organizing a reader's understandings about the material. Frames are sequences of blanks linked by transition words that reflect a line of thought. Frames like the ones in Example 5.7 can be used with a variety of selections. Oja (1996, p. 129) says, "Using story frames along with basic elements of story grammar directs both students' and teachers' attention to the actual structure of the story and how the content fits that structure."

Students can fill out story frames as they read or after reading. The frames can be the basis for the postreading class discussion of a story. Because the frames are open-ended, the discussion will include much varied input. The teacher should stress that the information used in subsequent blanks should relate logically to the material that

---

EXAMPLE 5.7   Sample Story Frames

Frame 1: Setting

The setting for the story is _____ (where) _____ (when).

I could tell where the story took place because the story said "_____
_____."

I could tell when it took place because the story said "_____
_____."

Frame 2: Characters

The main character in this story is _____ (name).

I could tell that _____ (name) was _____ (trait)

because the story said "_____."

I could tell that _____ (name) was _____ (trait)

because the story said "_____."

came before it. Students may use frames independently after the process has been modeled and practiced in class, and the class may also discuss the results. This technique is especially useful with primary-grade students and struggling readers (Fowler, 1982).

Norton (1992b) suggests several ways to help younger students understand plot structures, including acting out stories through creative drama, drawing plot diagrams, identifying the plot structures of wordless books, and writing stories based on wordless books. Acting out nursery rhymes that have logical sequences (for example, "Little Miss Muffett") allows students to identify characters, action, and sequence in a simplified setting. By asking the students to try to act out the events of the story in a different order, the teacher can show them how changing the order of events destroys the story.

Creative dramatics can help young students comprehend stories. The active reconstruction of a story through drama focuses children's minds on the characters, setting, and plot of the story. Students can resolve conflicts among different interpretations through discussion. Stories with a lot of dialogue are good for use with drama. As students read these stories, they must use their knowledge of such print conventions as quotation marks to interpret what each speaker is saying (Miller and Mason, 1983; Bidwell, 1992).

Older students, as well as younger ones, benefit from drawing plot diagrams and relating these diagrams to characterizations and themes. The plot diagram of *Mufaro's Beautiful Daughter* (Steptoe, 1987) in Example 5.8 on page 208 shows how the plot is related to the characters of the two daughters and to the overall theme that kindness and generosity are good and will be rewarded, whereas greed and selfishness are bad and will be punished (Norton, 1992b).

To help children comprehend stories that start and end at the same place, with a series of events in between, the *circle story* can be effective (Jett-Simpson, 1981; Smith and Bean, 1983). The teacher draws a circle on a large sheet of paper and divides it into a number of pie-shaped sections corresponding to the number of events in the story. The teacher reads the story to the children, who then decide which events need to be pictured in each section of the circle. Circle story completion can be done in small groups, with each child responsible for illustrating a different event. If the paper is large enough, all of the children can work at the same time.

TECHNOLOGY Teachers can improve understanding of story features such as plots, themes, characters, and setting by using movies, a medium in which students generally have high interest. For example, they can list types of plots that movies may have and let the students match movies to plots (Sawyer, 1994). This understanding can then be transferred to stories in books through parallel techniques.

Focus on Settings. Settings may serve simply as backdrops for stories, or they may be integral to the narrative, influencing characters, action, and theme. Use of sensory imagery by the author helps to make the setting clear. Pictures in the book also enhance the effect of the words in the text in clarifying setting (Watson, 1991).

Focus on Characters. To fully comprehend a story, the readers must understand the characters. Preadolescents often focus on what is happening in a story rather than on the reasons behind the actions. They may assume that story characters think and

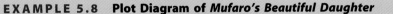

EXAMPLE 5.8 **Plot Diagram of *Mufaro's Beautiful Daughter***

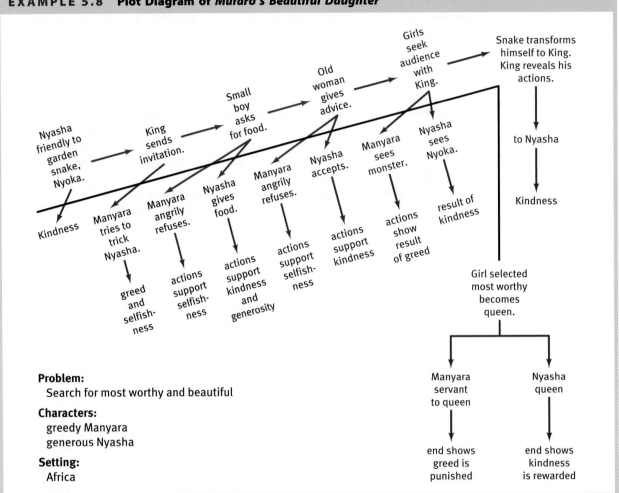

Problem:
  Search for most worthy and beautiful

Characters:
  greedy Manyara
  generous Nyasha

Setting:
  Africa

Source: Donna E. Norton, "Understanding Plot Structures," *The Reading Teacher*, 46 (3) (November 1992), pp. 254–258. Reprinted with permission of the International Reading Association.

feel the same way they do, even if the characters come from very different backgrounds. Younger children may focus on only part of a story and consider only the perspective of the main character. Story maps that include character perspectives that go with each story event can help students understand stories more fully (Emery, 1996). Having students create a collage of words describing a character's traits, drawn from both text and pictures and superimposed on a drawing of the character, can also be helpful (Golden, Meiners, and Lewis, 1992). Use of character interrogations, in which one student plays the character and other students question him or her, is another valuable way to work on understanding characterization, as is the use of character journals, which is discussed in the next section (Van Horn, 1997).

Awareness of story characters' emotions is particularly helpful in understanding cause-and-effect relationships in the stories. Students need instruction in understanding emotional words and finding clues to characters' emotional states, and they need to realize that story characters may experience several emotions simultaneously (Barton, 1996). Word lines, such as those described in Chapter 4, and word webs can be used to show the relationships among the words. Barton (1996) uses the categories "strong," "moderate," and "mild" to organize related emotion words in word webs. For example, *ecstatic* would be placed under "strong" in a web for the word *happiness.*

Teachers can ask students questions to help them make connections between their own emotions and those of story characters. One question that Barton (1996, p. 25) suggests is "Has anyone ever treated you like this character is being treated by the people around him/her? How did it feel?" Teachers can also alert students to clues that authors supply about characters' emotions, such as explicit character statements and actions, explicit plot events, text features, and emotional words. Implicit clues that need attention may come from the setting, the characters' thoughts, the story mood, or the author's style (Barton, 1996).

Focus on Themes.   Students need to be able to identify themes. Au (1992, p. 106) states that "themes are often implicit and emerge gradually as the story unfolds." The theme is "an idea that encompasses the text as a whole." (Some stories may have several themes.) The teacher can offer support through questions and comments as students work at constructing the theme of a story. Gradually, the students can take more responsibility for the construction. Students learn from opportunities to discuss themes with peers.

Cautions.   Even though there is much interest among educators in the use of story grammars, questions about this technique remain. Results of studies on the effectiveness of story grammar instruction in increasing reading comprehension have been contradictory (Dreher and Singer, 1980; Greenewald and Rossing, 1986; Sebesta, Calder, and Cleland, 1982; Spiegel and Fitzgerald, 1986). Some have shown positive effects, and others have shown no benefits. It must be remembered that story grammars describe only a limited set of relatively short, simple stories, ones derived from a fairy tale or folktale tradition, and are unable to describe stories that have characters with simultaneously competing goals (Fitzgerald, 1989; Mandler, 1984; Schmitt and O'Brien, 1986).

Reading-Writing Connection

Composition and comprehension both involve planning, composing, and revising. Although these steps may seem clear in composition, their equivalents in reading may be less obvious. Teachers may need to think of the prereading activities related to background building, schema activation, and prediction as the planning phase in comprehension; of developing tentative meanings while reading as the composing phase; and of revising the meanings when new information is acquired as the revision phase.

Writing can be involved with reading comprehension instruction at each phase. In the prereading phase, children can write story predictions based on questioning or prereading word webs. During reading, students can take notes in the form of outlines or series of summary statements. Macrocloze activities related to story grammars and the use of story frames are other ways to use writing to enhance reading. Interpretive reading activities, such as rewriting sentences that contain figurative expressions into literal forms and rewriting sentences that contain pronouns by using their referents instead, are composition activities.

Creating a *character journal* involves writing diary entries from the viewpoint of a character in a story. Students can be asked to write a diary entry for each chapter in a book. The entries are written in first person. Students are encouraged to write as the character might have written, without concern for mechanics and spelling. Personal comments not in the voice of the character can be allowed, but they should be put in parentheses or brackets to set them apart from regular entries. Teacher responses to the entries can help encourage the students and reassure them about their competence. When students are asked to compose diary entries for characters in the literature they are reading, they become more intensely involved in the reading. To accomplish this, the students must get inside the character's head and experience the events through his or her eyes. Taking a character's perspective in this way can improve comprehension (Hancock, 1993).

TECHNOLOGY ▣   Writing comments about reading may be facilitated through the use of a computer. Bernhardt (1994) suggests putting a reading passage on the computer and allowing students to interact with it by breaking it into meaningful or difficult chunks. Then they mark, number, or reorder these chunks and intersperse their own comments and questions in the text. Comments are written in all capital letters or in different colors or fonts so that they stand out from the original text. This active involvement with the text can promote better understanding.

Writing in cooperative groups works well for helping students understand the elements of a story. For example, after students have read a selection, the teacher can give each group a character to describe. He or she can instruct the children first to web the characters' characteristics and evidence from the story and then to write character descriptions based on the web (Avery and Avery, 1994).

More on the reading-writing connection appears in Chapters 1, 7, 8, and 10. Many writing activities are a part of instruction in creative reading, as described in Chapter 6.

TECHNOLOGY ▣ ## Educational Television

Reading Rainbow is a television program that presents books to children. It regularly tries to relate the topics in featured books to children's experiences, a procedure that facilitates comprehension. This modeling of a solid comprehension strategy may help students to apply the strategy in their own subsequent reading. Comprehension monitoring and summarizing of material also are modeled on this program (Wood and Duke, 1997).

Between the Lions (PBS Kids) is another program that focuses on reading. It is aimed at children from four to seven years old. The show features a family of lions and interesting characters, such as "Tiger Words," a sports figure who plays with vowels and consonants. Other characters, with similarly clever names, also promote literacy skills. The lions, the "mane" characters, have a library. In their library, books and story characters come alive. Each episode of the show starts with the lion family reading a story, poem, or other piece of writing together. The show embraces a balanced approach to reading instruction.

FAMILY

DIVERSITY

Parents can encourage their children to watch such sound programming instead of programs that are primarily for entertainment. It may be particularly helpful for ELL students (and perhaps for other members of their families).

Strategy Prompts

Physical objects can provide prompts to help readers who are learning new strategies or struggling to use particular strategies in their reading. The physical prompts provide scaffolding to support the students as they work on developing and integrating comprehension strategies. Fournier and Graves (2002) found that a scaffolded reading experience throughout prereading, during-reading, and postreading activities increased seventh graders' comprehension of short stories.

Strategy access rods are instructional aids for struggling readers (Worthing and Laster, 2002). Each rod has a one-sentence reading strategy printed on it. The strategies are written in first person. The reader has in front of him or her, for easy reference, a personalized collection of rods that represent different strategies. Comprehension strategies can be color-coded to represent before-, during-, and after-reading strategies. An example of a before-reading strategy is "I predict!" (Worthing and Laster, 2002, p. 123). Struggling readers who encounter comprehension difficulties can then choose, from available strategies, ones that are appropriate for the reading event.

Newman (2001/2002) developed comprehension strategy gloves that could serve a similar purpose for beginning and struggling readers, as well as more advanced ones. She had a prereading glove, a narrative structure glove, and an expository structure glove with icons on the gloves to prompt recall of questions that need to be answered by the students.

SUMMARY

The central factor in reading is comprehension. Since reading is an interactive process that involves the information brought to the text by readers, the information supplied by the text, and the reading situation, good comprehension depends on many factors. Among them are readers' experiential backgrounds, sensory and perceptual abilities, thinking abilities, and word recognition strategies, as well as their purposes for reading, their audience for the reading, the importance of the reading to them, and their facility with various comprehension strategies that will help them unlock the meanings within the text. Children's schemata, built through background experiences, aid comprehension of printed material and are themselves modified by input from this material.

Having a purpose for reading enhances comprehension. Teachers should learn how to set good purposes for children's reading assignments and discover how to help them learn to set their own purposes.

The audience for reading affects the reading strategies used. The audience may be the reader himself or herself, the teacher, or other children.

The importance that the reading has for the reader is also a factor. High-risk reading for a test may be done differently from low-risk reading in the classroom setting.

Features of the text itself also affect comprehension. Sentences that are complex, contain relative clauses, are in the passive voice, have missing words, or express negation may need special attention because students may have difficulty comprehending them. The meaning conveyed by punctuation in sentences should receive attention. Students also need help in understanding the functions of paragraphs and the organizational patterns of paragraphs and whole selections.

Prereading, during-reading, and postreading activities can foster children's comprehension of reading selections. Prereading activities such as previews, anticipation guides, semantic mapping, writing before reading, and creative drama can be helpful. Metacognitive strategies, questioning, and the cloze procedure are among the techniques that can be used during reading. Postreading activities usually involve questioning, making visual representations, using readers' theater, retelling, and application of concepts. Some activities—such as discussion; the K-W-L procedure; semantic webbing and story mapping; story grammar, story frame, and other story structure activities; writing activities related to reading; educational television; and strategy prompts from physical objects—may be involved in prereading, during-reading, *and* postreading activities at various times.

TEST YOURSELF

True or False

_____ 1. Each schema that a person has represents what the person knows about a particular concept and the interrelationships among the known pieces of information.

_____ 2. Anything that increases a reader's background knowledge may also increase comprehension.

_____ 3. An intelligence is the same as a learning style.

_____ 4. Previews for stories that build background related to the stories have a positive effect on comprehension.

_____ 5. Character journals are journals filled with character sketches.

_____ 6. Comprehension-monitoring techniques are metacognitive strategies.

_____ 7. Punctuation marks do not function as clues to sentence meaning.

_____ 8. Reading comprehension involves relating textual information to preexisting knowledge structures.

_____ 9. Comprehension strategies should be taught in a way that emphasizes their application when students are actually reading connected discourse.

_____ 10. Less able readers may rely too heavily on either text-based or knowledge-based processing.

_____ 11. Richard Rystrom argues that reading is exclusively a top-down process.

_____ 12. InQuest combines student questioning with creative drama.

_____ 13. Story grammar activities can increase children's understanding of story structure and serve as a basis for questioning.

_____ 14. Relative clauses cause few comprehension problems for children.

_____ 15. Punctuation marks are clues to pauses and pitch changes.

_____ 16. Semantic webbing involves systematically deleting words from a printed passage.

_____ 17. Think-alouds are useless in teaching metacognitive strategies.

_____ 18. The K-W-L teaching model for expository text is strictly a prereading strategy.

For your journal ...

❶ Choose a short selection about an uncommon subject. Question your classmates to find out how complete their schemata on this topic are, and give them copies of the selection to read. Later, discuss the difficulties that some of them had because of inadequate prior knowledge. In your journal, write your observations about this activity and indicate what you could have done to develop schemata before the reading took place.

❷ Read Margaret Egan's article "Capitalizing on the Reader's Strengths: An Activity Using Schema" (*Journal of Reading*, 37 [May 1994], pp. 636–640), and try the check activity "Travail in Nova Scotia" with a group of middle or upper elementary students. Write your results in your journal.

❸ The teacher in the video that accompanies this chapter on your CD uses a graphic organizer to help her students think about two pieces of literature. How might this organizer be used to compare and contrast story elements?

... and your portfolio

❶ Construct a time line for a chapter in a social studies text that has a chronological-order organizational pattern. Write a description of how you could use the time line with children to teach this organizational pattern.

❷ Construct an anticipation guide for a well-known folktale.

❸ Construct a story map for a story.

❹ Read the Egan article cited in item 2 of "For your journal…," and compose a check story to use with students in a specific grade.

6

Comprehension: Part 2

**KEY
VOCABULARY**

*Pay close attention to these
terms when they appear in the
chapter:*

anaphora

creative reading

critical reading

ellipsis

idiom

interpretive reading

literal comprehension

propaganda techniques

schema

story grammar

topic sentence

visualization

*In addition, when you read the
section on propaganda techniques, pay close attention to the
terms used there.*

SETTING OBJECTIVES

When you finish reading this chapter, you should be able to

- Describe ways to promote reading for literal meanings.
- Explain the importance of being able to make inferences.
- Discuss some of the things a critical reader must know.
- Explain what creative reading means.
- Explain how to construct questions for discussions and assessments.

Whereas Chapter 5 emphasized the role of the reader, the text, and the reading situation, as well as some comprehension strategies, Chapter 6 examines two types of comprehension—literal and higher-order—and describes approaches for developing each type. To take in ideas that are directly stated is literal comprehension; this is the most basic type. Higher-order comprehension includes interpretive, critical, and creative comprehension. To read between the lines is interpretive reading; to read for evaluation is critical reading; and to read beyond the lines is creative reading. Example 6.1 shows these types of comprehension and their elements. Regardless of the type of comprehension involved, "instructional methods that generate high levels of student involvement and engagement during reading can have positive effects on reading comprehension" (Williams, 2002, pp. 253–254).

This chapter also discusses questioning techniques that can be used to guide reading, enhance comprehension and retention, and assess comprehension. Three important activities related to effective questioning are discussed: preparing questions, helping students answer questions, and helping students question. Although the two chapters look at different aspects of comprehension, the material in both chapters is necessary to understanding the overall process.

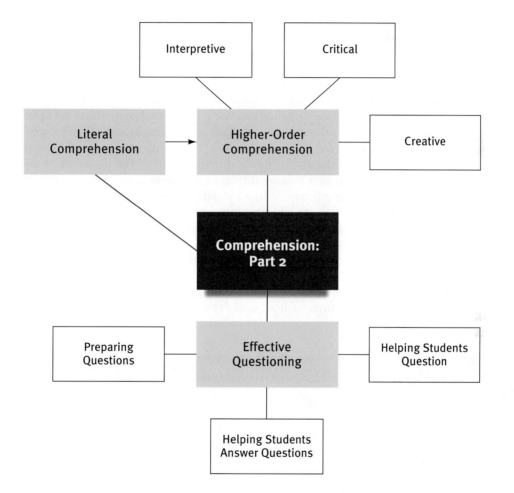

Interpretive

Critical

Literal
Comprehension

Higher-Order
Comprehension

Creative

**Comprehension:
Part 2**

Preparing
Questions

Effective
Questioning

Helping Students
Question

Helping Students
Answer Questions

Literal Comprehension

Reading for *literal comprehension*, or acquiring information that is directly stated in a selection, is important in and of itself and is also a prerequisite for higher-level comprehension. Recognizing stated information is the basis of literal comprehension. The specific, explicitly stated parts of a paragraph or passage that contain the basic information are the details on which main ideas, cause-and-effect relationships, inferences, and so on are built. For example, in the sentence "The man wore a red hat," the fact that a red hat was being worn is one detail that readers can note. Literal comprehension involves several skills, including locating details, understanding sequences, following directions, and recognizing cause-and-effect relationships. To locate details effectively, students may need some guidance as to the types of details signaled by specific questions. For example, a *who* question asks for the name or identification of a person, or sometimes an animal; a *what* question asks for a thing or an event; a *where* question asks for a place; a *when* question asks for a time; a *how* question asks for the way something is or was accomplished; and a *why* question asks for the reason for something. After discussing these question words and their meanings, the teacher can model for the students the locations of answers to each type of question in a passage displayed on the board or projected on a screen. Then the students can participate in an activity such as the one below to practice the skill. Newspaper articles are good for practice of this sort, since lead paragraphs tend to include information about *who, what, where, when, why,* and *how.* The teacher should provide feedback on the correctness of responses as soon as possible after the students complete the activity. Students may also practice finding details in newspaper articles at home, with family members.

 FAMILY

Sequence, the order in which events in a paragraph or passage occur, is signaled by time-order words such as *now, before, when, while, yet, after,* and so on. Children

---

MODEL ACTIVITIES   **Locating Details in a Newspaper Story**

Have the students read the following newspaper article and answer the questions in small groups, making sure that every group member agrees to each answer chosen.

The Live Wire Singers will be performing in concert at Lowe's Auditorium on First Street at 7:00 p.m. this Friday, to benefit the Children's College Fund. Admission is $10 per person or $15 per couple. This group presents programs of current pop songs and old standards. They have performed in thirty-six states to sell-out crowds during the past year.

1. Who is involved in this event?

2. What is about to take place?

3. Where will it take place?

4. When will it take place?

5. How or why will it take place?

Have a whole-class discussion of the article, with members from the different groups giving their groups' answers and the reasons for their answers.

EXAMPLE 6.1 Types of Comprehension

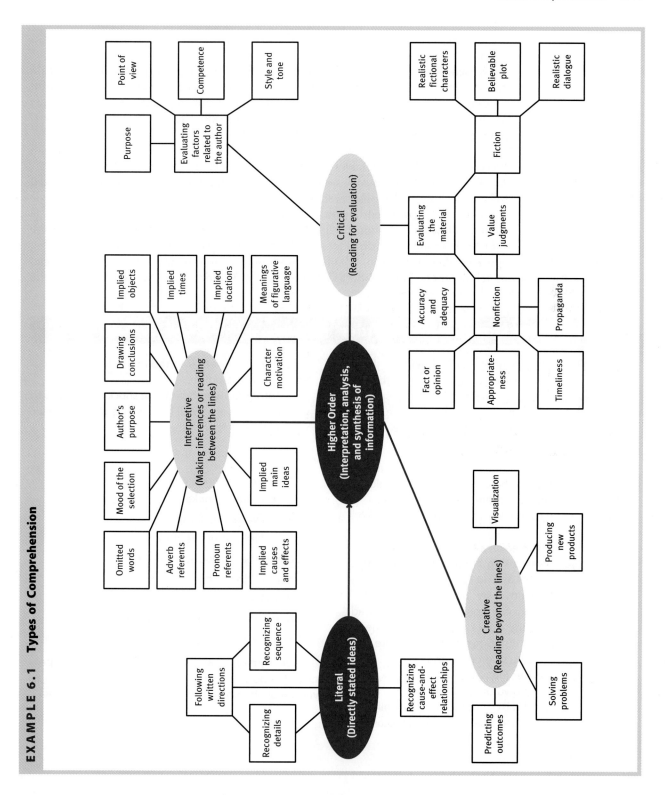

must learn to recognize straightforward chronological sequence, as well as flashbacks and other devices that describe events "out of order."

Teachers must model the process of finding the correct sequence of events in a passage before expecting students to locate such sequences independently. Helpful time-order words should be discussed and pointed out in selections. Then students need to engage in practice activities related to this skill, such as the one in the Model Activity "Placing Story Events in Order" below.

The ability to read and follow directions is a prerequisite for virtually all successful schoolwork. It involves understanding details and sequence.

The teacher should take a set of directions for performing a task and model following these directions carefully, reading the directions aloud as each step is completed and commenting on the meaning of each instruction. Then he or she should follow the directions again, leaving out a vital step. Class discussion about the results of not following directions carefully should then occur. After several modeling episodes, the teacher should consistently refer children to written directions instead of telling them how to do everything orally. Children can be asked to read the

---

MODEL ACTIVITIES   ## Placing Story Events in Order

Discuss the meaning of sequence with the children. Give an example of the sequence in a very familiar story such as "The Three Little Pigs." Then ask the children to read the following story and place the list of events in order.

We were all excited on Friday morning because we were going to go to the circus. We had trouble concentrating on eating breakfast, but Mother wouldn't allow us to leave the table before we were finished.

Immediately after breakfast, we piled into the van. Everyone was talking at once and bouncing around on the seats as Dad started the van and backed out of the driveway. We were making so much noise and moving around so much that Dad didn't hear or see the truck turn the corner. The truck driver honked his horn, but it was too late. Dad backed right into the side of the truck.

The angry driver jumped out of his truck, but when he saw the crowd of us in the van, he calmed down. He and Dad talked to each other awhile, staring at the damaged side of the truck occasion-

ally. Then they went into the house to report the accident to the police.

Mother recovered from the shock and told us to get out of the van. "We'll have a long wait before we will be able to leave," she said.

Story Events

The family got into the van.

The truck driver honked his horn.

The family ate breakfast.

Dad backed out of the driveway.

Dad and the truck driver talked.

Mother told the children to get out of the van.

Dad backed into the side of the truck.

Dad and the truck driver went into the house.

The driver jumped out of his truck.

After everyone has finished the exercise independently, discuss the children's results in class. Be sure to have the children give the reasons for their decisions.

FAMILY directions silently and then repeat them in their own words. There are numerous opportunities for children to practice following directions outside of school. With family members, they may read and follow directions for using public transportation, cooking, or even participating in games and crafts.

Recognizing and understanding a cause-and-effect relationship in a written passage is an important reading skill. It is considered a literal skill when the relationship is explicitly stated ("Bill stayed out because he was ill."); it is considered an interpretive skill if the relationship is implied.

Here are some activities for working with literal comprehension:

1. After students have read a paragraph, preferably from a book they have chosen themselves, ask them questions for which the answers are directly stated in the paragraph. These are often *who, what, where,* and *when* questions. Have them show where they found the answers in the paragraph.

2. Give the children a set of directions for a task that they need to complete, and have them number the important details (or steps), as has been done in the following example. Go through one or more examples before you ask them to work alone or cooperatively, with partners or in small groups.

   To make a good bowl of chili, first (1) sauté the onions for about ten minutes. Then (2) add the ground beef and brown it. (3) Stir the mixture frequently so that it will not burn. Finally, (4) add the tomatoes, tomato sauce, Mexican-style beans, salt, pepper, and chili powder. (5) Cook over low heat for forty-five minutes to one hour.

3. Make some copies of a menu. After modeling for the students how to locate items and prices, ask them to read the menu and answer specific questions such as these:

   a. What is the price of a soft drink?

   b. Can you order a baked potato separately? If so, under what heading is it found?

   c. What else do you get when you order a steak?

   d. How many desserts are available?

4. Using a description like the following one and reading each step aloud, draw an object on the board. Then give the children a written description of another object and ask them to draw it.

   The flower has five oval petals. The petals are red. The center, at which the petals meet, is brown. The flower has a long green stem. At the bottom of the stem are overlapping blade-shaped leaves, which are half as tall as the stem.

5. Display (by writing on the board or by projecting the material on a screen) a paragraph from a book the students have read that contains a cause-and-effect relationship. Model the process of locating the cause and the effect.

Point out clue words, such as *because*, if they are present, but make sure the children know they cannot always expect such clues to be present. Then show the children another paragraph from the same book or another book. State the cause of the action, and have them identify the effect. Discuss the children's responses. A paragraph similar to the following one could be used for instruction.

> Bobby, Jill, Leon, and Peggy were playing softball in Bobby's yard. Peggy was up at bat and hit the ball squarely in the direction of Bobby's bedroom window. As the group watched in horror, the softball crashed through the window, shattering the glass.

> Question: What happened when the softball hit the window?
> *or*
> What caused the window to break?

LITERATURE 6. Have the children read a selection such as the folktale "Lazy Jack." Then list the events in the story out of sequence, and show students how to reorder them, explaining why the events came in that order. Using another selection, such as that in the Model Activity "Placing Story Events in Order" on page 218, ask the children to list the events in sequence. (Use shorter selections for younger children.)

7. Discuss with the children the functions of such key words as *first, next, last,* and *finally*. Then give them a paragraph containing these words, and ask them to underline the words that help to show the order of events.

8. Use an activity similar to the Model Activity "Following Directions" below.

MODEL ACTIVITIES | **Following Directions**

Give the students handouts with the following information printed on them.

Directions: Read all the items before you begin to carry out each instruction. Work as quickly as you can; you have five minutes to finish this activity.

1. Write your name at the top of the paper.

2. Turn the paper over and add 15 and 25. Write the answer you get on this line: _____.

3. Stand up and clap your hands three times.

4. Count the number of times the word *the* is written on this page. Put the answer on this line: _____.

5. Go to the board and write your name.

6. Count the people in this room. Put the answer under your name at the top of the page.

7. Now that you have read all of the directions, take your paper to the teacher. It should have no marks on it.

After the children have finished the exercise, hold a discussion about why some of them made marks on the paper that they should not have made. Emphasize the importance of reading and following directions carefully to avoid errors.

9. Teach the children the meanings of words commonly encountered in written directions, such as *underline, circle, divide, color, example, left, right, below, over,* and *match*.

10. Write directions for an activity, and have the students perform it. Construction and cooking projects, as well as science experiments and magic tricks, can be used. Discussion can center on the results that occur if the correct sequence is not followed. Directions can be cut apart, scrambled, and reconstructed to give the children an opportunity to demonstrate their comprehension of the necessary sequence.

Perhaps because literal comprehension is the easiest to deal with in the classroom, teachers have given it a disproportionate amount of attention; but children also need to achieve higher-order reading comprehension to become thoughtful and effective citizens.

Higher-Order Comprehension

Higher-order reading comprehension goes beyond literal understanding of a text. It is based on the higher-order thinking processes of interpretation, analysis, and synthesis of information. In this chapter, we discuss the higher-order comprehension processes of interpretive reading, critical reading, and creative reading.

Good readers employ a variety of higher-order strategies. They interpret and evaluate the material that they read. They adjust the way they read to the type of text being read. They paraphrase ideas accurately, relate the ideas to their background knowledge, draw conclusions about the ideas, consider the author's purpose, and consider the accuracy of the material. They monitor their understanding as they read and adjust their reading strategies accordingly. In other words, they are very active readers (Pressley, 2002; Duke and Pearson, 2002).

Knowledge is necessary to higher-order thinking, but students do not always use the knowledge they possess to think inferentially, critically, and creatively (Beck, 1989). They may have the background knowledge needed for comprehending a text but may fail to use it, or they may have misconceptions about certain topics — misconceptions that are more detrimental to comprehension than no background knowledge at all. Students in all groups, regardless of socioeconomic level or ethnic origin, vary in background knowledge, but it is true that "membership in specific cultural groups goes far in determining what a reader knows that can be related to text—and thus goes far in determining a reader's interpretation of text" (Pressley, 2001, p. 8). Limited background knowledge about U.S. language and customs can negatively affect ELLs' comprehension (Ganske, Monroe, and Strickland, 2003). Semantic mapping (described in Chapter 5) accompanied by group discussion can help students who have little individual knowledge about a topic to pool their information and expand their knowledge (Maria, 1989).

DIVERSITY

Making predictions about reading material is an important higher-order reading strategy. Predicting what will happen in a story or other reading selection engages students' interest and leads them to organize their thinking. A hypothesis-testing process is initiated in which students make predictions and then read to confirm or reject them. If the predictions must be rejected, the students revise them. In all cases, they must be ready to explain why they made the predictions they did and why they believe the predictions can be accepted or must be rejected.

Students need to realize that any evidence that refutes a prediction is enough to show the prediction is not valid but that even a great deal of supporting evidence in favor of a prediction may not conclusively prove that it is true. They also need to realize that just because a prediction has not been refuted at one point in the reading does not mean that evidence to refute it will not appear later. Readers tend to overlook refuting evidence while noticing confirming evidence, and students must be taught to avoid doing this. By refuting unsupportable predictions, students reduce uncertainty about the story's outcome. Teachers should ask students if their predictions have been proved wrong yet, and other, similar questions, to encourage them to search for refuting evidence (Garrison and Hoskisson, 1989).

Asking for predictions when the text offers clues about what will happen helps make students aware of the usefulness of text information in making inferences. Asking for predictions when there are no text clues about what will happen encourages creative thinking on the part of the children. Both types of prediction activities are good to include in lessons over time (Beck, 1989). Before students are asked to make and verify predictions, the teacher should model the strategy with a variety of materials.

LITERATURE Reading response activities can also help students develop higher-order comprehension skills. Ollmann (1996) tried seven types of open-ended reading response formats with her middle-school students: literary letters to the teacher; reading response questions; two-column responses, in which quotations from a book are written on one side and personal responses to the quotations on the other; letters to an author asking questions about the development of a book; hexagonal essays, in which students respond to a book from the perspective of each of the six levels of Bloom's Taxonomy; buddy journals, in which partners who have read the same book write about it in a journal and respond to each other's entries; and character journals, in which each student writes a first-person diary entry as a main character in the book. The hexagonal essay worked best at promoting higher-order thinking: with it, students "summarize the plot, make a personal association with text, analyze the theme, analyze literary techniques, compare and contrast with other literature, and evaluate the work as a whole" (Ollmann, 1996, p. 579). The two-column response format was also effective. Character journals led to development of empathy with the characters.

● Interpretive Reading

Interpretive reading is reading between the lines or making inferences. It is the process of deriving ideas that are implied rather than directly stated. Interpretive reading includes making inferences about the main ideas of passages, cause-and-effect relationships that are not directly stated, referents of pronouns, referents of adverbs, and omitted words. It also includes detecting the mood of a passage, detecting the author's purpose in writing a selection, drawing conclusions, and interpreting figurative language.

Even young children can use their backgrounds of experience to make inferences, especially if teachers help them develop their schemata and model the process of making inferences.
(© Jean Claude LeJeune/ Stock Boston)

No text is ever fully explicit. Some relationships among events, motivations of characters, and other factors are left out, with the expectation that readers will figure them out on their own. Readers, therefore, must play an active role in constructing the meanings represented by the text. They must infer the implied information by combining the information in the text with their background knowledge of the world. Stories that require more inferences are more difficult to read (Carr, 1983; Pearson, 1985).

Lange (1981) has pointed out that "readers make inferences consistent with their *schemata*" (p. 443). Even very young children can, during their daily activities, make inferences by connecting new information to information they already possess. It is important to realize, however, that children have less prior knowledge than adults do and that, even when they possess the necessary background knowledge, they do not always make inferences spontaneously, without teacher direction.

Active involvement with the printed message enhances students' abilities to make inferences related to it. Comparing events in students' own lives with events that might occur in stories they are about to read is one way to help the students see the thinking processes they should use when they read. Even struggling readers show the ability to make inferences about the material they are reading when such a procedure is used (Hansen and Hubbard, 1984).

McIntosh (1985) suggests that teachers should ask first graders to make inferences based only on pieces of information located close together in the text.

When the information is not adjacent in the text, the teacher can use guiding questions to lead students to it. This type of instruction helps students become aware of the need to search actively for the meanings of written passages. Older children grow in their ability to make inferences, possibly because of their increased knowledge of the world.

Students are expected to make inferences about a number of things: locations, people who act in certain ways, time, actions, devices or instruments, categories, objects, causes and/or effects, solutions to problems, and feelings. To make these inferences, they can relate important vocabulary in the reading material to their backgrounds of experience. First, the teacher should explain how readers can use important words in a passage to help them make a particular inference about the passage. Then the teacher should have students practice and apply this procedure. During the application phase, students are asked to make an inference based on the first sentence and to then retain, modify, or reject it as each subsequent sentence is read (Johnson and Johnson, 1986).

Such instruction is needed because some students will make hypotheses about the reading material but will fail to modify them when additional information shows them to be incorrect. Instead, they may distort subsequent information in an attempt to make it conform to their original hypotheses. These children may have problems with passages that present one idea and follow it with a contrasting idea or passages that present an idea and subsequently refute it. They may also have difficulty with passages that give examples of a topic before the topic statement appears or with passages that give no topic statement (Kimmel and MacGinitie, 1985).

To help students learn to revise their hypotheses when reading, teachers can use a passage that contains a word with multiple meanings, asking students to hypothesize about possible meanings for the word on the basis of the initial sentences in the passage. Then they can have students read further to confirm or disprove these predictions. Reading stories written from unusual points of view can also help; for example, *The True Story of the 3 Little Pigs*, by Jon Scieszka (Viking Kestrel), is written from the wolf's point of view.

LITERATURE

Pearson (1985) succinctly describes a method related to teaching inference skills that was developed by Gordon and Pearson (1983). Children should: "(1) ask the inference question, (2) answer it, (3) find clues in the text to support the inference, and (4) tell how to get from the clues to the answer (i.e., give a 'line of reasoning')" (Pearson, 1985, p. 731). First, the teacher models all four steps; then the teacher performs Steps 1 and 2, while requiring the students to complete Steps 3 and 4; then the teacher performs Steps 1 and 3, requiring the students to complete Steps 2 and 4; and finally the teacher asks the question (Step 1) and the students perform all the other steps. The responsibility for the task is thus gradually transferred from teacher to students. This is an excellent procedure and can be used for other skills as well. Providing practice in answering inferential questions is important to helping the students improve in this skill.

Interpreting Anaphora

Interpreting anaphora is another task that requires students to make inferences. *Anaphora* refers to the use of one word or phrase to replace another one (Irwin,

TIME for REFLECTION

Some people believe that children intuitively know the referents for pronouns. Others say children need instruction to help them recognize referents. **What do *you* think, and why?**

1991). Examples include using pronouns in place of nouns (*he* for a noun such as *Bill*), using adverbs for nouns or noun phrases (*here* for a phrase such as *in the kitchen*), letting adjectives stand for the nouns that would have followed them (*several* for *several people*), using a superordinate term to stand for a subordinate one (*reptile* for *rattlesnake*), using an inclusive term to stand for an extended section of text (*this* for *a disturbance in the neighborhood* presented in an earlier sentence), and letting referents in another sentence or clause represent deleted items (*I will too*, following *Mom will bake brownies for the sale*. Here *bake brownies for the sale* is "understood").

DIVERSITY

At some point, teachers will probably need to address in class all forms of anaphora, but the approaches used can be similar. Modeling of the thought processes used is important. Because children, especially English language learners (Herrell, 2000), frequently have trouble identifying the noun to which a pronoun refers, they need practice in deciding to whom or to what pronouns refer. The Classroom Scenario on pronoun referents on page 226 offers ideas for instruction about and practice with pronouns. Some other forms of anaphora are discussed in subsequent sections.

Pronoun Referents.   Few, if any, pieces of writing explicitly state the connections between pronouns and their referents (anaphoric relationships), so the task of determining the referent is an inferential one. After reading, students recall structures in which the referent is a noun or a noun phrase more easily than they remember structures in which the referent is a clause or a sentence (Barnitz, 1979).

> Mark wanted an ice cream cone but did not have enough money for it. (noun phrase referent)

> Mike plays the guitar for fun, but he does not do it often. (sentence referent)

Similarly, children find it easier to remember structures in which the pronoun follows its referent than structures in which the pronoun comes first (Barnitz, 1979).

> Because it was pretty, Marcia wanted the blouse.

> Marcia wanted the blouse because it was pretty.

Teachers should call students' attention to the structures just described. They should use stories or content selections that the students are currently reading and explain the connections between the pronouns and referents in a number of examples before asking students to determine the relationships themselves. See the Classroom Scenario on page 226 for an example of such a procedure.

Adverb Referents.   At times, adverbs refer to other words or groups of words without an explicitly stated relationship. Teachers can explain these relationships, using examples such as the following, and then let children practice making the connections independently.

> I'll stay at home, and you come here after you finish. (The adverb *here* refers to *home*.)

CLASSROOM SCENARIO — Pronoun Referents

Mr. Stevens wrote the following sentence on the chalkboard: "Joan put the license plate on her bicycle." Then he read it to the class. After reading the sentence, he modeled the process involved in determining the referent in the sentence by saying, "*Her* is a pronoun that stands for a noun (or, with younger children, 'a word that stands for a person, place, or thing'). The noun usually comes before the pronoun that stands for it. The two nouns in this sentence that come before *her* are *Joan* and *plate*. *Her* indicates a woman or a girl. A plate isn't a woman or a girl, so *her* probably stands for *Joan*."

Then he wrote this second sentence on the chalkboard: "Since the book was old, it was hard to replace." He asked the children to determine the referent for *it* in this sentence in the way he had determined the referent for *her* in the other sentence.

Ronnie said, "*It* refers to *book*."

Mr. Stevens asked Ronnie, "How did you know?"

"You told us that *it* refers to a thing, and the book is the only thing mentioned in the sentence," Ronnie responded.

"That's good thinking," Mr. Stevens replied, as he wrote a new sentence on the board for further guided practice. After another student successfully dealt with this sentence, Mr. Stevens gave the students a handout that included several paragraphs from a book they were reading in class. Each paragraph included pronouns and referents. He asked the students to draw an arrow from each pronoun to its referent and be ready to explain their choices later in the day in small-group sessions.

Analysis of Scenario

Mr. Stevens followed a good instructional plan by first modeling the skill of determining pronoun referents, then offering the students guided practice in which they were asked to support their responses with reasons, and finally having students practice independently, using other sentences chosen from material they were currently reading.

I enjoy the swimming pool, even if you do not like to go there. (The adverb *there* refers to *swimming pool*.)

Omitted Words.　Sometimes words are omitted and said to be "understood," a structure known as ***ellipsis***. Ellipsis can cause problems for some students, so again teachers should provide examples, explain the structure, and then give children practice in interpreting sentences.

Are you going to the library? Yes, I am. (In the second sentence, the words *going to the library* are understood.)

Who is going with you? Bobby. (The words *is going with me* are understood.)

I have my books. Where are yours? (Here the second sentence is a shortened form of *Where are your books?*)

After this structure has been thoroughly discussed, students may practice by restating the sentences, filling in the deleted words.

Main Ideas

The main idea of a paragraph is the central thought around which the whole paragraph is organized. It is often, but not always, expressed in a **topic sentence** in expository writing; in narrative writing, fewer topic sentences are found.

To understand written selections fully and to summarize long selections, children must be able to determine the main ideas in their reading materials. Teachers should provide them with opportunities to practice recognizing main ideas and help them to realize the following facts:

❶ A topic sentence often states the main idea of the paragraph.

❷ The topic sentence is often, though not always, the first sentence in the paragraph; sometimes it appears at the end or in the middle.

❸ Not all paragraphs have topic sentences.

❹ The main idea is supported by all of the details in a well-written paragraph.

❺ When the main idea is not directly stated, readers can determine it by discovering the topic to which all the stated details are related.

❻ The main idea of a whole selection may be determined by examining the main ideas of the individual paragraphs and deciding to what topic they are all related.

The teacher should model the thought process that students need to follow in deciding on the main idea of a selection before asking them to try this task independently. For paragraphs with topic sentences, the teacher can show students that the topic sentence is the main idea and that the other sentences in the paragraph are related to it by taking a paragraph, locating the topic sentence, and showing the relationship of each of the other sentences to the topic sentence. Then the teacher can give the students paragraphs and ask them to underline the topic sentences and tell how each of the other sentences is related to each topic sentence.

To give students a concrete analogy for main ideas and details, a teacher can use a familiar object such as a bicycle. The whole bicycle can be identified as the main idea, and the handlebars, seat, pedals, gears, wheels, and chain can represent the supporting details that together make up the main idea.

Activities such as those illustrated in the Focus on Strategies on page 228 and described in the Model Activity on inferring unstated main ideas (page 229) can give students practice in locating main ideas in paragraphs.

Individual teachers mean different things when they request main ideas from students, and, when students are asked to give the main idea of a passage, some produce topics, some topic sentences, and some brief summaries. A description of the task expected, however, may be all that students need to prompt them to produce the desired response (Moore and Cunningham, 1984).

A topic merely identifies the subject matter; a main idea also includes the type of information given about the topic. For example, a topic of a paragraph or selection might be "football," whereas the main idea might be "There are several different ways to score in football."

Duffelmeyer and Duffelmeyer (1991) suggest the use of gamelike activities to show students that a topic and a statement about the topic combine to make a main idea statement. They encourage following these activities with modeling of the writing of details to support the main idea statements formed, and then arranging guided practice for the students in performing this task.

FOCUS ON STRATEGIES

Finding Main Ideas

Mrs. Braswell wrote the following paragraph on the chalkboard:

Edward Fong is a good family man. He is well educated, and he keeps his knowledge of governmental processes current. He has served our city well as a mayor for the past two years, exhibiting his outstanding skills as an administrator. Edward Fong has qualities that make him an excellent choice as our party's candidate for governor.

She said, "I am going to try to locate the topic sentence, the one to which all of the other sentences are related. The topic sentence provides one type of main idea for the paragraph. ... Now, let's see, is it the first sentence? No. None of the other sentences appears to support his being a good family man. ...

Is it the second sentence? No. That idea isn't supported by the first sentence. ... Is it the third sentence? No. That sentence may be supported by the second sentence, but not by the others. ... Is it the fourth sentence? Yes, I think it is. A candidate for governor would do well to be a good family man, to be well educated and knowledgeable about government, and to have experience as a city administrator. All the other sentences support the last one, which is broad enough in its meaning to include the ideas expressed in the other sentences."

After this demonstration, Mrs. Braswell let one student "think aloud" the reasoning behind his or her choice of a topic sentence for another paragraph. Finally, she had students work on this process in pairs, "thinking aloud" to each other.

In many selections, readers must infer the main idea from related details. Even in selections in which the main idea is directly stated, readers generally must make inferences about which sentence states the main idea. The teacher can help develop students' readiness to make such inferences by first asking them to locate the main ideas of pictures. Then the teacher can ask them to listen for main ideas as he or she reads to them. Finally, the teacher can have students look for the main ideas of passages they read themselves.

Finding the main idea in whole selections of nonfiction generally is a categorizing process in which the topic is located and the information given about the topic is then examined. In fiction, however, there is not a "topic" but a central problem, which is rarely stated explicitly.

Showing students how to infer unstated main ideas is more difficult than showing them how to decide which stated sentence represents the main idea. In situations such as the one shown in the Model Activity on page 229, the teacher could compare each of the possible choices to the details in the selection, rejecting those that fail to encompass the details. As students practice and become more proficient at identifying implied main ideas, the teacher should omit the choices and ask them to construct the main idea themselves. Teachers can also increase passage length as the children gain proficiency, beginning with paragraphs that include directly stated topic sentences, moving to paragraphs that do not have directly stated topic sentences, and finally moving gradually to entire selections. Because of their obvious morals, Aesop's fables are good for teaching implied main ideas. The teacher can give

LITERATURE

MODEL ACTIVITIES — Inferring Unstated Main Ideas

Model the generation of a main idea for a paragraph from one of the students' textbooks that has an unstated main idea. Be sure to show how each sentence in the paragraph supports the main idea you generated. Then display a copy of the following paragraph (or a similar one from one of their textbooks) and main idea choices on the board or a transparency.

The mayor of this town has always conducted his political campaigns as name-calling battles. Never once has he approached the basic issues of a campaign. Nevertheless, he builds himself up as a great statesman, ignoring the irregularities that have been discovered during his terms of office. Do you want a person like this to be reelected?

The main idea of this selection is:

1. The current mayor is not a good person to reelect to office.

2. The mayor doesn't say nice things about his opponents.

3. The mayor is a crook.

4. The mayor should be reelected.

Say: "In this selection, the main idea is implied but not directly stated. Choose the correct main idea from the list of possible ones. Try to use a thinking process similar to the one I used in the example that I gave for you. Be ready to explain the reason for your choice to your classmates."

---

students a fable and ask them to state the moral, then compare the morals given in the fables with the ones stated by the students, discuss any variations, and examine reasoning processes. Children may have fun using Arnold Lobel's *Fables* (Harper & Row, 1980) with this activity as well.

Finding main ideas in fiction is a somewhat different process. To help students learn to locate a central problem in a fictional work, the teacher should first activate their schemata for problems and solutions, perhaps by talking about background experiences or stories previously read. Then the class may identify and categorize types of problems. Finally, the teacher should model the process of identifying a central story problem, using a familiar, brief story. By pausing during reading to hypothesize about the central problem and to confirm or modify hypotheses, the teacher can show the students how to search for the thing the central character wants, needs, or feels—the thing that provides the story's problem. The teacher should let the children see how the story's events affect the hypotheses they have made. Events of a story may be listed on the board to be analyzed for the needs or desires of the main character (Moldofsky, 1983).

Two activities using newspaper articles can provide enjoyable practice in identifying main ideas:

1. Gather old newspapers and cardboard for mounting. Cut from the newspapers a number of articles that you think will interest the children, and separate the text of each article from its headline. Mount each article and title on cardboard. The children's task is to read each article and locate the most suitable headline for it. To make the task easier, have them begin by

matching captions to pictures, use very short articles, or use articles that are completely different in subject matter. Have the children discuss the reasons for their choices. Make the activity self-checking by coding articles and headlines. To follow up, you might use these ideas: (a) have children make pictures and captions to share in the reading center, or (b) have them try to match advertisements to pictures or captions to cartoons.

CLASSROOM SCENARIO

Inferring Cause-and-Effect Relationships

Mrs. Taylor stacked three books on the edge of her desk as the children watched. Then she said, "Cover your eyes or put your heads down on your desks so that you can't see the books anymore. Don't peek."

When all eyes were covered, Mrs. Taylor knocked the books off the desk. Then she said, "You can open your eyes now."

The children opened their eyes and saw the books on the floor.

"What caused the books to be on the floor?" Mrs. Taylor asked.

Rob immediately responded, "You knocked them off."

"How do you know that I knocked them off?" Mrs. Taylor persisted. "You didn't see me do it."

"Nobody except you was up there," Rob replied.

"How do you know that I didn't just lay them gently on the floor?" the teacher then asked.

"Because they made such a loud noise," Rob answered. "If you had put them down gently, there wouldn't have been much noise."

"Excellent thinking, Rob!" said Mrs. Taylor. "You used clues to figure out something that you didn't actually see. When you read, you can use that skill, too. Sometimes the author leaves clues about what he wants you to know, but he doesn't come right out and say it. You have to use clues he gives and 'read between the lines' to find out what happened. We're going to try doing that right now."

Mrs. Taylor passed out a handout with the following paragraphs on it. She said, "Read the following paragraphs and answer the question."

> Jody refused to go to bed when the baby sitter told her it was time. "This is a special occasion," she said. "Mom and Dad said I could stay up two hours later tonight."
>
> Reluctantly, the baby sitter allowed Jody to sit through two more hour-long TV shows. Although her eyelids drooped, she stubbornly stayed up until the end of the second show.
>
> This morning Jody found it hard to get out of bed. All day there was evidence that she was not very alert. "What is wrong with me?" she wondered.
>
> Question: What caused Jody to feel the way she did today?

When everyone had finished reading and had answered the question independently, Mrs. Taylor had one child answer the question aloud. The other children verified the answer, and several pointed out the clues in the material that helped them to decide on the answer.

Analysis of Scenario

Mrs. Taylor used a concrete experience to show the children how they made inferences about experiences every day. Then she had them try to apply the same kind of thinking to a reading experience. She asked them to analyze their thinking and to point out the clues they used, so that classmates who were having trouble with the skill could see how they processed the information.

2. Collect newspaper articles and cut off the headlines. Then have students construct titles using the information in the lead paragraph. Show them how to do this before you ask them to work on the task alone.

Cause and Effect

Sometimes a reader needs to infer a cause or an effect that has been implied in the material. Cause-and-effect relationships can be taught using cause-and-effect chains drawn from real life and from stories. Brainstorming out loud about causes and effects may help children develop more skill in this area. The teacher can ask, "What could be the effect when a person falls into the lake? What could be the cause of a baby crying?" Then the teacher should elicit the reasoning behind children's answers. The Classroom Scenario on page 230 describes a practice activity for this skill.

Detecting Mood

Certain words and ways of using words tend to set a mood for a story, poem, or other literary work. Teachers should have children discuss how certain words trigger certain moods—for example, *ghostly, deserted, haunted,* and *howling* convey a scary mood; *lilting, sparkling, shining,* and *laughing* project a happy mood; *downcast, sobbing,* and *dejected* indicate a sad mood. They should model for the children the process of locating mood words in a paragraph and using these words to determine the mood of the paragraph. Then they can give the children copies of selections in which they have underlined words that set the mood and let them decide what the mood is, judging on the basis of the underlined words. Finally, teachers can give the students a passage such as the one provided in the Classroom Scenario on page 232 and tell them to underline the words that set the mood. After the students complete the practice activity, they should discuss the mood that the words established.

Detecting the Author's Purpose

Writers always have a purpose for writing: to inform, to entertain, to persuade, or to accomplish something else. Teachers should encourage their students to ask, "Why was this written?" by presenting them with a series of stories and explaining the purpose of each one, and then giving them other stories and asking them to identify the purposes. The class should discuss reasons for the answers. The Model Activity on page 233 gives students practice in detecting purpose.

Drawing Conclusions

To draw conclusions, a reader must put together information gathered from several sources or from several places within the same source. Students may develop readiness for this skill by studying pictures and drawing conclusions from them. Answering questions like the following may also help. The teacher should model the process before having the students attempt it.

❶ What is taking place here?

❷ What happened just before this picture was taken?

❸ What are the people in the picture preparing to do?

Detecting Mood

Mrs. Vaden read to her class the following excerpt from *Homesick: My Own Story* by Jean Fritz (Dell, 1982, p. 138).

By the time we were at the bottom of the hill and had parked beside the house, my grandmother, my grandfather, and Aunt Margaret were all outside, looking exactly the way they had in the calendar picture. I ran right into my grandmother's arms as if I'd been doing this every day.

"Welcome home! Oh, welcome home!" my grandmother cried.

I hadn't known it but this was exactly what I'd wanted her to say. I needed to hear it said out loud. I was home.

Mrs. Vaden said, "In this passage, the mood of happiness is effectively developed by describing the girl running into her grandmother's arms, the cries of 'welcome' from her grandmother, and the statement 'I was home.' All these things combine to help us feel the happy mood. Some authors carefully choose words to help readers feel the mood they want to share. Read the paragraph on the board, decide what mood the author wanted to set, and be ready to tell the class which words helped you to decide about the mood."

The following paragraph was on the board:

Jay turned dejectedly away from the busy scene made by the movers as they carried his family's furniture from the house. "We're going away forever," he thought sadly. "I'll never see my friends again." And a tear rolled slowly down Jay's cheek, further smudging his unhappy face.

Steve raised his hand. When the teacher called on him, he said, "The mood is sad."

"That's right," Mrs. Vaden responded. "What clues did you use to decide that?"

"*Sadly, tear,* and *unhappy*," he replied.

Sharon chimed in, "I see another one. *Dejected* is a sad word, too."

"Very good," said Mrs. Vaden. "You both found clues to the mood of this paragraph. Next, we will look for the mood as we begin to read our story for this week. Jot down the clue words as you find them to help you decide on the mood."

Analysis of Scenario

Mrs. Vaden first showed the children how she decided about the mood of a passage in a literature selection with which they were familiar. Then she gave them an opportunity to determine the mood for another selection, under her supervision. Finally, she asked them to apply the skill in further purposeful reading activities.

Cartoons may be used to good advantage in developing this comprehension skill. The teacher can show the students a cartoon like the one on page 233 and ask a question that leads them to draw a conclusion, such as "What kind of news does Dennis have for his father?" Putting together the ideas that an event happened today and that Dennis's father needs to be relaxed to hear about it enables students to conclude that Dennis was involved in some mischief or accident that is likely to upset his father. The teacher can model the necessary thinking process by pointing out each clue and relating it to personal knowledge about how parents react. Then students can practice on other cartoons.

LITERATURE   In the early grades, riddles such as "I have a face and two hands. I go tick-tock. What am I?" offer good practice in drawing conclusions. Commercial riddle books, used in such a way as to allow readers to answer riddles and explain the reasoning behind their answers, may also be helpful for developing this skill.

DENNIS THE MENACE

"LET ME KNOW WHEN YOU'RE RELAXED ENOUGH TO HEAR ABOUT SOMETHIN' THAT HAPPENED TODAY."

Source: DENNIS THE MENACE® used by permission of Hank Ketcham Enterprises and © by North America Syndicate.

Another way to help children draw conclusions is to ask questions about sentences that imply certain information. For example, the teacher can write on the board, "The two men in uniforms removed a stretcher from the back of their vehicle." Then the teacher can ask, "What kind of vehicle were these men driving? What are your reasons for your answers?" Even though the sentence does not directly

---

MODEL ACTIVITIES   ## Detecting the Author's Purpose

Display the following list of reading selections on the board, or display the actual books. Ask the children to consider the selections and decide, for each selection, whether the author was trying to inform, entertain, persuade, or accomplish a combination of purposes.

The New Way Things Work by David Macaulay. New York: Houghton Mifflin, 1998.

The Long Road to Gettysburg by Jim Murphy. New York: Scholastic, 1992.

The Good, the Bad, and the Goofy by Jon Scieszka. New York: The Trumpet Club, 1992.

Puzzled Penguins: A Maze Adventure by Patrick Merrill. New York: Troll, 1999.

"Put Safety First." A pamphlet.

After each child has had time to make a decision about each selection, ask volunteers to share their responses and the reasons for each one. Clear up any misconceptions through discussion.

state that the vehicle is an ambulance, the details lead to this conclusion. With help, children can become adept at detecting such clues to implied meanings. The Model Activity on drawing conclusions below offers practice with this skill.

To draw conclusions about characters' motives in stories, children must have some knowledge about how people react in social situations. This knowledge comes from their backgrounds of experience. Teachers' questions can encourage inferences by requiring students to consider events from the viewpoints of different characters; to reflect on the characters' probable thoughts, feelings, and motives; and to anticipate the consequences of the actions of various characters.

Interpreting Figurative Language

Interpreting figurative language is an inferential task. Idioms abound in the English language. An **idiom** is a phrase that has a meaning different from its literal meaning. A person who "keeps his eyes peeled," for example, does not actually peel his eyes, but uses them intently. Idioms make language more difficult to comprehend, but they also add color and interest.

DIVERSITY   Students who are not part of the mainstream culture often lack the backgrounds of experience with that culture to help them interpret idioms. They may be confused over the idea that a word or phrase has different meanings in different contexts, and its meaning in an idiomatic context may be very different from any of its denotative meanings.

It may be helpful to teach idioms by defining and explaining them when they occur in reading materials or in oral activities. Studying the origins of the expressions may also be helpful. After an idiom's meaning has been clarified, students need to use

---

MODEL ACTIVITIES   Drawing Conclusions

Divide the class into small cooperative groups. Give each group a copy of a handout containing the following two paragraphs. Tell the children: "Read each paragraph and answer the question that follows it. After each person in your group has finished, discuss the answers with the members of your group and explain why you answered as you did. Modify your answers if you believe your thinking was wrong originally. Be ready to share your decisions with the rest of the class."

Ray went through the line, piling his plate high with food. He then carried his plate over to a table, where a server was waiting to find out what he wanted to drink. Where was Ray?

_____

_____

Cindy awoke with pleasure, remembering where she was. She hurried to dress so that she could help feed the chickens and watch her uncle milk the cows. Then she would go down to the field, catch Ginger, and take a ride through the woods. Where was Cindy?

_____

_____

Hold a whole-class discussion in which representatives from each small group share their groups' answers.

it in class activities. They may rewrite sentences to include newly learned idioms or replace these idioms with more literal language. Deaton (1992) found that doing writing that makes use of idioms can help students better understand the meanings. Illustrating idioms is another helpful activity. Students can also listen for idioms in class discussion or try using them. Creative writing about possible origins of idioms may elicit interest in discovering their real origins (Bromley, 1984).

One of the best ways to teach figurative language, as well as all interpretive reading strategies and skills, is through think-alouds. The following Focus on Strategies includes excerpts from a think-aloud used by a primary-grade

FOCUS ON STRATEGIES   Figurative Language Instruction

Evelyn Forbes was reading aloud from the story "The Big Green Umbrella" by Elizabeth Coatsworth while the students followed along in their books. As she read the paragraph of text that said that "the umbrella seemed to grow tired of keeping the rain off the Thomases on rainy days and standing in the dark corner. … It had heard the talk of the winds … whispering of raindrops, which had seen all the world. … the umbrella acted," she stopped and inserted her thoughts about the text. "Wind can't really talk, and raindrops can't whisper," she mused. "Umbrellas can't grow tired, hear, or act. People do. Why is the author making the umbrella have the characteristics of a person?" At this point she paused and discussed personification with the students, connecting it to previous reading they had done. After the discussion, she drew the accompanying diagram on the board and had the children tell what characteristics given to the umbrella were characteristics of a person. She wrote these characteristics on the raindrops falling from the umbrella.

Reading further, Mrs. Forbes came to the statement that "it soared upward like a kite" and "turned head-over-heels like a child at play." She repeated the similes and said, "These words paint a picture in my head of kites flying in a blue sky while children turn somersaults in the grass. What pictures are in your heads?" Then she called the children's attention to the use of *like* to compare the umbrella with things that she knew about that she could picture.

Later in the paragraph, the umbrella was said to be "dancing and bowing above the river," and the children were able to apply their knowledge of personification once more. Mrs. Forbes stopped reading after a few more paragraphs in which the story characters speculated about the plight of the umbrella. She said, "Mr. Thomas is wrong about the umbrella. What do you think is going to happen?" The students' predictions ended the lesson for that day, leaving them eager for reading time the next day, when they would discover whether or not their predictions were right.

classroom teacher in which she emphasized the figurative language in the selection. It shows how she followed up the think-aloud to focus attention specifically on personification.

More extensive coverage of figurative expressions appears in Chapter 4. That discussion identifies different types of figures of speech and offers teaching suggestions.

● Critical Reading

Critical reading is evaluating written material—comparing the ideas discovered in the material with known standards and drawing conclusions about their accuracy, appropriateness, and timeliness. The critical reader must be an active reader, questioning, searching for facts, and suspending judgment until he or she has considered all the material. Critical reading depends on both literal and interpretive comprehension; grasping implied ideas is especially important.

People must read critically to make intelligent decisions based on the material they read, such as which political candidate to vote for, which products to buy, which movies to attend, which charitable organizations to support, which television programs to watch, and so on. Since children face many of these decisions early in life, they should receive early instruction in critical reading.

Teachers can begin promoting critical reading in the first grade, or even kindergarten, by encouraging critical thinking. When reading a story to the class, they can ask, "Do you think this story is real or make-believe? Why do you think so?" If the children have difficulty in answering, questions such as the following can be helpful: "Could the things in this story really have happened? Do you know of any children who can fly? Have you ever heard of any real children who can fly? Have you ever heard of anyone who stayed the same age all of the time? Do all people grow up after enough years have passed?" By asking "Can animals really talk? Have you ever heard an animal talk?" teachers can help children understand how to judge the reality or fantasy in a story.

Critical thinking can also be promoted at an early stage through critical reading of pictures. If children are shown pictures that contain inaccuracies (for example, a car with a square wheel), they can identify the mistakes. Children's magazines often contain activities of this type, and illustrators of books often inadvertently include incorrect content. After the children have read (or have been read) a story containing such a picture, ask them to identify what is wrong in the picture, based on information in the story.

Critical listening instruction and critical reading instruction are appropriate for readers at all levels of proficiency. Such instruction has been effective with students in grades one through six, regardless of whether or not they have already mastered basic decoding skills, and instruction in critical listening has been shown to improve critical reading and general reading comprehension for low-performing readers in grades four through six (Boodt, 1984).

Critical reading is closely related to revision in writing. Both activities require critical thinking. Students must evaluate their own writing to improve it, just as they evaluate the writing of others as they read.

Group thinking conferences can help students become better critical readers and writers. In these small-group conferences, students read their own written materials aloud. After a piece has been read, the teacher motivates discussion by asking what the piece was about, what the students liked about it, and what questions or suggestions the students might have for the author. The students revise their own pieces after the group conferences. The same type of conference can be held about a published text by a professional author. This process gives student writers insight into what readers expect of writers. If students fail to respond in ways that alert their classmates to missing or inappropriate aspects of the written pieces, the teacher can ask questions aimed at helping them make these discoveries (Fitzgerald, 1989).

As Robertson and Rane-Szostak (1996) have done with older students, middle-school teachers can use short written dialogues between two people who have different positions on an issue being discussed to help students develop critical thinking skills. The students, in collaborative learning groups, can be asked to evaluate the dialogues by identifying each person's viewpoint, biases in the presentations, evidence for positions, evidence that was excluded, misstated facts, and mistaken reasoning. The groups then can choose the most reasonable position. Each group can act out its dialogue and explain its decision. The other class members can then add to the analysis.

Critical literacy instruction is sometimes avoided because it addresses issues that are controversial and potentially disturbing. Foss (2002, p. 402) said of her work with eighth graders that "although our critical conversations make students uncomfortable and push them to think more deeply, those discussions tend to be the ones students remember the most." Teachers, as well as students, may find these discussions uncomfortable, but ultimately valuable, educational experiences.

To foster critical reading skills in the classroom, teachers can encourage pupils to read with a questioning attitude and can lead them to ask questions such as the following when they are reading nonfiction.

1. Why did the author write this material?

2. Does the author know what he or she is writing about? Is he or she likely to be biased? Why or why not?

3. Is the material up to date?

4. Is the author approaching the material logically or emotionally? What emotional words does he or she use?

5. Is the author employing any undesirable propaganda techniques? If so, which ones? How does he or she use them? (Several propaganda techniques are described later in this chapter.)

Fiction can also be read critically, but the questions that apply are a little different.

1. Could this story really have happened?

2. Are the characters believable within the setting furnished by the story? Are they consistent in their actions?

3. Is the dialogue realistic?

❹ Did the plot hold your interest? What was it that kept your interest?

❺ Was the ending reasonable or believable? Why or why not?

❻ Was the title well chosen? Why or why not?

Groups may be used for discussion of the reading material, whether all of the children have read the same selection or some of them have read different selections on a common topic or from a common genre. The children compose questions to be discussed by the group, and the group decides about which questions to consider. When questions have been selected, the children prepare for the group meeting by reading and/or rereading material to answer the questions, taking notes about their findings, and marking (with strips of paper or sticky notes) passages in the book that support their answers. The group discussions that ensue are just that: children discuss without holding up their hands for a turn or being called on. They respond to the comments and questions of the other group members (Reardon, 1988). In this activity, analysis of the material is meaningful to the students. They decide what is significant in the material, and they relate the material to matters of importance to them—for example, how the author's use of language affects the story.

LITERATURE 📖 ## Critical Reading of Literature

Many excellent books for children are filled with themes of honesty and dishonesty, Msharing and selfishness, courage and cowardice, and others. Discussion of these themes in the context of the stories' characters, with consideration of alternatives available to them and of the appropriateness or inappropriateness of their actions, can build skill in critical reading (McMillan and Gentile, 1988). The students can be asked to compare the actions of the characters to standards of behavior set by the law, the school, parents, and so forth.

Resnick (1987) points out that "[h]igher order thinking often yields multiple solutions, each with costs and benefits, rather than unique solutions" and that "[h]igher order thinking involves imposing meaning, finding structure in apparent disorder" (p. 3). Literature analysis can help students become skillful in performing these tasks. One critical reading activity is to have children evaluate the evidence that Chicken Little had that the sky was falling and decide whether or not the other animals were right to just take her word for it. They can also be asked if the Little Red Hen used good strategies to elicit help from the other animals and what else she might have done (Beck, 1989).

Critical thinking is often important to the interpretation of humor (Whitmer, 1986). Therefore, humorous literature can be an enjoyable vehicle for teaching critical reading skills. It is especially good for determining the author's purpose (often to entertain, but sometimes also to convince through humor) and for evaluating content (especially distinguishing fact from fantasy and recognizing assumptions).

To analyze characterization in literature selections, students must be able to make inferences about characters. Norton (1992a) believes that teachers need to model the process of making inferences about characters for the students. They can read examples from a text, pause and verbalize a question that requires an inference, and answer the question, using supporting data from the text and making their reasoning process clear to the students. They can tell how their prior knowledge and beliefs affected the answer. Then students can be asked to attempt these same steps. Norton suggests the book *Shiloh* (Naylor, 1991) as a good one for helping students learn to make inferences about characters.

Norton (1992a, p. 65) says that students must understand that making inferences involves going beyond the information stated in the text and that "they must use clues from the text to hypothesize about a character's emotions, beliefs, actions, hopes, and fears. Students must also be aware that authors develop characters through dialogue, narration, thoughts, and actions." This activity leads directly into character analysis. Clyde (2003) uses a "subtext strategy" in which students both act out stories and imagine as they speak the characters' lines what these characters were thinking at the time. Teacher modeling preceded the activity, and the children learned to take the perspective of different characters.

Commeyras (1989) suggests the use of literature selections and a grid developed by Ashby-Davis (1986) to help students learn about character analysis. Example 6.2 on page 240 shows a completed grid based on the character of Tom Sawyer. Such a grid leads students to collect evidence about a character, interpret the evidence, and make a generalization about the evidence after all of it has been collected. Looking for commonalities and discrepancies in the data and considering the amount of evidence available for a conclusion drawn are important to good critical analysis. When readers draw evidence from the reactions of other characters in the story, they must evaluate the credibility of the sources before accepting that evidence.

DIVERSITY Careful questioning by the teacher to extend limited and stereotyped depictions of people in reading materials can help children develop expertise in critical reading. Children must be encouraged to relate their personal experiences to the materials. Children can examine stereotyped language in relation to stories in which it occurs, and teachers can point out the problems caused by looking at people and ideas in a stereotyped way (Zimet, 1983). For example, some books give the impression that certain nationalities have particular personality characteristics, but it should be easy to demonstrate that not all people of that nationality are alike, just as not all Americans are alike. Multicultural literature can be a vehicle through which teachers can create awareness of cultural variations and of negative biases that exist toward some groups, allowing progress to be made toward elimination of these biases (Barta and Grindler, 1996).

DIVERSITY Santino (1991) suggests having students compare different versions of folktales by constructing Venn diagrams and comparison charts. Such activities can improve comprehension and show commonalities in stories from different cultures. Example 6.3 on page 241 shows a comparison of a Russian folktale with an Appalachian one.

TECHNOLOGY Teachers can also encourage students to think critically by having them compare film versions of stories with the text versions. Analysis of the dramatic interpretation of a story can also provide students with a model of creative response to the narrative (Duncan, 1993). (Creative responses are discussed in more detail later in this chapter. See Chapter 11 for a Classroom Scenario involving comparisons of text and film versions of stories.)

EXAMPLE 6.2   Sample Grid on Tom Sawyer

	External clues	Student's interpretation

(1) Frequent kinds of statements made by this character

A. Fibs   A. Tom gets his way.

B. Commands   B. Tom is confident.

My summary of these interpretations of statements:

Tom is bold and daring.

(2) Frequent actions of the character

A. Mischievous   A. Tom likes to fool around.

B. Heroic   B. Tom isn't afraid.

My summary of these interpretations of actions:

Tom's good deeds are more important than his misbehavior.

(3) Frequent ways of thinking by this character:

A. He schemes.   A. Tom finds solutions.

B. He's optimistic.   B. Tom has confidence.

My summary of these interpretations of thought:

Tom is smart.

(4) What do others frequently say to the character:

A. What have you done?   A. Tom is unpredictable.

B. This is fun!   B. Tom has good ideas.

Summary of my interpretations of these statements:

Tom is independent in his actions.

(5) What do others do to this character:

A. They get mad at him.   A. Tom upsets people.

B. They follow his lead.   B. Tom gets respect.

Summary of my interpretation:

Tom gets to people one way or another.

(6) What do others say about the character:

A. He's stubborn.   A. Tom doesn't give up.

B. He's brave.   B. Tom helps others.

Summary of my interpretation:

Tom isn't all good or all bad.

My final generalization concerning the personality of Tom Sawyer:

Tom Sawyer is a boy who gets into trouble,
but ends up doing the right thing in the end.

Source: Michelle Commeyras, "Using Literature to Teach Critical Thinking," *Journal of Reading,* 32 (8) (May 1989), 703–707. Reprinted with permission of the International Reading Association and the author.

EXAMPLE 6.3   Comparison of Folktales

Comparison of Two Stories

	Hardy Hardhead	Fool of the World and the Flying Ship
QUEST	To break enchantment and marry King's daughter	To provide flying ship to Czar and marry Czar's daughter
CHARACTERS	Two older brothers (Tom & Will) favored by parents	Two older brothers favored by parents
	Younger brother (Jack) – thought to be foolish	Younger brother – Fool of the World
	Old Man ⟨ Tom and Will didn't share / Jack shared food / Gave Jack a flying ship and money (Take in everyone)	Old man ⟨ Fool shared food / Showed Fool how to get flying ship (Take in everyone)
	[1]Hardy Hardhead [2]Eatwell [3]Drinkwell [4]Runwell [5]Harkwell	[4]Man with bread [5]Man walking around lake [3]Man on one leg (other tied to head) [1]Man listening to all that is being done in the world
	[6]Seewell [7]Shootwell	[2]Man with gun [6]Man with wood on shoulders [7]Man with sack of straw
ACTION	Each person Jack picked up helped Jack win a bet with the witch.	Each person the Fool picked up helped him perform a seemingly impossible task for the Czar.
RESOLUTION	Jack paid back old man and kept ship. Enchantment on King's girl was broken.	Fool married princess. They fell in love with each other.

Note: The numbers beside the character names indicate the order in which the characters appear in the respective stories.

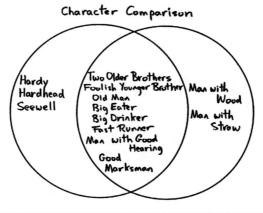

If the children have adequate schemata for understanding the text, it is better to have them read the text before seeing the film. Sometimes the children may be exposed to the story on film, but only a portion of the text version may be used in instruction. Then some students may be motivated to finish the text on their own. Most film versions are necessarily abbreviated versions. However, seeing an abbreviated presentation of a story that provides a knowledge of its basic structure may offer needed support for struggling readers, giving them the confidence to attempt to read the text (Duncan, 1993).

Students can use Venn diagrams to show how characters were alike and different in film and text versions of stories. They can also write film reviews, including notes about how true the film was to the book. *Sarah, Plain and Tall; Where the Red Fern Grows; The Secret Garden; Bridge to Terabithia; Tuck Everlasting;* and *Holes* are books that have film versions available for comparison.

Evaluating Factors Related to the Author

Krieger (1990) found that middle-school students were not aware of the authors of the material they read and the devices the authors used (flashbacks, foreshadowing, and so forth) for special purposes. She read to these students, modeling as she read her thinking processes concerning why the author included certain details. She asked them to make predictions about what might happen next from clues left by the author. Outside assignments based on the material allowed for further thinking about the story or the author; students might be asked to keep listening journals with reactions to the stories, for example. Through this listening experience, Krieger opens the students' minds to the ways that authors express ideas, making it more likely that they will be able to read stories with understanding later.

A critical literacy curriculum emphasizes discussion, both aloud and mental. "Students involved in a critical literacy curriculum read the world and the word, by using dialogue to engage texts and discourses inside and outside the classroom" (Cadiero-Kaplan, 2002, p. 377). Students who take this approach to reading history, for example, see it "as a record told from one perspective that can be examined from other perspectives" (p. 378). Acknowledging the bias that may be present in a particular point of view enables students to draw more valid conclusions from reading than they would if they accepted everything that is in print as true.

McKeown, Beck, and Worthy (1993) have developed a technique called Questioning the Author to help children access ideas in a text. They point out that someone wrote the ideas in the text and that some people do not write as clearly as others. Students are invited to figure out the ideas behind the author's words, to determine the author's reasons for presenting the particular information, and to decide whether the author has presented the ideas clearly. Then students are asked to state confusing material in a clearer way. Teachers should model this process for students before asking them to do it independently.

The mature critical reader must consider and evaluate factors related to the person who wrote the material, taking into account the following four categories.

Author's Purpose.   The critical reader will try to determine whether the author wrote the material to inform, to entertain, to persuade, or for some other purpose. This is an interpretive reading skill.

Author's Point of View.   The critical reader will want to know whether the writer belonged to a group, lived in an area, or held a strong view that would tend to bias any of her or his opinions about a subject in one way or another. Two accounts of the Revolutionary War might be very different if one author was from Canada and the other was from the United States.

Students can learn more about point of view by writing letters or essays about issues from different points of view. For example, they might imagine that a school dress code is being considered and take the point of view of an elementary school student, then that of a concerned parent, and finally that of a school principal.

Author's Style and Tone.   The author's style is the manner in which he or she uses vocabulary (vividness, precision, inclusion of emotional words, use of figurative language) and sentence structure (the order in which the elements of the sentence appear). Special attention should be given to use of figurative language, language that is not meant to be taken literally, and to the use of emotional words, which do much to sway the reader toward or away from a point of view or attitude. Note the effects of these two sentences:

Author 1: Next we heard the heart-rending cry of the wounded tiger.

Author 2: When the tiger was shot, it let out a vicious roar.

(More information on figurative language is found in Chapter 4.)

Teachers should be aware of undesirable aspects of the style or tone of some writers of material for children. A condescending tone, for example, is quickly sensed and resented.

Author's Competence.   The reliability of written material is affected by the author's competence to write about the subject in question. If background information shows that a star football player has written an article on the nation's foreign policy, intermediate-grade youngsters will have little trouble determining that the reliability of the statements in this article is likely to be lower than the reliability of a similar article written by an experienced diplomat.

To determine an author's competence, students should consider his or her education and experience, referring to books such as *Current Biography Yearbook: 2002* (H. W. Wilson, 2002) and *Eighth Book of Junior Authors and Illustrators* (H. W. Wilson, 2000) or to book jacket flaps to find this information. Teachers can give students a topic and ask them to name people who might write about it. Students can discuss which people might be most qualified, or they can compare two authors of books on the same subject and decide which one is better qualified.

TECHNOLOGY 🖥   In these days of heavy use of Internet sites, determining the competence of authors is made more difficult. Students should be taught to be wary of material posted on the Internet by unknown authors or on sites that do not screen the material and provide information about the authors.

Evaluating the Material

Besides comprehending the material literally, the critical reader needs to be able to determine and evaluate the following factors.

Timeliness. The critical reader will wish to check the date the material was published, because the timeliness of an article or a book can make a crucial difference in a rapidly changing world. An outdated social studies book, for example, may show incorrect boundaries for countries or fail to show some countries that now exist; similarly, an outdated science book may refer to a disease as incurable when a cure has recently been found.

Accuracy and Adequacy. Nonfiction material should be approached with this question in mind: "Are the statements presented here true?" The importance of a good background of experience becomes evident in this situation. A reader who has had previous experience with the material will have a basis of comparison not available to a reader who lacks this experience. A person with even a little knowledge of a particular field can often spot such indications of inadequacy as exaggerated statements, one-sided presentations, and opinion offered as fact. Readers without experience in the subject can always check reference books to see if the statements in the material are supported elsewhere.

TECHNOLOGY Material found on the Internet poses a problem. As Owens, Hester, and Teale (2002, p. 623) point out, "Just because a site is listed in the first set of hits that appear on the search screen does not mean it is a legitimate or useful site." In some cases, companies or organizations pay to ensure that their site turns up at or near the top of specific searches. Students need to be led to see the potential biases that might be associated with such sites. Double-checking information in other reference materials is highly advisable when material from Internet sites is used. Brainstorming about the biases that are most likely to appear on specific sites is a good classroom activity.

Appropriateness. Critical readers must be able to determine whether the material is suitable for their purposes. A book or an article can be completely accurate and yet not be applicable to the problem or topic under consideration. For example, a child looking for information for a paper entitled "Cherokee Ceremonies" needs to realize that an article on the invention of the Cherokee alphabet is irrelevant to the task at hand.

Inquiry Charts can be constructed in order to promote the use of critical reading strategies (Hoffman, 1992). First, the class identifies a topic and formulates the questions that will be the basis of the inquiry. The teacher records these on a large I-Chart (see Example 6.4 for a sample I-Chart). Materials, such as textbook selections, trade books, encyclopedia articles, magazine articles, and websites that pertain to the topic are also collected and listed on the I-Chart as they are used.

Next, the teacher questions the students to discover their prior knowledge about the topic and enters their responses, whether correct or incorrect, on the I-Chart under the identified questions. Information the students have that is not related to the identified questions is recorded under "Other Interesting Facts and Figures." If students have other questions that were not initially identified, these are listed under

EXAMPLE 6.4   I-Chart

I - CHART

GUIDING QUESTIONS

TOPIC: Columbus	1. Why did Columbus sail?	2. What did he find?	3. What important things did he do when he got there?	4. How was Columbus regarded by others?	Other Interesting Facts & Figures	New Questions
WHAT WE KNOW	to prove the world was round	America	... not sure	He was a hero	He sailed in 1492. He was Spanish	Did he have a family?
1. *Meet Christopher Columbus,* de Kay. New York; Random House, 1989	He was trying to find a new route to the Indies	He found friendly Indians... some pieces of gold... different islands. He found America	He named the islands. He claimed the land for Queen Isabella and King Ferdinand. He brought back gold for Isabella	At the beginning people regarded him as a normal person. Later, when he got back, they thought he was a great man.	C.C. had asked the King of Portugal for ships. He was turned down. When he came back he landed in Portugal and was taken to the King. The King was mad that he didn't help him.	Whatever happened to his son?
2. *The World Book Encyclopedia.* World Book Childcraft, Inc. 1979	to find riches... and a shorter route to the Indies. He wanted to be famous.... to be known as a great sailor and explorer.	He found America. Indians... new islands.	He named the islands. He captured some Indians as slaves. He became the governor.	He was an "understanding... dreamy" person. It sounds like he had a lot of friends	In other books I've read he wasn't very popular. He had 2 sons, not 1... Six brothers and a sister. He was born in Italy.	Whatever happened to his sons?
3. *Where do You Think You're Going Christopher Columbus?* Jean Fritz. New York; G.P. Putnam's Sons, 1980	Because he liked to travel and explore they said they would give a big reward for finding a new route to the Indies	He found Indians... Some small hunks of gold	He talked to the Indians. He asked for directions to the Palace of the Khan. He named the islands	Before he went he was wealthy because he had married a rich woman. He was famous after he sailed, but a couple of years later, everyone forgot about him.	Columbus sounded greedy in this book. He said he saw land first and claimed the prize money. He claimed that all of this was God's work.	Was he really cruel to the Indians? Whatever happened to the slaves he brought back to Spain?
SUMMARY	To find a new route to the Indies... He hoped to find riches and become famous as an explorer. He already knew the world was round.	He found America and the Indians living there. He found a little gold.	He claimed the new land for Spain. He named the islands. He met with the Indians. He took some back to Spain as slaves. He became Governor.	Before he sailed he was normal... a dreamer. After he came back he was famous and a hero. He seemed greedy. Everyone forgot about him after a while.	He claimed he was doing God's work. His family supported him. He tried to get money for his voyage from lots of people. He was born an Italian.	Find out more about his family and what happened to them. Was he cruel to the Indians? What happened to the slaves?

Source: James V. Hoffman, "Critical Reading/Thinking Across the Curriculum: Using I-Charts to Support Learning," *Language Arts,* February 1992. Copyright 1992 by the National Council of Teachers of English. Reprinted with permission.

"New Questions." Then the students read the source material independently or in a group, or the teacher reads it to them. Each source is discussed, and decisions are made about the appropriateness of the information in answering the identified questions. Information pertinent to the questions is recorded in the proper spaces. More "Interesting Facts" and "New Questions" may also be added.

After all sources have been read and information from them recorded, the students write summary statements to answer each question, considering the information from all of the sources. They also summarize the "Interesting Facts."

Then the students compare what they had listed as prior knowledge with the newly acquired information and note the differences, clarifying any misconceptions that they previously held. Unanswered "New Questions" are researched further by individuals or small groups, who must decide about appropriate sources for the information, and findings are reported to the class.

Differentiation of Fact from Opinion. This skill is vital for good critical reading. People often unquestioningly accept as fact anything they see in print, even though printed material is frequently composed of statements of opinion. Some authors intermingle facts and opinions, giving little indication that they are presenting anything but pure fact.

Some readers have trouble reading critically because they lack a clear idea of what constitutes a fact. Facts are statements that can be verified through direct observation, consultation of official records of past events, or scientific experimentation. The statement "General Lee surrendered to General Grant at Appomattox" is a fact that can be verified by checking historical records. For various reasons, opinions cannot be directly verified. For example, the statement "She is the most beautiful girl in the world" is unverifiable and is therefore an opinion. Even if all the girls in the world could be assembled for comparison, people's standards of beauty differ and a scale of relative beauty would be impossible to construct.

Many readers are not alert to clues that signal opinions. Knowledge of key words that signal opinions, such as *believe, think, seems, may, appears, probably, likely,* and *possibly,* can be extremely helpful to readers. By pointing out these clues and providing practice in discrimination, teachers can help students develop the ability to discriminate between facts and opinions.

Children must also understand that not all opinions are of equal value, since some have been based on facts, whereas others are unsupported. Critical readers try to determine the relative merit of opinions as well as to separate the opinions from the facts.

Newspaper editorials offer one good way for children to practice distinguishing fact from opinion, especially in the intermediate grades. Students can underline each sentence in the editorial with colored pencils, one color for facts and another for opinions. They can then be encouraged to discuss which opinions are best supported by facts.

Furleigh (1991) has students read and analyze an editorial for the subject or main idea, the writer's opinion about the subject, and their own opinions about the subject. The teacher or peers then evaluate the answers that each student provides. When peers do the evaluations, the evaluations offer them additional practice.

Activities similar to the Model Activity on page 247 may also be used to help children make this difficult differentiation.

Recognition of Propaganda Techniques. Elementary school children, like adults, are constantly deluged with writing that attempts to influence their thinking and actions. Some of these materials may be used for good purposes and some for bad ones. For example, most people would consider propaganda designed to persuade people to protect their health as "good" and propaganda intended to persuade people to do things that are harmful to their health as "bad." Since propaganda techniques

MODEL
ACTIVITIES **Fact and Opinion**

Give the students copies of the following paragraph, which opens the book *Homesick: My Own Story* by Jean Fritz (Dell, 1982, p. 9).

In my father's study there was a large globe with all the countries of the world running around it. I could put my finger on the exact spot where I was and had been ever since I'd been born. And I was on the wrong side of the globe. I was in China in a city named Hankow, a dot on a crooked line that seemed to break the country right in two. The line was really the Yangtse River, but who would know by looking at a map what the Yangtse River really was?

Ask students to read this opening paragraph carefully, underlining any parts that are statements of opinion, based on the definition of opinion that was discussed in class. Ask them to decide what they can tell about the main character from both the facts and the opinions revealed in this opening paragraph. Then have them decide how the opinion or opinions that they have located are likely to affect the story they are about to read.

Let the students share their reactions to this opening passage before they begin to read the book. After they have finished reading the book, have them discuss whether or not their initial reactions were accurate.

---

are often used to sway people toward or away from a cause or point of view, children should be made aware of these techniques so that they can avoid being unduly influenced by them.

The Institute for Propaganda Awareness has identified seven undesirable ***propaganda techniques*** that good critical readers should know about:

❶ Name calling—using derogatory labels (*reactionary, troublemaker*) to create negative reactions toward a person without providing evidence to support such impressions.

❷ Glittering generalities — using vague phrases to influence a point of view without providing necessary specifics.

❸ Transfer technique—associating a respected organization or symbol with a particular person, project, product, or idea, thus transferring that respect to the person or thing being promoted.

❹ Plain-folks talk—relating a person (for example, a politician) or a proposed program to the "common people" in order to gain their support.

❺ Testimonial technique — using a highly popular or respected person to endorse a product or proposal.

❻ Bandwagon technique—playing on the urge to do what others are doing by giving the impression that everyone else is participating in a particular activity.

❼ Card stacking—telling only one side of a story by ignoring information that favors the opposing point of view.

Teachers should describe propaganda techniques to the class and model the process of locating these techniques in printed materials such as advertisements. Then the children should practice this skill. Children can learn to detect propaganda techniques by analyzing newspaper and magazine advertisements, printed political campaign material, and requests for donations to various organizations.

LITERATURE   *Making Value Judgments.*   Readers need to be able to determine whether the actions of both fictional and real-life characters are reasonable or unreasonable. To help children develop this ability, teachers may ask questions such as the following:

> Was the Little Red Hen justified in eating all the bread she made, refusing to share with the other animals? Why or why not?
>
> Was it a good thing for Heidi to save bread from the Sessmans' table to take back to the grandmother? Why or why not?

Readers draw on their schemata related to right and wrong actions in order to complete this type of activity. Because of their varying schemata, not all children will answer in the same way.

Activities like the following ones can be used to provide children with practice in critical reading strategies.

ACTIVITIES

1. Have a propaganda hunt. Label boxes with the names of the seven propaganda techniques listed earlier. Then ask children to find examples of these techniques in a variety of sources and to drop their examples into the boxes. As a class activity, evaluate each example for appropriateness to the category in which it was placed.

2. Have students compare editorials from two newspapers with different viewpoints or from different areas. Have them decide why differences exist and which stand, if either, is more reasonable, based on facts.

3. Ask students to compare two biographies of a well-known person by answering questions such as "How do they differ in their treatment of the subject? Is either of the authors likely to be biased for or against the subject? Are there contradictory statements in the two works? If so, which one seems most likely to be correct? Could the truth be different from both accounts?"

TECHNOLOGY   4. Use computer simulation programs for practice in making critical judgments. These programs provide simulated models of real-life experiences with which students can experiment in a risk-free manner.

5. Ask students to examine newspaper articles for typographical errors and to determine whether or not each typographical error changed the message of the article.

6. Have the class interpret political cartoons from various newspapers.

7. Ask students to examine the headlines of news stories and decide whether or not the headlines fit the stories.

8. Ask students to write editorials about topics of interest. Their editorials should include facts, their own opinions, and their reasons for holding these opinions.

9. Locate old science or geography books containing statements that are no longer true, and use them to show the importance of using current sources. Let students compare old and new books to find the differences (new material included, "facts" that have changed, etc.), and discuss which types of material are most likely, and which least likely, to be dependent on recent copyright dates for accuracy (Ross, 1981).

10. Direct students to write material that will persuade their classmates to do something. Then examine the material for the techniques they used.

11. Discuss the nutritional aspects of sugar and chemical food additives and the foods that contain them. Then have students examine the ingredients lists from popular snacks, asking themselves what food value various snacks have, according to their labels (Neville, 1982).

● Creative Reading

Creative reading involves going beyond the material presented by the author. Like critical reading, creative reading requires readers to think as they read, and it also requires them to use their imaginations. Such reading results in the production of new ideas.

Teachers must carefully nurture creative reading, trying not to ask only questions that have absolute answers, since such questions may discourage the diverse processes characteristic of creative reading. To go beyond the material in the text, readers must make use of their background schemata, combining this prior knowledge with ideas from the text to produce a new response based on, but not completely dictated by, the text. Creative readers must be skilled in predicting outcomes, visualizing the things they read about, solving problems, and producing their own creations.

Predicting Outcomes

Predicting outcomes, discussed earlier as a good purpose-setting technique, is a creative reading skill. In order to predict outcomes, readers must put together available information, note trends, and then project these trends into the future, making decisions about what events might logically follow. A creative reader is constantly predicting what will happen next in a story, reacting to the events he or she is reading about, and drawing conclusions about their results.

An enjoyable way to work on this skill is to have students read one of the action comic strips in the newspaper for several weeks and then predict what will happen next, on the basis of their knowledge of what has occurred previously. The teacher can record these predictions on paper and file them; later, students can compare the actual ending of the adventure with their predictions. The teacher should be sure students can present reasons to justify what they predict. When judging their theories, the teacher should point out that some predictions may seem to be as good a way to end the story as the one the comic strip artist used. Other predictions may *not* make sense, given the evidence, and the reasons for this should be made clear.

LITERATURE 📖   Another way to work on prediction is to stop students at particular points in their reading of a literature selection and let them predict what will happen next. In the story "Stone Soup," for example, the teacher would stop before the first townsperson contributed food to the soup and ask what the students think will happen next. A similar pause and request for a prediction after the point in the story at which the first contribution was made to the soup would then be appropriate.

To help students acquire the skill of reading creatively, teachers should model the thought process involved. After the students practice on various texts, the teacher can ask them to explain their reasons for thinking as they did. Some questions they might answer for *Heidi*, for example, are as follows:

> What would have happened in the book if Peter had not pushed Klara's wheelchair down the side of the mountain?
>
> What would have happened if Herr Sessman had refused to send Heidi back to the Alm, even though the doctor advised it?

Visualization

Visualization is seeing pictures in the mind, and readers draw on their existing schemata to accomplish this. By vividly visualizing the events depicted by the author's words, creative readers allow themselves to become a part of the story; they see the colors, hear the sounds, feel the textures, taste the flavors, and smell the odors the writer describes. They will find that they are living the story as they read. By doing this, they will enjoy the story more and understand it more deeply.

Students can be encouraged to see pictures in their minds as they read silently, although training in visualization may be less effective with very young children, who may not be able to form images on command, than with third- through sixth-grade students (Tierney and Cunningham, 1984). Such *guided imagery* has been shown to enhance comprehension and can help with later recall of the events the student has read about. Guided imagery can be used before reading, as well as during or after reading. Guided-imagery activities before reading a story can help readers draw on their past experiences to visualize events, places, and things in a story. Creating such images before reading has been shown to result in better literal comprehension than is produced by creating the images after reading (Harp, 1988; Fredericks, 1986).

Dee Mundell suggests four steps for helping children develop techniques for visualization. First, teachers should lead students to visualize concrete objects after they have seen and closely examined them in the classroom. Then teachers can ask children to visualize objects or experiences outside the classroom. They can draw the objects they visualize and later compare their drawings to the actual objects. Next, teachers can read high-imagery stories to the children, letting individuals share their mental images with the group and having small groups illustrate the stories after the reading. Finally, teachers should encourage students to visualize as they read independently (Fredericks, 1986).

Open-ended questions can aid development of imagery. For example, if a child says she sees a house, the teacher can ask, "What does it look like?" If she replies that it is white with green trim, the teacher may ask, "What is the yard like?"

Following are activities that encourage visualization.

ACTIVITIES

1. Give students copies of a paragraph from a children's book that vividly describes a scene or a situation, and have them illustrate the scene or situation in a painting or a three-dimensional art project.

2. Using a paragraph or statement that contains almost no description, ask students questions about details they would need in order to picture the scene in their minds. An example follows.

    The dog ran toward Jane and Susan. Jane held out her hands toward it and smiled.

    Questions: What kind of dog was it? How big was it? Why was it running toward the girls? What happened when the dog reached the girls? Where did this action take place? Was the dog on a leash, behind a fence, or running free?

LITERATURE

3. Have the children dramatize a story they have read, such as the folktale "Caps for Sale."

TECHNOLOGY

4. Compare the characters, action, and scenery in a movie with mental images formed from reading a book or story.

Solving Problems

LITERATURE Creative readers relate the things they read to their own personal problems, sometimes applying the solution of a problem they encounter in a story to a different situation. For instance, after reading the chapter in *Tom Sawyer* in which Tom tricks his friends into painting a fence for him, a child may use a similar ruse to persuade a sibling to take over his or her chores or homework.

To work on developing this problem-solving skill, teachers need to use books in which different types of problems are solved, choosing an appropriate one to read or to let the children read. Then the teacher can ask the children questions such as the following:

❶ What problem did the character(s) in the story face?

❷ How was the problem handled?

❸ Was the solution a good one?

❹ What other possible solutions can you think of?

❺ Would you prefer the solution in the book or one of the others?

Literature selections abound with characters trying to solve problems in efficient and inefficient ways. Children can analyze these problem-solving situations. Problems in a story can be identified as they occur. Discussion of the situation can take place as each problem arises. Some element of the story can be changed, and the children can then be asked how the character would have handled the new situation (Beck, 1989). *Encyclopedia Brown* and *Nate the Great* mysteries offer good problem-solving opportunities for children in intermediate and primary grades, respectively (Flynn, 1989). Any of the *Amelia Bedelia* books would also work well for this activity.

Bransford and Stein's IDEAL approach to problem solving is good to use in conjunction with cooperative learning techniques (Bransford and Stein, 1984; Flynn, 1989). The *I* stands for *identifying* the problem, the *D* for *defining* the problem more clearly, the *E* for *exploration* of the problem, the *A* for *acting* on ideas, and the *L* for *looking* for the effects. Cooperative learning techniques encourage the development of problem-solving skills through discussion, negotiation, clarification of ideas, and evaluation of the ideas of classmates. These activities help students meet their group and individual goals.

TIME for REFLECTION

Some teachers believe that only literal-level thinking should be expected of young children when these children read. Others believe that the children can and should do higher-order thinking about their reading. **What do *you* think, and why?**

Producing New Creations

Art, drama, and dance can be useful in elaborating on what students read. By creating a new ending for a story, adding a new character, changing some aspect of a character, or inserting an additional adventure within the framework of the existing story, students approach reading creatively. Following are some possible activities; some of them involve responding to literature through writing. (More on the reading-writing connection appears in Chapter 8.)

1. Ask the students to illustrate a story they have read, using a series of pictures or three-dimensional scenes.

2. Have the students write plays or poems based on works of fiction they have read and enjoyed.

3. Have the students write prose narratives based on a poem they have read.

4. After the children have read several stories of a certain type (such as *Just So Stories*), ask each of them to write an original story of the same type.

5. Have the students transfer the story of *Heidi* to the Rocky Mountains or to Appalachia.

Effective Questioning

STANDARDS AND
ASSESSMENT

All teachers use both written and oral questions as a part of class activities. They may ask questions as a way of setting purposes for children's reading, in discussions, or on tests and quizzes. Regardless of when they are used, questions have been found to foster increased comprehension, apparently because readers give more time to the material related to answering them (Durkin, 1981). Students also remember best information about which they have been directly questioned. Additionally, the types of questions that teachers ask about selections affect the type of information that

The types of questions that teachers ask about selections affect the type of information that students recall about selections, and students remember best information about which they have been directly questioned.
(© Joel Gordon)

students recall about selections (Wixson, 1983). Research indicates, for example, that asking more inference questions during and after the reading of stories results in improved inferential comprehension (Hansen and Pearson, 1983; Pearson, 1985). Because questions have such a strong influence on student learning, teachers need to understand thoroughly the process of preparing questions.

Farrar (1984a) notes that the phrasing of questions should depend on the amount of challenge individual children need. Questions can be phrased differently and still address the same content. The phrasing can make questions easier or harder to answer and can require simple or complex answers. It may take several questions requiring simple responses to elicit all the information obtainable from one question that requires a complex response.

Wiggins and McTighe (1998, p. 28) assert, "To get at matters of deep and enduring understanding, we need to use provocative and multilayered questions that reveal the richness and complexities of a subject. We refer to such questions as 'essential' because they point to the key inquiries and the core ideas of a discipline." Wiggins and McTighe (1998) recommend using "essential questions" as the central focus of courses, units, and lessons. They suggest that teachers use relatively few (two to five) of these questions for a unit and that they plan concrete activities and inquiries related to each one. Teachers should word essential questions in such a way that children can understand them and should develop initial assessment tasks to show whether or not students understand the question focus. In addition, teachers should present questions about a central concept in the order of simple to complex. The questions asked early in the unit should always point toward the larger essential questions, and teachers should lead the students to ask broader questions prompted by their answers to questions more narrowly cast. Wiggins and McTighe (1998, p. 35) suggest introductory questions such as "In what ways is a fairy tale 'true'? In what ways is any documentary 'false'? (Can be used to compare myths, novels, biographies, histories, and docudramas.)" Guiding a unit of study by using essential questions can also help address diversity in academic ability in a classroom, since essential questions can prompt gifted and talented students to explore the central, significant ideas of a discipline through independent learning and inquiry.

DIVERSITY

● Preparing Questions

Teachers often ask questions that are devised on the spur of the moment. This practice no doubt results from the pressure of the many different tasks a teacher must perform during the day, but it is a poor one for at least two reasons. First, questions developed hastily, without close attention to the material involved, tend to be detail

---

EXAMPLE 6.5   Options for Questioning

Questions Based on Comprehension Factors

1. Main idea—identify the central theme or idea of the selection

2. Detail—identify directly stated facts

3. Vocabulary—define words to fit the context of the selection

4. Sequence—identify the order of events in the selection

5. Inference—infer information implied by the author

6. Evaluation—judge ideas presented, on the basis of a standard

7. Creative response—go beyond the material and create new ideas based on the material read

Questions Based on Source of Answers

1. Textually explicit—answers are directly stated in the text

2. Textually implicit—answers are implied by the text that require inferences on the part of the reader

3. Scriptually implicit—answers come from the reader's background knowledge

Questions Based on Story Grammar

1. Setting—when and where the story took place and who was involved

2. Initiating event—the event that started the story sequence

3. Reaction—the main character's reaction to the initiating event

4. Action—the main character's actions caused by the initiating event and subsequent events

5. Consequence—the result of the main character's actions

questions ("What color was the car? Where were they going?"), since detail questions are much easier to construct than most other types. But detail questions fail to measure more than simple recall. Second, many hastily constructed questions tend to be poorly worded, vague in intent, and misleading to students. Example 6.5 on page 254 shows some options on which to base questioning.

Questions Based on Comprehension Factors

One basis for planning questioning strategies is to try to construct specific types of questions to tap different types of comprehension and different factors related to comprehension. Seven major types of questions are generally useful in guiding reading: main idea, detail, vocabulary, sequence, inference, evaluation, and creative response questions.

Main Idea Questions.   Main idea questions ask the children to identify the central theme of the selection. These questions may give children some direction toward the nature of the answer. The question "What caused Susie to act so excited?" could direct readers toward the main idea of a passage in which Susie was very excited because she had a secret. An example of a question that offers no clues to the main idea is "What is a sentence that explains what this selection is about?" Main idea questions help children to become aware of the relationships among details.

Detail Questions.   Detail questions ask for bits of information covered by the material, such as "Who was coming to play with Maria? What was Betty bringing with her? What happened to Betty on the way to Maria's house? When did Betty finally arrive? Where had Betty left her bicycle?" Although it is important for students to assimilate the information these questions cover, very little depth of comprehension is necessary to answer them all correctly. Therefore, even though these questions are easy to construct, they should not constitute the bulk of the questions the teacher asks.

Vocabulary Questions.   Vocabulary questions check children's understanding of word meanings, generally as used in a particular selection. For discussion purposes, a teacher might ask children to produce as many meanings of a specific word as they can, but purpose-setting questions and test questions should ask for the meaning of a word as it is used in the selection being read.

Sequence Questions.   Sequence questions check the child's knowledge of the order in which events occurred in the story. The question "What did Alex and Robbie do when their parents left the house?" is not a sequence question, since children are free to list the events in any order they choose. The question "What three things did Alex and Robbie do, in order, when their parents left the house?" requires children to display their grasp of the sequence of events.

Inference Questions.   Inference questions ask for information that is implied but not directly stated in the material. These questions require some reading between the lines. The following is an example:

Margie and Jan were sitting on the couch listening to Linkin Park CDs. Their father walked in and announced, "I hear that there is a Linkin Park concert at the Municipal Auditorium next week." Both girls jumped up and ran toward their father. "Can we go? Can we go?" they begged.

Question: Do you think Margie and Jan liked to hear the music of Linkin Park? Why or why not?

Evaluation Questions.   Evaluation questions require children to make judgments about the material. Although these judgments are inferences, they depend on more than the information implied or stated by the story; the children must have enough experience related to the situations involved to establish standards for comparison. An example of an evaluation question is "Was the method Kim used to rescue Dana wise? Why or why not?" These questions are excellent for open-ended class discussion but hard to grade as test questions.

Creative Response Questions.   Creative response questions ask children to go beyond the material and create new ideas based on the ideas they have read. Questions requiring creative response are also good for class discussions. As a means of testing comprehension of a passage, however, they are not desirable, since almost any response could be considered correct. Examples of creative response questions include "If the story stopped after Jimmy lost his money, what ending would you write for it?" and "If Meg had not gone to school that day, what do you think might have happened?"

Other Categorizations of Question Types

Pearson and Johnson (1978) suggest three question types. They label questions as *textually explicit* when the questions have answers that are directly stated in the text, as *textually implicit* when they have implied answers (but the text contains clues for making the necessary inference), and as *scriptually implicit* when the reader must answer them from his or her background knowledge.

The reader's own characteristics interact with the text and the question to determine the actual demands of the question-answering task. A reader's interest, background knowledge, and reading skill affect the difficulty and even the type of question for each reader. The structure of a question may lead a teacher to expect a textually explicit response, whereas the student's background may cause him or her to give a scriptually implicit response (Wixson, 1983). For example, if the text tells readers how to construct a kite, a child who has actually made a kite before reading the material may answer the question on the basis of direct experience, rather than from information presented in the text.

Inability to take the perspective of another person can affect comprehension. Students who can take the perspective of another person do better on scriptually implicit questions than those who cannot (Gardner and Smith, 1987).

Story Grammar as a Basis for Questioning

Another basis for questioning deserves attention: the use of a story grammar. A story is a series of events that are related to one another in particular ways. As people hear and read many stories, they develop expectations, sometimes called story schemata, about the types of things they will encounter; these help them organize information. Related story schemata are described by a **story grammar**. As Sadow (1982) suggests, questions based on a story grammar may help children develop story schemata. The questions should be chosen to reflect the logical sequence of events.

David Rumelhart proposed a simple story grammar that "describes a story as consisting of a setting and one or more episodes" (Sadow, 1982, p. 519). The setting includes the main characters and the time and location of the events, and each episode contains an initiating event, the main character's reaction to it, an action of the main character caused by this reaction, and a consequence of that action, which may act as an initiating event for a subsequent episode. (Sometimes some of the elements of an episode are not directly stated.) Sadow suggests the following five generic questions as appropriate types to ask about a story.

❶ Where and when did the events in the story take place, and who was involved in them? (setting)

❷ What started the chain of events in the story? (initiating event)

❸ What was the main character's reaction to this event? (reaction)

❹ What did the main character do about it? (action)

❺ What happened as a result of what the main character did? (consequence) (Sadow, 1982, p. 520)

Such questions can help students see the underlying order of ideas in a story, but of course teachers should reword them to fit the story and the particular children. For example, Question 1 can be broken into three questions (*where, when, who*), and the teacher can provide appropriate focus by using words or phrases from the story. After students address these story grammar questions, which establish the essential facts, they should answer questions that help them relate the story to their own experiences and knowledge (Sadow, 1982).

STANDARDS AND ASSESSMENT

Marshall (1983) has also suggested using story grammar as a basis for developing comprehension questions and for evaluating student retellings, which can sometimes be used instead of questions. A checklist for story retellings can indicate if story parts were included and whether they were included with or without prompts. In Marshall's questioning scheme, *theme* questions are similar to main idea questions and ask about the major point or moral of the story. As in Sadow's questioning scheme, *setting* questions are *where* and *when* questions, but *character* questions ask about the main character and/or other characters. *Initiating events* questions often ask about a problem faced by a particular character. *Attempts* questions ask what a character did about a situation or what he or she will do. *Resolution* questions ask how a character solved the problem or what the reader would do to solve the problem. *Reaction* questions focus on what a character felt, the reasons for a character's actions or feelings, or the feelings of the reader.

STANDARDS AND ASSESSMENT

Guidelines for Preparation

Some guidelines for preparing questions may be useful to teachers who wish to improve their questioning techniques. The following suggestions may help teachers avoid some pitfalls that other educators have detected.

❶ In trying to determine overall comprehension skills, ask a variety of questions designed to reflect different types of comprehension. Avoid overloading the evaluation with a single type of question.

❷ Don't ask questions about obscure or insignificant portions of the selection. Such questions may make a test harder, but the children's responses to them are not realistic indicators of comprehension. "Hard" tests and "good" tests are not necessarily the same thing.

❸ Avoid ambiguous or tricky questions. If a question has two or more possible interpretations, more than one answer for it has to be acceptable.

❹ Avoid useless questions. Questions that a person who has not read the material can answer correctly offer you no valuable information about comprehension.

❺ Don't ask questions in language that is more difficult than the language of the selection the question is about. Otherwise, questions may be worded in a way that prevents a child who knows the answer from responding appropriately.

❻ Make sure the answers to sequence questions require knowledge of the order of events. Don't confuse questions that simply ask for lists with sequence questions.

❼ Don't ask for unsupported opinions when you are testing for comprehension. Have children give support for their opinions, by asking, "Why do you think that?" or "What in the story made you think that?" If you ask for an unsupported opinion, any answer will be correct.

❽ Don't ask for opinions if you want facts. Ask for the type of information you want to receive.

❾ Avoid questions that give away information. Instead of asking, "What makes you believe the boy was angry?", ask, "How do you think the boy felt? Why?" Questions may lead students to the answers by supplying too much information.

❿ Use precise terms in phrasing questions related to reading. Ask students to compare or contrast, to predict, or to draw conclusions about the reading (Smith, 1989b).

● Helping Students Answer Questions

DIVERSITY 🌐 Some children lack familiarity with the question-answer-feedback sequence often used for instructional purposes. Some children have not been exposed to this language pattern at home and find it strange and confusing that the teacher is asking for information he or she already knows. Teachers may need to teach the question-answer-feedback strategy directly, in oral and written situations, so that students will respond appropriately (Farrar, 1984b). Teacher modeling of the answers to questions is helpful. In the process, the teacher can explain how to interpret the question, how and where to find the information, and how to construct the answer after the information is located (Armbruster, 1992).

Raphael and Pearson (1982) taught students three types of Question-Answer Relationships (QARs). QAR instruction encourages students to consider both information in the text and their own background knowledge when answering questions (Raphael, 1986). The relationship for questions with answers that were directly stated in one sentence in the text was called "Right There." The students looked for the words in the question and read the sentence containing those words to locate the answer. The relationship for questions with an answer in the story that required information from multiple sentences or paragraphs was called "Think and Search," and the relationship for questions for which answers had to come from the reader's own knowledge was called "On My Own" (Raphael and Pearson, 1982). Modeling the decision about Question-Answer Relationships and correct answers based on them was an important part of the teaching. Supervised practice after the modeling, with immediate feedback on student responses, was also important. The practice involved gradually increased passage lengths, progressing from simpler to more difficult tasks (Raphael, 1982). Learning the three types of QARs enhanced students' success in answering questions. The training appeared to help average- and low-ability students most (Raphael, 1984). Primary-grade children needed more repetition to learn QARs than intermediate-grade children did (Raphael, 1986).

Raphael (1986) subsequently modified QAR instruction to include four categories, clustered under two headings. Example 6.6 illustrates this modification.

EXAMPLE 6.6   Question-Answer Relationships (QARs)

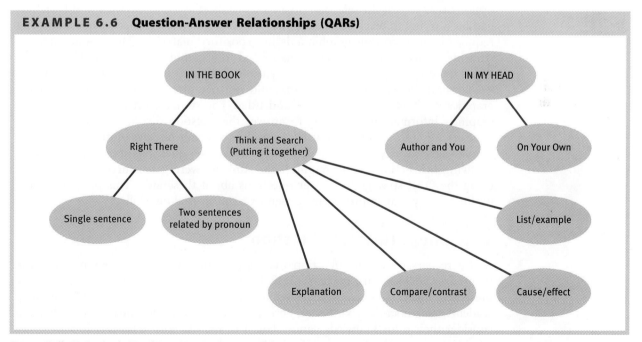

Source: Taffy E. Raphael, "Teaching Question Answer Relationships, Revisited," *The Reading Teacher*, 39 (6) (February 1986), 516–522. Reprinted with permission of the International Reading Association and the author.

In the modified scheme, the "In My Head" category is divided into questions that involve both the text information and the reader's background of experiences (Author and You) and those that can be answered from the reader's experience without information from the story (On My Own) (Raphael, 1986).

Discussing the use of the QAR categorization to plan questioning strategies, Raphael (1986) states:

> Questions asked prior to reading are usually On My Own QARs. They are designed to help students think about what they already know and how it relates to the upcoming story or content text. In creating guided reading questions, it is important to balance text-based and inference questions. For these, Think and Search QARs should dominate, since they require integration of information and should build to the asking of Author and You QARs. Finally, for extension activities, teachers will want to create primarily On My Own or Author and You QARs, focusing again on students' background information as it pertains to the text. (p. 521)

Mesmer and Hutchins (2002) discovered that a group of fifth-grade students had problems interpreting graphic aids in order to answer questions about them. (See Chapter 9 for a discussion of the attributes of graphic aids.) The educators realized that a complex, multistep process is involved in answering questions from the information in graphic aids. "Students must first read a related question, then read and analyze the graphic, determine the answer, locate the answer within a list of options, and record the selection on an answer sheet" (p. 22). Mesmer and Hutchins had been trying to teach students to use a QAR framework to answer questions that require them to consult graphic aids in expository materials. They found that the students tended to treat all questions related to a graphic aid as Right There types, when these questions could be any type, including those that require the use of background knowledge, and that they did not pay attention to the details on the graphics, such as units of measure and titles. The students often assumed that the graphic's information was going to answer the question directly and failed to pay close attention to the question itself. Learning the characteristics of different kinds of graphic aids was important to helping students answer questions about the aids. After receiving instruction about graphic aids, students were given direct instruction in using the QAR strategy to answer questions about these aids. This proved to be a useful strategy that improved metacognitive and test-taking skills.

● Helping Students Question

Active readers constantly question the text. As they construct meaning, they ask themselves, "Does this make sense?" Questions about why the material being presented makes sense, also referred to as "elaborative interrogation," can help students remember the texts better, perhaps because these questions cause students to consider their prior knowledge and relate it to the material (Pressley, 2001).

Many authorities advocate teaching the reader to generate questions throughout the reading process to enhance comprehension, and such training has proved effective. Students who are trained to ask literal questions about material being read have learned to discriminate questions from nonquestions and good literal questions from poor ones. After they practiced the production of good literal questions for paragraphs and then for stories that they read to answer the questions, their comprehension improved (Cohen, 1983). Other students who were taught (through modeling, with gradual phasing out of teacher involvement) to generate their own questions based on a story grammar also had enhanced comprehension (Nolte and Singer, 1985). Bristow (1985) believes that interspersing questions in the text to provide a transition from teacher questioning to self-questioning may be helpful.

Questioning and sharing responses in small groups can help children improve their critical insights into texts. Student-generated questions can motivate peers to respond and cause the questioner to have more interest in the response. Both Commeyras (1994, p. 519) and Simpson (1996, p. 124) conclude that "good discussion questions are the ones students want to discuss."

Kitagawa (1982, p. 43) encouraged children to become questioners by asking questions that had to be answered by a question, such as "What question did the author mainly answer in the passage we just read?" She also encouraged them to develop questions they wished to have answered through educational activities, such as field trips, and to construct preview questions, based on titles and pictures, for reading selections. Students were asked what questions they would ask the author of a selection or a character, if they could, and they were asked to predict what questions would be answered next in the selection.

TIME for REFLECTION

Under what conditions would you encourage students to construct their own questions, and under what conditions would you use teacher-generated questions in your classroom? What are the reasons for your choices?

Busching and Slesinger (1995) also led students to ask their own questions about what they read. The students wrote, in their reading response journals or notebooks, questions that selections raised. This preserved the questions for ongoing reflection. Busching and Slesinger (1995, p. 344) discovered that "[w]hether a question is about facts or concepts is less important than whether a question is a part of something significant. The outward form of the question may have little to do with the level, the depth, or the importance of thinking that has occurred." When reading *Rose Blanche*, middle-school students first raised factual questions because of their limited backgrounds of experience. Later, more of their questions were on higher levels. Some of their questions became "What if…" questions.

LITERATURE

SUMMARY

This chapter examines types of reading comprehension. Literal comprehension results from reading for directly stated ideas. Higher-order comprehension goes beyond literal comprehension to include interpretive, critical, and creative reading. Interpretive reading is reading for implied ideas; critical reading is reading for evaluation; and creative reading is reading beyond the lines. Teachers can generally teach strategies in all of these areas most effectively through explanation and modeling, guided student practice, and independent student practice.

Questioning techniques are important to instruction because teachers use questions to provide purposes for reading, to elicit and focus discussion, and to check comprehension of material read. Questions may be based on comprehension factors or story structure. Students may need to be taught how to approach answering questions. Self-questioning by the reader is also a valuable comprehension and comprehension-monitoring technique. Teachers can help students develop the skill of self-questioning.

TEST YOURSELF

True or False

_____ 1. Literal comprehension involves acquiring information that is directly stated in a selection.

_____ 2. Students must attend to details when they follow directions.

_____ 3. Critical reading is reading for evaluation.

_____ 4. Critical reading strategies are easier to teach than literal reading strategies.

_____ 5. Higher-order comprehension may involve determining the author's purpose.

_____ 6. Critical readers are not interested in copyright dates of material they read.

_____ 7. An inference is an idea that is implied in the material, rather than being directly stated.

_____ 8. Elementary school children are too young to be able to recognize propaganda techniques.

_____ 9. A bandwagon approach takes advantage of people's desire to conform to the crowd.

_____ 10. Critical thinking skills should first be given attention in the intermediate grades.

_____ 11. Critical readers read with a questioning attitude.

_____ 12. Creative reading involves going beyond the material presented by the author.

_____ 13. Teachers should give little class time to creative reading because it is difficult to assess.

_____ 14. In composing comprehension questions for testing purposes, teachers should use several types of questions.

_____ 15. A hard test is a good test, and vice versa.

_____ 16. Listing questions and sequence questions are the same thing.

_____ 17. The main idea of a paragraph is always stated in the form of a topic sentence.

_____ 18. Children make inferences that are consistent with their schemata.

_____ 19. Some children have difficulty determining the referents of pronouns and adverbs.

_____ 20. Young children are unable to make inferences.

_____ 21. Hexagonal essays promote higher-order thinking.

_____ 22. "Essential" questions, as defined by Wiggins and McTighe, point to the core ideas of a discipline.

For your journal . . .

❶ Using the seven question types based on comprehension factors that are described in this chapter, compose some questions about the content of this chapter or of another chapter in this book. Answer the questions.

❷ After you have read a novel written for children, write story grammar-based questions about the story. Answer the questions.

❸ Reflect on the video that accompanies this chapter on your CD. What type of comprehension—literal or higher-order—does each question asked by the teachers in the video promote? Explain why. Do teachers need to question for both types of comprehension? Why or why not?

. . . and your portfolio

❶ Make a board or folder game based on a favorite children's book for a grade of your choice.

❷ Gather examples of each propaganda technique listed in the chapter in order to create a file for each type. Describe instructional uses for your file.

7

Major Approaches and Materials for Reading Instruction

SETTING OBJECTIVES

When you finish reading this chapter, you should be able to

● Discuss the characteristics of different types of published reading series.

● Compare and contrast a directed reading activity with a directed reading-thinking activity.

● Discuss the characteristics of literature-based approaches to reading instruction.

● Explain the rationale behind the language experience approach.

● Discuss the place of computers in reading instruction.

● Discuss how a teacher might use elements of several approaches in a single classroom.

Over the years, educators have developed many approaches to teaching reading. This chapter discusses some of the more widely accepted approaches. These approaches are not mutually exclusive; many teachers use more than one method simultaneously. They often select the best techniques and materials from a number of approaches to meet the varied needs of individual students in their classrooms. We take the position that no one approach is best for all students or all teachers. Therefore, we attempt to acquaint teachers with the characteristics of different approaches so that they will be able to make an informed choice of which procedures to use in their classrooms.

Just as there are many approaches, there are many types of materials that can be used for reading instruction; they vary from teacher-made charts to published reading series, library books, and computers. All are tools to help teachers present reading instruction effectively.

Chapter 7 Organization

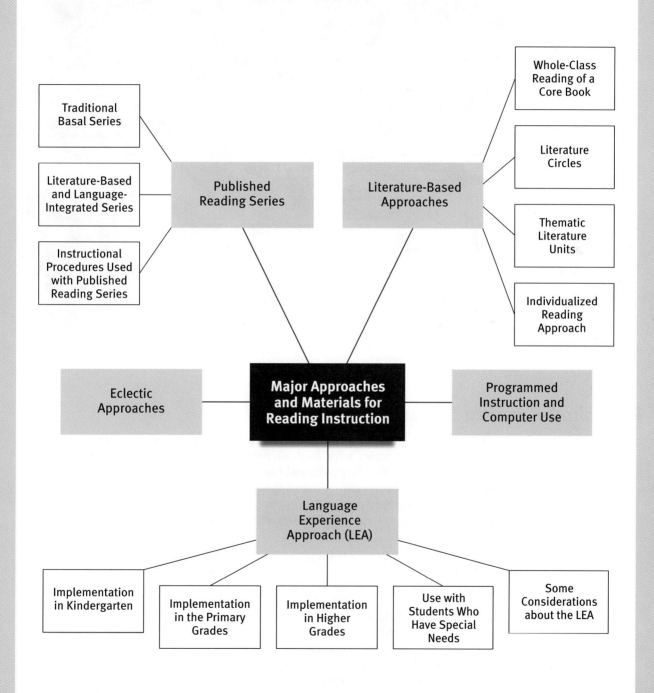

Basal readers are anthologies of stories, content area selections, poems, and plays.
(© Carol Palmer/INDEX-STOCK)

Published Reading Series

Many schools depend on published reading series for materials to support reading instruction. These series have evolved over time. For many years, the published reading series were like the traditional basal series described here. Recently, however, many publishers have been moving toward more literature-based and language-integrated series as they try to take into account both the criticisms of the traditional series and the current theory and research in reading.

● Traditional Basal Series

For many years, basal reader series have been the most widely used materials for teaching reading in the elementary schools of the United States. They begin with prereading materials and provide materials for development and practice of reading strategies in each grade.

In addition to the student books, basal reader series include teacher's manuals with detailed lesson plans to help teachers use the readers effectively. Teachers who follow these plans use what is called a *directed reading activity (DRA)*, described later in this chapter. Basal reader series also include workbooks and/or blackline duplicating masters of skillsheets that children can use to practice skills and strategies they have previously learned in class. Many publishing companies offer other supplementary materials to be used in conjunction with basal series, such as

- "big books"—chart-sized versions of books that are important tools in holistic teaching (see Chapter 2);

- student journals;

- read-aloud libraries for the teacher;

STANDARDS AND ASSESSMENT
- unit tests;

- puppets to go with some early stories;

TECHNOLOGY
- computer management, reinforcement, and enrichment activities.

LITERATURE
Basal reading series are quite useful for elementary school teachers. They provide anthologies of stories, content area selections, poems, plays, and so on that can be the basis for enriching classroom reading activities. Many of these pieces are whole selections or excerpts from high-quality literature. The new basals contain much literature because the publishers are trying to provide material that teachers want (Cullinan, 1992). Many newer basal reading programs are presenting integrated, thematic approaches to reading.

As Wiggins (1994) points out, when a basal reading program is used, teachers have an idea of what their students have been taught in past years. This can aid in curricular planning.

The teacher's manuals offer many valuable suggestions for teaching reading lessons and thus can save much lesson preparation time. Such suggestions offer positive guidance for teachers, helping them to include all aspects of reading (word recognition, comprehension, oral reading, silent reading, reading for information, and reading for enjoyment) in their reading lessons. Manuals allow for systematic

STANDARDS AND ASSESSMENT
teaching and reteaching of skills and strategies and for systematic review. They provide strategy and skill scope and sequence charts that show what strategies are introduced, taught, and reinforced at different grade levels throughout the series. They also offer ways to monitor the effectiveness of the instruction (Wiggins, 1994).

The wealth of material offered in the teacher's manuals allows teachers to implement the suggestions that fit their needs and discard those that do not. If teachers try to do everything suggested, however, they may use valuable time for activities that are inappropriate for some groups of children, leaving inadequate time for more suitable activities. Teachers should not use basal readers from front to back in their entirety without considering the special needs of the children in their classes. A teacher might use one set of activities from the basal one year and a different set the next year to accommodate the different needs of the two classes.

Teachers should also be aware that the workbooks in basal series are not designed to teach the skills and strategies and should not be used for this purpose. They are designed to provide practice in skills that have been taught. Some educators have pointed out that basal reader workbook pages may fail to be directly related to the story in the reader and may not give sufficient attention to higher-level comprehension skills. Therefore, teachers may want to have students write responses to the selections in reading logs and let students discuss the selections in literature circles, as described later in this chapter, or to use a variety of other literary response activities, such as drama, art, and story telling, rather than depending on workbook activities that are unrelated to the stories or that cover comprehension superficially.

Some people equate basal readers with the overly simplified texts that have received much negative media attention. Many publishers today, however, consider factors other than readability formulas to aid in placement, and vocabulary control may be accomplished by using traditional stories with repetitive lines and predictable formats, rather than by changing the stories to fit vocabulary goals.

LITERATURE ⬛ Publishers of basal readers are continually working to improve them. To provide stories with high quality, limited vocabulary, and extensive repetition, they include unaltered folktales in some of the early readers. They also include other good literature, often without adaptation, as well as more content area material. Unlike the language in earlier basal readers, the language in today's basal readers is more natural

DIVERSITY 🌎 and conversational. These readers have diversified characters, including people of various racial and ethnic groups, elderly people, and people with disabilities, and depict them in less stereotyped ways than in the past. Women are also portrayed in roles other than the traditional ones.

Basal publishers have put many research findings about reading into practice in a context that takes into account the pressures that classroom teachers face. Basal readers address considerations from diagnosis to reading appreciation and offer suggestions for both instructional techniques and guided practice. Teachers should make their instructional needs known to publishers. Publishers have been responsive to user reactions in the past and are likely to continue to be responsive.

Hoffman and McCarthey (1995) reported that studies of the first-grade materials of old and new basals of five companies show that the newer materials are very different from the old ones. The new materials have less vocabulary control, more diversity of genre, minimal adaptations, higher literary quality, increased predictability, and decreased decodability. Newer basals offer integrated reading and language instruction and often provide practice activities that go beyond worksheets alone.

Uses and Misuses of Basal Materials

Much of the criticism of basal readers has focused on less than desirable uses of the materials. Teachers have a responsibility to plan the use of all materials in their classrooms, including the basal readers, regardless of the presence or absence of guiding suggestions accompanying the materials.

If teachers perceive basals as *total* reading programs, they may fail to provide the variety of experiences that children need for a balanced program. Basals can never provide all of the reading situations a student needs to encounter.

Some teachers form basal reading groups based on achievement. They place the best readers in the top group, the average readers in a middle group or groups, and the poorest readers in the lowest group. These teachers believe that in this way, they can provide all of the children with basal materials that are appropriate for their reading levels. In actuality, however, the match of materials with children is not always good. Forell (1985) has pointed out that good readers are often placed in comfortable reading materials in which word recognition problems are not frequent and attention can be given to meaning, using context clues to advantage. Poor readers, however, are often placed in "challenging" material that causes frustration and is not conducive to comprehension, because so much attention is needed for word recognition—an arrangement that denies them a chance for fluent reading. All readers should be given material that is comfortable enough to allow reasonable application of comprehension skills. Teachers may be reluctant to place students in materials at as low a level as they need in order to allow this to happen, but doing so can be beneficial in the long run.

Blanton, Moorman, and Wood (1986) suggest that teachers use direct instruction in basal reader skill lessons by assessing the students' background knowledge related to the skill; explaining the skill in detail, including when it is needed and why it is important; having the students explain the skill in their own words; modeling the use of the skill for the students and then providing them with guided practice with the skill; having students apply the skill in regular reading materials; and leading the students in discussion of real-world encounters with the skill. Some of these steps may already be included in basal manual instructions. Teachers can add the other steps to create complete skills lessons. Of course, teachers need to provide much time for actual reading of connected text.

Teachers may ask students to illustrate scenes from the story, write questions to be answered by other class members, write other adventures for story characters, read books by the author of the story or books related to the story, or engage in many other activities that encourage active participation and interaction with the selection (Weiss, 1987; Fuhler, 1990).

Educators have expressed considerable concern about the misuse of workbooks or skillsheets that accompany basal readers; some teachers use them to keep children busy while they meet with other children or do paperwork. Wiggins (1994) decries the fact that some teachers assign all pages sequentially to all students, regardless of the appropriateness to the individual child's needs. It is important to note that the fault here is with the teachers' procedures and not with the workbooks. Workbook activities should always be purposeful, and teachers should never assign workbook pages simply to keep students occupied. Teachers should also grade and return completed workbook assignments promptly, since children need to have correct responses reinforced immediately and need to be informed about incorrect responses so that they will not continue to make them.

TIME for REFLECTION

Would you ask all students to complete all workbook pages, to ensure learning? Why, or why not? If not, what would *you* do?

In summary, teachers do not have to follow all suggestions in the manuals—or, indeed, *any* of the suggestions—in order to use basal materials to provide children with a variety of reading materials that would not otherwise be available in many schools. Likewise, they are not limited to using only the suggestions in the manuals. The manner in which basal materials are used, not the basals themselves, has often been the main concern about basal programs.

Variations in Basal Reading Programs

Although the preceding discussion of basal reading programs contained some generalizations about them, our intention is not to imply that all basal reader series are alike. On the contrary, these series differ in basic philosophy, order of presentation of strategies and skills, degree and type of vocabulary control, types of selections, and number and types of practice activities provided. Some supplement workbook/skillsheet material with student journals that call for more varied responses. Most are eclectic in approach, but some emphasize a single method, such as a linguistic or an intensive phonics approach.

Linguistic Series. *Linguistics* is the scientific study of human speech. Linguistic scientists (also called *linguists*), such as Leonard Bloomfield, have set forth principles that have affected the development of reading instructional materials. A number of these principles have been applied to many of the basal reading series. Some series have been based specifically on Bloomfield's ideas and have incorporated a number of his beliefs, including the following:

❶ Beginning readers should be presented with material that uses only a single sound for a letter at a time. Other sounds for the letter should not be presented until the first association is mastered.

❷ Irregularly spelled words should be avoided in beginning reading material, although some (for example, *a* and *the*) must be used to construct sentences that have relatively normal patterns.

❸ Word attack skills should be taught by presenting **minimally contrasting spelling patterns**, words that vary by only a single letter. For example, one lesson might contain the words *can, tan, man, ban, fan, ran,* and *pan.* This exposure to minimally contrasting patterns is designed to help the child understand the difference a certain letter makes in the pronunciation of a word.

❹ Sounds should not be isolated from words, however, because when sounds are pronounced outside the environment of a word, they are distorted. This is particularly true of isolated consonant sounds; *buh, duh,* and *puh* are sounds incorrectly associated with the letters *b, d,* and *p.*

These materials emphasize reading orally. Reading is viewed as turning writing back into spoken language.

Intensive Phonics Series. Series that focus on intensive phonics use a synthetic phonics approach to phonics instruction. (See Chapter 3 for a description of this approach.) The materials often look similar to the ones found in a linguistic series, but the sounds are not isolated from the words in a linguistic approach, whereas they are taught in isolation and then blended into words in a synthetic phonics approach.

LITERATURE ● **Literature-Based and Language-Integrated Series**

One of the most widely heralded changes that educational publishers have made is the creation of *literature-based* reading series. These programs offer quality literature selections for students to read, often in their entirety and without adaptation. In addition, some series are integrating instruction involving all the language arts, including listening, speaking, and writing activities to accompany the literature selections. These activities make the lessons true communication experiences. Having students write in journals and participate in unit studies that tie together selections with similar themes, by the same author, or of the same genre is common in the literature-based and language-integrated series.

These series often stress purpose setting by the students themselves, perhaps through predictions, and much attention is devoted to confirming or rejecting predictions after reading takes place. A "Theme at a Glance" section from one such series (Houghton Mifflin, 2001) is found in Example 7.1 on pages 272–273. It gives an idea of the breadth of coverage in these materials.

● Instructional Procedures Used with Published Reading Series

A number of instructional procedures can be used with published reading series. Some are built into the manuals included in the series, and some can be easily adapted to use with these materials.

Directed Reading Activity (DRA)

The *directed reading activity (DRA)* is a teaching strategy used to extend and strengthen a child's reading abilities. It can be used with a story from a published reading series or with any other reading selection, including content area materials and trade books. The DRA is the strategy that is generally built into basal reading series' teacher's manuals. The following five components are often included in the DRA.

STANDARDS AND ASSESSMENT

❶ *Motivation and development of background (activating and building schemata).* The teacher attempts to interest students in reading about the topic by helping them associate the subject matter with their own experiences or by using audiovisual aids to arouse interest in unfamiliar areas. It may not be necessary to work on motivation for all stories.

At this point, the teacher can determine whether the children have the backgrounds of experience and language needed for understanding the story, and, if necessary, he or she can develop new concepts and vocabulary before they read the story.

❷ *Directed story reading (silent and oral).* Before children read the story silently, the teacher provides them with purpose questions (or an anticipation guide or study guide) or helps them to set their own purposes (by questioning or predicting) to direct their reading (on a section-by-section basis at lower grade levels). Following the silent reading, the teacher may ask children to read aloud their answers to the purpose or study-guide questions, to read aloud to prove or reject their predictions, or to read orally for a new purpose. Oral reading is not always included in upper-grade lessons. This section of the lesson is designed to aid children's comprehension and retention of the material.

EXAMPLE 7.1   **Theme at a Glance in Published Series**

Theme 4

Theme at a Glance

Theme Concept: *Animals coexist with people in a variety of habitats.*

☑ **Indicates Tested Skills**
See page 10G for assessment options.

	Reading		Word Work
	Comprehension Skills and Strategies	**Information and Study Skills**	**Decoding Longer Words** Structural Analysis/Phonics
Anthology Selection 1: **Nights of the Pufflings** Science Link	☑ Fact and Opinion, *17C, 23, 39A* **Comprehension:** Topic, Main Idea, Supporting Details, *27;* **Making Generalizations,** *29;* **Genre:** Nonfiction Magazine Article, *38* **Strategy Focus:** Evaluate, *17B 22, 28*	How to Use SQRR, *36* ☑ Multimedia Resources, *39C*	☑ Structural Analysis: Syllabication and Review, *39E* **Phonics:** The Vowel + / r / Sound in *hair, 39F*
Anthology Selection 2: **Seal Surfer** Career Link	☑ Compare and Contrast, *45C, 49, 69A* **Visual Literacy:** Analyzing an Illustration, *53;* **Comprehension:** Sequence of Events, *57;* Author's Viewpoint, *61;* How to Read a Magazine Article, *66;* **Genre:** Magazine Article, *68* **Strategy Focus:** Summarize, *45B, 50, 60*	Skim and Scan, *69C*	☑ Structural Analysis: Word Endings *-ed* and *-ing* and Changing Final *y* to *i, 69E* **Phonics:** Consonant Clusters, *69F*
Anthology Selection 3: **Two Days in May** Poetry Link	☑ Making Judgments, *71C, 77, 99A* **Visual Literacy:** Foreground, *75;* **Writer's Craft:** Similies, *85;* **Comprehension:** Problem Solving, *87;* Predicting Outcomes, *91;* How to Read a Poem Aloud, *96;* **Genre:** Poetry, *98* ☑ **Strategy Focus:** Monitor/Clarify, *71B, 76, 90*	Adjusting Reading Rate, *99C*	☑ Structural Analysis: Prefixes *un, re,* and Suffixes *-ful, -ly, -er, 99E* **Phonics:** Digraphs *ch, sh, th, tch, wh, wr, 99F*
Theme Resources	Reteaching: Comprehension, *R8, R10, R12* Challenge/Extension: Comprehension, *R9, R11, R13*		Reteaching: Structural Analysis, *R14, R16, R18*
Special Theme Features	**Test Preparation** **Taking Tests: Vocabulary Items** • Anthology, *100* • Teacher's Edition, *100* • Practice Book, *53–54*		**Spelling** **Additional Lessons:** • Frequently Misspelled Wo • Spelling Review/Assessm

(10E)   THEME 4: **Animal Habitats**

Source: From Teacher's Edition: Animal Habitats, Grade 3, Theme 4 in *Houghton Mifflin Reading: a Legacy of Literacy* by J. David Cooper and John J. Pikulski, et al. Copyright © 2001 by Houghton Mifflin Company. Reprinted by permission of Houghton Mifflin Company. All rights reserved.

Pacing	Multi–age Classroom	Technology
• This theme is designed to take approximately 4 to 6 weeks, depending on your students' needs.	**Related themes—** • **Grade 2:** *Amazing Animals* • **Grade 4:** *Nature: Friend and Foe*	**Education Place: www.eduplace.com** Log on to Education Place for more activities relating to *Animal Habitats*. **Lesson Planner CD-ROM:** Customize your planning for *Animal Habitats* with the Lesson Planner.

Writing & Language

Spelling	Vocabulary Skills, Vocabulary Expansion	Grammar, Usage, and Mechanics	Writing	Listening/ Speaking/Viewing	Cross-Curricular Content Area
The Vowel +/r/ sounds in *hair*, 39G	Dictionary: Parts of Speech, 39I Words for Animal Homes, 39J	The Verb *be*, 39K	Taking Notes, 39M Choosing What's Important, 39N	Have a Literature Discussion, 39O	**Responding:** Science, Viewing, Internet, 35 **Theme Resources:** R26–R27
Added Endings, 69G	Dictionary: More Multiple-Meaning Words, 69I Words for Young Animals, 69J	Helping Verbs, 69K	Writing a Poem, 69M Using Exact Verbs, 69N	View and Evaluate Media, 69O	**Responding:** Music, Math, Internet, 65 **Theme Resources:** R26–R27
Prefixes and Suffixes, G	Dictionary: Base Words and Inflected Forms, 99I Sounds Around Us, 99J	Irregular Verbs, 99K	A Problem-Solution Essay, 99M Varying Sentence Types, 99N	Listen to and Make Announcements, 99O	**Responding:** Health, Listening and Speaking, Internet, 95 **Theme Resources:** R26–R27
	Challenge/Extension: Vocabulary Activities, R15, R17, R19	Reteaching: Grammar, R20–R22	Writing Activities, R23–R25		Cross-Curricular Activities, R26–R27

Teacher's Edition, 43F, 101
Practice Book, 20–22, 55–57

Reading-Writing Workshop: Research Report
• Anthology: Student Writing Model, 40–41
• Practice Book, 18, 19

• Teacher's Edition, 40–43G
Writing Process
Locating and Evaluating Information
Topic Sentences and Supporting Facts
Subject-Verb Agreement

Theme at a Glance 10F

❸ *Strategy- or skill-building activities.* At some point during the lesson, the teacher provides direct instruction in one or more word recognition or comprehension strategies or skills.

❹ *Follow-up practice.* Children practice strategies and skills they have already been taught, frequently by doing workbook exercises or playing skill-oriented games.

❺ *Enrichment activities.* These activities may connect the story with art, music, or creative writing or may lead the children to read additional material on the same topic or by the same author. Creative drama is often included as an enrichment activity that links the reading with speaking and listening.

Although the steps may vary from series to series, most basal reading lessons have parts that correspond to this list of components. Directed reading of a story generally involves the teacher asking questions and the children reading to find the answers, or the teacher asking the children to make predictions and read to confirm or reject them. Traditional basal readers tend to give the teacher responsibility for purpose setting. Literature-based and language-integrated series, in contrast, have moved toward giving students more responsibility for purpose setting and stress the making and confirming of predictions.

Adaptations of the DRA.   Rearranging a basal reading lesson so that the activities labeled *enrichment activities* are completed before, rather than after, the story is read can produce better results than presentation in the traditional order. These activities can help the students build and integrate background knowledge (Thames and Readence, 1988; Pearson and Fielding, 1991).

Comprehension monitoring (metacognitive activities) can be made a natural part of a DRA by using student *predictions,* rather than teacher questions, as the purpose-setting vehicle for the lessons. The title, pictures, and children's background information about the general topic that has been activated can be used as a basis for the predictions. The predictions are revised as necessary as the children read the material, much as is done in a directed reading-thinking activity (discussed in the next section). *Self-questioning* before and during the reading is encouraged. In addition, stops at logical story breaks can be made to allow *summarization* of main points as a check for continuing comprehension. Summarization of the entire selection can follow completion of the reading. The students may ask classmates questions that they have generated about story features (Schmitt and Baumann, 1986). Many basal series incorporate some of these activities into their teacher's manuals, and the newer literature-based and language-integrated readers tend to use the predicting and confirming techniques regularly.

Guided Reading

Guided reading, as developed in New Zealand, has become a popular method of reading instruction. According to Fawson and Reutzel (2000, p. 84), "When implementing guided reading in classrooms, children are matched with books that provide a level of challenge and familiarity that appropriately support the development of each child's self-extending reading strategies. In short, children receive instruction during guided reading that focuses on their use of specific reading strategies so that they are able to choose from and apply a variety of reading strategies." The groups for guided reading are flexible, just as we have advocated in this text for all grouping practices. Although guided reading is sometimes characterized by teachers as being very different from the use of DRAs, we believe that good teachers generally use DRAs in a very similar manner. Guided reading lessons begin with an introduction to the story that is focused on concepts important to the story. Just as in a DRA, the purpose is to build background for the material in the story. Then students read the story aloud quietly, while the teacher observes their application of reading strategies and provides support, just as a good teacher should do in a DRA. Finally, the students may take part in extension activities, such as additional instruction on strategies, dramatizations, writing, and the like, which serve the same purpose as extension activities in the DRA.

Because teachers do not always have access to as many "leveled" books as would be needed to carry out the required matching, basal reading anthologies can provide material. The stories in kindergarten through grade-two readers in five basal reading series have been leveled using the text gradient criteria of Fountas and Pinnell (1996, 1999). The basal stories covered levels A through L of the Fountas and Pinnell gradient. Other materials would be needed for levels M through R (Fawson and Reutzel, 2000). More information on guided reading can be found in Chapter 2.

The Directed Reading-Thinking Activity (DRTA)

One alternative to the DRA is the *directed reading-thinking activity (DRTA)*. The DRTA focuses on student control instead of primarily teacher guidance of the reading. The DRTA is a general plan for directing children's reading of stories in published reading series, trade books, or content area selections and for encouraging children to think as they read and to make predictions and check their accuracy. The steps in a DRTA are listed in Example 7.2 on page 276. Stauffer (1968) offered some background for understanding the DRTA:

> Children are by nature curious and inquiring, and they will be so in school if they are permitted to inquire. It is possible to direct the reading-thinking process in such a way that children will be encouraged to think when reading—to speculate, to search, to evaluate, and to use. (p. 348)

STANDARDS AND ASSESSMENT

Stauffer (1969) further pointed out that teachers can motivate students' effort and concentration by involving them intellectually and encouraging them to formulate questions and hypotheses, to process information, and to evaluate tentative solutions. The DRTA is directed toward accomplishing these goals. The teacher observes the children as they read, in order to diagnose difficulties and offer help (kidwatching time). (See Chapter 12.) Perhaps because the student is interacting with the material during reading, the DRTA is extremely useful for improving children's comprehension of selections. After the reading, skill-building activities take place.

Making predictions about what will occur in a text encourages children to think about the text's message. In making predictions, students use their background

EXAMPLE 7.2 Steps in a DRTA

Step 1: Making Predictions from Title Clues

Write the title of the story or chapter to be studied on the chalkboard, and have a child read it. Ask the children: "What do you think this story will be about?" Give them time to consider the question thoroughly, and let each child have an opportunity to make predictions. All student predictions should be accepted, regardless of how reasonable or unreasonable they may seem, but the teacher should not make any predictions during this discussion period.

Step 2: Making Predictions from Picture Clues

Have the students open their books to the beginning of the selection. If there is a picture on the first page, ask them to examine it carefully. After they have examined it, ask them to revise the predictions they made earlier, basing their new predictions on the additional information in the picture.

Step 3: Reading the Material

Have the students read a predetermined amount of the story to check the accuracy of their predictions.

Step 4: Assessing the Accuracy of Predictions and Adjusting Predictions

When all of the children have read the first segment, lead a discussion by asking such questions as "Who correctly predicted what the story was going to be about?" Ask the children who believe they were right to read orally to the class the parts of the paragraph that support their predictions. Children who were wrong can tell why they believe they were wrong. Let them revise their predictions, if necessary, and then ask them to predict what will happen next in the story.

Step 5: Repeating the Procedure Until All Parts of the Lesson Have Been Covered

Have the children read the next predetermined segment of the story to check the accuracy of their predictions. Have them read selected parts orally to justify the predictions they think were correct and tell why they believe other predictions were incorrect. Have them revise or adjust their predictions on the basis of their reading. Then repeat the making of predictions and the checking of predictions until all predetermined segments of the story have been read.

knowledge about the topic and their knowledge of text organizational patterns. This step provides purposes for reading: trying to confirm one or more predictions from others in the group and to confirm or reject their own. It also encourages students to apply metacognitive skills as they think through their lines of reasoning. When students are unable to make predictions as requested, the teacher can model his or her thinking in making a prediction, using a think-aloud, or can provide several possible predictions for the student to choose from and ask for the reason a particular one is chosen. The teacher should accept all predictions and encourage the students to reflect on their accuracy later. If students are new at making predictions, the teacher can use highly predictable materials, such as folktales, to encourage success. It

TIME for REFLECTION

Some teachers think a DRA is too prescriptive to use but consider a DRTA acceptable because it gives students some control over their own learning. Other teachers believe that there is a place for each technique. **What do** *you* **think, and why?**

may help to have the students summarize what has happened before making predictions (Johnston, 1993).

In preparing a DRTA, the teacher should select points at which to pause so that the children can make predictions. These points should probably be ones where the story line changes, points of high suspense, or other logical spots, and there should be no more than four or five stops in a story (Haggard, 1988). During pauses, the teacher may use one or more open-ended questions to elicit student predictions about the next part of the story. (See Chapter 10 for an example of the application of a DRTA to a content area lesson.)

Literature-Based Approaches

LITERATURE Most educators recognize the value of using quality literature as a basis for reading instruction. A *literature-based approach* places emphasis on connecting stories to children's personal background knowledge, on analyzing stories and selections for particular elements, and on monitoring students' understanding of the reading materials. In addition, "good literature offers readers opportunities to engage in life experiences that they would otherwise miss" (Barone, Eeds, and Mason, 1995, p. 31).

The foundation of a literature-based program is *trade books*—that is, books not written primarily for instructional purposes. Most teachers have always made use of trade books for children in their classrooms. They have read aloud to the children from these books, urged students to read the books in the classroom reading center or to check them out from the school library for recreational reading, and used them as supplements to basal instruction. In a literature-based program, the teacher uses knowledge of students' backgrounds and attempts to "hook" them on reading selections. The teacher may give book talks that are based on marketing procedures, as Shiflett (1998) suggests, finding a book that engages the students and focusing their attention on the book by applying techniques that are often used in advertising.

Teachers need to understand theoretical perspectives on literature and reading, and they also need to know the reasons for using a particular book and a particular instructional approach (McGee and Tompkins, 1995). They need a clear instructional plan and clear goals and expectations for students. Wordless picture books, for example, provide materials for the emerging literacy of young children. These children can learn to follow a plot without having to decode words, and they can learn to provide their own interpretations of the author's ideas. Patterned books can provide another level of literary exposure for beginning readers. Books of all types may be read aloud to students or be made available in reading corners for students to read independently.

Essential reading skills and strategies can be taught within the context of material the children are actively involved in reading. Baumann, Hooten, and White (1999) found that students understood material better and enjoyed reading more when they incorporated comprehension strategy instruction within the context of literature. During reading, students' strategy use is monitored by both teacher and students, who share the responsibility for the students' learning (Ruddell, 1992). After reading, students may participate in activities such as retelling stories with or without flannel boards, writing reactions to books, and conversing about books with the teacher and other students. Children can study the writers' styles and use them as models for their personal writing (Fuhler, 1990). For example, Lunsford (1997) found that mini-lessons based on literature enhanced her writing workshops.

DIVERSITY

Literature-based instruction has been successful with a wide range of students. Zucker (1993) found that applying a literature-based whole language teaching/learning philosophy in classes with students who had language and learning disabilities resulted in positive gains in listening, speaking, reading, and writing. Stewart and colleagues (1996, p. 476) found that literature-based developmental reading programs resulted in improved reading performance by seventh and eighth graders. They believe that "choice leads to interest and ownership, interest and ownership to practice, and practice to speed and fluency. Speed and fluency result in increased comprehension and retention (i.e., reading proficiency)." Time for reading is, of course, necessary for this model to work.

STANDARDS AND ASSESSMENT

On the other hand, Scharer and Detwiler (1992) point out some concerns regarding literature-based instruction. When it is used, teachers find it hard to be sure all needed strategies and skills are being covered, hard to know how to assess progress, and hard to know how to handle the poorer readers. Certainly, teachers need to be well prepared as language teachers to use the approaches effectively.

Literature-based programs may be conducted in a number of ways, and combinations of these approaches are common in most literature-based classrooms. Four such approaches are whole-class reading of a core book, use of literature circles with multiple copies of several books, use of thematic literature units, and individualized reading approaches (Henke, 1988; Zarillo, 1989; Hiebert and Colt, 1989). Each of these approaches will be discussed in turn. A common adjunct to all of them is Sustained Silent Reading (SSR), in which students and teachers alike are allowed time to read materials of their own choice without interruption. (SSR is described in detail in Chapter 8.) Cole (1998) found that, during SSR periods, beginner-oriented books—ones similar to primary-level basal stories of earlier years—may be helpful to struggling readers for whom more aesthetically constructed texts do not provide enough commonalities in text to facilitate development of decoding and fluency. A number of older trade books have these qualities and should be available, during SSR periods, for students who need these less complex texts with much high-frequency vocabulary.

● Whole-Class Reading of a Core Book

Generally, core books used for whole-class reading are acquired in classroom sets so that every student has a personal copy. Teachers usually select these books for the quality of the material and sometimes because they fit into the overall classroom curriculum by being related to topics under discussion in other curricular areas, such as social studies and science. It is a further advantage if the teacher personally likes the book, for the teacher's attitude is communicated to the children as the reading progresses.

Prereading Activities

Before a book is presented to the class, there may be prereading activities in which the students share personal experiences related to the book's content and activate information they possess about the topics or themes covered in it. (See Chapter 5 for information about techniques for schema activation.) The teacher may also present a minilesson on some literary element that is important in the book, such as characterization or flashbacks (Atwell, 1987). Purposes for listening to or reading the material are often set by having students predict what will happen in the story, based on the title and possibly on the picture on the book's cover or the first page of the story. At other times, purposes may be set by having students generate questions about the story that they expect to answer from reading. Occasionally, the teacher may suggest some purpose question that will focus the readers' attention on a key element in the book, such as "How is the setting of the story important to its plot?"

Some students may present the book or a portion of it in a readers' theater as an introduction for other students. Such a presentation can help the other students activate their schemata for the reading to come.

During-Reading Activities

Sometimes the teacher first presents the book to the students by reading aloud part or all of it, depending on the students' reading abilities and the difficulty of the book. A chapter book may be read in installments over a period of days. After the teacher's oral reading, silent reading of the book by the students generally follows. At other times, the students may read the book silently first.

At strategic points in the initial reading or independent rereading, there are usually pauses for small-group or whole-class discussion of the material. If the students initially made predictions, these discussions may focus on the predictions, which can be evaluated, retained for the time being, altered slightly, or changed completely, on the basis of the new information. The discussion may also focus on the purpose questions that were generated or on students' personal reactions to the story. To guide these discussions, the teacher may design questions that help the children to relate the story to their own experiences and to think critically and creatively about the material.

Between reading sessions, students may write reactions to the story in literature logs. The literature logs may be written just for the individual students, to help them think through what they are reading; or they may be dialogue logs, addressed to the teacher or a buddy. If the logs are a part of a written dialogue with the teacher, the teacher must respond to each entry with his or her own reaction to the story and/or to the student's reaction. Students should be free to write any honest response to the material without concern for negative teacher reaction. For example, a student who is bored by the story should feel free to say so in the log. Therefore, the teacher's comments should be encouraging, thought-provoking, and nonjudgmental. The teacher should not be looking for predetermined responses but should respond with genuine interest in the students' comments (Wollman-Bonilla, 1989; Fuhler, 1994). Students should be encouraged to link the reading material with personal experiences. The teacher should model such entries for students by sharing his or

EXAMPLE 7.3   Literature Log

EIGHT COUSINS   Read to 53
10-8-86
    Each time I read this book it seems to get easier to read. I guess it is because I'm getting used to the proper English used. I enjoy it a lot and feel so carried off when I read it. So far the story is very good and I just want to always know whats going to happen next.

                                    Anita

Anita,
    I haven't read *Eight Cousins*, but I sure would like to after reading your enthusiastic responses. I must confess that Louisa May Alcott is one author I've never read. I think I'll read *Eight Cousins* and give her a try.
    Can you discover what or how the author is creating such a wonderful feeling for you?

                                    Mrs. H.

Source: Jill Dillard, "Lit Logs: A Reading and Writing Activity for the Library/Media Center and the Classroom." Reprinted with permission of the author and the Ohio Educational Library/Media Association's *Ohio Media Spectrum* journal, from the Winter 1989 issue, Vol. 41, No. 4, p. 39.

her personal log entries orally. Students should also be encouraged to note phrases and expressions that appealed to them, statements that caused them confusion, and predictions about what will happen next. Many different learning goals may be met through this student-teacher interaction (Flitterman-King, 1988; McWhirter, 1990). An example of one type of literature log is presented in Example 7.3. Another type is presented in Example 7.4, in the section on literature circles.

Postreading Activities

After the book has been read, follow-up activities should be used to extend the children's understanding and to help them elaborate on the ideas they gained from the shared book. These activities often involve writing—for example, composing another episode for the characters in the story, another story of the same genre, or a character sketch of a favorite character. Swindall and Cantrell (1999) ask sixth graders to write questions for well-developed characters in the literature selections they are reading and then to impersonate characters of their choice and answer questions that their classmates, as interviewers, ask them. Retelling the story in various ways is a good follow-up activity, especially for young children. They may simply retell the story to a partner, who may ask questions about missing events or ideas; they may retell the story using a flannel board and appropriate pieces; or they may act out the story through creative dramatics or puppetry. Illustrating the story sequence or selected parts of the story is a good follow-up activity that causes the students to reflect on the story and provides the teacher with insight into the students' degrees of comprehension of the story. The students may construct group or individual story maps after the reading. The maps can be displayed in the classroom or shared during discussions or oral presentations. Students may apply information learned in the story (for example, how to do origami), or they may read related materials because their interest in the topic has been aroused.

Modifications of Whole-Class Reading of a Core Book

Teachers have made many individual modifications of the procedures for close, careful reading of a book by a class. Shaw (1988) had fifth graders keep narrative journals in which they wrote after reading each chapter of their book, taking the perspective of the main character to relate that character's adventures. Through this activity, they learned much about summarizing and the first-person narrative form. Journal writing is a powerful way to reflect and discover insights about material read. It encourages active reading and gives the teacher a glimpse of the students' personal transactions with the story (Fuhler, 1994).

Dugan (1997, p. 87) uses transactional literature discussions that include "getting ready, reading and thinking aloud, wondering on paper, and looking back." Getting ready includes reviewing and making predictions during the reading—predictions that the students then try to confirm or reject. Teachers need to model the think-aloud process and to encourage students to think aloud as they read. (This step eventually evolves into thinking silently as they read.) As they read, or just after they finish, students write responses to the reading on sticky notes that are placed on the pages to which they refer. These written responses can provide fodder for talk sessions in which students respond, question, listen to their classmates, and make links between the events in the story, between the story and their personal experiences, or between their ideas and their classmates' ideas. After their talk sessions, the students write in their journals. Finally, the students review what they have learned. Teachers offer scaffolding throughout this process, but scaffolds are not used when students no longer need them. This procedure has produced a positive effect on students' reading abilities and enhanced their pleasure in reading.

Wertheim (1988) created a personal teaching guide for the novels she had her students read by listing difficult vocabulary at the beginning of each chapter; underlining important vocabulary in the text; writing discussion questions on the pages to which they pertained (coded as literal, inferential, and critical); writing other, more inclusive, questions at ends of chapters; and listing follow-up activities at the end of the book. This plan can be efficient, but some educators feel that it is too structured.

The following Focus on Strategies describes one way to do close reading of a core book. This example is not a prescribed procedure; many variations are possible.

● Literature Circles

In *literature circles*, the teacher generally chooses several books for which multiple copies are available, introduces each one, lets children choose which book to read, and presents the books to the children if they are unable to read them independently first. The structured book choices lead students to try books in a variety of genres and

Whole-Class Reading of a Core Book

In this lesson, the teacher has chosen the book *Patchwork Quilt* because of the way it shows relationships among the characters. This book is good for use with younger readers; for older readers, teachers would probably choose chapter books, with the discussion times coming at the ends of chapters.

The teacher opens with a minilesson on character development, leading the children to see how authors reveal characterization through the things the character says and does, the things other characters say about the character, and the ways they react to him or her.

Next, the teacher asks the students to brainstorm their personal associations for the words *Grandma*, *quilt*, and *masterpiece*. Webs of these associations are written on the board or on a chart.

Now the teacher invites the children to predict what the story will be about. They write down their predictions or share them orally with partners or the whole group. The teacher tells the children that, as they read the story, they should look for clues that will either confirm or disprove their predictions and that they should also look for the characteristics of the characters (noticing what is said about and to them, what they say, and what they do).

The teacher may ask the students to read just the first two pages of the story and then stop to discuss these questions with others at their tables:

What is the relationship between Tanya and her grandmother like?

Do you have a relationship like that with some older person?

Now students may read the rest of the story, with the number of pages read each time varying with the maturity of the students. The following is a list of some possible stopping points and questions for discussion in the small groups.

After two more pages:

Did Tanya's mother understand why Grandma wanted to make the quilt?

How did the reaction of Tanya's mother to the quilt make Grandma feel? How could you tell?

After five more pages:

What did Grandma mean when she said, "A quilt won't forget. It can tell your life story"?

Can a quilt really tell stories? If so, how?

Did Mama find out what Grandma meant about the quilt telling stories? How do you know?

After four more pages:

When Grandma got sick, why didn't she tell the others at first?

How did she feel about leaving her quilt unfinished? How could you tell?

Why did each person who worked on the quilt do what he or she did?

Would you have wanted to work on the quilt if you had been one of them? Why or why not?

After the next page:

Was Tanya right to take squares out of Grandma's old quilt without asking permission? Why did she do it? What will Grandma think of it?

After the story is finished:

How did Grandma feel about her quilt pieces going into the quilt?

What did she say and do that makes you believe that?

Why did they give Tanya the quilt?

How will Tanya feel about this quilt when she is older?

Do you have anything that you feel that way about?

Follow-up activities after the reading may include some of the following:

1. Find another book that tells about a relationship between a child and a grandparent or

Continued

Continued

another older person. Compare and contrast the stories.

2. Design a get-well card that Tanya might have made for her grandmother when she was sick.

3. Write a diary entry that Tanya might have made on the third day after she saw how sick her grandmother was. Have Tanya tell her diary how she felt about her grandmother's illness.

4. Pick a character and describe him or her. List his or her characteristics and why you did or did not like him or her.

5. Make a small patchwork quilt for the classroom. (Students provide material scraps for it. The children design the quilt pattern after looking at books about quilts and pictures of quilts. Then they cut out the pieces, and sew them together.) The quilting may be done by a volunteer parent or group of parents, or a resource person may show quilts and demonstrate quilting.

by a variety of authors. On the basis of their choices, the teacher has the students form groups to hold discussions about the books, and he or she may participate as a member in these group discussions. Students respond in response journals or literature logs. The teacher then lets the children help decide about ways to share the experience of the books (Egawa, 1990; Heald-Taylor, 1996). In this process, teachers make a number of decisions that touch on many aspects of instruction, such as their own roles in the groups, when and how much teacher-directed instruction should be involved, how books will be chosen, how students can be helped to respond more effectively, and how groups should be structured (Spiegel, 1998).

DIVERSITY Groups should be formed after the teacher and students have established rapport, so that they feel comfortable exchanging thoughts and ideas. Usually there are four or five groups in a class, each consisting of four to six members. Martinez-Roldan and Lopez-Robertson (1999/2000) discovered that English language learners are capable of participating productively in literature circles in mainstream classrooms, so this activity can have groups that are heterogeneous in terms of cultural composition, as well as in terms of reading ability, as long as the children have chosen the same book.

Groups generally meet two to five times a week, with each group lasting about two to three weeks. When they meet, students look through their books, decide how far to read each time (in order to finish the reading by the deadline and to have enough material for good discussions at each meeting), and begin reading. During group sessions, a student leader can conduct the activities, which may consist of silent reading, writing in and sharing literature logs, asking open-ended questions, discussing what was read, and doing extension activities. In their groups, students initiate and sustain discussion topics, connect literature selections to their lives, compare literature selections and authors with each other, note authors' styles, and consider authors' intents. Discussions are directed by the insights and ideas that the students bring to the group, instead of a list of teacher-supplied questions (Brabham and Villaume, 2000). Personal responses to literature replace "correct" answers to questions about the stories. Participation in an interpretive community of readers allows half-formed ideas to be explored from different perspectives. Students are required to provide substantiation for their contributions to the group. They should be receptive to the interpretations of their classmates, but they should also feel free to disagree (Spiegel, 1996). (See Chapter 12 for a teacher's checklist for literature circles.)

STANDARDS AND
ASSESSMENT

Reading response journals or literature logs allow for the collection of reactions to the reading throughout the reading process, not just at the end, and can be the basis for small-group discussions. When writing in their literature logs, students record personal interpretations, strategies for constructing meaning, questions that arise, and issues they may want to discuss with others (Popp, 1997). Since spelling and grammar are not checked in any way, the students feel freer to communicate. One type of literature log or response journal was shown in the section on whole-class reading of a core book. Example 7.4 is another type that can be used.

From reading these entries, teachers not only become aware of ways in which students are reacting to literature but also gain insight into each student's literacy processes (Handloff and Golden, 1995). Supportive comments by the teacher can encourage students to react honestly to the material and to persevere in the reading. Sometimes students may need encouragement to be more specific in their entries (Hancock, 1992; Raphael et al., 1992; Fuhler, 1994). To provide such encouragement, Berger (1996, p. 381) had her students respond to these questions: "What do you notice? … What do you question? … What do you feel? … What do you relate to?" These questions led the students to do more than just summarize the reading.

Hancock (1992) believes that awareness of typical response patterns in literature response journals can help teachers encourage extensions of response types. Some possible response types involve interaction with the characters, empathy with the characters, prediction and validation of predictions, personal experiences that are related to the reading, and philosophical reflections.

To introduce students to literature circles, Jewell and Pratt (1999) encourage their second and third graders to think out loud about literature selections and then put their thoughts on paper. They offer the children "explicit feedback that validates their thoughts and ideas" (p. 843), which frees them to take risks in responding to the literature. During whole-class discussions, held once or twice a week, the teachers model literature response and discussion behaviors for the students. Although the teachers participate in the discussions, they endeavor to leave ownership of the discussion to the children. After several weeks they divide the class into two groups and let these smaller groups discuss the literature selections, basing the discussion on writing that they have done in response journals. Still later, smaller groups are formed on the basis of student choices of selections to read, and true literature circles are formed.

TECHNOLOGY

Technology can provide ways for students to respond to their reading. Margaret Moore (1991) had teachers in a graduate methods course take part in electronic dialogue journals with fifth-grade students (using computers and modems). The partners discussed the book *Superfudge* by Judy Blume. The teachers modeled good

EXAMPLE 7.4   Literature Log

Part 1

Amaroq, the Wolf

NAME: Katie Smith
DATE: September 11

TITLE OF BOOK: Julie of the wolves
PAGE STARTED: 20
PAGE STOPPED: 45

RETELL:

Miyax is still looking for food. No matter what she will not give up. Now she is communicating with the wolves. She talks and acts like them.

Jello, one of the wolves, brings food back from the hunt and Miyax gets offered some.

COMMENTS:

- p. 20 How many wolves? Have I missed missed something?
- p. 22 Does Miyax think the wolves can understand her? Can they?
- p. 23 Eelie? Excitement = Eelie?
- p. 24 Why does she try to make the wolves get food for her when she has an ulo?
- p. 25 Sunny Night?
- p. 27 "learn about her family" Does that mean her wolf family?

REACTION:

Exciting!

discussions of characters and setting through their entries, and the quality of students' entries improved. Both groups enjoyed the interaction. We conducted a similar project and had a high level of success (Roe and Smith, 1997). (See Chapter 11 for more details about the project.)

Art provides another option for responding. Whitin (2002) has her students try to show their ideas about the books through sketching. She says, "It's called sketch-to-stretch because as we sketch and talk about our sketches, our minds are stretched to think in new ways" (p. 445). Students use colors, shapes, lines, or complete pictures to represent their thinking and are asked to give reasons for their representations. They also write brief statements that explain their thoughts in words. Whitin emphasizes that story ideas can be represented in many ways; some students use colors and shapes, some more detailed drawings. Often, the symbolism that is used exhibits deep understanding.

As groups finish their books, the teacher can encourage students to create extension projects individually, in pairs, or as a group. Examples include reading a similar book or a book by the same author, creating a drama, and writing an epilogue for the story.

● Thematic Literature Units

Thematic literature units are structured around themes, based on topics such as homes, families, survival, taking care of our earth, wild animals, pets, specific geographic regions (for example, South America), or specific groups of people (for example, Japanese); genres, such as biography, science fiction, or folktales; authors, such as Cynthia Voigt, Judith Viorst, or Maurice Sendak; or single books. Shanahan, Robinson, and Schneider (1995, p. 718) urge development of units around such themes as "We all should try to make the world a better place," rather than just topics, such as "lupines." Barton and Smith (2000, p. 55) echo the idea of avoiding the use of simple topics that "organize content and activities together simply because they contain or mention a similar subject—bears, cats, dragons, leaves."

Thematic units allow students to delve more deeply into ideas and thus develop deeper understandings and see connections between ideas. With themes, students can support or challenge a position and think more deeply about it. Themes can help teachers and learners focus on meaning making. A theme offers a *focus* for instruction and activities, making it easier for students to see the reason for classroom activities, acquire an integrated knowledge base, achieve depth and breadth of learning, and connect with real audiences. The variety of materials used allows for these accomplishments (Lipson et al., 1993; Bergeron, 1996).

There are other values as well. The reflection involved in studying themes can enhance metacognition, but perhaps the biggest advantage of thematic teaching is the promotion of positive attitudes toward reading and writing. The range of topics covered and the opportunity for self-selection promote student interest and positive attitudes. Another advantage is that time is less fragmented in a classroom in which the teacher uses thematic units. The number of subjects to be taught is reduced by embedding one subject in another one (Lipson et al., 1993).

Norton (1993b) suggests a procedure for developing a unit. The first step is to identify a theme that can be enriched with literature. Then the teacher and students construct a web with subtopics that become the subjects of study for groups of students. Students locate books and other resources that will help them investigate their subjects; then they share their findings creatively with the rest of the class. Example 7.5 on page 288 shows another way to develop a literature-based, learner-centered thematic unit that is based on the K-W-L procedure (Ogle, 1989) described in Chapter 5.

A single book or story can be used as the focus for curricular integration (Lauritzen, Jaeger, and Davenport, 1996). (Example 7.6 shows a web for a unit based on the book *Number the Stars.*) *Webbing* is a technique that connects a central topic or perhaps a book to related ideas. A web is a framework that can cut across curricular areas. Emphasizing that no two webs are alike, Huck, Hepler, and Hickman (1997) recommend webbing as a plan for literature study that grows out of students' interests and the strengths of the books. During the process of creating a web, teachers become aware of the many directions in which books can lead children. Although the teacher uses the web as an overall plan, students contribute their own ideas as the theme unfolds, so the study becomes learner-centered.

Teachers can also develop literature units using books that share similar characteristics. *Textsets* are books that have the same author, theme, topic, genre, or some other characteristic. They can set the stage for critical thinking by students as they look for connections. Textsets encourage discussion and varied interpretations (Heine, 1991). A textset on Katherine Paterson's books might include *Bridge to Terabithia, Lyddie, The Great Gilly Hopkins, Jacob Have I Loved,* and *The Sign of the*

TECHNOLOGY 🖥️ *Chrysanthemum.* Textsets are available for computers on CD-ROM, as well. Obviously, use of textsets allows small-group discussion in which students can compare and contrast a variety of related books and write in response journals about the relationships they have discovered. Roser and colleagues (1992) incorporated literature comparison charts (which they called *language charts*) into thematic units to facilitate the making of connections among the stories. The charts seemed to enhance the students' reactions to the literature.

Gallagher (1995) suggests hooking the interest of adolescent readers with one or more young adult novels, then including in the textset a classic that is related in some way to the young adult literature. The connections made between or among the books can enrich the reading. For example, Katherine Paterson's *Park's Quest* could lead to the reading of Charles Dickens's *Great Expectations.* Both books are concerned with a young man's search for his own identity. S. E. Hinton's *The Outsiders* could also be paired with *Great Expectations;* Ponyboy even says he feels like Pip. Joan Lowery Nixon's *The Name of the Game Was Murder* could be paired with Agatha Christie's *And Then There Were None* (Pavonetti, 1996). Books may be paired according to theme, setting, mood, or some other element.

DIVERSITY Evans (1994) describes a bilingual thematic unit on fear, composed of scary stories from English and Spanish cultures. The focus can be on understanding fear and overcoming it. Since fear is a universal emotion, its use as a topic allows for

EXAMPLE 7.5 Thematic Unit: Immigrants

Topic: Immigrants must make adjustments to their new environments (adapted from the curriculum framework theme of multicultural studies)

Goal: To understand how immigrants adjust to a new environment

Initiating Activity: Read Allen Say's Caldecott winner *Grandfather's Journey* (Houghton Mifflin, 1993), the story of the author's grandfather, who lived in both Japan and the United States. Follow the reading with a discussion of how it feels to belong to two countries, and introduce the word *immigrant*.

What We Know: Ask the children what they know about immigrants. They respond by saying:

> People come to the United States from all over the world.
>
> Many of them speak different languages.
>
> They have special customs.

What We Want to Learn: Ask the children what they want to learn. They respond by saying:

> How do immigrants get to be citizens?
>
> How do they feel about leaving their homes?
>
> What are some problems they face in a new land?

How We Can Find Out: Ask the children how they will find the answers. They respond by saying:

> Read books about people who are immigrants.
>
> Invite an immigrant to speak to the class.
>
> Ask our families where *we* came from.

Resource Materials: With your help and that of the librarian, the children collect trade books and reference sources to learn about immigrants. Some of their favorites are

> *Coolies* by Yin (New York: Philomel, 2001). Chinese brothers come to America and find work helping to build a railroad across the West.
>
> *Immigrant Kids* by Russell Freedman (New York: Scholastic, 1980). Photographs tell the story of immigrant children at home, school, work, and play.
>
> *The Lotus Seed* by Sherry Garland (Orlando: Harcourt Brace Jovanovich, 1993). A Vietnamese family flees its homeland to escape a war and takes along a precious lotus seed.
>
> *Molly's Pilgrim* by Barbara Cohen (New York: Lothrop, 1983). A Jewish girl takes a doll to school dressed as her mother was dressed when she left Russia.
>
> *Refugees* by Carole Seymour-Jones (New York: New Discovery Books, 1992). People who believe they must leave their country face problems in the new land.
>
> *How My Family Lives in America* by Susan Kuklin (New York: Bradbury, 1992). Children of parents born in other countries tell what makes their families special.

Continued

> **EXAMPLE 7.5** **Thematic Literature Unit Plan** *(cont.)*
>
> **Activities:** The children
>
> 1. inquire about their family backgrounds and find books about their own cultures.
>
> 2. use reference books to discover how immigrants become U.S. citizens.
>
> 3. read independently each day from a theme-related book.
>
> 4. make displays of books that feature different cultures.
>
> 5. write travel diaries of their own real or imagined journeys to a new land.
>
> 6. discuss which prized possessions they would take with them.
>
> 7. choose one nationality that represents many of the children and divide into groups to study the contributions of that culture (prominent people, inventions and discoveries, songs and dances, folklore, games, foods, vocabulary words, and customs).
>
> 8. meet in groups to prepare projects on these topics.
>
> 9. write a play about emigrating to the United States on the basis of experiences and feelings understood from books they have read.
>
> **Culminating Activity:** The children invite another class to attend their play, view their book displays, and observe or participate in their group projects.
>
> **What We Learned:** Ask the children what they learned. They will give many answers, including these:
>
> > About our own heritages
> >
> > Contributions of different nationalities
> >
> > Some of the problems immigrants face

cultural comparisons of literary treatments of the topic. Thematic units are often opened with prereading activities for developing background, such as those mentioned earlier for the core book, in which children discuss what they already know about the focus of the unit. Students may brainstorm terms that they associate with the theme, and these terms may be organized into a semantic web. (See Chapters 4, 5, and 10 for more on semantic webs and literature webs.)

The teacher may read aloud one or more books that fit the focus of the unit before allowing students to form small groups to read from multiple copies of other related books. One fifth-grade teacher read aloud *Lincoln: A Photobiography* at the beginning of a unit based on the genre of biography and let the students form small groups to read such books as *What's the Big Idea, Ben Franklin?*; *Eleanor Roosevelt: First Lady of the World*; *A Weed Is a Flower: The Life of George Washington Carver*; and others for which she had secured multiple copies. Single copies of other biographies were also available for independent reading, as were short biographies in basal readers, anthologies, and periodicals (Zarillo, 1989).

Any *genre*, or type of literature, can be a focus for study (Tompkins and McGee, 1993). In Example 7.7 on page 292 the genre is folktales. Other viable genres are

EXAMPLE 7.6 **Literature Web**

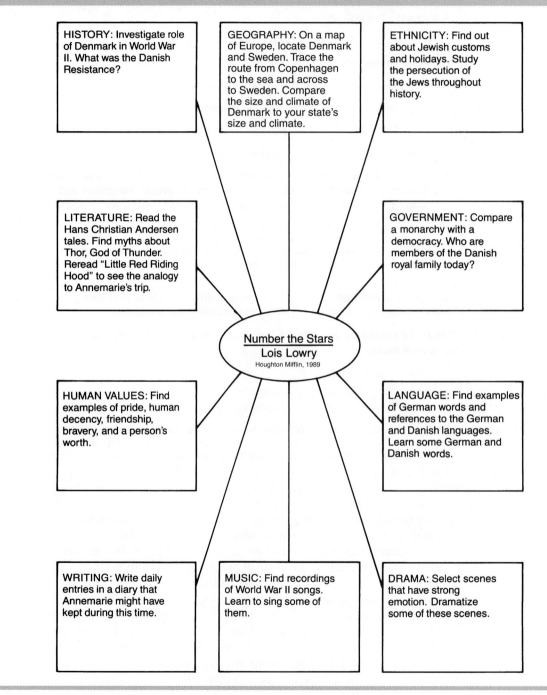

HISTORY: Investigate role of Denmark in World War II. What was the Danish Resistance?

GEOGRAPHY: On a map of Europe, locate Denmark and Sweden. Trace the route from Copenhagen to the sea and across to Sweden. Compare the size and climate of Denmark to your state's size and climate.

ETHNICITY: Find out about Jewish customs and holidays. Study the persecution of the Jews throughout history.

LITERATURE: Read the Hans Christian Andersen tales. Find myths about Thor, God of Thunder. Reread "Little Red Riding Hood" to see the analogy to Annemarie's trip.

GOVERNMENT: Compare a monarchy with a democracy. Who are members of the Danish royal family today?

Number the Stars
Lois Lowry
Houghton Mifflin, 1989

HUMAN VALUES: Find examples of pride, human decency, friendship, bravery, and a person's worth.

LANGUAGE: Find examples of German words and references to the German and Danish languages. Learn some German and Danish words.

WRITING: Write daily entries in a diary that Annemarie might have kept during this time.

MUSIC: Find recordings of World War II songs. Learn to sing some of them.

DRAMA: Select scenes that have strong emotion. Dramatize some of these scenes.

Source: Web based on *Number the Stars* by Lois Lowry (Boston: Houghton Mifflin, 1989).

poetry, historical fiction, biography, and fantasy, each of which may be divided into subtopics. For instance, the types of fantasy that may be studied include (1) modern literary tales based on folktales, (2) fantastic stories, which are basically realistic but contain elements of fantasy, (3) science fiction, and (4) high fantasy with heroes and heroines who confront evil for the sake of humanity.

TECHNOLOGY The teacher may read aloud to the entire class the selection or selections chosen to open the unit. Some selections may be presented through videotapes or audiotapes. Each reading should be accompanied by or followed by discussion of the material, writing in literature logs, and other activities, such as those listed for follow-up activities in the section on whole-class reading of a core book.

The teacher may then give book talks about the books that are available in multiple copies to help children make decisions about the groups in which they will work. Students should have choices regarding these books, although it may be necessary to ask them to list their top three choices and to assign a book from among these choices, because of the limited number of copies available for each book. Book talks may also be given for some of the single-copy books. In addition, as students finish reading certain books, they may give book talks to entice their classmates to read these books.

Some unit activities should be designed for whole-group participation (for example, the read-alouds), some for small-group participation (for example, activities related to the multiple-copy books), and some for independent work (for example, literature logs about books read individually). Whole-group activities are likely to include minilessons related to the reading that the children are doing. These minilessons may focus on literary elements or reading strategies.

When small groups meet about the books they are reading in common, activities such as those described in the section on literature circles can be used. As small-group and independent reading progress, students may continue to build on the webs they started during the introductory activities. At the end of the unit, culminating activities may include comparing and contrasting the books read and some elements of the books, such as characters, settings, plots, and themes; construction of time lines related to the unit theme; creative dramatics based on readings; writing related to the theme; and so on. For example, students may cooperatively write a story with the same theme that appears in the books they have read in the unit (Marzano, 1990).

Example 7.8 shows a thematic literature unit plan that is based on a theme focus from a core book.

● Individualized Reading Approach

The ***individualized reading approach*** encourages each student to move at her or his own pace through self-chosen reading material, rather than requiring students to move through teacher-prescribed material at the same pace as other students placed in the same group for reading instruction. With the individualized reading approach, which is designed to encourage independent reading, each student receives assistance in improving performance when the need for such assistance becomes apparent.

EXAMPLE 7.7 Thematic Unit on Folklore

1. Let children read and compare folktale variants, beginning with the Brothers Grimm tales and moving toward contemporary versions.

2. Encourage children to tell stories, repeating familiar favorites or creating new tales.

3. Read and/or tell classic folktales to the students.

4. Provide opportunities for discovering word origins and literary allusions, especially in myths (e.g., echo, Pandora's box, Mercury, Atlas).

5. Let children dramatize folktales using puppets, pantomime, readers' theater, or creative dramatics.

6. Encourage children to write creatively. Have them

   a. study the characteristics of a fable (brevity, animal characters, a moral) and create new fables.

   b. write modern versions of fairy tales.

   c. make up a ballad based on folklore and set it to music.

   d. make up original *pourquoi* tales, such as "Why the Rabbit Has Long Ears."

   e. write new endings for folktales after changing major events in the stories.

   f. select a newspaper story, find a moral for it (e.g., "theft doesn't pay"), and write a fable about this moral.

7. Help students find out how folktales were originally communicated and how they came to be written.

8. Invite storytellers for children to hear. Ask students to interview the storytellers about techniques and about the origins of the tales they tell.

9. Encourage students to compare similarities in characters and motifs of folktales from around the world (e.g., the Jackal in India, the Weasel in Africa, and Brer Rabbit in the United States).

10. Have students locate the origins of various versions of folktales on a map.

11. Ask students to compare the artwork used to illustrate folktales (e.g., compare the illustrations in Walt Disney's version of *Snow White and the Seven Dwarfs* with Nancy Burkert's illustrations).

12. Provide tapes of music and dance based on folktales, such as selections from Stephen Sondheim's *Into the Woods*.

Characteristics of an individualized reading approach include the following:

❶ *Self-selection.* Students are allowed to choose material they are interested in reading. Each student may choose a different book. The teacher may offer suggestions or give help if it is requested, but the decision ultimately rests with the student. Thus an individualized reading approach has built-in motivation: students want to read the material because they have chosen it themselves.

EXAMPLE 7.8 Thematic Literature Unit Plan

Pam Petty, a second-grade teacher at Carthage Elementary School in Carthage, Tennessee, developed a thematic unit around the reading of *Freckle Juice* by Judy Blume (Dell, 1971).

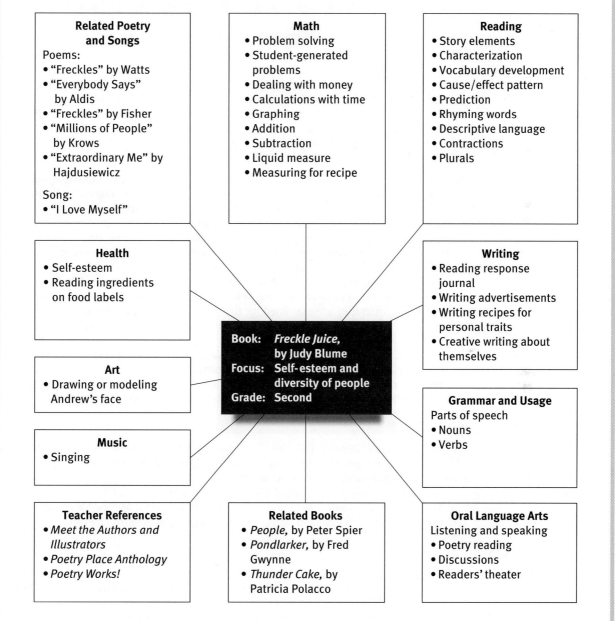

Related Poetry and Songs

Poems:
- "Freckles" by Watts
- "Everybody Says" by Aldis
- "Freckles" by Fisher
- "Millions of People" by Krows
- "Extraordinary Me" by Hajdusiewicz

Song:
- "I Love Myself"

Math
- Problem solving
- Student-generated problems
- Dealing with money
- Calculations with time
- Graphing
- Addition
- Subtraction
- Liquid measure
- Measuring for recipe

Reading
- Story elements
- Characterization
- Vocabulary development
- Cause/effect pattern
- Prediction
- Rhyming words
- Descriptive language
- Contractions
- Plurals

Health
- Self-esteem
- Reading ingredients on food labels

Art
- Drawing or modeling Andrew's face

Music
- Singing

Book: *Freckle Juice,* by Judy Blume
Focus: Self-esteem and diversity of people
Grade: Second

Writing
- Reading response journal
- Writing advertisements
- Writing recipes for personal traits
- Creative writing about themselves

Grammar and Usage

Parts of speech
- Nouns
- Verbs

Teacher References
- *Meet the Authors and Illustrators*
- *Poetry Place Anthology*
- *Poetry Works!*

Related Books
- *People,* by Peter Spier
- *Pondlarker,* by Fred Gwynne
- *Thunder Cake,* by Patricia Polacco

Oral Language Arts

Listening and speaking
- Poetry reading
- Discussions
- Readers' theater

Continued

EXAMPLE 7.8   Thematic Literature Unit Plan *(cont.)*

Pam's unit plan also uses other literature selections as it focuses on self-esteem and diversity among people. It has cross-curricular connections with a number of content areas: listening/speaking, reading, writing, health, math, art, and music, as shown in the diagram.

The unit covers ten days of instruction.

Day 1

The children are introduced to Judy Blume, the author of *Freckle Juice*. The teacher shares information gleaned from Scholastic's *Meet the Authors and Illustrators,* by Deborah Kovacs and James Preller. Other books by Judy Blume are displayed. The children examine the target book for information, such as title, author, copyright date, and publisher. They are asked to look at the cover picture and the picture at the beginning of Chapter 1 and make predictions on the basis of the title and pictures.

Day 2

The students read Chapter 1. They keep a word log of "neat" words and unknown words found in the chapter. In the search for "neat" words, students look for interesting language use. (This activity is repeated for each chapter.) The class begins to construct a story map on the board. The teacher diagrams the elements of the story as the students dictate. The students use the map to fill in data about the story on a story-frame handout that asks for main characters, setting, problem, and solution. They copy the map on the board onto the back of their story-frame handout.

The poems "Freckles" by Mabel Watts, "Everybody Says" by Dorothy Aldis, and "Freckles" by Aileen Fisher (found in *Poetry Place Anthology*, Scholastic, 1983) are used for choral reading. Then they are examined for rhyming words, plurals, nouns, verbs, and contractions. The words in the poems are used to stimulate brainstorming about other words that share the same characteristics.

The students begin a reading response journal in which they respond each day to the reading. They also discuss their entries in small groups.

For each chapter (Chapter 1 on this day), on a cause-and-effect chart, one main action is chosen as the cause and entered on the left side of the chart, and the result or effect of this action is entered on the right side.

Day 3

The students read Chapter 2. They read the poem "Millions of People" by Jane W. Krows (*Poetry Place Anthology*), which is useful for promoting self-esteem. They also examine the poem for plurals, nouns, and rhyming words.

The students sing "I Love Myself" (Affective Enterprises).

The students do creative writing on "The Best Things About Me" or "What I Would Like to Change About Myself (and Why)," or they design flyers advertising Freckle Juice for sale.

Day 4

The students read Chapter 3.

The teacher reads aloud the book *People* by Peter Spier (Doubleday, 1980). This book illustrates global diversity among people.

The children write original recipes for curls, blue eyes, height, or other traits.

Continued

EXAMPLE 7.8   Thematic Literature Unit Plan *(cont.)*

Day 5

The students take one card per character and list that character's name, description, and traits on one side of the card. They draw a picture of the character on the back. Students hold up character cards to respond to questions in class.

For art, the students draw Andrew's face or make it out of clay, and they glue on popcorn or other materials for freckles.

Day 6

The students read Chapter 4. They do choral reading of the poem "Extraordinary Me" by Babs Bell Hajdusiewicz (*Poetry Works*, Modern Curriculum Press, 1990). The students use the descriptive language to draw a picture of the person. Then they compare their pictures with the one on the poem chart.

The students make lists of words to describe themselves. Classmates read the lists and try to guess who is being described.

Day 7

The students read Chapter 5. They finish the story map and story frame.

The teacher gives the students a handout with a boy's face on it, laminating film, and markers. The students listen to the teacher read descriptions of three story events: being embarrassed at school, drawing blue spots on face, and being sad and sick after drinking juice. The students color laminating film and hold it on the boy's picture to show which event is being read about.

Day 8

The students do math problems related to Andrew's allowance and saving to buy the juice, problems related to telling time (connected with events in the story), problems about adding or multiplying quantities of liquid (quarts of freckle juice), and problems related to making and reading graphs. The teacher reads *Pondlarker* by Fred Gwynne to the students to stimulate further discussion of self-esteem.

Day 9

The students retell the story or perform it through readers' theater.

The teacher reads *Thunder Cake* by Patricia Polacco to the children. This book involves both self-esteem and a recipe.

Day 10

The teacher shows the students cans and boxes of food or juice and tells them to write down the expected ingredients for Thunder Cake. Then the class follows the recipe for Thunder Cake and compares the actual list of ingredients to the students' expected list. The students discuss "surprise" ingredients (such as tomatoes).

---

❷ *Self-pacing.* Each student reads the material at his or her own pace. Slower students are not rushed through material in order to keep up with the faster ones, and faster students are not held back until others have caught up with them.

❸ *Strategy and skill instruction.* The teacher helps students as needed, either on an individual basis or in groups, to develop their word recognition and comprehension strategies and skills.

STANDARDS AND
ASSESSMENT

❹ *Recordkeeping.* The teacher keeps records of each student's progress. He or she must know the levels of a student's reading performance to know which books the student can read independently, which are too difficult or frustrating, and which can be read with the teacher's assistance. The teacher must also be aware of each student's reading strengths and weaknesses and should keep a record of the strategies introduced and the skills help given to each one. Each student should keep records of books read, new words encountered, and new strategies learned.

STANDARDS AND
ASSESSMENT

❺ *Student-teacher conferences.* One or two times a week, the teacher schedules a conference with each student; its length may vary from three to fifteen minutes, depending on the purpose. Teachers act as collaborators in the reading of text, as demonstrators of strategies, and as observers and assessors of reading behaviors during conferences (Gill, 2000).

❻ *Sharing activities.* The teacher plans some time each week for the students to share books they have read individually. The students may share with the entire class or with a small group. Sharing can sometimes take the form of book auctions in which the students bid with play money on the opportunity to read a book next. The "auctioneer" tries to interest the students in bidding by telling about the book (Bagford, 1985).

❼ *Independent work.* The students do a great deal of independent work at their seats, rather than spending most of the assigned reading period in a group with the teacher. Better readers and older students can benefit more from time spent in individualized reading than can poorer readers and younger students, who need more teacher direction (Bagford, 1985).

Exposure to different types of literature can help students build schemata for these types and should thus increase their efficiency in processing texts. Reading a variety of material also provides them with vicarious experiences that help build other schemata and thus enhance future comprehension. Encountering words in a variety of meaningful contexts extends the students' vocabulary knowledge.

To set up an individualized reading program, a teacher must have available a large supply of books, magazines, newspapers, and other reading materials, covering a variety of reading levels and many different interest areas. This collection will need to be supplemented continuously after the program begins, for many students will quickly read all the books that are appropriate for them.

STANDARDS AND
ASSESSMENT

The teacher should have read a large number of the books available in the classroom, since doing so makes it much easier to check the students' comprehension. Starting a file of comprehension questions and answers for books being used in the program is a good idea; these questions will be available year after year and will help refresh the teacher's memory of the books. The teacher will also find it convenient to have a file of strategy- and skill-developing activities, covering the entire spectrum of word recognition and comprehension strategies and skills and a wide range of difficulty levels.

When starting an individualized program, the teacher should determine the students' reading levels and interests in order to choose books for the program that cover a sufficiently broad range of topics and difficulty levels. Two articles that can be helpful in choosing materials on appropriate levels are "Caldecott Medal Books and Readability Levels: Not Just Picture Books" (Chamberlain and Leal, 1999) and "A Newbery Medal-winning Combination: High Student Interest Plus Appropriate Readability Levels" (Leal and Chamberlain-Solecki, 1998), both of which provide readability information for excellent book choices. There are many sources that can help teachers find books appropriate for various cultural backgrounds, such as books featuring Hispanic culture or characters (Smolen and Ortiz-Castro, 2000; Martinez-Roldan and Lopez-Robertson, 1999/2000).

DIVERSITY

Before initiating an individualized program, the teacher can plan routines to follow in the classroom, considering questions such as (1) How are books to be checked out? (2) How will conferences be set up? (3) What should students who are working independently at their desks do when they need assistance? The room arrangement can also be planned in advance to allow for good traffic flow. If books are categorized and located in a number of places instead of bunched together in a single location, students will have less trouble finding them, and the potential noise level in the room will be lower.

STANDARDS AND ASSESSMENT

The teacher may find that having a file folder for each student helps in organizing and recordkeeping. Each file folder can contain both checklists on which to record that student's strengths and weaknesses in applying particular skills and strategies and a form noting conference dates and instructional help given. Students can keep their own records in file folders that are accessible both to them and to the teacher. These records will have different content and more or fewer specific details, depending on the maturity of the children.

Student-teacher conferences serve a variety of purposes, including the following:

❶ *To help with book choices.* Teachers should spend some time showing children how to choose appropriate books. Teachers can encourage them to read one or two pages of the books they think might appeal to them and to consider the number of unfamiliar words they encounter. If there are more than five unfamiliar words per page, the book might be too difficult, whereas if there are no unfamiliar words, the child should consider the possibility that he or she could read more difficult material. A teacher can suggest potentially interesting books to students who find it hard to make a choice. Student-written book reviews may be provided for students who are having trouble deciding about books. Students can learn to write good reviews by examining models of written reviews and receiving assistance from the teacher or librarian (Jenks and Roberts, 1990).

STANDARDS AND ASSESSMENT

❷ *To check comprehension.* Conferences help determine how well the children are comprehending the books and other materials they are reading. Much of the time, the teacher and students may have authentic discussions about issues in the book during the conferences. Sometimes, however, the teacher may ask a student to retell all or part of the story or may ask a variety of types of comprehension questions. (See Chapter 6 for information on question types.)

STANDARDS AND ASSESSMENT

❸ *To check word recognition strategies and oral reading skills.* The teacher can ask a student to read orally, observing his or her methods of attacking unfamiliar words and using oral reading skills, such as appropriate phrasing and good oral expression.

4 *To give assistance in applying strategies and skills.* If a student is the only one in the room who needs help with a particular strategy or skill, the teacher can help that student on a one-to-one basis during a conference.

5 *To plan for sharing.* Some conferences are designed to help students prepare for sharing their reading experiences with others. If a student wishes to read a portion of a book to the class, the teacher might use a conference to listen to that student practice audience reading and to give help with the presentation.

There is nothing contradictory about using group instruction in an individualized reading program. A teacher can group students with similar difficulties to give help. The important thing is to be sure that all students get the instruction they need when they need it and are not forced to sit through instruction they do not need.

In an individualized reading program, each student is expected to be involved in independent silent reading a great deal of the time. This time should not be interrupted by noisy surroundings or non-task-oriented activities. The teacher should make the rules for the reading time very clear and should indicate acceptable activities, such as taking part in student-teacher conferences, selecting a book, reading silently, giving or receiving specific reading assistance, taking part in a reading group, completing a strategy or skill-development practice activity, and keeping records concerned with reading activity.

Individualizing a reading program is a huge undertaking, but such a program can be introduced gradually by using it only one day a week, while using the basal program the other four days, and then increasing the time spent in the individualized program one day at a time over a period of weeks until all five days of the week are devoted to it. An alternative is to introduce the program to one reading group at a time while the remaining groups continue the basal program. After one group has become familiar with the approach, other groups can be introduced to it, until the entire class is participating in the individualized reading program. Teachers whom Harris (1996) worked with thought that using the basal for part of the week and literature-based instruction for the other part of the week would be a good way to start.

The main advantages of an individualized reading approach follow.

1 Students have built-in motivation to read books they have chosen themselves.

2 Students are not compared negatively with one another because every student has a different book and because the books are primarily trade books, which have no visible grade designations.

3 Each student has an opportunity to learn to read at his or her own rate.

4 Student-teacher conferences create a great deal of personal contact between the teacher and students.

5 Reading books at comfortable reading levels develops fluency and can contribute to improved reading rates.

6 Students realize that reading is enjoyable.

TIME for REFLECTION

Some teachers believe that literature-based instruction using trade books should completely replace the use of published reading series that contain anthologies of literature. Others believe that using both results in the best instruction. **What do *you* think, and why?**

The characteristics of this approach that some educators have considered to be disadvantages are as follows:

❶ The teacher must amass and continually replenish a large quantity of reading material.

❷ The need to schedule many individual conferences and small-group meetings can create time difficulties.

❸ An enormous amount of recordkeeping is necessary.

❹ The program lacks a sequential approach to strategy and skill development.

Language Experience Approach (LEA)

The *language experience approach* interrelates the different language arts and uses the children's experiences as the basis for reading materials. The rationale for this approach has been stated very concisely by one of its leading proponents, R. V. Allen:

What I can think about, I can talk about.

What I can say, I can write—or someone can write for me.

What I write, I can read.

I can read what I write, and what other people can write for me to read (1973, p. 158).

A child's background may be limited, but every child has experiences that can be converted into stories. In addition, the teacher can plan interesting firsthand experiences that can result in the creation of reading material that is meaningful for all students.

This approach to reading is obviously not new, although its implementation has changed over the years. Today the experience charts used in the approach may be either group or individual compositions; stories about field trips, school activities, or personal experiences outside school; or charts that contain directions, special words, observations, job assignments, questions to be answered, imaginative stories or poems, or class rules. Current applications are often found in whole language classrooms, since this approach gives the children control over the content and language used in the stories. (See Chapter 2 for more about experience charts.)

DIVERSITY 🌐 Because the stories used in the language experience approach are developed by the children, they are motivational, and because these stories use the language of the children, the reading material is meaningful to them. The language experience approach has been used effectively with students who speak English as a second language; it provides material for reading instruction that they can understand (Moustafa and Penrose, 1985; Moustafa, 1987).

The language experience approach is consistent with schema theory. Because it uses the child's experiences as the basis for written language, the child necessarily has adequate schemata to comprehend the material and can thus develop a schema for

Individualized Reading Approach

Mr. Neal is sitting at a table with Paul, a student who has been reading the book *Maniac Magee*. They are having a lively discussion about which characters in the story value reading and how they show that they do. Mr. Neal is able to tell from this discussion how well Paul has comprehended various aspects of the book, but he is also engaged in a valid discussion of the content about which he has a personal opinion with a boy who has his own opinion, feels free to share it, and knows how to use events from the book to back up his ideas.

In the meantime, most of the other class members are reading from self-selected books at their desks or on the carpeted area of the reading center. When Megan has problems with a word in her book, she quietly leans over and asks for assistance from her assigned buddy, Tracy. When Tracy fails to be of help, Megan lists the word, page, and paragraph and reads on in her book.

Trey, who has a great deal of trouble sustaining independent reading over a period of time, is sitting at the computer, reading from a book on CD-ROM that allows him to click on words he doesn't know to obtain both pronunciations and definitions. With this assistance, Trey is able to remain focused on his reading for the entire period.

Jason and Joshua are sitting close together discussing the mock interview they plan to use during the book-sharing time on Friday. Both have read *Hatchet*, and they have decided to share with the rest of the class by having Jason play a reporter and Joshua play Brian. They are intently listing interview questions and answers to use for this purpose.

As Mr. Neal finishes the conference with Paul, he asks who needs some help. Megan and Mark hold up their hands, and Mr. Neal moves to their desks to offer assistance. Then he returns to the conference table and calls Michael, who is scheduled for the next conference, to come up. Michael has been having difficulty with word recognition skills, and Mr. Neal asks him to read orally from some new material in the book that he is currently reading, in order to assess the particular difficulties that he is having.

After Michael's conference, Mr. Neal will meet with a small group of students who need help in making inferences when they read. He will model the process for them and have them engage in some directed practice activities.

Each student in Mr. Neal's class has self-selected material to read when he or she is not involved in a teacher-student conference, a peer-planning session, or a needs-group session. The students know the procedures to use when they have trouble, and they know they can receive individual attention during conferences or at intervals during class time if they follow accepted procedures. The fact that they have chosen their reading material heightens their motivation to read it and makes student engagement more likely.

reading that includes the idea that written words have meaning (Hacker, 1980). Children can use compound and complex sentences and a wide vocabulary in their stories, and they seem to find their own language patterns much easier to read than those in basal readers, probably because clues in a familiar context are easier to use. In fact, students often pick up the long, unusual words in experience stories faster than many of the short service words, probably because the distinctive configurations of these words contribute to recognition.

With the language experience approach, reading grows out of natural, ongoing activities. Students can see the relationships between reading and their oral language. This approach offers good opportunities for developing the concepts of *writing, word,* and *sentence.* During the language experience process, children see the transformation from oral language to print take place, including directionality, spacing between words, and punctuation and capitalization. Framing the individual language units with the hands helps teachers illustrate their meanings to students. Another benefit is that observations made during the dictation and reading of a language experience story and during the follow-up activities can provide the teacher with diagnostic insights into children's reading difficulties (Waugh, 1993).

STANDARDS AND ASSESSMENT

● Implementation in Kindergarten

Chapter 2 describes the use of language experience charts in kindergarten and also provides an example of a chart. At this level, teachers often use the charts to emphasize that oral language can be recorded and reconstructed, rather than focusing on having the children read the charts. Others, such as Karnowski (1989), involve kindergarten students in activities more like those described for the primary grades in the next section. Karnowski uses the language experience approach with process writing (discussed in Chapter 8), having the children choose their topics for writing from among their previous experiences. Discussion and sometimes dramatic play and/or drawing precede the writing of the story. The initial dictation of the story is revised and edited according to the children's direction, to show that first drafts are not the only drafts. The teacher reads and rereads charts before the children read them independently. Then the teacher uses the charts to teach vocabulary, decoding, and comprehension skills. Of course, the charts are "published" for reading by the children and their peers. This approach fits perfectly with the current belief in emergent literacy.

Individual stories may be solicited by asking the children to write something they want the class to know, a kind of written show-and-tell. The writing should include invented spellings such as those described in Chapter 2 (Coate and Castle, 1989).

The children who have started to recognize many words may move into a program similar to the one described next for use in the primary grades.

● Implementation in the Primary Grades

Implementation of the language experience approach with a group of primary-grade students may take a number of forms, but the following steps are typical.

❶ Participating in a shared experience

❷ Discussing the experience

❸ Cooperative writing of the story on a chart, the board, or a computer

❹ Participating in extension activities related to the story

After the children have participated in a shared experience and have talked it over thoroughly, they are ready to compose a group experience story. First, the teacher may ask for suggestions for a title, allowing the students to select their favorite by voting. Then the teacher records the title on the chalkboard or a transparency. Each child offers details to add to the story, and the teacher records these details. She or he may write "Joan said" by Joan's contribution or may simply

During the creation of a language experience chart, children see the transformation from oral language to print taking place.
(© Elizabeth Crews)

write the sentence, calling attention to capitalization and punctuation while doing so. After recording each idea, the teacher reads it aloud. When all contributions have been recorded, the teacher reads the entire story to the class, sweeping his or her hand under each line to emphasize the left-to-right progression. Then the teacher asks the class to read the story with him or her as he or she moves a hand under the words. Under cover of the group, no child will stand out if he or she does not know a particular word.

If the children have had numerous experiences with this type of activity, the teacher may proceed to other activities involving the story. If this is a very early reading experience for the group, the teacher will probably stop at this point until the next day. On the second day, the class can be divided into three or four groups with which the teacher can work separately. To begin each group session, the teacher rereads the story to the children, using a master chart made the day before. Then the group rereads it with him or her. Next, a volunteer may read the story with the teacher, filling in the words he or she knows while the teacher supplies the rest. After each child in the group has had a chance to read, the teacher asks students to find certain words on the chart. The teacher may also show the children sentence strips (prepared the day before) and have them match these strips with the lines on the chart, either letting volunteers reconstruct the entire chart from the sentence strips or using this as a learning-center activity to be completed individually while other groups are meeting. Group charts can be useful in developing many skills and are commonly used for lessons in word endings, compound words, long and short vowels, rhyming words, initial consonants, capitalization, punctuation, and other areas.

If the teacher makes a copy of the story for each student, it is possible to underline, on that copy, the words that the student recognizes while reading the story. The teacher may then make word cards of these words, which serve as the beginnings of the children's *word banks.* (Word cards containing the words a child has used in stories can eventually be used to practice sight vocabulary, to work on word recognition skills, and to develop comprehension skills.) As a group of students finishes meeting with the teacher, the students may be given the opportunity to illustrate their stories individually.

TECHNOLOGY After this first attempt, students will write most experience stories in small groups, sometimes working on a story together and sometimes producing and sharing individual stories. At times, some children may dictate their stories to helpers from higher grades. Some teachers use audiotape recorders for dictation.

Class stories do not always have to be in the same format. They may take the form of reports, newspaper articles, descriptive essays, or letters, or they can be creative in content while incorporating a particular writing style to which the children have been exposed. It is important that teachers use the children's own language in language experience stories, even if the children's language does not fit the teacher's idea of basic words and sentence patterns for reading. If they do not do so, students are not likely to reap the full benefits of this approach.

TECHNOLOGY Computers can be useful in a language experience lesson. The teacher can enter into the computer student-dictated material and modify it as the students direct. A large monitor or projection device is needed for this approach. The teacher can give students individual printed copies to illustrate or include in reading notebooks.

At some point the students may be able to enter their stories into the computer themselves. Several word-processing programs are easy enough for even primary students to learn to use.

Children can write stories on the computer most effectively when several students work together. The group of children can collectively decide what to say, taking turns entering sentences as they are composed, or some students can be in charge of keyboarding and others in charge of content and mechanics, spelling, and grammar.

Sharing stories, whether orally or in written form, is very important, since group members will soon see that certain words occur over and over again and that they can read the stories their classmates write. The experience stories written by the group as a whole may be gathered into a booklet under a general title chosen by the group, and individuals may also bind their stories into booklets. Children will enjoy reading one another's booklets, and a collection of their own stories provides both a record of their activities and evidence of their growth in reading and writing.

In some schools students write language experience stories, illustrate them, make them into books, and set them up in a classroom library with library pockets and checkout cards, just as they might have in a regular library. Children assume jobs as librarians.

As time passes and the children learn to write and spell, they may wish to write experience stories by themselves, asking the teacher or turning to their word banks or dictionaries for help in spelling. Teachers should allow children to use invented spellings when they are writing, since they can go back and correct spelling and rewrite the story in a neater form later if others are to read it.

Rereading and editing require children to make judgments about syntax, semantics, and the topic and about whether or not others will understand the written account. These activities provide ways to emphasize comprehension when using language experience stories. The Classroom Scenario below presents the language experience approach in a primary-grade classroom.

Word banks offer many opportunities for instructional activities. When children have accumulated a sufficient number of word cards in their word banks, they can use them to compose new stories or to play word-matching or visual and auditory discrimination games. To develop comprehension skills, a teacher can use classification games, asking questions such as "How many of you have a color

CLASSROOM SCENARIO

Language Experience Approach

A lifelike raccoon puppet was shown to the children in a first-grade classroom. The presenter introduced the puppet as Rocky Raccoon and proceeded to tell them about his personality, including his preferences (for example, Rocky Road ice cream and rock music). The children looked at Rocky, touched his fur, and discussed him thoroughly. Then they dictated the following story:

Rocky Raccoon

Rocky is beautiful. Rocky is soft. Rocky is funny. Rocky is a nice raccoon. Rocky can do tricks. Rocky is cuddly. Rocky is fluffy.

The presenter read the story to the class and allowed them to read it with her. Then she posed this question: "Does your story sound like the ones that you have been listening to your teacher read to you?"

After thinking about it, the children said it did not sound like the books they had heard being read. The presenter then asked them, "What could you do to the story to make it sound more like the stories in books?"

Several children said, "Not repeat *Rocky* so many times. Use longer sentences. Put stuff from sentences together."

Step by step, the presenter questioned them about which mentions of *Rocky* to change and what to change them to and about which sentences went together and how they should be combined. The children's revisions were recorded one at a time, and the story was reread each time to see if they liked it better. They also decided to add a sentence. The final version that met with their approval went like this:

Rocky Raccoon

Rocky is beautiful. He is soft. He is funny. Rocky is a nice raccoon. He can do tricks. He is cuddly and fluffy. Rocky looks like he is wearing a mask.

Analysis of Scenario

This activity was the children's first experience with revising their own writing. They liked the fact that they could change the writing around to make it sound better to them. Even though they did not end up with classic literature, they had taken a step in their literacy development.

word? A word that shows action? A word that names a place?" When each student has as many as ten word cards, the children can begin to alphabetize them by the first letter, which gives them a practical reason to learn alphabetical order. They can also develop picture dictionaries representing the words on their cards, or they can search for their words in newspapers and magazines. After they recognize that their words appear in books, they will realize that they can read the books. The uses for word banks seem to be limited only by the teachers' and children's imaginations.

● Implementation in Higher Grades

The language experience approach has many applications above the primary grades. These applications are often in content area instruction: writing the results of scientific experiments; comparing and contrasting people, things, or events; writing directions for performing a task; and so forth.

Text structures found in content area textbooks, such as comparison-and-contrast patterns, can initially be taught through language experience activities. Then students will be more likely to understand these structures when they encounter them in content materials. First, the teacher can present students with two items and ask them how these items are alike. Then the teacher can ask how the items are different. The class can construct a chart of these likenesses and differences during the discussion. After the discussion, the students can dictate a language experience story based on the information listed on their chart. The teacher can encourage them to write first about likenesses and then about differences. Heller (1988) has pointed out that direct teaching of story structure can be helpful during language experience activities that are used with older remedial learners. She also emphasizes the inclusion of revision and editing as natural extensions of experience story writing.

TECHNOLOGY 🖥 Many computer applications lend themselves to upper-grade activities, for they allow children to enter their stories easily and provide ease of revision without the drudgery of recopying. A good computer application is the production of a newspaper based on experiences around the school. Programs are available that make the production of a nice-looking newspaper relatively easy for children. Students can be reporters, who initially enter the stories into the computer; editors, who edit the work of the reporters; and "typesetters," who format the edited material (Mason, 1984).

DIVERSITY 🌐 ## ● Use with Students Who Have Special Needs

The language experience approach can be used to help students with special needs learn how to read. Teachers must weigh the general benefits and drawbacks of this approach for these students, as well as for other students in the class. It offers something for students regardless of the modes through which they learn best, because it incorporates all modes. For instance, the learners use the auditory mode when stories are dictated or read aloud, the kinesthetic (motor) mode when they write stories, and the visual mode when they read stories.

The language experience approach promotes a good self-concept. It shows students that what they have to say is important enough to write down and that others are interested in it. It also promotes close contact between teachers and students. As the example in the Classroom Scenario below shows, this approach has been highly successful as a remedial technique, allowing low-achieving readers to read material that interests them rather than lower-grade-level materials that they quickly recognize as being designed for younger children.

DIVERSITY

The LEA is a good approach to use with English language learners (Heald-Taylor, 1989). Students who know very little English, however, need to acquire additional vocabulary and knowledge of oral language before they dictate sentences (Moustafa and Penrose, 1985). To increase students' vocabularies, teachers can ask them to touch, name, label, and talk about concrete objects.

The language experience approach also offers many advantages as a method for teaching reading to students whose dialect differs considerably from Standard English. A *dialect* is a variation of a language that is sufficiently different from the original to be considered a separate entity but not different enough to be classified as a separate language. Dialectal variations are usually associated with socioeconomic level, geographical region, or national origin. In truth, we all speak a dialect of some sort, and differences exist even within a regional pattern.

Each dialect is a complete and functional language system, and no dialect is superior or inferior to another for purposes of communication. However, for individuals to be readily accepted in some social classes and to attain certain career goals, use of Standard English is desirable. Teachers should accept and respect children's dialects as part of their cultures and environments but should also make them aware of Standard English as an important alternative. Perhaps the most widely accepted view among linguists and educators is support of *bidialectalism*, which affirms both the value of the home dialect and its use within the community and the value of teaching students Standard English (Ovando and Collier, 1985).

Critics point out that the language experience approach might simply reinforce students' dialects without providing contact with Standard English. Gillet and Gentry

---

CLASSROOM SCENARIO

Language Experience Approach with Struggling Readers

During her third-grade practicum, Molly Johnson had been assigned to work with three boys who hated to read and were reading at a first-grade level. After deciding to use a language experience chart with them, Molly began by reading Tomie de Paola's *The Quicksand Book* (Holiday House, 1977). After a discussion about quicksand, she involved the students in making quicksand in a large tub. The children made several charts related to the experience on such topics as what to do if trapped in quicksand, where quicksand is found, and the steps in conducting the experiment. When the three boys finished their work, Molly arranged for them to share their information with the rest of the class. They stood in the front of the classroom and read their charts to their peers, who were visibly impressed by what these boys had done.

Analysis of Scenario

By choosing an interesting topic and holding high expectations, Molly had found a way to motivate these students. They became excited about their special project and looked forward to the reading and writing activities related to their study of quicksand. By reading their charts in front of the room, they gained self-esteem and a measure of respect from their classmates.

(1983) propose a variation of this approach that values children's language but also provides exposure to Standard English. The teacher transcribes the children's story exactly as dictated. The process continues in the traditional way, but later the teacher writes another version of the dictated chart in Standard English with conventional sentence structure, using the same format and much of the same vocabulary. The teacher presents it as another story, not a better one, and children compare the two versions. The students then revise the original chart, making their sentences longer, more elaborate, and more consistent with Standard English. They then practice echo reading and choral reading with this version until they can read it fluently and have acquired additional sight words.

● Some Considerations About the LEA

If the LEA is the only reading approach used, development of reading skills in a predetermined sequence is not likely. However, there is no single correct sequence for presenting reading skills, and students learn from a variety of programs that provide different skill sequences.

Using only the LEA would also result in lack of systematic repetition of new words and a lack of vocabulary control in general. Still, structure words, which are important and need to be learned in context, are generally repeated quite often.

With the LEA as the exclusive approach to reading instruction, the limitations of the students' backgrounds of experience might drastically limit reading content, and the materials used in reading would also rarely be of good literary quality. However, since the LEA is generally used along with other approaches, such problems are unlikely to develop.

Programmed Instruction and Computer Use

Two other related approaches are particularly helpful for individualizing instruction — programmed instruction and computer use. *Programmed instruction* is sometimes used to offer individualized instruction. Programmed materials instruct in small, sequential steps, each of which is referred to as a *frame*. The student is required to respond in some way to each frame and is instantly informed of the correctness (or inaccuracy) of his or her response (given immediate reinforcement). Because the instruction is presented to an individual student, rather than to a group, each student moves through the material at his or her own pace, thereby benefiting from some individualization. Branching programs provide an even greater degree of individualization by offering review material to students who respond incorrectly to frames, thereby indicating that they have not mastered the skills being presented.

Programmed instruction in print or electronic form can also provide follow-up reinforcement for instruction presented by the teacher, freeing the teacher from many drill activities and allowing him or her more time to spend on complex teaching tasks. The programmed materials are designed to be self-instructional and do not require direct teacher supervision.

Programmed instruction does not, however, lend itself to teaching many complex comprehension skills, such as those involving analysis and interpretation, nor does it promote flexibility of reading rate. It also does not encourage student-to-student interaction (Wood, 1989). Word analysis and vocabulary-building skills are most prominently treated in programmed materials, so teachers may wish to use other materials (for example, basal texts) or techniques (for example, semantic webbing) to present and provide practice in the complex comprehension skills.

TECHNOLOGY 🖥 Materials used with programmed instruction may consist of print materials such as programmed texts, or they may exist in electronic format, presented on computers. The delivery of programmed instruction on a computer is known as computer-assisted instruction (CAI). Because of the interactive characteristics of the computer—it can provide immediate responses to input from student users—teachers find that it is a good tool for individualizing instruction. Because of its ability to repeat instructions patiently without showing irritation or judging students negatively, it is also useful for remedial instruction.

TECHNOLOGY 🖥 Computers are valuable tools for the reading teacher in ways other than CAI, as well. Word processing, database applications, and computerized literature presentations enable teachers to plan many meaningful learning experiences for students. LITERATURE 📖 Literature-oriented teachers often use computer programs, such as interactive fiction programs, that are more open-ended than drill-and-practice programs. Also especially popular are programs that allow construction of semantic maps, story maps, and interactive branching stories, as well as programs that offer onscreen activities tied in with popular trade books. Web browsers that give students access to information on the Internet can be powerful research tools. There is also a great deal of software available to help teachers with recordkeeping and other class-management tasks. Information about all of these applications is offered in Chapter 11.

Eclectic Approaches

Eclectic approaches combine the desirable aspects of a number of different methods, rather than strictly adhering to a single one. Research has not found one method that works for everyone but, rather, has repeatedly pointed to the teacher as the key factor in effective programs. An effective teacher integrates materials and methods as is appropriate to meet students' needs. As Duffy and Hoffman (1999) point out, current laws that mandate a single method of reading instruction keep teachers from adjusting instruction for students who would learn better from another approach. They downgrade the professional nature of teaching and discourage innovation in the field. Duffy and Hoffman have in fact concluded that "effective teachers are eclectic" (p. 11), echoing findings of Shanahan and Neuman (1997) and Stahl (1997). Thoughtful eclecticism is based on experience, professional studies and research, and analysis and reflection, and it requires teachers who are adaptive decision makers (Duffy and Hoffman, 1999).

Teachers often take an eclectic approach in choosing instructional materials and techniques to fit their unique situations and provide a variety of reading experiences for students. The following examples are only possibilities, and teachers should remember that the only limitations are school resources and their own imaginations.

LITERATURE **1** Language experience stories can be based on characters, events, or ideas in either trade books or stories in a basal reader. The teacher can plan an experience related to the story, lead a discussion of the experience, and record the students' dictated account. If an experience such as this is used prior to reading the book or basal story, it can help to activate the students' schemata related to the story. It will also probably involve use of some of the vocabulary found in the story, providing an introduction to this vocabulary in context. The story may be used as a basis for skills instruction suggested in the basal reader, as well (Jones and Nessel, 1985).

2 Grabe (1981) also suggests having the teacher supplement the basal reader approach by having students write "books about the book": they dictate stories about the basal selection using the new vocabulary. This approach has been found to enhance comprehension and vocabulary skills.

LITERATURE **3** In a class in which whole-class reading of a core book is taking place, the children can write language experience stories based on material from the particular book being read. For example, if the core book is *The Cay* by Theodore Taylor (Avon, 1969), the experience might be to try to weave a mat while blindfolded. The students could write a story about the experience and, in the process, develop a better understanding of the difficulty Phillip had when Timothy asked him to weave a mat, even though he was blind.

TECHNOLOGY 🖥 **4** Computers can be used with any approach. Word-processing software, for example, makes the computer a natural tool for implementing the language experience approach.

5 Teachers can use the individualized reading approach for two or three days each week and the basal program for the rest of the week, or they can alternate

---

CLASSROOM SCENARIO

An Eclectic Approach

Ms. Gray, a teacher who embraces an eclectic approach to reading instruction, is working with one reading group in a corner of the room during her scheduled reading time. At the same time, children from another reading group are illustrating a language experience story that they wrote on the previous day. As they finish their illustrations, pairs of children from this group are forming sentences with their word-bank words. Several other children are busy reading self-selected library books at their seats.

Three children have returned to the room from the library and have seated themselves together to discuss some research reading they have been doing on space travel. One of them is holding the printout from a database query she made during the library trip.

In another corner of the room, two girls are reading an interactive text story on a computer, discussing each decision and coming to a consensus about it before indicating their choices through keyboard commands.

Analysis of Scenario

In this classroom, all of the students are busy at reading tasks, but the tasks involve many different approaches to reading instruction. The teacher has chosen activities that fit the children's individual instructional needs.

weeks, using the individualized reading approach one week and the basal program the next. They may supplement either or both with occasional language experience activities, either on or off the computer.

LITERATURE

TECHNOLOGY

❻ Teachers can use a thematic literature unit approach to reading instruction, making use of pertinent basal reader stories as they are available and using language experience activities as appropriate to the planned curriculum. They may use database software to store information about the unit on the computer in an organized way, and they may use word-processing software to produce written reports about aspects of the theme.

LITERATURE

❼ Walker-Dalhouse and colleagues (1997) conducted a literature-based reading program that employed basal themes with middle-school students. Some of the selections were from the Houghton Mifflin literature-based reading program; others were theme-related trade books. Writing, language, oral reading, and independent reading were taught in the communications area. Writing and grammar lessons were related to the literature theme, although a grammar textbook was used. Oral-reading groups read a common book and discussed it. Students also chose independent books from a group designated by the teachers, and the teachers developed instructional packets for each group. Students chose books, completed the activities in the packets, and had conferences with the teachers about the reading. Students responded well to the program.

TIME for REFLECTION

Some teachers believe that they should stay with a single approach to reading instruction. Others believe that using the best ideas from all approaches is preferable. **What do *you* think, and why?**

SUMMARY

Published reading series are the most widely used materials for teaching reading in elementary schools in this country. Basal readers have been improved in recent years and provide teachers with anthologies of reading materials, detailed teacher's manuals, and many supplementary materials. Some published series are being called literature-based and/or language-integrated series because of their greater focus on quality literature selections and their integration of other types of language activities with the reading. Literature-based and language-integrated series focus on more student-generated prediction and more instructional options for the teacher than are found in traditional basal reader manuals.

The directed reading activity (DRA) is the teaching strategy presented in traditional basal manuals. This strategy can be used with other reading materials as well. Teachers can use the *enrichment activities* of the DRA before the story to help build and integrate background. Comprehension monitoring can also be made a natural part of a DRA. An alternative to the DRA is the directed reading-thinking activity (DRTA). Another alternative, guided reading, involves steps similar to those of a DRA but focuses on matching students with reading material in leveled books.

Literature-based reading approaches include whole-class reading of a core book, literature circles reading several books for which there are multiple copies, thematic literature units, and the individualized reading approach. Whole-class reading of a core book, thematic literature units, and the individualized reading approach all include the use of minilessons. Thematic literature units focus on a theme, a genre, an author, or a book. All of these approaches include various types of responses to literature. The individualized reading approach allows students to move at their own paces through reading material that they have chosen. Student-teacher conferences help the teacher monitor progress and build rapport with the students. Sharing activities allow group interaction.

The language experience approach interrelates the different language arts and uses children's experiences as the basis for reading materials. This approach has many advantages: it incorporates the visual, auditory, and kinesthetic modes of learning; it promotes a positive self-concept and fosters close contact between teachers and students; and it serves as an effective remedial technique in the upper grades. This approach can be introduced in kindergarten, but it continues to have applications for all students in higher grades, especially in conjunction with content area activities.

Some approaches are particularly helpful for individualizing instruction. Among these are programmed instruction and computer use, in addition to the individualized reading approach. Programmed instruction is administered through materials that present information in small, sequential steps. The student responds at each step and receives immediate feedback about whether her or his response was correct or incorrect. Students are allowed to learn at their own paces.

An eclectic approach combines desirable aspects of a number of different methods. The only limitation to possible combinations is the teacher's imagination.

TEST YOURSELF

True or False

_____ 1. All published reading series are alike.

_____ 2. Teacher's manuals in basal reading series generally provide detailed lesson plans for teaching each story in a basal reader.

_____ 3. Basal reader workbooks are designed to teach reading skills and do not require teacher intervention.

_____ 4. Workbook activities are useful only for keeping children busy while the teacher is engaged in other activities.

_____ 5. The language experience approach (LEA) is not useful above first grade.

_____ 6. The language experience approach uses student-created material for reading instruction.

_____ 7. A word bank is a collection of words that the teacher believes children should learn.

_____ 8. The language experience approach promotes a better self-concept in many children.

_____ 9. The individualized reading approach utilizes self-selection and self-pacing.

_____ 10. The individualized reading approach involves no direct skills instruction.

_____ 11. Student-teacher conferences are an integral part of the individualized reading approach.

_____ 12. When literature-based reading programs are used, children interact with texts in meaningful ways.

_____ 13. Close reading of core books, discussion, and writing related to the reading take place in many literature-based classrooms.

_____ 14. Thematic literature units involve the reading of a single book by all class members and the writing of a book report on the book.

_____ 15. Programmed instruction presents instructional material in small, sequential steps.

_____ 16. An eclectic approach combines features from a number of different approaches.

_____ 17. The language experience approach is not consistent with schema theory.

_____ 18. The directed reading-thinking activity is a good alternative to the directed reading activity when the teacher wishes to provide a more student-centered experience.

_____ 19. Word processing on the computer is useful for writing language experience stories.

For your journal...

❶ Visit an elementary school classroom and then write about the instructional materials used in the reading program.

❷ Visit a school and watch an experienced teacher use a DRA. Write your reactions.

... and your portfolio

❶ Plan an individualized reading approach for a specific group of children. Explain what materials will be used (include reading levels and areas of interest) and where they will be obtained. Outline the recordkeeping procedures; explain how conferences will be scheduled and the uses to which they will be put; and describe the routines students will follow for selecting books, checking out books, and receiving help while reading.

❷ Develop a directed reading-thinking activity (DRTA) for a trade book.

❸ Choose a basal reader for a grade level you might teach. Examine it for variety of writing types (narrative, expository, poetry). Make a chart showing the frequency of the various types. Note also the frequency of different types of content (language skills, social studies, science, art, mathematics, music, and so on).

❹ Plan a thematic literature unit for a grade level of your choice. Think about ways that you can actively involve the students with the books.

🕮 Language and Literature

SETTING OBJECTIVES

When you finish reading this chapter, you should be able to

- Explain the importance of integrating instruction in the language arts for all students.

- Identify some relationships between reading and writing.

- Understand how to implement the writing process, and list the major steps in this process.

- Discuss procedures for using journals and for implementing writing and reading workshops.

- Design a classroom environment conducive to reading and writing for a diverse population of students.

- Select appropriate literature of good quality and high interest, and read or tell stories expressively.

- Discuss a variety of ways to respond to literature.

- Identify the characteristics of a variety of literary genres.

This chapter opens with a brief discussion of some principles for facilitating language development, which are the basis for many of the strategies and procedures that follow. The chapter also presents reasons for connecting the language arts, particularly reading and writing, and discusses the value of literature as a vehicle for integrating the curriculum. Connections between reading and writing are demonstrated through discussions of process writing, journal writing, and reading and writing workshops. The chapter also supports the concept of enabling all students to make choices and assume responsibility for their learning.

The second part of the chapter focuses on the use of literature to integrate the curriculum. It provides ideas for creating a classroom environment where children support one another's efforts and experience a sense of ownership in their reading and writing. That section also offers suggestions for selecting appropriate literature for children, as well as for helping children choose books for themselves. It contains a discussion of literary genres. Many ways to respond to literature, including

Chapter 8 Organization

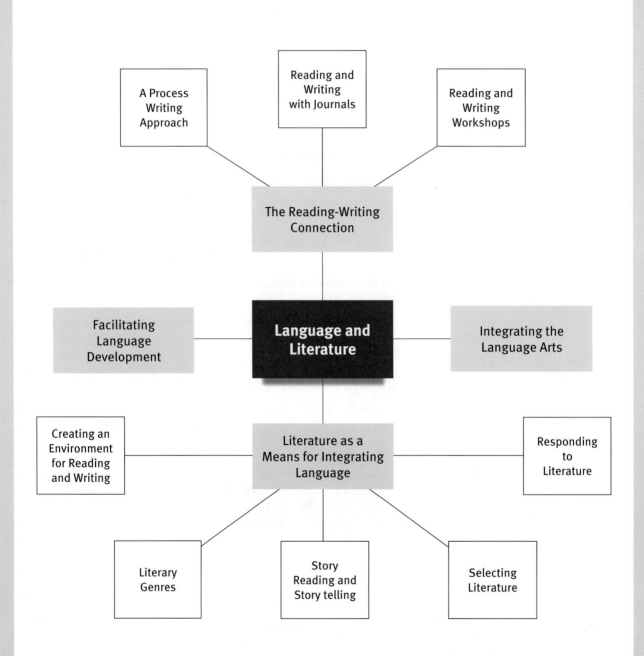

participation in literature circles, oral interpretation, drama, written expression, art, music, and the creation of multimedia presentations, are presented.

Facilitating Language Development

STANDARDS AND
ASSESSMENT

Teachers today encourage children to use language in authentic, integrated situations. Learning is centered on the child, and the child learns communication skills through verbal interaction with others. The following basic tenets for facilitating language development are congruent with the *Standards for the English Language Arts* (1996).

- *Learning is integrated.* Students learn more effectively when they can see connections and relationships among ideas and subjects than when they learn bits and pieces of information in isolation.

- *Tasks are authentic.* Authentic activities are those that are related to real-world tasks such as writing letters and reading for information. When students can see the purpose and meaning of the work they do, they understand why it is important to do it.

- *Learning is social.* The purpose of language is to communicate with others. Students therefore learn to use language by sharing ideas, working cooperatively, and becoming part of a community of learners.

- *Classrooms are learning-centered.* To feel a commitment to learning language, students need to be actively involved in the learning process by accepting such responsibilities as making choices, taking part in negotiating decisions about procedures and curriculum, and self-evaluation.

- *Learning is holistic.* Reading skills and strategies are learned in meaningful context. Students are actively engaged in tasks that promote understanding and meaning-making. For example, instead of learning phonics by filling out worksheets, children learn phonics by observing letter-sound patterns during shared reading.

LITERATURE

- *Literature is an integral part of the curriculum.* Because the premise that children learn to read by reading is widely accepted, classrooms should offer a large variety of books and related materials. Good books can be used across the curriculum as sources of information and pleasure and can provide the tools necessary to meet the specific instructional needs of struggling readers.

Integrating the Language Arts

STANDARDS AND
ASSESSMENT

TECHNOLOGY

Integration means coordinating activities so that children can see the natural connections among the various forms of language as they work to achieve goals. Listening, speaking, reading, and writing have long been accepted as the language arts, but developers of the *Standards for the English Language Arts* have expanded the concept to include viewing and visually representing. "Being literate in contemporary society means being active, critical, and creative users not only of print and spoken language but also of the visual language of film and television, commercial and political advertising, photography, and more" (*Standards*, 1996, p. 5). As teachers challenge students to integrate visual communication with other language forms, students are learning to use, interpret, and create illustrations, graphs, charts, videos, and electronic displays.

The integration of language arts in the classroom is not a new idea; indeed, curriculum designers have advocated it from time to time for decades. In many classrooms, however, the practice of scheduling a specific amount of time for spelling, handwriting, reading groups, grammar, and so forth has prevailed. If each of these is transmitted as a separate, unrelated item, such segmentation of the language arts can interfere with children's natural, purposeful use of language in real situations, and it may result in their failure to apply what they already know about oral language to reading and writing.

For the classroom teacher, integration may mean setting aside a large block of time for language arts. This time period allows for flexible scheduling and freedom to develop special projects fully. During this extended time period, children may engage in a variety of language activities, such as pursuing research projects, responding creatively to stories, preparing a school newspaper, or working at a poetry center. With a little guidance from the teacher, they become aware of the interrelationships among the language arts. They see, for instance, how the stories they read can serve as models for the stories they want to write, how the information they need for writing reports can be found by using research materials, and why good handwriting and correct spelling are important for publishing their own books.

Even though a specific time period may be allocated for language arts instruction, integrated language experiences extend throughout the day into every area of the curriculum. For example, reading, writing, speaking, listening, and viewing are essential for learning about ideas that have changed history and about science concepts that have resulted in new discoveries. In the Model Activity below, the teacher provides an integrated language arts lesson by reading a book and then allowing the students to pursue their natural curiosity. During this lesson, children become involved in listening, speaking, reading, writing, and problem solving.

The Focus on Strategies on page 317–318 shows how a single book can become the center for learning in many areas. As seen here, the teacher may introduce a book that so intrigues the students that they assume an active role in developing

---

MODEL ACTIVITIES | **Integrated Language Arts Lesson**

After reading Katherine Paterson's *Park's Quest* to the class, ask: "What do you think the title means? What is a quest?" Discuss responses. If the students wish to pursue various aspects of the book, form groups to investigate topics that interest them. These topics may lead to such activities as a debate over U.S. involvement in the Vietnam War, a student-made book that connects the quest of King Arthur with that of Park, a diary in which students write from Park's perspective after each day on the farm, a report on the causes of strokes and the effects of a stroke on a person's health, or an annotated bibliography of books about the Vietnam War.

Developing a Literature-Based Thematic Unit That Integrates the Language Arts

Ms. Brison introduced Chris Van Allsburg's *The Wretched Stone* to her students by asking them to listen for clues that tell what the stone represents. This story was one of her favorites, and she hoped the students would like it too. When she finished reading it aloud, the students eagerly raised their hands to tell what they thought the stone really was. Isaac, the class scientist, thought it was malachite, and Katrina said it must be a mirror. Others thought it was an object from outer space.

The students begged Ms. Brison to reread the story, and she agreed to do so if they would listen again for clues. This time Janis solemnly said, "I believe it's a television because that's how television makes some people act." The others quickly agreed as they noted the similarities between a television set and the stone in the story.

Still fascinated, the students wanted to know more about the story, so Ms. Brison asked them what they would like to do with it. Mike suggested finding other books by Chris Van Allsburg to read, and Beth wanted to learn more about the way sailors lived and worked long ago. Tim said he could teach a group how to make sailors' knots, and Molly said they could write logs as if they were sailors on the ship.

Ms. Brison recorded the ideas on the chalkboard and then placed each idea at the top of a piece of chart paper. She wrote *Other* at the top of one chart to allow the students to come up with other creative responses. She told the students to think about what they would like to do and then sign up to work on a topic. Those responsible for finding other books by Van Allsburg checked the school library, the neighborhood branch library, and the downtown library. They found *The Widow's Broom*, *The Stranger*, and *Two Bad Ants*. They also borrowed books that Ms. Brison checked out at the Teacher Center. Each day the children read a different story until they became quite familiar with Van Allsburg's style. "His books always have something mysterious in them," Jack said. "Yes," Connie continued, "and they start like it's for real, and

then something happens that makes you know it has to be fantasy."

The students who signed up to research the lives of sailors years ago collected books about sailing, took notes, and compiled an illustrated informational book that told of the hardships of sea travel—the food sailors ate, the length of their journeys, weather signs, the consequences of storms at sea, and the stars they used to chart their courses. Some students, intrigued by pirates on the high seas, found stories and legends about pirates, particularly Blackbeard. Van Allsburg's detailed illustrations intrigued many children, who compared his black-and-white drawings in earlier books with the colored ones in more recent books. Students who had read *Jumanji* decided to make their own board game with penalties and rewards. As their projects neared completion, most groups decided to put their work at a center so that they could see what others were doing. Another group showcased their work when they dramatized *The Wretched Stone* for the class next door.

This had been a truly integrated language arts unit: the thoughtful listening as the students tried to identify the elements of mystery, the well-supported points they made while defending their views about Van Allsburg's use of fantasy, the reading of related storybooks and reference materials, and the incredible informational book they wrote that portrayed the harsh life at sea. Perhaps the logs they wrote as sailors impressed Ms. Brison most of all. The students had used such vivid descriptive words to express their feelings as they moved from being lively, active sailors to being entranced viewers of the stone.

Ms. Brison reflected on how her teaching had changed over the years. As they became involved with the book, students used authentic language strategies instead of the workbooks she used to rely on. Instead of planning a unit herself and providing all the resource materials, she shared this responsibility with her students. Both she and the students seemed to enjoy their shared task tremendously.

Continued

Continued

Ms. Brison also realized that while the students were having fun investigating Chris Van Allsburg, they were actually learning a great deal about language and literature. She got out her curriculum guide and checked off several language skills for her grade level: making inferences, differentiating reality from fantasy, recognizing an author's style, locating information, and using reference materials. Of course, there were other skills as well.

meaningful related activities. They contribute their own ideas so that their investigation is truly learner-centered rather than teacher-directed. More on the development of thematic units can be found in Chapter 7.

DIVERSITY Culturally diverse students come from many regional cultures, ethnic groups, and religions. In recent years the enrollment of culturally diverse students in schools has increased dramatically (Wood, 1993), and the ethnic and racial composition of the student bodies in most schools has changed. Classrooms are now composed of children whose values, orientations toward school, and speech patterns may differ greatly. Both the cultural and the linguistic divergences influence how children learn and how they should be taught.

Multicultural education involves developing an understanding and appreciation of various cultural groups. However, simply being aware of this and having good intentions to be just and fair are not enough to achieve the level of changes necessary in today's classrooms. Children should be taught with sensitivity to their cultural heritages, their language preferences, and their lifestyles. Teachers need to concentrate on teaching the strategies and content necessary for all students to achieve success in American society.

The use of multicultural literature merits special attention because it affirms and legitimizes various cultures (Diamond and Moore, 1995). It helps children connect with people of different cultures and provides them with information and insights about their own heritage. Because it implicitly acknowledges individuals' rights to be who they are, multicultural literature increases understanding of and respect for differences. Ultimately, literature can help to reduce fear and prejudice.

The following are some general guidelines for creating a learning environment inclusive of students with diverse cultural backgrounds (Au, 1993; Coelho, 1994; Wood, 1993).

TIME for REFLECTION

Some teachers believe they need to teach each language art separately (i.e., fifteen minutes for handwriting, twenty minutes for spelling, etc.) each day in order to be sure to cover each subject. Other teachers feel that integration of the language arts is more meaningful and that, with planning, every subject will be adequately covered. **What do *you* think, and why?**

❶ *Learn about the students' cultures.* Find out about the children's language and learn cultural variations in word meanings. Learn about children's living conditions and what things are important to them. Try to discover cultural traits that affect how students learn. Show that you accept and value their cultures, even though these cultures may differ from your own.

FAMILY ❷ *Value their contributions.* Take an interest in what children bring to share, and listen to what they say. Create opportunities for their families to share their cultural heritages through learning experiences in the curriculum.

❸ *Provide a supportive classroom environment.* Let the environment reflect the various cultures represented in the classroom by displaying multicultural literature and materials and by including instruction related to multicultural education.

❹ *Provide opportunities for cooperative learning.* Let students work collaboratively to develop social and academic skills, to understand and appreciate the diversity among themselves, and to learn strategies to use in their interactions outside of school.

LITERATURE   ❺ *Use multicultural literature.* When possible, choose stories related to students' cultural backgrounds. Exposure to such stories benefits all children. They gain self-esteem as they read about their own heritage and broaden their concepts of the world and the people in it as they read about other cultures.

The Reading-Writing Connection

Reading and writing are both composing processes. On the basis of prior knowledge, attitudes, and experiences, the reader constructs meaning from text and the writer composes meaningful text. Both reading and writing require the use of similar thinking skills, such as analyzing, selecting and organizing, making inferences, evaluating, problem solving, and making comparisons.

Reading and writing tend to reinforce each other. According to Smith (1983), children must learn to read like writers in order to write like writers. By offering a model, good literature instructs young authors through example and inspires them to try their hand at creating stories of their own (Lancia, 1997). Children quickly detect patterns in predictable and repetitive books, and they imitate these patterns as they write themselves (Saccardi, 1996a). By carefully observing an author's use of dialogue while reading a story, a child begins to learn how to create dialogue when writing a story. Or in trying to write a description of the setting for a piece of writing, a child may read and reread the setting from another selection to get ideas.

Table 8.1 shows examples of links between reading and writing (based on Butler and Turbill, 1987; Hornsby, Sukarna, and Parry, 1986). Stotsky (1983) warns, however, that although similarities exist in the ways in which reading and writing are learned, research shows there are sufficient differences to warrant attention to each independently, as well as in combination.

Educators have explored many ways of utilizing the linkage between reading and writing. A literacy program that integrates direct instruction and holistic approaches emphasizes reading and writing with many regular opportunities for students to be actively engaged. Involving students in authentic tasks is motivating and promotes their understanding of reading and writing as meaning-making processes. The functional situations given in Example 8.1 are appropriate for any learner, but particularly for struggling readers and writers.

TECHNOLOGY   Teachers and children have used message boards, or centrally located bulletin boards, for sending and receiving messages, and some students correspond with other students through pen-pal programs. Pen-pal programs are sometimes conducted

TABLE 8.1 **Links Between Reader and Writer**

Reader	Writer
Brings and uses prior knowledge about topic	Brings and uses prior knowledge about topic
Reconstructs another's meaning	Constructs own meaning
Predicts what comes next	Predicts what should come next
Has expectations for text based on experiences	Has expectations for how text might develop
Modifies comprehension of text while reading	Develops and changes meaning while writing continues
Engages in "draft reading"—skimming, making sense	Engages in "draft writing"—getting ideas, writing notes
Rereads to clarify	Rewrites to clarify
Uses writer's cues to help make sense of reading	Uses writing conventions to assist reader
Responds by talking, doing, and/or writing	Gets response from readers

EXAMPLE 8.1 **Imaginary Functional Situations**

Your dog is sick. What number do you call for help? Where could you take your dog?

Choose a magazine you would like to order. Fill out the order form.

Your mother is coming home on the bus, but you forget what time she is supposed to arrive. Look it up in the schedule.

You want to watch a television special, but you can't remember the time or channel. Find it in the newspaper or media guide.

Look through a catalogue and choose four items you would like to have for less than $100 in all. Fill out the order blank.

If a house is on fire, what number would you call? What are some other emergency phone numbers?

You want to write a lost-and-found ad for the bicycle you lost. Write the ad and find the address and phone number of the newspaper.

You want to order a game that is advertised on the back of a cereal box. Follow the directions for placing the order.

Look at a menu and order a meal for yourself. Find out how much it costs.

You want to go to a football game in a nearby town. Find the stadium on the map and be able to give directions.

electronically. These are generally referred to as keypal programs. Computers make it possible, too, for young authors to share their work on electronic bulletin boards, class websites, and other maintained sites. Several types of young authors' programs exist for various purposes, including encouraging children to write illustrated bound books and to share their writing with other authors outside their schools (Harris-

Sharples, Kearns, and Miller, 1989). Following are some class activities for combining writing with reading.

ACTIVITIES

1. Provide opportunities for students to publish: (a) news stories that are modern adaptations of fairy tales and Mother Goose rhymes, (b) news stories reported as if they were written at the same time and place as the setting of the book the teacher is reading to the class, (c) a literary digest of news about books, or (d) advertisements for favorite books.

TECHNOLOGY 🖥

2. Encourage students to write a radio or television script based on a story they have read. (First, they should read some plays to become familiar with directions for staging and appropriate writing style for dialogue.) Students could videotape the performance of their created script or record it as a digital movie and share it on their class website.

3. Arrange for students to correspond with pen pals or key pals from other regions of the country through either regular or electronic mail. As they interact, they are likely to become interested in those geographical areas, so provide resource materials for them to read about their pen pals' homes.

4. Organize a young authors' conference in which children display and read from books they have published. The conference could take place among classes within a single school, or it could be district-wide.

TECHNOLOGY 🖥

5. Facilitate opportunities for students to develop multimedia presentations about their favorite books. The presentations could be shared in class or posted and shared electronically on a class website.

Struggling readers and writers benefit from personalized reading and writing strategies (Walker, 2000). An effective strategy for struggling readers is repeated shared readings of predictable and repetitive stories and poetry, a procedure that enables students to sense language patterns (Ford and Ohlhausen, 1988; Wicklund, 1989). Students may then compose their own pieces based on the now familiar patterns. Repeated readings encourage students to use overall contextual meaning and sentence structure to help increase the accuracy of their word recognition (Walker, 2000). Semantic mapping (explained in Chapters 4 and 5) is another particularly useful strategy for struggling readers because it helps them visualize relationships among concepts, as well as providing practice in reading and writing.

● A Process Writing Approach

A *process writing approach* is a learning-centered approach to writing in which students create their own pieces of writing based on their choice of topic, their awareness of audience, and their development of ideas from initial stages through revisions to final publication. The process is ongoing and recursive, with writing in some form generally occurring every day and with pieces in various stages of

DIVERSITY 🌐

development. The first and final drafts of a composition written during process writing instruction by an English language learner (ELL) from Swedon, Jonas Lindgren, appear on page 322.

EXAMPLE 8.2 Process Writing Drafts by an ELL Student

The soccer final

It is year 2001 and Italy and Gurmeny is in the soccer final. Five minits in the game Gurmeny gets a very good clans, they kik the ball right outsid the gol. then Gurmeny gets a new clans 44 minits in the game. They cros it over to the mit spot of the penalty eria where ther mit for word is to hit it right in the kworner of the gol. (then the first hafe finich) The sakend hafe was Italis hafe the started with a gol in the 23 met and the finiched with a gol in the 43 menit. I italy won the world campion agen.

Jonas Lindgren ③

The world champion soccer game

It is year 2009, and Italy and Germany are in the world champion soccer final. Five minuts in the game Germany, gets a very good chance, they kick the ball right outside the gol. Then Germany gets a new chance 44 minuts in the game, they crossed the ball over to the mit spot, in the middle of the penelty area, where there striker was standing wating to hit it in the corner of the gool, and he did it. (Then the first half was finiced.

The second half was Italys half, they started with a gool in the 23ed minute and then they finiched with a gool in the 43ed.

ITALY WON THE WORLD CUP AGAIN.

Cross-Grade Process Writing

During a cross-grade writing project at Crossville Elementary School, Austin Hamby's fifth graders were preparing to give their completed books to Ann Norris's second graders who were their partners. It was the fifth graders' first attempt at process writing, and most of them were somewhat amazed at how well their stories had developed with input from classmates and teachers during conferences. One boy said, "This is a good story. I'd really like to keep it for myself." Nevertheless, he gave his book to his partner, who was delighted with it and told the story to anyone who would listen. A couple of times, fifth graders excitedly showed the program director their writing, saying, "Look what I wrote for my partner! It wasn't part of an assignment; I just wanted to do it."

Analysis of Scenario

Awareness of their audience for the stories caused students to devote much attention to the development process. The students were much more concerned about revising their stories to improve them and about copying them neatly for their partners than they had been about polishing stories that were written before the project began. The fifth graders produced whole books for their young partners, complete with title pages, copyright dates, dedications, and "About the Author" sections. Writing for authentic purposes obviously made a difference in the quality of these students' writing.

Cross-grade process writing programs provide opportunities for older students to act as literary advisors and/or attentive audiences for younger children and for younger children to act as audiences for older writers. Roe (1990) conducted such a program involving partnerships between fifth graders and second graders.

Stages of the Writing Process

The *writing process* consists of the following major stages: prewriting, drafting, revising, editing, and publishing and/or sharing. These stages may be used at any grade level, although, of course, first graders' writing will be very simple, and their bookmaking will require a great deal of guidance from the teacher. In fact, in some cases the teacher may write stories from student dictation. As children progress through the grades, they will become capable of producing more complex, more carefully edited works. The stages of the writing process may be briefly described as follows:

Prewriting.   The author prepares for writing by talking, drawing, reading, and thinking about the piece and by organizing ideas and developing a plan.

Drafting.   The author sets ideas on paper without regard for neatness or mechanics.

Revising.   After getting suggestions from others, the author may wish to make some changes in the initial draft. These changes may include adding dialogue, deleting repetitious parts, adding depth to a character, clarifying meaning, providing needed information, or changing the ending of the story.

Editing.   With careful proofreading and the help of peers and the teacher, the author corrects spelling and mechanics.

Sharing and Publishing. After thoughtful revisions, the authors are eager to share their finished pieces with real audiences. Pages can be fastened with brads, taped together, sewn, or professionally bound. Finished books may be kept in the classroom or taken to the school library, fitted with pockets, and made available for checking out.

TECHNOLOGY 🖥 Word-processing programs simplify the writing process. They enable students to enter rough drafts quickly, revise frequently, and print their final copies. Students revise by inserting or deleting material and moving chunks of text, and they edit by correcting spelling and mechanics.

The process approach to writing provides a supportive format for struggling readers and writers. The revision and editing stages provide opportunities for all students to produce material for others to read. Of special benefit during the writing process is peer conferencing, in which students help one another by offering suggestions and asking questions that lead to better composition (Wong-Kam and Au, 1988).

● Reading and Writing with Journals

Students write in *journals* to record their thoughts and ideas, without concern for correctness of form or mechanics. Writers determine the audience, for sometimes journals or designated pages within them are personal, and other times they are meant TECHNOLOGY 🖥 to be shared. Journals may be spiral notebooks or simply papers stapled together with student-decorated construction-paper covers, or they may be kept in word-processing files or folders. To develop writing fluency, students must have time for journal writing, preferably on a daily basis. A child of any age can do journal writing; younger children can use invented spellings and pictures to express their ideas.

To introduce students to journal writing, the teacher might discuss diary writing and read to the children books written in letter or journal form, such as Joan Blos's *A Gathering of Days: A New England Girl's Journal, 1830–32* or Beverly Cleary's *Dear Mr. Henshaw*. The teacher should write in a journal as the children write, to model FAMILY 👥 the importance of recording thoughts and ideas. Teachers can also encourage parents and family members who write in journals to model their writing habits at home. If students have trouble finding topics, the teacher might offer such suggestions as an important event, a perplexing problem, or a really good friend. Writers should understand that journals are a place where they can complain, ask questions, or express their true feelings.

Journal writing can take many forms:

- *Dialogue journals* are interactive, with the teacher or other reader responding to the student's writing. The responder should never "correct" the student's writing but can model proper spelling and writing conventions in the response.

- *Reading or literary journals* enable students to write responses to what they have read and to receive the teacher's supportive feedback as a guide for further reading (Wollman-Bonilla, 1989).

- In *buddy journals* (see Example 8.3 on page 325), student pairs "converse" in writing on a continuing basis, thus engaging in a meaningful writing and reading exchange (Bromley, 1989).

- A *double-entry journal* enables the student to respond to a passage of particular interest. The student writes what the author says on one side of the page and enters a personal response on the other side. Responses may be drawings, opinions, questions, reflections, or connections to personal experiences (Popp, 1997). In Example 8.4 on page 326, sixth grader Madyson Burgess responds to *The Westing Game* by Ellen Raskin.

DIVERSITY   Journal writing is an effective strategy for all learners but is especially beneficial for those students who are acquiring English. Teachers should encourage English language learners to write for authentic purposes even before they are proficient in English. Students may use a combination of symbols, drawings, and invented

---

EXAMPLE 8.3   Buddy Journal Entries

Fri, 16, Feb, 1990

Erin,
    You are a very good reader. You are going to be a better reader if you keep practicing.
    do you like school? What is your favorite subject? My favorite subject is spelling.
                        Your partner,
                        Lesley Ann Richards

Wed. 21, 1990

Lesley,
    I do not like school very much. My favorite subject is scisce.
            do you like school?
                        Your Partner,
                        Erin Young

Source: Leslie Ann Richards and Erin Young, Crossville Elementary School, Crossville, Tennessee.

EXAMPLE 8.4 **Double-Entry Journal**

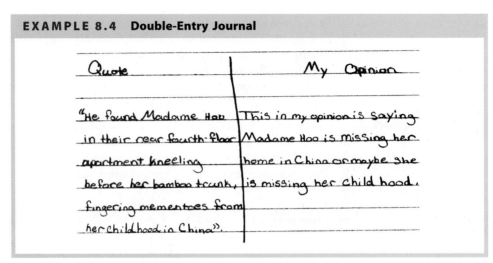

Quote	My Opinion
"He found Madame Hoo in their rear fourth-floor apartment kneeling before her bamboo trunk, fingering mementoes from her childhood in China".	This in my opinion is saying Madame Hoo is missing her home in China or maybe she is missing her childhood.

Source: Madyson Burgess, Prescott Central Middle School, Cookeville, Tennessee, 1997. Used with permission.

TIME for REFLECTION

What are the advantages and disadvantages of encouraging all students to write freely in journals without regard for mechanical accuracy?

spellings to communicate their ideas. Dialogue journals enable teachers to move English language learners toward competency by providing them a nonthreatening, nonstructured medium for exchanging ideas.

● Reading and Writing Workshops

Reading and writing workshops provide opportunities for teachers to teach specific strategies directly during brief minilessons and for students to spend most of their time actually reading and writing.

Although formats differ, most reading workshops operate in a similar manner, beginning with a minilesson that might be about comprehension strategies, literary appreciation, or genres. After the teacher records student-selected tasks on the status-of-the-class record sheet, students spend most of their time with self-selected reading and responses. During this time, the teacher may hold conferences with some of the students. Before the end of class, students spend five to ten minutes sharing their activities, books, or projects with one another (Atwell, 1985, 1987; Ross, 1996). Such workshops promote inquiry by letting students reflect on literature, interpret it, seek deeper meanings for it, and respond to it in various ways (Heald-Taylor, 1996).

Ross (1996) describes the four steps of the writing workshops as a minilesson, a status-of-the-class report, the actual writing process, and sharing time. The minilesson lasts only a few minutes and deals with issues such as following procedures, writing realistic dialogue, and using mechanics correctly, starting with good leads (Clemmons and Laase, 1995). The status-of-the-class check is made as the teacher calls each student's name and records what the student will be doing during the workshop. The writing workshop, when most students write and/or confer, consumes most of the class time. Group sharing occurs during the last few minutes

Lively responses to literature are likely to occur in classrooms with nurturing environments that provide an abundance of high-quality books, opportunities for library visits, adequate time for selecting and reading, introductions of new books, daily reading aloud, book discussions, and creative experiences with literature. *(© Elizabeth Crews/Stock Boston)*

when students share their writing, try out ideas, and respond to one another's writing.

Literature as a Means for Integrating Language

Literature can be the basis for learning to read and write and for developing positive attitudes toward further language learning for all students. Teachers who integrate literature with language arts give children purposes and opportunities for reading and writing throughout the day and across all areas of the curriculum. They read aloud to students daily from various genres of children's literature and provide a variety of good books for classroom library shelves.

TIME for REFLECTION

In reading and writing workshops, teachers present skills and strategies during five- or ten-minute minilessons and then allow students to read or write during the remaining class time. Other teachers may spend an entire class period (forty-five minutes or so) teaching skills and strategies, believing they need this much time to provide instruction. What do *you* think should be done, and why?

● Creating an Environment for Reading and Writing

The classroom environment should be supportive and free from the risks that inhibit honest expression. To help children feel a sense of ownership in their reading, teachers should allow some time for them to choose books or for partner reading or reading aloud to others. Children should have input into how they are to respond to what they have read and how their own related work is to be displayed or published. They may choose to share their writing by sitting in an author's chair and reading orally, by displaying a copy in the classroom or school library, or by electronically mailing copies of their written work to others.

Effective teachers encourage children to read by arranging portable, freestanding bulletin boards and dry-erase boards, sets of shelves, and other furniture to create nooks and crannies for reading. They provide carpet scraps and cushions that allow children to read comfortably and privately. Bookshelves and containers filled with books should be within easy reach. Writing materials, including lined and unlined paper, pencils with erasers, colored pens for revising and editing, and folders for completed work, are readily available. Backs of furniture become spaces for showing children's work and for creating inviting displays about books. Teachers set up writing centers with activities that encourage children to make written responses to books, and they provide enough time for such reading and writing to take place. Working together, the teacher and students can design bulletin boards and arrange displays that are related to a theme, represent a genre (such as poetry or biography), or focus on books by a popular author.

Sustained Silent Reading (SSR), or Drop Everything and Read (DEAR), occurs in classrooms where children are given time, a wide selection of books, and encouragement to read. The teacher sets aside a period of time each day, usually from fifteen to thirty minutes, for silent reading. SSR can be used by a single classroom or by the entire school (students, faculty, and staff). The teacher also reads to model the value of reading for everyone. There is no formal reporting or assessment at the conclusion of SSR periods, so students feel no pressure as they read. Nevertheless, students who engage in SSR and who have teachers who read to them score significantly higher on standardized tests than students who are deprived of these benefits (Trelease, 1995).

SSR can be effective with kindergartners and first graders, but it may consist mostly of looking at books and pretend reading, and it tends to be noisier (with children reading and speaking aloud to themselves) and of shorter duration (five to ten minutes) (Kaisen, 1987; McCracken and McCracken, 1987). This strategy is easily modified for students with special needs. During Sustained Silent Reading, students are encouraged to choose familiar, predictable, or high-interest books that are easy to read. They may be encouraged to read their books orally to partners and to discuss them in pairs (Ford and Ohlhausen, 1988; Rhodes and Dudley-Marling, 1988). Adding Sustained Silent Writing and encouraging the use of invented spelling can also be effective for struggling readers and writers, because it includes the same element of student choice as SSR.

DIVERSITY

● Literary Genres

A teacher's knowledge of literary genres is essential for selecting literature and for establishing an environment that supports both reading and writing. Harris and Hodges define *genre* as "a category used to classify literary works, usually by form, technique, or content" (1995, p. 94). Following are characteristics of a number of literary genres or categories.

Fiction consists of made-up stories written in a narrative style designed to entertain. Characters, setting, plot, authors' style, and theme are elements that are often identified in fictional writing. Fantasy stories, folklore, realistic fiction, and mysteries are all types of fiction. Harris and Hodges (1995, p. 82) define *fantasy* as a "highly imaginative story about characters, places, and events that, while sometimes believable, do not exist."

Traditional literature, or folklore, may include *folktales, cumulative tales*, pourquoi *tales, fables, myths*, and *legends*. Traditional tales are often passed from generation to generation through oral narration and have no identifiable author (Norton, 1999). Folklore presents many possibilities for introducing different literary forms. Many young children are familiar with the repetitive plot sequence in **cumulative tales** such as "The Gingerbread Boy" and "The House That Jack Built." Intermediate-grade children are often entertained by **tall tales**, which feature individuals who accomplish astonishing feats. Students especially enjoy locating the exaggerations in tall tales, such as those about Paul Bunyan or Pecos Bill.

Another form of folklore is the *fable*, which is usually characterized by brevity, a moral, and use of animal characters. Students can practice identifying the morals of the fables before they read the ones stated in the books.

Myths, pourquoi ("why") tales, some Native American folklore, and Rudyard Kipling's *Just So Stories* provide explanations of universal origins. **Legends** are historical tales that originated orally; later many were put in written form. These are all excellent stories for helping children to understand different cultures and become familiar with literary classics.

Teachers can introduce children to *poetry* by reading selections of all kinds and asking them to respond freely and with feeling. The children should then have opportunities to read much poetry for themselves and to participate in choral reading/speaking of poetry. Galda (1989) suggests following the reading of poems to which children respond positively with a focus on rhythm and rhyme, alliteration and onomatopoeia, and metaphors and imagery, to name only a few elements.

Nonfiction may include biographies and informational books. The purpose of nonfiction literature is to inform and/or to instruct. Nonfiction selections are especially helpful for developing curriculum ties with various content areas.

Reading *play scripts* is quite different from reading the narrative and expository material discussed previously. Bringing a play to life involves many interpretive and creative decisions about the elements of setting, action, and characters. Discussion about the way dialogue should be delivered helps students become more sensitive to language styles and usages that fit the context and the characters. Engaging students in the reading of play scripts can also help demonstrate the relationship between print and spoken language (Manna, 1984).

Comparisons of narrative and script versions of the same stories can help students identify differences in the writing styles and help them learn to look for information in the appropriate places (Manna, 1984). Many plays based on children's stories are readily available. Basal readers often include play selections, as do some trade books.

Understanding different genres helps readers recognize text structure and story elements. Readers who successfully identify common elements can use this knowledge to construct their own stories, strengthening the connection between reading and writing (Buss and Karnowski, 2000).

● Story Reading and Storytelling

Reading aloud to children of all ages serves many purposes. Oral reading by the teacher serves as a model and allows students to experience literature that they might not be able or inclined to read for themselves. It can encourage students to read more on their own, since hearing an exciting chapter or section of a book often stimulates children to read the entire book themselves. Besides providing exposure to specific books, reading to children can introduce them to creative and colorful use of language in prose and poetry, can present new vocabulary and concepts, and can acquaint them with the variety of language patterns found in written communication. DIVERSITY Hearing literature read aloud gives English language learners opportunities to hear the intonation and rhythm of the English language in meaningful contexts and to become familiar with the structure of the language.

Research supports the benefits of reading aloud to students. In *Becoming a Nation of Readers*, Richard Anderson and colleagues (1985) conclude, "The single most important activity for building the knowledge required for eventual success in reading is reading aloud to children" (p. 23). In addition, Michener (1988) finds research support for the following benefits of reading aloud to students:

❶ Helps them get off to a better start in reading.

❷ Improves their listening skills.

❸ Increases their ability to read independently.

❹ Expands their vocabularies.

❺ Improves their reading comprehension.

❻ Helps them to become better speakers.

❼ Improves their abilities as writers.

❽ Improves the quantity and quality of independent reading.

DIVERSITY Teachers approach read-aloud events in different ways (Barrentine, 1996). Some limit interactions during story reading and then conduct reflective after-reading discussions. Other teachers read stories interactively, encouraging children to respond verbally to their peers, to the text, and to the teacher as they listen. During interactive read-alouds, teachers ask questions to guide students in constructing meaning and making personal responses. Both approaches enable students to connect stories to their lives, explore layers of meaning, develop knowledge about literary elements, and personalize story meanings.

Just before reading a story aloud to the class, the teacher might ask students to listen to how the author uses a lead sentence to create interest in the story or uses dialogue to develop characterization. During the story, the teacher can stop occasionally to point out a literary technique or to ask students to close their eyes and DIVERSITY visualize a descriptive passage. It can be very helpful to provide ELL students with printed copies of the book that is being read aloud, or to read from a big book. ELL students benefit from observing English print characteristics and directional patterns, making predictable stories into big books, and developing an awareness and

CLASSROOM SCENARIO — Reading Aloud to Students

Kim Yunker calls her students to a corner of the classroom that has been set up to resemble a room in pioneer days. She asks a child to turn off the lights while she lights a kerosene lamp. Seated in a rocker, she shares a book that is related to the unit theme, "Little House in the Big Woods." She introduces Cynthia Rylant's *When I Was Young in the Mountains* and then begins reading aloud. Occasionally she interjects questions such as "What is okra?" and "What do you think a johnny house is?" After she finishes the book, she asks questions about life in pioneer days, and the children browse quietly through some of the other books. As the children leave, they return to illustrating spelling words related to the unit (e.g., *maple, wagon, slate*) or building a model fort from Lincoln Logs.

Analysis of Scenario

In Kim Yunker's class, story reading is integrated with the theme so that children are able to make connections between the stories and the work they are doing in other subjects.

appreciation of literature (Heald-Taylor, 1989). During shared big book reading, the teacher can help all students learn to read English by reinforcing reading strategies, modeling good reading, and inviting the children to read along (Lukasevich, 1996a).

After completing the story or chapter, the teacher might ask students what they specifically liked or disliked about the way the author wrote. When they discuss their likes and dislikes with the teacher, students learn to evaluate material, and this makes them more critical readers and can improve their writing abilities as well. The Classroom Scenario above shows how one teacher reads aloud to her third graders.

Teachers should read in natural tones and with expression, providing time for sharing the illustrations, exploring key words and phrases, and evaluating reactions. The best stories to read aloud are those that children cannot easily read by themselves, that the teacher personally likes and is thoroughly familiar with, and that possess the qualities characteristic of the best literature. Jim Trelease's *The New Read-Aloud Handbook* (1995) is an excellent source of information about how and what to read aloud to children.

In a balanced reading program, Doiron (1994) recommends reading aloud nonfiction as well as fiction. When reading nonfiction, teachers can consider children's special interests, relate books to thematic units, respond to student-initiated inquiries, read high-interest excerpts selectively, and expand students' knowledge of a variety of topics. As children listen to informational books and discuss ideas from them, they may find it easier and more natural to read expository text for their own pleasure. More middle-school educators have begun to recognize the importance of including nonfiction trade books for self-selection during in-class reading, and as a result, students often respond more favorably to reading and demonstrate a greater interest in reading (Moss and Hendershot, 2002).

Storytelling, like story reading, acquaints children with literature and provides good listening experiences. Listeners visualize the story through a "transfer of imagery" (Lipman, 1999). The storyteller uses oral language to prompt the listener to develop his or her own images of the story. Folktales are especially good for telling, because they were told and told again long before they were captured in print.

Either teachers or students can tell stories. Students who participate as storytellers can develop fluency and expression in oral language. By preparing and telling stories, they also can develop poise and build self-esteem. As storytellers, students must be aware of pitch, volume, timing, and gesture, as well as the responsiveness of the audience. A logical progression is for students to move from hearing, reading, and telling stories to writing original stories, which are often based on literary patterns they already know (Peck, 1989; Roe, Alfred, and Smith, 1998).

● Selecting Literature

From the thousands of books published annually for children, teachers and media specialists must select quality literature that they think children will want to read. Making such decisions is a challenge and a responsibility. Fortunately, there are several sources that teachers can use for reference when they choose literature. A useful source in selecting children's books is a listing of Newbery and Caldecott Award winners. The John *Newbery Award* is presented annually to the author whose book is selected as the year's most distinguished contribution to American literature for children. Excellence in the illustration of picture books for children is the criterion used in selecting the winner of the annual Randolph *Caldecott Award*.

LITERATURE   Some educators advocate classics, quality books that exhibit enduring excellence, as the foundation for reading. Not all classics are popular with students, however, so it is important to choose appropriate works and avoid those that may discourage students from reading. Some favorite classics are *Charlotte's Web; The Borrowers; Peter Pan; The Secret Garden; Where the Red Fern Grows; The Lion, the Witch, and the Wardrobe;* and *Little House in the Big Woods.*

DIVERSITY   Another consideration in choosing books is their social significance in relation to human values, cultural pluralism, and aesthetic standards (Norton, 2003). For minority children, multicultural literature based on familiar traditions and values can be a mirror that reflects and validates their own cultural experiences. For all children, such books can be revealing windows into less familiar cultures (Cox and Galda, 1990). Teachers can ask themselves the following questions to help them choose books that promote cultural pluralism and avoid portraying negative stereotypes:

❶ Do the illustrations and text depict the character in the story as a distinct individual or as a stereotype of a particular ethnic group?

❷ Is dialect used as a natural part of the story or contrived to reinforce a stereotype?

❸ Is the culture treated respectfully or portrayed as inferior?

❹ Are the people and the settings described authentically?

One valuable instructional resource that teachers can consult when searching for multicultural literature is the *Coretta Scott King Awards* presented annually by the American Library Association. The recipients are authors and illustrators of African descent whose books promote peace and world brotherhood.

Hadaway and Florez (1990) point out several ways to use multicultural literature. Teachers, with the help of librarians or media specialists, should select books that represent cultural groups realistically and integrate these books into literature and social studies programs. As they tell or read the stories to the class, teachers can promote vocabulary, comprehension, and writing skills, along with values education. Despite adult critics' recommendations, many children prefer to make their own choices. Each year, the International Reading Association–Children's Book Council Joint Committee publishes an annotated list of "Children's Choices," which appears in the October issue of *The Reading Teacher.* Each list is compiled by approximately 10,000 children who, working in teams, read new books and vote for their favorites. Since children are the ultimate critics of their literature, teachers and librarians should consider their choices seriously when purchasing and recommending books.

STANDARDS AND ASSESSMENT In helping children select books, teachers need to know both the books that are available and their children's needs and interests. Teachers can assess children's personal reading interests by simply asking them to list three things that interest them or by administering an interest inventory. Teachers can guide children's choices by helping them locate books on special topics, by sampling new books to pique their interest, by allowing time for children to browse in the library, and by suggesting titles on occasion. Regardless of this assistance, however, most children will value the freedom to choose their own books.

LITERATURE Selecting appropriate poetry for children is especially difficult. Suitable poems will amuse, inspire, emotionally move, or intellectually stimulate children, but poorly chosen poems can prejudice children against poetry. Children prefer poems with rhyme, rhythm, humor, and narration; works by Shel Silverstein (*Where the Sidewalk Ends, Light in the Attic*) and Jack Prelutsky (*The New Kid on the Block, Something Big Has Been Here*) are natural favorites. The humor they use comes from alliteration, plays on words, or highly exaggerated situations, as in "Sarah Cynthia Sylvia Stout Who Would Not Take the Garbage Out" (from *Where the Sidewalk Ends*). Kupiter and Wilson (1993) contend, however, that teachers must sensitively cultivate an interest in poetry that goes beyond Silverstein and Prelutsky; they must build bridges from these popular poems to the rich array of diverse poetry waiting to be discovered.

Not to be overlooked are the intriguing nonfiction selections that can supplement textbooks or even substitute for them. So many appealing, well-illustrated informational books are available on nearly every topic that choosing the best books can be difficult. When selecting nonfiction, teachers should look for the following characteristics:

- content that is accurate and current

- organization and layout that facilitate easy use

- cohesive text in which ideas are arranged logically

- specialized vocabulary that is clearly defined

- attention-grabbing content and illustrations (Sudol and King, 1996).

LITERATURE Because informational books can be read or viewed at varying levels, most are appropriate for many ages. Young readers can examine illustrations in David

With teacher guidance, children read and respond to information found in a weekly newspaper. *(© Elizabeth Crews/Stock Boston)*

Macaulay's *Cathedral* and *Pyramid*, for example, whereas more mature students can read those books to find out how these structures were built. Worthy (1996) found that nonfiction selections, particularly those dealing with sports, animals, drawing, or cars, are popular with reluctant readers. Joanna Cole's Magic School Bus series, a mixture of fact and fiction, appeals to children who enjoy the characters and their escapades, as well as to children seeking information. Fascinating books about animals — books useful for enriching a thematic unit — include *Summer Ice: Life Along the Antarctic Peninsula*, a combination of text and photographs about animal life in Antarctica; *Raptor Rescue: An Eagle Flies Free*, detailing the work of Minnesota's Raptor Center in rehabilitating injured raptors; and *Dolphin Man: Exploring the World of Dolphins*, a photobiography of Randy Wells, an authority on dolphins.

Many teachers prefer paperback books, because multiple copies of one book cost the same as a single library edition, allowing teachers to order enough for small groups of children to read and use in follow-up activities and discussions. Paperback books are often available at special reduced rates through numerous book clubs.

Children's magazines and newspapers are available for different reading levels and different areas of interest. These periodicals are excellent classroom resources and offer several benefits for the reading program: (1) the material is current and relevant; (2) the reading range varies in level of difficulty and in content presented; (3) several genres usually appear in a single issue; (4) language activities, such as crossword puzzles, contests, and children's writings, are often included; (5) the illustrations and photographs are excellent and can improve comprehension; (6) their low cost makes them easily accessible; and (7) they are popular with reluctant readers (Seminoff, 1986; Worthy, 1996). Classroom subscriptions to two or three favorites will enrich the reading program. Some popular choices are listed in Stoll's *Magazines for Kids and Teens* (1997).

● Responding to Literature

According to reader response theory, readers are actively constructing meaning as they read. Because all readers differ in background experiences and preformed attitudes, each interprets the text somewhat differently (Cox, 1997).

Rosenblatt (1978) proposed that any text can be read efferently (for information) and/or aesthetically (as a lived-through experience), as explained in Chapter 1. Usually readers move back and forth along a continuum between an efferent stance and an aesthetic stance until they settle on a single predominant stance (Cox, 1997). They may be getting information as they read, but they may also be experiencing the emotions of the characters, the mood of the story as the plot unfolds, or a sense of morality in relation to an episode in history. For example, Lloyd Alexander's *The King's Fountain* offers a historical perspective on village life, but the courageous poor man's efforts to save his village tug at the heart. Both types of responses are important, but teachers tend to ask questions that call for efferent responses (Zarillo and Cox, 1992), even though in some cases aesthetic responses may be more meaningful and more enduring. Students need to be able to choose their types of responses and to have adequate time for reflecting on and responding to books (Cox and Many, 1992; Hickman, 1995).

Children can express their responses in a variety of ways, such as answering teacher questions, participating in literature circles, interpreting literature orally, dramatizing reading selections, writing, or creating art or music. For English language **DIVERSITY** 🌐 learners, reader response is especially beneficial because it allows the student to respond to literature uniquely in terms of his or her own cultural background and level of English proficiency (Cox and Boyd-Batstone, 1997).

Responding to Questions

Teachers can prepare generic questions to encourage children to respond thoughtfully to literature. These questions may be used during conferences, for written responses, for group activities, or during class discussions. Questions should be open-ended, not limited to a single correct answer. Popp (1997) suggests four categories of questions, which are given here with sample prompts for each category.

Evaluation

What did you like or dislike about this book? Why?

Why do you think the main character acted in such a way?

Connection

How did a character make you think of someone you know?

Has anyone you know faced a similar challenge? What was it?

Comprehension

What is a theme of this story?

What does this story mean to you?

Strategy

How did you figure out an unfamiliar word in this story?

What special features helped you understand this story?

Literature Circles

An organized procedure for responding to literature is the use of *literature circles* (Bell, 1990; Strube, 1996; Zogby, 1990). These groups give students opportunities to read and respond to good literature, to engage in high-level thinking about books, and to do extensive and intensive reading. Information on establishing and implementing literature circles appears in Chapter 7.

Oral Interpretation of Literature

Fluent oral reading with intonation and phrasing that accurately reflect the mood and tone of the story or poem is another way to respond to literature. Oral reading is more difficult than silent reading, because in order to convey the author's message to an audience, the reader must pronounce words correctly, phrase appropriately, enunciate distinctly, use proper intonation, and pace the reading appropriately. To accomplish these goals, the oral reader should have an opportunity to read silently first to become acquainted with the author's style of writing, determine the author's message, and check the correct pronunciation of unfamiliar words. If the passage is particularly difficult, the reader may need to practice it aloud to ensure proper phrasing and intonation.

STANDARDS AND ASSESSMENT

Oral reading skills require special attention. The teacher may demonstrate fluent and poor oral reading, let the children analyze these performances, and then help students develop a rubric or draw up a list of standards or guidelines such as the following:

❶ Be sure you can pronounce each word correctly before you read your selection to an audience. If you are not sure of a pronunciation, check the dictionary or ask for help.

❷ Say each word clearly and distinctly. Don't run words together, and take care not to leave out word parts or add parts to words.

❸ Pause in the right places. Pay attention to punctuation clues.

❹ Emphasize important words. Help the audience understand the meaning of the selection by the way you read it. Read slowly enough to allow for adequate expression, and speak loudly enough to be easily heard.

5 Prepare carefully before you read to an audience.

When well-rehearsed oral reading occurs, there should be one or more people with whom the reader is attempting to communicate through reading. Audience members should not have access to the book from which the performer is reading so that they cannot follow the reading with their eyes. Instead, they should listen to the reader to grasp the author's meaning and, if the reader is reading to prove a point, to agree or disagree. The reader must attempt to hold the audience's attention through oral interpretation of the author's words. A stumbling performance will lead to a restless, impatient audience and a poor listening situation.

Here are some examples of purposes for audience reading:

1 Confirming an answer to a question by reading the portion of the selection in which the answer is found.

2 Sharing a part of a published story, a poem (most poems are written to be read aloud), or an experience story that the reader has enjoyed.

3 Participating in choral reading or readers' theater.

4 Sharing riddles, jokes, and tongue twisters to entertain classmates.

5 Reading stories aloud to children in lower grades.

6 Reading the part of a character in a play or the narration for a play or other dramatic presentation.

LITERATURE Books by Paul Fleischman contain poems for two voices that invite students or groups of students to collaborate in reading aloud. Sometimes passages are to be read singly and sometimes in unison, but students must read expressively and fluently to achieve the proper effect. *Joyful Noise* contains poems about insects that think and act as humans; *I Am Phoenix* consists of poems that celebrate a variety of birds.

Responses Through Drama

Dramatic interpretations of literature are aesthetic responses, and they help children find success because there are no right or wrong answers (Fennessey, 1995). Through drama, children can deepen their responses to literature and discover underlying meanings. Drama helps children become aware of different points of view and develops imagination and critical thinking.

DIVERSITY Through creative drama, bilingual students can interpret the stories they hear, thereby clarifying their understanding of story structure and vocabulary. Role playing enables them to experiment with vocabulary and sentence structure as they explore their feelings.

Drama can take many forms. In *pantomime*, children speak no lines but show what is happening through their gestures and body movements. Simple nursery rhymes and fables are good for pantomiming. *Characterization* focuses on revealing the way characters feel, act, and relate to other characters in the story, and children attempt to speak, to move, and to modify their facial expressions as they "become" the story characters. *Creative dramatics* means acting out a story without using a script, and *choral speaking* or *choral reading* is the dramatic interpretation of poetry

EXAMPLE 8.5 **Book Recommendation**

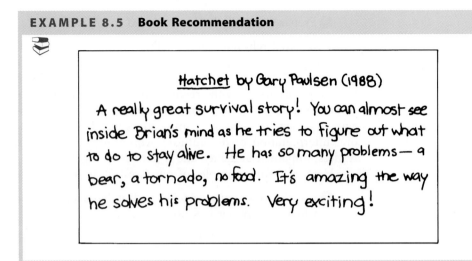

> <u>Hatchet</u> by Gary Paulsen (1988)
>
> A really great survival story! You can almost see inside Brian's mind as he tries to figure out what to do to stay alive. He has so many problems — a bear, a tornado, no food. It's amazing the way he solves his problems. Very exciting!

or other literature with two or more voices. In *readers' theater*, students read aloud in dramatic style from scripts; no sets, costumes, or props are necessary, and the emphasis is on interpretive oral reading (Cullinan and Galda, 1994; Savage, 1994).

Responses Through Written Expression

Traditional written book reports in which students merely summarize the plots of stories have in many cases been replaced by more authentic responses to literature. Students are encouraged to react thoughtfully to what they read by writing in literature logs or critically reviewing books on note cards that are filed for other students to read. In one class, students place on a bulletin board minireviews of favorite books they want to recommend. Example 8.5 above is a sample of a child's recommendation.

Several ideas for activities that combine reading and writing were presented earlier in this chapter. Here are some additional activities that focus on written responses to literature.

LITERATURE

ACTIVITIES

1. Ask students to collect as many Newbery Award books and Honor books (runners-up to Newbery Award books) as they can find, read several of them, and ask their friends to read others. After making up and filling out an evaluation checklist for each book, including such criteria as characterization, author's style, authenticity of setting, and plot development, they may add to the checklist comments about the merit of each book.

2. Let each student read a biography of a famous historical figure and write a story about what would happen if that person lived today — for example, how he or she would bring peace to the world, solve medical problems, or protect the environment. The popular *Lincoln: A Photobiography*, by Russell Freedman, would be a good choice.

3. Choose an environmental book, such as Chris Van Allsburg's *Just a Dream*, and have students discuss the issues it raises. Ask them each to choose one issue that especially concerns them and write letters to their congressperson describing the issue and recommending solutions.

4. Read Byrd Baylor's *I'm in Charge of Celebrations*, and discuss the meaning of *celebration* as used in this book. Then ask the children to keep journals of their own special celebration days over a period of two or three months. Students may wish to share their celebrations by reading from their journals.

5. Read to the class Mem Fox's *Wilfred Gordon McDonald Partridge* or a similar book about elderly people, and discuss both the contributions and the special needs of older people. Ask each child to identify an elderly person to whom he or she can write a letter or send a story. Help the children follow through with their plans.

6. After reading several selections of multicultural literature, keep on a world map a continuing record of the settings featured in the selections. Encourage students to identify the sites of their family origins.

Responses Through Art and Music

Many children who have difficulty expressing themselves with words prefer to respond to literature in other ways (Hoyt, 1992). Art and music offer creative options for these children.

TECHNOLOGY 🖥️   Through exposure to well-illustrated picture books, children learn to appreciate the artists' work and begin to see themselves as illustrators capable of creating their own art (Galda and Short, 1993). They can interpret stories through many art media, including clay, paint, papier-mâché, scraps of felt and ribbon, colored pencils and pens, computer drawing programs, and three-dimensional objects. Using such media, they can create collages and montages, dioramas and puppet figures, mobiles and stabiles, and illustrations for their own storybooks (Russell, 1994).

LITERATURE 📖   Children have a natural tendency to respond to the rhythm and melody of music, so it can be effective to combine music with literature and language activities (Kolb, 1996). Many picture books of children's story songs and singing games are available, and these books help children connect the words they sing with the words they see in print (Beaty, 1994). Some examples are

- *The Wheels on the Bus* by Maryann Kovalski (Boston: Little, Brown, 1987). An action song with movements and sounds that accompany the wheels, wipers, horns, and so forth.

- *Old McDonald Had a Farm* by Glen Rounds (New York: Holiday House, 1989). A familiar song with repetitive phrases such as "With a MOO-MOO here" and a chorus of "EE-AY, EE-AY, OH."

- *Abiyoyo* by Pete Seeger; Michael Hays, illustrator (New York: Macmillan, 1986). A story song based on a South African lullaby in which a little boy and his father make a monster disappear.

- *THUMP, THUMP, Rat-a-Tat-Tat* by Lois Ehlert's (Singapore: Harper & Row, 1989). By picturing the instruments and simulating the sounds of a marching band, this book can provide the stimulus for creating a rhythm band.

SUMMARY

Some basic tenets of facilitating language development are that learning is integrated, tasks are authentic, learning is social, classrooms are learning-centered, and literature is an integral part of the curriculum. Applications of these principles are found throughout the text.

Instead of separating the language arts into discrete time periods, teachers should integrate instruction in reading, writing, listening, and speaking. When children learn language as an integrated whole, they are likely to view reading and writing as meaningful events.

Many similarities exist between reading and writing. Both are composing processes in which meaning is constructed. Teachers can use this natural connection by guiding children into activities that call for both reading and writing. Process writing is a child-centered approach to writing that consists of five steps: prewriting, drafting, revising, editing, sharing and publishing. Journal writing and reading enable students to record their ideas and, in many cases, to read responses from their teacher. Writing and reading workshops provide minilessons and large blocks of time for students to concentrate on actual writing and reading.

Literature is useful for integrating language. Story reading and storytelling provide multiple benefits by enticing children to read and providing them with knowledge. Teachers should be aware of the characteristics of a variety of literary genres, and they should consider both literary merit and children's interests when helping children choose books. Teachers should also establish environments with an abundance of interesting books and attractive displays that create interest in reading.

Children may respond to literature aesthetically (by making emotional responses) or efferently (by seeking information). Their responses may be communicated in literature circles or through oral reading, drama, written expression, art, and/or music.

TEST YOURSELF

True or False

_____ 1. Ideally, language arts instruction should be integrated throughout the curriculum.

_____ 2. Reading and writing are both composing processes.

_____ 3. The writing process refers to the way children use punctuation, grammar, and spelling.

_____ 4. Children generally prefer poems with thoughtful, serious themes.

_____ 5. During the drafting stage, students must be careful to observe correct use of spelling and mechanics.

_____ 6. Children must work alone when doing revisions.

_____ 7. In dialogue journals, usually the student writes some thoughts and the teacher responds in writing.

_____ 8. Their review of journal writing is a good opportunity for teachers to correct students' handwriting, spelling, and grammar.

_____ 9. In writing and reading workshops, students complete workbook exercises.

_____ 10. Elementary students are capable of using word processors to write and edit compositions.

_____ 11. Literature can be an effective vehicle for integrating the instruction in language arts across the curriculum.

_____ 12. When readers take an aesthetic stance as they respond to literature, they read to gain information.

_____ 13. When reading aloud, teachers should speak in natural tones and with expression.

_____ 14. In a double entry journal, the student writes on one side of the page and the teacher writes on the other.

_____ 15. The Newbery Award is given for excellence in illustration.

_____ 16. Many high-quality children's magazines are being published.

_____ 17. Silent reading is more difficult than oral reading.

_____ 18. Performers in readers' theater memorize their parts.

_____ 19. When writing responses to literature, a student should give first priority to the mechanics of writing.

_____ 20. There is no need for teachers to read aloud to children after children learn to read for themselves.

_____ 21. Award-winning trade books can be found for nearly every period in history.

_____ 22. The Coretta Scott King Award is given to outstanding selections by authors and illustrators of African descent.

For your journal ...

1. Read a junior novel, such as *Little House in the Big Woods* or *The Sign of the Beaver*, and respond to it either aesthetically or efferently.

2. If you could choose, how would you prefer to respond to literature — through writing, oral expression, art, music, drama, or some other way? Why?

3. Reflect on the video that accompanies this chapter on your CD. What steps in the writing process are demonstrated? In your opinion, which steps of the writing process support the basic tenets for facilitating language development, described in Chapter 8?

... and your portfolio

1. Begin an annotated list of books you would like to have in your classroom library, and add to the list as you find other selections you wish to include.

2. When you are visiting schools, jot down literature-related ideas that you see teachers using. These might include bulletin-board displays, classroom library corners, theme-related book collections, and children's responses to literature.

3. As you come across books you might like to use during thematic units, copy their bibliographic information and brainstorm ways to connect each book to different areas of the curriculum.

Reading/Study Techniques

KEY VOCABULARY

Pay close attention to these terms when they appear in the chapter.

bar graphs

circle or pie graphs

database

graphic organizers

guide words

legend (of a map)

line graphs

metacognition

picture graphs

reading rate

reading/study techniques

scale (of a map)

SQ3R

SQRQCQ

SETTING OBJECTIVES

When you finish reading this chapter, you should be able to

● Discuss the features of the SQ3R study method.

● Explain the importance of developing flexible reading habits.

● Name some skills students need in order to locate information in a variety of print and nonprint sources.

● Describe how to help students learn to organize, outline, and summarize information.

● Discuss metacognitive strategies that students need.

● Explain how to teach students to use graphic aids in textbooks.

I t is important that all students develop the reading and study skills necessary to gather information, organize it, and evaluate it in a variety of contexts. *Reading/ study techniques* are strategies that enhance comprehension and retention of information in print and nonprint sources and thus help students cope successfully with assignments in content area classes and with informational reading throughout their lives. To succeed in their schoolwork, students need a variety of skills. They need to use study methods that can help them retain material they read, take tests effectively, exercise flexibility in their reading habits, locate and organize information effectively, and use metacognitive strategies when studying. They also need to learn the skills necessary to derive information from graphic aids (maps, graphs, tables, and illustrations) in content area reading materials.

Teaching study techniques is not exclusively the job of the intermediate-grade teacher, although the need for such instruction is more obvious at this level than at the primary level. Primary-grade teachers must lay the foundation for this instruction and make the children aware of the need for study skills. They can do this in a number of ways. They can have the children begin to keep assignment books in which to record all school assignments, along with related instructions and due dates. Teachers can introduce children to such activities as making free-form outlines related to stories they have heard or read and occasionally writing group experience charts in outline form. Primary teachers can also let the children see them using

Chapter 9 Organization

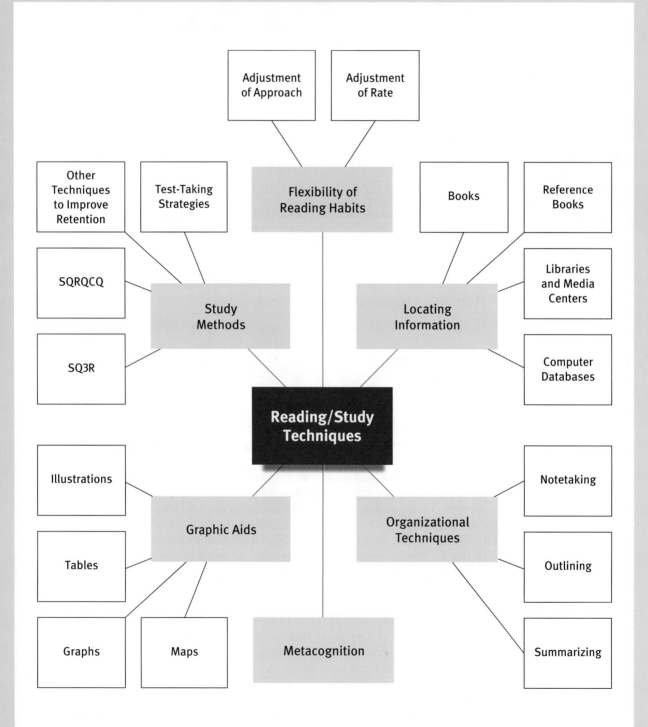

Adjustment of Approach

Adjustment of Rate

Flexibility of Reading Habits

Other Techniques to Improve Retention

Test-Taking Strategies

Books

Reference Books

SQRQCQ

Study Methods

Locating Information

Libraries and Media Centers

SQ3R

Computer Databases

Reading/Study Techniques

Illustrations

Notetaking

Graphic Aids

Organizational Techniques

Tables

Outlining

Graphs

Maps

Metacognition

Summarizing

indexes and tables of contents of books to find information that they need, and they can begin actual study skill instruction in the use of some parts of books, such as tables of contents and glossaries. They can read aloud information related to content area study from a variety of reference books and can start teaching children some principles of dictionary use, including alphabetical order, through use of picture dictionaries. Primary teachers can also help their students use the library by showing them the locations of the easy-to-read books and explaining the check-in and check-out procedures. Children in the primary grades can start to learn to read maps (titles, directional indicators, legends), graphs (picture graphs, circle graphs, simple bar graphs), and pictures.

Teachers may present study techniques during a content class when the need arises or during a reading class, but they should be sure the strategies are applied to content promptly if they are taught during a reading class. Children will retain study techniques longer if they apply them, and they will see these skills as useful tools, rather than as busywork exercises. They are more likely to apply their new knowledge if they practice the techniques in the context in which they will use them. Therefore, a teacher may find it very effective to set aside time during a content class to teach a study strategy that students will need to use immediately in that class.

Study Methods

Study methods are techniques that help students read, listen to, or view material in a way that enhances comprehension and retention. Unlike the directed reading activities (DRAs) found in teacher's manuals in basal reading series, study methods are student-directed, rather than teacher-directed. (See Chapter 7 for a description of a DRA.)

● SQ3R

Probably the best-known study method is Robinson's *SQ3R* method: Survey, Question, Read, Recite, Review (Robinson, 1961). For this method, the steps given to the students are as follows:

- *Survey.* As you approach a reading assignment, you should notice the chapter title and main headings, read the introductory and summary paragraphs, and inspect any visual aids such as maps, graphs, or illustrations. This initial survey provides a framework for organizing the facts you later derive from the reading.

- *Question.* Formulate a list of questions you expect to be answered in the reading. The headings may give you some clues.

- *Read.* Read the selection in order to answer the questions you have formulated. Since this is purposeful reading, making brief notes may be helpful.

- *Recite.* After reading the selection, try to answer each of the questions you formulated earlier, without looking back at the material.

- *Review.* Reread to verify or correct your recited answers and to make sure that you have the main points of the selection in mind and that you understand the relationships among the various points.

Using a study method such as SQ3R will help a student remember content material better than simply reading the material would. Consequently, it is worthwhile to take time in class to show students how to go through the various steps. Teachers should have group practice sessions on SQ3R (as on any study method) before expecting the children to perform the steps independently.

Material chosen for SQ3R instruction should be content material on which the students should normally use the method. The teacher should ask all the students to survey the selection together — reading aloud the title and main headings and the introductory and summary paragraphs, and discussing the visual aids — in the first practice session.

The step that needs most explanation by the teacher is the Question step. The teacher can show children how to take a heading, such as "Brazil's Exports," and turn it into a question: "What are Brazil's exports?" This question should be answered in the section, and trying to find the answer provides a good purpose for reading. A chapter heading, such as "The Westward Movement," may elicit a variety of possible questions: "What is the Westward Movement?" "When did it take place?" "Where did it take place?" "Why did it take place?" "Who was involved?" The teacher can encourage children to generate questions like these in a class discussion during initial practice sessions.

After they have formulated questions, students read to find the answers. The teacher might make brief notes on the board to model behavior the children should acquire. Then he or she can have students practice the Recite step by asking each child to respond orally to one of the purpose questions, with the book closed. During the Review step, the children reread to check all the answers they have just heard.

In subsequent practice sessions, the teacher can merely alert the children to perform each step and have them all perform the step silently at the same time. It will probably take several practice sessions before the steps are thoroughly set in the students' memories.

● SQRQCQ

Another method that seems simple enough to use with good results at the elementary level is one developed especially for use with mathematics materials: *SQRQCQ* (Fay, 1965). *SQRQCQ* stands for Survey, Question, Read, Question, Compute, Question. This approach may be beneficial because youngsters frequently have great difficulty reading statement problems in mathematics textbooks. For this method, the steps given to the students are as follows:

- *Survey.* Read through the problem quickly to get an idea of its general nature.

- *Question.* Ask, "What is being asked in the problem?"

- *Read.* Read the problem carefully, paying attention to specific details and relationships.

- *Question.* Make a decision about the mathematical operations to be carried out and, in some cases, about the order in which they are to be performed.

- *Compute.* Do the computations you decided on in the preceding step.

Reading/study techniques should be taught using the students' textbooks.
(Elizabeth Crews)

- *Question.* Decide whether or not the answer seems to be correct, asking, "Is this a reasonable answer? Have I accurately performed the computations?"

As with SQ3R, the teacher should have the whole class practice the SQRQCQ method before expecting students to use it independently. Teaching the SQRQCQ method takes little extra time, since it is a good way to manage mathematics instruction. (You may wish to refer to this section again as you read the section in Chapter 10 on mathematics materials.)

● Other Techniques to Improve Retention

In addition to providing students with effective study strategies, a teacher can improve their ability to retain content material by following these suggestions:

❶ Conduct discussions about all assigned reading material. Talking about ideas that they have read helps to fix these ideas in students' memories.

❷ Teach students to read assignments critically. Have them constantly evaluate the material they read, and avoid giving them the idea that something is true "because the book says so" by encouraging them to challenge any statement in the book if they can find evidence to the contrary. The active involvement with the material that is necessary in critical reading aids retention. (See Chapter 6 for a thorough discussion of critical reading.)

❸ Encourage students to apply the ideas about which they have read in authentic situations. For example, after reading about parliamentary procedure, students can conduct a club meeting; after reading about a simple science experiment, they can actually conduct the experiment. Children learn those things they have applied in real life better than those they have only read about.

❹ Always be certain that students have in mind a purpose for reading before they begin each reading assignment, since this increases their ability to retain material. You may supply them with purpose questions or encourage them to state their own purposes. (Information about purpose questions is found in Chapters 5 and 6.)

❺ Use audiovisual aids to reinforce concepts presented in the reading material.

❻ Read background material to students to give them a frame of reference to which they can relate the ideas they read.

❼ Prepare study guides for content area assignments. Study guides help children retain their content area concepts by setting purposes for reading and providing appropriate frameworks for organizing material. (Study guides are discussed extensively in Chapter 10.)

❽ Teach students to look for the author's organization of material. Have them outline the material or construct a diagram of the organizational pattern. (Outlining is discussed later in this chapter.)

TECHNOLOGY ❾ Encourage children to picture the ideas the author is describing. Visualizing information will help them remember it longer. Some children will find it helpful to draw, graph, or chart the ideas they visualize. Semantic webs are particularly useful. (See Chapter 10 for a description of the use of webs with content material.) *Inspiration* (Inspiration) and *Kidspiration* (Kidspiration) are programs that facilitate webbing of ideas.

❿ Teach note-taking procedures and encourage note taking. Writing down information often helps children retain it. (Note taking is discussed later in this chapter.)

⓫ After children have read the material, have them paraphrase and summarize the information in either written or oral form. (Later in this chapter we discuss summarizing skills in more detail.)

⓬ Have children use spaced practice (a number of short practice sessions extended over a period of time) rather than massed practice (one long practice session) for material you wish them to retain for a long time.

⓭ Encourage *overlearning* (continuing to practice a skill for a while after it has been initially mastered) of material you wish students to retain for long periods of time.

⓮ When appropriate, teach some simple mnemonic devices (short phrases or verses used as memory aids)—for example, "there is *a rat* in the middle of sep*arate*."

⓯ Offer positive reinforcement for correct responses to questions during discussion and review sessions.

⓰ Encourage students to look for words and ideas that are mentioned repeatedly, because they are likely to be important ones.

⓱ Encourage students to study more difficult and less interesting material when they are most alert (Memory and Yoder, 1988).

⓲ Teach students to ask and answer *why* questions about each factual statement in an informational passage (Menke and Pressley, 1994).

STANDARDS AND
ASSESSMENT

● Test-Taking Strategies

Students need to retain what they have read in order to do well on tests, but sometimes students who know the material fail to do as well as they could because they lack good test-taking strategies. Students may study in the same way for essay tests and objective tests, for example. Helping them understand how to study for and take different types of tests can improve their performance.

DIVERSITY

Teachers can help students prepare for taking essay tests by helping them understand the meanings of certain words, such as *compare, contrast, describe,* and *explain,* that frequently appear in essay questions. This is especially important for English language learners. The teacher can state a potential question that uses one of these terms and then model the answer to the question, explaining what is important to include in the answer. If a contrast is requested, the differences between the two things or ideas should be explained. If a comparison is requested, likenesses should be included. The use of visual/graphic aids such as Venn diagrams can support the concept of comparison/contrast relationships.

To prepare for objective tests, teachers should encourage students to learn important terms and their definitions, study for types of questions that have been asked in the past, and learn to use mnemonic devices to help in memorizing lists.

Providing students focused instruction on taking standardized tests can help them perform better on these tests. Teachers should discuss with the children the purpose of the tests and the special rules that apply during testing well before the standardized tests are to be given. They should provide practice in completing test items within specified time limits. A practice test with directions, time limits, and item formats as similar as possible to those of the actual test should be given to familiarize the children with the overall testing environment.

Children need to learn to follow the directions for testing exactly, including those related to recording answers. They should learn to answer first those items they can answer quickly and to check answers if they have time left. Teachers can also encourage students to consider the words *always*, *never*, and *not* carefully when answering true-false questions, since these words have a powerful effect on the meaning. They can make sure students realize that if any part of a true-false statement is false, the answer must be false. They can also caution students to read and consider all answers to a multiple-choice question before choosing an answer and can encourage them to guess rather than leave an answer blank if there is not a severe penalty for guessing.

Flexibility of Reading Habits

Flexible readers adjust their approaches and rates to fit the materials they are reading. Good readers continually adjust their reading approaches and rates without being aware of it.

● Adjustment of Approach

Flexible readers approach material according to *their purposes for reading* and the *type of material.* For example, they may read poetry aloud to get the full effect of the rhythms and the sound of the words, or they may read novels for relaxation in a leisurely fashion, savoring descriptive passages that evoke visual imagery and taking time to think about the characters and their traits. If they are reading novels simply to be able to converse with friends about the story lines, they may read less carefully, wishing only to discover the novels' main ideas and basic plots.

Flexible readers approach informational reading with the goal of separating the important facts from the lesser details and paying careful attention in order to retain what they need from the material. Rereading is often necessary if the material contains a high density of facts or very difficult concepts and interrelationships. With such material, reading every word may be highly important, whereas it is less important with material that contains few facts or less difficult concepts. Flexible readers approach material for which they have little background with greater concentration than material for which their background is extensive.

Some reading purposes do not demand the reading of every word in a passage. Sometimes *skimming* (reading selectively to pick up main ideas and general impressions about the material) or *scanning* (moving the eyes rapidly over the selection to locate a specific bit of information, such as a name or a date) is sufficient. Skimming is the process used in the Survey step of SQ3R, when students are trying to orient themselves to the organization and general focus of the material. Scanning is useful when searching for names in telephone books or entries in dictionaries or indexes.

● Adjustment of Rate

Children often make the mistake of trying to read everything at the same rate. Some of them read short stories as slowly and carefully as they read science experiments, and they may not enjoy recreational reading because they have to work so hard and it takes them so long to read a story. Other children read everything rapidly, often failing to grasp essential details in content area reading assignments, even though they complete the reading. *Reading rate* should not be considered as separate from comprehension. The optimum rate for reading a particular piece is the fastest rate at which the reader maintains an acceptable level of comprehension.

Students will use study time more efficiently if they are taught to vary their rates to fit their reading *purposes* and *materials*. Students should read light fiction for enjoyment much more rapidly than a mathematics problem that must be solved. When reading to find isolated facts such as names and dates, a student will do better to scan a page rapidly for key words than to read every word of the material. When reading to determine the main ideas or organization of a selection, he or she will find skimming more practical than reading each word of the selection.

One way to help children fit appropriate rates to materials is to give them various types of materials and purposes, allow them to try different rates, and then encourage them to discuss the effectiveness of different rates for different purposes and materials. This will be particularly helpful if regular classroom materials are used for the practice. Emphasis on increasing reading speed is best left until children have well-developed basic word recognition and comprehension skills. By the time they reach the intermediate grades, some will be ready for help in increasing their reading rates. It is important to remember that speed without comprehension is useless, so the teacher must be sure students maintain satisfactory comprehension levels as they keep working to increase their reading rates. Techniques that teachers can use with students to help them increase their reading rates include the following:

ACTIVITIES

1. To encourage students to try consciously to increase their reading rates, time their reading for three minutes. At the end of that period, have the students count the total words read, divide by three, and record the resulting number as their rate in average words per minute. To ensure that they are focusing on understanding, follow the timed reading with a comprehension check. The students can graph the results of these timed readings over a period of time, along with the comprehension results. Ideally, students will see their rates increase without a decrease in comprehension. If the children's comprehension does decrease, encourage them to slow down enough to regain an appropriate comprehension level.

2. To help students cut down on unnecessary regressions (going back to reread), have them use markers to move down the page, covering the lines just read.

3. To help decrease children's anxiety about comprehension, which could impede their progress, give them material written at their independent reading levels for practice in building their reading rates. (Information about independent reading levels is presented in Chapter 10.)

TIME for REFLECTION

Some teachers spend time on development of reading rate but do not address flexibility. Other teachers address flexibility but give little attention to increasing rate. Some teachers work on both aspects. Still others dismiss rate considerations entirely, as inappropriate for elementary school instruction. **What do *you* think, and why?**

Locating Information

To engage in many study activities, students need to be able to locate the necessary material. Inquiry learning, for example, requires students to locate applicable information. A recent review of exemplary elementary classrooms and teachers concluded that in these classes students were encouraged to view themselves as researchers and to approach learning through inquiry (Allington, 2002). Teachers who create inquiry-based classrooms do more than just pose carefully designed questions; they also encourage students to approach learning in an inquisitive manner. They facilitate independent learning and provide opportunities for students to discover knowledge. Tower (2000) emphasized the need for students to have experience with nonfiction reading and writing before the inquiry process can be a successful strategy for gathering information. A teacher can help prepare students by pointing out the location aids in textbooks, reference books, and libraries and by showing them how to access databases.

● Books

Most books offer students several special features that are helpful for locating needed information, including prefaces, tables of contents, indexes, appendices, glossaries, footnotes, and bibliographies. Teachers should not assume that children can adjust from the basal reader or trade book format to the format of content area textbooks without assistance. Basal readers have a great deal of narrative (storylike) material that, unlike most content material, is not packed with facts to be learned. When the trade books used in a program are primarily fiction, they will also be narrative in format. Although most basals have a table of contents and a glossary, they may not contain as many helpful special features as content textbooks; and, although some nonfiction trade books have tables of contents and/or glossaries, not all do. DIVERSITY 🌐 Therefore, teachers should present content textbooks to children carefully. Such instruction is particularly important for struggling readers and English language learners.

Preface/Introduction

When presenting textbooks to students in the intermediate or upper grades, the teacher can ask them to read the preface or introduction to get an idea of why the book was written and of the manner in which the author or authors plan to present the material.

Table of Contents

On the day a new textbook is distributed, the teacher can lead students in an examination of the table of contents in the textbook. All students at the primary and intermediate levels can learn that the table of contents lists the topics the book discusses and the pages on which they appear, making it unnecessary to look through the entire book to find a specific section. The teacher can help students discover information about their new textbooks by asking questions such as the following:

What topics are covered in this book?

What is the first topic discussed?

On what page does the discussion about _____ begin?
(This question can be repeated several times with different topics inserted in the blank.)

Indexes

Students in the intermediate and upper grades should become familiar with indexes. They should understand that an index is an alphabetical list of items and names mentioned in a book, along with the pages where these items or names appear, and that some books contain one general index and some contain subject and author indexes as well as other specialized ones (for example, a first-line index in a music or poetry book). Most indexes contain both main headings and subheadings, and students should be given opportunities to practice using these headings to locate information within their books. The teacher can lead children to examine the index of a book in order to make inferences about which topics the author considers to be important, judging on the basis of the amount of space devoted to them. The Focus on Strategies on page 354 illustrates the use of the index to locate information.

In using an index, thinking skills become important when the word being sought is not listed. Readers must then think of synonyms for the word or another form of the word that might be listed. Brainstorming possibilities for alternative listings for a variety of terms could be a helpful class activity to prepare students to be flexible when such situations occur.

Appendices

Students can also be shown that the appendices of books contain supplementary information that may be helpful to them—for example, bibliographies or tabular material.

Glossaries

Primary-grade children can be shown that glossaries, which are often included in their textbooks, are similar to dictionaries but include only the words presented in the book in which they are found. Textbooks often contain glossaries of technical terms that can greatly aid students in understanding the books' content. The skills necessary for proper use of a glossary are the same as those needed for using a dictionary. (See Chapters 3 and 4 for discussions of dictionary use.)

Footnotes and Bibliographies

Footnotes and bibliographies refer students to other sources of information about the subject being discussed in a book, and teachers should encourage students to turn to these sources for clarification, for additional information on a topic for a report, or simply for their own satisfaction.

● Reference Books

Elementary school children often need to find information in such reference books as encyclopedias, dictionaries, almanacs, and atlases. Unfortunately, many students reach high school still unable to use such aids effectively. Although some skills related

Using the Index to Locate Information

Several children in Ms. Rand's class needed to find out how to check addition problems that they had completed the previous day, but they had trouble locating the part of the book they wanted and spent too much time on the task. Ms. Rand noticed that none of the children used the index to find the pages. When she questioned a couple of them, she found out that they had only a hazy concept that the index was in the back of the book and that they didn't know how to use it.

The next day, Ms. Rand set out to remedy this situation. "Turn to page 315 of your math books," she told her class. "Tell me what you find there."

Here is a portion of what the children found:

Sample Index

Addition

 checking, 50–54

 meaning of, 4

 on number line, 10–16, 25–26

 number sentences, 18–19

 regrouping in, 80–91, 103–104

Checking

 addition, 50–54

 subtraction, 120–125

Circle, 204–206

Counting, 2–4

Difference, 111–112

Dollar, 35

Dozen, 42

Graph, 300–306

 bar, 303–306

 picture, 300–303

"It's called the *index*," Tommy replied, as he located the page.

"Right, Tommy," said Ms. Rand. "The index is a part of the book that can help you find information that you need to locate in the book. It lists the topics in the book in alphabetical order, and after each topic it has the pages on which that topic is discussed in the book. For example, in your index, you can see that information about graphs is found on pages 300 through 306. The dash shows that all the pages in between 300 and 306 are about graphs too. If it had been written this way — (*She writes on chalkboard.*) 300, 306 — that would mean the information would just be on those two pages. Who can tell me which pages have information about circles?"

"Pages 204 and 206," Tamara said.

"What about page 205?" asked Ms. Rand.

Ramon broke in: "It is about circles, too. You said the dash meant all of the pages between the ones listed."

"Oh, yeah," agreed Tamara, "205 is part of it, too."

"Very good," Ms. Rand replied. "Now look under the listing for Graph, and notice that there are some words indented there. These are types of graphs, and the particular types are listed with their own page numbers. When there is a list of indented terms under the main term, those terms are related to the main term, but they are there to help you find more specific topics. If I wanted to find out about bar graphs, I could look on pages 303 through 306. I wouldn't have to look at the other pages about graphs, because bar graphs wouldn't be discussed there. What if I wanted to read about picture graphs?"

"You would read pages 300 through 303," Penny replied.

"Right! And what if I wanted to find out about regrouping in addition?" Ms. Rand asked.

"Pages 80 through 104," said Morgan.

"All of them?" asked Ms. Rand.

"Well, there are dashes," Morgan replied.

"What else do you see besides the dashes?" Ms. Rand asked.

"There is a comma between the 91 and the 103," Morgan reported.

"What do you think that tells you?" Ms. Rand asked.

Continued

Continued

"I guess that 92 through 102 don't have anything about regrouping on them," Morgan answered hesitantly.

"Good thinking," Ms. Rand replied. "You are getting that punctuation figured out."

Then she told the class, "Now get in your math work groups and see if you can answer the questions on this sheet about the index in your math text." (The sheet asked the students to locate pages on which specific math topics were covered.)

After the small groups had all reached agreement on the answers, the whole class discussed the items to ensure that everyone had been successful in understanding the process.

At the end of the lesson, Ms. Rand said, "Find the meaning of addition and read it to me."

Mark did so.

"Did you look in the index to find the page number?" she asked.

"Yes, I did," Mark said proudly.

"Do you think you found it more quickly by looking in the index than you would have by turning through the book to find it?"

"Yes," Mark replied.

"When you need to look things up in your textbooks, remember that the index can be helpful to you," Ms. Rand reminded the group as the lesson ended.

to the use of reference books can be taught in the primary grades (for example, use of picture dictionaries), the bulk of the responsibility for teaching use of reference books rests with the intermediate-grade teacher.

Important skills for the effective use of reference books include the following:

General

❶ Knowledge of alphabetical order and understanding that encyclopedias, dictionaries, and some atlases are arranged in alphabetical order

❷ Ability to use guide words, knowledge of their location on a page, and understanding that they represent the first and last entry words on a dictionary or encyclopedia page

❸ Ability to determine key words under which related information can be found

Encyclopedias

❶ Ability to use cross references

❷ Ability to determine which volume of a set of encyclopedias will contain the information needed

Dictionaries

❶ Ability to use pronunciation keys

❷ Ability to choose, from several possible word meanings, the one that most closely fits the context in which a word is found

Atlases

❶ Ability to interpret the legend of a map

❷ Ability to interpret the scale of a map

❸ Ability to locate directions on maps

Glossaries are similar to dictionaries.
(© Kalman/The Image Works)

Because encyclopedias, almanacs, and atlases are often written at much higher readability levels than other materials used in the classroom, teachers must use caution when assigning work in these reference books. Children are not likely to profit from looking up material in books that are too difficult for them to read. When asked to do so, they tend to copy the material word for word without trying to understand it.

However, teachers should keep in mind the difference between *assigning* students to use a particular reference work and letting the students *choose* to use any work that interests them. Readers can handle much more difficult levels of high-interest material than of low-interest material. Therefore, a student who is intensely interested in the subject matter of an encyclopedia article may be able to glean much information from it, even if his or her usual reading level for school materials is lower. For this reason, teachers should never forbid students to try to use material that *may be* too difficult for them. They should, however, avoid *forcing* students to struggle with material that is clearly beyond their range of understanding.

Many skills related to the use of an atlas are included in the section on map reading in this chapter. Some factors related to dictionary and encyclopedia use are discussed in the following sections.

Dictionaries

Before a child can use a dictionary for any of its major functions, he or she must be able to locate a designated word with some ease. Three important skills are necessary

MODEL ACTIVITIES **Alphabetizing for a Picture Dictionary**

Have first graders who are studying a science or social studies topic make a picture dictionary of words they encounter that are related to the topic. For example, if the class is studying animals in science, the children might construct a picture dictionary that includes *bears, deer, lions, tigers, elephants,* and so on. The teacher can list each animal that enters the study on the board, and a child can find a picture of the animal, write the word on a page for the picture dictionary, and illustrate the page. The students can also write or dictate a factual statement about each animal. After a number of pages have been constructed, a small group of students can alphabetize them and place them in a loose-leaf notebook. As more animals are studied, pages can be added for each one. Pages can be constructed by one child and alphabetized in the class picture dictionary by another child. Of course, throughout the study, all students can use the picture dictionary for spelling help or just to browse.

to do this: using alphabetical order, using guide words, and locating variants and derivatives.

Using Alphabetical Order. Since the words in a dictionary are arranged in alphabetical order, children must learn to use alphabetical order to find the words they seek. Beginning with the first letter of the word, they gradually learn alphabetization by the first two or three letters, discovering that sometimes it is necessary to work through every letter in a word in the process.

The Model Activity above offers an idea for developing and strengthening students' knowledge of alphabetical order.

Using Guide Words. Children need to learn that the ***guide words*** at the top of a dictionary page tell them the first and last words on that page. If they are proficient in using alphabetical order, they should be able to decide if a word will be found on a certain page by checking to see if the word falls alphabetically between the two guide words.

Another suggestion for practice with guide words appears on page 358.

Locating Variants and Derivatives. Variants and derivatives are sometimes entered alphabetically in a dictionary, but more often they either are not listed or are listed in conjunction with their root words. If they are not listed, the reader must find the pronunciation of the root word and combine the sounds of the added parts with that pronunciation. This procedure requires advanced skills in word analysis and blending.

An exercise on determining the correct entry word in the dictionary appears on the top of page 359.

DIVERSITY ⊕ ***Bilingual Dictionaries.*** English language learners would benefit from instruction in the use of bilingual dictionaries. English speakers, as well, could gain in vocabulary understanding from use of these resources.

TECHNOLOGY ▪ ***Using Electronic Dictionaries.*** Some dictionaries are available on computer disks, CD-ROMs, or DVD-ROMs. They may provide definitions, spellings, pronunciations,

MODEL ACTIVITIES **Guide Words**

Divide the group into two or more teams. Write the word pair *brace—bubble* on the board or a chart. Ask the children to pretend that these words are the guide words for a page of the dictionary. Explain that you would expect the word *brick* to be on this page because *bri* comes after *bra* and *r* comes before *u*. Then write words, one at a time, from the following list on the board below the word pair. Let each team in turn tell you if the word would be found on the page with the designated guide words. Ask them to tell why they answered as they did. The team gets a point if the members can answer the questions correctly. The next team gets a chance to answer if they cannot. The reason for the answer is the most important part of the response.

1. beaker	5. brave
2. boil	6. border
3. break	7. bypass
4. braid	8. bud

Variation: Write four guide words and the two dictionary pages on which they appear on the board or a chart. For example, you could write

Page 300 *rainbow—rapid*

Page 301 *rapport—raven*

Write the words from the following list below the two sets of guide words, one at a time. Ask each team in turn to indicate on which page the displayed word would be found, or if the word would be found on neither page. Have them tell why they answered as they did. (Of course, you would model the decision-making process for them, as described earlier, before the activity starts.) If the team answers the questions about a word correctly, it is awarded a point. If the team answers incorrectly, the next team gets a chance to answer.

1. rare	5. rave
2. ramble	6. ratio
3. ranch	7. range
4. rabbit	8. raw

and idioms. Some feature interactive multimedia. Users may be able to hear words pronounced when they click on them with the mouse, hear sound effects related to the words, and play word games. In addition to the standard definitions, there may be color illustrations for many words, sentences using the words, syllabic breakdowns, spellings, pronunciations, and plural forms (Johnson, 1994). Other aspects of dictionary use are discussed in Chapters 3 and 4.

Encyclopedia Use

Since encyclopedias vary in content and arrangement, students should be exposed to several different sets. Teachers should have them compare the entries from different encyclopedias on a specified list of topics. The Model Activity on the bottom of page 359 can provide children with instruction and practice in the use of the encyclopedia as they work on a thematic unit on the Revolutionary War.

Encyclopedia articles are often very difficult for many intermediate-grade readers to comprehend. This makes it harder for them to put the information they find into their own words. To encourage appropriate encyclopedia use, the teacher can work

MODEL ACTIVITIES: Determining the Correct Entry Word

As the students are reading a story that contains many words with affixes, call their attention to the affixed words as they occur in the text. Tell the students that, if they wanted to look up the words in the dictionary, they might not be able to find them listed separately. These words have prefixes, suffixes, and inflectional endings added to root words, so students might need to locate their root words to find them. Choose one word from the text, perhaps *happily*. Point to the word and say: "I recognize the *-ly* ending here. The rest of the word is almost like *happy*. The *y* was changed to *i* when the ending was added. So the root word is *happy*." Repeat this procedure for one or two other words from the text.

Later, as a follow-up activity, write on the board the list of words presented below. Then, for each word, ask the students to find the root word and tell about the other word parts that made the root word hard to find. They may also discuss the spelling changes made in the root word when endings were added.

1. directness
2. commonly
3. opposed
4. undeniable
5. gnarled
6. customs
7. cuter
8. joyfully
9. comradeship
10. concentrating

MODEL ACTIVITIES: Encyclopedia Skills

Have students find the correct volume for each of the following topics, without opening the volume:

    Revolutionary War
    George Washington
    Declaration of Independence
    Muskets
    British Parliament
    Battle of Bunker Hill

Have them check their choices by actually looking up the terms. If they fail to find a term in the volume where they expected to find it, ask them to think of other places to look. Let them check these possibilities also. Continue the process until each term has been located. Here is a possible dialogue between teacher and student:

Teacher: In which volume of the encyclopedia would you find a discussion of George Washington?

Student: In Volume 23.

Teacher: Why did you choose Volume 23?

Student: Because *W* is in Volume 23.

Teacher: Why didn't you choose Volume 7 for the *G*s?

Student: Because people are listed under their last names.

Teacher: Look up the term and check to see if your decision was correct.

Student: It was! I found "George Washington" on page 58.

Teacher: Very good. Now tell me where you would find a description of the Battle of Bunker Hill.

Student: In Volume 2 under "Battle."

Teacher: Check your decision by looking it up.

Student: It's not here. It must be under "Bunker."

Teacher: Good idea.

Student: Here it is. It's under "Bunker Hill, Battle of."

with the students to construct a list of things the students should look for about their topics, and the students can list what they already know about each category of information. Next, the children can examine the graphic aids in the encyclopedia article to gather information. Then they can skim the written material to gather main ideas. Finally, they should read the material carefully and put it into their own words. They should be encouraged to consult other sources to check their facts and obtain additional information.

TECHNOLOGY 🖥   Electronic encyclopedias have become widely available and are located in many school settings. These encyclopedias are available in a CD-ROM or DVD-ROM format that is accessed by a computer. Some of these encyclopedias have text, pictures, sound, and animation. They can be searched by using key words and phrases, alphabetical title searches, and topical searches. They are motivational and easy to use (Roe, 2000).

Other Reference Materials

Children are often asked to use materials other than books, such as newspapers, magazines, catalogues, transportation schedules, and pamphlets and brochures, as reference sources. For a thematic unit on pollution, for example, students might search through newspapers, magazines, and government pamphlets for stories and information about pollution and groups that are trying to do something about it, in addition to using trade books related to this problem.

To help students learn to locate information in newspapers, teachers can alert them to the function of headlines and teach them how to use the newspaper's index. Teachers also should devote some class time to explaining journalistic terms, which can help children better understand the material in the newspaper, and to explaining the functions of news stories, editorials, columns, and feature stories. Some of this instruction could actually be a part of a thematic unit on the newspaper. Children are often fascinated by the procedures involved in publishing a newspaper and the techniques used to design and produce a good newspaper. Activities such as the one on using a newspaper's index would be appropriate. Whenever possible, teachers should use real newspapers as a basis for activities similar to the Model Activity on "Using a Newspaper's Index." (See page 361.)

Other instruction could take place as an integral part of other units being used in the classroom. For example, before the students search the newspaper for information on pollution for the unit mentioned earlier, the teacher could introduce activities related to developing the concept of *main idea* (see Chapter 6) to sensitize youngsters to the function of headlines. This could help make their newspaper searches more efficient and meaningful.

In helping children to obtain information from magazines, teachers can call attention to the table of contents and give the children practice in using it, just as they do with textbooks. Distinguishing between informational and fictional materials is important in reading magazines, as is analyzing advertisements to detect propaganda. Chapter 6 contains activities related to these critical reading skills.

To obtain information from many catalogues, children again need to be able to use indexes. Activities suggested in this chapter for using indexes in newspapers and

MODEL ACTIVITIES | **Using a Newspaper's Index**

Hand out copies of the following newspaper index, or write the example on the board or a chart.

Index

Classified Ads B-5–10

Comics B-11–12

Crossword B-11

Editorials A-2–3

Entertainment B-3–4

Finance A-4–7

Horoscope A-8

Obituaries A-11

Have a class discussion based on the following questions:

1. Where in the newspaper would you find information about the stock market? Why would you look there?

2. In what section would you look to find a movie that you would like to see or to find the television schedule? How did you know that you should look there?

3. On what page is the crossword puzzle found? How did you know?

4. How many pages have comics on them? How did you know?

5. Where would you look to find the names of people who have died recently? How did you know that you should look there?

textbooks can be profitably used here as well. The ability to read charts giving information about sizes and about shipping and handling charges may also be important in reading catalogues.

A variety of transportation schedules, pamphlets, and brochures may be used as reference sources in social studies activities. Since their formats vary greatly, teachers will need to provide practice in reading the specific materials they intend to use in their classes.

● Libraries and Media Centers

Libraries or media centers are key locations in schools. Teachers and librarians/media specialists should work together as teams to help the students develop the skills they need to use libraries effectively. (The librarian/media specialist will hereafter be referred to as *librarian* for the sake of easy reference, but the expanded role this person plays in dealing with multimedia should be kept in mind.)

Librarians can be helpful in many ways. They can show students the locations of books and journals, card catalogs, and reference materials (such as dictionaries, encyclopedias, atlases, and the *Reader's Guide to Periodical Literature*) in the library; explain the procedures for checking books in and out; and describe the rules and regulations for expected behavior in the library. Demonstrations of the use of the card catalog (either print or electronic version) and the *Reader's Guide* and explanations of the arrangement of books in libraries are also worthwhile.

LITERATURE

Prominently displayed posters can remind children to observe checkout procedures and library rules.

Currently, librarians are more often using library periods, not only to help children locate and select books, but also to share literature with them. Librarians may introduce students to book reviews that can guide them in their selection of materials. The children can also be guided to write reviews that they can share with other students.

By familiarizing children with reasons for using the library and explaining to them why they may need to use such aids as manual and computerized card catalogs and the *Reader's Guide*, teachers can prepare students for a visit to the library. While they are still in the classroom, the children can learn that cards in the manual card catalog are arranged alphabetically and that the card catalog contains subject, author, and title cards. Sample cards of each type can be drawn on posters and placed on the bulletin board. In addition, fifth and sixth graders will benefit from a lesson on the use of cross-reference cards.

TECHNOLOGY

If the school has a computerized card catalog, students will be able to search for books by title, author, and subject, just as they do with the manual card catalog. They can choose the type of search they need, type in the keywords necessary for the search, and view a list of the available books on the monitor.

Here are two other suggestions for practice with library skills:

1. Send the children on a scavenger hunt that requires using the library by dividing the class into teams and giving the teams statements to complete or questions to answer. (Example: The author of *The Secret Garden* is…)

2. Give students questions and ask them to show, on a map of the library, where they would go to find the answers (Muller and Savage, 1982).

The Classroom Scenario on locating information on page 363 shows how one class puts their research skills to work.

The librarian is an important ally for the teacher as thematic units are planned, because no unit will be successful if the necessary reading materials are not available in a reasonable supply. Both books and other media are needed for these units, and the books need to be on a variety of levels. The librarian is also a valuable helper when children search the library for this related material as the unit progresses. Librarians have useful input for teachers and students alike about books that are good for reading aloud, for sustained silent reading, and for reference sources. Cooperative planning between teachers and librarians can ensure that what goes on in the library and what goes on in the classroom are connected (Lamme and Ledbetter, 1990; Hughes, 1993). In many schools, children are moving in and out of the library all the time. The library is used as "an extension of the classroom" (Hughes, 1993, p. 294).

Many children use the library to find books, to read, to write, and to interact with classmates about books. Many also use it to do research on questions they need to answer, and their research is specific and of personal interest (Hughes, 1993). When students need a research skill, librarians now often teach it or direct them to other students who can help

TIME for REFLECTION

Some teachers think that the librarian should have the complete responsibility for teaching library skills. Others think the teaching of library skills should be a team effort. What do *you* think, and why?

CLASSROOM SCENARIO

Locating Information

Students in a fifth-grade classroom are about to begin a study of World War II. They have formed into groups, each of which will research a different topic related to the war. One group is going to research transportation methods for troops.

When the children in Keith's group meet, Keith says, "First we need to know the different types of transportation that were used. I think we can find that in the encyclopedia under 'World War II.' Who would like to check that out?"

"I will," replies Elaine. "I'll look in all of the different encyclopedias and see if they all have the same information or if they have different stuff. That will help us when we divide up jobs later."

"Good," Keith says. "Then we can make a list of the types of transportation, and each one of us can look up one or two of them and get more details. We can use the dictionary for a basic definition and the encyclopedia for more details on the type of transportation we are looking for, like 'jeeps.' Where else will we get information?"

"We can check the card catalog," Tammy suggests. "The subject cards on 'World War II' and things like 'jeeps' would give us some leads."

"I have a book at home on airplanes," Randy says. "Some of them were from World War II. Can I draw some for our report?"

"Great!" Keith says. "We need some visuals for our report, and you are better at drawing than the rest of us. We'll want some drawings of those planes and tanks and probably some other stuff. We'll all be on the lookout for examples that you can use for models. I'll also ask my Great Uncle Joe about it. He was in the Army in World War II."

Analysis of Scenario

These students have received instruction that made them aware of places to find information for class studies, and they are putting that information to use as they work in their research group. Randy does not immediately have ideas about where to find things in the library, but he recognizes that he has a valuable personal resource and offers it for the study. The children have been taught that there are sources of information other than school materials, and they freely plan to use personal books and even primary sources.

TECHNOLOGY   with that skill. The library frequently remains open to students all day, allowing access when need exists (Hansen, 1993). Valenza (1996) points out that since multimedia production is a research process, it belongs in the school library, where audiovisual and print resources are located, most schools have Internet connections, and librarians are available. (See Chapter 11 for more information on multimedia production.)

TECHNOLOGY   ● **Computer Databases**

In today's schools, students need to be able to locate and retrieve information from computer *databases*, in addition to performing more traditional activities. A computer database is a collection of related information that has been organized to facilitate retrieval through an electronic search. Each database is somewhat like a filing cabinet or several filing cabinets, with separate file folders for the different articles in the database. The information is categorized and indexed for easy retrieval. Users may create their own databases or use existing ones. Using databases, students pose questions, decide on keywords to access the data, read, follow directions, collect and categorize data, summarize material, and make comparisons and contrasts

(Layton and Irwin, 1989; Roe, 2000). The electronic encyclopedias discussed earlier are examples of databases that are available in some schools. In addition, many databases can be accessed through the Internet.

Organizational Techniques

When engaging in such activities as writing reports, elementary school students need to organize the ideas they encounter in their reading. Too often teachers at the elementary level give little attention to organizational techniques such as note taking, outlining, and summarizing, and too many students enter secondary school without knowing how to perform these tasks.

● Note Taking

Teachers may present note-taking techniques in a functional setting when children are preparing written reports on materials they have read. Children should be taught the following note-taking techniques:

❶ Include key words and phrases in the notes they take.

❷ Include enough of the context to make the notes understandable after a period of time has elapsed.

❸ Include a bibliographical reference (source) with each note.

❹ Copy direct quotations exactly.

❺ Indicate carefully which notes are direct quotations and which are reworded.

Key words—the words that carry the important information in a sentence—are generally nouns and verbs, but they may include important modifiers. Example 9.1

EXAMPLE 9.1   Sample Paragraph and Notes

A restaurant is not as easy a business to run as it may appear to be to some people, since the problem of obtaining good help is ever-present. Cooks, servers, and cleaning personnel are necessary. Cooks must be able to prepare the food offered by the restaurant. Servers need to be able to carry out their duties politely and efficiently. Cleaning personnel need to be dependable and thorough. Poorly prepared food, inadequately cleaned dishes, and rude help can be the downfall of a restaurant, so restaurant owners and managers must hire with care.

SAMPLE NOTE CARD

> Problem for restaurant owner or manager—good help: good cooks; polite, efficient servers; dependable, thorough cleaning personnel. Hire with care.

shows a sample paragraph and a possible set of notes based on this paragraph. Laase (1997) suggests using sample paragraphs and an overhead projector to model note taking. Seitz (1997) also uses the overhead projector to model note taking for his middle-school students.

After reading the paragraph shown in Example 9.1, the note taker first thinks, "What kind of information is given here?" The answer, "Problem for restaurant owner or manager—good help," is the first note. Then the note taker searches for key words to describe the kind of help needed. For example, cooks who "are able to prepare the food offered by the restaurant" can be described as "good cooks"—ten words condensed into two that carry the idea. In the case of the nouns *servers* and *cleaning personnel,* descriptive words related to them are added; condensation of phrases is not necessary (although the *ands* between the adjectives may be left out) because the key words needed are found directly in the selection. The last part of the paragraph can be summed up in the warning "Hire with care." It is easy to see that notes based on key words carry the message of the passage in a very condensed or abbreviated form.

A teacher can go through an example like this one with the children, telling them what key words to choose and why, and then provide another example, letting the children decide as a group which key words to write down and having them give reasons for their choices. Finally, each child can do a selection individually. After completing the individual note taking, the children can compare their notes and discuss the reasons for their choices.

Students can take notes in outline form, in sentences, or in paragraphs. Beginners may even benefit from taking notes in the form of semantic webs or maps. (See Chapters 4, 5, and 10 for information on these techniques.)

● Outlining

Teachers can lead children to understand that outlining is writing down information from the material they read in a way that shows the relationships among the main ideas and the supporting details. To create an outline, the children must already know how to recognize main ideas and details. Two types of outlines that are important for children to understand are the *sentence* outline, in which each point is a complete sentence, and the *topic* outline, which is composed of key words and phrases. Since choosing key words and phrases is in itself a difficult task for many youngsters, it is wise to present sentence outlines first.

The first step in forming a traditional outline is to extract the main ideas from the material and to list these ideas beside capital Roman numerals in the order in which they occur. Supporting details are listed beside capital letters below the main idea they support and are slightly indented to indicate their subordination. Details that are subordinate to the main details designated by capital letters are indented still further and are preceded by Arabic numerals. The next level of subordination is indicated by lower-case letters, although elementary students will rarely need to make an outline that goes beyond the level of Arabic numerals. A model outline form like the one shown in Example 9.2 may help students understand how outlines are arranged.

EXAMPLE 9.2 Sample Outline

TITLE
I. Main idea
  A. Detail supporting I
  B. Detail supporting I
    1. Detail supporting B
    2. Detail supporting B
      a. Detail supporting 2
      b. Detail supporting 2
    3. Detail supporting B
  C. Detail supporting I
II. Main idea
  A. Detail supporting II
  B. Detail supporting II
  C. Detail supporting II

The teacher can supply students with partially completed outlines of chapters in their content textbooks and ask them to fill in the missing parts, gradually leaving out more and more details until the students are doing the complete outline alone. To develop students' readiness for outlining, the teacher can use the Model Activity below called "Readiness for Outlining."

This activity can be used as a first step in teaching the concept of outlining to first and second graders. The next step might be to have the students make free-form

MODEL ACTIVITIES **Readiness for Outlining**

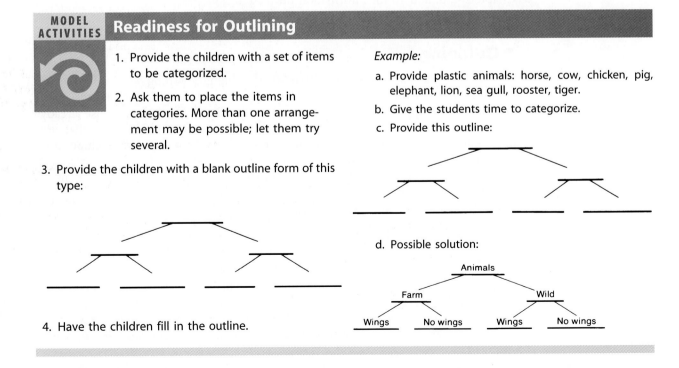

1. Provide the children with a set of items to be categorized.

2. Ask them to place the items in categories. More than one arrangement may be possible; let them try several.

3. Provide the children with a blank outline form of this type:

4. Have the children fill in the outline.

Example:

a. Provide plastic animals: horse, cow, chicken, pig, elephant, lion, sea gull, rooster, tiger.

b. Give the students time to categorize.

c. Provide this outline:

d. Possible solution:

Animals
Farm
Wild
Wings
No wings
Wings
No wings

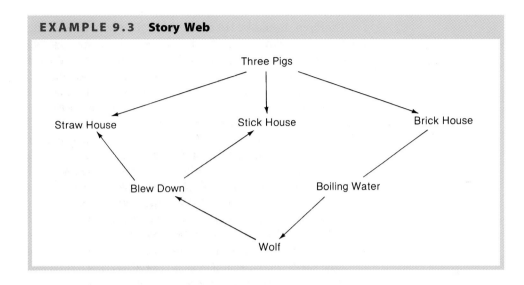

EXAMPLE 9.3 Story Web

outlines, or story webs, in which they use words, lines, and arrows to arrange key words and phrases from the story in a way that shows their relationships. Using simple, very familiar stories enables children to concentrate on arranging the terms logically rather than on locating the details. Example 9.3 shows a web based on the familiar story "The Three Little Pigs." (See Chapter 5 for more information on webbing or mapping stories.)

Teacher modeling of web construction should come first. Then one or more story webs may be constructed cooperatively by the whole class. The teacher may need to provide the key words and phrases in early experiences with webbing. The children can then cooperatively develop webs in small groups with help from the teacher's probing questions about connecting lines, directions of arrows, and positions of phrases. The children may also ask the teacher questions about their decisions. As they develop proficiency with the task, the teacher can allow them to choose key words and phrases themselves, at first with assistance and then independently. After mastering this step, the children can move on to forming webs without assistance (Hansell, 1978).

TECHNOLOGY   Children can obtain outlining practice by outlining material the teacher has entered into a computer file. The children can move phrases and headings around with a word-processing program and create an outline in relatively painless fashion. Computer programs such as *Kidspiration, Inspiration,* and *Power Point* also provide support for the students' creation of outlines of information.

● Summarizing

In a summary, a student is expected to restate what the author has said in a more concise form. Main ideas of selections should be preserved, but illustrative materials and statements that merely elaborate on the main ideas should not be included.

Children should be led to see that, when they are making summaries, they should delete trivial and redundant material. Superordinate terms can be used to replace lists of similar items or actions (for example, *people* for *men, women, and children*). Steps in an action may be replaced by a superordinate action (*baked a cake* for *took flour, butter, … and then placed it in an oven*). Each paragraph can be represented with its topic sentence or implied main idea sentence (Brown and Day, 1983; Brown, Day, and Jones, 1983; Recht, 1984).

The teacher should model the deletion of nonessential material when constructing summaries and then should have students practice this activity under supervision. Choosing superordinate terms and actions and choosing or constructing topic sentences should also be modeled and practiced. Teachers can use a think-aloud process to demonstrate how to delete "redundant, trivial, and subordinate information" (Allington, 2002, p. 744). Easy material should be used for beginning instruction, and paragraphs should be summarized before proceeding to longer passages. The think-aloud process is discussed in more detail in Chapter 5.

One way the teacher can build children's experience with summarizing is to give them a long passage to read and three or four summaries of the passage. The teacher can let the students examine the summaries and decide which one is best and why each of the others was not satisfactory. The teacher can help in this exploration process by asking appropriate questions if the students appear confused about what to consider. For example, the teacher may ask, "Does this sentence tell something different, or is it just an example?" After the children have been successful in differentiating between the satisfactory and unsatisfactory summaries, the teacher can refer them to a passage in one of their textbooks, along with several possible summaries, and have them choose the best summary and tell why they did not choose each of the others. In addition, the Model Activity below on single-sentence summaries can provide practice with summarizing.

Metacognition

Metacognition involves knowing what is already known, knowing when understanding of new material has been accomplished, knowing how that understanding was reached, and knowing why something is or is not known (Guthrie, 1983).

MODEL ACTIVITIES **Single-Sentence Summaries**

Have the children read a short passage like the following one and try to summarize its content in a single sentence.

Sometimes your hair makes a noise when you comb it. The noise is really made by static electricity. Static electricity collects in one place. Then it jumps to another place. Rub your feet on a rug. Now touch something. What happens? Static electricity collects on your body, but it can jump from your finger to other places. Sometimes you can see a spark and hear a noise.

Have students compare their answers and then revise them as they discuss the merits of different answers.

Metacognitive strategies are important in reading for meaning and in reading for retention. Students who monitor their own comprehension and use fix-up strategies such as rereading, self-questioning, retelling, predicting and verifying, and reading further while withholding judgment are more likely to comprehend and retain the information they read. Recognizing important ideas, checking mastery of the information read, and developing effective strategies for study are metacognitive techniques involved in reading for retention (Paris, Wasik, and Turner, 1991; Baumann, Jones, and Seifert-Kessell, 1993). Schwartz (1997, p. 43) points out that "monitoring strategies involve checking one's attempts to coordinate the variety of cues found in texts." Self-correction behaviors are indications that monitoring strategies are occurring.

The RAND Reading Study Group report (Perkins-Gough, 2002) reinforces the importance of metacognitive strategies to comprehension. Students who approach their reading with a purpose, and who actively monitor their understanding as they read, comprehend the material that they are reading better than those who do not. The report suggests that explicit instruction in the use of metacognitive strategies, such as creating and understanding graphic organizers, questioning, and summarizing, can help students develop their abilities to locate, organize, and analyze information. (More information on instruction in metacognition skills appears in Chapter 5.)

Research indicates that comprehension monitoring is a developmental skill that is not fully mastered until adolescence. Ann Brown and Sandra Smiley discovered that low-ability students did not always benefit from instruction in monitoring strategies. These strategies may be beneficial only if students have the background and understanding to use them effectively. With attention to students' levels of maturity, however, aspects of comprehension monitoring can be taught. It is important for teachers to guide students toward actually using these strategies, rather than just to teach them *about* the strategies (Meir, 1984). Rhoder (2002) describes a model of strategy instruction designed to promote "mindful reading" during which students understand, select, and monitor strategies. The model involves instruction within the students' zone of proximal development (the area of skills they are capable of learning with the help of an expert), explicit modeling, practice, and opportunities to transfer their use of metacognitive strategies into new situations.

To help children develop metacognitive strategies, the teacher must convince them of the need to become active learners. Children need to learn to set goals for their reading tasks, to plan how they will meet their goals, to monitor their success in meeting their goals, and to remedy the situation when they do not meet their goals.

To plan ways to meet their goals, children need to know certain techniques, such as relating new information to their background knowledge, previewing material to be read, paraphrasing ideas presented, and identifying the organizational pattern or patterns of the text. Students should learn the value of periodically questioning themselves about the ideas in the material to see if they are meeting their goals (Babbs and Moe, 1983). They need to learn to ask if the information they have read makes sense. If it does not make sense, they need to learn to ask why it does not make sense. They should decide whether they have a problem with decoding a word, understanding what a word means, understanding what a sentence is saying, understanding how a sentence is related to the rest of the passage, or grasping the focus or purpose of the passage (Wilson, 1983). If they have not met their goals because they did not recognize certain words, they need to use context clues, structural analysis, phonics, and possibly the dictionary. If word meaning is the problem, they can again use any of these techniques (except phonics). If sentence structure or sentence relationships are the problem, they can try identifying key words, breaking down sentences into separate meaning units, locating antecedents for pronouns, and other such techniques.

Teachers often use *graphic organizers* (visual depictions of text material, such as webs) before, during, or after reading to assist students in the comprehension of expository material. (Chapter 10 includes a discussion of the value of graphic organizers in helping students understand content material.) Combined with other metacognitive strategies, graphic organizers can help students activate their recall of background information, identify essential information in the reading, and recognize relationships among concepts. Reviewing the research on the growth and development of graphic organizers, Merkley and Jefferies (2000/2001) suggest the following guidelines for teachers who plan to use graphic organizers:

Conduct a prereading dialogue to discuss the relationships illustrated by the graphic,

Encourage student input throughout the discussion,

Connect to previous learning by correcting errors in understanding and challenging thinking,

Reference the upcoming text as a source for additional information,

Reinforce decoding and structural analysis without distracting from the emphasis on comprehension.

Teachers should teach specific strategies for students to use when they do not comprehend material. Moderately difficult material should be used for this instruction so that the children will have some actual comprehension problems to confront, although the material should not be too difficult to be useful. Teachers should present background information before the children read so that they have the information needed to apply comprehension strategies (Fitzgerald, 1983).

Teacher modeling and student practice of "think-alouds" can help students learn metacognitive strategies. "Think alouds require a reader to stop periodically, reflect on how a text is being processed and understood, and relate orally what reading strategies are being employed" (Baumann, Jones, and Seifert-Kessell, 1993, p. 185). Students have to be told what each strategy is and why it is important. Then the teacher can model strategies for monitoring comprehension by reading a passage aloud and "thinking aloud" about his or her own monitoring behaviors and hypotheses. Noting things that are currently known and things that are still unknown, and modifying these notes as more information is added, can be helpful. Students should be drawn into the process in subsequent lessons by practicing the think-aloud strategy with the teacher's guidance at first and then independently. Eventually they need to apply the monitoring strategy independently (Fitzgerald, 1983; Baumann, Jones, and Seifert-Kessell, 1993; Oster, 2001).

TIME for REFLECTION

Some teachers begin work on comprehension monitoring in the primary grades. Others believe that it is best taught beginning in the intermediate grades. What do *you* think, and why?

To check students' monitoring of their own comprehension, teachers can ask students to read difficult passages and then ask questions about them. The children write their answers and indicate their degree of confidence in the answers. Incorrect answers should have low confidence ratings, and correct answers should have high ratings in order to indicate good comprehension monitoring (Fitzgerald, 1983).

Graphic Aids

Textbooks contain numerous reading aids that children often disregard because they have had no training in how to use them. We have already discussed glossaries, footnotes, bibliographies, and appendices in this chapter, but we also need to consider graphic aids such as maps, graphs, tables, and illustrations. Teachers should explain how these aids function, model their use for the students, and provide students with supervised practice in extracting information from them. Making their own graphic aids also helps students develop their communication abilities.

● Maps

Many maps appear in social studies textbooks, and they are sometimes found in science, mathematics, and literature books. As early as the first grade, children can begin developing skills in map reading, which they will use increasingly as they progress through school and maps appear with greater frequency in reading materials.

A first step in map reading is to examine the title (for example, "Annual Rainfall in the United States") to determine what area is being represented and what type of information is being given about the area. The teacher should emphasize the importance of determining what information is conveyed by the title before moving on to a more detailed study of the map. The next step is to teach children how to determine directions by helping them to locate directional indicators on maps and use these indicators to identify the four cardinal directions.

Interpreting the map's *legend* is the next reading task. The legend contains an explanation of each symbol used on the map, and, unless a reader can interpret these symbols, he or she will be unable to understand the information the map contains.

Learning to apply a map's *scale* is fairly difficult. Because it would be highly impractical to draw a map to the actual size of the area represented (for instance, the United States), maps show areas greatly reduced in size. The scale shows the relationship of a given distance on the map to the same distance on the earth.

Upper-elementary school students can be helped to understand about latitude and longitude, the Tropic of Cancer and the Tropic of Capricorn, the north and south poles, and the equator. Students should also become acquainted with map terms such as *hemisphere, peninsula, continent, isthmus, gulf, bay,* and many others.

Each time children look at a map of an area, the teacher should encourage them to relate it to a map of a larger area—for example, to relate a map of Tennessee to a map of the United States. This points out the position of Tennessee within the entire United States.

Students need practice in thinking critically about the information that maps can provide (Mosenthal and Kirsch, 1990). For example, the teacher may give students a map of the United States in the early 1800s that shows waterways, bodies of water, and population distributions and ask the students to draw conclusions about the population distributions. The effect of the bodies of water should be evident to the children.

Some suggestions for teaching map-reading skills follow. These skills are best taught when the students are being asked to read maps for a purpose in one or more of their classes. Map skills should be applied to these authentic materials immediately after instruction takes place.

ACTIVITIES

1. To teach children to apply a map's scale, help them construct a map of their classroom to a specified scale. Provide step-by-step guidance.

2. Model the use of a map's legend. Then have the children practice using the map's legend by asking them questions such as the following:

   Where is there a railroad on this map?

   Where is the state capital located?

   Where do you see a symbol for a college?

   Are there any national monuments in this area? If so, where are they?

3. Give the children a map of their county or city, and let them locate their homes on the map.

4. Give the children maps such as the one presented in Example 9.4, and have them answer questions about them.

DIVERSITY

5. Have English language learners label parts of maps to become familiar with map terminology.

LITERATURE

6. Have students map the locale in a piece of literature that they are reading.

● Graphs

Graphs often appear in social studies, science, and mathematics books to clarify written explanations. Four basic types of graphs are described as follows and are illustrated in Example 9.5.

❶ *Picture graphs* express quantities through pictures.

❷ *Circle or pie graphs* show relationships of individual parts to the whole.

❸ *Bar graphs* use vertical or horizontal bars to compare quantities. (Vertical bar graphs are easier to read than horizontal ones.)

❹ *Line graphs* show changes in amounts.

Students can learn to discover from the graph's title what comparison is being made or what information is being given (for example, time spent in various activities during the day or populations of various counties in a state), to interpret the legend of a picture graph, and to derive needed information accurately from a graph.

EXAMPLE 9.4 **Sample Map and Questions: Number of American Indians by Counties of the U.S., 1970**

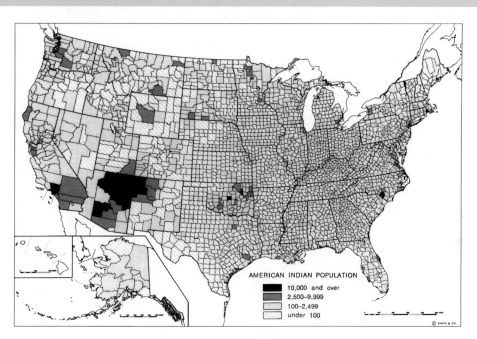

Multiple-Choice Questions

1. What is this map about?

   a. American Indian tribes of the United States

   b. Number of American Indians in United States counties in 1970

   c. Number of American Indians in United States counties today

2. The example shows a main map and two inset maps. What is true about these three maps?

   a. They are all drawn to the same scale.

   b. Two of them are drawn to the same scale.

   c. They are all drawn to different scales.

3. What indicates the densest population?

   a. Solid white

   b. Gray and white stripes

   c. Solid black

4. What was the Indian population in most of Tennessee?

   a. Under 100

   b. 100–2,499

   c. 2,500–9,999

5. The Indian population in Nevada varied from what to what?

   a. 100–2,499

   b. 2,500–10,000

   c. Under 100–10,000 and over

6. In what portion of the United States was there the largest concentration of Indians?

   a. Southwest

   b. Southeast

   c. Northeast

Source: Rand McNally and Company. Reprinted with permission.

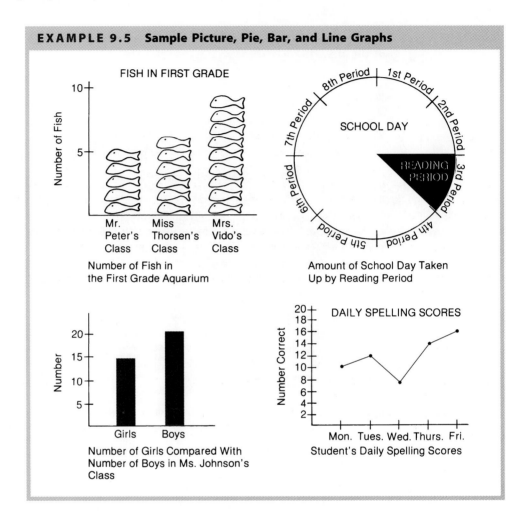

EXAMPLE 9.5 **Sample Picture, Pie, Bar, and Line Graphs**

FISH IN FIRST GRADE

Number of Fish in the First Grade Aquarium

SCHOOL DAY

Amount of School Day Taken Up by Reading Period

Number of Girls Compared With Number of Boys in Ms. Johnson's Class

DAILY SPELLING SCORES

Student's Daily Spelling Scores

One of the best ways to help children learn to read graphs is to have them construct meaningful graphs (Hadaway and Young, 1994). Following are some examples of graph construction activities:

❶ A picture graph showing the number of festival tickets sold by each class. One picture of a ticket could equal five tickets.

❷ A circle graph showing the percentage of each day that a child spends sleeping, eating, studying, and playing.

❸ A bar graph showing the number of books read by class members each week for six weeks.

❹ A line graph showing the weekly arithmetic or spelling test scores of one child over a six-week period.

LITERATURE ❺ A picture graph, bar graph, or circle graph of students' predictions about a story (McDonald, 1999).

● Tables

Tables, which may appear in reading materials of all subject areas, can present a problem because children have trouble extracting specific facts from a large mass of available information. The great amount of information that tables offer in a small amount of space can confuse children unless the teacher provides a procedure for reading tables.

Just as the titles of maps and graphs contain information about their content, so do the titles of tables. In addition, since tables are arranged in columns and rows, the headings can provide information. To discover specific information, students must locate the intersection of an appropriate column with an appropriate row. The teacher can model reading tables, verbalizing the mental processes involved in locating the information. Then the children can be asked to read a table, such as the multiplication table shown in Example 9.6, and answer related questions. Some sample questions are provided.

● Illustrations

Various types of illustrations, ranging from photographs to schematic diagrams, are found in textbooks. Too often children see illustrations merely as space fillers, reducing the amount of reading they will have to do on a page. As a result, they tend to pay little attention to illustrations, even though illustrations are a very good source of information. A picture of a jungle, for example, may add considerably to a child's understanding of that term; a picture of an Arabian nomad may illuminate the term

---

EXAMPLE 9.6   Sample Table and Questions

Multiplication Table

×	1	2	3	4	5	6	7	8	9
1	1	2	3	4	5	6	7	8	9
2	2	4	6	8	10	12	14	16	18
3	3	6	9	12	15	18	21	24	27
4	4	8	12	16	20	24	28	32	36
5	5	10	15	20	25	30	35	40	45
6	6	12	18	24	30	36	42	48	54
7	7	14	21	28	35	42	49	56	63
8	8	16	24	32	40	48	56	64	72
9	9	18	27	36	45	54	63	72	81

Questions

1. What is the product of 5×6?
2. What is the product of 9×3?
3. Is the product of 5×4 the same as the product of 4×5?
4. Which number is greater: the product of 3×8 or the product of 4×7?
5. When a number is multiplied by 1, what will the product always be?
6. Why does 24 appear where the 4 row and the 6 column meet?
7. How do the numbers in the 2 row compare with the numbers in the 4 row?

DIVERSITY *Bedouin* in a history class. Diagrams of bones within the body can show a child things that cannot readily be observed firsthand. Having English language learners and students with special needs label illustrations is particularly helpful to their comprehension of content material.

SUMMARY

Reading/study techniques enhance students' comprehension and retention of printed material. Study methods, such as SQ3R and SQRQCQ, can help students comprehend and retain material that they read. A number of other techniques can also help students with organization and retention.

Developing test-taking strategies can allow students to show more accurately what they have learned. Students need strategies for taking objective and essay tests, and they need special strategies for standardized testing situations.

Flexible reading habits can help children study more effectively. Children need to be able to adjust their approaches to the reading and to adjust their reading rates.

Children need to learn strategies for locating information in trade books and textbooks, using the important parts of the books; in reference books, such as dictionaries and encyclopedias; in the library; and in computer databases. They need to learn how to design and use graphic organizers. They also need to learn how to organize the information when they find it and how to monitor their comprehension and retention of material (metacognition).

In addition, students need to know how to obtain information from the graphic aids found in textbooks. They must be able to read and understand maps, graphs, tables, and illustrations.

TEST YOURSELF

True or False

_____ 1. SQ3R stands for Stimulate, Question, Read, Reason, React.

_____ 2. SQ3R is a study method useful in reading social studies and science materials.

_____ 3. SQRQCQ is a study method designed for use with mathematics textbooks.

_____ 4. Students remember material better if they are given opportunities to discuss it.

_____ 5. Study guides are of little help to retention.

_____ 6. Writing information often helps children to fix it in their memories.

_____ 7. Massed practice is preferable to spaced practice for encouraging long-term retention.

_____ 8. Students should read all materials at the same speed.

_____ 9. Rereading is often necessary for materials that contain a high density of facts.

_____ 10. Many content area textbooks offer glossaries of technical terms as reading aids.

_____ 11. Index practice is most effective when children use their own textbooks rather than a worksheet index that has no obvious function.

_____ 12. Elementary school students have no need to learn how to take notes, because they are not asked to use this skill until secondary school.

_____ 13. Subordination in outlines is indicated by lettering, numbering, and indentation.

_____ 14. The legend of a map tells the history of the area represented.

_____ 15. A good way to help children develop an understanding of graphs is to assist them in constructing their own meaningful graphs.

_____ 16. Children may use newspapers, magazines, catalogues, and brochures as reference sources.

_____ 17. Teachers do not need to teach journalistic terms to elementary-level students; this is a higher-level activity.

_____ 18. Using catalogues often requires the ability to read charts.

_____ 19. Key words are the words that carry the important information in a sentence.

_____ 20. The ability to recognize main ideas is a prerequisite skill for outlining.

_____ 21. Guide words indicate the first two words on a dictionary page.

_____ 22. When making a summary, it is important to retain all details in the material.

_____ 23. Some children fail to do well on essay tests because they do not understand such terms as *compare* and *contrast*.

_____ 24. Children need to practice under standardized testing conditions so that they will be familiar with the testing situation when they take a standardized test.

_____ 25. Comprehension monitoring is a skill that can be fully developed in first grade.

_____ 26. Rereading can be a useful metacognitive strategy.

_____ 27. Graphic organizers are designed to provide visual representations of key concepts or terms.

_____ 28. In an inquiry-based learning environment, locating and organizing information is primarily the responsibility of the teacher.

For your
journal ...

1. Visit an elementary school library and listen as the librarian explains the reference materials and library procedures to students. In your journal, evaluate the presentation and decide how you might change it if you were responsible for it.

2. Choose a textbook from a subject area and grade level of your choice. Examine closely the material on twenty consecutive pages, and list the study skills needed to obtain information from these pages effectively.

3. Reflect on the video that accompanies this chapter on your CD. Can reading or creating maps and other graphic aids help students organize information? Explain your answer.

... and your
portfolio

1. Using materials of widely varying types, develop and document a procedure to help elementary students learn to be flexible in their rates of reading.

2. Choose a content area textbook at the elementary level, and plan procedures to familiarize children with the parts of the book and the reading aids the book offers.

3. Collect materials that students can use as supplementary reference sources (newspapers, magazines, catalogues, brochures, etc.), and develop several short lessons to help the children learn to read these materials effectively.

4. Make a variety of types of graphs into a display that you could use in a unit on reading graphs. Photograph the display.

5. Collect pictures and diagrams that present information. Ask several children to study these pictures and extract as much information from them as possible. Provide a written summary of your analysis.

Reading in the Content Areas

10

KEY VOCABULARY

Pay close attention to these terms when they appear in the chapter.

content area textbooks

directed reading-thinking activity

expository style

figurative language

frustration level

guided reading procedure

independent level

instructional level

language arts

language experience approach

narrative style

readability

study guides

SETTING OBJECTIVES

When you finish reading this chapter, you should be able to

- Describe several general techniques for helping students read content area materials.

- Describe some procedures and resources that are helpful to students in understanding material in language arts, social studies, mathematics, and science and health books.

Reading in *content area textbooks*, such as those for social studies, science, mathematics, and other curricular areas, and in supplementary materials used in content classes is often difficult for students. Content area textbooks and other informational materials contain *expository* (explanatory) text that can be more difficult for children to read than *narrative* (story) text. These materials also contain many new concepts. As Yopp and Yopp (2000) point out, the different text features and structures found in informational text pose different problems from those found in narrative text, and the ability to read narrative text is no guarantee that students can read informational text with the same competence.

Reading strategies are often initially acquired in reading class, using basal readers. Because content area books and supplementary materials present special reading problems, however, teachers should be aware that simply offering their students instruction in basal readers, even though today's basal readers contain more content-oriented text, is not sufficient if the children are to read well in content area texts and other nonfiction materials.

To read well in content area textbooks, children need good general reading strategies, including word recognition and comprehension, and reading/study strategies. If they cannot recognize the words they encounter, they will be unable to take in the information from the material. Without good literal, interpretive, critical, and creative reading comprehension strategies, as described in Chapter 6,

Chapter 10 Organization

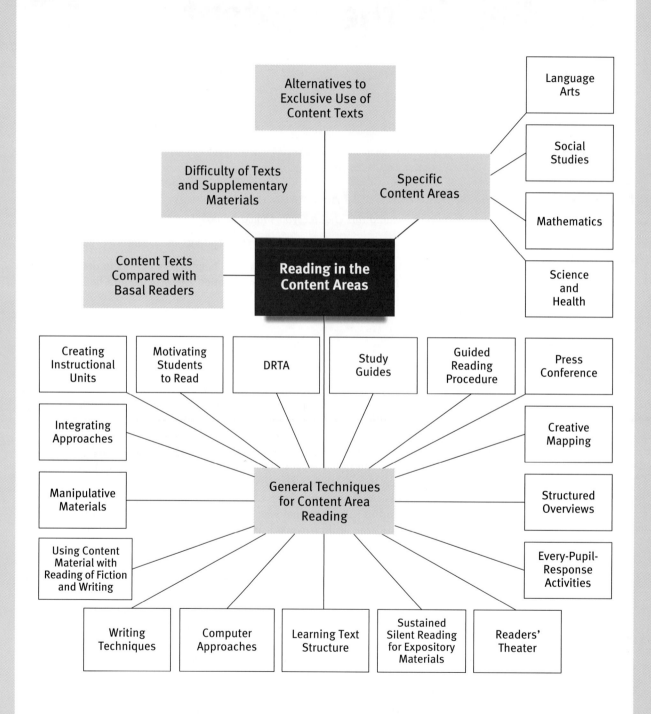

Alternatives to Exclusive Use of Content Texts

Difficulty of Texts and Supplementary Materials

Specific Content Areas

Content Texts Compared with Basal Readers

Reading in the Content Areas

Language Arts

Social Studies

Mathematics

Science and Health

Creating Instructional Units

Motivating Students to Read

DRTA

Study Guides

Guided Reading Procedure

Press Conference

Integrating Approaches

Creative Mapping

Manipulative Materials

General Techniques for Content Area Reading

Structured Overviews

Using Content Material with Reading of Fiction and Writing

Every-Pupil-Response Activities

Writing Techniques

Computer Approaches

Learning Text Structure

Sustained Silent Reading for Expository Materials

Readers' Theater

they will not understand the textbook's message. And if they lack good reading/study strategies, they will be less likely to comprehend and retain the material. Special help with content area reading, at the time children are expected to do such reading, is important, for this is when children most effectively learn how to apply the strategies and techniques. Classrooms in which the teachers integrate learning activities across the curriculum, rather than scheduling separate periods for language, science, social studies, and so on, will offer opportunities throughout the day to help children read and comprehend the expository texts generally used in content areas.

We will see later in this chapter that, instead of relying solely on textbooks, teachers may choose nonfiction trade books (library books), newspapers, brochures, and other factual materials to supplement the curriculum in some classes and as the core of the curriculum in others. Students often need to apply the same strategies to reading many of these informational materials as they do to reading content area textbooks.

Because of the special challenges posed by reading in content area textbooks, teachers need to know a variety of techniques for helping students understand their reading. Teachers often use concrete manipulatives (such as maps and pictures) to develop concepts. Manipulatives are especially helpful with young children and struggling readers. The teachers encourage students to visualize information, which can be enhanced by use of manipulatives, and to brainstorm about the topics; they often provide narratives on the same topic and use audiotaped, videotaped, or computer-based materials to aid comprehension. Teachers may also require retellings of text material and have students summarize the material to check understanding. Semantic mapping of the main topic, use of the K-W-L procedure, and use of expository paragraph frames are other good techniques. This chapter concludes with an examination of several content areas—language arts, social studies, mathematics, and science and health—along with the specific difficulties that can confront students in reading in these areas, as well as activities to promote readiness and good comprehension. In addition, it presents general content area reading strategies to use in conjunction with the many strategies already described in Chapters 5 and 6 as comprehension aids in reading content area material.

Content Texts Compared with Basal Readers

Much material in basal readers is written in a narrative style that describes the actions of people in particular situations. Basal readers do not have the density of ideas typical of content textbooks, which are generally written in an expository style, with heavy concentrations of facts. Children find narrative material easier to read than expository material. Narrative selections often have entertaining plots that children can read for enjoyment. Content selections rarely offer this enticement.

Many children are unfamiliar with the organizational structures of expository texts. Therefore, these students are left without a predictable structure to use when they are asked to read such materials. Students must give attention to each sentence in a content book, for nearly every one will carry important information that they must acquire before they can understand later passages. This is rarely true of basal readers, in which each selection is generally a discrete entity.

Whereas basal readers may have planned repetition of key words to encourage their acquisition, content area texts present many new concepts and vocabulary terms with little planned repetition. Content area textbooks are likely to define new terms at their first appearance and then to assume that the students will remember their meanings.

All of the content areas have specialized and technical vocabularies that students must acquire. Generally, basal readers contain little specialized or technical vocabulary. (See Chapter 4 for a discussion of specialized and technical vocabulary.)

Content textbooks contain a large number of graphic aids that students must interpret, whereas basal readers contain much smaller numbers of these aids. The illustrations in basal readers above first-grade level are often included primarily for interest value, but those in content books are designed to help clarify concepts and need to be studied carefully.

Whereas content area textbooks have abundant headings that signal the organization of the selections, few such headings are used in basal readers, and the ones that are used may be less informative than those in the content books. As they begin to read content books, children should be helped to see that sometimes the headings outline the material for them, indicating main ideas and supporting details.

Organizational patterns of some newer content textbooks are changing, however, and these changes may signal even more reading difficulties for students, if they are not properly prepared for the reading by their teachers. Walpole (1998/1999) examined a traditional and a newer science textbook and found them to be organized differently. The newer text had a less linear, less predictable format and did not lend itself as well to traditional outlining. Subheads in the newer text did not have a hierarchical order, and the format was more varied. Compared with the newer text, the traditional text had more signal words to help students make connections between ideas. The newer text posed more unanswered questions and more often asked the reader to perform actions or think about something. Captions for pictures in the traditional text generally paraphrased the main text, whereas in the newer text the captions contained new information. Teachers must adjust instruction to fit the formats and organizational patterns of the textbooks they must use.

Difficulty of Texts and Supplementary Materials

STANDARDS AND
ASSESSMENT

The teacher's first step in helping children to read content material is to be aware of the level of difficulty of the textbook and other reading assignments they make. Teachers must adjust their expectations for each student according to that student's reading ability, so that no child is assigned work in material on his or her *frustration level*—that is, the level at which the material is so difficult that it will immediately be frustrating and the student will be unable to comprehend it. Trying to read from material that is too hard for them can prevent students from learning the content. If children are forced to try to read a book or other material at this difficulty level, they may develop negative attitudes toward the subject, toward the teacher, and even toward school in general. Students will probably learn best from printed material that is written on their *independent levels*, or the levels at which they read with ease and comprehension. They can also learn from textbooks written on their *instructional levels*, or the levels at which they read with understanding when given sufficient help by the teacher. (See Chapter 12 for further discussion of independent, instructional, and frustration levels and of techniques for determining readability.)

After determining each student's ability to benefit from the class textbook and chosen supplementary materials, the teacher has the information needed to make instructional decisions. For some students, the content area reading assignments will be on their independent level. They will be able to read the assignments and prepare for class discussion independently, and they will often be able to set their own purpose questions to direct their reading. For other students, the material will be at their instructional level. These students will need to have the teacher introduce material carefully, build concepts and vocabulary gradually, and assign purpose questions. For still other students, the material will be at their frustration level. These students will need to be introduced to the subject and, in order to understand the concepts and information involved, should be given some simpler materials with a lower readability level than that of the text or supplementary material being used with their classmates.

All students can participate together in discussing the material, and the teacher can record significant contributions on the board in the same way as in recording a language experience story. (Detailed discussions of the language experience approach appear later in this chapter and in Chapter 7.) When the teacher asks students to read the contributions from the board at the end of the discussion period, even poor readers may be able to read fairly difficult contributions because they have heard the sentences being dictated and have seen them being written down. Before the next class, the teacher can duplicate the class summary for each student to use in reviewing for tests. During study periods, he or she can help the children who are at their frustration levels to reread the notes, emphasizing the new words and concepts.

Not only are many content area textbooks written at much higher *readability levels* than basal readers for the corresponding grades, but subject matter textbooks also often vary in difficulty from chapter to chapter. If teachers are aware of various levels of difficulty within a text, they can adjust their teaching methods to help students gain the most from each portion of the book, perhaps by teaching easier chapters earlier in the year and more difficult chapters later on. Of course, this technique is not advisable for teaching material in which the concepts in an early, difficult chapter are necessary for understanding a later, easier chapter.

A good way to decrease the difficulty of content passages for students is to teach the content vocabulary thoroughly before the material containing that vocabulary is assigned to be read. The more unfamiliar content vocabulary is a major factor in the higher difficulty levels of many content area materials.

Alternatives to Exclusive Use of Content Texts

Some students find textbooks difficult to read or are unmotivated to read them because they find them dull and dry. For such students, supplementary trade books offer one viable option for learning content area material. Many children experience their first serious difficulties with reading as they begin reading textbooks, but the

These first graders, who are looking at a book about Martin Luther King, Jr., illustrate how even young children become involved in content area reading. *(© Joseph Schuyler/Stock Boston)*

continued use of high-interest trade books along with textbooks may ease the transition.

Regardless of whether or not the students have trouble reading the textbooks, teachers can use trade books to enhance the study of textbook topics and help students learn more about the content. Trade books can be chosen to coincide with students' reading levels, easing one typical problem. These books can be visually appealing to students and therefore can arouse their interest. They can also cover a topic in greater depth than the length limits of a textbook would allow, and they frequently have very coherent organizational patterns. Newer books ensure access to timely information.

Some nonfiction books make use of a narrative format, with which students are often more familiar than they are with nonfiction organizational patterns, although others will have topical, comparison-contrast, problem-solution, cause-and-effect, or other expository patterns. Regardless of the organizational pattern, the nonfiction selections can provide more elaboration on a single topic than can a standard textbook description.

In selecting and using appropriate trade books, teachers should follow certain steps: identify concepts for further development; locate suitable trade books to help teach these concepts; present books to students by reading them aloud or making copies available for independent reading prior to textbook assignments; use trade books during and after reading of the text to extend concept acquisition; and provide follow-up activities in the forms of creative writing, drama, and interviewing (Brozo and Tomlinson, 1986).

LITERATURE

Camp (2000) suggests use of "Twin Texts" of fiction and nonfiction to present content. Such trade books are available on a wide variety of topics—for example, the fiction selection *Stellaluna* by Janell Cannon could be paired with the nonfiction *Bats* by Celia Bland, or the fiction selection *Hiroshima* by Laurence Yep could be paired with the nonfiction *Sadako and the Thousand Paper Cranes* by Eleanor Coerr. Each book presents pertinent information that helps children build a framework for understanding content lessons. The fiction selection has factual material woven into a fictional setting and narrative format, and many fiction selections are less packed with new concepts and vocabulary than are nonfiction books. Teachers must be aware, however, as Guillaume (1998) cautions, that the fiction selected should help students understand the topics and should not perpetuate faulty concepts.

Use of the Twin Texts before the textbook material is read will lead to better understanding of the material because students will have activated or expanded their schemata before reading the textbook and because the Twin Texts provide elaboration on the topic. Teachers may wish to use Venn diagrams (see Chapter 6 for an example) to compare and contrast the fiction and nonfiction selections on the same topic. The K-W-L technique (see Chapter 5) could also be used when students read the Twin Texts. A DRTA (discussed in Chapter 7 and this chapter) could be employed in guiding the reading of the trade books. Writing about the central topic and webbing key vocabulary in the books are good follow-up activities (Camp, 2000).

TECHNOLOGY

Information from Internet sites can supplement the textbook information. Teachers may wish to bookmark appropriate sites and provide guidance for the students in how to use them. (See Chapter 11 for more on use of the Internet.)

Videotapes, CDs, and DVDs, too, can provide supplementary information. Teachers may want to suggest appropriate videotapes, CDs, and DVDs for the school librarian or media specialist to purchase. (See Chapter 11 for information on use of these materials.)

General Techniques for Content Area Reading

When working with students who are reading in the content areas, teachers should do many of the things suggested in earlier chapters for directing the reading of any material, such as developing vocabulary knowledge, activating background knowledge about the topic, and providing purposes for reading. They should also suggest use of a study method, such as SQ3R or another appropriate method, encourage note taking, and offer suggestions to promote retention of the material. Prior knowledge can be accessed and/or developed through such techniques as provision of firsthand experiences, discussion, brainstorming, mapping, and the K-W-L procedure. (Information about these activities appears in Chapters 4, 5, 6, and 9.) Teachers may also use a number of other techniques, such as the ones described in this section, to help their students read in content areas more effectively.

The teacher should make reading materials available at a variety of difficulty levels, so that all students can participate in acquiring information from print sources. They should also systematically include nonfiction selections in their daily read-aloud sessions in order to expose students to nonfiction material, organizational patterns, and authors. Dreher (1998/1999) suggests keeping a log of read-aloud selections to help in balancing types of material read.

● Motivating Students to Read

Mathison (1989) has found that teachers can stimulate interest in reading content area materials in a number of ways. Two effective strategies are using analogies to help give new ideas familiar connections and telling personal anecdotes that can help personalize reading material. For example, study of arteries and veins in a sixth-grade class could be motivated by drawing an analogy to roads leading into the downtown area; or, in a study of a particular climate, the teacher might share a personal anecdote about a camping trip in such a climate. Teachers should examine each reading assignment for possibilities for motivational introductions. Glynn (1996) also suggests ways to use analogies in science instruction.

Stories can help children see the connections that exist among people across time and from different places because of the needs that all people have in common. Participation in storytelling sessions helps the students develop shared experiences that create bonds among classmates (Combs and Beach, 1994). Such bonds enable the students to cooperate more freely as they work toward common goals in the classroom.

● Directed Reading-Thinking Activity (DRTA)

The *Directed Reading-Thinking Activity (DRTA)* can be used to direct children's reading of either basal reader stories or content area selections. (A complete discussion of the DRTA is found in Chapter 7.) In this activity students predict, read, and prove predictions as the teacher asks them what they think, why they think that, and how they can prove their points.

● Study Guides

Study guides are prepared by the teacher to guide expository reading in content fields. They can set purposes for reading, as well as provide aids for interpreting material through suggestions about how to apply reading strategies. These guides also serve as vehicles for group discussions and cooperative learning activities. Discussion of the questions or points from the study guide after reading the material is very important to the learning process. There are many kinds of study guides, and the nature of the material and the reason for reading it can help teachers determine which kind to use.

Content-process guides, as shown in Example 10.1 on page 388, focus on both the content and process aspects of reading. The study guide in Example 10.1 directs students' reading in the following way. First, the overview question offers an overall purpose for the reading, helping students read the material with the appropriate mental set. The first item after the overview question gives students content purposes for reading the first section. Notice that the questions are phrased to elicit thought about the information in the passage. Following the purposes are two questions about vocabulary meanings. The students are encouraged to use their skills in structural analysis to help them understand the vocabulary presented. This is process guidance. The second item offers purposes for reading the second main section. Notice that it specifies the groups under consideration. It is followed by a vocabulary question and a process suggestion to use context clues.

Pattern guides are study guides that stress the relationship among the organizational structure, the reading-thinking skills needed for comprehension, and the important concepts in the material. The first step in constructing such a guide is to identify the important concepts in the material. Then information about each concept must be located within the selection, and the author's organizational pattern must be identified. The teacher then integrates the identified concepts, the writing pattern, and the skills necessary for reading the material with understanding in a guide that offers as much direction as specific students need — whether it be the section of text in which the information is located; the page number; or the page, paragraph, and line numbers.

Conrad (1989) found that her students were able to work more effectively with cause-and-effect relationships if the effects were listed on the left side of the page and the causes on the right side. She believed this was because students tend to want to tell what happened and then add a *because* phrase.

Example 10.2 on page 389 shows a completed complex cause-and-effect pattern guide that also has an implicit comparison-contrast element, since effects on three populations are compared. This pattern guide is based on the text selection in Example 10.1. The guide listed the two causes for the students, and they had to fill in the multiple effects.

Anticipation guides, which are used before students read a selection, require them to react to a series of statements related to the selection to be read. The children can react to the anticipation guide again when they have finished reading to see the differences, if any, between their initial opinions and the correct responses. When the teacher asks for responses both before and after reading, the guide is often referred to as an anticipation/reaction guide.

The statements in an anticipation guide should be related to major concepts and significant details in the reading material. They may reflect common misconceptions about the topic, challenging students' beliefs. They should link students' prior knowledge with text concepts, and they should be general (Duffelmeyer, 1994). The guide may be used in a group setting, with students discussing and justifying their responses (Wood and Mateja, 1983). See Chapter 5 for an example of an anticipation/reaction guide.

Duffelmeyer and Baum (1992) suggest extending the anticipation guide by having students decide if the text supported each of their choices and having them indicate why their choices were correct or incorrect by citing evidence from the text.

EXAMPLE 10.1 **Sample Selection and Content-Process Study Guide**

[*Note*: The material in this passage is part of a discussion of the Seven Years' War.]

The Proclamation of 1763   With the French defeat, many colonists eagerly prepared to move across the Appalachian Mountains. However, the British were worried. They knew that new settlements would anger the Iroquois, Delaware, Shawnee, and other Indian tribes who already lived there. To prevent fighting, the British issued the Proclamation of 1763. This act saved all land west of the Appalachians for Indians. Colonists could not settle there.

The Proclamation upset many colonists. Earlier, the French had blocked new settlements. The French had been defeated. Now, though, the British also stopped people from moving west. Many colonists wondered why they had fought the war.

The Cost of Victory   Colonial anger at Britain's Proclamation of 1763 was just one hardship the war caused. The British, the Indians, and the colonists each faced new troubles.

In Britain, the war had caused the government to borrow money. Between 1754 and 1763, the money Britain owed doubled. The country needed money to pay back its many loans.

Britain also had to pay the 10,000 soldiers it sent to North America. These troops were needed to protect the large new British empire. Britain now had to spend three times as much to defend its American empire as it did before the war.

For many Indian tribes, the war brought a loss of power. They could no longer use the French to help them against the British. And even 10,000 British soldiers could not stop settlers from moving onto Indian lands.

In the colonies, the war caused great suffering. Boston, a city of about 2,200 families, lost 700 men during the war. These deaths left many widows and orphans who needed help just to buy food.

Study Guide

Overview Question: What were the effects of the war on the people of America and Great Britain?

1. Read the section titled "The Proclamation of 1763" to find out what effect this action had on the colonists. Were the colonists pleased with the effect? How can you tell?
    What is a settlement? What is a proclamation? If you don't know, locate the root words to help you figure this out.

2. Read the section titled "The Cost of Victory" to discover other hardships the war caused. Look for hardships faced by the British, the Indian tribes, and the people of the colonies.
    What is a synonym for *hardship*? Look for a context clue to this word's meaning.

This seems to be a good addition to the procedure. Merkley (1996/1997) suggests adding a prereading "I'm Not Sure" option to the "True and False" or "Yes and No" choices if the questions involve factual information. In postreading use of the items, "I'm Not Sure" should no longer be an option.

EXAMPLE 10.2 Cause-and-Effect Pattern Guide

Causes	Effects		
	On British	**On Indians**	**On Colonists**
Proclamation of 1763	Drew colonists' anger	Land west of Appalachians saved for them	Denied right to settle on land west of Appalachians
Seven Years' War	Needed money to pay back loans Had to pay larger numbers of soldiers	Loss of power Not enough British soldiers to keep settlers off their lands	Widows and orphans who needed help to buy food

● Guided Reading Procedure

Anthony Manzo's *guided reading procedure (GRP)*, designed to help readers improve their organizational skills, comprehension, and recall, is appropriate for content area reading at intermediate grades and above. The steps in the procedure follow.

❶ Set a purpose for reading a selection of about 500 words, and tell the children to remember all they can. Tell them to close their books when they finish reading.

❷ Have the students tell everything they remember from the material, and record this information on the board.

❸ Ask students to look at the selection again to correct or add to the information they have already offered.

❹ Direct the children to organize the information in an outline (see Chapter 9), semantic web (see Chapter 5), or some other arrangement.

❺ Ask synthesizing questions to help students integrate the new material with previously acquired information.

❻ Give a test immediately to check on the children's short-term recall.

❼ Give another form of the test later to check medium- or long-term recall (Ankney and McClurg, 1981).

● Press Conference

Press conference is a strategy in which some students take the parts of characters in material that has been read (literature, science, social studies, current events) and others take the parts of reporters interviewing the characters. The interviews must have carefully planned questions, and the interviewers must take detailed notes from which they compose news stories about the interviewees and/or the events in which they have been involved. These stories are taken through a process writing approach, and the final versions are published in a class newspaper (Dever, 1992).

● Creative Mapping

Naughton (1993/1994) suggests *creative mapping* to enhance content area reading. Creative mapping combines semantic mapping with pictures to display material in a way that helps students see relationships and also helps them recall it.

First, a picture that represents the topic or main idea is drawn. Then supporting details are arranged on or around the image in an organized manner. Students use both their background knowledge and the text to complete the map.

● Structured Overviews

Structured overviews of the vocabulary from a content area reading assignment can help students learn the terms and concepts. At first, the teacher can present an overview on an overhead projector, with students answering questions about how the vocabulary is related to the concepts in the assignment as the overview is developed in front of them, or the overview can be placed on strips on the bulletin board. Later the students can work cooperatively in small groups to form overviews, or they can make individual overviews from a chapter they read (Wolfe and Lopez, 1992/1993).

● Every-Pupil-Response Activities

Gaskins and her colleagues (1994) found that *every-pupil-response activities*, such as engaging in written responses to text, facilitated participation in discussion about the text. These responses were not graded but were used to help students assess their own understanding of the text and sometimes of its organizational structure. Partner discussions followed the writing and in turn were followed by whole-class discussions. The students helped one another to clarify their understandings and to see alternative interpretations.

Teachers reminded the students to support their positions with evidence from the text. Teachers also presented the students with real-life problems to which they could apply information from the text, eliciting enthusiastic small-group discussions. They talked about the strategies that would best fit the solution of the particular problem, why these strategies should help, when they should be used, and how to use them. Teachers modeled strategy use for the students before asking them to participate in guided practice.

● Readers' Theater

Young and Vardell (1993) suggest using *readers' theater* (a dramatic reading of a text in parts by two or more readers) with nonfiction trade books to increase active involvement with the material and add to enjoyment of it. Books with dialogue are especially easy to adapt to readers' theater scripts. Some other types of text may be rewritten as dialogue, or multiple narrators may be assigned. Prologues may be added to introduce the material in the scripts, and/or postscripts may be added to bring some scripts to a close. Students should have an active part in developing the scripts, so that producing them is as much of a learning experience as performing in them. Suggestions of books to use for readers' theater include David M. Schwartz's *How Much Is a Million?* for math; Joanna Cole's books about the Magic School Bus for science; and Joan Anderson's *The First Thanksgiving Feast,* Russell Freedman's *Buffalo Hunt,* and Jean Fritz's *And Then What Happened, Paul Revere?* for social studies.

LITERATURE

● Sustained Silent Reading (SSR) for Expository Materials

In regular sustained silent reading periods, children have free choice of materials to read, and they generally choose narrative materials. Teachers can encourage students to read both fiction and nonfiction during SSR periods; there may even be separate SSR periods for the two types of text. Having many nonfiction titles easily accessible to students in the classroom, school library, or media center facilitates nonfiction reading (Dreher, 1998/1999; Joranko, 1990). This approach should help students become familiar with many expository text structures, without the pressure that accompanies assigned reading. When they have opportunities to interact with informational text, young children increase their facility with it (Duke and Kays, 1998; Yopp and Yopp, 2000).

● Learning Text Structure

Many students do not use text structure to help them comprehend and retain information from content area textbooks, but research has shown that use of text structure can be taught (McGee and Richgels, 1985). Systematic attention to clues about the organizational structure of a text and creation of visual representations of the relationships among ideas aid both comprehension and retention (Pearson and Fielding, 1991). Five of the more common expository text structures are cause-and-effect, comparison-contrast, problem-solution, description, and collection. Description and collection (a series of descriptions about a topic presented together) are more common in elementary-level texts than are the other three types.

Using Graphic Organizers

Using graphic organizers (such as webs), teachers can show how passages with the same text structure can have different content. Then they can prepare a graphic organizer for each structure to be taught. Focusing on one structure at a time, they can present students with the graphic organizer for a passage and have them construct a passage based on this organizer (see the section "Webs Plus Writing" in this chapter), which will include appropriate clue words, such as *because, different from,* and so forth. Teachers should emphasize how the clue words help both readers and writers. After revising and refining their passages, students can compare them with the passage on which the graphic organizer was based (McGee and Richgels, 1985).

Hadaway and Young (1994) encourage the use of visual representations to help students grasp organization and content. They suggest using index cards to assist in the construction of time lines, especially when multiple sources are used. Venn diagrams can help students see common elements of concepts and can help them visualize similarities and differences in order to make comparisons and contrasts. Flow charts help students visualize a sequence of events, such as the sequence of steps in a science experiment. (See Chapter 9 for more information on graphic organizers.)

Maps of the content may be used before, during, and/or after students read it. (See Chapter 5 for a discussion and some examples of semantic mapping.) Sometimes the teacher can construct the maps, and at other times students can do so (Flood, 1986). The teacher should also ask appropriate questions before, during, and after the students read. (See Chapter 6 for a discussion of questioning techniques.)

Using Paragraph Frames

Another way to work on students' knowledge of text structure is through the use of expository paragraph frames. *Expository paragraph frames* are similar to the story frames described in Chapter 5. They provide sentence starters that include signal words or phrases to fit the paragraph organization. The sequential pattern appears to be an easy one for young children to recognize and use. The teacher can write a sequential paragraph that uses the cue words for sequence: *first, next, then, finally.* The sentences can be copied on sentence strips, the sequential nature of the material can be discussed in the group, and the students can be asked to arrange the sentences in sequential order in a pocket chart. The children can read the arranged sentences together. Then they can arrange the sentences individually and copy them on their papers in paragraph form. Finally, they can illustrate the information. The teacher can show the children a frame with the signal words and can model filling in the frame with responses elicited from students. At this point, the meanings of signal words can be clarified.

Any expository structure can be used with appropriate frames. Lewis and her colleagues (1994) have found sequential, enumeration, comparison, contrast, and reaction frames to work well. They also have had success with getting children to draw pictures depicting sequential text after they read, but before they write about, the material; having them transform the information in the text into a graphic form (for example, a chart or a map); and having them rewrite material in another genre, such as a job advertisement.

Cudd and Roberts (1989) suggest the use of reaction frames that are elaborations of enumeration frames. One type leads the children to tie prior knowledge to new information. Here is an example:

Before I started reading about trucks, I knew _____

_____ .

In the book I read, I learned that _____ .

I also learned _____ .

The thing that surprised me most was _____ .

Cairney (1990) says that these frames provide probes that encourage text recall.

TECHNOLOGY 🖳 ● **Computer Approaches**

Teachers can incorporate computer technology with other strategies for helping students with their content reading. Dowd and Sinatra (1990) point out, for example, that there are three kinds of computer software designed to help students learn about text structure. One type models the different text structures and then has the students write something based on the model. Another type includes interactive/prompt tutorials on particular types of discourse. Some of these allow students to write working outlines for papers; others allow them to process a complete draft, revise it, and edit it. The last type lets students use their knowledge of text structure to do real-life activities requiring use of that knowledge, such as writing a class newspaper.

Wepner (1992b) has described cross-curricular units on endangered species, which use books, software, magazines, and musical recordings. Some teachers overlook software when planning thematic units. Wepner (1992a, 1992c) makes suggestions for using technology with a variety of content area units. Internet projects that pertain to various content areas are discussed in Chapter 11.

● Writing Techniques

A number of writing techniques may be used to advantage in helping students learn to read effectively in the content areas. Probably the best known is the language experience approach. Others include feature analysis plus writing, webs plus writing, and keeping learning logs.

Language Experience Approach (LEA)

The *language experience approach (LEA)* is a good basic method to use in content area teaching. Expository text structure can be taught through the LEA. For example, a teacher who wishes to have students learn the comparison-and-contrast pattern of writing can have them discuss how two objects are alike and how they are different, make a chart showing the likenesses and differences, and dictate a written selection based on the chart. The teacher can ask first for likenesses and then for differences as the dictation takes place. Then the children can use their own written selection to locate the two related parts of a comparison or contrast and do other activities that involve the structure. (This chapter contains several examples of applying the language experience approach to specific content areas to promote learning of the content.)

Feature Analysis Plus Writing

A *feature matrix* can be helpful for gathering, comparing, and contrasting information about several items in the same category (Cunningham and Cunningham, 1987). The teacher first reads through the material and selects the members of the category and specific features that some, all, or none of them have. Then he or she forms them into a matrix like the one in Example 10.3 on page 394 and displays the matrix to the class. The students fill in the matrix in the same way that the semantic feature analysis chart in Chapter 4 was completed, leaving blanks when they are unsure about a feature. Then the students read the assigned material to confirm or

---

EXAMPLE 10.3 **Semantic Feature Matrix for Geometric Shapes**

	Straight lines	Curved lines	Four sides	Three sides	All sides must be equal in length
Triangle Rectangle Circle Square					

---

revise their original markings and to fill in any empty spaces. They are encouraged to erase and change marks if the information they read refutes their initial ideas. During class discussion after the reading, the students and teacher complete the class matrix cooperatively. If there is disagreement, students return to the text to find support for their positions. Some points may require library research.

The information on the feature matrix can then be used as a basis for writing about the reading material. For instance, in Example 10.3 above, the teacher can choose one geometric shape and can model the writing of a paragraph about it. Students and teacher can then cooperatively write another paragraph about another shape. Then each student or small group of students may choose other shapes to write about. (Note that the matrix can be expanded to include many more shapes and features.) Using the information from a feature matrix for paragraph writing promotes retention of information covered in the matrix.

Webs Plus Writing

Webs are useful organizers in the content areas. Before the students read the content material, the teacher records the information the students think they know about the topic of the chapter in the form of a web like the one shown in Example 10.4 on page 395.

The students may make individual webs, containing only the points they think are correct. Then they read the material, checking the information on the web and adding the new information they find. In class discussion that follows the reading, the class web is revised and disagreements are settled by consulting the text. The class can write paragraphs about different strands of the web—for example, about famous leaders from Tennessee.

Keeping Learning Logs

Using *learning logs* or journals to promote content area learning is a very effective technique. Students can follow the reading or discussion of a content topic by writing summaries, comments, or questions related to the reading or class discussion. The content teacher can read the comments and adjust future lessons in response to the degree of understanding or confusion reflected in the logs.

EXAMPLE 10.4 Web for Content Material

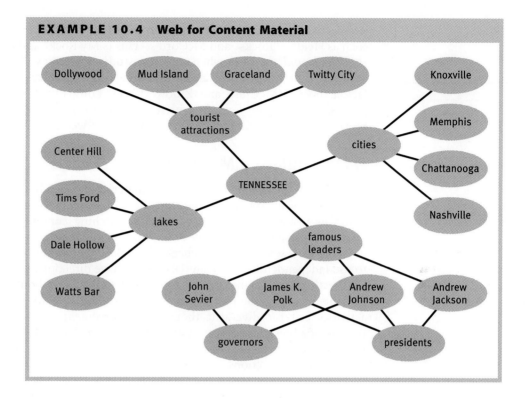

In social studies and science classes, students can be encouraged to observe things around them, record their observations (in pictures or writing), and associate what they observe with their past experiences and prior knowledge. When students keep observation notebooks, the teacher can lead them to draw conclusions about word parts in words chosen from their notebooks, thereby allowing them to work with words they can already identify. This enhances students' decoding skills while they are engaged in content learning (Sullivan, 1986).

LITERATURE ● **Using Content Material with Reading of Fiction and Writing**

Ollmann (1991) suggests using factual content material as part of the prereading phase to prepare students for reading literature that involves content concepts. Encyclopedia articles, travel magazines and brochures, *National Geographic,* or other material can often provide background information related to settings or to scientific concepts involved in stories. When the prereading material is being examined, the teacher can emphasize strategies needed for reading content material, such as skimming, scanning, and use of alphabetical order and guide words in a realistic setting.

Besides reading factual content material, students can read poems and other literature related to the content, think about the content from an aesthetic perspective, and write poetry related to the topic. For example, they can read poems such as Heide's "Rocks" and McCord's "This Is My Rock" and Peters's book *The Sun, the Wind, and the Rain* when they are studying geology. Then they can write in descriptive or poetic form about the things they have discovered from the more factual books (McClure and Zitlow, 1991). Long (1993) suggests using acrostic poems, rather than formal written reports, to share information gained from researching a topic. She found that they worked well for third graders.

● Manipulative Materials

Teachers can use *manipulative* learning materials to teach both content objectives and the reading skills necessary to attain these objectives. An example of manipulative materials would be puzzles that require matching content vocabulary terms with pictures representing the terms. After introducing and demonstrating these materials in whole-class sessions, the teacher should place them in learning centers for students to use independently. The materials should have directions for easy reference, should be directly related to the content area being studied, and should include a way for the students to determine the accuracy of their answers or to receive reinforcement. If activities call for divergent thought, reinforcement is usually provided through sharing of a report or project. Activities include matching technical vocabulary terms with illustrations of their meanings in a puzzle format, matching causes with effects, and following directions to produce an art product (Morrow, 1982).

● Integrating Approaches

Because no single technique will enable all students to deal with the many demands of content material, a teacher must know many approaches, teach them directly, and let the students know why they help. Children need to be able to pick out an appropriate approach for a particular assignment.

A procedure similar to the DRA may provide structure. First, the teacher may plan activities to motivate the students to read the material and build their background for reading it, including teaching vocabulary through context clues or by relating the words to words that the children already know. Students may discuss what they already know about the topic, web this information, and survey the material to be read. After the survey, they may be asked to predict what information is going to be presented. Then purposes for reading need to be set by the students, the teacher, or both cooperatively. The teacher may provide a study guide to guide the reading, focusing attention on important concepts and/or appropriate reading processes. Students may read to answer *who, what, when, where, how,* and *why* questions; to verify hypotheses; or to discover important material to add to information they have already collected about a topic. After the students have completed the reading, the teacher should plan activities that lead students to organize and synthesize information. They may write content-based language experience stories on the material or make graphic representations of the content (graphs, charts, diagrams), for example; for some material the students may be able to *apply* the concepts presented.

● Creating Instructional Units

LITERATURE Two types of instructional units that are often used in conjunction with content instruction are thematic units, in which the theme is a concept or a topic, and literature-based units across the curriculum, in which a piece of literature is the central focus. Literature should be an integral part of both types. Smith and Johnson (1994) say, "Literature can become the lens through which content is viewed." It puts the content into context and perspective. Reading aloud or Sustained Silent Reading (SSR), paired reading and discussion, guided reading, and literature circles are a part of much content area instruction. The Classroom Scenario below shows students working in a small group on a thematic unit.

Thematic Content Units

LITERATURE The use of thematic units was discussed as one approach to literature-based reading instruction in Chapter 7. The same concept can apply to teaching content units.

CLASSROOM SCENARIO

Thematic Unit on Survival

The children in Ms. Parker's sixth-grade class had been reading books related to the theme of *survival*. Several of them were seated around a table, beginning to discuss how their books were related to the theme.

"In *Julie of the Wolves,* Miyax has to survive by herself on the Alaskan tundra," Tonya began.

"In *Hatchet,* Brian has to survive by himself after his plane crashes in the Canadian wilderness," David said.

"Karana was left alone on an island off the coast of California," Zack said, referring to the main character in *Island of the Blue Dolphins.*

"Well, Phillip wasn't all alone on the Caribbean island in *The Cay* at first, but he did need help because he was blind after the blow to his head," David said. "Timothy, the black man, was really the one who made sure Phillip would survive. He used a lot of survival techniques."

"Let's list the survival techniques the characters used," Bruce said. "We could web them like Ms. Parker had us do with settings last month. We could use headings like 'Food' and 'Clothing.' "

"That's a good idea!" Tonya chimed in. "How about 'Shelter' for another heading?"

"Karana ate abalones and scallops from the sea," Zack said, "and she made herself a fenced-in house and a shelter in a cave."

"That's a good start," said Tonya. "Let's get that down on paper before we go on." She went to the storage shelf and returned with a piece of drawing paper and a black marker. She handed the materials to Bruce, the group member with the best handwriting skills. "Put your ideas and Zack's down before we forget them," she said. "Then we'll add more things from other people."

As Bruce began to write on the drawing paper, several other children began to take notes on their own papers about contributions they wanted to make.

Analysis of Scenario

The children in Ms. Parker's class had worked in discussion groups many times and were ready to participate when they came to the table. Tonya acted the part of a good leader by getting the discussion started and by collecting materials for the webbing and delegating the task of actually constructing the web to another student. Ms. Parker had taught a valuable skill, webbing, in earlier lessons, and these children remembered it and put it to use.

Thematic content units involve linking the reading of fiction and nonfiction about a content topic in order to help the children get a more comprehensive picture of the topic. As Doiron (1994) points out, facts can be embedded in fiction, and narrative structures can be used to convey facts presented in nonfiction. Therefore, both types of books are useful, and children need to be able to read both types. Text sets (sets of books on one topic, by the same author, of the same genre, about the same culture, or that share some other attribute) are useful in unit instruction. After students read the related texts, they can share and extend their understanding of each text in a different way than would have been possible if they had read only one text (Harste, Short, and Burke, 1988). Nonfiction trade books need to be available on a number of difficulty levels, and teachers need to show students how to locate them and use them to find information. Assignments involving these books should require synthesis and critical thinking (Palmer and Stewart, 1997).

Teachers should not overlook the possible value of picture books in content units for the upper grades. These books are often relegated to the primary grades, but many are appropriate for older students, and they add motivation and variety to lessons (Danielson, 1992). Eve Bunting has written a number of books that would be appropriate for these students, although they can be used with younger students, too. They include *How Many Days to America?* (Clarion, 1988), *Terrible Things* (The Jewish Publication Society, 1989), and *The Wall* (Clarion, 1990). Thematically focused alphabet books by Jerry Pallotta, George Ella Lyon, Gisela Jernigan, Abbie Zabar, Malka Drucker, Red Hawk, and John Agard are also good. They cover a variety of topics, and many focus on science and social studies concepts. For example, books by Zabar, Drucker, Red Hawk, and Agard introduce other cultures. Many of Pallotta's books have science and social studies themes (Chaney, 1993; Thompson, 1992). (See Example 10.5 on page 399.)

Children's magazines, such as *National Geographic World, Cobblestone, Appleseeds, Odyssey,* and *Ranger Rick,* are also useful (Short, 2002). Nonfiction offers information in many forms, including text, pictures, and maps. It frequently has useful headings and subheadings, as well as other typographic aids (Harvey, 2002).

Some thematic units are related to a single discipline; some are interdisciplinary, linking content and skills from different disciplines through authentic tasks; and some are integrative, in which the theme is the focus, and boundaries between the disciplines are not evident. (Students may collaborate with the teacher in theme selection, or the content may be mandated by the school district.) Teachers should choose broad themes that lend themselves to good instructional activities (Lapp and Flood, 1994). Good themes can focus on such wide-ranging areas as horrors of the Holocaust and life long ago contrasted with life today. A web for the content topic can be elaborated with fiction and nonfiction selections, textbooks, magazines, newspapers, videos, and software for use with each subtopic.

After resources have been located and organized, the classroom activities to be used in the unit can be planned, with a web of resources as a helpful reference. Such a web is not a complete plan. Teachers still must decide on goals and objectives for their units, because not all concepts presented in all of the sources can possibly be used. Then they must choose instructional procedures and related activities to meet these goals, gather related materials, schedule unit activities, and decide how to assess the outcomes. Shanahan (1997) points out that the teacher needs to have a clear idea

EXAMPLE 10.5 Page from Thematic Alphabet Book

K k K is for Kulan. Kulans have incredible endurance. People have seen them run without stopping for more than twenty miles. They could easily run a marathon. Kulans are not only found in the desert. They are also found in areas called steppes. A steppe is a huge grassland or plain often found on the edge of a desert.

How many miles are in a marathon? The alphabet is a clue.

Source: Jerry Pallotta, *The Desert Alphabet Book* (Watertown, Mass.: Charlesbridge Publishing, 1994). Copyright © 1994 by Jerry Pallotta. Illustration copyright © 1994 by Mark Astrella. Used with permission by Charlesbridge Publishing. All rights reserved.

of the desired learning outcomes, since thematic unit instruction does not automatically result in learning. He also cautions that instruction in the separate fields, accompanied by drill and practice, is still needed when integration is implemented, because "a common problem in integrated instruction can be that the focus is so much on relevance that students never practice anything enough to get good at it" (p. 18).

Thematic units connect information from language arts, science, social studies, math, art, music, and drama. Shanahan (1997) indicates that the different disciplines involved all need sufficient attention; some disciplines may not fit into a particular thematic study. At times a discipline such as math may need to be taught separately from the thematic unit to give it appropriate attention. During thematic studies, the ways in which text is used in the different disciplines should receive attention, because scientists, mathematicians, historians, and practitioners in other fields think and write differently.

To set reading purposes, students can brainstorm questions about a topic. The children learn to read selectively to answer their questions. They can sort their questions into categories, discovering that by doing so, they can find answers to more than one question at a time by locating the proper sections of books and becoming aware of the organization of nonfiction. When they share information with the class, they may refer to the text to prove points (Hess, 1991).

Schmidt (1999) suggests a modification of the K-W-L procedure—KWLQ—to help students form questions for inquiry during thematic units. The first three steps are the same as K-W-L (which is described in Chapter 5). The Q step asks for more questions, to show that learning is continuous. Students are not likely to be successful with inquiry procedures if they are not explicitly taught the steps in such procedures and if they have not seen how the procedures work. They may first need much exposure to nonfiction writing and to the differences in the ways in which fiction and nonfiction are organized and used (Tower, 2000).

Literature-Based Units Across the Curriculum

LITERATURE   A single piece of literature can be the basis of a unit that will include activities from many curricular areas. Related science, social studies, math, art, and drama content may be taught with the piece of literature as the focal point. Language learning can take place along with reading, discussion, and writing done in relation to the literature selection. Example 10.6 on page 401 shows one such unit.

Specific Content Areas

Special reading challenges are associated with each of the content areas. It is best to teach skills for handling these challenges at a time when students need the skills in order to read their assignments.

● Language Arts

The *language arts* block of the elementary school curriculum involves instruction in listening, speaking, reading, writing, viewing, and visually presenting. It includes the subjects of reading, literature, and English. Since basal readers that may be used during reading class were discussed in other chapters of this textbook, they will not be considered here. Although literature is treated briefly in this chapter, more thorough coverage is found in Chapter 8.

LITERATURE   **Literature**

Ideally, a literature program should encourage students to learn about their literary heritages and the heritages of others, to expand their imaginations, to develop reading preferences, to evaluate literature, to increase their awareness of language, and to grow socially, emotionally, and intellectually. These goals can be reached through a well-planned program in which the teacher reads aloud to students daily and provides them with opportunities to read and respond to literature. Teachers may teach literary skills directly through a unit on poetry or a novel, or they may integrate these skills with basal reader and language arts lessons.

Teaching Literature Skills. When developing literature programs, teachers can organize instruction by genres (forms or categories), literary elements, or topics in

EXAMPLE 10.6   Literature-Based Unit Across the Curriculum

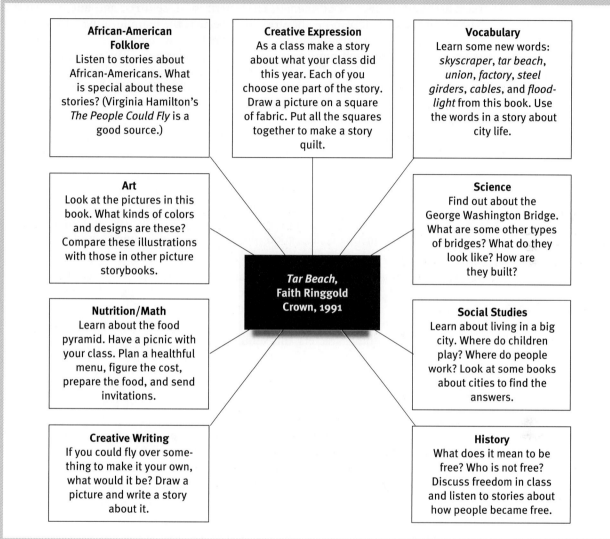

African-American Folklore
Listen to stories about African-Americans. What is special about these stories? (Virginia Hamilton's *The People Could Fly* is a good source.)

Creative Expression
As a class make a story about what your class did this year. Each of you choose one part of the story. Draw a picture on a square of fabric. Put all the squares together to make a story quilt.

Vocabulary
Learn some new words: *skyscraper*, *tar beach*, *union*, *factory*, *steel girders*, *cables*, and *flood-light* from this book. Use the words in a story about city life.

Art
Look at the pictures in this book. What kinds of colors and designs are these? Compare these illustrations with those in other picture storybooks.

Science
Find out about the George Washington Bridge. What are some other types of bridges? What do they look like? How are they built?

Nutrition/Math
Learn about the food pyramid. Have a picnic with your class. Plan a healthful menu, figure the cost, prepare the food, and send invitations.

Tar Beach,
Faith Ringgold
Crown, 1991

Social Studies
Learn about living in a big city. Where do children play? Where do people work? Look at some books about cities to find the answers.

Creative Writing
If you could fly over something to make it your own, what would it be? Draw a picture and write a story about it.

History
What does it mean to be free? Who is not free? Discuss freedom in class and listen to stories about how people became free.

Source: Web based on *Tar Beach* by Faith Ringgold (New York: Crown, 1991).

order to vary students' experiences, and they should introduce students to the specialized vocabulary and skills they need to develop an appreciation of literature.

In literature classes, children are asked to read and understand many literary forms, including short stories, novels, plays, poetry, biographies, and autobiographies. One characteristic of all these forms is the frequent occurrence of ***figurative language,*** or nonliteral language. Figurative language is sometimes a barrier to understanding, because children tend to interpret such language literally. Chapter 4 covers teaching children to deal with figurative expressions.

Literary Elements. To understand literary passages, children need to be able to recognize and analyze plots, themes, characterization, settings, and authors' styles. The *plot* is the overall plan for the story; the *theme* is the main idea the writer wishes to convey; and *characterization* is the way in which the writer makes the reader aware of the characteristics and motives of each person in the story. The *setting* consists of time and place, and the *style* is the writer's mode of expressing thoughts. Teacher-directed questioning can make students aware of these literary elements and help children understand the interrelationships among them. Following are some points related to major story elements:

❶ *Setting.* Teachers should point out how time and place affect the plot, characterization, and mood of a story. Stories must be true to their settings; characters behave differently today from the way they behaved a hundred years ago, and city life involves situations different from those that occur in country life. All of these facts make understanding the setting of a story important. *Bud, Not Buddy* by Christopher Paul Curtis and *Madeline* by Ludwig Bemelmans are good books to use in helping children see the importance of setting.

❷ *Characterization.* Children who examine literature with strong characterization find that writers develop their characters through dialogue, actions, interactions with others, and insights into their thoughts and feelings, as well as through description. Looking for these clues will make the children more attuned to the characters and should increase their overall understanding of the piece of literature. Children can also take note of how characters grow and change as the story progresses (Galda, 1989). The characterizations in Cynthia Voigt's *Dicey's Song* make good discussion material. In addition, the children can read *Miss Nelson Is Missing* by Harry Allard and James Marshall and compare and contrast the two identities of Miss Nelson. They could write dialogue for "Miss Nelson" and "Miss Swamp" and use this dialogue in a puppet show, imitating the way each character would speak, as well as using appropriate lines (Dreher, 1989).

❸ *Plot.* Children may analyze short, simple stories to see how writers introduce their stories, develop them through a series of incidents, create interest and suspense, and reach satisfying conclusions. Awareness of the ways in which plots are developed can increase understanding of narratives. Picture books with predictable plots are good places to start. Mem Fox's *Hattie and the Fox* is a good choice for picture-book plot analysis (Galda, Carr, and Cox, 1989). *Doctor Desoto* by William Steig is another good book for examining plot with children (Sharp, 1984).

❹ *Style.* Children should examine written material to analyze the authors' choices of words, sentence patterns, and manners of expression. Teachers and students can discuss and compare the styles of writing in Maurice Sendak's *Chicken Soup with Rice*, Cynthia Rylant's *When I Was Young in the Mountains*, and Patricia MacLachlan's *Sarah, Plain and Tall*.

❺ *Theme.* The concept of *theme* is abstract. Smit (1990) suggests selecting two stories that have the same theme but differ in setting, plot, and other elements to enable students to see how the same theme can be developed in different ways. She suggests *Why the Chimes Rang* by Raymond MacDonald Alden and *The Grateful Statues,* a Japanese folktale, for helping the students discover the theme of *giving.*

One way that teachers may work on these elements is through journal writing. (See Chapters 7 and 8 for more on journal writing.) The children may be asked to respond to a story by selecting a character from the story and writing a journal entry as though that character were writing it. The entries can be dated according to the time in which the book takes place. The journal writers can leave clues in their entries to the identities of the characters doing the writing. These entries can then be shared orally, and the other children can try to decide which character wrote each entry. Such an activity encourages attention to characterization, point of view, and mood (Jossart, 1988).

Webbing literary elements related to a story can help students clarify their concepts of these elements. The teacher can read the story and have the students listen for the elements that need to be added to the web.

Literary Forms. Children's literature consists of a variety of genres, or literary forms, including historical and realistic fiction, biographies, poetry, plays, informational books, and fantasy and folklore. Historical fiction, biographies, and informational books are all useful for integrating with content areas, whereas good realistic fiction serves as a model for helping children to understand others and solve problems in their own lives. Nonfiction selections give students a way to investigate and understand the world, offering a wide range of subjects and ideas to explore (Harvey, 2002). Poetry encourages children to explore their emotions, and plays offer the pleasure of acting out favorite stories. Both modern fantasy and folklore allow children to escape into worlds of imaginary characters and events. Teachers should use all of these forms in their literature programs, and they can enhance children's understanding of them by reading literature of all forms aloud and pointing out the characteristics of each genre. More information on literary genres appears in Chapter 8.

English

English textbooks cover the areas of listening, speaking, and writing. They generally consist of a series of sections of instructional material followed by practice exercises. The technical vocabulary includes such terms as *noun, pronoun, cursive,* and *parliamentary procedure.* The concepts presented in the informational sections are densely packed; each sentence is usually important for understanding, and examples are abundant. Children need to be encouraged to study the examples, because they help to clarify the information presented in the narrative portion of the textbook.

Teachers are wise to plan oral activities in class to accompany the listening and speaking portions of the English textbook, since such practice allows students to apply the concepts immediately and helps them retain the material. Similarly, to enhance retention, it is wise to ask students to apply the concepts encountered in the writing section as soon as possible in relevant situations.

Writing instruction can form the basis for reading activities. Children read to obtain information to include in their compositions, and they read to learn different styles of writing. For example, they read poems to absorb the style of writing before attempting to write poetry, and they read informational books for ideas about the structure they will need to use to write their own books. Children can also read their own material in order to revise it to enhance accuracy, improve clarity, or ensure correct use of language conventions. They may read it aloud to peers for constructive criticism, or their peers may read it themselves.

LITERATURE Much of a student's formal vocabulary instruction takes place in English classes. Trade books can be the basis for vocabulary lessons. Fred Gwynne's *The King Who Rained* and *A Chocolate Moose for Dinner* offer good examples of figurative expressions, homonyms, and words with multiple meanings that can be used to interest students in word study. In the Amelia Bedelia books by Peggy Parish, Amelia takes everything literally, with disastrous results: her sponge cake is made of sponges! Emily Hanlon's *How a Horse Grew Hoarse on the Site Where He Sighted a Bare Bear* offers examples of homonyms in nonsense verses.

● Social Studies

Social studies texts in particular have been criticized for being difficult to read, often requiring more reading ability than prospective readers have, and varying four or more years in difficulty from passage to passage. Social studies texts have often been found to assume unrealistic levels of background knowledge on the part of the students and to lack coherence (Stetson and Williams, 1992; Beck and McKeown, 1991a), interest, and meaning for them (Guzzetti, Kowalinski, and McGowan, 1992).

Social studies materials are generally written in a very precise and highly compact expository style in which many ideas are expressed in a few lines of print. Authors may discuss a hundred-year span in a single page or even a single paragraph; they may cover complex issues in a few paragraphs, even though whole books could be devoted to these issues. Study guides are recommended for helping students read social studies materials with understanding and purpose.

Social studies materials are organized in a variety of ways, including cause-and-effect relationships, chronological order, comparisons and/or contrasts, and topical order (for example, by regions, such as Asia and North America, or by concepts, such as transportation and communication). The content selection in Example 10.1 on page 388 illustrates the cause-and-effect pattern, but it also offers comparisons and contrasts of the effects of the war on different groups. Knowing the organizational pattern of the selection enables children to approach the reading with an appropriate mental set, which aids greatly in comprehension of the material. To help children deal with cause-and-effect and chronological order arrangements, teachers can use the ideas found in Chapter 6 for helping students determine such relationships and sequences. Drawing time lines is one good way to work with chronological order, and pattern guides such as the one in Example 10.2 on page 389 are ways to work on cause-and-effect or comparison-contrast relationships.

In social studies reading, students encounter such technical terms as *democracy, tropics, hemisphere, decade,* and *century,* as well as many words with meanings that differ from their meanings in general conversation. When children first hear that a candidate is going to *run* for office, they may picture a foot race—an illusion that is furthered if they read that a candidate has decided to enter the *race* for governor. If the term *race* is applied to people in their texts, the children may become even more confused. Children who know that you *strike* a match or make a *strike* when bowling may not understand a labor union *strike.* Discussions about the *mouth* of a river could bring unusual pictures to the minds of children. The teacher is responsible for seeing that the students understand the concepts that these terms represent.

Harmon and Hedrick (2000) have developed a technique called "Zooming In and Zooming Out" to enhance vocabulary and conceptual learning in social studies. Zooming Out refers to situating the term or concept within a larger context, and Zooming In refers to looking closely at the concept itself. The procedure begins with the students brainstorming about their current knowledge about the concept, while the teacher lists their ideas. Then the students read to find out more about the concept and confirm the brainstormed ideas, making notes as they read. Discussion about their findings then ensues, with the students identifying the most and least important facts about the concept, after the teacher models this process. The discussion also involves concepts or people and places that are similar to, related to, or unrelated to the target concept. At the end of the discussion, the students summarize information about the concept in a single statement. Harmon and Hedrick (2000) suggest putting this information into a web that provides a visual display of the information collected.

Social studies materials also present children with maps, charts, and graphs to read. Ways of teaching the use of such reading aids are suggested in Chapter 9. Social studies materials must be read critically. Students should be taught to check copyright dates to determine timeliness and to be alert for such problems as outdated geography materials that show incorrect boundaries or place names.

LITERATURE 📖 Using Literature in Social Studies

Social studies materials are frequently written in a very impersonal style and may be concerned with unfamiliar people or events that are remote in time or place. Students may also lack interest in the subject. For these reasons, teachers should use many interesting trade books to personalize the content and to expand on topics that are covered very briefly in the textbook. Biographies of famous people who lived during different historical periods add spice to textbook accounts, and using literature about different peoples is one way to approach multicultural issues (Rasinski and Padak, 1990; Martinez and Nash, 1990a; Pugh and Garcia, 1990). Walker-Dalhouse (1992) believes that the use of multicultural literature can decrease negative stereotyping of people from other cultures.

DIVERSITY 🌐

Trade books provide causal relationships between concepts and give students a chance to answer their own questions about the content from their reading. Trade books offer opportunities to meet curricular objectives for both reading and social studies simultaneously. For example, maps in trade books can be used to teach map-reading skills, to locate the places being studied, and to identify the features of the land in these places. When students are using such books, brainstorming about prior knowledge and forming semantic maps can be helpful. Then teachers can have students use "think sheets" on which they list their questions about a central question posed by the teacher, their ideas about how these questions would be answered, and how the text answered the questions. They may eventually produce their own question-and-answer books about the topic (Guzzetti, Kowalinski, and McGowan, 1992).

The five fundamental themes in geography are location (where a story takes place and why); place (what the place is like); relationships within places (including relationships between humans and the environment); movement of people, materials, and ideas (descriptions and consequences); and regions (including how they change) (Norton, 1993a; Committee on Geographic Education, 1983; *GEONews Handbook,* 1990). Norton (1993a) shows how the books *People of the Breaking Day* by Marcia Sewell, *Christopher Columbus: Voyager to the Unknown* by Nancy Smiler Levinson, *Encounter* by Jane Yolen, and *The Other Fourteen Ninety-Two: Jewish Settlement in the New World* by Norman H. Funkelstein can help students learn about these five themes in the context of literature rather than textbook discussions. This treatment, supplemented with other books about the period, offers diverse perspectives on the geographical concepts being studied.

Picture books can be valuable for presenting many social studies concepts to middle- and upper-elementary students, as well as primary-level students. These books elaborate on topics that would otherwise get limited attention. Sensitive issues that are ignored in textbooks can often be treated effectively in fictional accounts. Children become emotionally involved with other people and historical situations through these books (Farris and Fuhler, 1994).

Fictionalized biographies and diaries used for social studies instruction are excellent for teaching children to evaluate the accuracy and authenticity of material, since authors have invented dialogue and thoughts for the characters to make the material seem more realistic. Teachers should lead children to see that these stories try to add life to facts but are not completely factual, perhaps by having them check reference books for accuracy of dates, places, and names. Sometimes, reading an author's foreword or postscript will offer clues to the fictional aspects of a story; for example, at times only the historical events mentioned are true. Students should also be aware that authors use first-person narrative accounts to make the action seem more personal, but that in reality the supposed speaker is not the person who did the writing. Also, any first-person account offers a limited perspective, because the person speaking cannot know everything that all the characters in the story do or everything that is happening at one time. Teachers should alert students to look for the author's bias and, if a bibliography of sources is given, should ask them to check to see how much the author depended on actual documents (Storey, 1982; Zarnowski, 1988).

Another approach to reading biographical material is to have students choose a famous person; read that person's biography; do additional research on the person, using multiple sources; make time lines of events in the person's life; and take on the role of that person in role-playing sessions. Since reading research strategies should be taught in context, this procedure provides fertile ground for such teaching. Such studies can also naturally link social studies with science and language.

Reading biographies can help students think about social issues and individuals' involvement with them, assessing the importance of events and understanding the objective and subjective dimensions of the events. This can lead to lessons on determining fact and opinion (Miller, Clegg, and Vanderhoff, 1992).

Children can also be drawn into historical periods and issues through historical fiction. Historical fiction transforms a series of events into an interpretation of these events, providing humanizing details. It can help students understand the times in which historical events occurred. Children are able to become emotionally involved with people from the past. As they identify with the actual historical characters in the books they read, they face conflicting viewpoints that require them to do critical thinking. They read to interpret the moral and ethical issues that the characters faced during these events. They see multiple perspectives and can make informed judgments (Johnson and Ebert, 1992; Levstick, 1990). As students study these materials, teachers can read related materials to them to build background. Then the students can do activities such as making time lines based on their readings, marking maps to show where events in the reading occurred, classifying characters in terms of their beliefs or allegiances, producing mock newspapers from the times, illustrating events and places described, writing diaries for characters in the reading, or writing letters to characters to offer comments and advice (Johnson and Ebert, 1992).

LITERATURE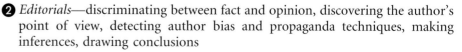

DIVERSITY

Award-winning trade books can be found for nearly every period of history. Elizabeth Speare's *The Bronze Bow* is a novel about a boy who encounters Jesus in Rome; Marguerite De Angeli's *The Door in the Wall* treats the situation of a boy with a physical disability in fourteenth-century England; *The Courage of Sarah Noble,* by Alice Dalgliesh, describes a young girl who must face the difficulties of living in Connecticut in early pioneer days; *The Sign of the Beaver,* by Elizabeth Speare, is the story of a boy's struggle to survive in the Maine wilderness in the 1700s; Carol Brink's *Caddie Woodlawn* draws the reader into the excitement of living on the Wisconsin frontier during the last half of the nineteenth century; Paula Fox's *The Slave Dancer* tells about a boy who becomes involved in the slave trade with Africa during pre–Civil War days; and Patricia MacLachlan's *Sarah, Plain and Tall* unites a woman from the East with a motherless family on a prairie farm during pioneer days.

Using the Newspaper to Teach Social Studies

Teachers may use special student newspapers or regular newspapers in class. The newspaper is a living textbook for social studies through which students learn about tomorrow's history as it is happening today. Different parts of the newspaper require different reading skills, as noted here:

❶ *News stories* — identifying main ideas and supporting details (who, what, where, when, why, how), determining sequence, recognizing cause-and-effect relationships, making inferences, drawing conclusions

❷ *Editorials*—discriminating between fact and opinion, discovering the author's point of view, detecting author bias and propaganda techniques, making inferences, drawing conclusions

❸ *Comics*—interpreting figurative language and idiomatic expressions, recognizing sequences of events, making inferences, detecting cause-and-effect relationships, drawing conclusions, making predictions

❹ *Advertisements*—detecting propaganda, making inferences, drawing conclusions, distinguishing between fact and opinion

❺ *Entertainment section*—reading charts, such as the TV schedule, and evaluating material presented

❻ *Weather*—reading maps

Each of these skills is discussed fully in either Chapter 6 or Chapter 9.
The following activities offer practice in reading newspapers more effectively.

1. Have students locate the *who, what, where, when, why,* and *how* in news stories.

2. Using news stories with the headlines cut off, have students write their own headlines and then compare them with the actual headlines.

3. Give children copies of news stories about the same event from two different newspapers. Then ask them to point out and discuss similarities and differences.

4. Using copies of conflicting editorials, have students underline facts in one color and opinions in another color and then discuss the results. Also, have them locate emotional language and propaganda techniques in each editorial.

5. Discuss the symbolism and the message conveyed by each of several editorial cartoons. Then ask students to draw their own editorial cartoons.

6. Have students compare an editorial and a news story on the same topic. Discuss differences in approach.

7. Tell students to locate some comics that are funny. Then ask them to explain why these comics are funny.

8. Have students study the entertainment section and decide which movies or plays would be most interesting to them or locate time slots for certain television programs.

9. Encourage children to try to solve crossword puzzles.

10. Have students compare human interest features with straight news stories to discover which type of writing is more objective, which has more descriptive terms, and so on. Have them dramatize appropriate ones.

11. Ask students to search grocery advertisements from several stores for the best buy on a specified item or to study the classified advertisements to decide what job they would most like to have and why. Then ask them to write their own classified ads.

12. Have the students study the display advertisements for examples of propaganda techniques.

13. Ask students to use the index of the paper to tell what page to look on for the television schedule, the weather report, the classified ads, and so on.

14. Ask the children to search through the newspaper for typographical errors. Then discuss the effects of these errors on the material in which they appear.

15. Have students search the sports page for synonyms for the terms *won* and *lost*. Ask them why these synonyms are used.

● Mathematics

Mathematics material is very concise and abstract in nature and involves complex relationships. A high density of ideas per page characterizes this kind of material, and understanding each word is very important, for one word may be the key to understanding an entire section. Yet elementary teachers too often approach a math lesson in terms of developing only computational skill, overlooking the fact that reading skills can be advanced during arithmetic lessons and that arithmetic statement problems would be more comprehensible if attention were given to reading skills.

Reading in mathematics poses a number of special difficulties. First is the technical and specialized vocabulary. Young children have to learn terms like *plus, minus, sum,* and *subtraction,* whereas older children encounter such terms as *perimeter* and *diameter.* Words with multiple meanings also appear frequently. Discussions about *planes, figures,* finding the *difference,* or raising a number to the third *power* can confuse children who know other, more common meanings for these words. Nevertheless, many mathematics terms have root words, prefixes, or suffixes that children can use in determining their meanings. (For example, *triangle* means "three angles.")

Mountain (1993) suggests constructing stories that require the use of math synonyms in context to help students build concepts. Here is an example:

Mother needed *one yard* of material to make the cover.

"Mr. Huffer sells the material by the foot," Jamie complained.

"Then buy *three feet* of material," said Mother. "You're lucky he doesn't sell it by the inch. Then you'd have to remember to get *thirty-six inches.*"

Some of the synonyms in the story can be provided and others left out, to be filled in by the students from the context. Whitin and Whitin (1997) encourage teachers to postpone the use of technical mathematics vocabulary until students have had a chance to explain significant concepts in their own words.

Difficulties with words are not the only problems children have with math textbooks. They are also required to understand a different symbol system and to read numerals as well as words, which involves understanding place value. Children must be able to interpret such symbols as plus and minus signs, multiplication and division signs, symbols for union and intersection, equals signs and signs indicating inequalities, and many others, as well as abbreviations such as *ft., lb., in., qt., mm,* and *cm.*

Symbols are often particularly troublesome to children, perhaps partly because some symbols mean other things in other contexts; for example, - means *minus* in math but is a hyphen in regular print. Matching exercises such as the one described in the Model Activity on page 411 encourage students to learn the meanings of symbols.

To read numbers, students must understand place value. They must note, for example, that the number 312.8 has three places to the left of the decimal point (which they must discriminate from a period) and that this positioning of the decimal point means that the leftmost numeral indicates a particular number of hundreds, the next numeral tells how many tens, and the next numeral tells how many ones (in this case, three hundreds, one ten, and two ones, or three hundred twelve). To determine the value to the right of the decimal, they must realize that the first place is tenths, the second place is hundredths, and so forth. In this example, there are eight tenths; therefore, the entire number is three hundred twelve and eight tenths. This is obviously a complex procedure, involving not merely reading from left to right but also reading back and forth.

Mathematical sentences also present reading problems. Children must recognize numbers and symbols and translate them into verbal sentences, reading $9 \div 3 = 3$, for example, as "nine divided by three equals three."

Students will need help in reading and analyzing word problems as well. Teachers should arrange such problems according to difficulty and should avoid assigning too many at one time. Story problems can present special comprehension difficulties. They require all of the basic comprehension skills (determining main ideas and details, seeing relationships among details, making inferences, drawing conclusions, analyzing critically, and following directions). Chapter 9 contains a description of the SQRQCQ study method for mathematics, which takes these requirements into account.

Sometimes children find it useful to draw a picture of the situation a problem describes or to manipulate actual objects, and teachers should encourage such approaches to problem solving when they are appropriate. Teachers should watch their students solve word problems and decide where they need the most help: with computation, with problem interpretation (understanding of problems that they are not required to read for themselves), with reading, or with integration of the three skills in order to reach a solution. Small groups of students who need help in different areas of problem solving can be formed (Cunningham and Ballew, 1983).

Since story problems are not written in a narrative style, children often lack the familiarity with the text structure that is needed for ease of comprehension. The pattern of writing for story problems is procedural, with important details provided at the beginning and the topic sentence appearing near the end. This pattern fails to offer children an early purpose for their reading (Reutzel, 1983).

Braselton and Decker (1994) suggest that teachers have students think of word problems as short stories that they could comprehend by using their prior knowledge. They suggest the use of a graphic organizer to help students visualize the steps in

Matching Activity for Symbols

Place the symbols =, ≠, >, <, −, +, and ÷ on separate index cards. Write *equals, is not equal to, is greater than, is less than, minus, plus,* and *divided by* on other individual cards. Shuffle the cards and give them out randomly to students. Then let one student with a symbol card go to the front of the room and hold up his or her card. The student with the matching card should go up to join the first student. If nobody moves, the students with the definition cards all hold them up where the first student can see them, and he or she calls the student with the matching card to the front. If the student at the front cannot choose correctly, a student without a card may volunteer to make the match. After the match is made, the pair (or the trio if outside help was used) watches as other matches are made. Then each pair or trio thus formed makes up a math problem, using its own symbol, for the rest of the class to solve. These problems are written on the board. All students go to their seats and work the problems on their own papers. Then students who were not involved in constructing the problems volunteer to work them on the board, with the original pairs or trios acting as verifiers.

problem solution. The use of the organizer can be taught through modeling by the teacher, followed by guided practice and then independent practice by the students.

Hadaway and Young (1994) suggest that children will benefit from creating story problems related to their own experiences after a group language experience approach with classroom-related math problems. A research study showed that students who made up their own math story problems to solve performed better on tests of application skills than did those who practiced textbook word problems. Children are likely to interpret a story problem more successfully if they have constructed a similar problem (Ferguson and Fairburn, 1985). Fortescue (1994, p. 576) says, "To write about a mathematical problem, one must separate the problem into a series of steps that lead to a solution. So, in writing about math problems or activities, students become familiar with analytical writing while gaining and displaying a deeper understanding of the math concept."

Donna Strohauer uses a technique called "mathematician's circle" in which students (one at a time) share problems they have generated with a group and invite other students to solve the problems. Answers and explanations of answers follow, and peers of the students presenting the problems are asked to make suggestions about the problems (Winograd and Higgins, 1994/1995).

Study guides can be useful for working with mathematics materials. Students may be given a reaction guide composed of statements about the mathematics material that are either true or false. Then, working in cooperative groupings, they can complete the guide by agreeing or disagreeing with each statement and providing their reasons (Wood, 1992).

Fortescue (1994) gave third graders math task cards and asked them to complete the activities on the cards, record the results, and describe what they did during the activity. Each activity and the way to talk and write about it were modeled for the whole group before the activity was completed by the students. The students completed the activities, talked to one another about them, and then wrote about them. They had other students and then the teacher read their descriptions to verify that they were clear. These activities clarified their thinking about math processes.

Graphs, maps, charts, and tables, which often occur in mathematics materials, were discussed in Chapter 9. Students need help with these graphic aids in order to perform well on many mathematics assignments.

LITERATURE ⬙ **Using Literature in Mathematics**

Teachers can use literature to help them teach mathematical material. Counting books, for example, can provide material for teaching addition and subtraction. Bell (1988b) suggests the books *Animals One to Ten* by Deborah Manley and *Anno's Counting House* by Mitsumasa Anno for working with addition and subtraction. Through the humorous situations in Rod Clement's *Counting on Frank,* readers can begin to think like mathematicians—experimenting, calculating, and estimating. An excellent book for developing concepts of large numbers is *How Much Is a Million?* by David M. Schwartz, and a good one for encouraging students to work with division is *The Doorbell Rang* by Pat Hutchins. This book can also be used for addition with younger children. Carr and others (2001) suggest the use of Demi's *One Grain of Rice* when studying how numbers that are doubled grow rapidly. Children's literature can also help students learn to tell time. Bell (1988a) suggests using *The Scarecrow Clock* by George Mendoze for this purpose and the book *Chicken Soup with Rice* by Maurice Sendak for motivating children to learn to read the calendar. The Focus on Strategies on page 413 shows a mathematics lesson that is based on literature.

A good way to teach mathematics includes presenting mathematics content in ways that are like real-life uses. Therefore, the mathematics program would have problems related to students' everyday experiences, and the problems could be written by teachers and students. Language and mathematics strategy lessons would be interwoven as students performed such tasks as shopping for groceries within a budget, figuring the tax on purchases, conducting surveys, and constructing graphs.

● Science and Health

Scientific literacy involves asking and finding answers to questions about experiences and being able to describe and explain natural phenomena. "Observing, questioning, predicting, describing, explaining, and investigating" are scientific practices that are related to literacy (Ebbers, 2002, p. 40). Ebbers (2002, p. 41) points out that "[a] current emphasis on inquiry encourages the participation of students in genuine scientific activity, gradually developing their abilities to test theories and construct explanatory models." El-Hindi (2003) stresses the importance of getting students to reason out loud about scientific concepts during inquiry learning activities. This process will promote instructional conversations that develop both understanding of the science concepts and their linguistic competence. Writing about scientific concepts, such as keeping logs of observations, can also be helpful.

Having students brainstorm questions about material read in the science text, categorize the questions, and work as cooperative groups to investigate them can result in children interacting with the text as a group and sharing information

Mathematics Lesson Based on Literature

Ms. Barnes opened the class by displaying the book *The Doorbell Rang* by Pat Hutchins. "From the picture on the cover of this book and the title *The Doorbell Rang*, what do you think it will be about?" she asked the children.

"There are lots of people in the picture," Sammy said. "I think a lot of people have come to visit. The doorbell rings every time somebody comes. We have a doorbell that people ring when they come."

"What else does the picture make you think?" Ms. Barnes asked.

"They've tracked up the kitchen," said Monica. "The mom is going to have to clean it up. She'll send them all out."

"Does anybody else have something to add?" Ms. Barnes asked.

"The children don't look happy. Maybe she is running them out," Tasha suggested.

"They are looking out the slot in the door. Maybe the person that just rang the bell is someone they don't like," Jimmy said.

"Or maybe the kids don't want anyone else to come," Don added.

"Listen carefully as I read the story to see if your predictions were right," Ms. Barnes said. "Also listen to see what this book has to do with math."

Ms. Barnes read the story. When she finished, she asked, "Were your predictions right?"

"I was right that lots of people came, and the bell rang every time," Sammy said.

"Mom didn't send them out of the kitchen, so Tasha and I were wrong," Monica said.

"I was wrong," Jimmy said. "They acted like they liked the people who came."

"But I'll bet they really didn't want all of those people to come and share the cookies. I think I was right, even though they don't act bad about it," Don said.

"How does all of this fit into a math problem?" asked Ms. Barnes.

"They have to decide how many cookies to give each person," Don replied.

"That's right. Now we are going to see how they figured it all out," Ms. Barnes said as she handed out stacks of plastic chips to each set of math partners in the room.

"Now," she said, "listen carefully and use your chips to answer my questions as I go back through the story."

She read the first two pages. "How many children were there?" she asked.

"Two," the children chorused.

"How many cookies did each one get?" she asked.

"Six," answered the children.

"We need to know how many cookies there were in all," she said. "What do we do to get this answer?"

"We add them," answered Joey.

"Who can write out an addition problem on the board that we have to solve?" she asked.

Benny went to the board and wrote "6 + 6 =".

"Now solve the problem," she told them.

The children, who had used the chips to solve problems before, worked with their partners to form two rows of six chips each and count them. Soon hands were up all over the room. When all were finished, Ms. Barnes called on Billy, who proudly answered, "Twelve."

"Did anyone get any other answer?" she asked. A sea of shaking heads answered her. "Good job," she said. She let Sean go to the board and write the answer to the problem after the equals sign. Then she read further in the book.

"How many children were there after Tom and Hannah came?" she asked. Hands went up immediately, without use of the chips.

Ms. Barnes let Sammy give the answer, "Four," and go to the board and write the entire problem and answer: "2 + 2 = 4."

"Show with your chips how Sam and Victoria knew that each one would get three cookies," Ms.

Continued

Continued

Barnes directed. The children arranged their chips into four rows of three chips each.

"Now write an addition problem to show how putting these cookies back on the plate would give us the twelve we started with," she told them. Children wrote on their own papers and consulted with their partners before holding up their hands. Ms. Barnes let Laticia write "3 + 3 + 3 + 3 = 12" on the board. She asked if everyone agreed, and they did.

She repeated the above procedure for the entrance of Peter and his brother and again for the entrance of Joy and Simon and their four cousins, with the added step of asking how many people were at the door when Joy and Simon came. The children quickly did the addition of two plus four without the aid of chips.

At the end of the lesson, the children counted the cookies on the tray that Grandma brought, added that number to twelve by combining the chips from several sets of partners, and put the total number of chips into twelve rows to see how many each one would have before they let in that last person at the door.

(Sampson, Sampson, and Linek, 1994/1995). Such active involvement tends to facilitate learning.

Extremely heavy use of technical vocabulary is typical in science and health textbooks, in which students will encounter such terms as *lever, extinct, rodent, pollen, stamen, bacteria, inoculation,* and *electron*. Again, some of the words that have technical meanings also have more common meanings—for example, *shot, matter, solution,* and *pitch*. In these classes, as in all content area classes, the teacher is responsible for seeing that students understand the concepts represented by the technical and specialized terms in their subjects. For example, a science teacher might bring in a flower to explain what *stamens* are and where they are located. Although diagrams are also useful, a diagram is still a step removed from the actual object, and the more concrete an experience students have with a concept, the more likely it is that they will develop a complete understanding of the concept.

Comprehension strategies, such as recognizing main ideas and details, making inferences, drawing conclusions, recognizing cause-and-effect relationships, classifying items, recognizing sequence, and following directions, are important in reading science and health materials, as are critical reading strategies. The scientist's inquiring attitude is exactly the same as that of the critical reader. Students must determine the author's purpose for writing, must assess the completeness and timeliness of the information presented, and must check the accuracy of the material (Casteel and Isom, 1994). Because material can rapidly become outdated, it is very important that students be aware of the copyright dates of these materials.

Armbruster (1992/1993) points out that students need to learn how to read scientific material in order to obtain valid scientific information. She says, "The same skills that make good scientists also make good readers" (p. 347). Casteel and Isom (1994) have clearly illustrated the relationship of literacy processes to understanding of scientific material. The literacy processes form the root system, which supports the branches that represent the parts of the scientific method, which in turn support the scientific facts, concepts, laws, and theories of science. (See Example 10.7.)

Science and health materials must be read slowly and deliberately, and rereading may be necessary to fully grasp the information presented (Mallow, 1991). These

EXAMPLE 10.7   Relationship of Literacy Processes and Scientific Content

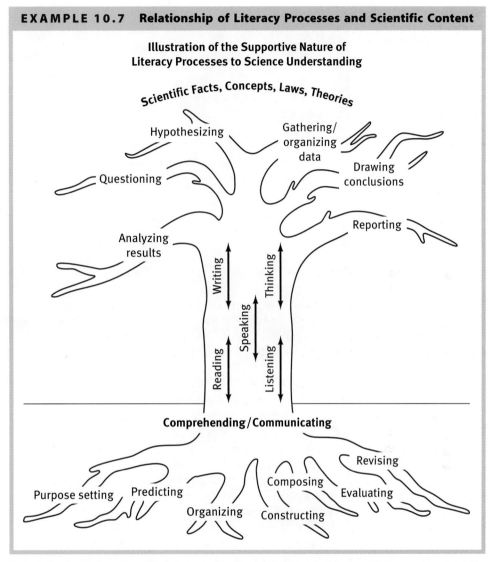

Illustration of the Supportive Nature of
Literacy Processes to Science Understanding

Scientific Facts, Concepts, Laws, Theories

Hypothesizing

Gathering/
organizing
data

Questioning

Drawing
conclusions

Reporting

Analyzing
results

Writing

Thinking

Speaking

Reading

Listening

Comprehending/Communicating

Revising

Composing

Purpose setting   Predicting

Evaluating

Organizing   Constructing

Source: Carolyn P. Casteel and Bess A. Isom, "Reciprocal Processes in Science and Literacy Learning," *The Reading Teacher,* 47 (7) (April 1994), 538–545. Reprinted with permission of the International Reading Association and the author.

materials, like social studies materials, are written in a highly compact, expository style that often involves classification, explanations, and cause-and-effect relationships. The suggestions in Chapter 9 for teaching outlining skills can be especially useful in working with classification, which involves arranging information under main headings and subheadings. The suggestions given in Chapter 6 for recognizing cause-and-effect relationships will help children handle this type of arrangement when it occurs in science textbooks.

These students use many diverse reading and study skills in their science class as they follow directions, interpret diagrams, and relate text exposition and description to scientific materials and models. *(© David S. Strickler/Indexstock)*

The ability to use such reading aids as maps, tables, charts, and graphs is also necessary. Explanations in science and health materials often describe processes, such as the pasteurization of milk, that may be illustrated by pictures, charts, or diagrams designed to clarify the textual material. Teachers might apply the material in Chapter 9 on reading diagrams and illustrations or the material in Chapter 6 on detecting sequence, because a process is generally explained in sequence.

Science textbooks often contain instructions for performing experiments. Readers must be able to comprehend the purpose of an experiment, read the list of materials to determine what must be assembled before the experiment is performed, and determine the order in which the steps must be followed. The suggestions in Chapter 6 on locating main ideas and details, on recognizing sequential order, and on learning to follow directions should be useful when reading material of this nature. Before they perform an experiment, children should attempt to predict the outcome on the basis of their prior knowledge. Afterward they should compare their predicted results with the actual results and investigate the reasons for any differences. Did they perform each step correctly? Can they check special references to find out what actually should have happened?

Because science textbooks are often written at higher difficulty levels than the basal readers for the same grade level, some children will need alternative materials for science instruction. Trade books are available on all levels of difficulty to meet this need.

Keeping a science log or journal is a traditional practice for scientists and makes a natural connection to language instruction. Children can enter a short science-related passage in a journal each day. The passage can vary from a single sentence about a nature observation to a complete explanation of an experiment and its results. Students can also write reports on science projects, detailing the procedures and the findings. These reports may be taken through the writing process from initial drafts and revisions to the finished products (Rubino, 1991).

Science activities that involve direct experiences, such as using manipulative materials, doing experiments, or making observations of phenomena, can be used as the basis for language experience stories or charts that will provide reading material in science. The experience is accompanied and/or followed by class discussion, after which the children produce a chart or a story about the experience. Reading of related concept books, such as the ones mentioned later in this chapter, may provide children with material to use in expanding their stories.

LITERATURE ## Using Literature in Science and Health

Teachers can use children's trade books that deal with scientific concepts to help students distinguish between real and make-believe situations. Both fiction and nonfiction selections can help teachers clarify scientific information (Cerullo, 1997; El-Hindi, 2003). Ebbers (2002) identifies seven nonfiction genres that can help students learn about science: reference books, explanation books, field guides, how-to books, narrative expository books (these books give information through a story format), biographies, and journals. *The Magic School Bus* series by Joanna Cole uses multiple genres. Discussion of the books offers children a chance to ask questions, share their opinions and background knowledge, make predictions, and engage in inferential and critical thinking. Literature circles and book club discussions that focus on books about scientific topics could be very effective (El-Hindi, 2003).

Teachers should make a wealth of science trade books available for Sustained Silent Reading (SSR) or Drop Everything and Read (DEAR) periods, so that students can discover the books for themselves. Some books that can be useful for particular scientific concepts and topics are

Aliki. *Fossils Tell of Long Ago.* New York: HarperCollins, 1990. (fossils)

Carle, Eric. *The Very Hungry Caterpillar.* New York: Philomel, 1969. (animal changes)

de Paola, Tomie. *The Cloud Book.* New York: Holiday House, 1985. (clouds)

DeRegniers, Beatrice. *Shadow Book.* New York: Harcourt Brace Jovanovich, 1960. (shadows)

Kramer, Stephen. *Hidden Worlds: Looking Through a Scientist's Microscope.* Boston: Houghton Mifflin, 2001. (microscience)

Pringle, Laurence. *An Extraordinary Life: The Story of a Monarch Butterfly.* New York: Orchard, 1997. (monarch butterfly)

Provensen, Alice, and Martin Provensen. *A Year at Maple Hill Farm.* New York: Atheneum, 1978. (seasons)

Weatherford, C. B. *The Sound That Jazz Makes.* New York: Walker, 2000. (sound)

Presenting scientific ideas and common misconceptions in narrative, or story, format, rather than in a straight expository format, can help students learn scientific information (Maric and Johnson, 1990; Schumm, 1991).

The color photographs and realistic illustrations found in many science books enhance a child's enjoyment and understanding (Norton, 1995). Science informational books, such as Laurence Pringle's *Into the Woods: Exploring the Forest Ecosystem,* help children understand the laws of nature. Lynne Cherry's beautifully illustrated *A River Ran Wild: An Environmental History* documents the story of the Nashua River — its pollution and revitalization — and her *The Great Kapok Tree* relates how the animals of a Brazilian rain forest convince a man not to cut down their home. Jeannie Baker has written two thought-provoking environmental books: *Window,* which shows how a wilderness evolves into a crowded city, and *Where the Forest Meets the Sea,* in which a boy explores a prehistoric rain forest and ponders its future. In Chris Van Allsburg's *Just a Dream,* Walter's dream helps him realize the importance of caring for the environment (Galda, 1991; Galda and MacGregor, 1992; Pierce and Short, 1993/1994). *Tree of Life: The World of the African Baobab* by Barbara Bash and *The Hidden Life of the Desert* by Thomas Wiewandt emphasize the interrelatedness of plant and animal life. Another type of ecosystem is explored in *Life in a Tidal Pool* by Alvin and Virginia Silverstein (Martinez and Nash, 1990b). Animal life in general is depicted in Doris Gove's *A Water Snake's Year,* in Miriam Schliess's *Squirrel Watching,* and in Jan Sterling's *Bears* (Galda and MacGregor, 1992).

Endangered species are discussed in *No Dodos: A Counting Book of Endangered Animals* by Amanda Wallwork, in *Saving Endangered Mammals: A Field Guide to Some of the Earth's Rarest Animals* by Thane Maynard, in *The Endangered Florida Panther* by Margaret Goff Clark, and in *On the Brink of Extinction: The California Condor* by Caroline Arnold. *Four Against the Odds: The Struggle to Save Our Environment* by Stephen Krensky and *The Fire Bug Connection* by Jean Craighead George are biographies of environmental activists. *Earthways: Simple Environmental Activities for Children* by Carol Petrash and *What To Do About Pollution* by Anne Shelby contain environmental activities for children (Pierce and Short, 1993/1994). Rule and Atkinson (1994) have analyzed books about ecology to help teachers choose books that show realistic

TIME for REFLECTION

Some teachers believe that literacy instruction should take place only during reading or language arts classes. Others believe it should also take place whenever students need literacy skills in content areas. What do *you* think, and why?

ecology problems, address possible solutions, have positive tones, avoid stereotypes, and are appropriate for the intended audience.

SUMMARY

Teachers must be aware that basal reading instruction alone is not likely to prepare children thoroughly to read in the content areas. Students need to learn reading skills that are appropriate to specific subject areas, as well as general techniques that are helpful in reading expository text. Content texts present more reading difficulties than do basal reader materials. They have a greater density of ideas presented, and they lack the narrative style that is most familiar to the children. They may also contain many graphic aids that have to be interpreted. Teachers need to be aware of the readability levels of the materials they give children to read, and they must adjust their expectations and reading assignments on the basis of the students' reading levels in relation to the readability of available instructional materials.

Many techniques can be used to help children read content area materials more effectively. Among them are the Directed Reading-Thinking Activity, the guided reading procedure, Press Conference, the language experience approach, feature analysis plus writing, keeping learning logs, webbing, creative mapping, structured overviews, every-pupil-response activities, readers' theater, use of study guides, use of manipulative materials, computer approaches, integrated approaches, thematic content units, and literature-based units across the curriculum.

Each content area presents special reading challenges, such as specialized vocabulary. Reading in literature involves comprehending many literary forms, including short stories, novels, plays, poetry, biographies, and autobiographies. English textbooks cover the areas of listening, speaking, and writing. The techniques presented in these areas need to be practiced through authentic oral and written experiences. Social studies materials abound with graphic aids to be interpreted and require much application of critical reading skills. The newspaper is a good teaching aid for the social studies area. Mathematics has a special symbol system to be learned, but perhaps the greatest difficulty in this content area is the reading of story problems. Children need to learn a procedure for approaching the reading of such problems. Science and health materials contain many graphic aids. They also often include instructions for performing experiments, which must be read carefully to ensure accurate results.

Using literature selections to work with content area concepts is effective in every content area. In addition, including real-life activities and connections to the students' backgrounds of experiences enhances learning.

TEST YOURSELF

True or False

_____ 1. Content area textbooks are carefully graded in terms of difficulty and are generally appropriate to the grade levels for which they are designed.

_____ 2. One difficulty encountered in all content areas is specialized vocabulary, especially common words that have additional, specialized meanings.

_____ 3. All children in the fifth grade can benefit from the use of a single science textbook designated for the fifth grade.

_____ 4. Students often must acquire concepts and vocabulary that are introduced early in content textbooks before they can understand later content passages.

_____ 5. Offering students instruction in basal readers is sufficient to teach reading skills needed in content area textbooks.

_____ 6. Story problems in mathematics are generally extremely easy to read.

_____ 7. Mathematics materials require a child to learn a new symbol system.

_____ 8. Concrete examples are helpful in building an understanding of new concepts.

_____ 9. Science materials need not be read critically, since they are written by experts in the field.

_____ 10. An expository style of writing is very precise and highly compact.

_____ 11. The cause-and-effect pattern of organization is found in many social studies and science and health materials.

_____ 12. Social studies materials often exhibit a chronological organizational pattern.

_____ 13. All parts of the newspaper require identical reading skills.

_____ 14. Study guides may set purposes for reading.

_____ 15. The Directed Reading-Thinking Activity is a general plan for teaching either basal reader stories or content area selections.

_____ 16. Expository text structure can be taught through the language experience approach.

_____ 17. Anticipation guides are used before reading a selection and can be the basis for discussion after reading has taken place.

_____ 18. Children's literature can be used to teach social studies and science concepts.

_____ 19. Real-life mathematics problems produced by children are effective teaching tools.

_____ 20. Expository paragraph frames can scaffold children's attempts to write about content area topics.

_____ 21. Passages using math synonyms can help students build concepts.

_____ 22. Use of picture books should be avoided above the third grade.

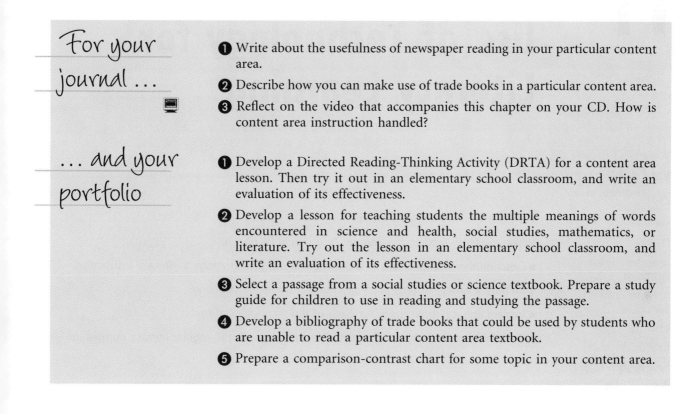

For your journal ...

1. Write about the usefulness of newspaper reading in your particular content area.

2. Describe how you can make use of trade books in a particular content area.

3. Reflect on the video that accompanies this chapter on your CD. How is content area instruction handled?

... and your portfolio

1. Develop a Directed Reading-Thinking Activity (DRTA) for a content area lesson. Then try it out in an elementary school classroom, and write an evaluation of its effectiveness.

2. Develop a lesson for teaching students the multiple meanings of words encountered in science and health, social studies, mathematics, or literature. Try out the lesson in an elementary school classroom, and write an evaluation of its effectiveness.

3. Select a passage from a social studies or science textbook. Prepare a study guide for children to use in reading and studying the passage.

4. Develop a bibliography of trade books that could be used by students who are unable to read a particular content area textbook.

5. Prepare a comparison-contrast chart for some topic in your content area.

11

Use of Technology for Literacy Learning

KEY VOCABULARY

Pay close attention to these terms when they appear in the chapter.

CD-ROM

computer-assisted instruction

computer-managed instruction

database

database programs

desktop publishing

digital literacy

DVD-ROM

electronic bulletin boards

electronic mail

electronic mailing list

hypermedia

hypertext

Internet

media literacy

multimedia

newsgroups

technological literacy

videoconferencing

videodisc

word-processing software

World Wide Web (WWW)

SETTING OBJECTIVES

When you finish reading this chapter, you should be able to

● Describe the teacher's role in choosing and using technology in literacy instruction.

● Identify a variety of technological tools for literacy instruction.

● Explain literacy applications for each of the technological tools.

● Describe how to integrate the use of technology into the regular literacy curriculum.

Today's classrooms are likely to be filled with technology that can enhance instruction in all subjects, including literacy instruction. Some of this technology has become familiar over the years, and most teachers are comfortable using it. Some emergent technology is so complex and unfamiliar that it intimidates many teachers—yet teachers should realize that all of the now-familiar technologies were once new and strange to some educators.

Indeed, teachers must learn what technological tools exist to help them with their literacy instruction, what strengths and weaknesses each of these tools has, and how best to integrate their use into the literacy curriculum. No application should be chosen just because it is novel or popular. Each one must serve a legitimate purpose in the classroom. Used properly, technological tools can offer students instruction in a range of literacy activities, from low-level drill-and-practice to the higher-order thinking activities involved in simulations. They can serve as vehicles for presenting material in class, for providing instruction, and for recording class activities for the purpose of evaluation. They can be used with whole classes or with individuals, and they can be used to individualize instruction.

Technology can be used to help students learn traditional literacy skills, which are reading and writing, as well as other language skills, but increased use of

Chapter 11 Organization

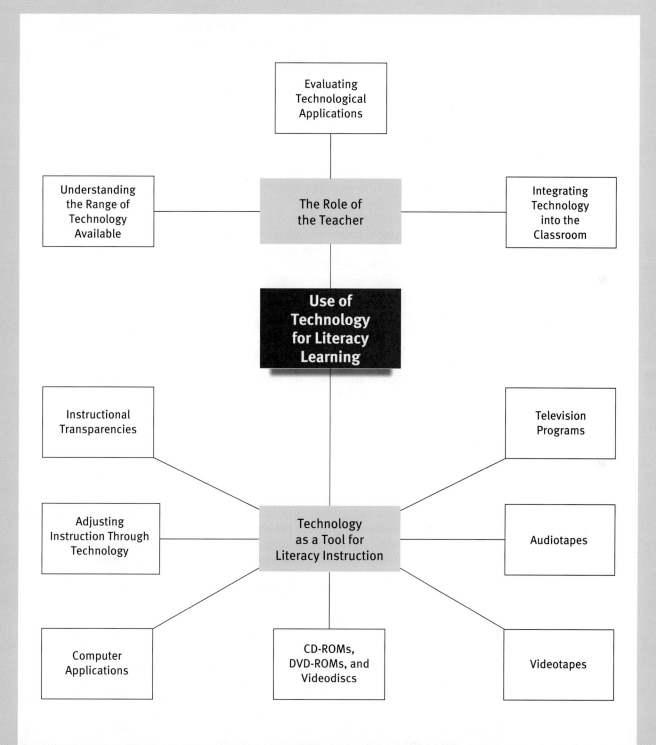

TECHNOLOGY 💻 technology has also expanded the traditional definitions of literacy to include new skills. The U.S. Department of Education (1997) defines **technological literacy** as "the ability to use computers and other technology to improve learning, productivity, and performance."

Students in one middle-school web-design course were presented with authentic tasks and software tools to learn about web design. The students worked in small groups to make decisions about how to complete real-world tasks—including planning, creating, and publishing on the Web an electronic tour of their school. They used digital cameras, computers with web authoring software, and school blueprints. Students acquired technological skills as well as improving other language skills through activities such as speaking and listening in groups, reading blueprints, and writing (Basden, 2001).

Media literacy includes questioning information that you view and read. Critical reading is hardly a new concept, and some attention has been given in the past to critical viewing of television, but critical viewing has more recently become a prominent concern. The area of media literacy incorporates consideration of "how media messages are created, marketed, and distributed" and how they can affect attitudes and behavior (Scharrer, 2002/2003, p. 355). Since students "spend an average of six-and-a-half hours per day with all media, including computers, videogames, radio, and CD players" (Scharrer, 2002/2003, p. 357), concern with media literacy is certainly well-founded.

Digital literacy is a subset of media literacy. It is the ability to understand, evaluate, and integrate information "in multiple formats that the computer can deliver" (Gilster, cited in Pool, 1997, p. 6). Valmont (2003, p. 92) points out that digital literacy involves both "active interpretation of nonverbal symbolic systems" found in electronic messages and "construction of sounds, images, graphics, photos, videos, animations, and movements to add nonverbal components to electronic messages."

The Role of the Teacher

The teacher has a critical role to play in the application of technology to literacy instruction. He or she is the decision maker about the technological tools that will be used, but a teacher cannot make valid decisions about the best technological applications for classroom use without knowing which ones are available.

● Understanding the Range of Technology Available

Overhead projectors, televisions, and audiotape recorders are so commonly available in classrooms that sometimes they are overlooked and sit unused when they would actually be ideal for particular teaching applications. Videotape recorders, CD-ROM, DVD-ROM, and videodisc players, and computers are less pervasive in schools; most schools have them, but many do not have them in the quantities that would make them be considered standard classroom equipment. In some situations, they have to be checked out of the media center; in the case of computers, some schools require that students go to scheduled labs to use the equipment. The situation is improving yearly, but by no means do all classrooms have all of this equipment. Teachers need to know what is available in their schools, not only in the way of hardware, but also in the materials to use with it: a videodisc player, for example, is useless without appropriate discs. Computer software must be available for the particular type of computer (PC or Macintosh, for example) that is in the classroom and also must be compatible with the computer's operating system (for instance, Windows, Linux, or the Macintosh OS).

Combining a number of different media, such as audio, print, graphic, and video items, results in a *multimedia* lesson or presentation. Computer systems often facilitate such use. Teachers should be aware of the possibilities of using multimedia. Using videos related to a book before students begin reading the book seems to increase understanding of and aesthetic responses to the material. Other media have also had positive effects on understanding. Students may view videos along with readings, produce videos based on readings, and use information from CD-ROMs, DVD-ROMs, and the Internet to enhance understanding (Lapp, Flood, and Fisher, 1999; Flood, Heath, and Lapp, 1997; Roe, 2000).

● Evaluating Technological Applications

All applications of technology in the classroom need to be evaluated for appropriateness and effectiveness, just as other materials should be. Teachers should not decide to use material or equipment simply because it is there. Example 11.1 shows some questions that a teacher may wish to ask about any potential application of technology in the curriculum.

Teachers have been evaluating the use of transparencies with overhead projectors, television programs, audiotapes, and films for a long time. Videotape and some videodisc evaluations are similar to those for films. There are, however, some more specific concerns in evaluating computer software, such as the ones listed in Example 11.2. on page 426.

Some of the considerations in Example 11.2 are appropriate only for software that would be considered computer-assisted instructional software, but most of them apply to any software. The best practice is to try out software before purchasing it, if

---

EXAMPLE 11.1   Evaluation of Technological Applications

To evaluate technological applications for your classroom, answer the following questions:

1. Does the application address content that is needed in this curriculum?
2. Does the application motivate students to learn the content?
3. Does the application clarify the concept for the student in some way?
4. Does the application lend itself to use in your classroom structure?
5. Is the application easy to implement?
6. Is the application instructionally sound?
7. Is the application cost-effective?
8. Is the application more effective than other possible approaches to the task?

> ### EXAMPLE 11.2 Evaluating Computer Software
>
> When evaluating computer software, ask the following questions:
>
> 1. Is the program compatible with the available hardware and operating system?
> 2. Does the program meet a curricular need better than another approach would?
> 3. Is the program well documented?
>   a. Are the objectives of the program clearly presented?
>   b. Are the steps involved in running the program clearly stated?
>   c. Are hardware requirements for the program clearly specified, and is this hardware available?
>   d. Are time requirements for program use described, and are they reasonable for classroom use? (If a program can be saved at any time and re-entered at the same place, some of the problems with time are alleviated.)
> 4. Is the program user-friendly?
> 5. Is there a management system that keeps up with a student's performance on the program, if that would be appropriate?
> 6. Are the screens well designed and readable?
> 7. Is the program essentially crash-proof?
> 8. Is feedback about performance offered to the students? Is the feedback appropriate for them?
> 9. Do the students have control over:
>   a. the speed of the program presentation?
>   b. the level of difficulty of the program?
>   c. the degree of prompting offered by the program (including seeing instructions for use)?
>   d. the sequence of presentation of material?
> 10. Is the program highly interactive, requiring more of the student than just page turning?
> 11. Is sound used appropriately, if at all? Can the sound be turned off without destroying the effectiveness of the program?
> 12. Is color used effectively, if at all?
> 13. Is the program adaptable for a variety of levels of students? Are your students within this range?
> 14. Is the material free of stereotypes and bias?
> 15. Is there a way that the teacher can modify the program for a particular class, set of data, or student? Is this procedure protected against student tampering?
> 16. Is the information presented in the program accurate and presented clearly and in grammatically correct form?

possible, because some pedagogically unsound, user-*un*friendly, and inflexible software is available, along with the many good programs. Reviews in professional periodicals such as *The Reading Teacher* can be helpful, but consulting them is less revealing than actually using the programs.

● Integrating Technology into the Classroom

Any application of technology—whether it is a television program, a videotape, or a computer program—should fit seamlessly into the teacher's curricular structure, or it should not be used. The application should present, reinforce, or teach a concept; offer tools for recording, collecting, and retrieving data; motivate students in their study; or provide assessment opportunities. The content should be appropriate to the subject area, grade level, and maturity level of the students. The presentation format should fit into the classroom organizational structure, and the use should be adaptable to the time available. Teachers must decide which applications fit these criteria and which do not. The evaluation questions found in Example 11.2, along with their knowledge of the students and the curriculum, can help teachers with this decision making.

Various technological applications are ideal for use with individual students, small groups, or whole classes. Teachers can choose the best applications for particular circumstances. Some people have the erroneous belief that working at a computer has to be a solitary activity; but, on the contrary, students' social interactions while working on some types of computer projects can be highly beneficial. Students in those situations have had a tendency to help each other spontaneously (Dwyer, 1994).

LITERATURE

Integration can take place across the curriculum. Morden (1994) reports an interdisciplinary simulation project in which she and a colleague involved students with literature selections about traveling, followed by the use of simulation software, such as *Oregon Trail* (MECC) and *Country Canada* (Didatech). Students chose travel destinations and gathered information about them, using letter writing with word processors and communication with people all over the world through *WorldClassroom*, a curriculum-based educational telecommunications network. Databases were used as organizational tools, and CD-ROMs and laserdiscs were viewed. Students had a budget, and they had to use a spreadsheet to plan an itinerary, staying within the budget. They "earned" money by doing jobs for the class or winning test review games. They planned a bon voyage party and even made invitations with *Print Shop* (Broderbund). As they "traveled" to their destinations, they collected information from people in those locations through telecommunications, CD-ROMs, laserdiscs, and even traditional print. They kept logs of their travels, one year on paper and the next year on audiotape, and developed a multimedia scrapbook.

DIVERSITY

DIVERSITY

STANDARDS AND ASSESSMENT

Smolin and Lawless (2003) describe activities in a second-grade bilingual classroom. The teacher asked students to interview bilingual business owners near their school about what it means to be bilingual. The activity was designed to meet "standards in language arts, social studies, and technology" (p. 570). To accomplish the task, students used computers, digital cameras, video recorders, and tape recorders. Instruction in the use of each of these tools focused on how they could be used to facilitate the process of interviewing and synthesizing the resulting

Integrating Technology into Classroom Activities

Students in a fifth-grade class in California needed funds to go to a science camp, and they also needed appropriate materials, on easy reading levels, about Hispanic leaders. They decided on a multimedia project to develop their own materials, not only about local Hispanic heroes, but also about African-American and Vietnamese-American community leaders as well. They planned to sell the materials to others to raise funds for science camp.

The fifth graders identified people whom they wished to interview; planned, conducted, and video-taped the interviews; and wrote up the main points from each one.

The students carried out their plans by first studying existing interviews of famous people to help them construct their questions; then they formed groups and practiced by interviewing each other. The actual interviews were conducted by collaborative groups, with one student videotaping, one asking questions, and one taking notes. The interviews were critiqued and transcribed, and the key points were summarized. This task involved much proofreading and editing. The teacher, Cliff Gilkey, moved from group to group, monitoring the students' progress and offering assistance.

Analysis of Scenario

The students were working on an authentic task to meet two real-life needs. The technology was used as a tool to help meet these needs. The process involved a number of important literacy skills as the students read interviews, composed questions, took notes, summarized material, and proofread and edited material. Cliff Gilkey acted as a coach and a facilitator of learning.

TIME for REFLECTION

Some people think that only "cutting edge" technology should be used in today's classrooms. They would discard applications that have been around a long time, referring to them as "anti-quated." In what ways can older technology accomplish curricular goals more effectively than newer applications?

information into an electronic slide show, which was shared with other students through e-mail. This process also enhanced students' visual literacy skills—understanding and producing visual messages (Smolin and Lawless, 2003; International Visual Literacy Association, 1998). Students gathered information from the World Wide Web, using websites that the teacher chose for age-appropriateness and sites located by using search engines designed for children, such as Yahooligans and Ask Jeeves for Kids (Smolin and Lawless, 2003).

Students should use technological tools to complete authentic tasks that involve both basic and advanced skills. They can work collaboratively, with the teacher monitoring and assisting in the activities. The work may take place over a period of time, as is true in unit studies. Means and Olson (1994) have described one such example of integration. A summary is found in the Classroom Scenario above on integrating technology into classroom activities.

Technology as a Tool for Literacy Instruction

This chapter, of course, is concerned primarily with the application of technology as a tool for literacy instruction, rather than for instruction in general. The following are ways in which many types of technology can be used for this purpose.

● Instructional Transparencies

Use of transparencies displayed on overhead projectors allows teachers who are not artistically inclined to present various types of material in an attractive way. Primary teachers, for example, might present sentences containing rebuses (pictures that represent words or syllables) to facilitate the reading of more advanced sentences early in the instructional program. Instructional transparencies may be produced manually, developed on a computer, or obtained from a commercial source.

Writing on blank transparencies as they present new material enables teachers to provide visual clarification or presentation of ideas without turning their backs to their classes, a plus for communication and for maintaining control. This use of transparencies is effective before reading a story or content selection when teachers want to record semantic webs of prior knowledge about a topic or entries for the *K* and *W* portions of a K-W-L chart. After reading, students can use transparencies to expand the web or to fill in the *L* portion of the K-W-L chart. (See Chapter 5 for more about these charts, including an example of one such chart.)

When describing the steps in a process, such as the steps in the process writing approach (see Chapter 8), the teacher can use a series of transparencies with overlays that show each step as it is mentioned. In the process writing approach, a blank transparency can be used to record the results of a brainstorming session. Students, individually or in groups, may organize the results of the brainstorming on other blank transparencies for display and discussion. Current student work can be displayed on transparencies, and students can discuss possible needs for revision, if the permission of the creators is obtained; or anonymous student work from previous classes may be used for this purpose.

● Television Programs

Many classrooms are equipped with televisions, making possible the incorporation of educational programming into instruction. "The National Council of Teachers of English and International Reading Association Standards for the English Language Arts (1996) mentions popular film and television as visual texts worthy of study in K–12 classrooms" (Morrell, 2002, pp. 74–75).

Some shows, such as *Reading Rainbow*, fit naturally into the literacy curriculum. In *Reading Rainbow* programs, books are read, illustrations are shared, and related activities are incorporated into the program to make the book presentations more meaningful. *Storytime, Wishbone,* and *Between the Lions* are other public broadcasting programs that fit the literacy curriculum. Other shows have less obvious connections, but any show that covers content currently being studied in a thematic unit would be likely to provide background information that would make reading and writing about that topic easier for students. If scheduling to fit the unit's prescribed time slot is a problem, it may be possible to videotape the program for later use, but teachers

must be careful to adhere to copyright laws. As a follow-up to viewing in class, teachers can encourage caregivers to watch episodes of the same programs at home with students.

Cable television connections are available in many schools. Special programming and teacher's guides are provided by some cable operators. *Cable in the Classroom* is "a noncommercial service aimed at in-school audiences" (Heinich et al., 1999, p. 338). Through it, local cable operators and national cable programmers "provide schools with free basic cable service and … commercial-free television programming" ("Cable in the Classroom Fact Sheet," 1999, p. 2).

Sharon Joseph tapes appropriate *Booknotes* episodes from C-SPAN and uses them as models for students who are creating presentations about books they are reading in class. She cites as a good example a *Booknotes* interview with Hillary Clinton about her book *It Takes a Village* (Butler, 1999).

LITERATURE

Taking notes on television programs is also a good way for students to apply literacy skills. The notes may provide source material for reports that will be written later or projects that are being undertaken as a part of unit study. Movies that have pertinent content may be viewed, and students may then write reviews related to their accuracy and effectiveness. Some movies are based on children's books and can serve as an introduction or follow-up to the reading of those books. Some books that have related movies are *Sarah, Plain and Tall; Holes;* and *Harriet, the Spy*. Films can also be discussed along with accompanying texts with similar themes. This can help the students hone their critical reading skills as they compare and contrast the books and films.

● Audiotapes

DIVERSITY

STANDARDS AND
ASSESSMENT

Sometimes a teacher may wish to use prerecorded audiotapes that provide information about a subject being studied in class. Prerecorded books on tape for read-alongs or prerecorded music that goes along with poetry that is being read may also be used. (This may be done by using listening stations at which several children can listen to the same tape at the same time.) Students who are having difficulty reading the material and English language learners can listen to the tape as they read, building sight vocabulary as they hear a fluent reader's correct phrasing and pronunciation. Teachers may tape the read-alouds that they do for the class and make them available to students who missed the reading or who wish to read along with the tapes. However, teachers most often use audiotape recorders to tape class activities. Tapes of group discussions or class presentations can be used for later evaluation of the activities. Audiotapes of a child reading orally over a period of time can be used as portfolio items for evaluation, since they provide convincing evidence of progress.

Many students have personal audiotape recorders. They may use these to tape themselves reading aloud or practicing an oral presentation and then listen to the tapes to decide if they are ready to perform for the class. They may also tape class lectures and discussions to review before tests or to use for note taking in a less stressful situation, with the time pressure removed.

● Videotapes

Many classrooms are equipped with videotape recorders, and others have them available for checkout from the media center. Videotapes are available for purchase,

Videotapes are available on most topics that are included in the school curriculum.
(© Bob Daemmrich)

for checkout from school and public libraries, and for rental from video stores. They have almost completely replaced films and filmstrips as educational tools in most classrooms. Videotape recorders are easier to operate than most film projectors, and the teacher can easily return to a part of the videotape to view it again.

Videotapes are available on most topics that are included in the school curriculum, and they are good for the following:

- Introducing new topics for discussion

- Making new concepts seem more concrete as they are presented in the context of real-life situations

- Providing a focus for follow-up discussion at the end of a unit of study

DIVERSITY Videotapes are particularly useful in illustrating text materials for less proficient readers or students with limited experiential backgrounds. They may help to bring a literary selection to life for students or help them understand a process that is described in a content-area textbook.

LITERATURE Movies based on children's books are often available on videotape or may be videotaped from television for use in the classroom. If the students have already read the book, they may compare and contrast the book and the movie. If they have not already read the book, they may view the movie first; and then students who choose to do so as an individual project may read the book and do the comparison. (See the Focus on Strategies on use of videotapes on page 432.) In some cases there are several

---

FOCUS ON STRATEGIES | Use of Videotapes

Two classes of middle-school students read the book *Bridge to Terabithia* and then viewed a videotape of a movie based on the book. They compared and contrasted the book and the video, coming out firmly in favor of the book. The students felt that the movie at times differed from the book "for no reason at all," although they saw that some changes had been made because of time constraints. They commented, too, that many important details had been left out of the movie, making the character portrayals weaker.

These classes later read the book *Tuck Everlasting* and then viewed a videotape of a movie based on it. Once again they compared and contrasted the movie and the book, with similar results. They found many changes to be unnecessary and inexplicable and even decided that the impact of the plot, as it unfolded, was lessened because the movie contained some foreshadowing that was not in the book (Roe and Smith, 1997).

---

movies based on the same book. *Heidi* is an example of such a book. The children could determine which of the movies portrayed the book most accurately, if videotapes of multiple versions were available.

A good application of videotape recorders in the classroom is having students make their own videotapes of class presentations or field trips. They can write scripts for skits or plays, do the casting, rehearse for the performances, videotape the productions, and edit the tapes until they have polished products. Creative drama and readers' theater performances can also be videotaped. Simulated newscasts can be written, dramatized, and videotaped, with editing as a final step. These activities involve many technological and higher-order thinking skills. A reference for teachers interested in creation of such tapes is *Creating Videos for School Use* by William Valmont (1995).

Today the prices of camcorders have dropped significantly, and their size has decreased, which makes them easier for small hands to manipulate. Special editing equipment still may not be available, but connecting two videotape recorders makes basic editing possible.

● CD-ROMs, DVD-ROMs, and Videodiscs

CD-ROMs, DVD-ROMs, and *videodiscs* can store large amounts of text, audio, and video information in relatively little space. They may be used to provide information for unit study, as videotapes do. They also generally offer high-quality images and sound. Some are interactive, allowing students to select words to be pronounced, defined, or pictured, for example. CD-ROMs and DVD-ROMs have the advantage over videotapes of holding much more information — whole reference books or works of fiction can be stored on them. Unlike videotapes, CD-ROMs, DVD-ROMs, and videodiscs make it easy for the user to access information from them in a nonlinear fashion, selecting particular information through keystrokes or mouse clicks with a CD-ROM or DVD-ROM or by a remote control unit or a bar code reader with a videodisc. Actually, CD-ROMs, DVD-ROMs, and videodiscs can all be controlled by a computer, and all are good instructional tools. However, these technologies may not be accessible for all teachers. Relatively few classrooms are routinely supplied with videodisc or DVD players, and not all classroom computers have CD-ROM or DVD-ROM drives.

Windows on Science (Optical Data Corporation) is an elementary-level videodisc program that integrates the use of videodiscs, reading, and writing. The videodiscs offer photographs, movie clips, animations, and diagrams to reinforce the science concepts. There are lesson plans to be used in conjunction with the discs (Rock and Cummings, 1994).

Among the materials most widely available on CD-ROM are electronic books. Some simply show the book pages on the screen, and the user "turns pages" by clicking a mouse or touching a key. These programs have little to recommend them over books, which are more portable and do not require hardware. For some students, they may increase motivation to read, but others find reading from the screen more of a strain and less satisfying than reading from a printed page. Other books on CD-ROM take better advantage of the capabilities of computers. (See the next section, on computer applications, for more about CD-ROMs.)

Reference works and movies are the educational resources most commonly found on DVD-ROM at the present time. One example is *The Complete National Geographic: 109 Years of National Geographic Magazine* (National Geographic Society), a natural literacy support for thematic studies in science and social studies.

● Computer Applications

The computer generation is indeed here. Leu (2000) points out that "the Internet is entering classrooms at a faster rate than books, newspapers, magazines, movies, overhead projectors, televisions, or even telephones." Today's children expect to use computers, which now pervade every aspect of life. Computers are found more frequently in classrooms today than they were in the past, although they still are not available in large enough quantities to offer every elementary school student substantial computer time each day. Even though not all classrooms have computers, most classes have some access, either through resident computers, computers on carts that can be checked out from a central location, or a computer lab that has scheduled times for use by various classes.

Even when only one computer is available in the classroom, there are many possible applications. With a projection device, the computer can be used for recording language experience stories (see Chapter 7) or any cooperative writing, including creative writing and report writing. These writing efforts can be printed for use by individual students or small groups. The computer can be used to display simulation programs, with children making joint decisions about required choices and a designated student entering data. It can be used to record in databases project information that can be printed out for class use. Or students can work in small groups to prepare sections of a multimedia presentation, which are then combined for sharing with the whole class and other classes.

When computers must be checked out of a media center for use in the classroom, careful planning and completion of off-computer preparation activities before the

There are many appropriate applications for computers in literary instruction. *(© Elizabeth Crews)*

TIME for REFLECTION

Some teachers believe that little can be accomplished when only one computer is available for a whole class. What useful applications for a single computer can you generate?

computers are brought to the classroom can facilitate effective use. Paper-and-pencil rough drafts may be developed for written products before students start using a word-processing or desktop-publishing program, for example.

Some teachers use authoring software or programming languages to produce their own programs. This option is extremely time-consuming, especially if programming languages are used, but authoring systems demand less computer expertise, and teachers can learn to use them within a shorter time frame to produce computer-based courseware. Some authoring systems are fairly user-friendly, containing English statements and menus, prompts, and help options to guide the teacher in choosing programming actions in a step-by-step manner. They provide, for example, lesson outlines that the teacher fills in with text, questions, answers, feedback, and prompts. Multimedia authoring tools may be used to combine text, graphics, and sound to present information.

Computer applications—whether produced commercially or by teachers—may be made basically linear or highly interactive. Anderson-Inman (1998, p. 679) points out that "any chunk of electronic text (e.g., a character, word, phrase, or paragraph) can be linked to any other chunk, allowing nonlinear movement through an electronic text document. ... This linking mechanism is the foundation for materials referred to as hypertext (or hypermedia)." With *hypermedia*, a variety of media—including text, full motion video, sound clips, graphics, and still images—can be viewed and/or heard in an order chosen by the user (Poole, 1997; Wilhelm, 2000). The term *multimedia* refers to the mixing of different media. Multimedia computer programs generally have interactive capabilities. For example, when reading an entry from a multimedia encyclopedia, a student may click on a word or symbol to view a picture, see a definition, watch a video clip, or hear an audio clip related to the topic.

Hypertext allows enhancements to text that assist comprehension; with hypertext and hypermedia applications, for example, a student can use a mouse pointer and click when the cursor is over boldfaced words in the material. This may cause the program to display a glossary text that defines the word, to provide a picture, and/or to read the word aloud. In this sense, hypertext is similar to footnotes in showing relationships between texts (Klein and Olson, 2001). (Some of the books on CD-ROM discussed in this chapter are examples of hypertext and hypermedia applications.) Hypertext applications may also provide graphic organizers or interspersed questions. They may offer options for taking notes as the reading progresses and later printing out notes for review or as a basis for developing essays.

Hypertext materials present new reading challenges. Readers may continue to click on keywords that lead them further away from the original text; then they may have trouble returning to their points of origin, a situation referred to as a "navigational problem" (Reinking, 1997). There is also the danger that hypertext and hypermedia will lead students to read about a large number of topics superficially, rather than reading in depth about any single topic (Leu, 1996). Obviously, hyperlinks and hypermedia found in electronic texts complicate the process of comprehending text material for those who are accustomed to reading traditional print, which is linear in nature (Coiro, 2000; RAND Reading Study Group, 2002).

Word Processing and Desktop Publishing

One of the most obvious applications of computers to literacy instruction is the use of *word-processing software* for both creative writing and writing of a functional nature, such as the writing of research reports. This software takes much of the dreaded labor out of editing and revising written products. Since words, sentences, and longer passages can be moved around with a few clicks of a mouse (or, with some older software, a few keystrokes), students are less reluctant to reconsider the content, organization, and mechanical aspects of their papers and to make needed changes. Freedom from recopying an entire document is a definite plus, especially for younger students who may still be laboring to perfect their handwriting. Roe (1987) and others have found that students who are allowed to do their creative writing on the computer, rather than with paper and pencil, tend to write longer pieces and to feel less resentful of making changes.

There are word-processing programs on many different levels of difficulty, so it is possible to find tools easy enough for primary students and tools powerful enough to meet the needs of older ones. The full facilitative effects of word processing on the quality of student writing may not be evident, however, until students become proficient in the use of the program and the equipment (Owston, Murphy, and Wideman, 1992; Schumm and Saumell, 1993). Peer assistance with computer tasks can help alleviate problems with the use of programs and equipment. It often appears to occur spontaneously, but teachers can capitalize on students' expertise by assigning peer tutors. There are particular advantages when lower-achieving students get the chance to be the experts (Sandholtz, Ringstaff, and Dwyer, 1997). Butler and Cox (1992) found that when first graders are allowed to work in pairs to compose stories on a computer, they discuss language usage, spelling, and punctuation, as well as the mechanics of computer use. They reread what they have written frequently, as a springboard to adding new text, as both children contribute to the story line.

Klein and Olson (2001, p. 233) point out that "electronic media intensify the functions of text by making them faster, denser, tidier, and more convenient," which makes these media especially useful for writing. Major word-processing programs include features that make mechanical aspects of writing, such as printing, spelling, and copying, easier. These features are most helpful to early elementary students and older ones with learning disabilities (Klein and Olson, 2001). When word-processing software is used, the students' written products can be printed in a neat, legible form to be read by class members. This feature may make students take more pride in their work.

Use of spelling checkers and grammar checkers alerts students to words that *may* be misspelled or constructions that *may* need modification, but the checkers do not make the decisions about what will actually be done. Students have to look at each comment and decide upon its merits. This is a critical reading activity that is a natural part of the writing process.

Many word-processing programs include dictionaries and thesauruses, which students can use to help them make decisions about their word choices. The dictionary can be used in deciding if a word has the correct meaning for the context; the thesaurus can be used in choosing a synonym when a word has been overused in a selection or in finding a word that fits the situation exactly.

Edinger (1994) reports that her school supplied inexpensive word processors (Tandy WP2s) for each child in her fourth-grade writing workshop. She found that the children were more willing to revise and to do multiple drafts of research papers than they had been previously, and that use of the spelling checker helped weak spellers find and correct spelling errors, with the aid of a conventional dictionary. Students polished their work more than they had in the past, and with the aid of the word processors, many began to write enthusiastically for the first time.

Teachers also benefit personally from use of word-processing programs to revise and edit their own written products (such as handouts, tests, and communications with parents) with more ease. Additionally, they can use projection devices to allow an entire group to see the material they have written on the computer, instead of writing on a chart or on the board.

In the past most teachers used **desktop-publishing programs** in order to integrate text and graphics in a document, flowing text around graphics, formatting text into columns, and using a number of styles and sizes of type, but now many word-processing programs will perform these functions. Students can write stories and research papers and can produce class newspapers and magazines with either word-processing software or desktop-publishing software. Multimedia programs such as *HyperStudio* (Roger Wagner) may also be used. With *HyperStudio*, students can create presentations that include audio or video clips, artwork, and buttons to lead to information about the authors of the presentations (Heide and Henderson, 1994; Robinette, 1995).

Desktop-publishing programs and multimedia programs are often used to set up special formats for such applications as banners and greeting cards. The programs may have clip art (ready-made images that can be used for illustrations), and students may be able to create their own illustrations or modify the available clip art. *The Print Shop Deluxe* (Broderbund) enables students to produce signs, posters, and banners, as well as to combine text and graphics to customize reports. With *Imagination Express* (EdMark) students can make electronic books with sound effects and animation. A variety of *Imagination Express Series* titles can be used in social studies and science classes. *Creative Writer* (Microsoft Corp.) is a creative-writing and desktop-publishing program, and *Classroom Publisher* (Staz Software) is an easy-to-use desktop-publishing program suitable for grades three and up (Cowan, 1996). Lee (2000) found that using desktop-publishing software helped fifth graders feel like "real writers" and that book reports posted on the World Wide Web caused sixth graders to care about the grammar, accuracy, and tone of their writing.

Multimedia Publishing

Multimedia publishing software enables students to "expand classroom publishing to include colorful graphics, moving images, sound effects …, music, and written and spoken words" (D'Ignazio, 1991, p. 250). Such options make high-interest projects possible. For example, *The Bank Street Writer for the Macintosh* (Scholastic Software) offers multiple fonts and has a hypertext function with buttons that allows students to provide additional explanations about their text, create databases of information about their subjects, or create sounds for their products. A graphic gallery, spelling checker, and thesaurus come with the package, and other Macintosh graphics can be imported. With today's multimedia programs, students can input text with the keyboard, draw onscreen (or draw on paper and scan the material into the computer), use predrawn pictures and backgrounds, record sounds to include in documents, or select sounds from prerecorded ones. This helps students with varied learning styles to approach compositions more easily (Rose and Meyer, 1994).

Students and teachers can develop multimedia presentations with a variety of special software, including Microsoft's *PowerPoint*, Multimedia Design's *mPower*, and *HyperStudio* (Roger Wagner). The Focus on Strategies on page 438 describes how two middle-school classes completed such a presentation.

STANDARDS AND ASSESSMENT

Teachers face a challenge in evaluating students' multimedia projects. They need to consider the planning (storyboarding); the variety, appropriateness, and documentation of sources; the organization and design; the clarity of navigation signals; and the choice and integration of media (Brunner, 1996). Slick presentation cannot be allowed to overshadow accuracy and organization.

Databases and Electronic Reference Works

Databases are organized collections of data that have the information filed in such a way that it can be retrieved by category. Databases are usually created and searched by special *database programs*. Students can create their own databases, or they may refer to a variety of databases prepared by others.

FOCUS ON
STRATEGIES
Multimedia Presentations

The two middle-school classes that are discussed in two other Focus on Strategies features in this chapter developed an *mPower* presentation on each of the books that they read along with their university e-mail partners, and the university partners viewed the presentations just before the end-of-semester meetings.

The middle-school classroom teachers organized their classes into cooperative groups to work on specific portions of the multimedia presentation and developed a schedule for the group assignments. Each group produced a rough draft to show what it planned to do. Then each group used the computer to create its portion of the presentation. To do this, the students had to decide what important incidents to include, what sequence to follow, what visual and sound features to incorporate, and what transitions to use. They used the *mPower* program to develop a series of carefully designed and sequenced slides that represented main events and characters in the books. They incorporated student-produced drawings, photography, and music to develop powerful presentations of content. The university students were impressed by the professional appearance and the thoroughness of the presentations. Such productions required a depth of understanding of the material that went far beyond the ability to describe the stories in words.

Database programs are valuable research tools and can be used to help students organize data for writing reports. Database programs make possible the categorization, storage, and orderly retrieval of data collected during research reading. When using databases, students perform such tasks as reading and following directions, taking notes, gathering and categorizing data, summarizing, posing questions, predicting outcomes, making comparisons and contrasts using collected information, using reference materials, identifying keywords for efficient data access, and testing hypotheses. All of these activities require them to be active, purposeful readers (Layton and Irwin, 1989). When creating databases, students also analyze and synthesize large amounts of information (Heide and Henderson, 1994).

Some libraries now have their holdings listed in computer databases that can be searched by author, title, and subject. Many elementary schools, however, still have traditional card catalogs.

Electronic reference works, such as electronic dictionaries, thesauruses, and encyclopedias, are elaborate databases that are searchable by keywords and categories. Such reference works take some of the manual labor out of library research, but they still require the same cognitive skills for location of information. Electronic reference works are available at different levels of difficulty. Teachers need to check the intended age groups for these tools when purchases are made.

DIVERSITY Electronic dictionaries for English language learners (ELLs), such as the *Longman Interactive English Dictionary (LIED)*, provide special aids that print dictionaries cannot offer (Butler-Pascoe and Wiburg, 2003). The *LIED* allows students to "compile and save pictures, audio, and video excerpts to contextualize the meanings of words and concepts" (Butler-Pascoe and Wiburg, 2003, p. 126). Help features include audio pronunciation, phonetic transcription, a grammar guide, verb formation, and many others.

Electronic Books

Labbo (2000, p. 542) says that "CD-ROM talking books are interactive, digital versions of stories that employ multimedia features such as animation, music, sound effects, highlighted text, and modeled fluent reading." More and more talking books are being produced as time passes.

The Living Books series from Broderbund offers many familiar children's books on CD-ROM, as well as some new selections. The pages contain text and illustrations, just as are found in printed books, but offer the reader a variety of options. The reader can choose to have the story read in English, Spanish, or Japanese. The child can read the story independently or have the computer read it aloud. In addition, if the reader clicks on objects in the pictures, some of the picture elements will become animated and may even produce sound effects. This interactivity makes the books highly motivational, but students may be distracted from actual reading by the special effects.

DIVERSITY 🌐

The Discis Books series is also available on CD-ROM. Students can click on words to get pronunciations, sound effects, syllable divisions, and explanations. The words that students click on for more information are saved in recall lists that the teacher can check. Students can also click on pictures to see labels, hear pronunciations, hear sound effects, and get syllable divisions. Words or phrases can be highlighted as the book is read; this helps to build word recognition. Students can hear the word used for that object or concept in another language if they wish. Online audio help is available to the user. Activity guides accompany the CD-ROMs to give teachers ideas for story preparation, story connections, and story extensions.

Teachers should model the use of the books' features so that the children will get the maximum benefit from such use. Children may also need teachers, paraprofessionals, or student assistants to offer some help with the software, especially when it is initially used. They may first listen to the story and then, in subsequent readings, read along with it or perhaps echo-read it. Labbo (2000) suggests many other approaches to these materials, from word-level activities, such as selecting rhyming words, to metacognitive- and story-response activities, including comparing the digital version of the story to the book version. Teachers must use their own creativity and knowledge of their students to guide the use of electronic books.

DIVERSITY 🌐

English language learners benefit from the "pictures, animation, and other context cues provided by interactive CD-ROM books. ... *Just Grandma and Me* and *Arthur's Teacher Trouble* from the Broderbund Living Books Series, for example, are excellent reading materials for young ELLs" (Butler-Pascoe and Wiburg, 2003, p. 125).

Electronic books are also available on the Internet. For example, there is an online version of *Alice's Adventures in Wonderland* at **www.megabrands.com/alice/indexx.html**.

The Internet

The ***Internet*** is a "network of networks" encompassing a multitude of computers throughout the world. Each of thousands of server computers supplies different information or services. The ***World Wide Web (WWW)*** is part of the Internet. The

Web has been reported to contain billions of pages (Thornburg, 2002). Hypermedia is "the platform of the World Wide Web" (Wilhelm, 2000, p. 4). The Web enables users to choose special words or symbols, with a mouse click or a keyboard stroke, and be automatically connected to related Web locations. Locating information on research topics in this way is much easier than having to know and enter each address for the locations of interest.

Students can also search the Internet, using special browsers (such as *Netscape Navigator* and *Microsoft Internet Explorer*) and search engines (such as AltaVista, Lycos, and WebCrawler) that allow keyword searches, to locate information to use for reports or unit studies. This information may be in the form of text, sound clips, video clips, and/or graphics. Students will need instruction in the use of browsers and search engines. They will probably also need practice in generating keywords to use with the search engines. An enjoyable way to practice searching for information on school topics is to participate in an Internet scavenger hunt for information specified by the teacher (Cotton, 1996). Another way is described in the Model Activity below.

Internet use causes teachers to look at literacy in new ways. According to El-Hindi (1998, p. 694), "being literate involves integrating reading and writing, navigating through information sources, discriminating between important and unimportant information, responding to e-mail, or engaging in electronic chat sessions." This Internet literacy view fits well into a constructivist perspective. The constructivist position that instruction should be organized around primary concepts is supported by the Internet, where a search may turn up hundreds of sites related to the topic of study, and the students can see how multifaceted the topic actually is. Current information on topics is also available, enhancing the students' ability to see the relevance of some studies. Inquiry learning, an approach consistent with a constructivist perspective, is facilitated by the ability of students to do extensive searches to answer questions they have generated (El-Hindi, 1998).

MODEL ACTIVITIES | **Internet Research for Making Books**

Read several informational alphabet books to your class. (See Chapter 10 for suggestions of thematic alphabet books.) Discuss the characteristics of these alphabet books.

Next, choose a topic, such as "Mammals," that you are studying in a particular content area. Discuss what has already been discovered about this topic.

Then divide the class into small groups, assigning one or more letters to each group. Let group members search the Internet for mammals that would fit the assigned letters. Have each group choose, from the mammals they locate, the ones to use for their book pages. Then have them write and print book pages for their assigned letters, using desktop-publishing software or word-processing software. Put the pages together to form a class book. Print multiple copies to use in the classroom, to share with other classes, and to send home to promote home-school communication. Finally, read the book to the class and let the group members responsible for each page tell about their search strategies.

Students may, however, need to overcome some of the challenges of using hypermedia, described earlier in the chapter, in order to develop the digital literacy needed to construct information from Internet sources. "Web-based texts are typically nonlinear, interactive, and inclusive of multiple media forms" (Coiro, 2003, p. 459). For example, on NASA's website for children, which is called StarChild: A Learning Center for Young Astronomers (**http://starchild.gsfc.nasa.gov/docs/ StarChild/StarChild.html**), a hyperlink in a passage about one topic may lead to a definition of the linked word, to a new passage on a related topic, to activities for the topic, or to a page for an e-mail message to the webmaster. Students need to decide whether or not to use the available links in their quest for information. If students try these links, they must be able to navigate back to the original location. In addition, web-based texts have many interactive aspects. For example, students may be asked to post comments on the material electronically and read the postings of others.

Web-based texts frequently combine texts with pictures, sounds, animations, and other representations. Sometimes video and audio clips must be deliberately downloaded before they are available for examination. Therefore, students are faced with accessing, as well as comprehending, these features.

When students conduct Internet research, teachers and students face some other challenges. One problem with letting students use the Internet for research is that the accuracy of material that is posted to electronic bulletin boards or placed on web pages is not monitored. Much inaccurate information is on the Internet, along with the useful material. Students should be encouraged to cross-check information that they find on the Internet in printed reference books, whenever possible. They need to see if the material is documented and to treat both undocumented and anonymous material as questionable. Santerre (2000, p. 37) believes that it is the teacher's responsibility "to help students learn to be critical readers of Web sites." Example 11.3 offers suggestions for evaluating websites. Rowlands (2000) also is concerned with discerning worthwhile and trustworthy sites. She points out that sites supported by governmental agencies, educational institutions, and professional organizations are best for use in developing curricula.

Teachers may want to supply students with a list of reliable sites that contain information related to the current topic of study. McVey (1997) suggests that teachers may want to perform Internet searches, compile a set of links, and use this material as a tailor-made textbook. The material can be made to fit specific course needs and the particular group of students. Students may also use a teacher-supplied list as a basis for class research. Reliable sites include the Library of Congress site at **www.loc.gov**, the NASA Quest Educational Web Site at **http://quest.arc.nasa.gov**, sites for the Appalachian Educational Laboratory at **www.ael.org** and the North Central Regional Educational Laboratory at **www.ncrel.org**, and the Smithsonian site at **www.si.edu**. The material in boldface gives the Internet addresses (called URLs, or Uniform Resource Locators) of the listed sites. The ones listed here are stable sites, but another hazard of providing students with a list of sites that you have found to have good information is that many sites are not stable. The World Wide Web is changing daily, and a site that you find today may not be there tomorrow. This situation can be frustrating for searchers. Example 11.4 is part of the NASA Quest Educational Web site.

> **EXAMPLE 11.3   Website Evaluation Questions**
>
> **Evaluating Websites**
>
> When you are evaluating websites, you must consider the reliability of the sources of the material, the accuracy of the content, the clarity of the material presented, and the purposes of the sites. Ask yourself the following questions when judging a website:
>
> 1. Can you determine who has developed the site? (If not, you may not want to place undue confidence in its contents.) If so, is the developer a reliable source for the information you are seeking? (A noted authority on the topic or an agency of the government would be considered reliable. Someone you have not heard of before may need to be investigated.)
>
> 2. Is there enough information given on the site developer that qualifications can be checked? (If not, be cautious.)
>
> 3. Are sources provided for information displayed on the site, so the user can cross-check information? If they are, this is a definite plus.
>
> 4. Does any of the information conflict with reliable sources that you have consulted? (If some of the information is in question, all of it is suspect.)
>
> 5. Is the layout of the site busy and confusing, making information difficult to evaluate? (Disorganization, particularly, is a bad sign.)
>
> 6. Is site navigation easy? (Sloppy navigational methods sometimes indicate a lack of attention to detail.)
>
> 7. Is the presented material grammatically correct, and is it free from errors in spelling and mechanics? (If it is not, the clarity is badly affected.)
>
> 8. Is the site free of advertising? (If not, look for possible bias of information presented, based on the advertising present.)
>
> 9. If currency of information is important, can you tell when the page was developed and last updated? (If not, be careful in accepting the information. If currency is not a factor —for example, for a Civil War site on which the material is not likely to become dated —this will not be a major concern.)

Source: Betty D. Roe, "Using Technology for Content Area Literacy." In *Linking Literacy and Technology: A Guide for K–8 Classrooms,* ed. Shelley B. Wepner, William J. Valmont, and Richard Thurlow (Newark, Delaware: International Reading Association, 2000), pp. 133–155.

Another problem with letting students use the Internet for research purposes is that many sites contain material that is not appropriate for students to read. To avoid having students access undesirable sites, either accidentally or intentionally, many schools have installed filter software, such as SurfWatch (**www1.surfwatch.com/**) (Zhao, Tan, and Mishra, 2000/2001).

TrackStar (**http://trackstar.hprtec.org**) is suggested by Smolin and Lawless (2003) as a site that helps teachers "organize and annotate websites, which can then be used to shape lessons" (p. 575), and Filamentality (**www.kn.pacbell.com/wired/**

EXAMPLE 11.4   Internet Site: "Welcome to Astro-Venture!"

Source: http://astroventure.arc.nasa.gov.

fil) is a site that contains templates to help teachers develop learning activities from Internet resources.

LITERATURE

There are sites that contain the full texts of some children's literature selections. This availability could make possible class activities that would ordinarily require multiple copies of the texts. The selections available are generally classics in the public domain.

Teachers may want to guide their classes in developing their own web home pages (Cotton, 1996). Many classes have done this, and the students have posted everything from creative writing to research reports and the results of scientific experiments. Class newspapers or magazines may be published on these web pages. It is possible to include text, graphics, photographs, and animations. Because web pages can be accessed from all over the world, the motivation for accuracy and clarity of information presented is great. Students may therefore be more inclined to revise and edit material.

Leu (2002) emphasizes that learning to learn is central to acquiring new literacy skills in our rapidly changing technological environment. Students must "continuously learn new skills and strategies required by the new technologies of literacy that will regularly emerge" (p. 466). To advance use of new Internet literacy skills, Leu and Leu (2000) suggest using Internet Workshop, which involves locating and bookmarking an Internet site related to a unit of study, designing an activity that requires students to use the site to reach unit goals (or letting advanced computer users develop their own inquiry projects), having students carry out the activity, and arranging for students to share results and reactions with classmates in a workshop session. This procedure is appropriate for all grade levels (Leu, 2002). Leu (2002) and a classroom teacher developed an Internet Workshop on the *Titanic* that is located at **http://sp.uconn.edu/~djleu/titanic.html**.

WebQuests are inquiry projects that also make use of links to online resources. See **http://sesd.sk.ca/teacherresource/webquests.htm**, for example WebQuests (Coiro, 2003). These WebQuests have well-defined purposes and lead students to try out new roles, such as scientist, as they attempt to construct "an understanding of the material by creating something that others can respond to, on-line or off" (Dodge cited in Coiro, 2003, p. 461).

The most common use of the Internet today is communication, which is discussed in the next section. Since communication is a language function, this use of the Internet is highly pertinent to literacy instruction.

Electronic Communications

There are a number of types of electronic communications that are useful for literacy instruction. Electronic mail (e-mail), electronic mailing lists (listservs), electronic bulletin boards (newsgroups), and electronic videoconferencing all have possible applications.

Electronic Mail. Writing can be exchanged among classrooms when *electronic mail* systems are available. Use of such experiences has resulted in more lengthy writing and improved attitudes toward and performance in reading and writing for middle-grade students (Riel, 1989; Moore, 1991). Newman (1989) found similar advantages for older students in length of text produced, attitudes toward writing, and language development (Moore, 1991).

LITERATURE   E-mail has many applications for literacy instruction. Students can e-mail other students in different classes, states, or countries. They can discuss the locales in which they live, customs in their countries, current events, topics being studied in school, and literature they are reading. Students in the Kentucky Telecommunications Writing Project read the same books as students at other Kentucky schools and communicate about their reading through e-mail (Bell et al., 1995; Holland, 1996). An Internet site designed to help children discuss literature with other children is Book Rap at **http://rite.ed.qut.edu.au/oz-teachernet/projects/book-rap/index.html** (Johnson, 1999). Students may also e-mail experts in different subjects about their areas of specialization to obtain information needed for study topics. Students have the opportunity to interact with published authors in the Kentucky Authors Project, sharing both personal information and works-in-progress. "Authors provide feedback to each student's work, share their own ideas and approaches to writing, and, on occasion, offer direct instruction. … Students also have a chance to read and discuss each author's work directly with the author through on-line 'literature conferences'" (Paeth et al., 1995, p. 1). In a number of programs, college classes and public school students have had e-mail exchanges about books (Roe and Smith, 1997; Sullivan, 1998; McKeon, 1999; Niday and Campbell, 2000), instruction, or general

DIVERSITY conversation. Stivers (1996) paired college methods students with middle-school students with special needs, for e-mail conversation and writing instruction. The

E-mail Conversations About Literature

During each of two semesters, students from Livingston Middle School, a rural public school, were paired with teacher education students enrolled in Betty Roe's reading and language arts methods classes at Tennessee Technological University to discuss literature selections that both groups were reading. In the fall semester both groups read *Bridge to Terabithia*, and in the spring semester both groups read *Tuck Everlasting*. The books were read on a predetermined schedule, and the partners communicated about their reading each week for seven weeks. During the fall semester, the university students also posted comments about literary features of the book to a newsgroup that was limited to the university students in the project. (Technical problems with the newsgroup caused its deletion from the second semester of the project.) After both groups viewed a videotape of the book that had been read, they communicated with partners by e-mail, comparing and contrasting the book and the video. (See the Focus on Strategies in the Videotapes section for more information about this facet of the project.) The middle-school students also prepared an *mPower* presentation about each book at the conclusion of the reading. (See the Focus on Strategies in the Multimedia Publishing section for more information on this part of the program.)

Evaluations of the program by public school and university teachers and students were positive.

The public school teachers felt that receiving e-mail motivated their students and enhanced the students' self-esteem. They felt that interacting with college students gave their students a sense of status and of doing high-level work. Some of the middle-school students had never read a novel before, but they read these books in order to communicate with their partners. Of course, they got additional reading practice when they read the e-mail correspondence from their partners in order to respond. These students had rarely done much writing, and the teachers saw the writing skills of many increase during the project. The university students had been encouraged to model good writing for their partners in their e-mail exchanges, and most did. Some partners continued to correspond after the semesters had ended. The e-mail communications reflected thinking on all levels of Bloom's taxonomy, and the university students were sometimes surprised at the higher-order thinking displayed by their partners.

The university students also gave the project high evaluations. One wrote, "This particular project not only introduced students to a good piece of literature; it introduced them to interactive technology, which is a skill that will be useful and probably necessary to their futures. It provided feedback that was fun and involving. I would definitely use this technique again" (Roe and Smith, 1997, p. 372).

public school students responded well, and the college students showed enhanced self-esteem as a result of the program. One e-mail project is described in the Focus on Strategies above (Roe and Smith, 1997).

Electronic Mailing Lists. *Electronic mailing lists* distribute messages to a group of readers who have "subscribed" to the list because of an interest in the topic. All "subscribers" receive all messages sent to the list until they "unsubscribe." The flow of mail to subscribers on these mailing lists is often exceedingly heavy, and the mail must be read and deleted frequently (usually every day).

A class may want to subscribe to a mailing list that is related to a topic of study while that study is going on and then cancel the subscription after the topic is covered in class. Jayne Everitt, for example, wanted her first graders to use the Internet to learn about effects of severe weather. She asked subscribers to the Kidsphere mailing list to send personal accounts of such effects. The children read the responses and charted the locations of the correspondents (Serim and Koch, 1996). Teachers should be careful to monitor the contents of mailing list communications, however, because some outside participants may send inappropriate comments and use objectionable language.

Electronic Bulletin Boards. *Electronic bulletin boards*, or *newsgroups*, differ from electronic mailing lists in that messages are posted to a network location, and readers who are interested in the topic can read the messages electronically by going to the newsgroup address. These messages may be posted and read by people from all over the world (Grabe and Grabe, 1998). Once again, teachers should monitor the content of newsgroups that students in class want to access, because inappropriate material may be posted. Some schools set up limited-access newsgroups to meet the needs of students who are studying a topic. These groups are less risky to use with elementary school students.

Electronic Videoconferencing. At present, most classrooms do not have the cameras and software needed for *videoconferencing*, but this may be an application on the horizon for literacy instruction. In videoconferences, individuals hold conferences over the Internet with others whom they can see on their computer monitors and hear through their speakers. The advantages of this method for bringing such people as authors of children's books, scientists, and historians into contact with elementary school students are obvious. Students could be responsible for researching the person, literature, or topic of conversation ahead of time, writing interview questions, conducting a controlled interview, taking notes on the discussion, and writing reports on the results — all valid literacy activities. This type of interaction could also take place between two groups of elementary students from different parts of the world. Maring (2002a) has used videoconferencing in his Cyber Mentoring projects at Washington State University. See **http://depts. washington.edu/wctl/cybermentor.htm** for information about these interactions between preservice education students and K–12 students (Maring, 2002b).

DIVERSITY 🌐 ## Interactive Internet Projects

There are many interactive Internet projects that enable students to work with other students from around the United States and even worldwide. El-Hindi (1998) describes how Patti Weeg, a Title I computer teacher in Maryland, involved her students in a project called the World Wide F. A. X. project that a second-grade teacher in Japan initiated. In this project, students write letters and greeting cards to (and draw pictures for) the international participants and read what the others have written. This experience encourages worldwide friendships.

Kidlink at **www.kidlink.org** is a site for an organization focused on enhancing global communication among children up through secondary school. The International Telementor Program (ITP) at **www.telementor.org** "facilitates electronic mentoring relationships between professional adults and students world-wide." The mentors communicate through "a secure Web-based messaging system" (**www.telementor.org/program.cfm**). There are even Internet sites where young writers can find resources to expand their writing abilities, such as **www.inkspot .com/young/** (El-Hindi, 1998).

To locate collaborative projects with schools in other countries, Leu, Karchmer, and Leu (1999) suggest checking out the Intercultural E-mail Classroom Connection at **www.iecc.org**. Global Schoolhouse Projects and Programs Main Page at **www.gsn.org** is a resource for permanent, ongoing Internet projects. Leu, Karchmer, and Leu (1999) list many other literacy-rich Internet projects that are worthy of attention.

iReap

Manzo, Manzo, and Albee (2002) suggest the use of the iREAP system for improving reading, writing, and thinking. It is based on the REAP (Read, Encode, Annotate, Ponder) system for text responses. The *i* in iREAP indicates the addition of the use of the Internet. The students read material, put it into their own words, respond in writing to the material with a variety of types of annotations, and finally think about the material and share reactions with others. The nature of the approach makes it appropriate to use with students "across a broad spectrum of student abilities, needs, and cognitive styles" (p. 45), such as you find in inclusion classrooms. Writing a variety of types of annotations makes it more likely that the students will attain new insights.

DIVERSITY Outstanding annotations may be posted on a web page with the author cited and will thus become available to students from differing cultures and backgrounds. Annotations about a single selection from a variety of students may be stored electronically in order to form a collection for use by future students. These collections could be printed for use in class or read from the computer. Manzo, Manzo, and Albee (2002, p. 47) say, "A global iREAP system could create meaningful cross-cultural cross-boundary dialogues on great books and great thoughts," and in the process could improve reading comprehension, higher-order thinking, writing, and content knowledge. (Visit **www.LiteracyLeaders.com** to learn more about this topic.)

Computer-Assisted Instruction (CAI)

Computer-assisted instruction refers to use of computers to promote learning. The heart of a CAI system is the software, the programs that actually provide the
DIVERSITY instruction. Computer software is available for developing many different literacy skills, including alphabet knowledge (*The Alphabet*), phonemic awareness (*Leap into Phonics*), and grammar (*Focus on Grammar Series*)—all areas of special need for English language learners (Butler-Pascoe and Wiburg, 2003).

Computer-assisted instructional programs can vary widely in quality, depending on the developers; the computer can only carry out the instructions its programmers have given it. To be instructionally sound, the program should present accurate information in a reasonable sequence with an appropriate amount of student interaction. It should not reward incorrect answers with clever messages or graphics, while not doing this for correct answers. It should be easy to use, providing clear instructions about what to do (1) to advance material on the screen, (2) to respond to questions (Should students use a letter or an entire typed-out answer to respond to a multiple-choice question? Should they touch the screen or click on or beside the correct answer?), and (3) to receive help when needed. Erroneous keystrokes should not "dump" a student out of the program; the program should allow him or her to recover in a clear and easy way.

The four most common types of computer-assisted instruction are drill-and-practice programs, tutorial programs, simulation programs, and educational game programs. Computer-assisted instructional programs often have a component that takes care of such tasks as recordkeeping, diagnosis, and prescription of individualized assignments. Such a component is a computer-managed system, and many packages of instructional materials contain both an instructional and a management component.

Drill-and-Practice Programs.   These programs consist of practice lessons on skills that students have previously been taught. They are the simplest types of computer applications and the ones most commonly found in classrooms. They generally focus on learning factual information. With drill-and-practice programs, students receive information in a programmed sequence of small, sequential steps; enter responses to the material; and receive immediate feedback on the correctness of their answers. Some programs give students more than one opportunity to respond to an item before telling them the correct answer.

Practice is important for developing accuracy in, and automaticity of, reading skills. Computer drill-and-practice programs help students do this by providing repetition without the impatience that teachers sometimes show. When the goal is developing accuracy, the computer can be used to present a few exercises accompanied by clear, immediate feedback, particularly for incorrect answers. After children have attained accuracy, the teacher can have them practice using computer programs with larger numbers of exercises, sometimes emphasizing speed, that are accompanied by less extensive feedback. Some drill-and-practice programs recirculate missed items for further practice, without requiring the teacher to plan or execute such repetition. These programs can take the place of worksheets, which are designed for the same purpose but lack the motivational advantage or interactive nature of computer use and the capability to give immediate reinforcement or planned repetition. Drill-and-practice programs can conserve a teacher's time while providing individualized instruction. Computer drills can also provide such things as graphics, animations, and sound that increase the appeal of the lessons and offer support for the textual material.

DIVERSITY ⊕ *Tutorial Programs.*   With these programs, the computer actually presents instruction and then follows it with practice activities. Some programs do not give students direct control over the sequence; others allow them to request review, remedial help, or additional practice.

Programs may be self-paced or computer-paced. Self-paced programs allow students to move at their own rates through the material, thereby providing more attention to individual differences than computer-paced programs, which progress through the material at a predetermined rate. Sometimes the programs are self-paced on a page-by-page basis; the student presses "Enter" or clicks to continue. Other programs are designed to allow the student to choose a pace for the entire program when the study session starts.

Programs can also be linear or branching. Linear programs take all students through the same sequence of material, although they generally allow the students to progress at their own rates. Branching programs, on the other hand, adjust the instructional sequence according to each student's performance. Depending on the correct and incorrect responses that a student makes as the program progresses, he or she may be branched to a remedial sequence of instruction, taken back through the initial instruction, directed through the typical sequence for the instruction, or skipped ahead in the program to avoid unnecessary practice. Branching programs are obviously more helpful for individualizing instruction.

Tutorial programs are available at a number of difficulty levels, and some provide a wide range of choices of difficulty level in one package, making them more versatile tools in a diverse classroom. They are particularly helpful for offering individual instruction to students who are far above or far below the instructional levels of the others in the class, allowing them to proceed through individually appropriate material. They also can offer make-up instruction for students who have missed that instruction in class, while leaving the teacher free for other tasks.

Some computer-based programs for teaching reading employ a multisensory approach. The IBM *Writing to Read* program, for example, attempts to teach reading through an approach that involves tactile, visual, and auditory senses. Hypertext and hypermedia applications offer many multisensory experiences, as well (Dillner, 1993/1994).

Simulation Programs.   These programs set up situations that simulate real-life activities, such as running a business or traveling west in a wagon train, that cannot be offered in other ways in the curriculum because of limited time, changed conditions (when the past is being simulated), or limited financial and physical resources. Geisert and Futrell (1995, p. 93) point out that such a computer model "is not a complete rendition of reality, but it can be made sufficient to enable users to examine events and study relationships, such as the behavior of objects when colliding." Simulations give students the opportunity to use critical reading skills as they examine the current situation, consider their options, and make decisions about how to proceed. The computer responds to the students' decisions and presents different outcomes, depending on these decisions. This practice in evaluating options and drawing conclusions often seems more like play than study to students.

Simulation programs are often time-consuming to use, but if the programs' status can be saved and the programs can be re-entered from the same place in a later session, students will be likely to stay with them until a conclusion is reached. Motivation for using these programs is often high.

Students enjoy joint work with simulation programs (with discussion about each needed decision and collaborative decision making). Even university students can feel the excitement as they work as a group to complete a simulation activity designed for elementary school children. Discussion becomes animated and thoughtful, and logic is applied in arguments framed in an effort to sway others toward a particular decision.

LITERATURE   Interactive fiction programs present stories that offer readers options for actions, as though they were characters in the story. The story lines are affected by the decisions of the students, so a story may unfold differently each time it is read. These simulation programs show the consequences of decisions based on critical reading. They closely resemble the printed Choose Your Own Adventure books. These programs are generally highly motivational, and because they can be used many times by each student, their use is cost-effective. Pairs of students may work with these programs together, making decisions collaboratively.

Educational Game Programs. These programs offer a variety of formats, often resembling arcade games. They are distinguished from other computer games in that they give students experiences related to educational goals, as well as providing a degree of entertainment. Computer graphics and sound effects make it possible to present informational material in a gamelike format; for example, the user might be asked to "shoot down" balloons containing words with long vowel sounds. Educational games offer one type of drill and practice, allowing students to work repetitively on fast, accurate responses, gaining automaticity.

Electronic games should be used to reinforce skills that have been taught. They should not be used only as a reward to students who finish their work early; otherwise, the students who need the practice most will be the ones least likely to get it. Rather, games that are found to be instructionally sound should be assigned as a regular part of the curriculum to students who are likely to benefit from the practice, and they can also be used as an option for free time for those who are not in particular need of practice but simply enjoy the games.

Adventure games can advance reading skills in some instances. Using them requires reading instructions and reading for clues (Downes and Fatouros, 1995).

STANDARDS AND ASSESSMENT ## Computer-Managed Instruction (CMI)

Computer-managed instruction (CMI) can help teachers keep track of students' performance and guide their learning activities. CMI systems vary greatly in complexity. CMI systems may provide computer-scored tests on specific objectives and then match the students' deficiencies to available instructional materials, suggest instructional sequences for the teacher to use, or assign material directly to the student. Some systems produce reports for parents and other caregivers on the objectives that their children have mastered. The computer may also perform tasks such as averaging grades on a series of tests, thereby relieving the teacher of quite a bit of burdensome recordkeeping. Many electronic gradebook programs are available, and they offer numerous options. Some even have family and student access possibilities, through which caregivers and students can dial in to the school computer and, using an identification number, access an individual student's grades and teacher comments. Electronic portfolios enable teachers to "save students' work in a variety of formats, such as text, graphics, audio, and video. They also provide a framework for organizing these collections" (Willis, Stephens, and Matthew, 1996, p. 153). Complete CMI systems are expensive programs, and they should be evaluated carefully (Willis, Stephens, and Matthew, 1996).

The Accelerated Reader (AR) Program, a type of reading management software, is widely used across the United States and beyond. The program is intended to motivate students to read more books. The books on which the program is based are ranked by reading difficulty level. "AR and its ancillary materials include computerized reading diagnostic tests and over 50,000 primarily literal-level quizzes; computer-based record-keeping systems for both students and teachers; and STAR Reading Program, a computerized, multiple choice, literacy skills objectives testing system" (Pavonetti, Brimmer, and Cipielewski, 2002/2003, p. 301). Pavonetti, Brimmer, and Cipielewski (2002/2003) conducted a study to determine whether AR turns children into lifelong readers. Their results were mixed but did not support such claims. Some concerns about use of the program include that teachers may not hold discussions of books, so that children will not learn answers to quizzes from discussion instead of reading; that some parents and teachers may limit the available books to AR books, reducing the students' opportunity to read more widely in books they like; that students may tell each other test answers, especially when AR points affect grades; and that some books on a particular reading level may not have appropriate material for some children who read at that level, and teachers may not know all the titles well enough to supply guidance.

Management components are built into some individual CAI programs. They allow the teacher to see how well children perform, and sometimes they indicate which items were answered incorrectly. The management components in some programs tell students when to move on to more difficult levels of the program and when to drop back to easier ones. Some of these management components, however, do not save results from session to session.

Combining Computer Applications

LITERATURE Many teachers use combinations of computer applications, along with other media, in their lessons regularly. Wepner and Ray (2000) tell about Mr. Xavier, a fifth-grade teacher, who uses the computer program *Reading Galaxy* to introduce two survival novels, *Hatchet* and *Julie of the Wolves*. These two novels are read by his students as part of a combined language arts/social studies unit. The computer "program is designed to stimulate interest in reading, using a game-show format to present character, setting, initial conflicts, and author backgrounds" (Wepner and Ray, 2000, p. 77) for these and other middle-school novels. The teacher is also using Internet and CD-ROM maps in the unit, as well as Internet sites to check on facts about Alaska. He also sets up Alaskan keypals for his students (Wepner and Ray, 2000).

Students could also read CD-ROM books and then use *Kidspiration* to web the stories just read and use word-processing software to write sequels to the books. They could post their webs and/or sequels on a class web page. Applications are limited only by the imaginations of creative teachers.

Some educators believe that extensive use of computers in classroom instruction will cause children to develop into social isolates, as they sit and interact with a computer screen instead of people. Others say that computers can be used by two or more students in collaborative ways that result in even more positive social interactions than are ordinarily found in a traditional classroom. Describe situations in which social interactions are likely to occur.

Cooperative Learning with Computers

Computer applications work well with cooperative learning. When pairs of students are allowed to work together at the computer, the language interactions are rich, whether the students are reading an electronic book, using a simulation program, or writing a story together. The computer screen appears to be a stimulus for interaction as children pass by or wait for turns (DeGroff, 1990; Cochran-Smith et al., 1988). The computer offers opportunities for reading their own writing and that of other students and enables teams of students to share in the preparation of presentations, each bringing her or his own strengths to the process, which can include searching for information, organizing information, designing a presentation, and implementing the planned design.

DIVERSITY ● **Adjusting Instruction Through Technology**

Technology can be used to help address the diverse needs of students in a classroom. Many computer applications, for example, can be used by students working at a variety of reading levels. Gifted and talented students can pursue independent inquiry through Internet research or creating their own websites — activities that often require both divergent and convergent thinking skills. Supportive technology can also help students overcome some reading problems. For example, audiotapes can be paired with printed text to build sight vocabulary and reading fluency. Computer-supported instruction can help "at-risk" students who have reading difficulties (McKenna et al., 1999).

Many computers are now capable of reading texts aloud, using synthetic speech. This enhances the utility of computer programs for young children, second language learners, and readers with visual disabilities. Computers can also provide larger print for visually impaired readers, and the color and typeface of print shown on the monitor can be changed.

With *Wiggleworks: Scholastic Beginning Literacy System* (Scholastic), a program that presents established children's books on CD-ROM, students can record sentences in their own voices, enter the sentences into the computer, have the computer read what has been entered in synthetic speech, and replay their recorded speech at any point for comparison. This capability makes it possible for students to self-monitor their writing — a feature that is useful for younger and less adept students, as well as English language learners (Rose and Meyer, 1994; Mike, 1994).

Other computer technologies are available for students who have physical problems. There are special pads that serve as input devices for young children who have not yet developed the fine-motor control necessary for keyboarding, and the same devices can be helpful for students with physical disabilities that affect motor control. Voice recognition programs are becoming more widely available and more effective, allowing speech input for students who lack motor control. Zorfass, Corley, and Remz (1994) describe a computer keyboard with Braille overlays on the keys,

Some people think that the motivational effect of using technology—particularly computers—will decline because of regular opportunities for such use. Others think the varied possibilities for using technological tools—especially computers—provide a constant stream of fresh motivation for using technology. **What do *you* think, and why?**

used in conjunction with a word-processing program with speech feedback to enable a blind girl with cerebral palsy to type and monitor her writing. An application referred to as *word prediction* allows students who have fine-motor difficulties to begin typing words, and, as they type, lists of words beginning that way appear, enabling the students to choose the desired words without having to type them in their entirety. Another application, called *abbreviation expansion*, allows whole messages to be encoded and retrieved with a given combination of keystrokes. Headsticks, mouthsticks, and customized hand-held pointers are also available for students with physical problems. If a student can make a consistent movement of some kind, the computer can be used. Braille translation programs are available to allow printouts on Braille printers (Zorfass, Corley, and Remz, 1994).

SUMMARY

Teachers are faced with a bewildering array of possible technological applications for their literacy classrooms. They need to understand the range of technology available, how to evaluate the different applications, and how to make technology an integral part of core learning.

Among the many technological tools that can be applied to literacy instruction are instructional transparencies, television programs, audiotapes, videotapes, CD-ROMs, DVD-ROMs, videodiscs, and other computer applications. Various combinations of technological tools are also used for multimedia applications. These tools can be used to present information and to enable students to do research and create presentations and written products. Computers are used in literacy instruction for word processing; for desktop publishing; to access databases, electronic books, electronic reference works, and the Internet; for electronic communications such as electronic mail, electronic mailing lists, electronic bulletin boards, and electronic videoconferencing; for computer-assisted instruction, including drill-and-practice, tutorial, simulation, and educational game programs; for computer-managed instruction; and for multimedia applications for classroom presentations and projects.

There are computer applications and materials that make possible the participation of students with special needs. Synthetic speech and large print on computer screens and printouts, as well as special input devices and output systems, are available today.

TEST YOURSELF

True or False

_____ 1. Overhead projectors are outdated and no longer have valid classroom uses.

_____ 2. All teachers now have computers with CD-ROM drives available in their classrooms.

_____ 3. Any computer software can be used on any computer that a teacher happens to have in the classroom.

_____ 4. Teachers should try out software before purchasing it.

_____ 5. Only one student at a time can work at a single classroom computer.

_____ 6. There are no television programs that fit comfortably into literacy instruction.

_____ 7. Videotaping and/or audiotaping student presentations can facilitate assessment.

_____ 8. Comparing a print version of a children's literature selection with a video version of the same story can be a good literacy experience for students.

_____ 9. CD-ROMs, DVD-ROMs, and videodiscs allow users to access information from them in a nonlinear fashion.

_____ 10. Many electronic books are available on CD-ROM.

_____ 11. Hypertext and hypermedia allow text and media, respectively, to be accessed in a nonsequential manner.

_____ 12. Hypertext and hypermedia usage may lead to "navigational problems" for users.

_____ 13. Teachers have to be programmers to use computers effectively in their classrooms.

_____ 14. CMI can help teachers keep track of students' performances on learning activities.

_____ 15. Management functions are built into some individual CAI programs.

_____ 16. Word-processing software takes much of the labor out of editing and revising written products.

_____ 17. Database programs allow the categorization, storage, and orderly retrieval of data collected during research reading.

_____ 18. Students can search the Internet using special browsers and search engines that allow keyword searches to locate information for reports or unit studies.

_____ 19. The accuracy of material that is posted to electronic bulletin boards or placed on web pages is carefully monitored and can be accepted as accurate without the students doing further checking.

_____ 20. World Wide Web home pages are too complicated for elementary teachers and students to develop and maintain.

_____ 21. Web pages can include only text; no use of sound or graphics is possible.

_____ 22. E-mail projects can allow students to discuss literature selections with authors and other students all over the world.

_____ 23. Most classrooms currently use electronic videoconferencing.

_____ 24. Computer-assisted instructional programs vary widely in quality.

_____ 25. Drill-and-practice programs offer initial instruction in skills.

_____ 26. CAI programs may be self-paced or computer-paced.

_____ 27. Simulation programs set up situations that simulate real-life adventures.

_____ 28. *Multimedia* refers to the mixing of different media.

_____ 29. Computers are now capable of reading texts aloud, enhancing their utility for young children and readers with visual disabilities.

_____ 30. If a student can make a consistent movement of some kind, the computer can be used.

For your journal ...

❶ Keep a section in your journal for reviews of pertinent videotapes, videodiscs, audiotapes, and computer programs that you might wish to use in your literacy program. If you can, try each one with students, and write an assessment of its effectiveness in the journal. You may want to include your reviews in your portfolio.

❷ Reflect on the video that accompanies this chapter. Would you say these teachers have integrated technology into their curricula in a seamless fashion? Why or why not? What must an application of technology do to fit seamlessly into the curriculum?

... and your portfolio

❶ Develop a multimedia presentation on a literacy topic of your choice for a grade level of your choice, and include a copy of it on disk or videotape in your portfolio.

❷ Produce a series of transparencies or a computer-driven slide presentation, using a computer program such as *PowerPoint* or *mPower*, to help explain a literacy topic, such as "Propaganda Devices in Advertising." Use the transparencies or slide show with a group of students to teach a lesson. Evaluate the results in your journal. Put a printout of your transparencies or slide show in your portfolio, along with the lesson plan that you taught.

12

Assessment of Student Progress and Text Difficulty

SETTING OBJECTIVES

When you finish reading this chapter, you should be able to

- Discuss current trends in assessment.
- Describe some appropriate multiple measures of assessment for young readers and writers.
- Identify some features and appropriate uses of formal assessment measures.
- Construct and interpret informal tests.
- Describe some ways in which authentic assessment differs from traditional assessment.
- Explain the importance of observation and identify some ways to record observations.
- Implement portfolio assessment in an elementary classroom.
- Recognize and analyze the significance of reading miscues.
- Identify some ways for students to assess their own progress.
- Use a cloze test to determine the difficulty of written materials.
- Identify some readability formulas that can be used to assess the difficulty of written materials.
- Discuss text "leveling."

Assessment is the collection and evaluation of data for the purpose of understanding the strengths and weaknesses of student learning (Harris and Hodges, 1995). Evaluating student progress is important because it enables the teacher to discover each student's strengths and weaknesses, to plan instruction accordingly, to communicate student progress, and to evaluate the effectiveness of teaching strategies. Assessing student learning is essential for effective teaching and

Chapter 12 Organization

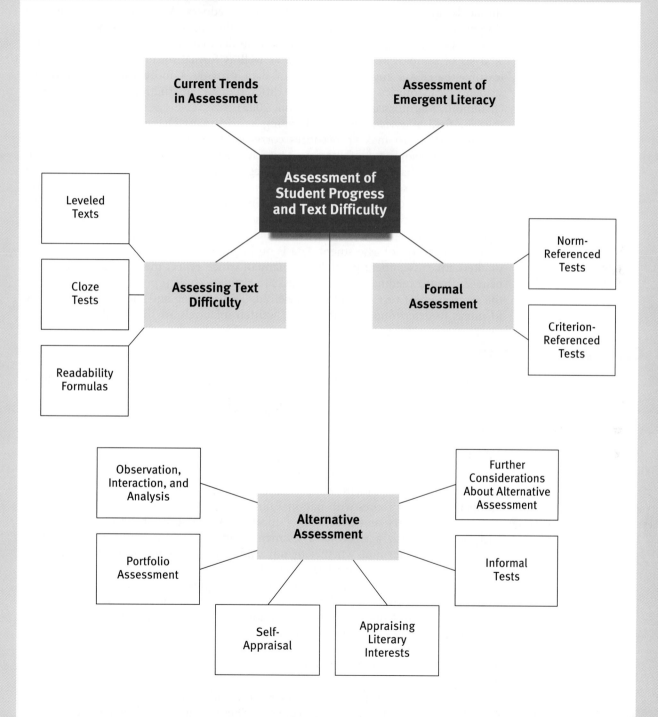

Assessment of Student Progress and Text Difficulty

Current Trends in Assessment

Assessment of Emergent Literacy

Assessing Text Difficulty
- Leveled Texts
- Cloze Tests
- Readability Formulas

Formal Assessment
- Norm-Referenced Tests
- Criterion-Referenced Tests

Alternative Assessment
- Observation, Interaction, and Analysis
- Portfolio Assessment
- Self-Appraisal
- Appraising Literary Interests
- Further Considerations About Alternative Assessment
- Informal Tests

should be an integral part of instructional procedures. Assessment should not be simply equated with testing. It should involve the collection of data from multiple measures—such as day-to-day observation, student conferences and interviews, and analysis of samples of students' work, as well as formal means. Profiles of student learning based on multiple sources of data provide a more valid evaluation of students' capabilities and facilitate differentiated instruction for all students (Brimijoin, Marquissee, and Tomlinson, 2003).

The field of assessment is undergoing a great many changes as researchers and educators strive to make procedures correspond more closely with current views about the development of literacy. This chapter first examines current trends in assessment that have resulted from federal legislation. Assessment is further discussed in terms of the use of data collection from multiple sources and the implementation of recent education reform movements. The assessment of emergent literacy and assessment techniques appropriate for use with young readers and writers are discussed. Formal assessment is defined, and a sampling of sources that provide multiple measures of assessment data is outlined. The chapter presents several types of alternative assessment procedures, many of which reflect the current emphasis on using authentic reading and writing tasks to evaluate student progress. In conclusion, the assessment of text difficulty is reviewed. Text leveling and the use of readability formulas to determine the difficulty of written materials are discussed.

Current Trends in Assessment

Assessment serves many purposes (Leslie and Jett-Simpson, 1997; Serafini, 1997; Walberg et al., 1994). Three primary reasons to evaluate students are (1) to provide accountability, (2) to classify students, and, most important, (3) to guide instruction.

Many formal assessment procedures are used as accountability instruments, although some provide indicators to teachers of overall strengths and weaknesses of students in a class. Standardized tests, for example, yield scores that school districts use for comparing student achievement with that from previous years and for comparing district scores with national norms.

DIVERSITY 🌐 The Elementary and Secondary Education Act (ESEA) of 2001 mandates that each state establish a rigorous assessment plan. States must plan annual testing programs that determine whether or not students in the state are making *adequate yearly progress* (AYP) toward learning objectives in key subjects. In addition, the annual tests must provide the states with *disaggregated data*, scores that show the progress of subgroups of students, including racial/ethnic groups, economically disadvantaged students, students with disabilities, and students with limited English proficiency (Tennessee State Department of Education, 2003). In order to demonstrate adequate yearly progress, states and school districts must set high academic achievement standards and outline measurable objectives in reading/language arts and math for all students.

Several assessment procedures, described in this chapter, can guide teachers and enable them to individualize instruction. These include observation, samples of students' work, and other informal techniques that help teachers to make classroom decisions. By reflecting on information from multiple sources, teachers can gain an understanding of each student's performance in order to plan long- and short-term instruction, determine lesson content, make instructional decisions, and decide which students need to be engaged in certain types of learning experiences (Parker et al., 1995).

Assessment should be a continuous process in which teachers observe and interact with students in various types of learning activities throughout the day. To provide a match between the strategies that students use when they read and the strategies and skills that are being assessed, many educators have turned to kidwatching (defined later in this chapter), the use of checklists, and the analysis of portfolios, response journals, and retellings. They are evaluating debates, collaborative activities, presentations, projects, journals, performances, exhibitions, process writing, and experiments (Sugarman, Allen, and Keller-Cogan, 1993; Wiggins, 1990). Assessment is part of good instruction when it occurs during typical learning activities, periods of social interaction, and times for reflection (Kapinus, 1994).

Assessment that corresponds with instruction should relate to students' prior knowledge, use complete text passages, accept different interpretations, and allow the reader to vary reading strategies. Many standardized tests, however, do not exhibit these features (Kapinus, 1994; Shepard, 1989). Large-scale standardized tests must be objective, formal, time- and cost-efficient, widely applicable, centrally processed, and presented in a form useful to policy makers. They usually consist of multiple-choice items that primarily measure literal comprehension and isolated skills. Although efforts have been made to create standardized tests that more closely resemble authentic assessment, few changes in standardized-test format have actually been implemented.

Current trends in assessment involve the development or revision of standards for what a student should know and be able to do in many subject areas. Numerous education agencies and professional associations are critically viewing curriculum and assessment through a standards lens. The International Reading Association (IRA) and the National Council for Teachers of English (NCTE) are two national organizations that have developed and published a set of reading and language arts standards (IRA/NCTE, 1996). (A copy of these standards appears in Chapter 1). Issues of accountability and effectiveness currently abound. The assessment method a teacher selects should match the desired standards and should accurately report how students perform. According to Snow, Burns, and Griffin (1998, p. 300), "Standards can serve as the common reference point for developing curricula, instructional materials, tests, accountability systems, and professional development."

Teachers must be able to rely on assessment to make informed instructional and curricular decisions (Serafini, 1997). It is extremely important that today's educator be familiar with a variety of assessment measures. It is even more important, in the current high-stakes testing atmosphere, that teachers use appropriate data to guide their instruction and to develop curricula. As faculty members work collaboratively in learning communities to implement school improvement plans and develop curricula, the understanding of assessment data and implications for classroom use is of paramount importance in helping students learn (Guskey, 2003).

Formal Assessment

Formal assessment is the use of published, ***standardized tests*** that have been constructed by experts in the field and are administered, scored, and interpreted according to specific criteria (Lipson and Wixson, 1997; Rubin, 1997).

For seventy years or longer, standardized tests have remained essentially the same (VanLeirsburg, 1993). Comprehension sections consist of series of short passages followed by multiple-choice questions, and tests require students to identify a single correct answer for each test item. Estimates of a child's reading ability are based on the number of correct answers as found in an answer key. Many educators believe these standardized tests fail to measure thinking and problem-solving skills, in-depth knowledge of subjects, and students' abilities to direct their own learning (Harp, 1994; Sugarman, Allen, and Keller-Cogan, 1993).

● Norm-Referenced Tests

Norm-referenced tests are standardized. They measure a student's relative standing in relation to comparable groups of students across the nation or locally. Authors of these tests sample large populations of children to determine the appropriateness of test items. They seek to verify the *validity* and *reliability* of test results so that schools can be confident that the tests measure what they are intended to measure and that results will not vary significantly if students take the same test more than once.

Norm-referenced tests can provide teachers with objective data about reading achievement, scholastic aptitude, and areas of strength and weakness. *(© Jean Claude LeJeune)*

Results of norm-referenced tests are most commonly expressed as standard scores, such as grade equivalents (or grade scores), percentile ranks, or stanines. A *grade equivalent* indicates the grade level, in years and months, for which a given score was the average score in the standardization sample. *Percentile rank* (PR) expresses a score in terms of its position within a set of 100 scores. The PR indicates the percentage of scores in a reference group that is equal to or lower than the given score; therefore, a score ranked at the fortieth percentile is equal to or better than the scores of 40 percent of the people in the reference group. On a *stanine scale*, the scores are divided into nine equal parts, with a stanine of 5 as the mean.

Schools administer standardized achievement tests in the spring or fall every year to assess the gains in achievement of groups of students. Most of these tests are batteries, or collections of tests on different subjects, and should be administered under carefully controlled conditions and often over the course of several days. Upon their completion, the tests are generally sent to the publisher for scoring.

Many standardized achievement tests contain subtests in reading and language that provide useful information for identifying students' general strengths and weaknesses in reading. However, these tests have limitations. In order to understand the limitations of standardized achievement tests, teachers should consider the following questions.

Do tests really reflect what we know about the reading process today? Some standardized tests do not reflect current thinking about reading comprehension as a strategic process because

❶ The test may check knowledge of vocabulary by asking students to find the one of several words that most closely matches an isolated key word, instead of asking students to identify vocabulary in context, in the manner in which readers nearly always encounter words.

❷ The test may assess reading comprehension on the basis of answers to series of short, unrelated paragraphs, instead of asking students to read longer passages as they would in real reading situations.

❸ The test may present material without regard for students' prior knowledge, instead of considering the way students' existing schemata interact with the text as students construct meaning.

DIVERSITY   *Is the test fair to diverse learners?* Test publishers have been giving increasing attention to the question of the fairness of their tests. They do not want to state questions in a way that will give certain children an unfair advantage or discourage some children so that they will not do their best. Many writers and editors from different backgrounds are involved in test construction, and members of several ethnic groups review questions to correct unintentional, built-in biases.

DIVERSITY   *How are test scores being used?* Too much emphasis is being placed on standardized test scores if they are the only source used to classify children as gifted or as having a learning disability, to group children according to achievement levels, to match materials designed for a particular reading level with children who scored at that level, or to place children in remedial classes. Although standardized tests may be one consideration, placements in special groups should be the result of evaluating multiple assessments (Eby, 1998; Flippo, 1997).

Some education agencies, such as the state of Tennessee and the Chicago public schools, include longitudinal achievement data as a value-added feature of their formal assessment programs. Whereas formal tests attempt to determine evidence of achievement in comparison with a normed sample of the population, value-added scores attempt to profile the academic growth of an individual student. By collecting value-added testing information over a period of time, teachers are better able to profile academic growth, identify learning trends, and note the impact on a student's performance of possible intervening variables, such as the school system, the school, and the individual teacher (Holloway, 2000).

TIME for REFLECTION

Many teachers believe that children should not have to take standardized tests, yet most administrators and legislators require them. **What do *you* think, and why?**

Researchers have been seeking to establish more authentic ways to assess reading ability by considering students' thought processes and reading strategies. Educators believe that because test scores often are used to direct instruction and predict performance, tests should measure the high-level thinking strategies that students actually employ when reading (Powell, 1989). Therefore, developers of standardized tests have been seeking ways to measure a student's ability to apply reading strategies in a variety of authentic reading tasks.

Rather than focusing on single correct answers, researchers have been considering the entire process of reading and the strategies used. Three ways that test developers have adapted new ideas about comprehension to their tests are (1) setting purposes for reading, (2) analyzing incorrect responses to multiple-choice questions to aid in diagnosing sources of difficulties, and (3) assessing vocabulary by asking readers to identify words embedded in text instead of words in isolation (Farr and Carey, 1986). Some tests attempt to evaluate students' use of the reading process, application of prior knowledge, and depth of understanding (Harp, 1994).

Despite efforts to include more authentic tasks on standardized tests, however, "there is little evidence of their wide-scale feasibility, practicality, and utility" (Walberg, Haertel, and Gerlach-Downie, 1994, p. 37). Difficulties arise from lack of information about technical characteristics of the new assessments; from the inability to establish consistent ratings among judges; and from the variability in a student's scores, depending on which performance task is given.

● Criterion-Referenced Tests

A *criterion-referenced test* (or objective-referenced test) is designed to yield scores that are interpretable in terms of specific performance standards—for example, to indicate that a student can identify the main idea of a paragraph 90 percent of the time. Criterion-referenced tests are designed to match the standards or expectations of what students should know at successive points, or benchmarks, throughout their school careers. Such tests, which may be commercially prepared or teacher-constructed, are intended to be used as guides for developing instructional prescriptions. For example, if a child cannot perform the task of identifying cause-

and-effect relationships, the teacher should provide instruction in that area. Such specific applications make these tests useful in day-to-day decisions about instruction. The National Assessment of Educational Progress (NAEP) uses criterion-referenced assessment data to report on what American students in public and private schools know and can do in a number of subject areas (Snow, Burns, and Griffin, 1998).

Criterion-referenced testing has both advantages and disadvantages. It is an effective way to determine what a student is able to do or to diagnose a child's knowledge of reading skills. Analyzing the results of a criterion-referenced assessment helps in prescribing appropriate instruction. Furthermore, students do not compete with other students but only try to achieve mastery of each criterion or objective. On the other hand, reading can appear to be nothing more than a series of skills to be taught and tested, and skills may be taught in isolation rather than in combination. Knowledge gained in this way may be difficult for children to apply to actual reading situations.

Another consideration in criterion-referenced assessment is establishing appropriate, yet challenging, standards. Establishing standards that are too high results in larger numbers of students who may fail to meet expectations. However, if standards are set too low, many students who are experiencing difficulty in reading will remain unidentified and may not receive appropriate instructional programs with interventions needed for success.

Assessment of Emergent Literacy

Tombari and Borich (1999, p. 101) state that "children should leave the early elementary grades able to read and write fluently—or automatically." As literacy develops, the teacher provides feedback and intervention when help is needed. Appropriate assessment can enable the teacher to provide scaffolding and support literacy development. Teachers sometimes administer formal tests at the end of kindergarten or at the beginning of first grade to predict a child's likelihood of success in reading. However, most teachers in the early grades rely heavily on various types of informal assessment.

A teacher in an emergent literacy classroom recognizes that most students arrive at school already knowing a great deal about literacy. Many teachers of young students are interested in investigating and documenting not only what a student knows but also what he or she can apply. Teachers can evaluate children's awareness of the function or purpose of writing by observing their responses to printed labels and messages. By noting their retellings (discussed in greater detail later in this chapter) or answers to questions about stories read to them, teachers can learn about children's comprehension strategies. Children reveal a great deal about their emergent literacy when they pretend to read books, especially by the way they structure stories or use pictures. Their use of invented spellings when they write and their perceptions of the connections between reading and writing as they "read" their writings also indicate their literacy development. Other indications include the ability to dictate coherent stories and to recognize environmental print (words on signs, for example).

Marie Clay's *Concepts About Print* is an assessment tool used by teachers to provide observation data to support the literacy development of young students. *Concepts About Print* is suggested for use during the first two years of literacy instruction and is one component of a more comprehensive tool, *An Observation Survey of Early Literacy Achievement* (1993). Authentic assessment methods are often employed successfully in a natural setting for the purpose of viewing the development of emergent literacy. Teachers can create their own informal checklists of literacy skills and behaviors. Periodically filling out and dating the checklist forms creates a written record of each child's progress. Example 12.1 provides a sample observation checklist for literacy development.

Alternative Assessment

Alternative assessment refers to all types of assessment other than formal, standardized tests. Concern about the inadequacies of standardized tests and about

---

EXAMPLE 12.1   Literacy Observation Checklist

Child's name: _____   Teacher's name: _____

Place a check beside each characteristic that the child exhibits.

Characteristics: **Dates:**

  1. Uses variety of comprehension strategies.   _____ _____ _____

  2. Expresses interest in reading and writing.   _____ _____ _____

  3. Reads voluntarily.   _____ _____ _____

  4. Applies word recognition skills.   _____ _____ _____

  5. Writes coherently.   _____ _____ _____

  6. Reads aloud fluently.   _____ _____ _____

  7. Expresses ideas well orally.   _____ _____ _____

  8. Listens attentively.   _____ _____ _____

  9. Enjoys listening to stories.   _____ _____ _____

10. Asks sensible questions.   _____ _____ _____

11. Makes reasonable predictions.   _____ _____ _____

12. Evaluates and monitors own work.   _____ _____ _____

13. Works well independently.   _____ _____ _____

14. Self-corrects errors.   _____ _____ _____

15. Shows willingness to take risks.   _____ _____ _____

the need to look carefully at students' work in order to evaluate student performance has caused educators to take more interest in alternative assessment. This type of assessment involves multiple progress indicators, includes authentic tasks, and reflects progress in terms of growth over time rather than in terms of a one-time performance (Cole, 1998). It involves students in creating and evaluating their own work, thus helping them develop a sense of responsibility and ownership.

Alternative assessment should be based on the following principles (Lipson and Wixson, 1997; Neill, 1997; *Standards for the Assessment of Reading and Writing*, 1994).

❶ The major purpose of assessment is improvement of student learning.

❷ Assessment is fair and equitable for all students.

❸ Assessment involves all members of the educational community (i.e., parents, students, administrators, the public).

❹ Communication about assessment is clear and regular.

❺ Assessment includes a variety of perspectives and data.

❻ Professional collaboration supports assessment.

❼ Activities assessed are meaningful and contextualized (within daily instruction rather than on tests).

❽ Assessment is continuous.

● Observation, Interaction, and Analysis

Three aspects of informal evaluation utilized by effective teachers are observation, interaction, and analysis (Goodman, Goodman, and Hood, 1989). During *observation*, the teacher carefully watches the activities of a single child, a group of children, or the whole class in order to evaluate language use and social behaviors. It is important for the observer to note that longer observations will reveal more information regarding students' progress. The observer may want to join or participate in a cooperative group activity in an effort to assess and analyze the depth of interaction informally. *Interaction* takes place when the teacher raises questions, responds to journal writing, and holds conferences with children in order to stimulate further language and cognitive growth. During *analysis*, the teacher gets information by listening to a child read or discuss and by examining a child's written work. The teacher then applies knowledge of learning principles to analyze the child's ability to use language.

Observation Strategies

Since much student assessment occurs informally, teachers need to interpret their observations with insight and accuracy. Johnston (1987) suggests several characteristics of teachers who successfully evaluate students' literacy development:

- Expert evaluators recognize patterns of behavior and understand how reading and writing processes develop. They notice, for example, that one child is unable to make reasonable predictions or that another uses invented spellings effectively.

- Observant teachers listen attentively, both at scheduled conferences and during the course of each day.

- Effective observers evaluate as they teach, and they accept the responsibility for assessing children's needs and responding to them, instead of relying only on test data.

On the basis of informal observations and even intuition, teachers can modify instructional strategies, clarify explanations, give individual help, use a variety of motivational techniques, adjust classroom management strategies, and provide reinforcement as needed. Two techniques to help teachers focus their observations are shadowing and kidwatching.

Shadowing is defined by Wilson and Corbett as "the process of following a student and systematically recording that student's instructional experiences" (1999, p. 47). It is a powerful descriptive method for collecting data through observation. It involves obtaining permission in advance and conducting an observation that extends throughout the school day. The teacher is attempting to experience an event or events from the student's point of view. Shadowing may involve the observation of one student at a time or of a group of students, and it includes debriefing with the students once the observations have been made (Sagor, 2000; Reed and Bergemann, 2001).

Kidwatching, a term introduced by Yetta Goodman (1978), is observation of a child in various classroom situations. Kidwatching allows teachers to explore two questions: (1) What evidence exists that language development is occurring? and (2) What does a child's unexpected production say about the child's knowledge of language? It is based on three premises (Y. Goodman, 1985):

1 Observers should use a theoretically sound framework to make meaningful and unbiased interpretations of what they see.

2 Observers should watch children in a wide variety of literacy situations.

3 Observers should consider the interactions between children and adults in language learning.

TIME for REFLECTION

How might observation data be more useful than test scores in guiding instruction?

Recordkeeping is an essential part of observation, and it may occur in different ways. Some teachers keep a notebook with a separate page to record observations for each child; others jot dated notes on sticky notes or on file cards that they later place in the students' files or portfolios. (See Example 12.2 for a sample observation card.) Use of anecdotal records, checklists, and rating forms can help to focus observations on important areas of literacy learning.

Anecdotal Records. *Anecdotal records* are written accounts of specific incidents in the classroom. The teacher records information about a significant language event: the time and place, the students involved, what caused the incident, what happened, and possibly the implications. Such records may be kept for individual students, groups, or the whole class. Anecdotal records are useful in evaluating

---

EXAMPLE 12.2   Observation Card

Denny   SSR   4/92

- self-selects books
- laughs softly to self
  (He was reading *Amelia
  Bedelia*)
- Whispered to Amanda
  (whom he sat near) to share
  a page in the book

Source: Reprinted by permission from Beverly Mackie, Jere Whitson Elementary School, Cookeville, Tennessee, 1994.

progress, individualizing instruction, planning instruction, informing others (including the students), noting changes in language development, and understanding attitudes and behaviors (*A Kid-Watching Guide*, 1984; Parker et al., 1995; Rhodes and Nathenson-Mejia, 1992). Anecdotal records are especially helpful when educators are discussing the progress of children with special needs, including English learners. Individualized Education Plan (IEP) team members often use anecdotal records to assist in the development of an initial IEP or in the revision of an existing one. Teachers who regularly keep anecdotal records become more sensitive to their students' special interests and needs than they were before they kept such records (Baskwill and Whitman, 1988). (See Example 12.3 for a sample anecdotal record.)

DIVERSITY 🌐

Checklists and Rating Scales.   Some teachers also keep checklists, such as the literacy observation checklist in Example 12.1 on page 464. Checklists are useful for recording information about student accomplishments and seeing at a glance what has been achieved and what needs further work. Rating scales provide additional information because teachers can assign numbers to each item, perhaps from 1 (lowest) to 5 (highest), according to each student's level of performance or achievement. Teachers can make several copies of the checklist or rating scale for each child and keep them in a folder. By filling out the forms periodically and dating each one, teachers have a written record of each child's progress over time.

EXAMPLE 12.3   Anecdotal Record

It was Lee's first day in our third-grade classroom. He appeared hesitant about joining the other students during our morning activities. I had previously asked another student, Steve, to partner with Lee and help him through the first day. Steve agreed, so I assigned Lee to the desk next to Steve. Steve and Lee ate lunch together, and Steve did help include Lee in a game of kickball during recess. Before independent reading time, another student showed Lee where the classroom library was located, and Steve suggested one of his own favorite books, *The Great Kapok Tree*. Even though Lee spoke and read little English, Steve partner-read with him, pointing to pictures and words and discussing the story. By the end of the day, Lee was smiling and interacting with small groups of students in the classroom. Before leaving at the end of the day, Steve told me that he thought Lee had had a good day.

An example of using a checklist for evaluation during literature circles, discussed in Chapters 7 and 8, comes from Natalie Knox's sixth-grade class. (See the Classroom Scenario below.) This was Ms. Knox's and the children's first time using multiple sets of books from quality literature instead of basal readers.

Rubrics

A *rubric* provides specific criteria for describing student performance at different levels of proficiency in different content areas (O'Neil, 1994). With this ***performance-based assessment***, students receive a number of points that represent minimal to high-quality work, depending on the type of response. For example, during group reading, the criterion for a high-quality response that would earn the greatest number of points might be "Carries on a meaningful conversation about reading," and the

---

CLASSROOM SCENARIO | **Evaluation of Literature Circles**

Natalie Knox reminds the students of their responsibilities for reading, discussing, writing in their literature logs, and planning for their next session while they are in their groups. She tries to meet with each group as both a participant and an evaluator. As she joins a group that is reading Lois Lowry's *Number the Stars*, she enters the discussion and also keeps a checklist of each student's status. One day's checklist is shown in Example 12.4.

students' interests and enthusiasm, ability to gain insights about characters and plot development, and skill in group interaction. From her observations, Natalie can make judgments about progress in student responses to literature and social interactions. The informal records of her observations can serve as a basis for parent conferences and entries on report cards.

Analysis of Scenario

As she visits different groups, Natalie is gaining a great deal of information over a period of time about

EXAMPLE 12.4 Checklist for Literature Response Groups

Number the Stars

Meeting # 1

Student	Attended	Read to page	Shared # of items	Asked questions for clarification	Made predictions &/or connections within the book (or other books)	Made connections to real situations	Responded to others in group	Read from response journal
Kristine Greer	✓	60	✓✓	-Ellen's family?		-Far away relatives	✓	hesitant
Marie Orly	✓	60	✓✓	-My star? -Buttons?	-Sister's death?		✓	excellent
Katie Smith	✓	125	✓✓✓	-Symbols? -Religion?		-Family, friends religious difference	✓ Missy Marie	thorough
Missy Bug	✓	65	✓✓✓	-Peter's involvement?	-Fishing? -Mom's ?s	-Aunt's death	✓ Marie	-detailed
Megan Clifton	✓	60	✓✓✓✓✓	-Symbols?				-skipped around -sequence?

Next meeting:
11/19
Read to: p. 94

criterion for a minimal response with low or no points might be "Unable to express thoughts or feelings about reading material" (Winograd, 1994, p. 421). Example 12.5 is a sample rubric.

A well-constructed rubric lets students know in advance what is expected of them and helps teachers grade students' work fairly. Then, when students receive their grades, they are more likely to understand them because they can refer to the criteria.

When constructing rubrics, teachers may invite students to suggest criteria to include (Batzle, 1992). Skillings and Ferrell (2000) reported a successful collaborative effort in the development and design of rubrics with second- and third-grade students. The involvement of the students began with the introduction of teacher-generated rubrics used for assessment and instruction, but with careful guidance, the students were encouraged to view rubrics critically and to generate components of

---

EXAMPLE 12.5   Rubric for Oral or Written Retelling of a Narrative

3	2	1
Characterization		
Accurately recalls both primary and secondary characters	Accurately recalls only primary or secondary characters, not both	Incorrectly identifies the characters
Uses vivid, appropriate descriptive words when discussing the characters	Provides limited, correct descriptions of the characters	Provides no descriptions or inaccurate descriptions of the characters
Setting		
Recalls the setting: both place and time	Recalls only the time or the place, not both	Provides minimal information or inaccurately describes the setting
Plot		
Recalls the action or plot in correct sequence as it happens in the story	Describes some of the events as they occur in the story sequence	Inaccurately describes events as they happen in the story sequence or describes events out of sequence
Conflict/Resolution		
Accurately discusses both the conflict and the resolution	Discusses only the conflict or the resolution, not both	Discusses fragmented sections of the story with little mention of a conflict or problem with a resulting resolution

Name of student: _____

Story: _____

Circle type of response: Written   Oral

their own. As the process continued, the students assumed more control in rubric design and development. The process of developing and implementing student-generated rubrics helped develop critical thinking and metacognitive skills.

When used correctly, rubrics are effective instructional and assessment tools (Andrade, 2000). The format of rubrics will vary, but all rubrics share two features: standards, which refer to the levels at which students perform tasks, and criteria, or what is being evaluated. In some cases, educators establish criteria for district- or statewide standards and train scorers to be consistent in their grading (Garcia and Verville, 1994). Here are some guidelines for writing rubrics:

- Base standards on samples of student work that represent each level of proficiency.

- Use precise wording that describes observable behaviors in terms that children can understand.

- Avoid negative statements, such as "Cannot make predictions."

- Construct rubrics with 3-, 4-, or 5-point scales, with the highest number representing the most desirable level.

- Limit criteria to a reasonable number.

Conferences and Interviews

Another type of informal assessment occurs when teachers have conferences with children (or interview them) about their attitudes, interests, and progress in reading. Conferences may be scheduled or may occur spontaneously when opportunities arise. Sample questions for teachers to ask include the following:

Do you like reading? Why or why not?

Do you think reading is important? Why or why not?

What books have you read recently? What did you like/dislike about them?

Are you a good reader? Why do you think that?

What do you do when you have a problem understanding what you are reading?

What do you do when you come to a word that you don't know?

Through interviews, teachers learn how students make interpretations and construct meaning. They also gain insights into the reasoning behind children's task performances as the children explain their answers (Seda and Pearson, 1991).

Retellings

LITERATURE Story *retelling* occurs when a student retells a story she or he has heard or read. Retellings can also be done with expository text and material from different genres, such as biographies, fables, and mysteries, so that the reader can explore different types of texts (Johnston, 1992). At first, the teacher encourages the student to retell without offering assistance, but when the student appears to have finished, the teacher may prompt by asking open-ended questions, or together they may complete a graphic organizer that might stimulate further retelling. By listening carefully and analyzing documentation, the teacher can learn much about a student's understanding and appreciation of the story. Retellings are effective assessment tools and may be used with either oral or written responses. As an instructional technique, retellings benefit students by improving their comprehension, sense of structure, and use of oral language (Fisette, 1993). Chapter 5 discusses the instructional use of retellings in greater detail. A rubric, such as the one in Example 12.5 on page 470, may be used to specify the criteria and standards for the retelling and can serve as documentation for the task.

● Portfolio Assessment

Many teachers are adopting a portfolio approach to assessment. A *portfolio* is defined as a purposeful recording of learning that focuses on the work of the student and involves his or her reflection on that work (National Education Association, 1993). Student portfolios may be kept in expandable file folders, three-ring binders, or storage boxes or saved digitally on hard drives or CD-ROMs. Some teachers currently take advantage of web-based technologies to maintain a classroom presence and display student portfolio artifacts. Some host websites, such as Homestead (**www.homestead.com**) and Teacherweb (**http://teacherweb.com**), allow students

TECHNOLOGY

Portfolios are helpful ways for teachers or students to share information about student progress with caregivers. Like this girl, many students enjoy sharing their work with family members. *(© Elizabeth Crews)*

FAMILY

and teachers to create personal or school sites using design templates. Web addresses are assigned and can be accessed easily with an Internet connection. Maintaining portfolio artifacts in this manner makes viewing and sharing the portfolio convenient. It also facilitates communication between the school and home.

Portfolios enable students and teachers to analyze and reflect on student work in order to evaluate progress. Danielson and Abrutyn (1997) believe that it is not the portfolio itself, but the process of portfolio implementation, that helps establish a classroom climate in which both teachers and students recognize that learning is valued. Portfolios should focus on what a student *can* do, unlike tests, which often spotlight areas where students have not yet developed competence.

Implementing portfolio assessment is not easy (Stowell and Tierney, 1995). Moving from traditional testing practices to assessing student progress with portfolios can be a difficult transition that may take several years. There is no single way to implement portfolios unless a district mandates procedures and inclusions, so teachers and students must decide what works best for them. Teachers face many difficult decisions, such as what to include in order to reflect the range of activities that students are pursuing and the extent of students' capabilities. They need to consider how to analyze the material, how to evaluate the contents for grading purposes, and how to guide students' selections of their best work. Teachers therefore must ask themselves: Who will see the portfolios? What should a portfolio look like? Who decides what to include? How should information be shared? Three types of portfolios are listed below (Batzle, 1992; Leslie and Jett-Simpson, 1997; Salinger, 1996).

1 A *working portfolio,* a sampling of student work usually chosen by the student in collaboration with the teacher

2 A *showcase portfolio,* student-selected samples of best work only, likely to be shared with family members during conferences

3 A *record-keeping portfolio,* records of evaluation and test scores kept by the teacher, often for purposes of accountability

Both students and teachers should decide on the artifacts to be included in the portfolio. Artifacts should be dated and will vary according to the purposes for using them and the criteria for selection. Possible inclusions are the following (Fiderer, 1995; Wiener and Cohen, 1997): writing samples (from first draft to published work, to show growth); literacy goals; accounts of classroom experiences; a variety of products that demonstrate purposeful use of language; communications with others; audiotapes and/or videotapes; multimedia presentations; reasons for selecting certain pieces; and reflections and self-evaluations.

Valencia (1990) suggests guiding principles, based on research and classroom practice, for implementing a working-portfolio approach. Assessment must be authentic, continuous, multidimensional (including a wide range of cognitive processes and literacy activities), and collaborative (involving reflection by both teacher and student). It should be aligned with curriculum and instruction (Valencia and Place, 1994).

Portfolios allow for innovative ways to reveal information that is not always revealed through traditional assessments. Some examples include evidence of community or service learning, culminating performances from an interdisciplinary unit, and creative student products that demonstrate proficiency in a particular subject or skill area (Danielson and Abrutyn, 1997).

Although it is important for teachers and students to review portfolios together periodically, such reviews can consume considerable time. Teachers should develop rotating schedules in order to have conferences with students at least once a month. The accompanying Focus on Strategies illustrates one teacher's procedure for conferences.

FOCUS ON STRATEGIES **Using Portfolio Assessment**

Although this was the first year that Mr. Fernandez had asked his students to prepare portfolios, he was quickly becoming aware of their usefulness. They were very helpful during parent conferences, because he could show the parents exactly what their children had done during a six-week period—the progress they had made or, in a few cases, their lack of progress. The parents seemed to understand better what their children were doing by looking at their work than by having him try to explain it.

Mr. Fernandez had also found the samples of students' work useful when it was time to give report card grades. He had always believed that grades should be more than averages of test scores, and now he could use students' work samples to supplement their test score averages. Quite often, an examination of their work told him that his students were capable of better work than their tests indicated. If anyone questioned his judgment about his grades, he would be able to show these samples, along with the test scores, to support his evaluation.

Perhaps best of all, many children liked working on their portfolios. They really enjoyed looking back through their papers, recalling different pieces they had worked on and realizing they were getting better. They also liked being able to choose which pieces to include, although sometimes Mr. Fernandez suggested additional pieces.

Mr. Fernandez moved throughout the room, visiting with the students at their desks while they were engaged in an independent reading assignment. The students had been asked to have their portfolios ready and to be prepared for the individual conferences. When Mr. Fernandez completed his visits for the morning, he realized how much he had learned about the students' work as they explained their portfolios to him. He learned that he would need to help students make judgments about their work so that they could decide which selections merited inclusion in their portfolios. He would need to spend more time with some students. Some needed help with organizing and completing work. He saw opportunities for peer coaching, integration of special interests, and use of technology and other resources. Mr. Fernandez realized that conducting periodic portfolio reviews was a fine way to get to know his students better, understand their work, and encourage them to think and reflect.

Next year, Mr. Fernandez thought, he would do a few things differently. He had heard of placing an audiotape in each portfolio and recording the children's oral reading periodically. That would be another way to measure their progress. He also needed a better system of weeding out some of their work; their portfolios would be quite bulky by the end of the year. He would try to get some ideas from teachers who were already using portfolios so that he could make the procedure run more smoothly next time. "We're off to a good start this year, though," Mr. Fernandez thought, "and next year will be even better."

● Self-Appraisal

Assessment should help students develop the ability to judge their own accomplishments—to set their own goals, decide how to achieve those goals, and evaluate their progress in meeting the goals—in order to experience a sense of ownership in the assessment process (Au, 1990). Teachers can guide students toward self-assessment in a number of ways (Hansen, 1992; Winograd, Paris, and Bridge, 1991). By sharing audiotapes or videotapes of oral reading, observation note cards, and checklists, and by debriefing after shadowing, teachers can help students become aware of their strengths and of the ways in which they might improve. Through interviews, they can help students focus on their own progress by asking such questions as "How has your reading improved in the last month?" and "What goals would you like to set for yourself in reading and writing?" By including student self-evaluations as part of report card grades, teachers show students that they value their judgments.

Students who display metacognition are aware of how they learn and of their personal strengths and weaknesses in relation to specific learning tasks. They ask themselves questions in order to assess the difficulty of an assignment, the learning strategies they might use, any potential problems, and their likelihood of success. While they are reading or studying, their self-questioning might proceed as follows:

❶ Do I understand exactly what I am supposed to do for this assignment?

❷ What am I trying to learn?

❸ What do I already know about this subject that will help me understand what I read?

❹ What is the most efficient way for me to learn this material?

❺ What parts of this chapter may give me problems?

❻ What can I do so that I will understand the hard parts?

❼ Now that I have finished reading, do I understand what I have read?

TIME for REFLECTION

Traditionally, teachers have felt that assessment was their job and that students should have little or nothing to say about their own work. **How might you encourage students to appraise their own work?**

The self-appraisal form in Example 12.6 on page 476 is designed primarily for intermediate and middle-school children. It enables them to assess their competency in various reading skills and to recognize areas of strength or weakness. Teachers can use the results to understand students' perceptions of their own needs and to plan appropriate instruction. Another application for self-appraisal is found in Natalie Knox's literature circles. (See the following Classroom Scenario on page 477.)

LITERATURE ● **Appraising Literary Interests**

An observant teacher who takes time to be a sensitive, yet constructively critical, evaluator of children's progress is probably the best judge of the quality of their reactions to literature. The following questions will help the teacher in the evaluation process:

EXAMPLE 12.6 **Self-Check Exercise**

Directions: Read the following sentences and put a number beside each one.
Put 1 beside the sentence if it is nearly always true.
Put 2 beside the sentence if it is sometimes true.
Put 3 beside the sentence if it is hardly ever true.

_____ I understand what I read.

_____ I can find the main idea of a paragraph.

_____ I think about what I read and what it really means to me.

_____ I can "read between the lines" and understand what the author is trying to say.

_____ I think about what I already know about the subject as I read.

_____ I can figure out new words by reading the rest of the sentence.

_____ I can figure out new words by "sounding them out."

_____ I can use a dictionary to figure out how to pronounce new words.

_____ I can use a dictionary to find word meanings.

_____ I know how to find information in the library.

_____ I can locate books I like to read in the library.

_____ I can read aloud easily and with expression.

_____ I know what is important to learn in my textbooks.

_____ I know how to use the indexes in my books.

_____ I know how to study for a test.

_____ I ask myself questions as I read to make sure I understand.

---

❶ Are the children gaining an appreciation of good literature? How do I know?

❷ Are the children making good use of time in the library and during free reading of books and periodicals?

❸ Are the children enjoying storytelling, reading aloud, choral reading, and creative drama?

Teachers can obtain answers to these questions through children's spontaneous remarks ("Do you know any other good books about space travel?"), through directed conversation with the class ("What books would you like to add to our classroom library?"), and during individual conferences, when children have opportunities to describe books they like and dislike.

An excellent device for showing changes in literary taste over a period of time is a *reading record,* in which children record each book they read, giving the author, title, kind of book, date of report, and a brief statement of how well they liked the book. Reading records are often maintained separately by (or for) each child. They may classify reading selections by topic, such as poetry, fantasy, adventure, mystery, myths and folklore, animals (or, more specifically, horses and dogs, for example), biography, other lands, and sports. By focusing on their various interests and noting

Literature Circle Self-Evaluation

The students have completed the book for their literature circle, and it is time to fill out the self-evaluations Natalie has given them. They rate themselves from 0 (not at all) to 3 (above average) on criteria related to their reading, their group responses, and their writing logs. After carefully rating themselves, they give themselves grades and justify their grades with reasons. Some of the children responded as follows:

The grade I think I deserve for this literature group is ___*A*___ because

most of the answers above are number threes. And I love discussing questions and other things about my book.

The grade I think I deserve for this literature group is *B* because

I think I deserve a B because I sometimes took my vocabulary folder home and left it and then didn't have it.

The grade I think I deserve for this literature group is ___*C*___ because

I think I can do better in keeping up with my journal. Mostly, I keep my voice level down and rarely get called down.

Analysis of Scenario

Such self-evaluation encourages children to reflect on their work and to become aware of their strengths and weaknesses. In so doing, they become independent learners.

what genres of literature the children read, teachers may encourage them to read about new topics and to expand their reading interests.

● Informal Tests

In addition to such informal assessments as observations, shadowing, checklists, rubrics, and portfolios, teachers may administer informal tests for specific purposes. Teachers may construct these tests or may find them commercially available in manuals or books.

Informal Tests of Specific Content or Skills

Sometimes the classroom teacher needs to administer an informal test to check students' knowledge and understanding of a specific skill or content area. For instance, the teacher might construct a vocabulary test from words students have studied during a thematic unit. Basal reader programs usually include tests to be used for determining how well students have learned the content of a specific unit of instruction. Workbooks also contain skill tests to be given periodically. Whenever such tests are given, they should be used for diagnosing students' strengths and weaknesses, deciding if reteaching is needed, and providing direction for future learning experiences.

Cloze Procedure

The *cloze procedure* is an instructional strategy that can also be used as a tool to assess student comprehension. It provides information regarding a student's use of semantics, syntax, and context clues. By filling in words that have been deleted from a textbook selection, the student reveals his or her familiarity with the subject and ability to read the text with understanding. Test results give information about the student's independent, instructional, and frustration levels for both narrative and expository material. Independent, instructional, and frustration levels are discussed further in the "Informal Reading Inventory" section that follows. Cloze tests are constructed as follows:

❶ Select a passage of approximately 250 consecutive words. The passage should be one the students have not read, or tried to read, before.

❷ Type the passage, leaving the first sentence intact and deleting every fifth word thereafter. In place of deleted words, substitute blanks of uniform length. Then leave the last sentence intact.

❸ Give students the passage and tell them to fill in the blanks. Allow them all the time they need.

❹ Score the test by counting as correct only the exact words that were in the original text. Determine each student's percentage of correct answers.

If a student had less than 44 percent of the answers correct, the material is probably at his or her frustration level and is therefore too difficult. Thus you should offer alternative ways of learning the material. If the student had from 44 to 57 percent of the answers correct, the material is probably at that student's instructional level, and he or she will be able to learn from the text if you provide careful guidance in the reading by developing readiness, helping with new concepts and unfamiliar vocabulary, and providing reading purposes to aid comprehension. If the student had more than 57 percent of the answers correct, the material is probably at that student's independent level, and he or she should be able to benefit from the material when reading it independently (Bormuth, 1968).

A teacher who uses the percentages given here must count *only* exact words as correct, since the percentages were derived using only exact words. Synonyms must be counted as incorrect, along with obviously wrong answers and unfilled blanks.

Maze Procedure

Originated by Guthrie (1974), the *maze procedure*, a modification of the cloze procedure, requires the reader to choose from alternatives rather than to fill in a blank. To construct a maze test, the teacher must first select appropriate text. The first and last sentences should be left intact. Beginning with the second sentence, every fifth or tenth word is deleted, and three alternatives are offered from which the reader must choose. One choice is the correct word; another is a word that is syntactically acceptable but semantically unacceptable; the final choice is both syntactically and semantically unacceptable. The order in which the three words are presented should vary for each deletion (Vacca and Vacca, 1987).

Multimedia and Computer Approaches

TECHNOLOGY ▣   Multimedia and computers provide motivational alternatives to traditional testing. Photographs of completed projects, audiotapes of children retelling stories or reading orally, and videotapes of student performances and students at work are useful for recording and evaluating children's learning experiences throughout the year. Multimedia computer presentations, prepared by students, show evidence of facility with a number of literacy skills.

Teachers can use computers for assessment in several additional ways. Online testing allows students to work at computers that have software that analyzes their responses. Sometimes computers are used to scan mark-sensitive answer sheets that students have completed while working with test booklets. The computer scores the tests, thus freeing the teacher from this task. Software is also available to help teachers modify test items and entire tests, perform test and item analysis, collect and analyze test scores and student grades, record grades for various assignments, and compute final grades. *Gradebook Plus* enables teachers to record grades daily and to compute a student's average grade at any time (McCarthy, 1994). Web-based technologies also allow teachers and students to create web pages that can be used to display and share portfolio artifacts.

Informal Reading Inventory

Teachers administer *informal reading inventories (IRIs)* to get a general idea of a child's reading levels and strengths and weaknesses in word recognition and comprehension. IRIs help teachers identify specific types of word recognition and comprehension difficulties so that they can use this information to plan appropriate instruction. An IRI can indicate a child's

❶ *Independent reading level* (level to be read "on his or her own").

❷ *Instructional level* (level of the material the child can read with teacher guidance).

❸ *Frustration level* (level that thwarts or baffles).

❹ *Listening comprehension level* (potential reading level).

An IRI typically consists of an analysis of oral and silent reading, as well as listening comprehension. The oral reading sequence in an informal reading inventory should begin on the highest level at which the child achieves 100 percent on a sight word recognition test. After the oral reading, the teacher asks questions about the selection; then the child reads the silent reading part and is asked questions about that selection.

Material is written at a child's *independent* reading level when he or she correctly pronounces 99 words out of 100 (99 percent correct) and correctly responds to at least 90 percent of the questions. The material for which the child correctly pronounces 95 percent of the words and correctly answers at least 75 percent of the questions is roughly at the child's *instructional* level, the level at which teaching may effectively take place.

If a student needs help on more than one word out of ten or responds correctly to fewer than 50 percent of the questions, the material is too advanced and is at the child's *frustration* level. After the frustration level has been reached, the teacher should read aloud higher levels of material until the child reaches the highest reading level for which he or she can correctly answer 75 percent of the comprehension questions. The highest level achieved indicates the child's probable *listening comprehension* level (potential reading level).

Teachers may make their own informal reading inventories, or they may use commercially prepared inventories. Example 12.7 shows a sample reading selection with comprehension questions and scoring aid from the *Burns/Roe Informal Reading Inventory*.

It is important to remember that the result of an informal reading inventory is an *estimate* of a student's reading levels. The percentages the child achieves are a significant indication of levels of performance, but the teacher's observations of the child taking the test are equally important.

Miscue Analysis

Similar in form and procedures to the informal reading inventory, the **reading miscue inventory (RMI)** considers both the quantity and the quality of **miscues**, or unexpected responses. Instead of simply considering the number of errors and giving equal weight to each, the teacher analyzes the RMI for the significance of each miscue. Knowing the type of miscue and what might have caused it provides more information about reading difficulties than knowing only the number of miscues. (Some commercial IRIs, such as the one in Example 12.7, also include a qualitative analysis.)

Miscue analysis helps teachers gain insight into the reading process and helps them analyze students' oral reading (Y. Goodman, 1995). Analysis of the types of miscues each student makes helps the teacher interpret why students are having difficulties. To some extent, miscues are the result of the thought and language the student brings to the reading situation. Therefore, analyzing miscues in terms of the student's background or schemata enables the teacher to understand why some miscues were given and to provide appropriate instructional strategies that build on the student's strengths.

Teachers should consider whether miscalled words indicate lack of knowledge about phonics or structural analysis, show inability to use context, reveal limited sight word knowledge, result from dialect differences, or suggest some other type of difficulty. Therefore, while listening to a child read, a teacher must evaluate the significance of different miscues. For example, the child who reads "The boys are playing" as "The boys is playing" may be a speaker of a nonstandard dialect and may be using his or her decoding ability to translate the printed text to meaning. This miscue does not interfere with meaning, but many miscues do reflect problems.

In studying the miscues, the teacher should check for specific items such as the following:

❶ Is the miscue a result of the reader's dialect? If the reader says *foe* for *four*, he or she may simply be using a familiar pronunciation that does not affect meaning.

EXAMPLE 12.7   Reading Selection and Questions from an Informal Reading Inventory

TEACHER 5 ☆

INTRODUCTORY STATEMENT: Read this story to find out about a harbor seal pup that has a special problem.

In the sea, a harbor seal pup learns to catch and eat fish by watching its mother. By the time it is weaned, at the age of four or five weeks, it is able to feed on its own.

Without a mother, and living temporarily in captivity, Pearson had to be taught what a fish was and how to swallow it. Eventually, he would have to learn to catch one himself.

Holly started his training with a small herring—an oily fish which is a favorite with seals. Gently, she opened his mouth and slipped the fish in headfirst. Harbor seals have sharp teeth for catching fish but no teeth for grinding and chewing. They swallow their food whole.

But Pearson didn't seem to understand what he was supposed to do. He bit down on the fish and then spit it out. Holly tried again. This time, Pearson got the idea. He swallowed the herring in one gulp and looked eagerly for more.

Within a week, he was being hand-fed a pound of fish a day in addition to his formula. This new diet made him friskier than ever. He chased the other pups in the outside pen. He plunged into the small wading pool and rolled in the shallow water, splashing both seals and people.

Source: Pearson, A Harbor Seal Pup, by Susan Meyers (New York: E. P. Dutton, 1980), pp. 15–16. [*Note*: Do not count as a miscue mispronunciation of the name Pearson. You may pronounce this name for the student if needed.]

FORM A

SCORING AID
Word Recognition %—Miscues
99–3
95–11
90–22
85–33
Comprehension %—Errors
100–0
90–1
80–2
70–3
60–4
50–5
40–6
30–7
20–8
10–9
0–10
214 Words (for word recognition)
217 Words (for rate)
WPM
∕13020

COMPREHENSION QUESTIONS

5 PASSAGE ☆

____ main idea 1. What is this story about? (teaching a harbor seal pup to catch and eat fish; teaching Pearson to catch and eat fish)

____ detail 2. How does a harbor seal pup learn to catch and eat fish in the sea? (by watching its mother)

____ vocabulary 3. What does the word "temporarily" mean? (for a short time; not permanently)

____ vocabulary 4. What does the word "captivity" mean? (the condition of being held as a prisoner or captive; confinement; a condition in which a person or animal is not free)

____ cause and effect/inference 5. What caused Pearson to need to be taught what a fish was and how to swallow it? (He didn't have a mother to show him.)

____ inference 6. What is an oily fish that seals like? (herring)

____ cause and effect/inference 7. What causes harbor seals to swallow their food whole? (They have no teeth for grinding and chewing.)

____ sequence 8. Name in order the two things that Pearson did the first time Holly put a fish in his mouth. (bit down on the fish and then spit it out)

____ inference 9. How fast did Pearson learn how to eat a fish? (He learned on the second try.)

____ detail 10. What made Pearson get friskier? (his new diet of fish and formula; his new diet)

Source: Betty D. Roe, *Burns/Roe Informal Reading Inventory*, Sixth Edition. Copyright © 1999 by Houghton Mifflin Company. Used with permission.

❷ Does the miscue change the meaning? If the reader says *dismal* for *dismiss*, the meaning is changed and the substitution would not make sense.

❸ Does the reader self-correct? If a student says a word that does not make sense but self-corrects, he or she is trying to make sense of what he or she is reading.

❹ Is the reader using syntactic cues? If a student says *run* for *chase*, the student still shows some use of syntactic cues, but if the student says *boy* for *beautiful*, he or she is probably losing the syntactic pattern.

❺ Is the student using graphic cues? Comparing the sounds and spellings of miscues and expected words in substitutions will reveal how a reader is using graphic cues. Examples of graphic miscues include *house* for *horse*, *running* for *run*, *is* for *it*, and *dogs* for *dog*.

Running Records

The *running record* is a detailed account of a student's reading behavior, which helps a teacher determine how well that student is reading (Clay, 1979; Harris and Hodges, 1995). The procedure for completing the running record is similar to that used with the IRI or RMI. While a child is reading, the teacher places a check above every word read correctly. When a child makes a miscue, the teacher uses a coding system to mark the type of miscue. After completing the running record, the teacher considers why the child made each miscue by asking, "What made him/her say that?"

Running records are particularly useful for classroom teachers because they can be made quickly and easily in any oral reading situation in which the teacher can see the text that a student is reading (Lipson and Wixson, 1997). Students' miscues offer insights into how well they use various reading strategies, construct meaning from text, and monitor their own reading (e.g., self-correct if something doesn't make sense). As a result, teachers become aware of students' strengths and weaknesses and gain information to guide their instruction (Salinger, 1996).

TIME for REFLECTION

Some educators believe that counting the total number of miscues a reader makes is sufficient for purposes of evaluation, but others consider it important to analyze miscues to find the reasons for unexpected responses. **What do *you* think, and why?**

● Further Considerations About Alternative Assessment

Even though alternative assessment gives a great deal of information about how well a child uses reading strategies, it has some limitations that teachers should consider. First, alternative assessment is subjective; that is, the teacher's personal biases may influence judgments about student performance. Therefore, it is possible for two teachers to assess the same work differently. Also, some teachers may not be knowledgeable about the use of informal strategies or may not have realistic expectations for students at a certain level, so their assessments may not be fair appraisals of student performance. Alternative assessment can also take a great deal of time if teachers write frequent narrative reports on student progress instead of simply assigning numerical or letter grades based on objective test results. In addition, teachers must know how to interpret and apply information from informal records to help children improve their reading strategies.

Assessing Text Difficulty

In planning instruction based on assessment, the teacher must not only be aware of the students' levels of performance but also be prepared to select materials that provide the appropriate scaffolding. In selecting materials to teach in the content areas, teachers must be aware of the level of difficulty of the textbook or literature assignments they make. Methods of identifying text difficulty include the use of readability formulas, cloze tests, and text-leveling techniques.

● Readability Formulas

Readability formulas often rank text by numerical values based on syntactic and semantic difficulty. When teachers have determined the students' reading levels with tests, they can obtain an approximate idea of whether a textbook or literature selection is appropriate by testing it with a standard measure of readability. Among widely used readability formulas, the *Spache Readability Formula* is designed for primary-grade books (Spache, 1966), the *Dale-Chall Readability Formula* is designed for materials from the fourth-grade through college levels (Dale and Chall, 1948), and the *Fry Readability Graph* (Fry, 1977b) can be used on material at all levels.

Because readability formulas are strictly text-based, they do not give information related to the interactive nature of reading. For example, they cannot gauge a reader's background knowledge about the topic, motivation to read the material, or interest in the topic, although these are important factors in determining the difficulty of a text for a particular student. In addition, they cannot separate reasonable prose from a series of unconnected words (Rush, 1985). They cannot measure the effects of an author's writing style or the complexity of concepts presented, and they do not consider the format of the material (typeface and type size, spacing, amount of white space on the page, numbers of illustrations and pictures, and so on). For these reasons, no formula offers more than an approximation of level of difficulty of material. Formulas do, however, generally give reliable information about the relative difficulty levels of textbook passages and other printed materials, and this information can be extremely helpful to teachers. Example 12.8 on page 484 shows a quick way to estimate readability. Computer programs designed to test readability can also ease the burden of making calculations by hand. Grammar and style checking programs may run several formulas.

Many content area textbooks are written at much higher readability levels than basal readers for the corresponding grades, and subject matter textbooks also often vary in difficulty from chapter to chapter, as discussed in Chapter 10. Unfamiliar content vocabulary is a major factor in the higher difficulty levels of many content area materials. A good way to decrease the readability levels of content passages for students, therefore, is to teach the content vocabulary thoroughly before the material containing the vocabulary is assigned to be read.

One way for the teacher to estimate the suitability of a textbook or literature selection for students is to construct and administer a cloze test. Because all the material in a given book is unlikely to be written on the same level, teachers should

EXAMPLE 12.8 Fry Readability Formula

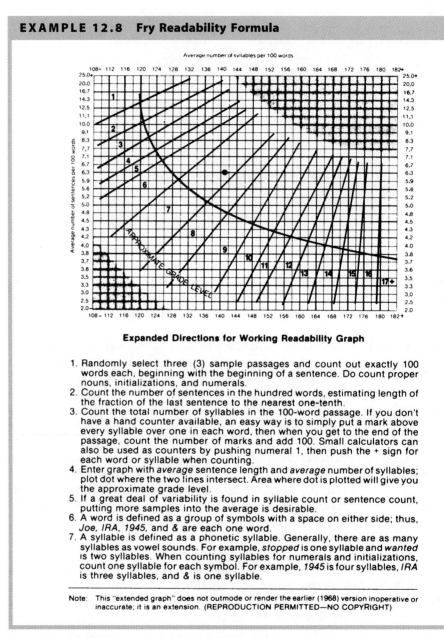

Expanded Directions for Working Readability Graph

1. Randomly select three (3) sample passages and count out exactly 100 words each, beginning with the beginning of a sentence. Do count proper nouns, initializations, and numerals.
2. Count the number of sentences in the hundred words, estimating length of the fraction of the last sentence to the nearest one-tenth.
3. Count the total number of syllables in the 100-word passage. If you don't have a hand counter available, an easy way is to simply put a mark above every syllable over one in each word, then when you get to the end of the passage, count the number of marks and add 100. Small calculators can also be used as counters by pushing numeral 1, then push the + sign for each word or syllable when counting.
4. Enter graph with *average* sentence length and *average* number of syllables; plot dot where the two lines intersect. Area where dot is plotted will give you the approximate grade level.
5. If a great deal of variability is found in syllable count or sentence count, putting more samples into the average is desirable.
6. A word is defined as a group of symbols with a space on either side; thus, *Joe, IRA, 1945,* and *&* are each one word.
7. A syllable is defined as a phonetic syllable. Generally, there are as many syllables as vowel sounds. For example, *stopped* is one syllable and *wanted* is two syllables. When counting syllables for numerals and initializations, count one syllable for each symbol. For example, *1945* is four syllables, *IRA* is three syllables, and *&* is one syllable.

Note: This "extended graph" does not outmode or render the earlier (1968) version inoperative or inaccurate; it is an extension. (REPRODUCTION PERMITTED—NO COPYRIGHT)

Source: "Fry's Readability Graph: Clarifications, Validity, and Extension to Level 17," *Journal of Reading,* 21 (December 1977), p. 249.

choose several samples for a cloze test from several places in the book in order to determine the book's suitability for a particular child.

Example 12.9 on page 485 shows a cloze passage for a social studies textbook. This passage contains 283 words. No words have been deleted from the first sentence

EXAMPLE 12.9 Cloze Test

Directions: Read the following passage and fill in each blank with a word that makes sense in the sentence.

The first battle in July 1861 began like a holiday outing. Union supporters packed picnic _____ (1) and followed soldiers from _____ (2), D.C., into Virginia. Newspaper _____ (3) also came to get _____ (4) story.
Armies from the _____ (5) and the South met _____ (6) a stream called Bull _____ (7), about 25 miles from _____ (8), D.C. At first Confederates _____ (9) the Union soldiers back. _____ (10) the Confederates attacked. Fierce _____ (11) broke out, and the _____ (12) army won the battle.
_____ (13) Battle of Bull Run _____ (14) the North that it _____ (15) not win the war _____ (16). Congress passed laws calling _____ (17) troops to serve three _____ (18). President Lincoln's generals had _____ (19) plan to save the _____ (20). The Union's "anaconda plan" _____ (21) named for the snake _____ (22) squeezes its prey to _____ (23). The Union planned to _____ (24) the strength out of _____ (25) South by a blockade, _____ (26) closing of southern ocean _____ (27). Union ships would stop _____ (28) and keep Southerners from _____ (29) money by selling cotton _____ (30) other countries.
Under the _____ (31) plan, Union ships would _____ (32) control of the Mississippi _____ (33). Confederate states would then _____ (34) unable to send boats _____ (35) supplies and soldiers to _____ (36) Confederate states. Finally, Union _____ (37) would try to capture _____ (38), the Confederate capital.
The _____ (39) also had plans. One _____ (40) to destroy Union ships. _____ (41) 1862, the South sent _____ (42) iron-sided steamship, *Merrimack*, up _____ (43) James River. (The South _____ (44) the ship the *Virginia*.) _____ (45) *Merrimack* was far stronger _____ (46) the Union's wooden ships. _____ (47) Union ships fired at _____ (48), the cannonballs could not _____ (49) the ship's sides.
The _____ (50) day, the Union sent its own iron ship, the *Monitor*, to attack the *Merrimack*. The two ships battled, with no clear winner.

Answers: (1) lunches, (2) Washington, (3) reporters, (4) the, (5) North, (6) near, (7) Run, (8) Washington, (9) held, (10) Then, (11) fighting, (12) Confederate, (13) The, (14) showed, (15) would, (16) easily, (17) for, (18) years, (19) a, (20) Union, (21) was, (22) that, (23) death, (24) squeeze, (25) the, (26) or, (27) ports, (28) supplies, (29) earning, (30) to, (31) anaconda, (32) take, (33) River, (34) be, (35) with, (36) other, (37) forces, (38) Richmond, (39) South, (40) was, (41) In, (42) its, (43) the, (44) renamed, (45) The, (46) than, (47) When, (48) it, (49) pierce, (50) next.

in order to give the student an opportunity to develop an appropriate mental set for the material that follows, and the entire paragraph in which the fiftieth blank occurs has been included in order to complete the thought that was in progress. A score of fewer than 22 correct responses indicates that the material is too difficult; a score of

22 to 28 indicates that the child can manage the material if the teacher gives assistance; and a score of more than 28 indicates that the child can read the material independently.

Some authorities prefer cloze tests to informal reading inventories, or IRIs, for matching textbooks to students because these tests put the child in direct contact with the author's language without having the teacher as a mediator (through the written questions). Frequently a child can understand the text but not the teacher's questions related to it, which can cause the teacher to underestimate the child's comprehension of the material. On the other hand, some children react with frustration to cloze materials; these children would fare better if tested with an IRI. Children should have experience with cloze-type exercises before teachers use this procedure to help match students with textbooks at the appropriate levels.

● Leveled Texts

Text leveling involves organizing texts according to a defined continuum of characteristics so that teachers can match students with appropriate materials (Fountas and Pinnell, 1996; Fry, 2002; Walker, 2004). Whereas readability is determined in an objective manner, leveling of texts occurs more subjectively. In some cases, individual teachers or teams of teachers work collaboratively to level texts and compile a collection of appropriate reading materials. Fountas and Pinnell (1996) offer lists of texts that have been leveled and are suggested for use in the implementation of guided reading, described in Chapter 10. Characteristics of texts are first identified, and then decisions about the level of difficulty are made. Some characteristics or text factors that are often included in the process of leveling are

- format or size and layout of print,

- content, including concepts and vocabulary,

- length,

- illustration support,

- genre,

- predictability, and

- language structure

Readability may also be considered in the leveling process. The leveling of texts involves observation of students' reading behavior as they interact with the text over a period of time. Running records are maintained and provide information to identify benchmark texts for the various levels. Benchmark texts are those that remain reliable for the level for approximately 90 percent of the students. Although the leveling of texts does not rely only on a quantitative formula, it involves consideration of more text factors and is particularly appealing to teachers at the primary levels (Fountas and Pinnell, 1996; Fry, 2002).

SUMMARY

Assessment procedures are constantly changing as educators seek ways to measure student progress in reading that reflect current views of the reading process. More than ever before, assessment is merging with instruction as teachers continuously observe students, interact with them, and analyze their strengths and weaknesses.

Although teachers may sometimes use formal assessment techniques, they are more likely to evaluate young children's progress through alternative assessment procedures. As students engage in learning experiences, the teacher collects and analyzes data to determine appropriate instructional strategies to scaffold and support the development of emergent literacy.

Formal assessment consists of standardized tests that are administered, scored, and interpreted according to designated procedures. Norm-referenced tests compare students with other students across the nation on the basis of standard scores. Most schools require that achievement tests be administered annually to measure the progress students have made in overall academic achievement. Most traditional standardized tests measure mastery by requiring students to answer multiple-choice questions. Test developers are seeking ways to include more authentic tasks on standardized tests, but progress has been slow.

The teacher can use criterion-referenced tests to determine how well a student has mastered a specific skill. Skill mastery, however, does not always indicate whether or not the student can apply the skill to actual reading situations.

Alternative assessment can take many forms, and teachers can learn much about their students by using observation strategies. Daily observation, or "kidwatching," is a key to effective assessment, and teachers can record their observations in a variety of ways, including anecdotal records and checklists and rating scales. Rubrics make students aware of expectations by giving specific criteria for scoring their work, and teachers gain insight into students' reading abilities through shadowing, conferences, interviews, and retelling. Portfolios are useful for keeping samples of student work, and self-appraisal helps students evaluate their own accomplishments.

Informal tests that cover specific areas, including teacher-made tests on content or skills, provide information about student mastery of specific detail. Cloze procedures and maze procedures enable teachers to assess a student's comprehension of material, and multimedia and computers are also used in various ways to assess students' knowledge. The informal reading inventory, reading miscue inventory, and running records are similar informal measures that help the teacher identify students' strengths and weaknesses.

The teacher's most useful assessment tool is day-to-day observation. Informal tests may be used to reinforce or supplement such observation, whereas standardized tests are generally given only as mandated by the school system. The following chart summarizes the purposes and characteristics of alternative and formal assessment.

Alternative Assessment	*Formal Assessment*
Gives teacher useful day-to-day information about student progress	Compares students with other students across the nation

Alternative Assessment	Formal Assessment
Informs teacher about planning instruction to meet students' needs	Provides accountability for school systems
Identifies individual strengths and weaknesses	Gives scores that can be interpreted statistically
Occurs continuously	Occurs once or twice a year
Uses classroom-based materials and procedures	Uses standardized materials and procedures

Teachers use various readability formulas and cloze tests to determine whether a text or written material is too easy or too difficult for students so that appropriate materials can be selected for instruction. Leveling is also a method of determining text difficulty according to predetermined characteristics or text factors, which may include, as one criterion used for the rankings, readability based on a formula.

TEST YOURSELF

True or False

_____ 1. Current practices in formal assessment correspond closely with what is known about the reading process.

_____ 2. Traditional standardized tests are more helpful than alternative multiple measures of assessment for guiding instruction.

_____ 3. Instruction and assessment should be separate procedures.

_____ 4. Teachers must devise their own informal reading inventories, since none are commercially available.

_____ 5. Most standardized tests consist primarily of multiple-choice items.

_____ 6. Material written on a child's independent reading level is less difficult than material written on his or her instructional level.

_____ 7. Miscue analysis can help a teacher understand the nature of a child's unexpected responses in reading.

_____ 8. Self-questioning is an effective tool for reading and studying.

_____ 9. Standardized tests that use authentic tasks are highly feasible and practical to use at this time.

_____ 10. A criterion-referenced assessment relates an individual's test performances to absolute standards rather than to the performances of others.

_____ 11. At present there are no computer programs for assessing reading skills.

_____ 12. Major changes have been occurring in standardized testing for much of the past seventy years.

_____ 13. Authentic assessment focuses on small, separate skills.

_____ 14. Three significant aspects of informal evaluation are observation, interaction, and analysis.

_____ 15. The term *kidwatching* refers to professional baby-sitting.

_____ 16. Recordkeeping is an essential part of observation.

_____ 17. Anecdotal records are written accounts of specific classroom incidents.

_____ 18. Story retelling enables teachers to learn about a child's comprehension of a story.

_____ 19. A rubric is used for scoring cloze tests.

_____ 20. It is considered desirable for students to assess their own progress.

_____ 21. In evaluating the results of a reading miscue inventory, the teacher focuses on the types of miscues rather than on the total number of miscalled words.

_____ 22. A running record is a narrative report of a child's overall progress.

_____ 23. Rubrics consist of standards (levels of proficiency) and criteria (skills or behaviors being evaluated).

_____ 24. The cloze procedure is an example of a norm-referenced test.

_____ 25. When portfolios are used, samples of a student's work should be collected and reviewed by both the student and the teacher.

_____ 26. The best questions for a teacher to ask during a student conference or interview are those that can be answered with *yes* or *no*.

_____ 27. Formal tests are the most appropriate form of assessment for young children.

_____ 28. Shadowing involves the important feature of debriefing, or discussing the observation with the student.

_____ 29. Web-based technologies enable teachers and students to maintain portfolios that can be accessed via the Internet.

_____ 30. Readability formulas and leveling are similar in that they both attempt to rank written materials on the basis of characteristics that contribute to text difficulty.

For your journal . . .

❶ Reflect on the various types of alternative assessment discussed in this chapter. Which of them do you consider most useful? Why?

❷ How can the misuse of standardized tests hurt both students and teachers? What can be done to avoid their misuse?

❸ What do you think it means to merge instruction and assessment? How can one support the other?

❹ Reflect on the video on your CD that accompanies this chapter. How might a running record be used as an artifact that shows progress or growth over time?

. . . and your portfolio

❶ Collect samples of student work that you could use as examples for each proficiency level, or standard, of a rubric. Be sure to focus on what you intend to measure.

❷ Start an annotated list of recent journal articles that present current views of assessment. Consider how you can apply these views to your classroom.

❸ Plan ways to use portfolio assessment in your classroom. Consider your purposes, a desirable format, ways to involve students in the selection and maintenance of portfolios, and ways to organize and store them.

Classroom Organization and Management

KEY
VOCABULARY
Pay close attention to these terms when they appear in the chapter.

Americans with Disabilities Act (ADA)

community of learners

cooperative learning

dynamic grouping

IEP (Individual Education Plan)

IEP team

Individuals with Disabilities Education Act (IDEA)

integrated language arts curriculum

interest grouping

learning center

learning contract

paraprofessional

peer tutoring

project or research grouping

skills or needs groups

student pairs

thematic unit

SETTING OBJECTIVES

When you finish reading this chapter, you should be able to

● Explain some benefits of an integrated language arts curriculum and how to implement it.

● Discuss some strategies for cooperative learning.

● Identify various ways that teachers might group students for reading-related purposes.

● Identify ways to create a supportive physical and social-emotional environment in the classroom.

● Outline the essential basics of the 4-Blocks Literacy Model for the language arts classroom.

● List several guidelines for creating an inclusive classroom in which all students can learn.

● Explain how the teacher can function as facilitator and manager of instruction, decision maker, researcher, and learner.

● Describe some ways that teachers can communicate with families.

● Explain the roles that paraprofessionals and tutors play within the reading program.

Classroom organization does not directly involve the reading process or materials, methods, or approaches to teaching reading. Yet without supportive classroom organization and management, reading instruction may be ineffective. It is not enough for teachers to know what to teach; they must also know what organizational patterns and management techniques are conducive to learning.

This chapter presents various types of organizational patterns and practical suggestions for forming and managing different kinds of groups. It considers an integrated language arts curriculum, a way to provide large blocks of time for students to learn and use language arts — reading, writing, listening, speaking,

Chapter 13 Organization

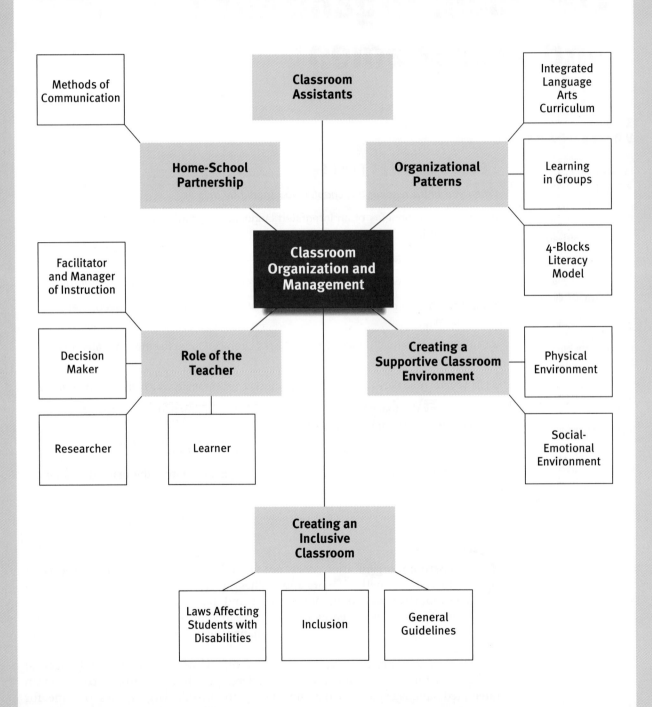

Methods of Communication

Home-School Partnership

Classroom Assistants

Integrated Language Arts Curriculum

Organizational Patterns

Learning in Groups

4-Blocks Literacy Model

Facilitator and Manager of Instruction

Classroom Organization and Management

Decision Maker

Role of the Teacher

Creating a Supportive Classroom Environment

Physical Environment

Researcher

Learner

Social-Emotional Environment

Creating an Inclusive Classroom

Laws Affecting Students with Disabilities

Inclusion

General Guidelines

viewing, and visually presenting—meaningfully. It examines cooperative learning, the 4-Blocks Literacy Model, and various grouping arrangements. The importance of creating inclusive classroom environments that are supportive of all students is discussed, and suggestions are outlined.

Next, the chapter recognizes the teacher as the most important variable in the classroom and introduces four major roles of the teacher: the teacher as facilitator and manager of instruction, as decision maker, as researcher, and as learner. The chapter also considers the influence of the home environment on students' reading attitudes and achievement. Finally, the chapter explains the value of paraprofessionals and tutors in the school program.

Organizational Patterns

DIVERSITY It is no secret that students within a single class vary a great deal in chronological age, maturity, physical and cognitive abilities, interests, and cultural and personal experiences. When attempting to provide the most appropriate instruction for each learner, teachers must give careful consideration to plans that adjust for individual differences and create a sense of community. Students should be given the opportunity to participate in small-group, individualized, partner, and whole-class activities.

Following are some general guidelines for classroom organization of a learning-centered classroom.

❶ Remember that no single classroom organization is best for all situations.

❷ Consider many criteria in deciding on a particular organizational plan, including students' needs and interests, your own strengths and weaknesses, your educational philosophy, and the specific goals of instruction.

❸ Keep organizational plans and scheduling flexible; alter them as you become aware of opportunities for improvement.

❹ Organize your classroom so that it is structured and orderly, but provide a supportive emotional climate.

❺ Offer opportunities for individualized learning, making sure to manage independent activities for the benefit of all students.

❻ Whenever appropriate, provide whole-class instruction so that all students experience a sense of community.

❼ Provide opportunities for students to cooperate and collaborate in a broad range of learning experiences.

● Integrated Language Arts Curriculum

An *integrated language arts curriculum*, described in Chapter 8, emphasizes relationships among reading, writing, listening, speaking, viewing, and visually presenting in authentic situations. Growth in one area is likely to result in growth in the others, and the language arts become the foundation for content area learning. As language learning extends into the various subject areas, teachers can create a holistic and connected curricular approach to learning (Tchudi, 1994). A well-developed integrated curriculum also encourages students to examine their own learning process while they are engaged in studying a particular subject or discipline (Tomlinson et al., 2002). Integration of subjects is supported by the associative theory of learning, which states that students learn by associating material with other information, rather than by practicing isolated skills and memorizing facts (Cunningham and Allington, 1994). They learn by drawing on material from different but related sources to solve problems and reach goals. Routman (1994) cautions, however, that teachers will find it difficult to achieve a fully integrated curriculum in which language, content, and concepts are interrelated across the entire curriculum all of the time.

For an integrated language arts classroom to work, teachers, along with their students, must develop and implement a basic management and organizational plan. Such a plan considers the needs of students, the room arrangement, the availability and location of resources, and time allocations. Resources consist of authentic reading and writing materials arranged so that students can access them easily. Reading materials may include newspapers and magazines, a large quantity of trade books (fiction and nonfiction), electronic books, print and electronic reference materials (atlases, dictionaries, almanacs, and so forth), computer software, student-published books, tape-recorded stories with accompanying books, scrapbooks, and textbooks. Writing materials include lined and unlined paper, simply constructed booklets, computer paper, mailboxes to hold individual correspondence, a variety of writing tools (felt-tipped markers, pencils, and pens), and a message board for students' messages. Because students often participate in organizing, storing, and maintaining these materials, they may feel responsible for them and thus tend to take good care of them.

In an integrated language arts curriculum, the language arts, along with the content areas, are taught in purposeful ways during flexible blocks of time. Children read and write throughout the day as they work independently, with partners, or in small groups. The Classroom Scenario on page 495 illustrates the importance of the teacher's preparation to the organization of an integrated language arts classroom.

Themes in an Integrated Curriculum

Thematic units, discussed in Chapter 7, integrate instruction meaningfully across the curriculum, thus enabling students to see connections among different subjects. Most subjects can be integrated with a theme, although some subjects must receive additional attention if they do not fit naturally into the theme. During theme studies, students often extend their learning by pursuing ideas or concepts in depth. They are using information for meaningful purposes instead of simply memorizing facts for test taking (Shanahan, Robinson, and Schneider, 1995). A theme study is the core of the curriculum for an extended period of time. "A thematic approach provides an organizational framework for students to learn language as well as to learn through language" (Pike, Compain, and Mumper, 1994, p. 272).

Themes should be broadly based, should provide a focus for the study, and should give the students an opportunity to enter the integration process (Erickson, 2001). Themes should be selected by considering curriculum standards, students'

STANDARDS AND
ASSESSMENT

Integrated Language Arts Classroom

The students in Melanie Childress's third grade are busily involved in a variety of reading and writing activities. Most students are working independently or with one another, while Ms. Childress acts as a consultant to students who need help. On the board, Ms. Childress has written "mystery questions" for which the students must find answers by searching through newspapers. She has also given them the option of either writing friendly letters to acquaintances, Miss Beth and Ms. Ann, or completing the following assignment: You are a pioneer. You can have three animals. What three animals would you choose, and why?

Other students are getting ready to publish books they have been working on for several weeks. Ms. Childress is helping them with their final drafts, while classmates also offer editorial advice.

One girl approaches a visitor and eagerly reads the book she has written. She points out that her book is patterned after another story but uses different names for the characters and a slightly different sequence of events. Another student enthusiastically shows the classroom library to a visitor and points out a milk crate full of books by Robert Munsch. Meanwhile, three boys excitedly approach a visitor and offer to act out a play that a fourth member of their group has written.

Analysis of Scenario

In Ms. Childress's classroom, students are enthusiastic about a multitude of reading and writing experiences. Ms. Childress's integrated language arts classroom may appear disorganized to the casual observer, but in reality, she has carefully planned and prepared purposeful activities in an environment in which students are free to choose, take risks, and explore their own interests in reading and writing.

interests and areas of expertise, school-wide themes, parental concerns, and the teacher's own sense of what is worth knowing. At the beginning of the school year, students might brainstorm topics they want to study, and the teacher can try to match their ideas with topics suggested in the curriculum framework.

Teachers and students may work together to *negotiate* the curriculum. Teachers bring their knowledge and experiences from encounters with experts and fields of study, and students bring their knowledge and experiences with life and learning. Together they plan what to study, make webs of "What We Know" and "What We Want to Know," and create lists of resources for obtaining information. As students explore a theme, they continue acquiring new information until they are ready to share their new knowledge with their classmates. The teacher's role is to help organize individual and group learning and to encourage students to consider new questions, search for resources, model and demonstrate effective learning strategies, and discover different ways to present their ideas to their peers. Students generally find a negotiated curriculum to be motivational, relevant, and meaningful (Davenport, Jaeger, and Lauritzen, 1995).

Scheduling

Scheduling is unique for each classroom. For an integrated language arts curriculum, large blocks of time may be needed, instead of small, fragmented, 15- or 20-minute

In an integrated language arts classroom, teachers should have brief conferences with most or all students daily or should schedule regular conferences as well as holding occasional unscheduled ones. *(© Jean Claude LeJeune)*

chunks each for handwriting, spelling, grammar, and so forth. This designated block of time should occur without interruption, providing time for a variety of language experiences, including conference time with students.

LITERATURE

Language arts instruction includes such activities as journal writing, process writing (including prewriting, drafting, revising, editing, and sharing and publishing), shared reading, author studies, reading and writing workshops, and literature circles. Whenever possible, the language arts should be related to the theme or topic; that is, spelling words may be theme-related words, and reading, research, and writing activities may center on the theme as well. Students continue using language arts to investigate the theme, while also learning about social studies, science, and other areas of the curriculum.

STANDARDS AND
ASSESSMENT

Teachers may hold conferences with individual students any time during the day that students are working independently, to offer help and evaluate progress. Since students are not always aware that they need conferences and therefore do not request them, teachers should have brief conferences with students daily or schedule regular conferences, as well as sometimes holding unscheduled ones. Scheduled conferences enable both teacher and student to prepare in advance by gathering and reviewing pertinent materials. Although the length of time varies depending on the needs of the students, conferences usually average about five minutes per student. Thus, in a class of thirty students, a teacher could schedule conferences with six students each day within a half-hour's time. Teachers may go to students' desks or work areas, meet with students by calling them one by one to a designated area, or assemble the group scheduled for that day at a conference table.

STANDARDS AND
ASSESSMENT ## Program Evaluation

In moving toward an integrated language arts classroom, teachers might ask themselves some of the following questions to determine their progress:

- Am I using themes to integrate instruction in the language arts?

- Am I valuing students' ideas in choosing and developing themes?

- Am I involving students in language arts activities that extend into various subject areas?

- Am I helping students find authentic purposes for using language arts throughout the day?

- Am I teaching the language skills that enable students to pursue theme studies?

- Am I providing the tools and resources that students need for exploring ideas in depth?

- Am I scheduling large blocks of time, to increase flexibility?

- Am I evaluating progress in terms of students' ability to use language arts effectively in pursuit of goals?

FAMILY
- Am I informing parents of the reasons for integrating the language arts?

- Am I modeling appropriate language usage for students?

Affirmative answers to these questions may take time to achieve, but they are worth working toward in order to provide a meaningful, authentic learning environment.

Learning in Groups

Students learn from one another as well as from the teacher and on their own. In many classrooms, students have opportunities throughout the day to work in different kinds of groups that may vary in purpose, format, and materials (Flood et al., 1992). Purposes for groups may be skill development or shared interest; formats may be teacher- or student-led with varying numbers of participants; and materials may be the same for all groups or differ according to levels and themes. Grouping should be *dynamic,* or flexible, with students moving in and out of groups as their needs and interests change, and should facilitate the acquisition of the student's knowledge and skills (Salinger, 1996; Tomlinson et al., 2002).

Cooperative Learning

In *cooperative learning,* students approach tasks cooperatively by working in mixed-ability groups to achieve certain goals. The organization of cooperative learning groups is generally highly structured, with students working in teams and assuming responsibility for their own learning, as well as for that of their teammates. Students must use social skills that enable them to interact productively, and they are accountable both individually and as a group.

Before initiating cooperative learning groups, the teacher should help children acquire the necessary social skills: speaking softly, showing respect for others, avoiding negative comments, appreciating other points of view, establishing trust, communicating accurately, and so forth (Johnson and Johnson, 1989/1990; Madden, 1988). The teacher is then ready to form mixed-ability groups of three to six students and present the guidelines, such as equal participation by group members and attention to the task.

One language arts–related model of cooperative learning for upper elementary grades is Cooperative Integrated Reading and Composition (CIRC). This model features integrated language arts with basal or literature-based readers. It involves teacher presentation, partner and independent practice activities, and testing. While the teacher works with one group, pairs of students from two different reading groups may engage in activities such as the following:

❶ Partner reading, in which students first read silently and then take turns reading aloud, with the listener correcting the reader when necessary

❷ Story structure and story-related reading, with students answering questions about story elements and making predictions about how the problem will be resolved

❸ Story retellings, in which students summarize stories for their partners

❹ Peer conferencing during writers' workshops (Slavin, Madden, and Stevens, 1989/1990; Slavin, 1991)

STANDARDS AND ASSESSMENT As measured by standardized and informal tests, students engaged in CIRC showed significant growth in decoding and comprehension, as well as consistently positive growth in writing and language (Roehler and Duffy, 1991).

Another popular model for cooperative learning is Jigsaw, in which six-member heterogeneous teams investigate academic material that has been divided into sections. Each team member is assigned a different section to study. During preparation time, students work individually to find the information they need. Those who have the same assignment are then placed together into "expert groups" to discuss their sections. Then the students are regrouped into their original teams to teach their teammates about their sections. Learning is evaluated by testing or through a team project, and teams receive recognition for their achievement (Slavin, 1991).

There is evidence that many students benefit from opportunities to learn together in mixed-ability groups (Pearson and Fielding, 1991). Research supports the use of cooperative learning for improving thinking skills, retaining information, earning higher achievement test scores, making decisions, and accepting responsibility for learning. There are also claims that cooperative learning increases students' eagerness to learn and helps struggling students develop positive attitudes toward learning (Augustine, Gruber, and Hanson, 1989/1990; Slavin, 1991; Kagan, 1994).

DIVERSITY Cooperative learning is especially effective for English language learners due to the amount of peer interaction that takes place during efforts to complete tasks as a group (Herrell, 2000). The Classroom Scenario on page 499 demonstrates one form of cooperative learning for reading instruction.

Cooperative Learning

Barbara Eldridge was using the CIRC model of cooperative learning with her fifth graders for the basal reader lesson, in which each student would work with a partner. During the teacher-presentation segment of the lesson, she led into the story by asking the students to share their experiences with animals and then to read the introductory paragraph and look at the pictures to predict what the story might be about. Ms. Eldridge went over the word mastery list of eleven words by pronouncing each word clearly and distinctly, having the students say the word, asking them to define it if they could, clarifying the definition, and once again pronouncing the word with the class.

Before the students moved into the partner activities, Ms. Eldridge reminded them that they would read silently to a predetermined page and then read orally with a partner in their "one-inch voices." The students found comfortable places in the room to read, some sitting on the floor, others in chairs with their feet up. As they finished reading, each student sat beside a partner, with the partners facing opposite directions, and read softly into the partner's ear. Partners discussed the answers to a short list of comprehension questions and then wrote their answers separately. Before resuming the same procedure for the second part of the story, the students made further predictions. During the silent reading and partner reading time, Ms. Eldridge monitored the pairs, collected observation notes, and randomly participated in some of the pairs' discussions following the readings of the segments.

Analysis of Scenario

Ms. Eldridge had formed partnerships randomly except for her three lowest-performing readers, whom she had paired with patient, better readers. The students thoroughly enjoyed reading with partners, and their teacher felt that they were doing very well in reading.

TIME for REFLECTION

Many educators support the concept of cooperative learning, believing that students learn better when they interact socially and share ideas. Others, however, believe all students need to work individually in order for the teacher to make sure that each student is learning necessary skills. What do *you* think, and why?

Grouping for Reading

To accommodate a wide range of reading levels and make efficient use of time and resources, many teachers group children within their classrooms as a compromise between whole-class and totally individualized instruction. Sometimes it is appropriate to engage students with the curriculum through whole-class groupings, whereas other times it is best to require students to work independently and individually. The grouping of students in small configurations should be an alternative organizational pattern based on the needs of the students and the curricular goals. Fountas and Pinnell (2001) suggest the following guidelines for grouping students for guided reading.

❶ Monitor the instructional level of the group members, gradually increasing the difficulty of the text. As students progress and instructional levels change for individual students, teachers should change the membership of the group.

❷ If only some students need to learn a particular concept and are ready to do so, assemble a small skill or needs group to instruct those students.

❸ When all students need and are ready to learn a concept, plan a minilesson in a whole-group setting with opportunities for guided application.

Literature circles, discussed in Chapters 7 and 8, book buddies or clubs, guided reading groups, and reading workshops are examples of effective groupings. Teachers may also form many other types of groups for reading-related purposes, including interest groups, project or research groups, and skills or needs groups, or they may let students work in pairs.

Interest Groups. Based on shared interests, *interest grouping* is recommended for investigating topics through reading, writing, and literature. Students who are familiar with a topic and have a special interest in it can usually read material about it at higher levels than they normally read (G. Anderson, Higgins, and Wurster, 1985).

Project or Research Groups. Another type of grouping is based on *projects or research*, usually related to a theme. Students of varying ability levels work together by investigating a topic, pooling their information, and planning a presentation.

Skills or Needs Groups. As students show areas of need in their use of reading strategies, the teacher may form *skills or needs groups* for direct instruction. Each group includes students who need help with the same strategy. A teacher can assemble such groups on a temporary basis and present minilessons, followed by student applications of the strategy. Skills or needs groupings are based on a teacher's knowledge of the skills level of each student and are maintained only for a brief period of instructional time (Herrell, 2000).

Student Pairs or Partners. Yet another type of grouping involves *student pairs or partners*, who may work cooperatively on such activities as

❶ reading orally and listening to stories from trade books.

❷ revising and editing stories.

❸ corresponding through buddy journals.

❹ providing assistance when one partner is a more proficient reader than the other.

Often student pairs or partners are formed to help students who are struggling academically. *Peer tutoring* occurs when one student tutors another student of the same age, whereas *cross-age tutoring* involves students of different ages. Results of peer tutoring reveal improvements for both partners in academic achievements, self-concepts, social interactions, and attitudes toward reading (Pearson and Fielding, 1991; Foster-Harrison, 1997).

When matching peer tutors with students, teachers must consider both the academic strengths and the emotional behavior of each student and peer tutor so that the two will work well together. Each tutor should receive training in planning appropriate lessons, selecting materials, following acceptable teaching procedures, and using strategies for assessing progress. During peer conferences, students learn how to interact by observing the teacher's modeling so that they can ask one another helpful questions (Forman and Cazden, 1994).

Individualized and Whole-Class Activities

Although much learning takes place in groups and partnerships, students also need time to work both individually and as part of a whole-class community. Individualizing instruction allows students to make choices, pursue personal goals, explore special interests, move at their own paces, and work up to their capacity levels. Independent activities may take place as students work at computers, engage in Sustained Silent Reading (SSR), and publish their own books.

Many teachers begin and end each day with whole-class participation. Early morning is a good time for making announcements, letting students share, and reading aloud. When teachers become aware of specific skills that students need to learn, they teach minilessons to the whole class, often at the beginning of reading and writing workshops. Just before students go home, teachers may remind them of homework assignments and review what they have accomplished during the day. Among whole-class language activities are creative dramatics and choral reading, listening to stories read by the teacher or other students, learning about reading/study skills, going to the library, watching educational television, writing a class newspaper, creating a language experience chart, watching and discussing a video of a story, sharing multiple copies of a student magazine or newspaper, and participating in a poetry hour.

● 4-Blocks Literacy Model

Cunningham and Hall's 4-Blocks Literacy Model provides a framework for the organization of the language arts classroom. Implementing the 4-Blocks model in a school or district involves a commitment to a focused staff development plan and possibly reorganization of classroom schedules. Teachers implementing the 4-Blocks model attend an initial three-day orientation where they are introduced to the framework, which includes blocks of time designated as follows:

- *Guided Reading Block.* During the guided reading block (30–45 minutes) the focus is on developing comprehension and fluency. First students receive direct, whole-class instruction. Then flexible groupings and pairings are formed, and a variety of literature selections are read by the students. Next come closure activities directed by the teacher.

- *Self-selected Reading Block.* The goals of the self-selected reading block (25–40 minutes) are to develop fluency and confidence by modeling through a read-aloud, then allowing students time to choose texts that are at their independent reading level and then share briefly and discuss what they have read in a follow-up activity.

- *Words Block.* The words block (10–15 minutes) begins with a teacher-directed activity in which students are encouraged to focus on print processing or on decoding and spelling. Strategies such as Word Walls and Word Sorts are included during this block.

- *Writing Block.* The writing block (30–40 minutes) devotes time to establishing the connection between reading and writing. During this block, teachers present a minilesson in which authentic writing is modeled. Students are then encouraged to self-select a topic, write about it, and share what they have written with their peers.

The 4-Blocks Literacy Model provides an organizational pattern whereby the essential components of the integrated language arts program can be incorporated every day. By planning and implementing the 4-Blocks model, teachers provide numerous and varied opportunities for all students to be successful. The model provides a plan for teachers to scaffold reading instruction before, during, and after reading, as well as making the connection between reading and writing (Cunningham, Hall, and Cunningham, 2000; Sigmon, 1997).

Creating a Supportive Classroom Environment

The physical environment and social-emotional climate of a classroom can significantly affect students' literacy development. By understanding what students need, teachers are able to create supportive environments that facilitate learning and promote positive attitudes (Prosise, 1996).

● Physical Environment

A classroom's furnishings and arrangement reflect a teacher's philosophy about how students learn (Wilson et al., 1991). Teachers who believe students learn from and with one another provide areas where they can work in pairs and small groups. Teachers who understand that students have individual interests to pursue arrange quiet areas for independent work, and teachers who know that students need to work in groups of differing sizes and composition provide flexible room arrangements.

Teachers should consider many factors in creating a classroom's physical environment. Furniture should be arranged so that traffic flows easily, there are no safety hazards, and the teacher is able to see each student. Teachers may need to

DIVERSITY 🌐 arrange furniture to accommodate students who use wheelchairs or have other special physical needs. Young children need well-defined areas, perhaps set off by a rug, marked with colored tape, or identified with bookcases and shelves set perpendicular to the walls. Classrooms for young children may also need book racks for storing big books and easels for displaying them. The library area should be attractive, with comfortable chairs, large cushions, and displays of books and magazines. Many teachers have students sitting at tables rather than at individual desks. This facilitates group work but necessitates setting up storage areas for students' books and supplies (Lukasevich, 1996b; Pike, Compain, and Mumper, 1994).

Many classrooms have *learning centers*, which are areas of the classroom that contain sets of materials related to a theme. Learning centers should contain attractive, varied, and interesting materials that are inviting to children and are related to the theme. All centers should provide the supplies necessary for carrying out activities and should include a comfortable place for students to work.

Learning centers require careful preparation and planning by the teacher. Students need to understand when they may go to the centers, how to use them, and

Teachers should create classroom arrangements that can accommodate the needs of all students in a classroom. *(© Elizabeth Crews/The Image Works)*

where to place their completed work. They should be able to work independently or with classmates. Teachers need to provide protective coverings for frequently used materials, replenish supplies regularly, and replace center activities before they cease

TECHNOLOGY 🖥 to be effective. Some types of learning centers that teachers may provide are computer centers, audiovisual stations, centers for puppet shows and creative drama, writing centers, and classroom library centers. (More information on learning centers appears in Chapter 2.)

Many teachers have acquired large numbers of trade books to place in classroom libraries, but keeping track of these books can be a problem. Hollie Brooks (1995) suggests separating books into categories, such as mystery, science, and reference; alphabetizing them by authors' last names within each category or section; using the computer to enter data in such fields as title, author, subject, and section; letting students enter in a spiral notebook the books they check out; and choosing students to be class librarians. An organizational plan such as this provides students with real-life applications, lets them use the computer, and instills a sense of responsibility.

TECHNOLOGY 🖥 Many schools face the challenge of how to use a limited number of computers to best advantage. The number of computers in schools has increased rapidly in recent years; but even so, there are many schools with limited technology resources where few students get sufficient exposure to computers. In some cases, teachers allow more aggressive students to dominate the computers, thereby limiting their use by less assertive students. One solution to inequitable distribution of resources is to create a lab in which an entire school may share the available computers. This requires scheduling and sometimes fragmented integration into the curriculum. Dockterman

(1998) suggests grouping students to maximize the integration of technology into the curriculum—certainly in settings with limited resources, but even in those settings with greater accessibility. Technology can facilitate the creation of a group environment where students interact and are actively engaged in learning.

● Social-Emotional Environment

Perhaps even more important than the physical environment is the social-emotional environment within the classroom. In this section, we consider three aspects of this environment: establishing a community of learners, creating a learning-centered classroom, and providing motivation.

Developing a sense of community begins by encouraging students to get to know one another well, perhaps exchanging points of view through class meetings or dialogue circles (Letts, 1994). Together, teacher and students establish the rules they perceive as necessary for reaching the goals for learning in their class (Roberts, 1993). When students feel part of a *community of learners*, they are likely to take reasonable risks, support one another, and control their behavior.

A community of learners flourishes in a learning-centered classroom where the environment supports the interests and needs of all students. The characteristics of a learning-centered classroom are detailed in Chapter 8. Here students display their work, interact with one another, collaborate on projects, and explore issues that interest them. The teacher confers with students, works among them, shows warmth and respect, and manages several different activities simultaneously. Students find a learning-centered classroom nonthreatening, so they feel comfortable making decisions, expressing ideas, and asking questions that may ultimately drive much of the curriculum (Kohn, 1996).

Effective, mature readers must have both the *skill* and the *will* to read (Gambrell, 1996). Motivated readers choose to read for different purposes, such as acquiring knowledge or enjoying a good story. They spend more time reading and are better readers, whereas students who are not motivated may be at risk of failure (Palmer, Codling, and Gambrell, 1994).

The elementary school years are critical for developing motivated readers, so teachers must take steps to create environments that encourage children to read, such as the following:

- Be a reading model; make your love of reading visible.
- Let children interact with classmates about their reading.
- Give them opportunities to become acquainted with a wide variety of books.
- Allow students the freedom to choose the books they read.
- Challenge them with moderately difficult tasks.
- Let students share control over their learning.
- Encourage them to discover how literacy tasks can be meaningful and purposeful.

Creating an Inclusive Classroom

DIVERSITY ⊕ Teachers should be aware of their legal responsibilities and their roles in making an inclusive classroom a welcoming place that supports the learning of all students.

● Laws Affecting Students with Disabilities

The *Americans with Disabilities Act of 1990 (ADA)* was intended to eliminate discrimination against all individuals with disabilities. Its implications for school-aged children include enabling them to participate more fully in all school programs and to learn more effectively by using telecommunication systems.

In 1975 Congress passed Public Law 94-142, the Education for All Handicapped Children Act, which altered the placement of students with disabilities in the public schools. Reauthorized in 1997, PL 94-142 was renamed the *Individuals with Disabilities Education Act (IDEA)*. The *Improving Education Results for Children with Disabilities Act of 2003* is a reauthorization of the IDEA and continues to provide federal guidance for the education of students with disabilities.

A major provision of the IDEA is the development of an *individual education plan (IEP)* for each elementary and secondary student with disabilities who is eligible for support. The IEP states the student's present levels of educational performance, the projected starting date of the program, and the duration of the special services. It sets annual goals for the student's level of educational performance as well as short-term instructional objectives, and all of these must be defined in measurable terms. The IEP also specifies educational services, transition service needs, and special instructional media for the student. These plans outline assessment, program modifications, reporting of progress, and parent and family involvement. A statement describing the extent to which the student will not participate in the regular school program is also included.

The IEP is developed collaboratively by members of the *IEP team*, which includes family members and school personnel who are involved in the decision-making process for designing the instructional program for a student, based on his or her individual needs. When appropriate, the student and other professional personnel may also be included.

● Inclusion

In an inclusive delivery system, students with disabilities participate in age-appropriate general education settings in neighborhood schools for the entire day, and appropriate supports are provided to the students and teachers. Supports may include physical accommodations, sufficient personnel, staff development and technical assistance, and collaboration among personnel involved. Successful inclusion of students with disabilities is dependent on cooperation, collaboration, careful planning, and preparation. According to Richey and Wheeler (2000), the research available indicates that a successfully implemented and maintained inclusive environment can affect all participants positively. The Focus on Strategies on pages 506 and 507 and Classroom Scenario on page 507, both of which are based on actual situations, show the effects of inclusion in two classrooms.

Inclusion

Long after the children had left, Faye sat at her desk reflecting on the year she had spent with this group of students. She remembered surveying her class of twenty-six second graders at the beginning of the year and thinking that this year would be quite a challenge. "It certainly has been," she thought, "and there was no way I could have predicted how it would turn out. I've had some very stressful experiences. It hasn't been easy."

Just before school started, Faye learned she would have two students in wheelchairs, Mickey with muscular dystrophy and Adam with spina bifida; Carlotta, with attention-deficit/hyperactivity disorder (ADHD); Yvonne, who was brain-traumatized; and Leslie, who had been identified as seriously emotionally disturbed (SED). Ruby, a support teacher, would spend most of her time with Mickey but part of her time with Adam. Both children needed considerable help in completing their work.

One problem that demanded immediate attention was how to manage two wheelchairs and one or two additional adults in an already crowded classroom. Faye had tried several arrangements until she settled on one that seemed to work best. Maneuvering the wheelchairs to reading groups, learning centers, and special instructional areas had created some serious traffic jams! Faye had also found that she had to allow more time when preparing to leave the classroom for lunch and recess; it took time to position the wheelchairs and move them through the hallways.

It had been interesting to watch the students' relationships with Mickey and Adam develop. At first, they had eyed the two boys in wheelchairs somewhat suspiciously. Then they approached them cautiously, and finally they warmed up to them. Mickey, with his bright, alert eyes, showed that he was eager to participate, and the students soon considered it a privilege to help him. Adam was more reticent, showing dependence on his mother, who often sat with him in class, and the students found it more difficult to communicate with him.

Believing that both boys were bright enough to do second-grade work, Faye held the same expectations for them that she did for the other students. Adam could speak well enough to answer her questions, but she found she had to modify his assignments because he was unable to track the work on the board to the paper on his tray. Mickey, on the other hand, could usually respond with only one or two words, so Ruby generally interpreted Mickey's answers for him. In small groups Mickey could speak more easily, perhaps as much as a sentence or two at a time.

Having another teacher in the room with her hadn't been easy at first, either, Faye thought. Sometimes hearing another adult speaking at the same time she was talking had been quite disturbing: it was something she had to get used to. Mickey needed Ruby's attention almost constantly in order to participate in the lessons. The only way he could take a spelling test was to spell the words to her so that she could write them down for him. Recalling some of the better times, Faye thought of the way the class had interacted with Mickey. "I really like the way the children took to Mickey," she thought. "They would bring him those toy trucks and stuffed animals to play with on his tray. Of course, he'd hit at them and knock them down when he'd try to pick them up because he couldn't control his arm movements, but the children didn't mind; they'd just pick them up for him. Mickey had a sparkle in his eye and was fun to be with."

One of the best ways the children worked with Mickey was as peer tutors during his therapy sessions. Pat, the physical therapist, would ask a couple of the students to accompany Mickey to therapy and would teach them how to help Mickey with his body movements. On a few occasions, Mickey and his peer tutors went swimming at a nearby indoor pool during therapy sessions. That had been a real treat for the peer tutors as well as for Mickey.

Adam, however, hadn't benefited from the experience as much as Mickey had, Faye observed.

Continued

Continued

Perhaps the students felt intimidated by his mother's presence, or maybe it was Adam's reluctance to participate in class activities. In any case, they seemed to prefer being with Mickey and spent little time with Adam voluntarily. Of course, they willingly pushed Adam's wheelchair when it was time for him to move to a different location.

Thinking back, Faye was well aware that Mickey and Adam hadn't been the only students with special needs. Carlotta, Leslie, and Yvonne had been taking medication to help them control their behavior, but occasionally Carlotta's mother forgot to give her the medicine. On those days, Faye had to spend extra time helping Carlotta focus on her work.

Leslie's problems were more serious, sometimes causing her to be hospitalized for treatment for days or weeks at a time. After her first long-term hospitalization, Leslie had been reassigned to a special education self-contained classroom. Even though Leslie was included in Faye's room for periods of time each day, Faye recalled how much easier it had been to manage the class without Leslie's disruptive behaviors.

Getting the class to pay attention to her had been a constant struggle, too. The children were so easily distracted! Faye remembered the day she had used Mickey as an example of attentive behavior because of his eagerness and alertness. She recalled saying, "I really like the way Mickey is paying attention. Look at his eyes — they are always watching me when I'm talking." Looking over at Mickey, one of the children had said, "I know. Let's call him 'Eagle Eyes,'" and the nickname had stuck.

This year had been a learning experience for them all, Faye observed — probably even more for herself than for the students. She had made it through somehow, but she hoped that accommodations would be made if she had so many students with special needs another year. A smaller class size would help, as would additional support teachers, even on a part-time basis. She would have also benefited from some additional training on how to select and implement appropriate modifications.

CLASSROOM SCENARIO | **Inclusion**

Danny, who has cerebral palsy, has been admitted to Alan Stanton's third-grade class. Danny can move only his head and is unable to speak, but his IQ has been placed at 110. By moving his head and using his eyes, Danny indicates his wishes and answers questions. He also holds a stylus in his teeth to type written work, which is displayed along with the work of his peers, and he reads from an open book placed on a music stand.

Alan's positive attitude toward Danny and the students' eagerness to include him in *everything* they did created a positive learning environment. A larger child pushed his wheelchair so that Danny could go with them on field trips, take his turn as class leader, and participate in activities on the playground. When paired with a student of lower academic ability, Danny supplied the "brains" for a project while the other student carried out the plan. When the class learned some folk dances, Danny was the hub of the wheel and a classmate turned his chair. The students were protective, respectful, and accepting.

Analysis of Scenario

As a result of this experience, Danny benefited by being accepted as part of the class. Perhaps even more important, his classmates gained an appreciation of how much a student with disabilities can do.

Inclusion without adequate supplementary aids and services can create a situation such as the one Faye experienced in the first vignette. *Responsible* inclusion, however, which occurs when regular and special educators are properly trained and supported (Lombardi and Ludlow, 1996), can positively affect achievement of educational objectives, communication skills, and social interactions. Schools, therefore, should offer the necessary support and services to students with disabilities within the regular classroom so that all the children can learn (Fisher, Sax, and Pumpian, 1996; Lombardi and Ludlow, 1996).

As the two vignettes on inclusion indicate, classmates play an important role in terms of offering acceptance and support to the included child. It is important that the child who is included be fully accepted as an integral part of the class and not just occupy space in the classroom. Teachers should pay careful attention to creating a community of learners in which all students are fully participating members.

Cooperative learning strategies, such as those discussed earlier in this chapter, provide a wide range of learning experiences and allow groups of students with varied abilities to work together on projects. Kagan (1994, p. 15) suggests cooperative learning as a good way to prepare students "to adapt to and modify their social and physical environment." Being included in these groups enables students with disabilities to contribute to the activities, thereby improving their self-concepts, and to learn from their peers. Other effective strategies for including children with special needs are workshops, described in Chapter 8 (Caldwell, 1997; Roller, 1996), and integrated, theme-centered activities, described earlier in this chapter as well as in Chapters 7, 8, and 10.

TIME for REFLECTION

What can regular and special education teachers do to help all students learn in an inclusive environment?

● General Guidelines

The following general practices, which apply to all learners, are crucial in teaching and motivating students who have special needs.

❶ *Maintain a positive attitude.* Students with special needs require a great deal of encouragement and understanding. Show that you are interested in them: talk with them about their interests, have high but reasonable expectations, and note things they have done.

❷ *Consider learning styles and modalities when planning instruction.* A student might be an auditory learner who readily associates sounds with symbols, a visual learner who remembers sight words easily, or a kinesthetic-tactile learner who needs to touch, manipulate, and move in order to learn to read. Such factors as lighting, space, time of day, and temperature may also affect students' ability to learn.

❸ *Provide appropriate materials and direct instruction as needed.* Supply high-interest materials that the students are capable of using successfully. Do not use the types of reading materials with which the students have previously failed. Provide explicit instruction to teach necessary skills and strategies that students need.

FAMILY

❹ *Communicate with others who work with students who have special needs.* Be sure to coordinate efforts with all others involved in the delivery of the IEP. Get to know students' family members to learn more about their interests, learning styles, strengths, and needs.

❺ *Provide a positive, inclusive classroom environment.* Help all members of the class to accept and appreciate the unique qualities of others by carefully planning activities and providing opportunities for all members to make worthwhile contributions.

TECHNOLOGY

❻ *Use varied instructional and assessment techniques.* Present concepts by means of concrete objects, manipulative devices, software, and multimedia presentations (television, videotapes, recordings) to maximize all students' understanding.

❼ *Provide opportunities for success in tasks.* Provide scaffolding by assigning tasks at appropriate levels to ensure reasonable success. Set short-term goals and give immediate feedback to encourage good work. Use progress charts to make growth apparent, and have students compete against their own records, not against those of their classmates.

Role of the Teacher

Establishing a supportive and inclusive classroom environment is only one of a teacher's many important responsibilities in the classroom. A competent, effective teacher makes a major difference in students' learning. Researchers have found that effective teachers balance authentic literacy experiences with direct teaching through minilessons, modeling, and explanations (Wharton-McDonald et al., 1997). They integrate skills instruction with authentic activities and avoid teaching skills in isolation. In addition to providing balanced instruction, highly effective primary literacy teachers use scaffolding extensively, integrate reading and writing, manage their classrooms competently, are aware of their purposes for instruction, encourage students to be self-regulated learners, and hold high expectations for all students.

● The Teacher as Facilitator and Manager of Instruction

As a facilitator of instruction, the teacher must provide conditions that enable students to learn. The teacher should employ a variety of methods to meet the needs of a diverse student population. Through such procedures as modeling and direct instruction, the teacher can help students acquire the strategies and knowledge they need to succeed. By providing a learning-centered environment, the teacher can support students in their efforts to become responsible, independent learners.

Classroom management is a crucial factor in learning, especially when instruction is individualized or conducted in groups. Clear, sensible, consistent procedures can contribute to an orderly classroom. Near the beginning of the year, teacher and students should agree on rules of behavior, which should be stated positively whenever possible. Students must know exactly what they are to do to be able to work well independently and with their peers.

One way that teachers manage their classrooms effectively is by modeling appropriate behavior and learning strategies. Their actions and words set expectations for students, and these expectations become powerful motivators. Teachers model by *inference* as they read along with students during SSR, and they model with *talk-alouds* by asking themselves questions out loud while performing academic tasks. When they use *think-alouds*, they model their reasoning by describing aloud their thought processes (Roehler and Duffy, 1991).

Tomlinson (1999) describes a variety of organizational strategies, including **learning contracts**, which facilitate differentiating instruction and engage students in meaningful tasks. Through learning contracts, students may "contract" to complete certain projects designed to help them with their individual needs. The agreement, formalized through the use of a written contract and signed by teacher and child, simply states what the student is to do and when the task is to be completed. A teacher can prepare and have available contracts that call for a variety of assignments and tasks, from which students can select those that best suit their needs, or a student can propose a contract and negotiate it with the teacher. Once the terms have been agreed on, the student should complete the contract as specified. Example 13.1 below illustrates one such contract.

EXAMPLE 13.1   Sample Learning Contract Form

1. After listening to the librarian read aloud *The Cay* by Theodore Taylor, read one of the following to learn more about the idea of survival.
    a. *Island of the Blue Dolphins* by Scott O'Dell
    b. *Stranded* by Matt Christopher
    c. *Hatchet* by Gary Paulsen
    d. *Call It Courage* by Armstrong Sperry
    e. *The Summer I Was Lost* by Philip Viereck

2. Share your research in one of these ways:
    a. Illustrate one incident in the story.
    b. Write a play dramatizing one incident.
    c. Make a model of an object that may be useful for survival.
    d. Interview an authority on the subject of some sort of survival technique, and write a report.
    e. Compare the character(s) of your story with Robinson Crusoe in terms of self-reliance.

Choose one book from Number 1 and one method from Number 2 for your contract.
I plan to do (1) _____ and (2) _____.
I will have this contract completed by _____.
Student's signature _____.
Teacher's signature _____.

EXAMPLE 13.2 **Sample Learning Center Record**

Name _____

I worked at the _____ center or station.

Time in: _____ Time out: _____

The work was _____. (good, fair, poor)

Activity:

I read _____

I worked on _____

I listened to _____

I read aloud with _____

I wrote _____

I also _____

STANDARDS AND
ASSESSMENT

Teachers also need a record of the activities that students complete at learning centers. Since students do this work independently and check their own answers, teachers may not know exactly what the students are doing unless they keep an account of their activities in some way. Example 13.2 above presents one way for a student to record learning center work.

TECHNOLOGY

STANDARDS AND
ASSESSMENT

DIVERSITY

Computer-managed instruction (CMI) simplifies teachers' work by providing grade books and test-development software (Yellin and Blake, 1994). Grade book programs enable teachers to develop class lists, enter grades, and average grades quickly; test construction programs allow teachers to create test banks from which they may select items to include on assessments. There are also programs available to assist teachers in the development and maintenance of IEPs. More information on the role of technology in instruction appears in Chapter 11.

● The Teacher as Decision Maker

Classroom teachers make countless decisions daily as they manage their classrooms. Some decisions are made quickly and intuitively, but others require conscious reflection. Teachers may ask themselves:

- How can I prevent potential behavior problems?
- What is the best way to motivate these students?
- What are the most appropriate materials to use?
- What types of classroom organization will be most effective?
- What teaching strategies are most appropriate to use?
- What assessment techniques will tell me how well the students are learning?
- What are the best ways to keep my students working productively?
- How can I best meet individual needs?
- How can I establish an inclusive classroom environment?

● What are the most effective ways to communicate with children, family members, and administrators?

Although the teacher has the final authority in the classroom, students should also assume some responsibility for making decisions about their learning (Garan, 1994; Sumara and Walker, 1991). When students internalize the behavior and reading strategies modeled by the teacher, they are able to direct their own learning within certain limits. For example, classroom teachers may retain control of the kinds of tasks and of when they are to be completed but may give students choices about how, with whom, and where to do them.

● The Teacher as Researcher

Many teachers have become involved in research in order to improve their own educational practices by gaining a better understanding of how their students learn. Education today is focusing on the process of learning—how students approach a learning task, how they self-correct misunderstandings, and what strategies they use as they read and write. As teachers carefully observe and record what their students are doing, they gain insights into effective educational procedures (Sagor, 2000).

● The Teacher as Learner

One of the most refreshing, yet challenging, aspects of being a teacher is that the role is constantly evolving. Changing situations and different groups of students each year call for modifications of teaching strategies to meet students' needs. Teachers who view themselves as learners ask questions and *want* to learn more about new ideas that may be useful to them in the classroom.

TECHNOLOGY 🖥 Teachers can continue to learn and develop professionally in a variety of other ways. They can network with other teachers through e-mail, share teaching ideas on classroom websites, and take college courses for advanced degrees and recertification; they may participate in in-service activities; and they may join professional organizations. Through these associations, they can subscribe to publications and participate in conferences to learn about and apply new ideas. Some professional organizations related to the interests of reading teachers are listed here, along with their addresses and major publications.

Children's Book Council, 568 Broadway, New York, NY 10012. *CBC Features.* **www.cbcbooks.org**

International Reading Association, 800 Barksdale Road, P.O. Box 8139, Newark, DE 19714-8139. *The Reading Teacher, Journal of Adolescent & Adult Literacy, Reading Research Quarterly.* **www.reading.org**

National Association for the Education of Young Children, 1509 16th Street, N.W., Washington, DC 20036-1426. *Young Children.* **www.naeyc.org**

National Council of Teachers of English, 1111 W. Kenyon Road, Urbana, IL 61801-1096. *Language Arts, Primary Voices K–6,* and *Voices from the Middle.* **www.ncte.org**

Home–School Partnership

FAMILY Caregivers and teachers should work together to create a positive learning environment for children. A child's first learning experiences occur in the home, and the home continues to provide educational opportunities that supplement learning activities in the classroom. Therefore, it is important that teachers understand a child's home environment and communicate with those responsible for the child's well-being.

Schools that value parent participation have more effective programs, more positive attitudes, and higher achievement than schools that do not encourage parents to participate (Jones, 1991). Parents usually want to know the goals of the school and the teacher, what the child is learning and how it is taught, attendance and homework policies, and the child's progress.

● Methods of Communication

It is important to establish and maintain communication between the school and the home. There are various forms of communication that a teacher may use.

Written Communication

Much of the written communication sent to students' homes comes from the teacher. Teachers often create newsletters, carefully written letters, and bulletins to keep caregivers informed about happenings at school. The classroom teacher may write a personal note to a parent or caregiver, especially to praise a student's performance; send home, at the end of the school year, a calendar of reading-related activities for each day of the summer; provide families with activities to do with children that correspond to current reading objectives; or send a form letter, such as the one in Example 13.3, that applies to a group or whole class of children. Sometimes students themselves may write letters to their families about forthcoming events.

Caregivers also get written information from the school and even from organizations outside the school. The school may publish brochures or booklets informing families of school policies and special events. These publications help caregivers learn about rules and regulations and other information they need to know

---

EXAMPLE 13.3 Letter to Parents

Dear _____,

During the past six weeks, your child has been working on a folklore unit in reading class. Your child has studied the characteristics of tall tales and has attempted to write an original tall tale of his or her own after reading several examples and hearing other examples read by the teacher. The story is attached to this report. You may wish to read it and discuss it with your child. All the children produced tall tales that indicated an understanding of this form of literature.

                                        Sincerely,

before and after sending their children to school. Public or school libraries may provide lists of recommended recreational reading suitable for various age levels. Professional societies may have helpful bulletins or pamphlets for teachers to send home.

STANDARDS AND
ASSESSMENT

Progress Reports. Progress reports are a frequently used method of communication. The report card is the traditional way to inform families about the student's performance in school, but report cards often give information that is incomplete and can be misunderstood. Simple A, B, or C grades for each subject tell very little about a student's interests, attitudes, and effort. Another option for communicating with families is to use portfolios that contain samples of the students' work (Flood and Lapp, 1989; Tomlinson, 1999). Caregivers often have difficulty understanding percentiles and standardized achievement test scores, but they may be able to see the progress students have made (or their lack of progress) over time on informal measures such as writing samples. The portfolio should contain a broad array of students' work, including informal assessments, voluntary reading activities, self-evaluations, standardized test scores, and writing samples.

Personal Communication

Personal communication between teachers and parents or caregivers can happen at parent-teacher association meetings, telephone calls, conferences, home visits (which give the parent or caregiver a chance to discuss particular problems and acquaint the teacher with the student's home environment), and Open House days (when parents or caregivers visit in the student's classroom to familiarize themselves with the materials, schedules, and routines of the school day).

Many schools schedule conferences two or three times throughout the school year, but teachers can arrange conferences whenever they are necessary. During a conference, the teacher needs to listen to the caregiver's concerns, share samples of the student's schoolwork, show records of achievement (test scores, for example), and offer constructive suggestions for ways of working together for the child's benefit. Conferences can include students; in fact, students sometimes lead them. They prepare by evaluating their own work, assembling selected pieces in portfolios, reflecting on their areas of strength and weakness, and role-playing conferences in order to be ready (Austin, 1994; Lenski, Riss, and Flickinger, 1996).

A fall conference or Open House is a good time to introduce parents to the reading materials used in the school and to describe the reading experiences and skills being emphasized that year. A teacher may want to explain how the reading program is organized and the general approaches he or she uses. The teacher may also point out what (if anything) will be required of the student in terms of homework, as well as what the family can do when the student requests help.

Technological Communication

TECHNOLOGY

Currently, many teachers are creating and maintaining classroom websites that provide a wealth of information for families and students. Not only can text information be shared, but photos and authentic work samples may also be displayed for viewing. There are several sites that allow educators free web space or charge a minimal fee. Often these sites provide templates that make the development and maintenance of the pages possible for educators with minimal technological skills. Web pages and electronic mail are powerful and versatile communication tools for the school and home partnership.

DIVERSITY 🌐 ● **Overcoming Communication Challenges**

It is important that teachers communicate effectively with and provide information to all families. This may challenge the teacher who needs to communicate with parents or caregivers whose primary language is not English. Written communication should be translated into the first language of the home, and audiotapes or videotapes of information may also be necessary if the literacy level is not known or is inadequate for comprehending written material.

Although some language-minority families may not have the level of English proficiency to participate fully in some school activities and may be adjusting to the culture and the language, they can still be very effective in a true home and school collaborative relationship. Creating a home or family literacy program can increase the amount of family involvement. Family literacy emphasizes literacy development within the authentic context of daily life. Whenever possible, schools should encourage families to reinforce concepts taught at school by reviewing them at home in the student's native language. Schools should encourage language-minority families to use the language with which they are the most comfortable and should promote use of the home language. Often, families want to emphasize the use of English and feel that using their native language will negatively affect the student's ability to become more proficient in English. Teachers should point out that an increase in literacy through the student's native language will assist in the development of literacy in English (Appalachia Educational Laboratory, 1998).

TIME for REFLECTION

What are the advantages of strengthening the communication between school and home?

Classroom Assistants

Many adults work as paid or volunteer assistants in the classroom by helping with a variety of tasks. Tasks may include individual or small-group instruction, grading student work, making displays, supervising computer-assisted instruction, and performing clerical tasks. Successfully utilizing a classroom volunteer depends both on planning and on explicitly communicating expectations. Successful volunteer programs often provide initial training and orientation, along with a clearly outlined list of specific tasks to be completed. Volunteers should feel comfortable in the school and classroom setting. Instructional materials should be accessible to the volunteer, and the volunteer should engage in documentation of, or reflection on, the completed tasks (Roller, 1998).

Paraprofessionals work along with teachers to provide instruction and services. Included in the reauthorization of the Elementary and Secondary Education Act (ESEA), or the No Child Left Behind Act, of 2001 is the provision that paraprofessionals be highly qualified, either by completing two years of study at an institution of higher education, by obtaining an Associate's degree (or higher), or by demonstrating knowledge of and ability to assist in the instruction of reading, writing, and mathematics. Generally, the training of paraprofessionals includes strategies for how to relate to children positively, how to support the instructional program, and how to observe and assess student progress. Basically, the classroom teacher is responsible for the activities the assistant performs and for preparing the paraprofessional to carry out assigned activities. The teacher and paraprofessional must communicate regularly through structured conferences and shared planning times.

SUMMARY

Orderly, efficient classroom organization is an important component of effective reading instruction. Many teachers strive to implement an integrated language arts curriculum, which enables children to understand the relationships among reading, writing, listening, speaking, viewing, and visually presenting, as they use these skills in meaningful situations. Teachers, with student input, select worthy themes as the focus of an integrated curriculum, and they use blocks of time (as in the 4-Blocks Literacy Model) to schedule language arts and content-area activities.

Several other possibilities exist for organizing a classroom, including different ways of grouping students. Cooperative learning is an organizational plan that allows students to work with partners and in small groups to meet curricular goals. Types of reading-related groups include literature circles, dynamic groups, interest groups, project or research groups, special skills or needs groups, and pupil pairs or partners. Teachers create most of these arrangements for a limited time and a specific purpose. Students also benefit from individualized and whole-class instruction. Often pupil partners engage in peer tutoring activities that can encompass multiple grades and ages successfully.

The classroom's physical environment is an important factor in determining how well students learn. Some teachers use learning centers, classroom libraries, and computers in the instructional program. The classroom's social-emotional environment is also important. Teachers should establish a community of learners within a learning-centered classroom and plan activities that engage and motivate students to read.

All teachers should be especially aware of their legal responsibilities for students with special needs. They also need to understand their roles in creating inclusive classrooms where all students can learn.

The teacher is the key figure in the classroom and daily makes countless decisions that affect student learning. In some cases, the teacher assumes the role of researcher by making systematic observations and records of student behaviors. The teacher is also a learner, always alert to information supplied by research and theory, professional interactions, and the students themselves.

Teachers should communicate with families frequently in a variety of ways, including conferences, report cards, meetings, and publications. Many teachers are electing to create and maintain a classroom website that can be a powerful communication tool. Teachers can offer suggestions to families to help them create supportive reading environments and strengthen the school and home partnership.

Teachers can benefit from the help of both paraprofessionals and volunteer assistants in the classroom. Classroom assistants can provide a variety of reading-related services, including listening to children read, grading papers, preparing instructional materials, and helping children locate and use reference materials.

TEST YOURSELF

True or False

_____ 1. Once organizational patterns have been established, they should be maintained without changes.

_____ 2. *Community of learners* refers to children who live in the same part of the school district.

_____ 3. In a negotiated curriculum, the teacher considers children's ideas for planning and directing learning.

_____ 4. Most groups are formed for limited times and specific purposes.

_____ 5. If reading skills are adequately covered during the reading instructional period, there is no need for any other type of reading during the day.

_____ 6. Classroom management is an important factor in how well students learn.

_____ 7. Specific needs grouping puts together children who need to work on the same skill and/or concept.

_____ 8. Learning centers allow children to carry out activities independently.

_____ 9. Computer-assisted instruction can be used only with one student for each computer.

_____ 10. According to current research and theory, children learn better when they can associate new material with prior knowledge.

_____ 11. When implementing an integrated language arts curriculum, teachers allocate brief periods of time for teaching each of the language arts.

_____ 12. Preparing learning contracts with students is one way that teachers can manage individual activities.

_____ 13. The best time to hold teacher-student conferences is before or after school.

_____ 14. The organizational pattern of a classroom is more important than the teacher.

_____ 15. In cooperative learning, students learn in partnerships or as teams.

_____ 16. Effective teachers teach skills in isolation.

_____ 17. A child's first learning experiences occur in the home.

_____ 18. CIRC is a form of cooperative learning for upper elementary students in the area of language arts.

_____ 19. Active student participation in language learning is an important aspect of whole language classrooms.

_____ 20. Teachers who observe students and record information about them are acting as researchers.

_____ 21. Just as students learn from teachers, teachers learn from students.

_____ 22. Peer tutoring benefits both partners.

_____ 23. In reading to their children, parents provide a foundation for the school's reading program.

_____ 24. Sending bulletins or letters to parents is a valuable way for teachers to communicate about the school's reading program.

_____ 25. Paraprofessionals should do only clerical work in the classroom.

_____ 26. To promote literacy development, teachers should encourage parents of English language learners to speak only English at home.

_____ 27. Some teachers use classroom websites as an effective communication tool to share information with families.

_____ 28. An inclusive classroom is designed to benefit only the student with special needs.

_____ 29. The 4-Blocks Literacy Model offers an organizational framework that includes the connection between reading and writing.

_____ 30. IDEA is a federal law that outlines provisions that should be considered when constructing the education plan for students with disabilities.

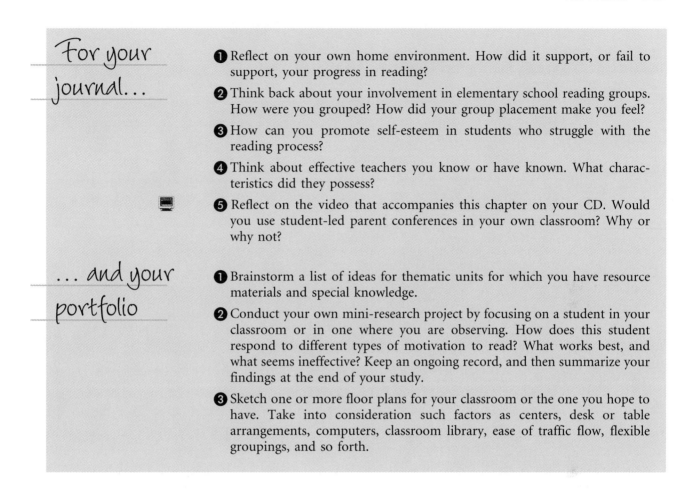

For your journal...

❶ Reflect on your own home environment. How did it support, or fail to support, your progress in reading?

❷ Think back about your involvement in elementary school reading groups. How were you grouped? How did your group placement make you feel?

❸ How can you promote self-esteem in students who struggle with the reading process?

❹ Think about effective teachers you know or have known. What characteristics did they possess?

❺ Reflect on the video that accompanies this chapter on your CD. Would you use student-led parent conferences in your own classroom? Why or why not?

... and your portfolio

❶ Brainstorm a list of ideas for thematic units for which you have resource materials and special knowledge.

❷ Conduct your own mini-research project by focusing on a student in your classroom or in one where you are observing. How does this student respond to different types of motivation to read? What works best, and what seems ineffective? Keep an ongoing record, and then summarize your findings at the end of your study.

❸ Sketch one or more floor plans for your classroom or the one you hope to have. Take into consideration such factors as centers, desk or table arrangements, computers, classroom library, ease of traffic flow, flexible groupings, and so forth.

APPENDIX A

Answers to "Test Yourself"

Chapter 1 *True or False*

1. F	11. T	21. T
2. T	12. T	22. T
3. F	13. F	23. F
4. T	14. F	24. T
5. T	15. T	25. F
6. T	16. T	26. T
7. F	17. T	27. F
8. F	18. F	28. T
9. T	19. T	
10. F	20. T	

Chapter 2 *True or False*

1. T	10. T	19. F
2. F	11. T	20. T
3. T	12. F	21. F
4. T	13. F	22. T
5. F	14. F	23. T
6. F	15. F	24. T
7. T	16. T	25. F
8. F	17. F	
9. F	18. F	

Chapter 3 *True or False*

1. F	13. T	25. T
2. F	14. T	26. F
3. T	15. T	27. F
4. F	16. T	28. T
5. T	17. T	29. F
6. T	18. F	30. T
7. F	19. T	31. T
8. T	20. F	32. T
9. F	21. F	33. T
10. T	22. T	34. F
11. T	23. T	35. T
12. F	24. T	

Chapter 3 *Multiple Choice*

1. a	5. c	9. b
2. c	6. a	10. b
3. a	7. c	11. a
4. b	8. b	

Chapter 4 *True or False*

1. F	11. T	21. T
2. T	12. F	22. F
3. F	13. T	23. T
4. F	14. T	24. T
5. T	15. T	25. T
6. T	16. T	26. F
7. T	17. T	27. T
8. T	18. T	28. F
9. T	19. T	29. T
10. T	20. F	30. F

Chapter 5 *True or False*

1. T	7. F	13. T
2. T	8. T	14. F
3. F	9. T	15. T
4. T	10. T	16. F
5. F	11. F	17. F
6. T	12. T	18. F

Chapter 6 *True or False*

1. T	9. T	17. F
2. T	10. F	18. T
3. T	11. T	19. T
4. F	12. T	20. F
5. T	13. F	21. T
6. F	14. T	22. T
7. T	15. F	
8. F	16. F	

Chapter 7 *True or False*

1. F	8. T	15. T
2. T	9. T	16. T
3. F	10. F	17. F
4. F	11. T	18. T
5. F	12. T	19. T
6. T	13. T	
7. F	14. F	

Chapter 8 *True or False*

1. T	9. F	17. F
2. T	10. T	18. F
3. F	11. T	19. F
4. F	12. F	20. F
5. F	13. T	21. T
6. F	14. F	22. T
7. T	15. F	
8. F	16. T	

Chapter 9 *True or False*

1. F	11. T	21. F
2. T	12. F	22. F
3. T	13. T	23. T
4. T	14. F	24. T
5. F	15. T	25. F
6. T	16. T	26. T
7. F	17. F	27. T
8. F	18. T	28. F
9. T	19.	
10. T	20. T	

Chapter 10 *True or False*

1. F	9. F	17. T
2. T	10. T	18. T
3. F	11. T	19. T
4. T	12. T	20. T
5. F	13. F	21. T
6. F	14. T	22. F
7. T	15. T	
8. T	16. T	

Chapter 11 *True or False*

1. F	11. T	21. F
2. F	12. T	22. T
3. F	13. F	23. F
4. T	14. T	24. T
5. F	15. T	25. F
6. F	16. T	26. T
7. T	17. T	27. T
8. T	18. T	28. T
9. T	19. F	29. T
10. T	20. F	30. T

Chapter 12 *True or False*

1. F	11. F	21. T
2. F	12. F	22. F
3. F	13. F	23. T
4. F	14. T	24. F
5. T	15. F	25. T
6. T	16. T	26. F
7. T	17. T	27. F
8. T	18. T	28. T
9. F	19. F	29. T
10. T	20. T	30. T

Chapter 13 *True or False*

1. F	11. F	21. T
2. F	12. T	22. T
3. T	13. F	23. T
4. T	14. F	24. T
5. F	15. T	25. F
6. T	16. F	26. F
7. T	17. T	27. T
8. T	18. T	28. F
9. F	19. T	29. T
10. T	20. T	30. T

APPENDIX B

Teaching Strategies Reference Guide

The PRAXIS II is a series of tests designed to assess the professional knowledge and skills of beginning teachers. A number of states have identified specific PRAXIS II series tests and established minimum scores as licensure requirements. The typical examinee has completed a teacher education program or must demonstrate competency through an alternative certification process.

The following are strategies that currently reflect "best practice" in reading instruction. Questions about them often appear on specialty tests designed to assess both knowledge of principles and familiarity with the processes. These strategies supplement or re-emphasize many of those more fully discussed in this edition of *Teaching Reading in Today's Elementary Schools,* and we have noted the chapters that you can review to learn more about each strategy or its applications.

Chunking

Reading Level: Intermediate and Middle levels

Appropriate Reading Material: Use with narrative or expository text.

Chapters: This is an additional technique for the development of oral reading fluency, which is discussed in Chapters 8 and 12.

- Choose a passage at the student's instructional level.

- Tape-record the student reading the passage before instruction.

- Chunk the sentences into meaningful phrases.
  (Chunking of the material can be modeled orally or can be visually displayed by drawing lines between specific words of text, providing visual cues for the meaningful phrases. The passage may also be cut into segments and mounted on index cards to provide manipulatives to support the chunking of the material.)

  Chunked example: The family's beloved pet / was / a brown and tan / basset hound.

- Model the reading of the passage, noting the chunked phrases (orally or with supporting manipulatives).

- Tape-record the student reading the passage.

- Repeat until the student's fluency improves.

Cloze Procedure

Reading Level: Primary, Intermediate, and Middle levels

Appropriate Reading Material: Use with content area reading or literature selections for comprehension instruction, matching reading materials to specific students, or testing

Chapter: 12

For comprehension instruction:

- Choose a selection of text approximately 200–250 words in length.

- Leave the first sentence and the last sentence of the passage intact.

- Beginning with the second sentence, delete every fifth word or select key terms or sight words.
  (If the procedure requires a written response from the student, blanks may be substituted for the deleted words. If the required response is oral, sticky notes may be placed over the target words as they appear in the text.)

- Instruct the student to read the entire passage and then to reread inserting each of the missing words.

- Students respond by writing words in the blanks or by responding orally to the deleted terms. Oral responses should be tape-recorded.

- Upon completion, the responses may be compared to the original text.

Directed Reading Activity

Reading Level: Primary, Intermediate, and Middle levels

Appropriate Reading Material: Use with textbooks, basal readers, or literature selections.

Chapter: 7

- Prior to instruction, introduce new vocabulary.

- Activate or establish background knowledge, using techniques such as discussion or webbing (see Chapter 5).

- Offer strategy or skill instruction as needed.

- Provide time for students to read the selection silently.

- Conduct follow-up activities, such as those described in Chapters 7 and 8.

Directed Reading-Thinking Activity

Reading Level: Primary, Intermediate, and Middle levels

Appropriate Reading Material: Use with textbooks, basal readers, or literature selections.

Chapters: 7 and 10

- Begin with development of background concepts, if necessary.

- Before reading, prompt students to make predictions on the basis of the title and any available pictures.

- During reading, model reading aloud or instruct students to read to strategic points; then stop to confirm or revise previous predictions. Continue this process throughout the text.

- After reading, discuss the selection as a whole and relate it to students' background knowledge and experiences and to the author's intended purpose. Discuss the strategies used throughout the process and review key vocabulary terms.

Echo Reading

Reading Level: Primary and Intermediate levels

Appropriate Reading Material: Easiest to use with literature selections

Chapters: This is an additional technique for the development of oral reading fluency, which is discussed in Chapters 8 and 12.

- Select a text that is approximately 150–200 words in length.

- Discuss the importance of fluency when reading.

- Read the first sentence of the text, modeling intonation, phrasing, and expression.

- Prompt the student to read the same line of text, imitating your intonation, phrasing, and expression. Tape-record student and teacher reading.

- Continue until the entire passage has been read.

- Play the tape, and discuss strengths as well as skills that need improvement.

Graphic Organizers

Reading Level: Primary, Intermediate, and Middle levels

Appropriate Reading Material: Use with textbooks, basal readers, and literature selections.

Chapters: 4, 5, 6, 9, and 10

● Select key concepts or vocabulary terms.

● Arrange the concepts or vocabulary terms visually so that the relationships among them can be viewed or the reader's background knowledge can be activated or established.

● Graphic organizers may be used before, during, or after reading.

K-W-L

Reading Level: Intermediate and Middle levels

Appropriate Reading Material: Use with expository text.

Chapter: 5

● Before reading a selection, introduce the students to the following organizer:

What I Know	*What I Want to Learn*	*What I Learned*

● Introduce the topic of the text and prompt responses from the students.

● Complete the organizer by recording the students' responses related to the first heading: What I Know.

● Before and/or during reading, record students' responses under the second heading: What I Want to Learn.

● After reading, record responses under the third heading: What I Learned.

● To summarize, conduct a class discussion reviewing responses related to the three headings in the diagram.

Language Experience Approach

Reading Level: Primary, Intermediate, and Middle levels

Appropriate Reading Material: Use to create students' own text.

Chapters: 2 and 7

- Create or lead the students through a shared experience, such as a field trip, class visitor or demonstration, or class project.

- Lead the class in a discussion about the shared experience. Prompt with questions, as needed.

- Record the authentic language used by the students to document their observations and reactions to the shared experience.

- Read the story together with the students.

- Conduct follow-up activities or minilessons, using the story as print material.

QAR

Reading Level: Intermediate and Middle levels

Appropriate Reading Material: Use with textbooks, basal readers, or literature selections.

Chapter: 6

- Select appropriate material.

- Introduce students to the following guides for locating information in the print material:
  - "Right There"—Information is in the print material, explicitly stated.
  - "Think and Search"—Information is distributed throughout the material. The student must combine information to identify the answer.
  - "Author and You"—Information from what the readers know and what they believe the author intended them to understand from the printed material is used to provide the answer.
  - "On My Own"—Information is related to the text, but the reader's own knowledge must be used to identify the answer.

- Discuss and model relationships between different types of questions.

Repeated Readings

Reading Level: Primary, Intermediate, and Middle levels

Appropriate Reading Material: Use with material at the appropriate instructional reading level.

Chapter: 12

- Select a text of interest to the student.
- Make a copy of the text.
- Discuss the importance of practice in developing a skill.
- Prompt the student to read aloud; tape-record and document miscues as they occur during the student's oral reading.
- Record the speed.
- Enter the miscues and the speed data on a graph.
- Provide scaffolding during minilesson sessions to address miscues.
- Prompt the student to reread the material.
- Record the new data and compare to the earlier performance.

Rate and word recognition accuracy should increase while maintaining comprehension.

Retelling

Reading Level: Primary, Intermediate, and Middle levels

Appropriate Reading Material: Easier to use with literature selections, although students can also "retell" informational text by summarizing it.

Chapters: 5 and 12

- Before reading narrative selections, prompt students to identify the following information as they read: *Characters, Setting, Plot, Conflict,* and *Solution.* If the students are reading expository material, they should create a list of key concepts. Ask students to identify the most important concepts in the selection, those that are supported by subordinate ideas.
- Following the reading of the material by you or the student, ask the student to retell the story or summarize the information, identifying the story elements or the key concepts as they appeared.

SQ3R

Reading Level: Intermediate and Middle levels

Appropriate Reading Material: Use with subject matter textbooks and readings.

Chapter: 9

- Select expository material at the appropriate readability level for the students.
- Introduce and demonstrate the SQ3R steps:
  - *Survey:* Model skimming the passage to locate important terms and headings.
  - *Question:* After skimming the passage, model questions about the material that might be answered in the passage. Prompt students to create questions of their own that they expect to be answered.
  - *Read:* Provide time for the students to read the material for the purpose of locating the answers to the questions posed during prereading.
  - *Recite:* Discuss orally the responses to the questions located in the chapter. Encourage the students to summarize and use their own language to express the answers.
  - *Review:* When the entire selection has been read and the questions and answers located, guide the students through an overall summary of the information.

GLOSSARY

adequate yearly progress (AYP) A component of the ESEA 2001 legislation that requires states and systems to collect annual data that represents the progress of students in meeting established assessment goals or progress in key subject areas.

affective Relating to attitudes, interests, values, appreciations, and opinions.

allusion An indirect reference to a person, place, thing, or event considered to be known to the reader.

alphabetic principle The concept that letters represent speech sounds.

alternative assessment All types of assessment other than standardized tests.

Americans with Disabilities Act (ADA) A law designed to eliminate discrimination against all individuals with disabilities.

analogies Comparisons of two similar relationships, stated in the form of the following example: *Author* is to *book* as *artist* is to *painting*.

analytic approach to phonics instruction Teaching the sounds of letters in already known words. Sight words are taught first and letter sounds second, in context.

anaphora Use of a word as a substitute for another word or group of words.

anecdotal record Written accounts of specific incidents or behaviors in the classroom.

anticipation guides Sets of declarative statements related to materials about to be read that are designed to stimulate thinking and discussion.

antonyms A pair of words that have opposite meanings.

appositive A word or a phrase placed beside another word or phrase as a restatement.

assessment The collection of data, such as test scores and informal records, to measure student achievement.

auditory acuity Sharpness of hearing.

auditory discrimination The ability to differentiate among sounds.

automaticity The ability to carry out a task without having to give it much attention.

bar graphs Graphs that use vertical or horizontal bars to compare quantities.

big books Large books that the entire class can share together, often characterized by predictability, repetition, and rhyme.

bottom-up models Models that depict reading as being initiated by examination of the printed symbols, with little input required from the reader.

categorization Classification into related groups.

CD-ROM Compact Disc–Read Only Memory. A digital data storage device from which information can be accessed in nonlinear fashion.

circle or pie graphs Graphs that show relationships of individual parts to a whole circle.

cloze procedure Method of estimating reading difficulty by omitting every *n*th (usually every fifth) word in a reading passage and observing the number of correct words a reader can supply; an instructional technique in which words or other structures are deleted from a passage by the teacher, with blanks left in their places for students to fill in by using the surrounding context.

cognitive development The acquisition of knowledge.

community of learners A cohesive group of class members who develop and pursue similar goals.

computer-assisted instruction Instruction that makes use of a computer to administer a programmed instructional sequence or other educational experience.

computer-managed instruction Use of the computer for such tasks as recordkeeping, diagnosis, and prescription of individualized assignments.

content area textbooks Textbooks in areas of information, such as literature, social studies, science, and mathematics.

context clues Clues to word meanings or pronunciations found in the surrounding words or sentences.

cooperative learning Learning through an instructional and grouping procedure that utilizes mixed-ability groups of students who work cooperatively to achieve certain goals.

creative dramatics Acting out stories spontaneously, without a script.

creative reading   Reading "beyond the lines."

criterion-referenced test   Test designed to yield measurements interpretable in terms of specific performance standards.

critical reading   Reading for evaluation.

cumulative tales   Traditional tales displaying rhythm and a pattern with a repetitive sequence of events or refrain.

database   An organized body of information that can be sorted and searched electronically.

database programs   Programs that facilitate the development of databases.

desktop publishing   Application of computers combining text and graphics for classroom publishing.

developmentally appropriate practice   A framework or an approach for working with young children in which the teacher considers each child's competencies and adjusts instruction accordingly.

dialect   Regional or social modifications of a language; distinguishing features may include pronunciation, vocabulary, and syntax.

digital literacy   The ability to understand, evaluate, and integrate digital or computerized information.

direct experience   Active participation in an event.

direct instruction   Teacher control of the learning environment through structured lessons, goal setting, choice of activities, and feedback.

directed reading activity   A strategy in which detailed lesson plans are followed to teach the reading of stories.

directed reading-thinking activity   A general plan for directing the reading of content area reading selections or basal reader stories and for encouraging children to think as they read, to predict, and to check their predictions.

disaggregated data   Scores that show the progress of subgroups of students, including racial/ethnic groups, economically disadvantaged students, students with disabilities, and students with limited English proficiency.

dramatic play   Simulating real experiences, such as playing the mother or father in a housekeeping center.

drite   A combination of drawing and writing.

DVD-ROM   Digital Video Disk–Read Only Memory. A disc the size of a CD that delivers excellent video and audio and holds more data than a videotape, videodisc, or CD.

dynamic grouping   Flexibly placing students into small groups on the basis of changing student needs such as achievement and student interest.

eclectic approaches   Approaches to teaching reading that combine desirable aspects of a number of different major approaches.

electronic bulletin boards   Network locations to which messages are posted so that readers who are interested in the topic can read the messages electronically. Sometimes referred to as newsgroups.

electronic mail   Messages sent electronically from one computer user to another.

electronic mailing list   Electronic distributor of messages on a particular topic to a group of readers who have "subscribed" to the list.

ellipsis   The omission of a word or group of words that are to be "understood" by the reader.

emergent literacy   A developing awareness of the interrelatedness of oral and written language.

environmental print   Words that children frequently see around them.

etymology   The origin and history of words.

euphemism   The substitution of a less offensive word or phrase for an unpleasant term or expression.

experience charts   Written accounts about common experiences, dictated by the student(s) and recorded by the teacher.

expository style   A precise, factual writing style.

fable   A brief moral tale in which animals or inanimate objects speak.

fantasy   A genre of literature that includes highly imaginative, fictional stories with fanciful or supernatural elements.

fiction   Stories that are not true, written in a narrative style, for the purpose of entertainment.

figurative language   Nonliteral language.

formal (standardized) assessment   The use of a testing instrument based on extensive normative data and for which reliability and validity can be verified.

frustration level   A level of reading difficulty with which a reader is unable to cope; when reading material is on this level, the reader usually recognizes 90 percent or less of the words he or she reads or comprehends 50 percent or less of what he or she reads.

genre   A category used to classify works of literature, such as historical fiction, biography, or folktales.

grapheme   A written symbol that represents a phoneme.

graphic organizers   Visual depictions of text material, such as webs.

guide words   Words printed at the top of each page in dictionaries, encyclopedias, and other reference books to aid users in finding entries. The first guide word names the first entry on the page; the second guide word names the final entry on the page.

guided reading procedure   A method designed to help readers improve their organizational skills, comprehension, and recall.

hearing impairment   A condition that exists when the sense of hearing is defective but is functional for ordinary purposes.

homographs   Words that have identical spellings but sound different and have different meanings.

homonyms   Pairs or groups of words that are spelled differently but are pronounced alike; homophones.

homophones   See **homonyms.**

hyperbole   An extreme exaggeration.

hypermedia   Text, sound, or pictures (still or animated) linked in a nonsequential manner, allowing access to the material in an order chosen by the user.

hypertext   Information that is linked in a nonsequential manner, allowing students to choose the paths they will take through the information.

idiom   A group of words that, taken as a whole, has a meaning different from that of the sum of the meanings of the individual words.

IEP (Individual Education Program)   A written individual plan that includes objectives, strategies, curriculum modifications, and classroom accommodations for a student with learning problems.

IEP Team   A multidisciplinary group of individuals who construct an IEP for a student with disabilities.

independent level   A level of reading difficulty low enough that the reader can progress without noticeable hindrance; the reader can ordinarily recognize at least 99 percent of the words and comprehend at least 90 percent of what he or she reads.

individualized reading approach   An approach to reading instruction that is characterized by pupils' self-selection of reading materials and self-pacing and by pupil-teacher conferences.

Individuals with Disabilities Education Act (IDEA)   A reauthorized version of the federal law PL 94-142 that modifies some of that law's provisions governing the education of students with disabilities and changes some terminology to show greater sensitivity for individuals with disabilities. *The Improving Education Results for Children with Disabilities Act of 2003* is the most recent reauthorized version of this federal law.

inflectional endings   Endings that when added to nouns change the number, case, or gender; when added to verbs change the tense or person; and when added to adjectives change the degree.

informal reading inventory   An informal instrument designed to help the teacher determine a child's independent, instructional, frustration, and capacity levels.

InQuest   Investigative Questioning, a comprehension strategy that combines student questioning with creative drama.

instructional level   A level of difficulty at which the reader can read with understanding with teacher assistance; the reader can ordinarily recognize at least 95 percent of the words in a selection and comprehend at least 75 percent of what he or she reads.

integrated language arts curriculum   The integration of purposeful reading, writing, listening, speaking, viewing, and visually presenting activities.

interactive theories   Theories that depict reading as a combination of reader-based and text-based processing.

interest grouping   Placing pupils into various groups on the basis of common interests.

Internet   International "network of networks" that links a multitude of computers.

interpretive reading   Reading between the lines.

invented spellings   Unconventional spellings resulting from children's attempts to associate sounds with letters.

journals   Written records of reflections, events, and ideas.

K-W-L Teaching Model   A teaching model for expository text; stands for What I *Know,* What I *Want* to Learn, What I *Learned.*

kidwatching   Observing children to gain insights into their learning.

kinesthetic   Pertaining to body movement and muscle feelings.

knowledge-based processing   Bringing one's prior world knowledge and background of experiences to the interpretation of the text.

language arts   Listening, speaking, reading, writing, viewing, and visually presenting skills.

language experience approach   An approach in which reading and the other language arts are interrelated in the instructional program and the experiences of children are used as the basis for reading materials.

learning center   An area containing several independent learning activities based on a theme.

learning contract   Negotiated agreement about what the pupil is to do and when the task is to be completed.

legend (of a map)   The map's key to symbols used.

legends   Unverified historical stories that originated orally.

line graphs   Graphs that show changes in amounts by connecting, with line segments, points representing the amounts.

linguistics   The scientific study of human speech.

listening comprehension level   Potential reading level.

literal comprehension   Understanding of ideas that are directly stated.

literature circles   Groups established to allow students to exchange ideas about books they are reading.

literature-based approaches   Approaches to teaching reading that use quality literature as a basis for reading instruction.

maze procedure   A procedure, similar to the cloze procedure, that requires the reader to complete missing sections of text by choosing among three provided alternatives.

meaning vocabulary   Words for which meanings are understood.

media literacy   Critical evaluation of materials in various media that incorporates consideration of how media messages are created, marketed, and distributed and how they can affect attitudes and behavior.

metacognition   A person's knowledge of the functioning of his or her own mind and his or her conscious efforts to monitor or control this functioning.

metacognitive strategies   Techniques for thinking about and monitoring one's own thought processes.

metaphor   A direct comparison not using the word *like* or *as.*

minimally contrasting spelling patterns   Words that vary in spelling by only a single letter.

miscue   An unexpected oral reading response (error).

modality   A sensory system for receiving and processing information (visual, auditory, kinesthetic, tactile).

morphemes   The smallest units of meaning in a language.

motivation   Incentive to act.

multimedia   Characterized by the use of a number of different media (graphics, text, moving images, sound effects, etc.) in the same application.

multiple intelligences   Several distinct areas of potential that readers possess to different degrees.

myths   Traditional literature selections that feature characters such as gods, heroes, or supernatural beings.

narrative style   Storylike presentation.

newsgroups   Network locations to which messages are posted so that readers who are interested in the topic can read the messages electronically. Sometimes referred to as electronic bulletin boards.

nonfiction   True stories or expository selections designed to inform or instruct.

norm-referenced test   Test designed to yield results interpretable in terms of a norm, the average or mean results of a sample population.

onsets and rimes   Word parts, onsets being the consonants or consonant clusters at the beginning of a syllable and rimes being the vowels, or vowel combinations and any consonants that follow.

paraprofessional   A teacher's assistant or other adult with some professional training who works in the classroom to assist the teacher.

peer tutoring   One student helping another student learn.

perception   The interpretation of sensory impressions.

performance-based assessment   Measurement of a student's ability to create an assigned response or product to demonstrate her or his level of competence.

personification   Giving the attributes of a person to an inanimate object or abstract idea.

phoneme   The smallest unit of sound in a language.

phonemic awareness   An understanding that speech consists of a series of small sound units.

phonics   The association of speech sounds with printed symbols.

picture graphs   Graphs that express quantities with pictures.

portfolio   A collection of a child's work over a period of time.

pourquoi tales   Traditional literature selections that often explain "why."

predictable books   Books that use repetition, rhythmic language patterns, and familiar concepts.

preoperational stage   Piaget's second stage of cognitive development, extending from age two to age seven.

print conventions   Generally accepted concepts about writing.

programmed instruction   A method of presenting instructional material in which small, sequential steps; active involvement of the learner; immediate reinforcement; and self-pacing are emphasized.

project or research grouping   Placing students of varying ability levels together so that they may investigate a topic.

propaganda techniques   Techniques of writing used to influence people's thinking and actions, including bandwagon technique, card stacking, glittering generalities, name calling, plain-folks talk, testimonials, and transfer techniques.

readability   An objective measure of the difficulty of written material.

readers' theater   Reading aloud from scripts in a dramatic style.

reading workshop   Instructional procedure consisting of a minilesson, a status-of-the-class report, reading, and sharing.

reading miscue inventory (RMI)   An informal instrument that considers both the quality and the quantity of miscues made by the reader.

reading rate   Speed of reading, often reported in words per minute.

reading/study techniques   Techniques designed to enhance comprehension and retention of written material.

reciprocal teaching   A technique to develop comprehension and metacognition in which the teacher and students take turns being "teacher." They predict, generate questions, summarize, and clarify ideas.

regressions   Eye movements back to a previously read word or phrase for the purpose of rereading.

reinforcement   Any event or condition that increases the likelihood that a response will or will not recur.

relative clauses   Clauses that refer to an antecedent (may be restrictive or nonrestrictive).

retelling   A student's recounting of a story or other material that he or she has read.

rime   See **onsets and rimes.**

rubric   A set of criteria used to describe and evaluate a student's level of proficiency in a particular subject area.

running record   A strategy for recording miscues during a student's oral reading.

scaffolding   Offering support through modeling or feedback, and then withdrawing support gradually as the learner gains competence.

scale (of a map)   The part of a map that shows the relationship of a given distance on a map to the same distance on the area represented.

schema   A preexisting knowledge structure developed about a thing, place, or idea.

schemata   The clusters of information that people develop about things, places, and ideas.

self-concept   Opinion of oneself.

semantic clues (or cues)   Meaning clues.

semantic feature analysis   A technique in which the presence or absence of particular features in the meaning of a word is indicated through symbols on a chart, making it possible to compare word meanings.

semantic maps   Graphic representations of relationships among words and phrases in written material.

semantic webbing   Making a graphic representation of relationships in written material through the use of a core question, strands (answers), strand supports (facts and inferences from the story), and strand ties (relationships of the strands to each other).

shadowing   An involved descriptive method used to collect data through observation.

shared-book experience   Reading and rereading books in a group activity for understanding and enjoyment.

sight words   Words that are recognized immediately, without having to resort to analysis.

simile   A comparison using *like* or *as*.

skills or needs groups   Placing pupils into various groups on the basis of deficiencies in skills.

SQ3R   A study method consisting of five steps: Survey, Question, Read, Recite, Review.

SQRQCQ   A study method consisting of six steps: Survey, Question, Read, Question, Compute, Question.

standardized test   A published test that has been constructed by experts in the field and is administered, scored, and interpreted according to specific criteria.

story grammar   A set of rules that define story structures.

story mapping   Making graphic representations of stories that make clear the specific relationships of story elements.

structural analysis   Analysis of words by identifying prefixes, suffixes, root words, inflectional endings, contractions, word combinations forming compound words, and syllabication.

student pairs   Partners who work cooperatively on activities.

study guides   Duplicated sheets prepared by the teacher and distributed to the children to help guide reading in content fields and alleviate some difficulties that interfere with understanding.

subskill theories   Theories that depict reading as a set of subskills that children must master and integrate.

Sustained Silent Reading (SSR)   A program for setting aside a certain period of time daily for uninterrupted silent reading.

synonyms   Groups of words that have the same, or very similar, meanings.

syntactic clues (or cues)   Clues derived from the word order in sentences.

synthetic approach to phonics instruction   Teaching pupils to blend together individual known letter sounds in order to decode written words. Letter sounds are taught first; then they are blended into words.

tactile   Pertaining to the sense of touch.

tall tales   Humorous folktales displaying a great deal of exaggeration.

technological literacy   The ability to use computers and other technology to improve learning, productivity, and performance.

text leveling   The categorization of books on a continuum based on a set of criteria that may include readability, genre, interest, format, links across the curriculum, or other characteristics.

text-based processing   Trying to extract the information that resides in the text.

thematic unit   An integrated learning experience with a topic or concept that is the core of the curriculum for an extended period of time.

think-alouds   Verbalizing aloud the thought processes present as one reads a selection orally.

top-down models   Models that depict reading as beginning with the generation of hypotheses or predictions about the material by the reader.

topic sentence   A sentence that sets forth the central thought of the paragraph in which it occurs.

trade book   A book marketed to the general public.

traditional literature   A literary genre of stories, without identified authors, that are passed from generation to generation through oral narration.

transactive theories   Theories based on Rosenblatt's idea that every reading act is a transaction that involves a reader and a text and occurs at a particular time in a specific context, with meaning coming into being during the transaction between the reader and the text.

vicarious experiences   Indirect experiences.

videoconferencing   The holding of conferences over the Internet with others who can be seen on their computer monitors and heard through the speakers.

videodisc   An analog data storage device from which information can be accessed in nonlinear fashion.

visual acuity   Sharpness of vision.

visual discrimination   The ability to differentiate among shapes.

visual impairment   The condition of being partially sighted but able to read print.

visualization   Picturing events, places, and people described by the author.

word bank   A collection of sight words that have been mastered by an individual pupil, usually recorded on index cards.

word configuration   Word shape.

word sorts   Categorization activities that involve classifying words into categories.

word webs   Graphic representations of the relationships among words that are constructed by connecting the related terms with lines.

word-processing software   Computer software designed to allow the entry, manipulation, and storage of text (and sometimes images).

World Wide Web (WWW)   A part of the Internet that allows users to choose special words or symbols with a mouse click or keyboard stroke and be automatically connected to related Web locations.

writing process   A child-centered procedure for writing that consists of prewriting, drafting, revising, editing, and publishing.

writing workshop   A support framework for teaching writing that includes a minilesson designed to improve writing skills, a writing and conference time when students are authentically engaged in composing while the teacher meets individually with each student, and a sharing time when students read or listen to the sharing of a student's written selection.

zone of proximal development   The span between a child's actual skill level and potential level when assistance is given.

REFERENCES

Aaron, Ira E., Jeanne S. Chall, Dolores Durkin, Kenneth Goodman, and Dorothy Strickland. "The Past, Present, and Future of Literacy Education: Comments from a Panel of Distinguished Educators, Part II." *The Reading Teacher,* 43 (February 1990), 370–380.

Adams, Marilyn Jager. *Beginning to Read: Thinking and Learning About Print.* Cambridge, Mass.: M.I.T. Press, 1990.

Adams, Marilyn Jager. "Modeling the Connections Between Word Recognition and Reading." In *Theoretical Models and Processes of Reading,* 4th ed., edited by Robert B. Ruddell, Martha Rapp Ruddell, and Harry Singer. Newark, Del.: International Reading Association, 1994, 838–863.

Adams, Marilyn Jager, et al. "Beginning to Read: A Critique by Literacy Professionals and a Response by Marilyn Jager Adams." *The Reading Teacher,* 44 (February 1991), 370–395.

Agnew, William J., ed. *Standards Based Language Arts Curriculum.* Boston: Allyn and Bacon, 2000.

Aiken, Adel G., and Lisa Bayer. "They Love Words." *The Reading Teacher,* 56 (September 2002), 68–74.

Airasian, Peter W., and Mary E. Walsh. "Constructivist Cautions." *Phi Delta Kappan,* 78 (February 1997), 444–449.

Allen, Linda. "An Integrated Strategies Approach: Making Word Identification Instruction Work for Beginning Readers." *The Reading Teacher,* 52 (November 1998), 254–268.

Allen, R. V. "The Language-Experience Approach." In *Perspectives on Elementary Reading: Principles and Strategies of Teaching,* edited by Robert Karlin. New York: Harcourt, 1973.

Allington, Richard L. "What I've Learned About Effective Reading Instruction from a Decade of Studying Exemplary Elementary Classroom Teachers." *Phi Delta Kappa,* 83 (June 2002), 740–747.

Anderson, Gary, Diana Higgins, and Stanley R. Wurster. "Differences in the Free-Reading Books Selected by High, Average, and Low Achievers." *The Reading Teacher,* 39 (December 1985), 326–330.

Anderson, Nancy A. "Teaching Reading as a Life Skill." *The Reading Teacher,* 42 (October 1988), 92.

Anderson, Richard C., Elfrieda H. Hiebert, Judith A. Scott, and Ian A. G. Wilkinson. *Becoming a Nation of Readers: The Report of the Commission on Reading.* Washington, D.C.: National Institute of Education, 1985.

Anderson, Richard C., J. Mason, and L. Shirey. *The Reading Group: An Experimental Investigation of a Labyrinth.* Technical Report No. 271. Urbana-Champaign, Ill.: Center for the Study of Reading, University of Illinois, 1983.

Anderson, Richard C., and William E. Nagy. "Word Meanings." In *Handbook of Reading Research,* Vol. II, edited by Rebecca Barr, Michael L. Kamil, Peter Mosenthal, and P. David Pearson. New York: Longman, 1991, 690–724.

Anderson-Inman, Lynne. "Electronic Text: Literacy Medium of the Future." *Journal of Adolescent & Adult Literacy,* 41 (May 1998), 678–682.

Andrade, Heidi G. "Using Rubrics to Promote Thinking and Learning." *Educational Leadership,* 57, no. 5 (February 2000), 13–18.

Ankney, Paul, and Pat McClurg. "Testing Manzo's Guided Reading Procedure." *The Reading Teacher,* 34 (March 1981), 681–685.

Armbruster, Bonnie B. "On Answering Questions." *The Reading Teacher,* 45 (May 1992), 724–725.

Armbruster, Bonnie B. "Science and Reading." *The Reading Teacher,* 46 (December 1992/January 1993), 346–347.

Armbruster, Bonnie, Fran Lehr, and Jean Osborn. *Put Reading First: The Research Building Blocks for Teaching Children to Read.* Jessup, Md.: National Institute for Literacy at ED Pubs, September 2001.

Armbruster, Bonnie B., and William E. Nagy. "Vocabulary in Content Area Lessons." *The Reading Teacher,* 45 (March 1992), 550–551.

Armstrong, Thomas. *Multiple Intelligences in the Classroom.* Alexandria, Va.: Association for Supervision and Curriculum Development, 1994.

Artley, A. Sterl. "Controversial Issues Relating to Word Perception." *The Reading Teacher,* 50 (September 1996), 10–13.

Ashby-Davis, Claire. "Improving Students' Comprehension of Character Development in Plays." *Reading Horizons,* 26, no. 4 (1986), 256–261.

Ashton-Warner, Sylvia. *Teacher.* New York: Simon & Schuster, 1963.

Atwell, Nancie. *In the Middle: Writing, Reading, and Learning with Adolescents.* Upper Montclair, N.J.: Boynton/Cook, 1987.

Atwell, Nancie. "Writing and Reading from the Inside Out." In *Breaking Ground: Teachers Relate Reading and Writing in the Elementary School,* edited by Jane Hansen, Thomas Newkirk, and Donald Graves. Portsmouth, N.H.: Heinemann, 1985.

Au, Kathryn. *Literacy Instruction in Multicultural Settings.* Fort Worth: Harcourt, 1993.

Au, Kathryn H. "Constructing the Theme of a Story." *Language Arts,* 69 (February 1992), 106–111.

Au, Kathryn H. "An Overview of New Concepts of Assessment: Impact on Decision Making and Instruction." Paper presented at the International Reading Association Convention, Atlanta, May 6, 1990.

Augustine, Dianne, Kristin Gruber, and Lynda Hanson. "Cooperation Works!" *Educational Leadership,* 47 (December 1989/January 1990), 4–8.

Austin, Terri. *Changing the View: Student-Led Parent Conferences.* Portsmouth, N.H.: Heinemann, 1994.

Avery, Charles W., and Beth Faris Avery. "Merging Reading and Cooperative Strategies Through Graphic Organizers." *Journal of Reading,* 37 (May 1994), 689–690.

Babbs, Patricia J., and Alden J. Moe. "Metacognition: A Key for Independent Learning from Text." *The Reading Teacher,* 36 (January 1983), 422–426.

Bagford, Jack. "What Ever Happened to Individualized Reading?" *The Reading Teacher,* 39 (November 1985), 190–193.

Bailey, Mildred Hart. "The Utility of Phonic Generalizations in Grades One Through Six." *The Reading Teacher,* 20 (February 1967), 413–418.

Baker, Linda, and Ann L. Brown. "Metacognitive Skills and Reading." In *Handbook of Reading Research,* edited by P. David Pearson et al. New York: Longman, 1984.

Ball, E. W., and B. A. Blachman. "Does Phoneme Awareness Training in Kindergarten Make a Difference in Early Word Recognition and Developmental Spelling?" *Reading Research Quarterly,* 26, no. 1 (1991), 49–66.

Barnitz, John G. "Developing Sentence Comprehension in Reading." *Language Arts,* 56 (November/December 1979), 902–908, 958.

Barone, Tom, Maryann Eeds, and Kathleen Mason. "Literature, the Disciplines, and the Lives of Elementary School Children." *Language Arts,* 72 (January 1995), 30–38.

Baroni, Dick. "Have Primary Children Draw to Expand Vocabulary." *The Reading Teacher,* 40 (April 1987), 819–820.

Barrentine, Shelby. "Engaging with Reading Through Interactive Read-Alouds." *The Reading Teacher,* 50 (September 1996), 36–43.

Barta, Jim, and Martha Crouthers Grindler. "Exploring Bias Using Multicultural Literature for Children." *The Reading Teacher,* 50 (November 1996), 269–270.

Barton, James. "Interpreting Character Emotions for Literature Comprehension." *Journal of Adolescent and Adult Literacy,* 40 (September 1996), 22–28.

Barton, Keith C., and Lynne A. Smith. "Themes or Motifs? Aiming for Coherence Through Interdisciplinary Outlines." *The Reading Teacher,* 54 (September 2000), 54–63.

Basden, Jonathan C. "Authentic Tasks as the Basis for Multimedia Design Curriculum." *T.H.E Journal,* 29 (November 2001), 16–21.

Baskwill, Jane, and Paulette Whitman. *Evaluation: Whole Language, Whole Child.* Toronto: Scholastic, 1988.

Batzle, Janine. *Portfolio Assessment and Evaluation.* Cypress, Calif.: Creative Teaching Press, 1992.

Baumann, James F., Helene Hooten, and Patricia White. "Teaching Comprehension Through Literature: A Teacher-Research Project to Develop Fifth Graders' Reading Strategies and Motivation." *The Reading Teacher,* 53 (September 1999), 38–51.

Baumann, James F., Leah A. Jones, and Nancy Seifert-Kessell. "Using Think-Alouds to Enhance Children's Comprehension Monitoring Abilities." *The Reading Teacher,* 47 (November 1993), 184–193.

Baumann, James F., and Maribeth C. Schmitt. "The What, Why, How, and When of Comprehension Instruction." *The Reading Teacher,* 39 (March 1986), 640–646.

Beach, R., and S. Hynds. "Research on Response to Literature." In *Handbook of Reading Research,* Vol. II, edited by Rebecca Barr, Michael L. Kamil, Peter Mosenthal, and P. David Pearson. New York: Longman, 1991, 453–489.

Beaty, Janice J. *Picture Book Storytelling.* Fort Worth: Harcourt, 1994.

Beck, I., and C. Juel. "The Role of Decoding in Learning to Read." *American Educator,* 8 (Summer 1995), 8–23.

Beck, Isabel L. "Reading and Reasoning." *The Reading Teacher,* 42 (May 1989), 676–682.

Beck, Isabel L., and Margaret G. McKeown. "Learning Words Well—A Program to Enhance Vocabulary and Comprehension." *The Reading Teacher,* 36 (March 1983), 622–625.

Beck, Isabel L., and Margaret G. McKeown. "Research Directions: Social Studies Texts Are Hard to Understand: Mediating Some of the Difficulties." *Language Arts,* 68 (October 1991a), 482–490.

Beck, Isabel, and Margaret McKeown. "Conditions of Vocabulary Acquisition." In *Handbook of Reading Research,* Vol. II, edited by Rebecca Barr, Michael L. Kamil, Peter Mosenthal, and P. David Pearson. New York: Longman, 1991b, 789–814.

Beck, Isabel L., Charles A. Perfetti, and Margaret G. McKeown. "Effects of Long-Term Vocabulary Instruction on Lexical Access and Reading Comprehension." *Journal of Educational Psychology,* 74 (1982), 506–521.

Bell, Barbara. "Literature Response Groups." Presentation at Richard C. Owen Workshop "Whole Language in the Classroom." Oak Ridge, Tennessee, June 12, 1990.

Bell, Kathy. "Books for Telling Time." *The Reading Teacher,* 42 (November 1988a), 179.

Bell, Kathy. "Using Literature to Teach Addition and Subtraction." *The Reading Teacher,* 42 (October 1988b), 90.

Bell, Nancy, Debbie Cambron, Kathy Rey-Barreau, and Beverly Paeth. "Online Literature Groups." Handout at the National Council of Teachers of English Convention, San Diego, 1995.

Bellows, Barbara Plotkin. "Running Shoes Are to Jogging as Analogies Are to Creative/Critical Thinking." *Journal of Reading,* 23 (March 1980), 507–511.

Berger, Linda R. "Reader Response Journals: You Make the Meaning … and How." *Journal of Adolescent & Adult Literacy,* 39 (February 1996), 380–385.

Bergeron, Bette S. "Seeking Authenticity: What Is 'Real' About Thematic Literacy Instruction?" *The Reading Teacher,* 49 (April 1996), 544–551.

Bernhardt, Bill. "Reading and Writing Between the Lines: An Interactive Approach Using Computers." *Journal of Reading,* 37 (March 1994), 458–463.

Bertrand, John. "Children at Risk of School Failure." In *Empowering Children at Risk of School Failure: A Better Way,* edited by John Bertrand and Carole Stice. Norwood, Mass.: Christopher-Gordon, 1995, 1–15.

Between the Lions. PBS Kids. Boston: WGBH/Sirius Thinking, 2003.

Bidwell, Sandra M. "Ideas for Using Drama to Enhance Reading Instruction." *The Reading Teacher,* 45 (April 1992), 653–654.

Blachowicz, Camille L. Z. "Making Connections: Alternatives to the Vocabulary Notebook." *Journal of Reading,* 29 (April 1986), 643–649.

Blachowicz, Camille L. Z. "Vocabulary Development and Reading: From Research to Instruction." *The Reading Teacher,* 38 (May 1985), 876–881.

Blachowicz, Camille L. Z., and John J. Lee. "Vocabulary Development in the Whole Literacy Classroom." *The Reading Teacher,* 45 (November 1991), 188–195.

Blachowicz, Camille L. Z., and Barbara Zabroske. "Context Instruction: A Metacognitive Approach for At-Risk Readers." *Journal of Reading,* 33 (April 1990), 504–508.

Blanton, William E., Gary B. Moorman, and Karen D. Wood. "A Model of Direct Instruction Applied to the Basal Skills Lesson." *The Reading Teacher,* 40 (December 1986), 299–304.

Blanton, William E., Karen D. Wood, and Gary B. Moorman. "The Role of Purpose in Reading Instruction." *The Reading Teacher,* 43 (March 1990), 486–493.

Bloomfield, Leonard, and Clarence Barnhart, *Let's Read: A Linguistic Approach.* Detroit: Wayne State University Press, 1961.

Bluestein, N. Alexandra. "Comprehension Through Characterization: Enabling Readers to Make Personal Connections with Literature." *The Reading Teacher,* 55 (February 2002), 431–434.

Boodt, Gloria M. "Critical Listeners Become Critical Readers in Remedial Reading Class." *The Reading Teacher,* 37 (January 1984), 390–394.

Booth, David. *Classroom Voices.* Toronto: Harcourt, 1994.

Borkowski, J. G., and B. E. Kurtz. "Metacognition and Executive Control." *Cognition in Special Children:*

Comparative Approaches to Retardation, Learning Disabilities, and Giftedness, edited by J. G. Borkowski and J. D. Day. Norwood, N.J.: Ablex, 1987, 123–152.

Bormuth, J. R. "The Cloze Readability Procedure." In *Readability in 1968,* edited by J. R. Bormuth. Champaign, Ill.: National Council of Teachers of English, 1968.

Brabham, Edna Greene, and Susan Kidd Villaume. "Continuing Conversations About Literature Circles." *The Reading Teacher,* 54 (November 2000), 278–280.

Brabham, Edna Greene, and Susan Kidd Villaume. "Vocabulary Instruction: Concerns and Visions." *The Reading Teacher,* 56 (November 2002), 264–268.

Bransford, John D., and Barry S. Stein. *The IDEAL Problem Solver.* New York: Freeman, 1984.

Braselton, Stephania, and Barbara C. Decker. "Using Graphic Organizers to Improve the Reading of Mathematics." *The Reading Teacher,* 48 (November 1994), 276–281.

Breen, Leonard. "Connotations." *Journal of Reading,* 32 (February 1989), 461.

Brimijoin, Kay, Ede Marquissee, and Carol Ann Tomlinson. "Using Date to Differentiate Instruction." *Educational Leadership,* 60 (February 2003), 70–73.

Bristow, Page Simpson. "Are Poor Readers Passive Readers? Some Evidence, Possible Explanations, and Potential Solutions." *The Reading Teacher,* 39 (December 1985), 318–325.

Bromley, Karen D. "Buddy Journals Make the Reading-Writing Connection." *The Reading Teacher,* 43 (November 1989), 122–129.

Bromley, Karen D'Angelo. "Teaching Idioms." *The Reading Teacher,* 38 (December 1984), 272–276.

Brooks, Hollie. "'I Know That Book's Here Somewhere!': How to Organize Your Classroom Library." *The Reading Teacher,* 48 (April 1995), 638–639.

Brown, A. L., and J. D. Day. "Macrorules for Summarizing Texts: The Development of Expertise." *Journal of Verbal Learning and Verbal Behavior,* 22, no. 1 (1983), 1–14.

Brown, A. L., J. D. Day, and R. Jones. "The Development of Plans for Summarizing Texts." *Child Development,* 54 (1983), 968–979.

Brown, Kathleen. "What Kind of Text—For Whom and When? Textual Scaffolding for Beginning Readers." *The Reading Teacher,* 53 (December 1999/January 2000), 292–307.

Brozo, William G., and Carl M. Tomlinson. "Literature: The Key to Lively Content Courses." *The Reading Teacher,* 40 (December 1986), 288–293.

Bruck, Maggie, and Rebecca Treiman. "Learning to Pronounce Words: The Limitations of Analogies." *Reading Research Quarterly,* 27, no. 4 (1992), 374–388.

Brunner, Cornelia. "Judging Student Multimedia." *Electronic Learning,* 15 (May/June 1996), 14–15.

Burmeister, Lou E. "Usefulness of Phonic Generalizations." *The Reading Teacher,* 21 (January 1968): 349–356, 360.

Busching, Beverly A., and Betty Ann Slesinger. "Authentic Questions: What Do They Look Like? Where Do They Lead?" *Language Arts,* 72 (September 1995), 341–351.

Buss, Kathleen, and Lee Karnowski. *Reading and Writing Literary Genres.* Newark, Del.: International Reading Association, 2000.

Butler, Andrea, and Jan Turbill. *Towards a Reading-Writing Classroom.* Portsmouth, N.H.: Heinemann, 1987.

Butler, Syd, and Barbara Cox. "DISKovery: Writing with a Computer in Grade One: A Study in Collaboration." *Language Arts,* 69 (December 1992), 633–640.

Butler, Terri Payne. "Booktime." *Cable in the Classroom,* 9 (March 1999), 12–14.

Butler-Pascoe, Mary Ellen, and Karin M. Wiburg. *Technology and Teaching English Language Learners.* Boston: Allyn and Bacon, 2003.

Cable in the Classroom, "Cable in the Classroom Fact Sheet." 9 (March 1999), 2.

Cadiero-Kaplan, Karen. "Literacy Ideologies: Critically Engaging the Language Arts Curriculum." *Language Arts,* 79 (May 2002), 372–381.

Cairney, T. *Teaching Reading Comprehension.* Milton Keynes, U.K.: Open University Press, 1990.

Caldwell, JoAnne. "Critical Questions." *The Reading Teacher,* 50 (February 1997), 436–437.

Cambourne, Brian. "Why Do Some Students Fail to Learn to Read? Ockham's Razor and the Conditions of Learning." *The Reading Teacher,* 54 (May 2001), 784–786.

Camp, Deanne. "It Takes Two: Teaching with Twin Texts of Fact and Fiction." *The Reading Teacher*, 53 (February 2000), 400–408.

Carney, J. J., D. Anderson, C. Blackburn, and D. Blessing. "Preteaching Vocabulary and the Comprehension of Social Studies Materials by Elementary School Children." *Social Education*, 48 (1984), 71–75.

Carnine, Douglas W. "Phonics Versus Look-Say: Transfer to New Words." *The Reading Teacher*, 30 (March 1977), 636–640.

Carr, Eileen, and Karen K. Wixson. "Guidelines for Evaluating Vocabulary Instruction." *Journal of Reading*, 29 (April 1986), 588–595.

Carr, Joan A. "Verbalizing Character Roles in Novels." *Journal of Reading*, 35 (October 1991), 145–146.

Carr, Kathryn S. "The Importance of Inference Skills in the Primary Grades." *The Reading Teacher*, 36 (February 1983), 518–522.

Carr, Kathryn S., Dawna L. Buchanan, Joanna B. Wentz, Mary L. Weiss, and Kitty J. Brant. "Not Just for the Primary Grades: A Bibliography of Picture Books for Secondary Content Teachers." *Journal of Adolescent & Adult Literacy*, 45 (October 2001), 146–153.

Carroll, John B., Peter Davies, and Barry Richman. *The American Heritage Word Frequency Book.* Boston: Houghton Mifflin, 1971.

Casteel, Carolyn P., and Bess A. Isom. "Reciprocal Processes in Science and Literacy Learning." *The Reading Teacher*, 47 (April 1994), 538–545.

Ceprano, Maria A. "A Review of Selected Research on Methods of Teaching Sight Words." *The Reading Teacher*, 35 (December 1981), 314–322.

Cerullo, M. *Reading the Environment: Children's Literature in the Science Curriculum.* Portsmouth, N.H.: Heinemann, 1997.

Chamberlain, Julia, and Dorothy Leal. "Caldecott Medal Books and Readability Levels: Not Just 'Picture' Books." *The Reading Teacher*, 52 (May 1999), 898–902.

Chaney, Jeanne H. "Alphabet Books: Resources for Learning." *The Reading Teacher*, 47 (October 1993), 96–104.

Cheng, Pui-wan. "Metacognition and Giftedness: The State of the Relationship." *Gifted Child Quarterly*, 37 (Summer 1993), 105–112.

Church, Susan M. "Is Whole Language Warm and Fuzzy?" *The Reading Teacher*, 47 (February 1994), 362–370.

Clay, M. M. *The Early Detection of Reading Difficulties*, 3d ed. Auckland, New Zealand: Heinemann, 1993.

Clay, Marie. *The Early Detection of Reading Difficulties.* Auckland, New Zealand: Heinemann, 1979.

Clemmons, Joan, and Lois Laase. *Language Arts Mini-Lessons.* New York: Scholastic, 1995.

Clyde, Jean Anne. "Stepping Inside the Story World: The Subtext Strategy — A Tool for Connecting and Comprehending." *The Reading Teacher*, 57 (October 2003), 150–160.

Clymer, Theodore. "The Utility of Phonic Generalizations in the Primary Grades." *The Reading Teacher*, 50 (November 1996), 182–187.

Coate, Sheri, and Marrietta Castle. "Integrating LEA and Invented Spelling in Kindergarten." *The Reading Teacher*, 42 (March 1989), 516–519.

Cochran-Smith, M., J. Kahn, and C. L. Paris. "When Word Processors Come into the Classroom." In *Writing with Computers in the Early Grades*, edited by J. L. Hoot and S. B. Silvern. New York: Teachers College Press, 1988.

Coelho, Elizabeth. *Learning Together in the Multicultural Classroom.* Markham, Ontario: Pippin, 1994.

Cohen, Ruth. "Self-Generated Questions as an Aid to Reading Comprehension." *The Reading Teacher*, 36 (April 1983), 770–775.

Coiro, Julie. "Reading Comprehension on the Internet: Expanding Our Understanding of Reading Comprehension to Encompass New Literacies." *The Reading Teacher*, 56 (February 2003), 458–464.

Cole, Ardith Davis. "Beginner-Oriented Texts in Literature-Based Classrooms: The Segue for a Few Struggling Readers." *The Reading Teacher*, 51 (March 1998), 488–501.

Combs, Martha, and John D. Beach. "Stories and Storytelling: Personalizing the Social Studies." *The Reading Teacher*, 47 (March 1994), 464–471.

Come, Barbara, and Anthony Fredericks. "Family Literacy in Urban Schools: Meeting the Needs of At-Risk Children." *The Reading Teacher*, 48 (April 1995), 566–570.

Commeyras, M. "Were Janell and Neesie in the Same Classroom? Children's Questions as the First Order of Reality in Storybook Discussion." *Language Arts,* 71 (1994), 517–523.

Commeyras, Michelle. "Using Literature to Teach Critical Thinking." *Journal of Reading,* 32 (May 1989), 703–707.

Committee on Geographic Education. *Guidelines for Geographic Education: Elementary and Secondary Schools.* Washington, D.C.: National Council for Geographic Education and the Association of American Geographers, 1983.

Conrad, Lori L. "Charting Effect and Cause in Informational Books." *The Reading Teacher,* 42 (February 1989), 451–452.

Cooper, Charles R., and Anthony R. Petrosky. "A Psycholinguistic View of the Fluent Reading Process." *Journal of Reading,* 20 (December 1976), 184–207.

Cordts, Anna D. *Phonics for the Reading Teacher.* New York: Holt, 1965.

Cornett, Claudia E. "Beyond Retelling the Plot: Student-Led Discussions." *The Reading Teacher,* 50 (March 1997), 527–528.

Cotton, Eileen Giuffre. *The Online Classroom: Teaching with the Internet.* Bloomington, Ind.: ERIC Clearinghouse on Reading, English, and Communication, 1996.

Cowan, Hilary. "Software at-a-Glance: New and Hot!: *Classroom Publisher.*" *Electronic Learning,* 15 (May/June 1996), 61–62.

Cox, Carole. "Literature-Based Teaching: A Student Response–Centered Curriculum." In *Reader Response in Elementary Classrooms,* edited by Nicholas Karolides. Mahwah, N.J.: Lawrence Erlbaum, 1997.

Cox, Carole, and Joyce Many. "Toward an Understanding of the Aesthetic Response to Literature." *Language Arts,* 69 (January 1992), 28–33.

Cox, Carole, and Paul Boyd-Batstone. *Crossroads.* Upper Saddle River, N.J.: Merrill, 1997.

Cox, Susan, and Lee Galda. "Multicultural Literature: Mirrors and Windows on a Global Community." *The Reading Teacher,* 43 (April 1990), 582–589.

Criscuolo, Nicholas P. "Creative Vocabulary Building." *Journal of Reading,* 24 (December 1980), 260–261.

Cudd, Evelyn T., and Leslie L. Roberts. "A Scaffolding Technique to Develop Sentence Sense and Vocabulary." *The Reading Teacher,* 47 (December 1993/January 1994), 346–349.

Cudd, Evelyn T., and Leslie Roberts. "Using Writing to Enhance Content Area Learning in the Primary Grades." *The Reading Teacher,* 42 (February 1989), 392–404.

Cullinan, Bernice E. "Whole Language and Children's Literature." *Language Arts,* 69 (October 1992), 426–430.

Cullinan, Bernice E., and Lee Galda. *Literature and the Child,* 3d ed. Fort Worth: Harcourt, 1994.

Cunningham, James W., and Hunter Ballew. "Solving Word Problem Solving." *The Reading Teacher,* 36 (April 1983), 836–839.

Cunningham, James W., and Lisa K. Wall. "Teaching Good Readers to Comprehend Better." *Journal of Reading,* 37 (March 1994), 480–486.

Cunningham, Pat. "Knowledge for More Comprehension." *The Reading Teacher,* 36 (October 1982), 98–101.

Cunningham, Patricia M. "A Compare/Contrast Theory of Mediated Word Identification." *The Reading Teacher,* 32 (April 1979), 774–778.

Cunningham, Patricia M. "Decoding Polysyllabic Words: An Alternative Strategy." *The Reading Teacher,* 21 (April 1978), 608–614.

Cunningham, Patricia M. *Phonics They Use: Words for Reading and Writing.* New York: HarperCollins, 1991.

Cunningham, Patricia, Dorothy Hall, and James Cunningham. *Guided Reading the Four-Blocks Way: The Four-Blocks Literacy Model Book Series.* Greensboro, N.C.: Carson-Dellosa, 2000.

Cunningham, Patricia M., and James W. Cunningham. "Content Area Reading-Writing Lessons." *The Reading Teacher,* 40 (February 1987), 506–512.

Cunningham, Patricia M., and James W. Cunningham. "Making Words: Enhancing the Invented Spelling-Decoding Connection." *The Reading Teacher,* 46 (October 1992), 106–115.

Cunningham, Patricia, and Richard Allington. *Classrooms That Work: They Can All Read and Write.* New York: HarperCollins, 1994.

Cunningham, Patricia M., and Richard L. Allington. *Classrooms That Work: They Can All Read and Write.* New York: Longman, 1999.

Dahl, Karin L., and Patricia L. Scharer. "Phonics Teaching and Learning in Whole Language Classrooms: New Evidence from Research." *The Reading Teacher,* 53 (April 2000), 584–594.

Dailey, Kathleen, and Kimberly Owen. "Dramatic Play and Literacy Development." Presentation at International Reading Association Convention, Toronto, Canada, May 1994.

Daisey, Peggy. "Three Ways to Promote the Values and Uses of Literacy at Any Age." *Journal of Reading,* 36 (March 1993), 436–440.

Dale, Edgar, and Jeanne S. Chall. "A Formula for Predicting Readability." *Educational Research Bulletin,* 27 (January 21, 1948), 11–20, 28; (February 18, 1948), 37–54.

Daneman, Meredyth. "Individual Differences in Reading Skills." In *Handbook of Reading Research,* Vol. II, edited by R. Barr, M. L. Kamil, P. Mosenthal, and P. D. Pearson. New York: Longman, 1991, 512–538.

Danielson, Charlotte, and Leslye Abrutyn. *An Introduction to Using Portfolios in the Classroom.* Alexandria, Va.: Association for Supervision and Curriculum Development, 1997.

Danielson, Kathy Everts. "Picture Books to Use with Older Students." *Journal of Reading,* 35 (May 1992), 652–654.

Davenport, Ruth, Michael Jaeger, and Carol Lauritzen. "Negotiating Curriculum." *The Reading Teacher,* 49 (September 1995), 60–62.

Davis, Anita P., and Thomas R. McDaniel. "An Essential Vocabulary: An Update." *The Reading Teacher,* 52 (November 1998), 308–309.

Davis, Susan J. "Synonym Rally: A Vocabulary Concept Game." *Journal of Reading,* 33 (February 1990), 380.

Davis, Zephaniah T., and Michael D. McPherson. "Story Map Instruction: A Road Map for Reading Comprehension." *The Reading Teacher,* 43 (December 1989), 232–240.

Deaton, Cheryl D. "Idioms as a Means of Communication: Writing in the Middle Grades." *The Reading Teacher,* 45 (February 1992), 473.

DeGroff, Linda. "Is There a Place for Computers in Whole Language Classrooms?" *The Reading Teacher,* 43 (April 1990), 568–572.

DeSerres, Barbara. "Putting Vocabulary in Context." *The Reading Teacher,* 43 (April 1990), 612–613.

Dever, Christine T. "Press Conference: A Strategy for Integrating Reading with Writing." *The Reading Teacher,* 46 (September 1992), 72–73.

Diamond, Barbara, and Margaret Moore. *Multicultural Literacy.* White Plains, N.Y.: Longman, 1995.

Dickerson, Dolores Pawley. "A Study of Use of Games to Reinforce Sight Vocabulary." *The Reading Teacher,* 36 (October 1982), 46–49.

Dickinson, David K. "Oral Language, Literacy Skills, and Response to Literature." In *The Dynamics of Language Learning,* edited by James R. Squire. Urbana, Ill.: ERIC Clearinghouse on Reading and Communication Skills, 1987.

D'Ignazio, Fred. "DISKovery: The Starship Enterprise: New Opportunities for Learning in the 1990's." *Language Arts,* 68 (March 1991), 248–252.

Dillner, Martha. "Using Hypermedia to Enhance Content Area Instruction." *Journal of Reading,* 37 (December 1993/January 1994), 260–270.

Dixon-Krauss, Lisbeth. "Using Literature as a Context for Teaching Vocabulary." *Journal of Adolescent & Adult Literacy,* 45 (December 2001/January 2002), 310–318.

Dixon-Krauss, Lisbeth. *Vygotsky in the Classroom.* White Plains, N.Y.: Longman, 1996.

Dockterman, David. *Great Teaching in the One-Computer Classroom,* 5th ed. Watertown, Mass.: Tom Snyder Productions, 1998.

Doiron, Ray. "Using Nonfiction in a Read-Aloud Program: Letting the Facts Speak for Themselves." *The Reading Teacher,* 47 (May 1994), 616–624.

Dowd, Cornelia A., and Richard Sinatra. "Computer Programs and the Learning of Text Structure." *Journal of Reading,* 34 (October 1990), 104–112.

Dowhower, Sarah L. "Supporting a Strategic Stance in the Classroom: A Comprehension Framework for Helping Teachers Help Students to Be Strategic." *The Reading Teacher,* 52 (April 1999), 672–688.

Downes, Toni, and Cherryl Fatouros. *Learning in an Electronic World.* Portsmouth, N.H.: Heinemann, 1995.

Downing, John. "How Children Think About Reading." In *Psychological Factors in the Teaching of Reading,* compiled by Eldon E. Ekwall. Columbus, Ohio: Merrill, 1973.

Downing, John. "Reading—Skill or Skills?" *The Reading Teacher,* 35 (February 1982), 534–537.

Dreher, Joyce. "Character Contrast." *The Reading Teacher,* 42 (March 1989), 551–552.

Dreher, Mariam Jean. "Motivating Children to Read More Nonfiction." *The Reading Teacher,* 52 (December 1998/January 1999), 414–416.

Dreher, Mariam Jean, and Harry Singer. "Story Grammar Instruction Unnecessary for Intermediate Grade Students." *The Reading Teacher,* 34 (December 1980), 261–268.

Drucker, Mary J. "What Reading Teachers Should Know About ESL Learners." *The Reading Teacher,* 57 (September 2003).

Duchein, M. A., and D. L. Mealey. "Remembrance of Books Past ... Long Past: Glimpses into Aliteracy." *Reading Research and Instruction,* 33, no. 1 (1993), 12–28.

Duffelmeyer, Frederick A. "Effective Anticipation Guide Statements for Learning from Expository Prose." *Journal of Reading,* 37 (March 1994), 452–457.

Duffelmeyer, Frederick A. "The Influence of Experience-Based Vocabulary Instruction on Learning Word Meanings." *Journal of Reading,* 24 (October 1980), 35–40.

Duffelmeyer, Frederick A. "Introducing Words in Context." *The Reading Teacher,* 35 (March 1982), 724–725.

Duffelmeyer, Frederick A. "Teaching Word Meaning from an Experience Base." *The Reading Teacher,* 39 (October 1985), 6–9.

Duffelmeyer, Frederick A., and Dale D. Baum. "The Extended Anticipation Guide Revisited." *Journal of Reading,* 35 (May 1992), 654–656.

Duffelmeyer, Frederick A., and Barbara Blakely Duffelmeyer. "Developing Vocabulary Through Dramatization." *Journal of Reading,* 23 (November 1979), 141–143.

Duffelmeyer, Frederick A., and Barbara Blakely Duffelmeyer. "Topic and Main Idea: Clearing Up the Confusion." *The Reading Teacher,* 45 (November 1991), 252–254.

Duffy, Gerald G., and James V. Hoffman. "In Pursuit of an Illusion: The Flawed Search for a Perfect Method." *The Reading Teacher,* 53 (September 1999), 10–16.

Duffy, Gerald G., Laura R. Roehler, and Beth Ann Herrmann. "Modeling Mental Processes Helps Poor Readers Become Strategic Readers." *The Reading Teacher,* 41 (April 1988), 762–767.

Dugan, Jo Ann. "Transactional Literature Discussions: Engaging Students in the Appreciation and Understanding of Literature." *The Reading Teacher,* 51 (October 1997), 86–96.

Duke, N., and J. Kays. "'Can I Say Once "Upon a Time"?' Kindergarten Children Developing Knowledge of Information Book Language." *Early Childhood Research Quarterly,* 13 (1998), 295–318.

Duke, Nell K., and P. David Pearson. "Effective Practices for Developing Reading Comprehension." In *What Research Has to Say About Reading Instruction,* edited by Alan E. Farstrup and S. Jay Samuels. Newark, Del.: International Reading Association, 2002, 205–242.

Duncan, Patricia H. "I Liked the Book Better: Comparing Film and Text to Build Critical Comprehension." *The Reading Teacher,* 46 (May 1993), 720–725.

Durkin, Dolores. "What Classroom Observations Reveal About Reading Comprehension Instruction." *Reading Research Quarterly,* 14 (1978/1979), 481–533.

Durkin, Dolores. "What Is the Value of the New Interest in Reading Comprehension?" *Language Arts,* 58 (January 1981), 23–43.

Dwyer, David. "Apple Classrooms of Tomorrow: What We've Learned." *Educational Leadership,* 51 (April 1994), 4–10.

Dwyer, Edward J. "Solving Verbal Analogies." *Journal of Reading,* 32 (October 1988), 73–75.

Dymock, Susan. "Reading But Not Understanding." *Journal of Reading,* 37 (October 1993), 86–91.

Eads, Maryann. "What to Do When They Don't Understand What They Read—Research-Based Strategies for Teaching Reading Comprehension." *The Reading Teacher,* 34 (February 1981), 565–571.

Eastern Stream Center on Resources and Training, Region IV Comprehensive Center at AEL, and Region XIV Comprehensive Center/Center for Applied Linguistics. *Help! They Don't Speak English Starter Kit for Primary Teachers: A Resource Guide for Educators of*

Limited English Proficient Migrant Students, Grades Pre-K–6, 3d ed. Charleston, W. Va. 1998.

Ebbers, Margaretha. "Science Text Sets: Using Various Genres to Promote Literacy and Inquiry." *Language Arts,* 80 (September 2002), 40–50.

Eby, Judy. *Reflective Planning, Teaching, and Evaluation K–12,* 2d ed. Upper Saddle River, N.J.: Merrill, 1998.

Edinger, Monica. "Empowering Young Writers with Technology." *Educational Leadership,* 51 (April 1994), 58–60.

Edwards, Anthony T., and R. Allan Dermott. "A New Way with Vocabulary." *Journal of Reading,* 32 (March 1989), 559–561.

Egawa, Kathy. "Harnessing the Power of Language: First Graders' Literature Engagement with *Owl Moon.*" *Language Arts,* 67 (October 1990), 582–588.

Ehri, L. C., and C. Robbins. "Beginners Need Some Decoding Skill to Read Words by Analogy." *Reading Research Quarterly,* 27, no. 1 (1992), 13–26.

El-Hindi, Amelia E. "Beyond Classroom Boundaries: Constructionist Teaching with the Internet." *The Reading Teacher,* 51 (May 1998), 694–700.

El-Hindi, Amelia E. "Integrating Literacy and Science in the Classroom: From Ecomysteries to Readers Theatre." *The Reading Teacher,* 56 (March 2003), 536–538.

Elkind, David. "Developmentally Appropriate Practice: Philosophical and Practical Implications." *Phi Delta Kappan,* 71 (October 1989), 113–117.

Emans, Robert. "The Usefulness of Phonic Generalizations Above the Primary Grades." *The Reading Teacher,* 20 (February 1967), 419–425.

Emery, Donna W. "Helping Readers Comprehend Stories from the Characters' Perspectives." *The Reading Teacher,* 49 (April 1996), 534–541.

Englot-Mash, Christine. "Tying Together Reading Strategies." *Journal of Reading,* 35 (October 1991), 150–151.

Enz, Billie, ed. "Strategies for Promoting Parental Support for Emergent Literacy Programs." *The Reading Teacher,* 49 (October 1995), 168–170.

Erickson, H. Lynn. *Stirring the Head, Heart, and Soul: Redefining Curriculum and Instruction,* 2d ed. Thousand Oaks, Calif.: Corwin Press, 2001.

Evans, Carol. "*Monstruos, Pesadillas,* and Other Frights: A Thematic Unit." *The Reading Teacher,* 47 (February 1994), 428–430.

Fallon, Irmie, and JoBeth Allen. "Where the Deer and the Cantaloupe Play." *The Reading Teacher,* 47 (April 1994), 546–551.

Farr, Roger, and Robert F. Carey. *Reading: What Can Be Measured?,* 2d ed. Newark, Del.: International Reading Association, 1986.

Farr, Roger, and Nancy Roser. *Teaching a Child to Read.* New York: Harcourt, 1979.

Farrar, Mary Thomas. "Asking Better Questions." *The Reading Teacher,* 38 (October 1984a), 10–15.

Farrar, Mary Thomas. "Why Do We Ask Comprehension Questions? A New Conception of Comprehension Instruction." *The Reading Teacher,* 37 (February 1984b), 452–456.

Farris, Pamela J., and Carol J. Fuhler. "Developing Social Studies Concepts Through Picture Books." *The Reading Teacher,* 47 (February 1994), 380–387.

Fawson, Parker C., and D. Ray Reutzel. "But I Only Have a Basal: Implementing Guided Reading in the Early Grades." *The Reading Teacher,* 54 (September 2000), 84–97.

Fay, Leo. "Reading Study Skills: Math and Science." In *Reading and Inquiry,* edited by J. Allen Figurel. Newark, Del.: International Reading Association, 1965.

Felber, Sheila. "Story Mapping for Primary Students." *The Reading Teacher,* 43 (October 1989), 90–91.

Fennessey, Sharon. "Living History Through Drama and Literature." *The Reading Teacher,* 49 (September 1995), 16–19.

Ferguson, Anne M., and Jo Fairburn. "Language Experience for Problem Solving in Mathematics." *The Reading Teacher,* 38 (February 1985), 504–507.

Fiderer, Adele. *Practical Assessments.* New York: Scholastic, 1995.

Fielding, L. G., R. C. Anderson, and P. D. Pearson. *How Discussion Questions Influence Story Understanding* (Technical Report No. 490). Urbana-Champaign, Ill.: University of Illinois, Center for the Study of Reading, January 1990.

Fields, Marjorie, and Deborah Hillstead. "Whole Language in the Play Store." *Childhood Education,* 67 (Winter 1990), 73–76.

Finn, Patrick. *Helping Children Learn to Read.* New York: Random House, 1985.

Fisette, Dolores. "Practical Authentic Assessment: Good Kid Watchers Know What to Teach Next." *The California Reader,* 26 (Summer 1993), 4–7.

Fisher, Bobbi. "The Environment Reflects the Program." *Teaching K–8,* 20 (August/September 1989), 82, 84, 86.

Fisher, Bobbi. *Joyful Learning.* Portsmouth, N.H.: Heinemann, 1991.

Fisher, Douglas, Caren Sax, and Ian Pumpian. "From Intrusion to Inclusion: Myths and Realities in Our Schools." *The Reading Teacher,* 49 (April 1996), 580–584.

Fitzgerald, Jill. "Enhancing Two Related Thought Processes: Revision in Writing and Critical Reading." *The Reading Teacher,* 43 (October 1989), 42–48.

Fitzgerald, Jill. "Helping Readers Gain Self-Control over Reading Comprehension." *The Reading Teacher,* 37 (December 1983), 249–253.

Fitzgerald, Jill. "Research on Stories: Implications for Teachers." In *Children's Comprehension of Text: Research into Practice,* edited by K. Denise Muth. Newark, Del.: International Reading Association, 1989.

Flippo, Rona. *Reading Assessment and Instruction: A Qualitative Approach to Diagnosis.* Fort Worth: Harcourt, 1997.

Flitterman-King, Sharon. "The Role of the Response Journal in Active Reading." *The Quarterly of the National Writing Project and the Center for the Study of Writing,* 10, no. 3 (1988), 4–11.

Flood, James. "The Text, the Student, and the Teacher: Learning from Exposition in the Middle Schools." *The Reading Teacher,* 39 (April 1986), 784–791.

Flood, James, and Diane Lapp. "Reporting Reading Progress: A Comparison Portfolio for Parents." *The Reading Teacher,* 42 (March 1989), 508–514.

Flood, James, Diane Lapp, Sharon Flood, and Greta Nagel. "Am I Allowed to Group? Using Flexible Patterns for Effective Instruction." *The Reading Teacher,* 45 (April 1992), 608–616.

Flood, James, S. B. Heath, and Diane Lapp, eds. *Handbook of Research on Teaching Literacy Through the Communication and Visual Arts.* New York: Macmillan, 1997.

Flynn, Linda L. "Developing Critical Reading Skills Through Cooperative Problem Solving." *The Reading Teacher,* 42 (May 1989), 664–668.

Flynn, Rosalind M., and Gail A. Carr. "Exploring Classroom Literature Through Drama: A Specialist and a Teacher Collaborate." *Language Arts,* 71 (January 1994), 38–43.

Ford, Michael, and Marilyn Ohlhausen. "Tips from Reading Clinicians for Coping with Disabled Readers in Regular Classrooms." *The Reading Teacher,* 42 (October 1988), 18–23.

Forell, Elizabeth. "The Case for Conservative Reader Placement." *The Reading Teacher,* 38 (May 1985), 857–862.

Forman, Ellice A., and Courtney B. Cazden. "Exploring Vygotskian Perspectives in Education: The Cognitive View of Peer Interaction." In *Theoretical Models and Processes of Reading,* 4th ed., edited by Robert Ruddell, Martha Rapp Ruddell, and Harry Singer. Newark, Del.: International Reading Association, 1994.

Fortescue, Chelsea M. "Using Oral and Written Language to Increase Understanding of Math Concepts." *Language Arts,* 71 (December 1994), 576–580.

Fortson, Laura, and Judith Reiff. *Early Childhood Curriculum.* Boston: Allyn and Bacon, 1995.

Foss, Abigail. "Peeling the Onion: Teaching Critical Literacy with Students of Privilege." *Language Arts,* 79 (May 2002), 393–403.

Foster-Harrison, Elizabeth. *Peer Tutoring for K–12 Success.* Bloomington, Ind.: Phi Delta Kappa, 1997.

Fountas, Irene C., and Gay Pinnell. *Guided Reading: Good First Teaching for All Children.* Portsmouth, N.H.: Heinemann, 1996.

Fountas, Irene, and Gay Su Pinnell. *Guiding Readers and Writers: Grades 3–6.* Portsmouth, N.H.: Heinemann, 2001.

Fountas, Irene C., and Gay Su Pinnell. *Matching Books to Readers: Using Leveled Books in Guided Reading, K–3.* Portsmouth, N.H.: Heinemann, 1999.

Fournier, David N. E., and Michael F. Graves. "Scaffolding Adolescents' Comprehension of Short Stories." *Journal of Adolescent & Adult Literacy,* 46 (September 2002), 30–39.

Fowler, Gerald. "Developing Comprehension Skills in Primary Students Through the Use of Story Frames." *The Reading Teacher,* 36 (November 1982), 176–179.

Fox, Barbara J. *Word Recognition Activities: Patterns and Strategies for Developing Fluency.* Upper Saddle River, N.J.: Merrill-Prentice Hall, 2003.

Frager, Alan M. "Affective Dimensions of Content Area Reading." *Journal of Reading,* 36 (May 1993), 616–622.

Fredericks, Anthony D. "Mental Imagery Activities to Improve Comprehension." *The Reading Teacher,* 40 (October 1986), 78–81.

Freedman, Glenn, and Elizabeth G. Reynolds. "Enriching Basal Reader Lessons with Semantic Webbing." *The Reading Teacher,* 33 (March 1980), 667–684.

French, Joyce, Nancy Ellsworth, and Marie Amoruso. *Reading and Learning Disabilities: Research and Practice.* New York: Garland, 1995.

Fresch, Mary Jo. "Self-Selection of Early Literacy Learners." *The Reading Teacher,* 49 (November 1995), 220–227.

Fry, Edward. *Elementary Reading Instruction.* New York: McGraw-Hill, 1977a.

Fry, Edward. "Fry's Readability Graph: Clarifications, Validity, and Extension to Level 17." *Journal of Reading,* 21 (December 1977b), 249.

Fry, Edward. "Readability versus Leveling." *The Reading Teacher,* 56 (November 2002), 286–291.

Fry, Edward. "The Most Common Phonograms." *The Reading Teacher,* 51 (April 1998), 620–622.

Fuhler, Carol J. "Let's Move Toward Literature-Based Reading Instruction." *The Reading Teacher,* 43 (January 1990), 312–315.

Fuhler, Carol J. "Response Journals: Just One More Time with Feeling." *Journal of Reading,* 37 (February 1994), 400–405.

Furleigh, Mary A. "Teaching Comprehension with Editorials." *The Reading Teacher,* 44 (March 1991), 523.

Galda, Lee. "Children and Poetry." *The Reading Teacher,* 43 (October 1989), 66–71.

Galda, Lee. "Saving Our Planet, Saving Ourselves." *The Reading Teacher,* 45 (December 1991), 310–317.

Galda, Lee, Emily Carr, and Susan Cox. "The Plot Thickens." *The Reading Teacher,* 43 (November 1989), 160–166.

Galda, Lee, and Pat MacGregor. "Nature's Wonders: Books for a Science Curriculum." *The Reading Teacher,* 46 (November 1992), 236–245.

Galda, Lee, and Kathy G. Short. "Visual Literacy: Exploring Art and Illustration in Children's Books." *The Reading Teacher,* 46 (March 1993), 506–516.

Gale, David. "Why Word Play?" *The Reading Teacher,* 36 (November 1982), 220–222.

Gallagher, Janice Mori. "Pairing Adolescent Fiction with Books from the Canon." *Journal of Adolescent and Adult Literacy,* 39 (September 1995), 8–14.

Gambrell, Linda. "Creating Classroom Cultures That Foster Reading Motivation." *The Reading Teacher,* 50 (September 1996), 14–25.

Ganske, Kathy, James K. Monroe, and Dorothy S. Strickland. "Questions Teachers Ask About Struggling Readers and Writers." *The Reading Teacher,* 57 (October 2003), 118–128.

Garan, Elaine. "Who's in Control? Is There Enough 'Empowerment' to Go Around?" *Language Arts,* 71 (March 1994), 192–199.

Garcia, Mary, and Kathy Verville. "Redesigning Teaching and Learning: The Arizona Student Assessment Program." In *Authentic Reading Assessment: Practices and Possibilities,* edited by Sheila Valencia, Elfrieda Hiebert, and Peter Afflerbach. Newark, Del.: International Reading Association, 1994.

Gardner, Howard. "Reflections on Multiple Intelligences: Myths and Messages." *Phi Delta Kappan,* 77 (November 1995), 200–209.

Gardner, Michael K., and Martha M. Smith. "Does Perspective Taking Ability Contribute to Reading Comprehension?" *Journal of Reading,* 30 (January 1987), 333–336.

Garrison, James W., and Kenneth Hoskisson. "Confirmation Bias in Predictive Reading." *The Reading Teacher,* 42 (March 1989), 482–486.

Gaskins, I. W., L. C. Ehri, C. Cress, C. O'Hara, and K. Donnelly. "Analyzing Words and Making Discoveries About the Alphabetic System: Activities for Beginning Readers." *Language Arts,* 74 (March 1997), 172–184.

Gaskins, I. W., M. A. Downer, R. C. Anderson, P. M. Cunningham, R. W. Gaskins, M. Schommer, and the Teachers of Benchmark School. "A Metacognitive

Approach to Phonics: Using What You Know to Decode What You Don't Know." *Remedial and Special Education*, 9 (1988), 36–41.

Gaskins, Irene West, et al. "Classroom Talk about Text: Learning in Science Class." *Journal of Reading*, 37 (April 1994), 558–565.

Gaskins, Irene West, et al. "Procedures for Word Learning: Making Discoveries About Words." *The Reading Teacher*, 50 (December 1996/January 1997), 312–327.

Gaskins, Robert W. "The Missing Ingredients: Time on Task, Direct Instruction, and Writing." *The Reading Teacher*, 41 (April 1988), 750–755.

Gaskins, Robert W., Jennifer C. Gaskins, and Irene W. Gaskins. "A Decoding Program for Poor Readers — And the Rest of the Class, Too!" *Language Arts*, 68 (March 1991), 213–225.

Geisert, Paul G., and Mynga K. Futrell. *Teachers, Computers, and Curriculum: Microcomputers in the Curriculum*, 2d ed. Boston: Allyn and Bacon, 1995.

GEONews Handbook, November 11–17, 1990, 7.

Gestwicki, Carol. *Developmentally Appropriate Practice.* Albany, N.Y.: Delmar, 1995.

Gill, J. Thomas, Jr. "Development of Word Knowledge As It Relates to Reading, Spelling, and Instruction." *Language Arts*, 69 (October 1992), 444–453.

Gill, Sharon Ruth. "Reading with Amy: Teaching and Learning Through Reading Conferences." *The Reading Teacher*, 53 (March 2000), 500–509.

Gillet, Jean Wallace, and J. Richard Gentry. "Bridges Between Nonstandard and Standard English with Extensions of Dictated Stories." *The Reading Teacher*, 36 (January 1983), 360–365.

Gipe, Joan P. "Use of a Relevant Context Helps Kids Learn New Word Meanings." *The Reading Teacher*, 33 (January 1980), 398–402.

Glass, Gerald G. "The Strange World of Syllabication." *The Elementary School Journal*, 67 (May 1967), 403–405.

Glynn, Shawn. "Teaching with Analogies: Building on the Science Textbook." *The Reading Teacher*, 49 (March 1996), 490–492.

Golden, Joanne M. "Children's Concept of Story in Reading and Writing." *The Reading Teacher*, 37 (March 1984), 578–584.

Golden, Joanne M., Annyce Meiners, and Stanley Lewis. "The Growth of Story Meaning." *Language Arts*, 69 (January 1992), 22–27.

Goldenberg, Claude. "Instructional Conversations: Promoting Comprehension Through Discussion." *The Reading Teacher*, 46 (December 1992/January 1993), 316–326.

Goodman, Kenneth S. "Reading: A Psycholinguistic Guessing Game." In *Perspectives on Elementary Reading*, edited by Robert Karlin. New York: Harcourt, 1973.

Goodman, Kenneth S. "Reading, Writing, and Written Texts: A Transactional Sociopsycholinguistic View." In *Theoretical Models and Processes of Reading*, 4th ed., edited by Robert B. Ruddell, Martha Rapp Ruddell, and Harry Singer. Newark, Del.: International Reading Association, 1994, 1093–1130.

Goodman, Kenneth S. "Unity in Reading." In *Theoretical Models and Processes of Reading*, 3d ed., edited by Harry Singer and Robert B. Ruddell. Newark, Del.: International Reading Association, 1985.

Goodman, Kenneth S. *What's Whole in Whole Language?* Portsmouth, N.H.: Heinemann, 1986.

Goodman, Kenneth S. "Why Whole Language Is Today's Agenda in Education." *Language Arts*, 69 (September 1992), 354–363.

Goodman, Kenneth S., and Catherine Buck. "Dialect Barriers to Reading Comprehension Revisited." *The Reading Teacher*, 50 (March 1997), 454–459.

Goodman, Kenneth S., Yetta M. Goodman, and Wendy J. Hood, eds. *The Whole Language Evaluation Book.* Portsmouth, N.H.: Heinemann, 1989.

Goodman, Yetta. "Kid Watching: An Alternative to Testing." *National Elementary Principal*, 57 (June 1978), 41–45.

Goodman, Yetta. "Kidwatching: Observing Children in the Classroom." In *Observing the Language Learner*, edited by Angela Jagger and M. T. Smith-Burke. Newark, Del.: International Reading Association, 1985.

Goodman, Yetta. "Miscue Analysis for Classroom Teachers: Some History and Some Procedures." *Primary Voices K–6*, 3 (November 1995), 2–9.

Gordon, Christine, and P. David Pearson. *Effects of Instruction in Metacomprehension and Inferencing on Students' Comprehension Abilities* (Technical Report No. 269). Urbana-Champaign, Ill.: University of Illinois, Center for the Study of Reading, 1983.

Gough, Philip B. "Word Recognition." In *Handbook of Reading Research,* edited by P. David Pearson et al. New York: Longman, 1984.

Gove, Mary. "Clarifying Teachers' Beliefs About Reading." *The Reading Teacher,* 37 (December 1983), 261–268.

Grabe, Mark, and Cindy Grabe. *Integrating Technology for Meaningful Learning.* Boston: Houghton Mifflin, 1998.

Grabe, Nancy White. "Language Experience and Basals." *The Reading Teacher,* 34 (March 1981), 710–711.

Graves, Michael F., and Maureen C. Prenn. "Costs and Benefits of Various Methods of Teaching Vocabulary." *Journal of Reading,* 29 (April 1986), 596–602.

Graves, Michael F., and Susan M. Watts-Taffe. "The Place of Word Consciousness in a Research-Based Vocabulary Program." In *What Research Has to Say About Reading Instruction,* edited by Alan E. Farstrup and S. Jay Samuels. Newark, Del.: International Reading Association, 2002.

Greenewald, M. Jane, and Rosalind L. Rossing. "Short-Term and Long-Term Effects of Story Grammar and Self-Monitoring Training on Children's Story Comprehension." In *Solving Problems in Literacy: Learners, Teachers, and Researchers,* edited by Jerome A. Niles and Rosary V. Lalik. Rochester, N.Y.: National Reading Conference, 1986.

Griffith, Priscilla, and Mary Olson. "Phonemic Awareness Helps Beginning Readers Break the Code." *The Reading Teacher,* 45 (March 1992), 516–523.

Groff, Patrick. "The Maturing of Phonics Instruction." *The Reading Teacher,* 39 (May 1986), 919–923.

Groff, Patrick. "Where's the Phonics? Making a Case for Its Direct and Systematic Instruction." *The Reading Teacher,* 52 (October 1998), 138–141.

Guillaume, Andrea M. "Learning with Text in the Primary Grades." *The Reading Teacher,* 51 (March 1998), 476–486.

Gunderson, Lee. "Voices of the Teenage Diasporas." *Journal of Adolescent and Adult Literacy,* 43 (May 2000), 692–706.

Gunning, Thomas G. "Word Building: A Strategic Approach to the Teaching of Phonics." *The Reading Teacher,* 48 (March 1995), 484–488.

Guthrie, John. "The Maze Technique to Assess, Monitor Reading Comprehension." *The Reading Teacher,* 28 (1974), 161–168.

Guthrie, John T. "Children's Reasons for Success and Failure." *The Reading Teacher,* 36 (January 1983), 478–480.

Guthrie, John T. "Models of Reading and Reading Disability." *Journal of Educational Psychology,* 65 (1973), 9–18.

Guskey, Thomas R. "How Classroom Assessments Improve Learning." *Educational Leadership,* 60 (February 2003), 7–11.

Guzzetti, Barbara J., Barbara J. Kowalinski, and Tom McGowan. "Using a Literature-Based Approach to Teaching Social Studies." *Journal of Reading,* 36 (October 1992), 114–122.

Hacker, Charles J. "From Schema Theory to Classroom Practice." *Language Arts,* 57 (November/December 1980), 866–871.

Hadaway, Nancy L., and Terrell A. Young. "Content Literacy and Language Learning: Instructional Decisions." *The Reading Teacher,* 47 (April 1994), 522–527.

Hadaway, Nancy, and Viola Florez. "Teaching Multi-ethnic Literature, Promoting Cultural Pluralism." *The Dragon Lode,* 8 (Winter 1990), 7–13.

Hafner, Lawrence E., and Hayden B. Jolly. *Teaching Reading to Children,* 2d ed. New York: Macmillan, 1982.

Haggard, Martha Rapp. "Developing Critical Thinking with the Directed Reading-Thinking Activity." *The Reading Teacher,* 41 (February 1988), 526–533.

Haggard, Martha Rapp. "The Vocabulary Self-Collection Strategy: Using Student Interest and World Knowledge to Enhance Vocabulary Growth." *Journal of Reading,* 29 (April 1986), 634–642.

Hall, Nigel. *The Emergence of Literacy.* Portsmouth, N.H.: Heinemann, 1987.

Hamann, Lori S., Loree Schultz, Michael W. Smith, and Brian White. "Making Connections: The Power of Autobiographical Writing Before Reading." *Journal of Reading,* 35 (September 1991), 24–28.

Hancock, Marjorie R. "Character Journals: Initiating Involvement and Identification Through Literature." *Journal of Reading,* 37 (September 1993), 42–50.

Hancock, Marjorie R. "Literature Response Journals: Insights Beyond the Printed Page." *Language Arts,* 69 (January 1992), 36–42.

Handloff, Elaine, and Joanne Golden. "Writing as a Way of 'Getting to' What You Think and Feel About a

Story." In *Book Talk and Beyond,* edited by Nancy Roser and Miriam Martinez. Newark, Del.: International Reading Association, 1995.

Hansell, Stevenson F. "Stepping Up to Outlining." *Journal of Reading,* 22 (December 1978), 248–252.

Hansen, Jane. "Students' Evaluations Bring Reading and Writing Together." *The Reading Teacher,* 46 (October 1992), 100–105.

Hansen, Jane. "Synergism of Classroom and School Libraries." *The New Advocate,* 6 (Summer 1993), 201–211.

Hansen, Jane, and Ruth Hubbard. "Poor Readers Can Draw Inferences." *The Reading Teacher,* 37 (March 1984), 586–589.

Hansen, Jane, and P. David Pearson. "An Instructional Study: Improving the Inferential Comprehension of Fourth Grade Good and Poor Readers." *Journal of Educational Psychology,* 75, no. 6 (1983), 821–829.

Hare, Victoria Chou. "What's in a Word? A Review of Young Children's Difficulties with the Construct 'Word.'" *The Reading Teacher,* 37 (January 1984), 360–364.

Harmon, Janis M. "Vocabulary Teaching and Learning in a Seventh-Grade Literature-Based Classroom." *Journal of Adolescent & Adult Literacy,* 41 (1998), 518–529.

Harmon, Janis M., and Wenda B. Hedrick. "Zooming In and Zooming Out: Enhancing Vocabulary and Conceptual Learning in Social Studies." *The Reading Teacher,* 54 (October 2000), 155–159.

Harp, Bill. "Principles of Assessment and Evaluation in Whole Language Classrooms." In *Assessment and Evaluation for Student Centered Learning,* 2d ed., edited by Bill Harp. Norwood, Mass.: Christopher-Gordon, 1994, 47–66.

Harp, Bill. "When the Principal Asks, 'Why Are You Doing Guided Imagery During Reading Time?'" *The Reading Teacher,* 41 (February 1988), 588–590.

Harp, Bill. "When the Principal Asks, 'Why Are You Doing Piagetian Task Testing When You Have Given Basal Placement Tests?'" *The Reading Teacher,* 41 (November 1987), 212–214.

Harp, Bill. "When the Principal Asks, 'Why Aren't You Using the Phonics Workbooks?'" *The Reading Teacher,* 42 (January 1989b), 326–327.

Harris, Albert J., and Edward R. Sipay. *How to Increase Reading Ability,* 8th ed. New York: Longman, 1985.

Harris, Sandra. "Bringing About Change in Reading Instruction." *The Reading Teacher,* 49 (May 1996), 612–618.

Harris, Theodore L., and Richard E. Hodges, eds. *The Literacy Dictionary: The Vocabulary of Reading and Writing.* Newark, Del.: International Reading Association, 1995.

Harris-Sharples, Susan D., Gail Kearns, and Margery Miller. "A Young Authors Program: One Model for Teacher and Student Empowerment." *The Reading Teacher,* 42 (April 1989), 580–583.

Harste, J. C., K. G. Short, and C. Burke. *Creating Classrooms for Authors: The Reading-Writing Connection.* Portsmouth, N.H.: Heinemann, 1988.

Harvey, Stephanie. "Nonfiction Inquiry: Using Real Reading and Writing to Explore the World." *Language Arts,* 80 (September 2002), 12–22.

Heald-Taylor, B. Gail. "Three Paradigms for Literature Instruction in Grades 3 to 6." *The Reading Teacher,* 49 (March 1996), 456–466.

Heald-Taylor, Gail. *Whole Language Strategies for ESL Students.* San Diego: Dormac, 1989.

Heide, Ann, and Dale Henderson. *The Technological Classroom: A Blueprint for Success.* Toronto: Trifolium Books, 1994.

Heilman, Arthur W. *Phonics in Proper Perspective.* Upper Saddle River, N.J.: Merrill/Prentice-Hall, 2002.

Heimlich, Joan E., and Susan D. Pittelman. *Semantic Mapping: Classroom Applications.* Newark, Del.: International Reading Association, 1986.

Heine, Patricia. "The Power of Related Books." *The Reading Teacher,* 45 (September 1991), 75–77.

Heinich, Robert, Michael Molenda, James D. Russell, and Sharon E. Smaldino. *Instructional Media and Technologies for Learning.* Upper Saddle River, N.J.: Prentice-Hall, 1999.

Heller, Mary F. "Comprehending and Composing Through Language Experience." *The Reading Teacher,* 42 (November 1988), 130–135.

Henke, Linda. "Beyond Basal Reading: A District's Commitment to Change." *The New Advocate,* 1, no. 1 (1988), 42–51.

Herman, Patricia A., Richard C. Anderson, P. David Pearson, and William E. Nagy. "Incidental Acquisition of Word Meaning from Expositions with Varied Text

Features." *Reading Research Quarterly,* 22, no. 3 (1987), 263–284.

Herrell, Adrienne L. *Fifty Strategies for Teaching English Learners.* Columbus, Ohio: Merrill, 2000.

Herrell, Adrienne I. *Fifty Strategies for Teaching English Language Learners.* Upper Saddle River, N.J.: Merrill, 2002.

Herrmann, Beth Ann. "Two Approaches for Helping Poor Readers Become More Strategic." *The Reading Teacher,* 42 (October 1988), 24–28.

Hess, Mary Lou. "Understanding Nonfiction: Purpose, Classification, Response." *Language Arts,* 68 (March 1991), 228–232.

Hickman, Janet. "Not by Chance: Creating Classrooms That Invite Responses to Literature." In *Book Talk and Beyond,* edited by Nancy Roser and Miriam Martinez. Newark, Del.: International Reading Association, 1995.

Hiebert, Elfrieda H., and Jacalyn Colt. "Patterns of Literature-Based Reading Instruction." *The Reading Teacher,* 43 (October 1989), 14–20.

Hoffman, James V. "Critical Reading/Thinking Across the Curriculum: Using I-Charts to Support Learning." *Language Arts,* 69 (February 1992), 121–127.

Hoffman, James V., and Sarah J. McCarthey. "Ongoing Research: Teachers' Practices and the New Basals." *NRRC News* (May 1995), 6–7.

Holdaway, Don. *The Foundations of Literacy.* Portsmouth, N.H.: Heinemann, 1979.

Holland, Holly. "Way Past Word Processing." *Electronic Learning,* 15 (May/June 1996), 22–26.

Holloway, John H. "A Value-Added View of Pupil Performance." *Educational Leadership,* 57 (February 2000), 84–85.

Hornsby, David, Deborah Sukarna, and Jo-Ann Parry. *Read On: A Conference Approach to Reading.* Portsmouth, N.H.: Heinemann, 1986.

Howell, Helen. "Language, Literature, and Vocabulary Development for Gifted Students." *The Reading Teacher,* 40 (February 1987), 500–504.

Hoyt, Linda. "Many Ways of Knowing: Using Drama, Oral Interactions, and the Visual Arts to Enhance Reading Comprehension." *The Reading Teacher,* 45 (April 1992), 580–584.

Huck, Charlotte S., Susan Hepler, and Janet Hickman. *Children's Literature in the Elementary School,* 6th ed. Fort Worth: Harcourt, 1997.

Huff-Benkoski, Kelly Ann, and Scott C. Greenwood. "The Use of Word Analogy Instruction with Developing Readers." *The Reading Teacher,* 48 (February 1995), 446–447.

Hughes, Melissa, Kristen Oakes, Caroline LenZo, and Jackie Carpas. *The Elementary Teacher's Guide to Conferences and Open Houses.* Greensboro, N.C.: Carson-Dellosa, 2001.

Hughes, Sandra M. "Impact of Whole Language on Four Elementary School Libraries." *Language Arts,* 70 (September 1993), 393–399.

Hunter-Grundin, Elizabeth. "Spoken Language in Emergent Literacy Learning." *Reading Today,* 7 (February/March 1990), 22.

International Reading Association & National Council of Teachers of English. *Standards for the English Language Arts: A Project of National Council of Teachers of English and International Reading Association.* Newark, Del.: International Reading Association; Urbana, Ill.: National Council of Teachers of English, 1996.

International Visual Literacy Association. *Frequently Asked Questions: What Is Visual Literacy?* 1998. (http://www.ivla.org/organization/whatis.htm)

Irwin, Judith Westphal. *Teaching Reading Comprehension Processes,* 2d ed. Englewood Cliffs, N.J.: Prentice-Hall, 1991.

Iwicki, Ann L. "Vocabulary Connections." *The Reading Teacher,* 45 (May 1992), 736.

Jasmine, Julia. *Addressing Diversity in the Classroom.* Westminster, Calif.: Teacher Created Materials, 1995.

Jenkins, Barbara L., et al. "Children's Use of Hypothesis Testing When Decoding Words." *The Reading Teacher,* 33 (March 1980), 664–667.

Jenks, Carolyn, and Janice Roberts. "Reading, Writing, and Reviewing: Teacher, Librarian, and Young Readers Collaborate." *Language Arts,* 67 (November 1990), 742–745.

Jett-Simpson, Mary. "Writing Stories Using Model Structures: The Circle Story." *Language Arts,* 58 (March 1981), 293–300.

Jewell, Terry A., and Donna Pratt. "Literature Discussions in the Primary Grades: Children's Thoughtful Discourse About Books and What Teachers Can Do to

Make It Happen." *The Reading Teacher,* 52 (May 1999), 842–850.

Johnson, Dale D., and James F. Baumann. "Word Identification." In *Handbook of Reading Research,* edited by P. David Pearson et al. New York: Longman, 1984.

Johnson, Dale D., and P. David Pearson. *Teaching Reading Vocabulary,* 2d ed. New York: Holt, 1984.

Johnson, Dale D., Susan D. Pittelman, and Joan E. Heimlich. "Semantic Mapping." *The Reading Teacher,* 39 (April 1986), 778–783.

Johnson, Dale D., and Bonnie von Hoff Johnson. "Highlighting Vocabulary in Inferential Comprehension Instruction." *Journal of Reading,* 29 (April 1986), 622–625.

Johnson, David, and Roger Johnson. "Social Skills for Successful Group Work." *Educational Leadership,* 47 (December 1989/January 1990), 29–33.

Johnson, Denise. "Electronic Collaboration: Children's Literature in the Classroom." *The Reading Teacher,* 53 (September 1999), 54–60.

Johnson, Lori Beckmann. "Windows Computing: Finding the Right Words: Dictionaries, Thesauruses, and Quotations." *PC Novice,* 5 (September 1994), 21–23.

Johnson, Nancy M., and M. Jane Ebert. "Time Travel Is Possible: Historical Fiction and Biography—Passport to the Past." *The Reading Teacher,* 45 (March 1992), 488–495.

Johnson, Terry D., and Daphne R. Louis. *Literacy Through Literature.* Portsmouth, N.H.: Heinemann, 1987.

Johnston, Francine R. "Improving Student Response in DR-TAs and DL-TAs." *The Reading Teacher,* 46 (February 1993), 448–449.

Johnston, Francine R. "The Reader, the Text, and the Task: Learning Words in First Grade." *The Reading Teacher,* 51 (May 1998), 666–675.

Johnston, Francine R. "The Timing and Teaching of Word Families." *The Reading Teacher,* 53 (September 1999), 64–75.

Johnston, Peter H. *Constructive Evaluation of Literate Activity.* New York: Longman, 1992.

Johnston, Peter H. "Teachers as Evaluation Experts." *The Reading Teacher,* 40 (April 1987), 744–748.

Jolly, Hayden B., Jr. "Teaching Basic Function Words." *The Reading Teacher,* 35 (November 1981), 136–140.

Jones, Linda L. "An Interactive View of Reading: Implications for the Classroom." *The Reading Teacher,* 35 (April 1982), 772–777.

Jones, Linda T. *Strategies for Involving Parents in Their Children's Education.* Bloomington, Ind.: Phi Delta Kappa, 1991.

Jones, Margaret B., and Denise D. Nessel. "Enhancing the Curriculum with Experience Stories." *The Reading Teacher,* 39 (October 1985), 18–22.

Joranko, Joyce. "Reading and Writing Informational Texts." *The Reading Teacher,* 44 (November 1990), 276–277.

Jossart, Sarah A. "Character Journals Aid Comprehension." *The Reading Teacher,* 42 (November 1988), 180.

Juel, Connie. "Beginning Reading." In *Handbook of Reading Research,* Vol. II, edited by R. Barr, M. L. Kamil, P. Mosenthal, and P. D. Pearson. New York: Longman, 1991, 759–787.

Juel, Connie. "Learning to Read and Write: A Longitudinal Study of Fifty-four Children from First Through Fourth Grade." *Journal of Educational Psychology,* 80 (1988), 437–447.

Kachuck, Beatrice. "Relative Clauses May Cause Confusion for Young Readers." *The Reading Teacher,* 34 (January 1981), 372–377.

Kagan, Spencer. *Cooperative Learning.* San Clemente, Calif.: Kagan Cooperative Learning, 1994.

Kaisen, Jim. "SSR/Booktime: Kindergarten and 1st Grade Sustained Silent Reading." *The Reading Teacher,* 40 (February 1987), 532–536.

Kane, Sharon. "Teaching Decoding Strategies Without Destroying Story." *The Reading Teacher,* 52 (April 1999), 770–772.

Kane, Sharon. "The View from the Discourse Level: Teaching Relationships and Text Structure." *The Reading Teacher,* 52 (October 1998), 182–184.

Kapinus, Barbara. "Looking at the Ideal and the Real in Large-Scale Reading Assessment: The View from Two Sides of the River." *The Reading Teacher,* 47 (April 1994), 578–580.

Kaplan, Elaine M., and Anita Tuchman. "Vocabulary Strategies Belong in the Hands of Learners." *Journal of Reading,* 24 (October 1980), 32–34.

Karnowski, Lee. "Using LEA with Process Writing." *The Reading Teacher,* 42 (March 1989), 462–465.

A Kid-Watching Guide: Evaluation for Whole Language Classrooms. Tucson, Ariz.: TAWL (Tucsonans Applying Whole Language), 1984.

Kimmel, Susan, and Walter H. MacGinitie. "Helping Students Revise Hypotheses While Reading." *The Reading Teacher,* 38 (April 1985), 768–771.

Kitagawa, Mary M. "Improving Discussions or How to Get the Students to Ask the Questions." *The Reading Teacher,* 36 (October 1982), 42–45.

Klein, Perry D., and David R. Olson. "Texts, Technology, and Thinking: Lessons from the Great Divide." *Language Arts,* 78 (January 2001), 227–236.

Kohn, Alfie. "What to Look for in a Classroom." *Educational Leadership,* 54 (September 1996), 54–55.

Kolb, Gayla. "Read with a Beat: Developing Literacy Through Music and Song." *The Reading Teacher,* 50 (September 1996), 76–77.

Koskinen, Patricia S., Linda B. Gambrell, Barbara A. Kapinus, and Betty S. Heathington. "Retelling: A Strategy for Enhancing Students' Reading Comprehension." *The Reading Teacher,* 41 (May 1988), 892–896.

Koskinen, Patricia S., Robert M. Wilson, Linda B. Gambrell, and Susan B. Neuman. "Captioned Video and Vocabulary Learning: An Innovative Practice in Literacy Instruction." *The Reading Teacher,* 47 (September 1993), 36–43.

Kotrla, Melissa. "What's Literacy?" *The Reading Teacher,* 50 (May 1997), 702–703.

Krieger, Evelyn. "Developing Comprehension Through Author Awareness." *Journal of Reading,* 33 (May 1990), 618–619.

Kupiter, Karen, and Patricia Wilson. "Updating Poetry Preferences: A Look at the Poetry Children Really Like." *The Reading Teacher,* 47 (September 1993), 28–35.

Kuta, Katherine Wiesolek. "Teaching Text Patterns to Remedial Readers." *Journal of Reading,* 35 (May 1992), 657–658.

Laase, Lois. "Study Skills: Note-Taking Strategies That Work." *Instructor,* 106 (May/June 1997), 58.

Labbo, Linda D. "12 Things Young Children Can Do with a Talking Book in a Classroom Computer Center." *The Reading Teacher,* 53 (April 2000), 542–546.

LaBerge, David, and S. Jay Samuels. "Toward a Theory of Automatic Information Processing in Reading." In *Theoretical Models and Processes of Reading,* 3d ed., edited by Harry Singer and Robert B. Ruddell. Newark, Del.: International Reading Association, 1985.

Lamme, Linda Leonard, and Linda Ledbetter. "Libraries: The Heart of Whole Language." *Language Arts,* 67 (November 1990), 735–741.

Lancia, Peter. "Literary Borrowing: The Effects of Literature on Children's Writing." *The Reading Teacher,* 50 (March 1997), 470–475.

Lange, Bob. "Making Sense with Schemata." *Journal of Reading,* 24 (February 1981), 442–445.

Lapp, Diane, and James Flood. "Integrating the Curriculum: First Steps." *The Reading Teacher,* 47 (February 1994), 416–419.

Lapp, Diane, and James Flood. "Where's the Phonics? Making the Case (Again) for Integrated Code Instruction." *The Reading Teacher,* 50 (May 1997), 696–700.

Lapp, Diane, James Flood, and Douglas Fisher. "Intermediality: How the Use of Multiple Media Enhances Learning." *The Reading Teacher,* 52 (April 1999), 776–780.

Lauritzen, Carol, Michael Jaeger, and M. Ruth Davenport. "Integrating Curriculum: Contexts for Integrating Curriculum." *The Reading Teacher,* 49 (February 1996), 404–406.

Layton, Kent, and Martha E. Irwin. "Enriching Your Reading Program with Databases." *The Reading Teacher,* 42 (May 1989), 724.

Lazear, David. *Teaching for Multiple Intelligences.* Bloomington, Ind.: Phi Delta Kappa, 1992.

Leal, Dorothy L. "The Power of Literary Peer-Group Discussions: How Children Collaboratively Negotiate Meaning." *The Reading Teacher,* 47 (October 1993), 114–120.

Leal, Dorothy J., and Julia Chamberlain-Solecki. "A Newbery Medal–Winning Combination: High Student Interest Plus Appropriate Readability Levels." *The Reading Teacher,* 51 (May 1998), 712–714.

Lee, Gretchen. "Technology in the Language Arts Classroom: Is It Worth the Trouble?" *Voices from the Middle,* 7 (March 2000), 24–32.

Lenski, Susan, Marsha Riss, and Gayle Flickinger. "Honoring Student Self-Evaluation in the Classroom Community." *Primary Voices K–6,* 4 (April 1996), 24–32.

Leslie, Lauren, and Mary Jett-Simpson. *Authentic Literacy Assessment.* New York: Longman, 1997.

Letts, Nancy. "Building Classroom Unity." *Teaching K–8,* 25 (August/September 1994), 106–107.

Leu, Donald J., Jr. "Exploring Literacy Within Multimedia Environments." *The Reading Teacher,* 50 (October 1996), 162–165.

Leu, Donald J., Jr. "Internet Workshop: Making Time for Literacy." *The Reading Teacher,* 55 (February 2002), 466–472.

Leu, Donald J., Jr. "Our Children's Future: Changing the Focus of Literacy and Literacy Instruction." *The Reading Teacher,* 53 (February 2000), 424–427.

Leu, Donald J., Jr., and Deborah Diadiun Leu. *Teaching with the Internet: Lessons from the Classroom.* Norwood, Mass.: Christopher-Gordon, 2000.

Leu, Donald J., Jr., Rachel A. Karchmer, and Deborah Diadiun Leu. "The Miss Rumphius Effect: Envisionments for Literacy and Learning That Transform the Internet." *The Reading Teacher,* 52 (March 1999), 636–642.

Levstick, Linda S. "Research Directions: Mediating Content Through Literary Texts." *Language Arts,* 67 (December 1990), 848–853.

Lewis, Maureen, David Wray, and Patricia Rospigliosi. "…And I Want It in Your Own Words." *The Reading Teacher,* 47 (April 1994), 528–536.

Lightbrown, Patsy A., and Nina Spada. *How Languages Are Learned.* Oxford: Oxford University Press, 1999.

Lipman, Doug. *Improving Your Storytelling: Beyond the Basics for All Who Tell Stories in Work or Play.* Little Rock: August House, 1999.

Lipson, Marjorie Y., Sheila W. Valencia, Karen K. Wixon, and Charles W. Peters. "Integration and Thematic Teaching: Integration to Improve Teaching and Learning." *Language Arts,* 70 (April 1993), 252–263.

Lipson, Marjorie, and Karen Wixson. *Assessment & Instruction of Reading and Writing Disability,* 2d ed. New York: Longman, 1997.

Lombardi, Thomas, and Barbara Ludlow. *Trends Shaping the Future of Special Education.* Bloomington, Ind.: Phi Delta Kappa, 1996.

Long, Emily S. "Using Acrostic Poems for Research Reporting." *The Reading Teacher,* 46 (February 1993), 447–448.

Loughlin, Catherine E., and Mavis D. Martin. *Supporting Literacy.* New York: Teachers College Press, 1987.

Lukasevich, Ann. "Meeting Special Needs in the Whole-Language Classroom." In *Whole Language,* 2d ed., edited by Victor Froese. Boston: Allyn and Bacon, 1996a, 306–337.

Lukasevich, Ann. "Organizing Whole-Language Classrooms." In *Whole Language Practice and Theory,* 2d ed., edited by Victor Froese. Boston: Allyn and Bacon, 1996b, 362–388.

Lundberg, I., J. Frost, and O. Peterson. "Effects of an Extensive Program for Stimulating Phonological Awareness in Preschool Children." *Reading Research Quarterly,* 23 (1988), 263–284.

Lunsford, Susan H. "'And They Wrote Happily Ever After': Literature-Based Mini-Lessons in Writing." *Language Arts,* 74 (January 1997), 42–48.

Lyon, G. Reid. *Research in Learning Disabilities: Research Directions (Technical Report).* Bethesda, Md.: National Institutes of Child Health and Human Development, 1991.

Maclean, Rod. "Two Paradoxes of Phonics." *The Reading Teacher,* 41 (February 1988), 514–517.

Madden, Lowell. "Improve Reading Attitudes of Poor Readers Through Cooperative Reading Teams." *The Reading Teacher,* 42 (December 1988), 194–199.

Mallow, Jeffry V. "Reading Science." *Journal of Reading,* 34 (February 1991), 324–338.

Mandler, J. M. *Stories, Scripts, and Scenes: Aspects of Schema Theory.* Hillsdale, N.J.: Erlbaum, 1984.

Mandler, Jean M., and Nancy S. Johnson. "Remembrance of Things Parsed: Story Structure and Recall." *Cognitive Psychology,* 9 (January 1977), 111–151.

Mangieri, John N., and Michael S. Kahn. "Is the Dolch List of 220 Basic Sight Words Irrelevant?" *The Reading Teacher,* 30 (March 1977), 649–651.

Manna, Anthony. "Making Language Come Alive Through Reading Plays." *The Reading Teacher,* 37 (April 1984), 712–717.

Manzo, Anthony, Ula Manzo, and Julie Jackson Albee. "iReap: Improving Reading, Writing, and Thinking in the Wired Classroom." *Journal of Adolescent & Adult Literacy,* 46 (September 2002), 42–47.

Maria, Katherine. "Developing Disadvantaged Children's Background Knowledge Interactively." *The Reading Teacher,* 42 (January 1989), 296–300.

Maric, K., and J. M. Johnson. "Correcting Misconceptions: Effect of Type on Text." In *Literacy Theory and Research: Analyses from Multiple Paradigms,* edited by

S. McCormick and J. Zutell. Chicago: National Reading Conference, 1990.

Maring, Gerald H. "Video Conferencing." International Reading Association Convention, San Francisco, California, May 1, 2002.

Marshall, Nancy. "Using Story Grammar to Assess Reading Comprehension." *The Reading Teacher,* 36 (March 1983), 616–620.

Martinez, Miriam. "Motivating Dramatic Story Reenactments." *The Reading Teacher,* 46 (May 1993), 682–688.

Martinez, Miriam, and Marcia F. Nash. "Bookalogues: Talking About Children's Literature." *Language Arts,* 67 (October 1990a), 599–606.

Martinez, Miriam, and Marcia F. Nash. "Bookalogues: Talking About Children's Literature." *Language Arts,* 67 (December 1990b), 854–861.

Martinez-Roldan, Carmen M., and Julia M. Lopez-Robertson. "Initiating Literature Circles in a First-Grade Bilingual Classroom." *The Reading Teacher,* 53 (December 1999/January 2000), 270–281.

Marzano, Lorraine. "Connecting Literature with Cooperative Writing." *The Reading Teacher,* 43 (February 1990), 429–430.

Marzano, Robert J. "A Cluster Approach to Vocabulary Instruction: A New Direction from the Research Literature." *The Reading Teacher,* 38 (November 1984), 168–173.

Mason, George. "The Word Processor and Teaching Reading." *The Reading Teacher,* 37 (February 1984), 552–553.

Mathison, Carla. "Activating Student Interest in Content Area Reading." *Journal of Reading,* 33 (December 1989), 170–176.

Maudeville, Thomas F. "KWLA: Linking the Affective and Cognitive Domains." *The Reading Teacher,* 47 (May 1994), 679–680.

Mavrogenes, Nancy A. "What Every Reading Teacher Should Know About Emergent Literacy." *The Reading Teacher,* 40 (November 1986), 174–178.

McCarthy, Robert. "Assessing the Whole Student." *Instructor Special Supplement* (May/June 1994), 18.

McClure, Amy A., and Connie S. Zitlow. "Not Just the Facts: Aesthetic Response in Elementary Content Area Studies." *Language Arts,* 68 (January 1991), 27–33.

McConaughy, Stephanie H. "Word Recognition and Word Meaning in the Total Reading Process." *Language Arts,* 55 (November/December 1978), 946–956, 1003.

McCracken, Robert, and Marlene McCracken. *Stories, Songs & Poetry to Teach Reading & Writing.* Winnipeg, Canada: Peguis, 1987.

McDonald, Jacqueline. "Graphs and Prediction: Helping Children Connect Mathematics and Literature." *The Reading Teacher,* 53 (September 1999), 25–29.

McGee, Lea M. "Exploring the Literature-Based Reading Revolution." *Language Arts,* 69 (November 1992), 529–537.

McGee, Lea M., and Donald J. Richgels. "Teaching Expository Text Structure to Elementary Students." *The Reading Teacher,* 38 (April 1985), 739–748.

McGee, Lea M., and Gail E. Tompkins. "Literature-Based Reading Instruction: Who's Guiding the Instruction?" *Language Arts,* 72 (October 1995), 405–414.

McGee, Lea M., and Gail E. Tompkins. "The Videotape Answer to Independent Reading Comprehension Activities." *The Reading Teacher,* 34 (January 1981), 427–433.

McGill-Franzen, Anne. "'I Could Read the Words!': Selecting Good Books for Inexperienced Readers." *The Reading Teacher,* 46 (February 1993), 424–426.

McIntosh, Margaret E. "What Do Practitioners Need to Know About Current Inference Research?" *The Reading Teacher,* 38 (April 1985), 755–761.

McKenna, Michael C., David Reinking, Linda D. Labbo, and R. D. Kieffer. "The Electronic Transformation of Literacy and Its Implications for the Struggling Reader." *Reading & Writing Quarterly,* 15 (1999), 111–126.

McKeon, Christine A. "The Nature of Children's E-mail in One Classroom." *The Reading Teacher,* 52 (April 1999), 698–706.

McKeown, Margaret G., Isabel L. Beck, Richard C. Omanson, and Charles A. Perfetti. "The Effects of Long-Term Vocabulary Instruction on Reading Comprehension: A Replication." *Journal of Reading Behavior,* 15 (1983), 3–18.

McKeown, Margaret G., Isabel L. Beck, and M. Jo Worthy. "Grappling with Text Ideas: Questioning the Author." *The Reading Teacher,* 46 (April 1993), 560–566.

McKeown, Margaret G., Isabel L. Beck, Richard C. Omanson, and Martha T. Pople. "Some Effects of the

Nature and Frequency of Vocabulary Instruction on the Knowledge and Use of Words." *Reading Research Quarterly,* 20, no. 5 (1985), 522–535.

McLane, Joan, and Gillian McNamee. *Early Literacy.* Cambridge, Mass.: Harvard University Press, 1990.

McMillan, Merna M., and Lance M. Gentile. "Children's Literature: Teaching Critical Thinking and Ethics." *The Reading Teacher,* 41 (May 1988), 876–878.

McNutt, Gaye, and Nancy Bukofzer. "Teaching Early Reading at McDonald's." *The Reading Teacher,* 35 (April 1982), 841–842.

McVey, Michael. "The Death of the Textbook: Shaping a New Learning Environment." *Talking Points,* 8 (May/June 1997), 5–7.

McWhirter, Anna M. "Whole Language in the Middle School." *The Reading Teacher,* 43 (April 1990), 562–565.

Means, Barbara, and Kerry Olson. "The Link Between Technology and Authentic Learning." *Educational Leadership,* 51 (April 1994), 15–18.

Meir, Margaret. "Comprehension Monitoring in the Elementary Classroom." *The Reading Teacher,* 37 (April 1984), 770–774.

Meltzer, Nancy S., and Robert Herse. "The Boundaries of Written Words as Seen by First Graders." *Journal of Reading Behavior,* 1 (Summer 1969), 3–14.

Memory, David M., and Carol Y. Yoder. "Improving Concentration in Content Classrooms." *Journal of Reading,* 31 (February 1988), 426–435.

Menke, Deborah J., and Michael Pressley. "Elaborative Interrogation: Using 'Why' Questions to Enhance the Learning from Text." *Journal of Reading,* 37 (May 1994), 642–645.

Merkley, Donna J. "Modified Anticipation Guide." *The Reading Teacher,* 50 (December 1996/January 1997), 365–368.

Merkley, Donna M., and Debra Jefferies. "Guidelines for Implementing a Graphic Organizer." *The Reading Teacher,* 54 (December 2000/January 2001), 350–357.

Mesmer, Heidi Anne E. "Scaffolding a Crucial Transition Using Text with Some Decodability." *The Reading Teacher,* 53 (October 1999), 130–142.

Mesmer, Heidi Anne E., and Elizabeth J. Hutchins. "Using QARs with Charts and Graphs." *The Reading Teacher,* 56 (September 2002), 21–27.

Michener, Darlene M. "Test Your Reading Aloud IQ." *The Reading Teacher,* 42 (November 1988), 118–122.

Mike, Dennis G. "Interactive Literacy." *Electronic Learning,* 13 (May/June 1994), 50–52, 54.

Miller, Etta, Luther B. Clegg, and Bill Vanderhoff. "Creating Postcards from the Famous for Social Studies Class." *Journal of Reading,* 36 (October 1992), 134–135.

Miller, G. Michael, and George E. Mason. "Dramatic Improvisation: Risk-Free Role Playing for Improving Reading Performance." *The Reading Teacher,* 37 (November 1983), 128–131.

Moldofsky, Penny Baum. "Teaching Students to Determine the Central Story Problem: A Practical Application of Schema Theory." *The Reading Teacher,* 36 (April 1983), 740–745.

Moore, David W., and James W. Cunningham. "Task Clarity and Sixth-Grade Students' Main Idea Statements." In *Changing Perspectives on Research in Reading/Language Processing and Instruction,* edited by Jerome A. Niles and Larry A. Harris. Rochester, N.Y.: National Reading Conference, 1984.

Moore, Margaret. "Electronic Dialoguing: An Avenue to Literacy." *The Reading Teacher,* 45 (December 1991), 280–286.

Morden, Dawn L. "Crossroads to the World." *Educational Leadership,* 51 (April 1994), 36–38.

Morrell, Ernest. "Toward a Critical Pedagogy of Popular Culture: Literacy Development Among Urban Youth." *Journal of Adolescent & Adult Literacy,* 46 (September 2002), 72–77.

Morrow, Lesley Mandel. "Manipulative Learning Materials: Merging Reading Skills with Content Area Objectives." *Journal of Reading,* 25 (February 1982), 448–453.

Morrow, Lesley Mandel. "Using Story Retelling to Develop Comprehension." In *Children's Comprehension of Text: Research into Practice,* edited by K. Denise Muth. Newark, Del.: International Reading Association, 1989.

Morrow, Lesley Mandel, and Susan B. Neuman. "Introduction: Family Literacy." *The Reading Teacher,* 48 (April 1995), 550–551.

Mosenthal, P., and T. J. Na. "Quality of Children's Recall Under Two Classroom Testing Tasks: Toward a Socio-Psycholinguistic Model of Reading Comprehension." *Reading Research Quarterly,* 15 (1980a), 501–528.

Mosenthal, P., and T. J. Na. "Quality of Text Recall as a Function of Children's Classroom Competence." *Journal of Experimental Child Psychology*, 30 (1980b), 1–21.

Mosenthal, Peter B. "The Whole Language Approach: Teachers Between a Rock and a Hard Place." *The Reading Teacher*, 42 (April 1989), 628–629.

Mosenthal, Peter B., and Irwin S. Kirsch. "Understanding Documents: Understanding Thematic Maps." *Journal of Reading*, 34 (October 1990), 136–140.

Moss, Barbara, and Judith Hendershot. "Exploring Sixth Graders' Selection of Nonfiction Trade Books." *The Reading Teacher*, 56 (September 2002), 6–17.

Moss, Barbara, and Harry Noden. "Pointers for Putting Whole Language into Practice." *The Reading Teacher*, 47 (December 1993/January 1994), 342–344.

Mountain, Lee. "Flip-a-Chip to Build Vocabulary." *Journal of Adolescent & Adult Literacy*, 48 (September 2002), 62–68.

Mountain, Lee. "Math Synonyms." *The Reading Teacher*, 46 (February 1993), 451–452.

Moustafa, Margaret. "Comprehensible Input PLUS the Language Experience Approach: A Longterm Perspective." *The Reading Teacher*, 41 (December 1987), 276–286.

Moustafa, Margaret, and Elba Maldonado-Colon. "Whole-to-Parts Phonics Instruction: Building on What Children Know to Help Them Know More." *The Reading Teacher*, 52 (February 1999), 448–458.

Moustafa, Margaret, and Joyce Penrose. "Comprehensible Input PLUS the Language Experience Approach: Reading Instruction for Limited English Speaking Students." *The Reading Teacher*, 38 (March 1985), 640–647.

Muller, Dorothy H., and Liz Savage. "Mapping the Library." *The Reading Teacher*, 35 (April 1982), 840–841.

Munson, Jennie Livingston. "Story and Poetry Maps." *The Reading Teacher*, 42 (May 1989), 736–737.

Nagy, William E. *Teaching Vocabulary to Improve Reading Comprehension*. Urbana, Ill.: National Council of Teachers of English, 1988.

Nagy, William E., and Richard C. Anderson. "How Many Words Are There in Printed School English?" *Reading Research Quarterly*, 19, no. 3 (1984), 304–330.

Nagy, William E., Patricia A. Herman, and Richard C. Anderson. "Learning Words from Context." *Reading Research Quarterly*, 20, no. 2 (1985), 233–253.

National Education Association. *Student Portfolios*. Washington, D.C.: National Education Association, 1993.

National Reading Panel. *Teaching Children to Read: An Evidence-Based Assessment of the Scientific Research Literature on Reading and Its Implications for Reading Instruction*. Jessup, Md.: National Institute for Literacy at Ed Pubs, December 2000.

Naughton, Victoria M. "Creative Mapping for Content Reading." *Journal of Reading*, 37 (December 1993/January 1994), 324–326.

Neill, Monty. "Principles for 'Assessment.'" *Talking Points*, 8 (February–March 1997), 26–27.

Nelson-Herber, Joan. "Expanding and Defining Vocabulary in Content Areas." *Journal of Reading*, 29 (April 1986), 626–633.

Nessel, Denise D. "Storytelling in the Reading Program." *The Reading Teacher*, 38 (January 1985), 378–381.

Neuman, Susan, and Kathleen Roskos. *Language and Literacy Learning in the Early Years*. Orlando: Harcourt Brace Jovanovich, 1993.

Neuman, Susan B., and Patricia S. Koskinen. "Captioned Television as Comprehensible Input: Effects of Incidental Word Learning in Context for Language Minority Students." *Reading Research Quarterly*, 27 (1992), 95–106.

Neville, Rita. "Critical Thinkers Become Critical Readers." *The Reading Teacher*, 35 (May 1982), 947–948.

Newman, Gayle. "Comprehension Strategy Gloves." *The Reading Teacher*, 55 (December 2001/January 2002), 329–332.

Newman, Judith M. "Online: From Far Away." *Language Arts*, 66 (1989), 791–797.

Newman, Judith M., and Susan M. Church. "Myths of Whole Language." *The Reading Teacher*, 44 (September 1990), 20–26.

Nicholson, Tom. "The Flashcard Strikes Back." *The Reading Teacher*, 52 (October 1998), 188–192.

Niday, Donna, and Mark Campbell. "You've Got Mail: 'Near-Peer' Relationships in the Middle." *Voices from the Middle*, 7 (March 2000), 55–61.

Nistler, Robert J., and Angela Maiers. "Stopping the Silence: Hearing Parents' Voices in an Urban First-

Grade Family Literacy Program." *The Reading Teacher,* 53 (May 2000), 670–680.

Nolan, Thomas E. "Self-Questioning and Prediction: Combining Metacognitive Strategies." *Journal of Reading,* 35 (October 1991), 132–138.

Nolte, Ruth Yopp, and Harry Singer. "Active Comprehension: Teaching a Process of Reading Comprehension and Its Effects on Reading Achievement." *The Reading Teacher,* 39 (October 1985), 24–31.

Norton, Donna E. "Circa 1942 and the Integration of Literature, Reading, and Geography." *The Reading Teacher,* 46 (April 1993a), 610–614.

Norton, Donna E. "Modeling Inferencing of Characterization." *The Reading Teacher,* 46 (September 1992a), 64–67.

Norton, Donna E. *Through the Eyes of a Child,* 4th ed. Columbus, Ohio: Merrill, 1995.

Norton, Donna E. *Through the Eyes of a Child: An Introduction to Children's Literature,* 5th ed. Upper Saddle River, N.J.: Merrill, 1999.

Norton, Donna E. *Through the Eyes of a Child: An Introduction to Children's Literature,* 6th ed. Upper Saddle River, N.J.: Merrill, 2003.

Norton, Donna E. "Understanding Plot Structures." *The Reading Teacher,* 46 (November 1992b), 254–258.

Norton, Donna E. "Webbing and Historical Fiction." *The Reading Teacher,* 46 (February 1993b), 432–436.

Ogle, Donna M. "K-W-L: A Teaching Model That Develops Active Reading of Expository Text." *The Reading Teacher,* 39 (February 1986), 564–570.

Ogle, Donna M. "The Know, Want to Know, Learn Strategy." In *Children's Comprehension of Text: Research into Practice,* edited by K. Denise Muth. Newark, Del.: International Reading Association, 1989.

Oja, Leslie Anne. "Using Story Frames to Develop Reading Comprehension." *Journal of Adolescent & Adult Literacy,* 40 (October 1996), 129–130.

Oldfather, Penny. "Commentary: What's Needed to Maintain and Extend Motivation for Literacy in the Middle Grades." *Journal of Reading,* 36 (March 1995), 420–422.

Oldfather, Penny. "What Students Say About Motivating Experiences in a Whole Language Classroom." *The Reading Teacher,* 46 (May 1993), 672–681.

Oleneski, Sue. "Using Jump Rope Rhymes to Teach Reading Skills." *The Reading Teacher,* 46 (October 1992), 173–175.

Ollila, Lloyd O., and Margie I. Mayfield. *Emerging Literacy: Preschool, Kindergarten, and Primary Grades.* Boston: Allyn and Bacon, 1992, 166–195.

Ollmann, Hilda E. "Creating Higher Level Thinking with Reading Response." *Journal of Adolescent & Adult Literacy,* 39 (April 1996), 576–581.

Ollmann, Hilda E. "Integrating Content Area Skills with Fiction Favorites." *Journal of Reading,* 34 (February 1991), 398–399.

O'Neil, John. "Making Assessment Meaningful." *ASCD Update,* 36 (August 1994), 1, 4–5.

Oster, Lester. "Using the Think-Aloud for Reading Instruction." *The Reading Teacher,* 55 (September 2001), 64–69.

Ovando, Carlos J., and Virginia P. Collier. *Bilingual and ESL Classrooms.* New York: McGraw-Hill, 1985.

Owens, Roxanne Farwick, Jennifer L. Hester, and William H. Teale. "Where Do You Want To Go Today? Inquiry-Based Learning and Technology Integration." *The Reading Teacher,* 55 (April 2002), 616–625.

Owston, R. D., S. Murphy, and H. H. Wideman. "The Effects of Word Processing on Students' Writing Quality and Revision Strategies." *Research in the Teaching of English,* 26 (1992), 249–276.

Paeth, Beverly, et al. "Kentucky Telecommunication Writing Program." Handout presented at the National Council of Teachers of English Convention, San Diego, 1995.

Pahl, Michele M., and Robert J. Monson. "In Search of Whole Language: Transforming Curriculum and Instruction." *Journal of Reading,* 35 (April 1992), 518–524.

Palincsar, Annemarie Sullivan, and Ann L. Brown. "Interactive Teaching to Promote Independent Learning from Text." *The Reading Teacher,* 39 (April 1986), 771–777.

Palmer, Barbara. "Dolch List Still Useful." *The Reading Teacher,* 38 (March 1985), 708–709.

Palmer, Barbara, Rose Marie Codling, and Linda Gambrell. "In Their Own Words: What Elementary Students Have to Say About Motivation to Read." *The Reading Teacher,* 48 (October 1994), 176–178.

Palmer, Rosemary G., and Roger A. Stewart. "Nonfiction Trade Books in Content Area Instruction: Realities and Potential." *Journal of Adolescent & Adult Literacy,* 40 (May 1997), 630–641.

Paris, Scott G., Barbara A. Wasik, and Julianne C. Turner. "The Development of Strategic Readers." In *Handbook of Reading Research,* Vol. II, edited by Rebecca Barr, Michael L. Kamil, Peter B. Mosenthal, and P. David Pearson. White Plains, N.Y.: Longman, 1991, 609–640.

Parkay, Forrest W. *Becoming a Teacher.* Boston: Allyn and Bacon, 1998.

Parker, Emelie, Regla Armengol, Leigh Brooke, Kelly Carper, Sharon Cronin, Anne Denman, Patricia Irwin, Jennifer McGunnigle, Tess Pardini, and Nancy Kurtz. "Teachers' Choices in Classroom Assessment." *The Reading Teacher,* 48 (April 1995), 622–624.

Pavonetti, Linda M. "Joan Lowery Nixon: The Grande Dame of Young Adult Mystery." *Journal of Adolescent & Adult Literacy,* 39 (March 1996), 454–461.

Pavonetti, Linda M., Kathryn M. Brimmer, and James F. Cipielewski. "Accelerated Reader: What Are the Lasting Effects on the Reading Habits of Middle School Students Exposed to Accelerated Reader in the Elementary Grades?" *Journal of Adolescent & Adult Literacy,* 46 (December 2002/January 2003), 300–311.

Pearson, P. David. "Changing the Face of Comprehension Instruction." *The Reading Teacher,* 38 (April 1985), 724–738.

Pearson, P. David. "Focus on Research: Teaching and Learning Reading: A Research Perspective." *Language Arts,* 70 (October 1993), 502–511.

Pearson, P. David, et al. *The Effect of Background Knowledge on Young Children's Comprehension of Explicit and Implicit Information.* Urbana-Champaign, Ill.: University of Illinois, Center for the Study of Reading, 1979.

Pearson, P. David, and Kaybeth Camperell. "Comprehension of Text Structures." In *Comprehension and Teaching: Research Reviews,* edited by John T. Guthrie. Newark, Del.: International Reading Association, 1981, 815–860.

Pearson, P. David, and Linda Fielding. "Comprehension Instruction." In *Handbook of Reading Research,* Vol. II, edited by Rebecca Barr, Michael L. Kamil, Peter Mosenthal, and P. David Pearson. New York: Longman, 1991, 815–860.

Pearson, P. David, and Dale D. Johnson. *Teaching Reading Comprehension.* New York: Holt, 1978.

Peck, Jackie. "Using Storytelling to Promote Language and Literacy Development." *The Reading Teacher,* 43 (November 1989), 138–141.

Perkins-Gough, Deborah, reviewer. "Special Report: RAND Report on Reading Comprehension." *Educational Leadership,* 60 (November 2002), 92.

Petrick, Pamela Bondi. "Creative Vocabulary Instruction in the Content Area." *Journal of Reading,* 35 (March 1992), 481–482.

Peterson, B. "Selecting Books for Beginning Readers." In *Bridges to Literacy: Learning from Reading Recovery,* edited by D. Deford, C. Lyons, and G. S. Pinnell. Portsmouth, N.H.: Heinemann, 1991, 119–147.

Pettersen, Nancy-Laurel. "Grate/Great Homonym Hunt." *Journal of Reading,* 31 (January 1988), 374–375.

Pierce, Kathryn Mitchell, and Kathy G. Short, eds. "Children's Books: Environmental Issues and Actions." *The Reading Teacher,* 47 (December 1993/January 1994), 328–335.

Pigg, John R. "The Effects of a Storytelling/Storyreading Program on the Language Skills of Rural Primary Students." Unpublished paper. Cookeville, Tenn.: Tennessee Technological University, 1986.

Pike, Kathy, Rita Compain, and Jean Mumper. *Connections: An Integrated Approach to Literacy.* New York: HarperCollins, 1994.

Pikulski, John J. "Questions and Answers." *The Reading Teacher,* 42 (April 1989), 637.

Pool, Carolyn R. "A New Digital Literacy: A Conversation with Paul Gilster." *Educational Leadership,* 55 (November 1997), 6–11.

Poole, Bernard J. *Education for an Information Age.* Boston: WCB/McGraw-Hill, 1997.

Popp, Marcia. *Learning Journals in the K–8 Classroom.* Mahwah, N.J.: Erlbaum, 1997.

Powell, Janet L. "How Well Do Tests Measure Real Reading?" *ERIC Clearinghouse on Reading and Communication Skills* (June 1989), 1.

Powell, William R. "Teaching Vocabulary Through Opposition." *Journal of Reading,* 29 (April 1986), 617–621.

Pressley, Michael. *Advanced Educational Psychology.* New York: HarperCollins, 1995.

Pressley, Michael. "Comprehension Instruction: What Makes Sense Now, What Might Make Sense Soon." *Reading Online,* 5 (September 2001), retrieved from http://www.readingonline.org/articles/art_index. asp?HREF=/articles/handbook/pressley/index.html.

Pressley, Michael. "Metacognition and Self-Regulated Comprehension." In *What Research Has to Say About Reading Instruction,* edited by Alan E. Farstrup and S. Jay Samuels. Newark, Del.: International Reading Association, 2002, 291–309.

Probst, Robert E. "Transactional Theory in the Teaching of Literature." *Journal of Reading,* 31 (January 1988), 378–381.

Prosise, Roger. *Beyond Rules and Consequences for Classroom Management.* Bloomington, Ind.: Phi Delta Kappa, 1996.

Pugh, Sharon L., and Jesus Garcia. "Portraits in Black: Establishing African American Identity Through Non-fiction Books." *Journal of Reading,* 34 (September 1990), 20–25.

Quiocho, Alice. "The Quest to Comprehend Expository Text: Applied Classroom Research." *Journal of Adolescent & Adult Literacy,* 40 (March 1997), 450–455.

Rand, Muriel K. "Story Schema: Theory, Research and Practice." *The Reading Teacher,* 37 (January 1984), 377–382.

RAND Reading Study Group. *Reading for Understanding: Towards an R&D Program in Reading Comprehension,* 2002. (http://www.rand.org/multi/achievementforall/reading/readreport.html)

Raphael, Taffy E. "Question-Answering Strategies for Children." *The Reading Teacher,* 36 (November 1982), 186–190.

Raphael, Taffy E. "Teaching Learners About Sources of Information for Answering Comprehension Questions." *Journal of Reading,* 27 (January 1984), 303–311.

Raphael, Taffy E. "Teaching Question-Answer Relationships, Revisited." *The Reading Teacher,* 39 (February 1986), 516–522.

Raphael, Taffy E., and P. David Pearson. *The Effect of Metacognitive Awareness Training on Children's Question Answering Behavior* (Technical Report No. 238). Urbana-Champaign, Ill.: University of Illinois, Center for the Study of Reading, 1982.

Raphael, Taffy, et al. "Research Directions: Literature and Discussion in the Reading Program." *Language Arts,* 69 (January 1992), 54–61.

Rasinski, Timothy V. "The Role of Interest, Purpose, and Choice in Early Literacy." *The Reading Teacher,* 41 (January 1988), 396–400.

Rasinski, Timothy V., and Nancy D. Padak. "Multicultural Learning Through Children's Literature." *Language Arts,* 67 (October 1990), 576–580.

Readence, John E., R. Scott Baldwin, and Martha H. Head. "Direct Instruction in Processing Metaphors." *Journal of Reading Behavior,* 18, no. 4 (1986), 325–339.

Readence, John E., R. Scott Baldwin, and Martha H. Head. "Teaching Young Readers to Interpret Metaphors." *The Reading Teacher,* 40 (January 1987), 439–443.

Reardon, S. Jeanne. "The Development of Critical Readers: A Look into the Classroom." *The New Advocate,* 1, no. 1 (1988), 52–61.

Recht, Donna. "Teaching Summarizing Skills." *The Reading Teacher,* 37 (March 1984), 675–677.

Reed, Arthea, and Verna Bergemann. *A Guide to Observation, Participation, and Reflection in the Classroom.* Boston: McGraw Hill, 2001.

Reinking, David. "Me and My Hypertext: A Multiple Digression Analysis of Technology and Literacy (Sic)." *The Reading Teacher,* 50 (May 1997), 626–643.

Resnick, Lauren B. *Education and Learning to Think* (report). Washington, D.C.: National Academy Press, 1987.

Reutzel, D. Ray. "C6: A Reading Model for Teaching Arithmetic Story Problem Solving." *The Reading Teacher,* 37 (October 1983), 28–34.

Reutzel, D. Ray, and Robert Cooter. "Organizing for Effective Instruction: The Reading Workshop." *The Reading Teacher,* 44 (April 1991), 548–554.

Rhoder, Carol. "Mindful Reading: Strategy Training That Facilitates Transfer." *Journal of Adolescent & Adult Literacy,* 45 (March 2002), 498–512.

Rhoder, Carol, and Patricia Huerster. "Use Dictionaries for Word Learning with Caution." *Journal of Adolescent & Adult Literacy,* 45 (May 2002), 730–735.

Rhodes, Lynn K., and Curt Dudley-Marling. *Readers and Writers with a Difference.* Portsmouth, N.H.: Heinemann, 1988.

Rhodes, Lynn, and Sally Nathenson-Mejia. "Anecdotal Records: A Powerful Tool for Ongoing Literacy Assessment." *The Reading Teacher,* 45 (March 1992), 502–509.

Richards, Janet Clarke, and Joan P. Gipe. "Activating Background Knowledge: Strategies for Beginning and Poor Readers." *The Reading Teacher,* 45 (February 1992), 474–478.

Richek, Margaret Ann. "Relating Vocabulary Learning to World Knowledge." *Journal of Reading,* 32 (December 1988), 262–267.

Richey, David D., and John Wheeler. *Inclusive Early Childhood Education: Merging Positive Behavioral Supports, Activity-Based Interventions, and Developmentally Appropriate Practice.* Albany, N.Y.: Delmar Thomson Learning, 2000.

Richgels, Donald, Karla Poremba, and Lea M. McGee. "Kindergartners Talk About Print: Phonemic Awareness in Meaningful Contexts." *The Reading Teacher,* 49 (May 1996), 632–642.

Richler, Howard. "Word Play: You're Likely to Be Clipped." *Notes Plus* (March 1996), 11–12.

Riel, M. "The Impact of Computers in Classrooms." *Journal of Research on Computing in Education* (1989), 180–189.

Roberts, Patricia. *A Green Dinosaur Day: A Guide for Developing Thematic Units in Literature-Based Instruction, K–6.* Boston: Allyn and Bacon, 1993.

Robertson, Julie Fisher, and Donna Rane-Szostak. "Using Dialogues to Develop Critical Thinking Skills." *Journal of Adolescent & Adult Literacy,* 39 (April 1996), 552–556.

Robinette, Michelle. *Mac Multimedia for Teachers.* Foster City, Calif.: IDG Books Worldwide, 1995.

Robinson, Francis P. *Effective Study,* rev. ed. New York: Harper & Row, 1961.

Robinson, H. Alan, Vincent Faraone, Daniel R. Hittleman, and Elizabeth Unruh. *Reading Comprehension Instruction, 1783–1987.* Newark, Del.: International Reading Association, 1990.

Rock, Heidi Marie, and Alysa Cummings. "Can Videodiscs Improve Student Outcomes?" *Educational Leadership,* 51 (April 1994), 46–50.

Roe, Betty D. *Report on Non-Instructional Assignment.* Cookeville, Tenn.: Tennessee Technological University, 1990.

Roe, Betty D. *Use of the Computer to Improve Writing Instruction in the Second Grade.* Cookeville, Tenn.: Rural Education Research and Service Consortium, 1987.

Roe, Betty D. *Use of Storytelling/Storyreading in Conjunction with Follow-up Language Activities to Improve Oral Communication of Rural First Grade Students: Phase I.* Cookeville, Tenn.: Rural Education Consortium, 1985.

Roe, Betty D. *Use of Storytelling/Storyreading in Conjunction with Follow-up Language Activities to Improve Oral Communication of Rural Primary Grade Students: Phase II.* Cookeville, Tenn.: Rural Education Consortium, 1986.

Roe, Betty D. "Using Technology for Content Area Literacy." In *Linking Literacy and Technology: A Guide for K–8 Classrooms,* edited by Shelley B. Wepner, William J. Valmont, and Richard Thurlow. Newark, Del.: International Reading Association, 2000, 133–158.

Roe, Betty D., and Sandy H. Smith. "University/Public Schools Keypals Project: A Collaborative Effort for Electronic Literature Conversations." In *Rethinking Teaching and Learning through Technology.* Proceedings of the Mid-South Instructional Technology Conference. Murfreesboro, Tenn.: Mid-South Technology Conference, 1997.

Roe, Betty, Suellen Alfred, and Sandy H. Smith. *Teaching Through Stories: Yours, Mine, and Theirs.* Norwood, Mass.: Christopher-Gordon, 1998.

Roe, Mary F. "Reading Strategy Instruction: Complexities and Possibilities in Middle School." *Journal of Reading,* 36 (November 1992), 190–196.

Roehler, Laura, and Gerald Duffy. "Teachers' Instructional Actions." In *Handbook of Reading Research,* Vol. II, edited by Rebecca Barr, Michael L. Kamil, Peter B. Mosenthal, and P. David Pearson. White Plains, N.Y.: Longman, 1991, 861–884.

Roller, Cathy. *So…What's a Tutor to Do?* Newark, Del.: IRA, 1998.

Roller, Cathy. *Variability Not Disability.* Newark, Del.: International Reading Association, 1996.

Roney, R. Craig. "Background Experience Is the Foundation of Success in Learning to Read." *The Reading Teacher,* 38 (November 1984), 196–199.

Rose, David H., and Anne Meyer. "Focus on Research: The Role of Technology in Language Arts Instruction." *Language Arts,* 71 (April 1994), 290–294.

Rosenbaum, Catherine. "A Word Map for Middle School: A Tool for Effective Vocabulary Instruction." *Journal of Adolescent and Adult Literacy,* 45 (September 2001), 44–49.

Rosenblatt, Louise M. *Literature as Exploration.* New York: Noble & Noble, 1938/1983.

Rosenblatt, Louise M. "Literature — S.O.S.!" *Language Arts,* 68 (1991), 444–448.

Rosenblatt, Louise M. *The Reader, the Text, and the Poem: The Transactional Theory of the Literary Work.* Carbondale, Ill.: Southern Illinois University Press, 1978.

Rosenblatt, Louise M. "The Transactional Theory of Reading and Writing." In *Theoretical Models and Processes of Reading,* 4th ed., edited by Robert B. Ruddell, Martha Rapp Ruddell, and Harry Singer. Newark, Del.: International Reading Association, 1994, 1057–1092.

Rosenshine, Barak, and Carla Meister. "Reciprocal Teaching: A Review of the Research." *Review of Educational Research,* 64 (Winter 1994), 479–530.

Roser, Nancy L., James Hoffman, Linda D. Labbo, and Cindy Forest. "Language Charts: A Record of Story Time Talk." *Language Arts,* 69 (January 1992), 44–52.

Roser, Nancy, and Connie Juel. "Effects of Vocabulary and Instruction on Reading Comprehension." In *New Inquiries in Reading Research and Instruction,* Thirty-First Yearbook of the National Reading Conference, edited by J. A. Niles and L. A. Harris. Rochester, N.Y.: National Reading Conference, 1982.

Ross, Elinor. *The Workshop Approach: A Framework for Literacy.* Norwood, Mass.: Christopher-Gordon, 1996.

Ross, Elinor Parry. "Checking the Source: An Essential Component of Critical Reading." *Journal of Reading,* 24 (January 1981), 311–315.

Rosso, Barbara Rak, and Robert Emans. "Children's Use of Phonic Generalizations." *The Reading Teacher,* 34 (March 1981), 653–657.

Routman, Regie. *Invitations.* Portsmouth, N.H.: Heinemann, 1994.

Routman, Regie. *Transitions: From Literature to Literacy.* Chicago: Rigby, 1988.

Rowlands, Kathleen Dudden. "Alice in Web Wonderland: Internet Resources for Middle Schoolers and Their Teachers." *Voices from the Middle,* 7 (March 2000), 49–54.

Rubin, Dorothy. *Diagnosis and Correction in Reading Instruction,* 3d ed. Boston: Allyn and Bacon, 1997.

Rubino, Ann. "The Science/Language Connection: Why to Make It … How to Do It." *The Reading Teacher,* 45 (November 1991), 248–249.

Ruddell, Martha Rapp, and Brenda A. Shearer. "'Extraordinary,' 'Tremendous,' 'Exhilarating,' 'Magnificent': Middle School At-Risk Students Become Avid Word Learners with the Vocabulary Self-Collection Strategy (VSS)." *Journal of Adolescent & Adult Literacy,* 45 (February 2002), 352–363.

Ruddell, Robert B. "A Whole Language and Literature Perspective: Creating a Meaning-Making Instructional Environment." *Language Arts,* 69 (December 1992), 612–620.

Ruddell, Robert B., and Norman J. Unrau. "Reading as a Meaning-Construction Process: The Reader, the Text, and the Teacher." In *Theoretical Models and Processes of Reading,* 4th ed., edited by Robert B. Ruddell, Martha Rapp Ruddell, and Harry Singer. Newark, Del.: International Reading Association, 1994, 996–1056.

Rule, Audrey, and Joan Atkinson. "Choosing Picture Books About Ecology." *The Reading Teacher,* 47 (April 1994), 586–591.

Rumelhart, David E. "Schemata: The Building Blocks of Cognition." In *Comprehension and Teaching: Research Reviews,* edited by John T. Guthrie. Newark, Del.: International Reading Association, 1981.

Rupley, William H., John W. Logan, and William D. Nichols. "Vocabulary Instruction in a Balanced Reading Program." *The Reading Teacher,* 52 (December 1998/January 1999), 336–356.

Rush, R. Timothy. "Assessing Readability: Formulas and Alternatives." *The Reading Teacher,* 39 (December 1985), 274–283.

Russell, David L. *Literature for Children,* 2d ed. New York: Longman, 1994.

Sabey, Brenda, and Linda Squire. "Environmental Print: Trash or Treasure." *Contemporary Issues in Reading,* 9 (Fall 1993), 45–51.

Saccardi, Marianne. "Predictable Books: Gateways to a Lifetime of Reading." *The Reading Teacher,* 49 (April 1996a), 588–590.

Saccardi, Marianne C. "Predictable Books: Gateways to a Lifetime of Reading." *The Reading Teacher,* 49 (May 1996b), 632–642.

Sadow, Marilyn W. "The Use of Story Grammar in the Design of Questions." *The Reading Teacher,* 35 (February 1982), 518–522.

Sagor, Richard. *Guiding School Improvement with Action Research.* Alexandria, Va.: Association for Supervision and Curriculum Development, 2000.

Salinger, Terry S. *Literacy for Young Children,* 2d ed. Englewood Cliffs, N.J.: Merrill, 1996.

Sameroff, Arnold, and Susan McDonough. "Educational Implications of Developmental Transitions: The 5- to 7-Year Shift." In *Early Childhood Education 96/97,* edited by Karen Paciorek and Joyce Munro. Guilford, Conn.: Dushkin, 1996–1997, 40–44.

Sampson, Mary Beth, Michael R. Sampson, and Wayne Linek. "Circle of Questions." *The Reading Teacher,* 48 (December 1994/January 1995), 364–365.

Samuels, S. Jay. "Decoding and Automaticity: Helping Poor Readers Become Automatic at Word Recognition." *The Reading Teacher,* 41 (April 1988), 756–760.

Samuels, S. Jay. "Toward a Theory of Automatic Information Processing in Reading, Revisited." In *Theoretical Models and Processes of Reading,* 4th ed., edited by Robert B. Ruddell, Martha Rapp Ruddell, and Harry Singer. Newark, Del.: International Reading Association, 1994, 816–837.

Samuels, S. Jay, and Sumner W. Schachter. "Controversial Issues in Beginning Reading Instruction: Meaning Versus Subskill Emphasis." In *Readings on Reading Instruction,* edited by Albert J. Harris and Edward R. Sipay. New York: Longman, 1984.

Sandholtz, Judith Haymore, Cathy Ringstaff, and David C. Dwyer. *Teaching with Technology.* New York: Teachers College Press, 1997.

Santerre, Mary. "One Teacher's Use of Computers and Technology: A Look Inside a Classroom." *Voices from the Middle,* 7 (March 2000), 33–40.

Santino, Betsy H. "Improving Multicultural Awareness and Story Comprehension with Folktales." *The Reading Teacher,* 45 (September 1991), 77–79.

Savage, John F. *Teaching Reading Using Literature.* Madison, Wis.: WCB Brown & Benchmark, 1994.

Sawyer, John Michael. "Using Media Knowledge to Enhance the Literary Schema of Literarily Impoverished Students." *Journal of Reading,* 37 (May 1994), 683–684.

Scharer, Patricia L., and Deana B. Detwiler. "Changing as Teachers: Perils and Possibilities of Literature-Based Language Arts Instruction." *Language Arts,* 69 (March 1992), 186–192.

Scharrer, Erica. "Making a Case for Media Literacy in the Curriculum: Outcomes and Assessment." *Journal of Adolescent & Adult Literacy,* 46 (December 2002/January 2003), 354–358.

Schell, Leo M. "Teaching Decoding to Remedial Readers." *Journal of Reading,* 31 (May 1978), 877–882.

Schifini, Alfredo. "Language, Literacy, and Content Instruction: Strategies for Teachers." In *Kids Come in All Languages: Reading Instruction for ESL Students,* edited by Karen Spangenberg-Urbschat and Robert Pritchard. Newark, Del.: International Reading Association, 1994, 158–179.

Schmidt, Patricia Ruggiano. "KWLQ: Inquiry and Literacy Learning in Science." *The Reading Teacher,* 52 (April 1999), 789–792.

Schmitt, M. C., and D. O'Brien. "Story Grammars: Some Cautions About the Translation of Research into Practice." *Reading Research Quarterly,* 26, no. 1 (1986), 1–8.

Schmitt, Maribeth Cassidy, and James F. Baumann. "How to Incorporate Comprehension Monitoring Strategies into Basal Reader Instruction." *The Reading Teacher,* 40 (October 1986), 28–31.

Schmoker, Mike, and Robert J. Marzano. "Realizing the Promise of Standards-Based Education." *Educational Leadership,* 56 (March 1999), 17–21.

Schumm, Jeanne Shay. "Overcoming Students' Misconceptions About Science." *Journal of Reading,* 35 (October 1991), 161.

Schumm, Jeanne Shay, and Linda Saumell. "Aliteracy: We Know It Is a Problem, But Where Does It Start?" *Journal of Reading,* 37 (May 1994), 701.

Schumm, Jeanne Shay, and Linda Saumell. "Word Processors: Their Impact on Process and Product." *Journal of Reading,* 37 (November 1993), 190.

Schwartz, Robert M. "Learning to Learn Vocabulary in Content Area Textbooks." *Journal of Reading,* 32 (November 1988), 108–118.

Schwartz, Robert M. "Self-Monitoring in Beginning Reading." *The Reading Teacher,* 51 (September 1997), 40–48.

Schwartz, Robert M., and Taffy E. Raphael. "Concept of Definition: A Key to Improving Students' Vocabulary." *The Reading Teacher,* 39 (November 1985), 198–205.

Sears, Sue, Cathy Carpenter, and Nancy Burstein. "Meaningful Reading Instruction for Learners with Special Needs." *The Reading Teacher,* 47 (May 1994), 632–638.

Sebesta, Sam Leaton, James William Calder, and Lynne Nelson Cleland. "A Story Grammar for the Classroom." *The Reading Teacher,* 36 (November 1982), 180–184.

Seda, Ileana, and P. David Pearson. "Interviews to Assess Learners' Outcomes." *Reading Research and Instruction,* 31 (Fall 1991), 22–32.

Seitz, Ernest R., Jr. "Using Media Presentations to Teach Notetaking, Main Idea, and Summarization Skills." *Journal of Adolescent & Adult Literacy,* 40 (April 1997), 562–563.

Seminoff, Nancy Wiseman. "Children's Periodicals Throughout the World: An Overlooked Educational Resource." *The Reading Teacher,* 39 (May 1986), 889–895.

Sensenbaugh, Roger. "Reading Recovery." *ERIC Digest.* Bloomington: Indiana University Press, September 1995.

Serafini, Frank. "Stances to Assessment." *Talking Points,* 8 (February–March 1997), 2–4.

Serim, Ferdi, and Melissa Koch. *Netlearning: Why Teachers Use the Internet.* Sebastopol, Calif.: Songline Studios and O'Reilly & Associates, 1996.

Shanahan, T., and S. Neuman. "Conversations: Literacy Research That Makes a Difference." *Reading Research Quarterly,* 32 (1997), 202–211.

Shanahan, Timothy. "Reading-Writing Relationships, Thematic Units, Inquiry Learning … In Pursuit of Effective Integrated Literacy Instruction." *The Reading Teacher,* 51 (September 1997), 12–19.

Shanahan, Timothy, Bonita Robinson, and Mary Schneider. "Integrating Curriculum: Avoiding Some of the Pitfalls of Thematic Units." *The Reading Teacher,* 48 (May 1995), 718–719.

Shanklin, Nancy L., and Lynn K. Rhodes. "Comprehension Instruction as Sharing and Extending." *The Reading Teacher,* 42 (March 1989), 496–500.

Sharp, Peggy Agostino. "Teaching with Picture Books Throughout the Curriculum." *The Reading Teacher,* 38 (November 1984), 132–137.

Shaw, Evelyn. "A Novel Journal." *The Reading Teacher,* 41 (January 1988), 489.

Shepard, Lorrie. "Why We Need Better Assessments." *Educational Leadership,* 46 (April 1989), 4–9.

Shiflett, Anne Chalfield. "Marketing Literature: Variations on the Book Talk Theme." *Journal of Adolescent & Adult Literature,* 41 (April 1998), 568–570.

Shoop, Mary. "InQuest: A Listening and Reading Comprehension Strategy." *The Reading Teacher,* 39 (March 1986), 670–674.

Short, Kathy G. "Informational Magazines for Children." *Language Arts,* 80 (September 2002), 21.

Sigmon, Cheryl M. *Implementing the 4-Blocks Literacy Model.* Greensboro, N.C.: Carson-Dellosa, 1997.

Simpson, Anne. "Critical Questions: Whose Questions?" *The Reading Teacher,* 50 (October 1996), 118–127.

Singer, Harry, John D. McNeil, and Lory L. Furse. "Relationship Between Curriculum Scope and Reading Achievement in Elementary Schools." *The Reading Teacher,* 37 (March 1984), 608–612.

Sippola, Arne E. "K-W-L-S." *The Reading Teacher,* 48 (March 1995), 542–543.

Sippola, Arne E. "What to Teach for Reading Readiness — A Research Review and Materials Inventory." *The Reading Teacher,* 39 (November 1985), 162–167.

Skillings, Mary Jo, and Robbin Ferrell. "Student-Generated Rubrics: Bringing Students into the Assessment Process." *The Reading Teacher,* 53 (March 2000), 452–455.

Slavin, Robert. "Synthesis of Research on Cooperative Learning." *Educational Leadership,* 48 (February 1991), 71–82.

Slavin, Robert, Nancy Madden, and Robert Stevens. "Cooperative Learning Models for the 3R's." *Educational Leadership,* 47 (December 1989/January 1990), 22–28.

Slavin, Robert E., Nancy A. Madden, and Nancy L. Karweit, Lawrence J. Dolan, and Barbara A. Wasik. "Success for All: Getting Reading Right the First Time." In *Getting Reading Right from the Start,* edited by Elfrieda H. Hiebert and Barbara M. Taylor. Boston: Allyn and Bacon, 1994, 125–147.

Smagorinsky, Peter. "Standards Revisited: The Importance of Being There." *English Journal,* 88 (March 1999), 82–88.

Smit, Edna K. "Teaching Theme to Elementary Students." *The Reading Teacher,* 43 (May 1990), 699–701.

Smith, Carl B. "Prompting Critical Thinking." *The Reading Teacher,* 42 (February 1989b), 424.

Smith, Frank. *Essays into Literacy.* Exeter, N.H.: Heinemann, 1983.

Smith, Frank. *Understanding Reading,* 4th ed. Hillsdale, N.J.: Erlbaum, 1988.

Smith, J. Lea, and Holly Johnson. "Models for Implementing Literature in Content Studies." *The Reading Teacher,* 48 (November 1994), 198–209.

Smith, Marilyn, and Thomas W. Bean. "Four Strategies That Develop Children's Story Comprehension and Writing." *The Reading Teacher,* 37 (December 1983), 295–301.

Smith, Richard J., et al. *The School Reading Program.* Boston: Houghton Mifflin, 1978.

Smolen, Lynn Atkinson, and Victoria Ortiz-Castro. "Dissolving Borders and Broadening Perspectives Through Latino Traditional Literature." *The Reading Teacher,* 53 (April 2000), 566–578.

Smolin, Louanne Ione, and Kimberly A. Lawless. "Becoming Literate in the Technological Age: New Responsibilities and Tools for Teachers." *The Reading Teacher,* 56 (March 2003), 570–577.

Smolkin, Laura, and David Yaden, Jr. "O Is for Mouse: First Encounters with the Alphabet Book." *Language Arts,* 69 (October 1992), 432–441.

Snow, Catherine, M. Susan Burns, and Peg Griffin, eds. *Preventing Reading Difficulties in Young Children.* Washington, D.C.: National Academy Press, 1998.

Spache, George D. *Good Reading for Poor Readers,* 6th ed. Champaign, Ill.: Garrard Press, 1966.

Spiegel, Dixie Lee. "Blending Whole Language and Systematic Direct Instruction." *The Reading Teacher,* 46 (September 1992), 38–44.

Spiegel, Dixie Lee. "Comprehension Materials: Quality of Directions and Instructional Language." *The Reading Teacher,* 43 (March 1990a), 502–504.

Spiegel, Dixie Lee. "Reinforcement in Phonics Materials." *The Reading Teacher,* 43 (January 1990b), 328–329.

Spiegel, Dixie Lee. "The Role of Trust in Reader-Response Groups." *Language Arts,* 73 (September 1996), 332–339.

Spiegel, Dixie Lee. "Silver Bullets, Babies, and Bath Water: Literature Response Groups in a Balanced Literacy Program." *The Reading Teacher,* 52 (October 1998), 114–124.

Spiegel, Dixie Lee, and Jill Fitzgerald. "Improving Reading Comprehension Through Instruction About Story Parts." *The Reading Teacher,* 39 (March 1986), 676–682.

Spiro, Rand J. *Etiology of Comprehension Style.* Urbana-Champaign, Ill.: University of Illinois, Center for the Study of Reading, 1979.

Staal, Laura A. "The Story Face: An Adaptation of Story Mapping That Incorporates Visualization and Discovery Learning to Enhance Reading and Writing." *The Reading Teacher,* 54 (September 2000), 26–31.

Stahl, S. "Instructional Models in Reading: An Introduction." In *Instructional Models in Reading,* edited by S. Stahl and D. Hayes. Mahwah, N.J.: Erlbaum, 1997, 1–29.

Stahl, Steven A. "Saying the 'P' Word: Nine Guidelines for Exemplary Phonics Instruction." *The Reading Teacher,* 45 (April 1992), 618–625.

Stahl, Steven A. "Separating the Rhetoric from the Effects: Whole Language in Kindergarten and First Grade." In *Reading, Language, and Literacy: Instruction for the Twenty-first Century,* edited by F. Lehr and J. Osborn. Hillsdale, N.J.: Erlbaum, 1994, 101–114.

Stahl, Steven A. "Three Principles of Effective Vocabulary Instruction." *Journal of Reading,* 29 (April 1986), 662–668.

Stahl, Steven A., and Barbara A. Kapinus. "Possible Sentences: Predicting Word Meanings to Teach Content Area Vocabulary." *The Reading Teacher,* 45 (September 1991), 36–43.

Stahl, Steven A., Jean Osborn, and Fran Lehr. *Beginning to Read: Thinking and Learning About Print — A Summary.* Champaign, Ill.: University of Illinois, Center for the Study of Reading, 1990.

Stahl, Steven A., and Sandra J. Vancil. "Discussion Is What Makes Semantic Maps Work in Vocabulary Instruction." *The Reading Teacher,* 40 (October 1986), 62–67.

Standards for the Assessment of Reading and Writing. Prepared by the IRA/NCTE Joint Task Force on Assessment. Newark, Del.: International Reading Association, 1994.

Stanovich, Keith. "Romance and Reality." *The Reading Teacher,* 47 (December 1993/January 1994), 280–291.

Stauffer, Russell G. "Reading as a Cognitive Process." *Elementary English,* 44 (April 1968), 348.

Stauffer, Russell G. *Teaching Reading as a Thinking Process.* New York: Harper & Row, 1969.

Stetson, Elton G., and Richard P. Williams. "Learning from Social Studies Textbooks: Why Some Students Succeed and Others Fail." *Journal of Reading,* 36 (September 1992), 22–30.

Stevens, Kathleen C. "Can We Improve Reading by Teaching Background Information?" *Journal of Reading,* 25 (January 1982), 326–329.

Stewart, Roger A., Edward E. Paradis, Bonita D. Ross, and Mary Jane Lewis. "Student Voices: What Works in Literature-Based Developmental Reading." *Journal of Adolescent & Adult Literacy,* 39 (March 1996), 468–478.

Stivers, Jan. "The Writing Partners Project." *Phi Delta Kappan,* 77 (June 1996), 694–695.

Stoll, Donald R. *Magazines for Kids and Teens.* Newark, Del.: International Reading Association, 1997.

Storey, Dee C. "Reading in the Content Areas: Fictionalized Biographies and Diaries for Social Studies." *The Reading Teacher,* 35 (April 1982), 796–798.

Stotsky, Sandra. "Research on Reading/Writing Relationships: A Synthesis and Suggested Directions." *Language Arts,* 60 (May 1983), 627–642.

Stowell, Laura, and Robert Tierney. "Portfolios in the Classroom: What Happens When Teachers and Students Negotiate Assessment?" In *No Quick Fix,* edited by Richard Allington and Sean Walmsley. Newark, Del.: International Reading Association, 1995, 78–94.

Strange, Michael. "Instructional Implications of a Conceptual Theory of Reading Comprehension." *The Reading Teacher,* 33 (January 1980), 391–397.

Strickland, Dorothy. "Some Tips for Using Big Books." *The Reading Teacher,* 41 (May 1988a), 966–968.

Strickland, Dorothy, and Lesley Morrow. "Creating a Print Rich Environment." *The Reading Teacher,* 42 (November 1988), 156–157.

Strickland, Dorothy, and Lesley Morrow. "Family Literacy: Sharing Good Books." *The Reading Teacher,* 43 (March 1990), 518–519.

Strickland, Dorothy S., Rose M. Dillon, Leslie Funkhouser, Mary Glick, and Corrine Rogers. "Research Currents: Classroom Dialogue During Literature Response Groups." *Language Arts,* 66 (February 1989), 192–205.

Strube, Penny. *Getting the Most from Literature Groups.* New York: Scholastic, 1996.

Struggling Readers, Day 1: Closing the Decoding Crack. Bothell, Wash.: The Wright Group, 2000.

Sudol, Peg, and Caryn King. "A Checklist for Choosing Nonfiction Trade Books." *The Reading Teacher,* 49 (February 1996), 422–424.

Sugarman, Jay, James Allen, and Meg Keller-Cogan. "Make Authentic Assessment Work for You." *Instructor,* 103 (July/August 1993), 66–68.

Sullivan, Jane. "The Electronic Journal: Combining Literacy and Technology." *The Reading Teacher,* 52 (September 1998), 90–92.

Sullivan, Joanne. "The Global Method: Language Experience in the Content Areas." *The Reading Teacher,* 39 (March 1986), 664–668.

Sulzby, Elizabeth. "I Can Write! Encouraging Emergent Writers." In *Early Childhood Education 94/95,* 15th ed., edited by Karen M. Paciorek and Joyce H. Munro. Guilford, Conn.: Dushkin, 1994, 204–207.

Sulzby, Elizabeth, William H. Teale, and George Kamberelis. "Emergent Writing in the Classroom: Home and School Connections." In *Emerging Literacy,* edited by Dorothy Strickland and Lesley Morrow. Newark, Del.: International Reading Association, 1989.

Sumara, Dennis, and Laurie Walker. "The Teacher's Role in Whole Language." *Language Arts,* 68 (April 1991), 276–285.

Swindall, Vickie, and R. Jeffrey Cantrell. "Character Interviews Help Bring Literature to Life." *The Reading Teacher,* 53 (September 1999), 23–25.

"A Talk with Marilyn Adams." *Language Arts,* 68 (March 1991), 206–212.

Taylor, Barbara, D. Peterson, P. David Pearson, and Michael Rodriguez. "Looking Inside Classrooms: Reflecting on the 'How' As Well As the 'What' in

Effective Reading Instruction." *The Reading Teacher,* 56 (December 2002), 270–279.

Tchudi, Susan. *Integrated Language Arts in the Elementary School.* Belmont, Calif.: Wadsworth, 1994.

Teale, William, and Elizabeth Sulzby. "Emergent Literacy: New Perspectives." In *Emerging Literacy: Young Children Learn to Read and Write,* edited by Dorothy Strickland and Lesley Morrow. Newark, Del.: International Reading Association, 1989.

Tennessee State Department of Education. "Tennessee Plan for Implementing the Teacher and Paraprofessional Quality Provisions of the No Child Left Behind Act of 2001." Nashville, Tenn.: Tennessee State Department of Education, August 2003.

Thames, D. G., and J. E. Readence. "Effects of Differential Vocabulary Instruction and Lesson Frameworks on the Reading Comprehension of Primary Children." *Reading Research and Instruction,* 27, no. 2 (1988), 1–12.

Thelen, Judith N. "Vocabulary Instruction and Meaningful Learning." *Journal of Reading,* 29 (April 1986), 603–609.

Thompson, Deborah L. "The Alphabet Book as a Content Area Resource." *The Reading Teacher,* 46 (November 1992), 266–267.

Thornburg, David. *The New Basics: Education and the Future of Work in the Telematic Age.* Alexandria, Va.: Association for Supervision and Curriculum Development, 2002.

Tierney, Robert J., and James W. Cunningham. "Research on Teaching Reading Comprehension." In *Handbook of Reading Research,* edited by P. David Pearson et al. New York: Longman, 1984.

Tombari, Martin, and Gary Borich. *Authentic Assessment in the Classroom: Applications and Practice.* Upper Saddle River, N.J.: Prentice-Hall, 1999.

Tomlinson, Carol Ann. *The Differentiated Classroom: Responding to the Needs of All Learners.* Alexandria, Va.: Association for Supervision and Curriculum Development, 1999.

Tomlinson, Carol Ann, Sandra Kapan, Joseph Renzulli, Jeanne Purcell, Jann Leppien, and Deborah Burns. *The Parallel Curriculum: A Design to Develop High Potential and Challenge High-Ability Learners.* Thousand Oaks, Calif.: Corwin Press, 2002.

Tompkins, Gail E., and Lea M. McGee. *Teaching Reading with Literature.* New York: Merrill, 1993.

Tovey, Duane R. "Children's Grasp of Phonics Terms vs. Sound-Symbol Relationships." *The Reading Teacher,* 33 (January 1980), 431–437.

Tower, Cathy. "Questions That Matter: Preparing Elementary Students for the Inquiry Process." *The Reading Teacher,* 53 (April 2000), 550–557.

Trachtenburg, Phyllis. "Using Children's Literature to Enhance Phonics Instruction." *The Reading Teacher,* 43 (May 1990), 648–654.

Trelease, Jim. *The New Read-Aloud Handbook,* 4th ed. New York: Viking Penguin, 1995.

Turner, Julianne, and Scott Paris. "How Literacy Tasks Influence Children's Motivation for Literacy." *The Reading Teacher,* 48 (May 1995), 662–673.

Tyson, Eleanore S., and Lee Mountain. "A Riddle or Pun Makes Learning Words Fun." *The Reading Teacher,* 36 (November 1982), 170–173.

U.S. Department of Education. "No Child Left Behind Act, Public Law 107-110." Washington, D.C.: U.S. Department of Education, 2001.

U.S. Department of Education. *President Clinton's Call to Action for American Education in the 21st Century: Technological Literacy,* 1997. (http://www.ed.gov/updates/PresEdPlan/part11.html)

Vacca, Richard, and JoAnne Vacca. *Content Area Reading.* Glenview, Ill.: Scott, Foresman, 1987.

Valencia, Sheila. "A Portfolio Approach to Classroom Reading Assessment: The Whys, Whats, and Hows." *The Reading Teacher,* 43 (January 1990), 338–340.

Valencia, Sheila, and Nancy Place. "Portfolios: A Process for Enhancing Teaching and Learning." *The Reading Teacher,* 47 (May 1994), 666–669.

Valenza, Joyce Kasman. "Library as Multimedia Studio." *Electronic Learning,* 16 (November/December 1996), 56–57.

Valmont, William J. "Cloze Deletion Patterns: How Deletions Are Made Makes a Big Difference." *The Reading Teacher,* 37 (November 1983), 172–175.

Valmont, William J. *Creating Videos for School Use.* Boston: Allyn and Bacon, 1995.

Valmont, William J. *Technology for Literacy Teaching and Learning.* Boston: Houghton Mifflin, 2003.

Van Horn, Leigh. "The Character Within Us: Readers Connect with Characters to Create Meaning and Understanding." *Journal of Adolescent & Adult Literacy,* 40 (February 1997), 342–347.

VanLeirsburg, Peggy. "Standardized Reading Tests: Then and Now." In *Literacy: Celebration and Challenge,* edited by Jerry Johns. Bloomington, Ill.: Illinois Reading Council, 1993, 31–54.

Veatch, Jeanette. "From the Vantage of Retirement." *The Reading Teacher,* 49 (1996), 510–516.

Villaume, Susan Kidd, and Edna Greene Brabham. "Comprehension Instruction: Beyond Strategies." *The Reading Teacher,* 55 (April 2002), 672–675.

Vygotsky, Lev. *Thought and Language,* rev. ed., edited by Alex Kozulin. Cambridge, Mass.: M.I.T. Press, 1986.

Wagstaff, Janiel M. "Building Practical Knowledge of Letter-Sound Correspondences: A Beginner's Word Wall and Beyond." *The Reading Teacher,* 51 (December 1997/January 1998), 298–304.

Walberg, Herbert, Geneva Haertel, and Suzanne Gerlach-Downie. *Assessment Reform: Challenges and Opportunities.* Bloomington, Ind.: Phi Delta Kappa, 1994.

Walberg, Herbert J., Victoria Chou Hare, and Cynthia A. Pulliam. "Social-Psychological Perceptions and Reading Comprehension." In *Comprehension and Teaching: Research Reviews,* edited by John T. Guthrie. Newark, Del.: International Reading Association, 1981, 140–159.

Walker, Barbara. *Diagnostic Teaching of Reading: Techniques for Instruction and Assessment.* Upper Saddle River, N.J.: Prentice-Hall, 2000.

Walker, Barbara. *Diagnostic Teaching of Reading: Techniques for Instruction and Assessment.* Upper Saddle River, N.J.: Pearson, 2004.

Walker-Dalhouse, Doris. "Using African-American Literature to Increase Ethnic Understanding." *The Reading Teacher,* 45 (February 1992), 416–422.

Walker-Dalhouse, Doris, A. Derick Dalhouse, and Dennis Mitchell. "Development of a Literature-Based Middle School Reading Program: Insights Gained." *Journal of Adolescent & Adult Literacy,* 40 (February 1997), 362–370.

Waller, T. Gary. *Think First, Read Later! Piagetian Prerequisites for Reading.* Newark, Del.: International Reading Association, 1977.

Walmsley, Sean A., and Ellen L. Adams. "Realities of 'Whole Language.'" *Language Arts,* 70 (April 1993), 272–280.

Walpole, Sharon. "Changing Texts, Changing Thinking: Comprehension Demands of New Science Textbooks." *The Reading Teacher,* 52 (December 1998/January 1999), 358–369.

Walshe, R. D. "Donald Graves in Australia." In *Donald Graves in Australia — "Children Want to Write ...,"* edited by R. D. Walshe. Rozelle, NSW, Australia: Primary English Teaching Association, 1986.

Watson, Dorothy J. "Whole Language: Why Bother?" *The Reading Teacher,* 47 (May 1994), 600–607.

Watson, Jerry J. "An Integral Setting Tells More Than When and Where." *The Reading Teacher,* 44 (May 1991), 638–646.

Waugh, Joyce Clark. "Using LEA in Diagnosis." *Journal of Reading,* 37 (September 1993), 56–57.

Weaver, Phyllis, and Fredi Shonhoff. "Subskill and Holistic Approaches to Reading Instruction." In *Readings on Reading Instruction,* edited by Albert J. Harris and Edward R. Sipay. New York: Longman, 1984.

Weiss, Maria J. "Who Needs a Teacher's Guide?" *The Reading Teacher,* 41 (October 1987), 119–120.

Weissman, Kathleen E. "Using Paragraph Frames to Complete a K-W-L." *The Reading Teacher,* 50 (November 1996), 271–272.

Wepner, Shelley B. "Technology and Textsets." *The Reading Teacher,* 46 (September 1992a), 68–71.

Wepner, Shelley B. "Technology and Thematic Units: A Primary Example." *The Reading Teacher,* 46 (November 1992b), 260–263.

Wepner, Shelley B. "Using Technology with Content Area Units." *The Reading Teacher,* 45 (April 1992c), 644–646.

Wepner, Shelley B., and Lucinda C. Ray. "Using Technology for Reading Development." In *Linking Literacy and Technology: A Guide for K–8 Classrooms,* edited by Shelley B. Wepner, William J. Valmont, and Richard Thurlow. Newark, Del.: International Reading Association, 2000, 76–105.

Wertheim, Judy. "Teaching Guides for Novels." *The Reading Teacher,* 42 (December 1988), 262.

Wharton-McDonald, Ruth, Michael Pressley, Joan Rankin, Jennifer Mistretta, Linda Yokoi, and Shari Ettenberger. "Effective Primary-Grades Literacy Instruction = Balanced Literacy Instruction." *The Reading Teacher,* 50 (March 1997), 518–521.

Whaley, Jill Fitzgerald. "Story Grammars and Reading Instruction." *The Reading Teacher,* 34 (April 1981), 762–771.

"What's in Store Software Guide." *Family Computing,* March 1986, 82–91.

White, Thomas G., Joanne Sowell, and Alice Yanagihara. "Teaching Elementary Students to Use Word-Part Clues." *The Reading Teacher,* 42 (January 1989), 302–308.

Whitin, Phyllis. "Leading into Literature Circles Through the Sketch-to-Stretch Strategy." *The Reading Teacher,* 55 (February 2002), 444–450.

Whitin, Phyllis E., and David J. Whitin. "The Numbers and Beyond: Language Lessons for the Mathematics Classroom." *Language Arts,* 74 (February 1997), 108–115.

Whitmer, Jean E. "Pickles Will Kill You: Use Humorous Literature to Teach Critical Reading." *The Reading Teacher,* 39 (February 1986), 530–534.

"Why Multicultural Education?" *Program News.* Alexandria, Va.: Association for Supervision and Curriculum Development (May 1994), 4–5.

Wicklund, LaDonna. "Shared Poetry: A Whole Language Experience Adapted for Remedial Readers." *The Reading Teacher,* 42 (March 1989), 478–481.

Wiener, Roberta, and Judith Cohen. *Literacy Portfolios.* Upper Saddle River, N.J.: Merrill, 1997.

Wiesendanger, Katherine D. "Comprehension: Using Anticipation Guides." *The Reading Teacher,* 39 (November 1985), 241–242.

Wiggins, Grant. *The Case for Authentic Assessment.* Washington, D.C.: ERIC Clearinghouse, 1990 [ED328611].

Wiggins, Grant, and Jay McTighe. *Understanding by Design.* Alexandria, Va.: Association for Supervision and Curriculum Development, 1998.

Wiggins, Robert A. "Large Group Lesson/Small Group Follow-Up: Flexible Grouping in a Basal Reading Program." *The Reading Teacher,* 47 (March 1994), 450–460.

Wilhelm, Jeff. "Literacy by Design: Why Is All This Technology So Important?" *Voices from the Middle,* 7 (March 2000), 4–14.

Wilkinson, Phyllis A., and Del Patty. "The Effects of Sentence Combining on the Reading Comprehension of Fourth Grade Students." *Research in the Teaching of English,* 27 (February 1993), 104–125.

Williams, Joanna P. "Reading Comprehension Strategies and Teacher Preparation." In *What Research Has to Say About Reading Instruction,* edited by Alan E. Farstrup and S. Jay Samuels. Newark, Del.: International Reading Association, 2002, 243–260.

Willis, Jerry W., Elizabeth C. Stephens, and Kathryn I. Matthew. *Technology, Reading, and Language Arts.* Boston: Allyn and Bacon, 1996.

Wilson, Bruce, and H. Dickson Corbett. "Shadowing Students." *Journal of Staff Development,* 20, no. 3 (Summer 1999), 47–48.

Wilson, Cathy Roller. "Teaching Reading Comprehension by Connecting the Known to the New." *The Reading Teacher,* 36 (January 1983), 382–390.

Wilson, Lorraine, David Malmgren, Shirl Ramage, and Leanne Schulz. *An Integrated Approach to Learning.* South Melbourne, Australia: Nelson, 1991.

Winograd, Peter. "Developing Alternative Assessments: Six Problems Worth Solving." *The Reading Teacher,* 47 (February 1994), 420–423.

Winograd, Peter, and Karen W. Higgins. "Writing, Reading, and Talking Mathematics: One Interdisciplinary Possibility." *The Reading Teacher,* 48 (December 1994/January 1995), 310–318.

Winograd, Peter, Scott Paris, and Connie Bridge. "Improving the Assessment of Literacy." *The Reading Teacher,* 45 (October 1991), 108–116.

Wiseman, Donna L. "Helping Children Take Early Steps Toward Reading and Writing." *The Reading Teacher,* 37 (January 1984), 340–344.

Wixson, Karen K. "Questions About a Text: What You Ask About Is What Children Learn." *The Reading Teacher,* 37 (December 1983), 287–293.

Wolfe, Ronald, and Alice Lopez. "Structured Overviews for Teaching Science and Terms." *Journal of Reading,* 36 (December 1992/January 1993), 315–317.

Wollman-Bonilla, Julie E. "Reading Journals: Invitations to Participate in Literature." *The Reading Teacher,* 43 (November 1989), 112–120.

Wong-Kam, Jo Ann, and Kathryn Au. "Improving a 4th Grader's Reading and Writing: Three Principles." *The Reading Teacher,* 41 (April 1988), 768–772.

Wood, Delores, and Joanne Nurss. "Print Rich Classrooms Support the Development of Print Awareness." *Georgia Journal of Reading,* 14 (Fall/Winter 1988), 21–23.

Wood, Judy. *Mainstreaming,* 2d ed. Columbus, Ohio: Merrill, 1993.

Wood, Julie M., and Nell K. Duke. "Inside 'Reading Rainbow': A Spectrum of Strategies for Promoting Literacy." *Language Arts,* 74 (February 1997), 95–106.

Wood, Karen D. "Fostering Collaborative Reading and Writing Experiences in Mathematics." *Journal of Reading,* 36 (October 1992), 96–103.

Wood, Karen. "Using Cooperative Learning Strategies." *Middle School Journal,* 20 (May 1989), 23–26.

Wood, Karen D., and John A. Mateja. "Adapting Secondary Level Strategies for Use in Elementary Classrooms." *The Reading Teacher,* 36 (February 1983), 492–496.

Wortham, Sue. *The Integrated Classroom.* Englewood Cliffs, N.J.: Merrill, 1996.

Worthing, Bernadette, and Barbara Laster. "Strategy Access Rods: A Hands-On Approach." *The Reading Teacher,* 56 (October 2002), 122–123.

Worthy, Jo. "A Matter of Interest: Literature That Hooks Reluctant Readers and Keeps Them Reading." *The Reading Teacher,* 50 (November 1996), 204–212.

Wysocki, Katherine, and Joseph R. Jenkins. "Deriving Word Meanings Through Morphological Generalization." *Reading Research Quarterly,* 22, no. 1 (1987), 66–81.

Yatvin, J. *Developing a Whole Language Program.* Richmond, Va.: Virginia State Reading Association, 1991.

Yatvin, Joanne, Constance Weaver, and Elaine Garan. "Reading First: Cautions and Recommendations." *Language Arts,* 81 (September 2003), 28–33.

Yellin, David, and Mary Blake. *Integrating Language Arts: A Holistic Approach.* New York: HarperCollins, 1994.

Yopp, Hallie. "Read-Aloud Books for Developing Phonemic Awareness: An Annotated Bibliography." *The Reading Teacher,* 48 (March 1995a), 538–542.

Yopp, Hallie Kay. "Developing Phonemic Awareness in Young Children." *The Reading Teacher,* 45 (May 1992), 696–703.

Yopp, Hallie Kay. "A Test for Assessing Phonemic Awareness in Young Children." *The Reading Teacher,* 49 (September 1995b), 20–29.

Yopp, Ruth Helen, and Hallie Kay Yopp. "Sharing Informational Text with Young Children." *The Reading Teacher,* 53 (February 2000), 410–423.

Young, Terrell A., and Sylvia Vardell. "Weaving Readers Theatre and Nonfiction into the Curriculum." *The Reading Teacher,* 46 (February 1993), 396–406.

Zarillo, James. "Teachers' Interpretations of Literature-Based Reading." *The Reading Teacher,* 43 (October 1989), 22–28.

Zarillo, James, and Carole Cox. "Efferent and Aesthetic Teaching." In *Stance and Literary Understanding: Exploring the Theories, Research, and Practice,* edited by Joyce Many and Carole Cox. Norwood, N.J.: Ablex, 1992.

Zarnowski, Myra. "Learning About Fictionalized Biographies: A Reading and Writing Approach." *The Reading Teacher,* 42 (November 1988), 136–142.

Zhao, Yong, Sophia Hueyshan Tan, and Punya Mishra. "Teaching and Learning: Whose Computer Is It?" *Journal of Adolescent & Adult Literacy,* 44 (December 2000/January 2001), 348–353.

Zimet, Sara Goodman. "Teaching Children to Detect Social Bias in Books." *The Reading Teacher,* 36 (January 1983), 418–421.

Zogby, Grace. "Literature Groups: Empowering the Reader." Presentation at Whole Language Umbrella Conference, St. Louis, Missouri, August 4, 1990.

Zorfass, Judith, Patricia Corley, and Arlene Remz. "Helping Students with Disabilities Become Writers." *Educational Leadership,* 51 (April 1994), 62–66.

Zucker, Carol. "Using Whole Language with Students Who Have Language and Learning Disabilities." *The Reading Teacher,* 46 (May 1993), 660–670.

NAME INDEX

SUBJECT INDEX

CD-ROM(s) available at Reference Desk.

DATE DUE

About the Authors

Betty Roe is Professor Emerita at Tennessee Technological University. She is the former Director of Doctoral Studies for the College of Education and Professor of Reading and Language Arts. She earned her Ed.D. at the University of Tennessee (1969) in Curriculum and Instruction with Reading emphasis. She is the Senior Author of Roe/Stoodt/Burns, *Secondary School Literacy Instruction,* Eighth Edition (Houghton Mifflin, 2004) and Burns/Roe, *Informal Reading Inventory,* Sixth Edition (Houghton Mifflin, 2002). Dr. Roe is an active speaker at inservice workshops and at the annual International Reading Association convention and other professional conferences and conventions. Her most recent area of interest is the use of technology in the teaching of reading. She has received numerous awards for her scholarship and service to the profession, including the Tennessee Reading Association's Distinguished Professor Award and the TTU Chapter Phi Delta Kappa Educator of the Year Award. She is a past president of the Tennessee Reading Association, the founder and past president of the Tennessee Tech Council of IRA, and the past chair of two special interest groups of the International Reading Association. She has also served on a number of IRA Committees.

Sandra Hope Smith is an Assistant Professor in the Department of Curriculum and Instruction and serves as the Director of the Teacher Education Program at Tennessee Technological University. She received her MA in Special Education in 1981 and a Specialist in Education Degree in Reading/Curriculum from Tennessee Technological University in 1989. She is currently completing her doctoral studies at Tennessee State University. In 1997, she was awarded the Tennessee Reading Association's Distinguished Professor Award, and has received numerous other accolades over the last 20 years—including the TTU Chapter Phi Delta Kappa Educator of the Year Award, Overton County Teacher of the Year Award, and the Tennessee CEC Special Education Teacher of the Year Award. She has presented papers at numerous state and national conferences, including the annual International Reading Association convention.